COL. BRIGGS ALDEN.
BORN 1723 – DIED 1796.

A HISTORY
of the
TOWN *of* DUXBURY MASSACHUSETTS

with
Genealogical
Registers

Justin Winsor

HERITAGE BOOKS
2012

HERITAGE BOOKS
AN IMPRINT OF HERITAGE BOOKS, INC.

Books, CDs, and more—Worldwide

For our listing of thousands of titles see our website
at
www.HeritageBooks.com

A Facsimile Reprint
Published 2012 by
HERITAGE BOOKS, INC.
Publishing Division
100 Railroad Ave. #104
Westminster, Maryland 21157

Copyright © 1849 Justin Winsor

— Publisher's Notice —
In reprints such as this, it is often not possible to remove blemishes from the original. We feel the contents of this book warrant its reissue despite these blemishes and hope you will agree and read it with pleasure.

International Standard Book Numbers
Paperbound: 978-0-7884-1747-4
Clothbound: 978-0-7884-9153-5

TO

THE INHABITANTS

OF

THE TOWN OF DUXBURY,

THIS

𝔎ecord of their 𝔄ncestry and 𝔄ncestral 𝔎onor,

IS INSCRIBED.

PREFACE.

More than two years have now elapsed, since the writing of this work was commenced by the Author. That the matter which he then began to collect would ever, or at least in so short a time, be submitted to the press, was a thing unthought of. As no opportunity was passed by for adding to the stock, which soon became gradually to increase, he had accumulated at the end of this time such a store of historic and genealogical information, that it was deemed advisable by many to whom the manuscripts were shown, that they should be put into a more durable form in print. With their request he was induced to comply, and although conscious of its many imperfections, he now submits it to them in their desired form, and also to those for whom it was more especially designed, the inhabitants of the town, and to professed antiquaries elsewhere, it is now given emanating from himself alone, and entitled to what consideration each may be persuaded to confer upon it.

The work has been one of much care and research. To the Author it has been one of amusement, though oftentimes subjecting him to considerable labor and toil; yet it has been more than recompensed, when with feelings of pleasure he has traced the nearly obliterated and illegible records of the past, and discovered in the language of their writings the spiritual character and heroic nature of the actors, in their struggles for religious freedom and civil independence.

Where is the land that can look back to a race of founders worthy of a higher and truer distinction, than can the people of New England? and where should there be their existing influence, mightier and more effectual, than among the descendants of that Pilgrim band, in whose midst were the abodes of a Brewster, a Standish, and an Alden? May they cherish that natural character of their inheritance, may they preserve it in its original purity, guard it with the watchfulness of their christian fathers, make their lives, as theirs, an example, and their end a monument of worldly excellence, worthy to be cherished.

In regard to the arrangement of the work it seems scarcely necessary to say a word. The matter embraced on the first eighty-eight pages seemed to be better placed by itself, distinct from the General History, than embodied in the latter. The Ecclesiastical History has been arranged in a chronological order, and biographical sketches of the pastors introduced. Of the Genealogical Registers, which have been prepared with considerable care, more will be said hereafter.

My acknowledgments are due to many, who have cheered me by their countenance, and afforded me aid in the compilation of the work, as well as to those whose advice and counsel in matters relative to its publication have been of much and valuable service. To Messrs. SAMUEL G. DRAKE and JAMES S. LORING I have to express my indebtedness.

To the REV. BENJAMIN KENT, the present Librarian of the Roxbury Athenæum, I feel under great obligations for the loan of his MS. Notes on Duxbury, made during his ministry in the town, as also for the use of his volume of original MS. Collections.

To Messrs. CHARLES EWER, WILLIAM H. MONTAGUE and others, who have aided me in different portions of the work, and encouraged me in the undertaking, I return my thanks; and especially to the REV. JOSEPH B. FELT, the courteous Librarian of the Massachusetts Historical Society, and to DR. NATHANIEL B. SHURTLEFF, the accurate genealogist of the Old Colony. To many of the aged inhabitants of the town, to whose tales I have listened with interest, and whose words I have taken from their lips, I must express my indebtedness. In regard to others whose assistance I have received, my acknowledgments will be recorded in their proper places.

Where such a multitude of dates, and variety of matter is recorded, it would seem almost impossible that some mistakes should not occur, though it has been a special care, that everything erroneous in its nature, arising from carelessness or a mistake in facts should be excluded from the work. Traditional authority has been received for what it is worth, and in no case is credence allowed it, except it is corroborated and substantiated by unquestionable proof.

J. W.

Boston, October, 1849.

CONTENTS.

	PAGE
SETTLEMENT	9
INCORPORATION	11
NAME	11
BOUNDS	13
PATHS, HIGHWAYS AND BRIDGES	17
SURVEYORS OF HIGHWAYS	21
ANCIENT LANDMARKS	23
TOWN'S COMMONS	35
MILLS, DAMS, ETC.	43
BOUNTIES, FINES, ETC.	45
ORDINARIES	46
FIRST SETTLERS	48
SCHOOLS AND EDUCATION	71
INDIANS	74
TOWN OFFICERS	77
" REPRESENTATIVES	77
" SELECTMEN	79
" CONSTABLES	81
" TREASURERS	82
" CLERKS	82
" RECORDS	82
MISCELLANEOUS	83
GENERAL HISTORY (CIVIL AND MILITARY)	89
PHILIP'S WAR	103
CHARTER OF 1691	112
STAMP ACT	118
REVOLUTION	123

CONTENTS.

	PAGE
Biographies of Revolutionary Men	147
War of 1812	161
History of the Church	171
Formation	171
Rev. Ralph Partridge	171
Rev. John Holmes	178
Rev. Ichabod Wiswall	180
Rev. John Robinson	184
Rev. Samuel Veazie	191
Rev. Charles Turner	202
Rev. Zedekiah Sanger	205
Rev. John Allyn	207
Rev. Benjamin Kent	210
Rev. Josiah Moore	210
Genealogical Registers	213
Appendix I.	348
" II.	348
" III.	349
Index	353

HISTORY

OF THE

TOWN OF DUXBURY.

SETTLEMENT.

THE town was first settled about the year 1632, by the people of Plymouth. Twelve years had elapsed since the first settlement of New Plymouth, and their numbers had greatly increased by emigration from the mother land, and larger allotments were called for by the inhabitants, so that by degrees the circle of the bay was occupied. We find this early record of the settlement, under the date 1632;—

"This year the people of [Plymouth] begin to grow in their outward estates, by the flowing of many People into the country, especially into the M. C: [Mass. Colony.] By which means Cattle and Corn rise to a great price, Goods grow plentiful, and many are enriched. And now their Stock increasing, the Increase vendible; there is no longer holding them together. They must go to their great Lots: they can no otherwise keep their cattle; and having Oxen grown, they must have more land for Plowing and Tillage. By this means they scatter round the Bay [of Plymouth] quickly, and the Town wherein they lived till now compactly, is soon left very thin, and in a short time almost desolate. The Church also comes to be divided, and those who have lived so long together in Christian and Comfortable Fellowship must now part."

That before this period in 1630 or 1631, there were some settlers in Duxbury is most probable; but they returned to Plymouth in the winter to insure their better attendance at Public Worship, as well as on account of their exposed situation, which would be liable to the attacks of the Indians at that remote distance from immediate relief. Their cottages here, too, being probably of hasty construction for the summer, they wished to resign for their more substantial abodes at Plymouth. Alden, Standish, Brewster and Prence, and also Collier, Delano, and some others, were the earliest settlers, and they could not be spared from the Town, unless under a promise of return at winter. We find the following in the Colony records :—

"An° 1632 ⎰ The names of those which promise to remove Aprell 2 ⎱ their fam[ilies] to live in the towne in the winter time, that they m[ay] the better repair to the worship of God.
JOHN ALDEN,
CAPT. STANDISH,
JONATHAN BREWSTER,
THOMAS PRENCE."

The year previous to the incorporation of Duxbury, the question was agitated about uniting the two Churches of Plymouth and Duxbury at some convenient place between the two settlements; and there to build a town, for the purpose of uniting for prompt protection in time of danger. And at a Colony Court held at Plymouth, March 2, 1635-6, persons were appointed "to confer on reuniting with them of Duxburrow at Jones River or such place as shall be most convenient." And again there was a meeting of the Court on the 21st of March, and "At this meeting, after much conference about the neerer uniting of Plymouth and those on Duxburrough side, divers were apointed to view Jones his river and Morton's hole, wch were thought the fittest plac^s & to render a reason for their judgement. The pties for Duxburrow side were Mr. William Collier, Stephen Tracy, Mr. Joh Howland, Edm Chandler, Joshua Pratt; for the other side Capt. Myles Standish, Manasseh Kempton, George Kenrick, John Jenney, & Edward Bangs; All these but Edward Bangs went and conferred together, and on the 21st of s^d moneth of March brought in their opinions and rendered their reasons for the same, wch are many and still extant; seaven of the said nine holding Jones River * to be the fittest place for the uniting of both pts unto a neerer society & there to build a meeting house and towne. And the two preferred the other, wch is Morton's Hole † before Jones River.

* This region, for many years a part of Plymouth and Duxbury, seems first to have been made a district about 1641, when separate surveyors of roads were appointed. Many years after, the portion belonging to Plymouth was incorporated under the name of Kingston.

† Morton's Hole is the name given to a round and deep hole on the flats, to the west of Captain's Hill, and the vicinity thereabout was without doubt the situation here intended.

" Afterwards the Govr. & Council sumoned sd psons deputed as before had done, & read their reasons of their judgem^t. And after long debating of the thing it was at length referred to the two churches on each side as churches to agree upon and end the same."—Old Col. Rec. Ct. orders. I. 90.

What conclusion the churches came to, we know not, as nothing more concerning it appears on the records, and the matter was probably dropped.

INCORPORATION.

On the Colony Records we find the following relative to the incorporation.

"June 7, 1637. It is enacted by the Court that Ducksborrow shall become a towneship and unite together for their better securitie and to have the p^{r}veledges of a towne, onely their bounds & limmits shalbe sett and appoynted by the next Court."

This date is old style; and here again I must repeat the fact, so often announced by historians, that *style is old and new*. In 1582, Pope Gregory corrected the calendar, and this correction was not adopted by the English Parliament until 1751, when the 3d of September, 1752, was ordered to be called the 14th, thus dropping eleven days, for the purpose of bringing the vernal equinox on the 21st of March; and the year was to begin on the 1st of January, instead of March 25th. Hence arose the practice of double dating between January 1st and March 25th, before 1752; thus March 2d, 1635-6, would be 1635 O. S., but 1636 N. S. In these pages the latter, or N. S. date, for the year is generally given; but the O. S. for the day.

NAME.

It received the name of Duxbury out of respect to Captain Standish, from Duxbury Hall, the seat of the Standish family in England. Even as early as 1306, it appears from English works on Pedigree, that there was living at Duxbury, in Lancashire, Hugh Standish, (the son of Ralph, the son of Thurston de Standish, who was living 1222), and in 1677, Sir Richard Standish, the great grandson of Hugh, occupied the same domain in England, which was held in 1812 by Sir Frank Standish of Duxbury Park.

This undoubtedly is the origin of the name of the New England town, and not, as the author of the Notes on Duxbury (Mass. Hist. Coll. II.) derives it, viz. — "The probable etymology is Dux [the Latin for Leader] and borough or burrow, as it was then written. It being a grant to the Captain or leader, it was called his borough." *

The name is variously spelled among ancient writers. The spelling of the records is Duxborough and Duxburrow, and sometimes Ducksburrow. Johnson, in his "Wonder-working Providence," calls it "Dukes Berry," and says of it, that it is in the "Plimouth government, scituated upon the sea-coast." Captain Underhill, in his history of the Pequot war, calls it "Dukesbury," and says of it and "Cap Cod" and "New

---

* Various names have been given at different times to the several portions and villages, which are included within the bounds of Duxbury. Ashdod is the name given to a small village in the north-west part of the town. A portion of the south-east is called Weechertown, and sometimes Loringtown. The name Weechertown is said to have been derived from Abijah Sprague, who built a small hut here, and called it his "weecher," the Indian for wigwam. A village in the upper part is called Tarkiln, or Chandlertown, and forms a school district. Here, at the junction of the road from Plymouth to Boston with the road from Duxbury, was the "Tree of Knowledge," so called ; and a box nailed to this was the depository for the Duxbury letters, many years ago, when a regular conveyance was established between Plymouth and Boston. Here the towns-people repaired to obtain their letters and papers, or some one was despatched to get them and distribute them. The mail was afterwards conveyed here to meet the Plymouth stage for Boston. And before the establishment of a direct mail between Duxbury and Boston, the Duxbury mail was carried to Kingston, and there met the Plymouth. A guide-board is now standing on the place where the tree stood, bearing a representation of it. Tinkertown is another village in the upper part of the town. The portion of the main street of the town, to the south of the Methodist churches, is generally styled "the Village," and sometimes "Sodom." The occasion of the latter name is said to have been as follows :—On one of the roads leading from the inland towns, was situated the house of Dr. John Wadsworth, who was noted as rather an eccentric individual, and concerning whom some anecdotes of an amusing nature are still current. By his door frequently passed the adventuresome sons of farmers of the interior, eager to ship themselves on board some of the comparatively many fishing vessels, which were then often leaving Duxbury at the proper season. At one time a party of these going by, asked the Doctor the distance to "the village," and other questions concerning the prospects before them, who met them with the reply, "Ah, you are going there ; are you? That place is *Sodom*. I tell you it is going to be sunk ; it *is !* Well now do you want me to make you a rhyme? Well then—

> The Swampineers avoid all fears,
> A fishing they will go,
> If they 'scape h—ll, it will be well,
> But that they will n't, I know."

And with this most solemn warning he dismissed them.

Plimouth," that they are " well accommodated for the receiving of people, and yet few are there planted, considering the spaciousness of the place."

Indian Name. The Indian name was Mattakeeset; but the north-western part (now Pembroke,) was called generally Namasakeeset or Namasakiset.

BOUNDS.

1640. THE bounds between Duxbury and Plymouth are "from a little brooke, running from Stephen Tracy's, to another little brooke, falling into Blackwater from the commons left to Duxburrow and the neighborhood thereabouts." The bounds of the Town were fixed at a Court, held *March* 1, 1640-1. Ordered, "that the bounds of Duxburrow Towneship, shall begin where Plymouth bounds do end, namely at the brooke falling into Blackwater [ut supra] and so along Mattachusetts payth to the North River. The said payth to be the westerne bounds thereof; excepting and reserving all those lands granted wthin the said limmits to pticuler psons in Plymouth, Greens Harbour and Scituate, whose cattell may likewise depasture upon the said comons wth them." *

Between Duxbury and Green's harbor these bounds were fixed; — "It is concluded and agreed betwixt Captain Miles Standish, Mr. John Alden, Jonathan Brewster & William Basset, and Mr. Edward Winslow the xxviiith day of December, 1640, that from a great rock that is flatt on the topp, called parting rock, shalbe the p^{r}sent bounds betweene Greens harbour and Duxburrow and shall range from thence norwest to the South river, & on the contrary South East wth payth between Scituate and Duxburrow, and from thence the payth to divide them to the bridge over Greens harbour fresh." Soon after the town was ordered to appoint men to define the bounds with Marshfield.†

---

* The bounds of Duxbury originally included what is now within the limits of Duxbury, Marshfield, Pembroke, Hanson, and the Bridgewaters. Marshfield was bounded off in 1640 ; *Pembroke* incorporated in 1711-12 ; *Hanson* set off from Pembroke in 1820 ; and *Bridgewater* (now four towns) was incorporated in 1656, having been granted to the inhabitants in 1645. For the grantees of Bridgewater, see Appendix I. The " Major's Purchase," an earlier grant to the town, was the great cedar swamp in Hanson.

† *Marshfield* was incorporated March 2d, 1640, though its bounds were not fixed until 1642. It was first called Rexham and Green Harbor, and afterwards, from the characteristic nature of its surface, Marshfield. Its

1658. *Namasakeeset* was ordered to belong to Duxbury about this year.

1665. Robinson's Creek was ordered to be the bounds between Duxbury's land and *Scituate*.

1674. A difficulty, which for some time had existed between Duxbury and Major Winslow of Marshfield, in relation to the division of a piece of marsh between the towns, was this year settled. Marshfield sent an order for the final settlement of it to Duxbury, bearing date May 21, 1674. Thereupon the town appointed Mr. John Alden, Mr. Samuel Seabury, Wm. Pabodie, John Tracy, and John Soule, "or any three of them to treat with the said Winslow, and make a full issue and settlement of said controversy." They accordingly met, with the exception of Mr. Alden, on 16th June, 1674, and "after some agitation and treaty," concluded thus;—From the Easterly side of Careswell Creek to another creek, and along its banks to its mouth, where it flows into the Major's River; and then crossing the river pursues the bank of an opposite creek, which flows a little north of Little wood Island, and thence across to Gotum River, and along its banks to a creek on the Easterly side, and from its mouth across to Cut River. Duxbury was to make over to Marshfield a meadow at Cut River, near its mouth, and, say the Records, "this instrument being brought to publique record shalbe a finall and perpetuall isshue of the abovesaid controversy."

"June, 1678. This Court have settled the *easterly* bounds of ye towne of Duxburrow to be ye sea near Green harbour, Indian name was Missaucatucket. In 1639, the Court granted unto Mr. Winslow and the others of Green harbor "a competent pcon of uplands and medowe betwixt the rivers [Green harbor and South] for a farme for a minister, and one other competent porcon of land, nere unto the said lot for the minister, either for Nehemiah Smyth or some other as the said inhabitants shall place in." *Mr. Richard Blinman*, who arrived from Wales in 1642, was the first minister, and who soon after went to Gloucester, to New London in 1648, to New Haven in 1658, to Newfoundland in 1659, and then to England, and died in the ministry at Bristol in a good old age. *Rev. Edward Bulkley* was pastor from 1642 to 1658, when he removed to Concord, and succeeded his father Rev. Peter in 1659 (who was son of Rev. Edward, D. D., of England), and died at Chelmsford 2d January, 1696, and was buried at Concord. His son John died at Marshfield in 1658. The town purchased his house for a parsonage, which was occupied by his successor, *Rev Samuel Arnold*, who was settled near the close of 1659, and who received £40 salary per annum. The town agreed with Benjamin Church to build a new parsonage in 1667. There were no Church records kept during his ministry. He died Sept. 1, 1693, leaving a library valued at £7 10s., and bequeathing to Rowland Cotton "his great Laten Book called Augustine Marloret, being an exposition of the New Testament." It is said he was a carpenter by trade. His son Samuel received his divinity books. The town records of M. are extant; but the early volumes are in a fragmentary state.—*Miss M. A. Thomas's Communication; Deane's Scituate; Farmer's Register; Col. Records and Probate do.*

where ye line cutts betweene Marshfield and Duxburrow to ye Gurrnett's Nose, excepting ye Gurnett, Clarks Iland, and Saquaquash, wh are not to be within ye jurisdition of Duxborough; saveing also every man's property and right to him, y^t is now in possession of any lands or Meadowes within these bounds, whether by grant or purchase, without disturbance as touching property by vertue of this grant, yet to be within ye jurisdition off Duxborough townshipp."

1684. *Marshfield* and *Duxbury*. From a rock near Clement King's house, northwest to North River, ranging near Samuel Hach's house: and again from said rock southeast to a cartway between Samuel and Seth Arnold's, thence to Green's harbour path, thence to Edw. Bump's at Duck hill, including his land within Marshfield.

Signed Feb. 23, 1684.

WILLIAM PABODIE,   } for Duxbury.   NATHL. THOMAS,   } for Marshfield.
JOHN TRACY,   SAML. SPRAGUE,

This from the Colony Records: A confirmation of previous grants: 1685:

"Hinckley, Govr.
Duxbury Bounds.

At the Generall Court held at Plimouth the twelfth day of Jun, Ano Domini 1685.

Whereas, William Bradford, Esqr. & his asociats in the yeare 1637, did grant unto Capt. Miles Standish & others the inhabitants & proprietors of the lands within the townshipe of Duxborrough, from and after the said yeare, so called, besides the farmes formerly granted to them, a certaine Tract of land for the settleing A plantation & making of a Townshipp. [Here follows a recapitulation of the several bounds mentioned above.] This p^rsent Court doth hereby declare it so to bee, and doe hereby Ratifye, Establish & confirme all former grants of land made by the said William Bradford & his asociats to particular p^rsons there, before the said place became a Townshipp, & all other the Lands within the said Townshipp, to the respective owners thereof, wheather Inhabitants or otherwise, According to the true intents & meaning of the said grants. [Here follows a confirmation of a grant made in 1660, viz., of one half of a tract of land, bounded southerly by Plymouth line, and westerly by Jones River Pond and Indian head River; the other half being granted to Marshfield.] To have & to hold the said Lands & meadows or marishes to the said town in Generall, & owners & proprietors in particular, whether Inhabitants or not of the said town, & to their successours, heires & assignees for ever to bee holden of our Soverⁿ Lord, the King, as of his mannor & tenure of East

Greenwich in the county of Kentt, &c. They the grantees yeilding & payeing to our Soveraign Lord, the King, his heires & successors & to the president of the honorable councill, such part of the Gold and sillver oar as p^r our Charter is expressed.

{ The Seale of the Country. } { In Testimony whereof this Court have ordered the publicke seale of this colony to be afixed to these p^{r}sents."

1686. *Duxbury* and *Scituate.* This year there was a controversy between these towns about the division of a tract of land. June 24th, Francis Barker was empowered to treat with Scituate, and defend the rights of the town. John Wadsworth and Edw. Southworth petitioned against it.

1714. The following more particular bounds between *Duxbury* and *Plymouth*, are from the Town Records.

Beginning at the beach on the northerly end of the highland at the Gurnet, on the easterly side, and running due west to a rock at the north end of Clarks Island, thence to Clarks Island Channel, which comes from Powder point, and down that to Jones River Channel, thence up this channel and Jones River to Stoney Brook, up said brook, and thence up Tussock's creek to the head of the western branch, thence northerly across Mile brook, and thence westerly to the mouth of Jones River Pond.

Signed April 30, 1714.

JOHN BRADFORD, JAMES WARREN, NATHL. THOMAS,	Agents for Plymouth.	JOHN WADSWORTH, JOHN ALDEN, THOMAS LORING,	Selectmen of Duxbury.

1735. Voted, That the line between *Kingston* and *Duxbury* remain the same, as it was between Plymouth and Duxbury. Kingston, which had been previously known as Jones River Parish, was set off from Plymouth and incorporated in 1726, although no mention of the line between it and Duxbury appears before the above date.

1751. The line between Duxbury and Pembroke, established. Pembroke was set off from Duxbury in 1711–2; yet I find in the Records no mention of a line earlier than this.

POPULATION.

WE have no satisfactory means of ascertaining the population of the town at early periods. In 1643, however, there are eighty-two persons mentioned as able to bear arms, being between the ages of 16 and 60, and allowing that they were one in five, which is a fair estimate, we should judge the population at that time to have been over 400. We might also conclude that the town was less populous than many others of the colony, from the fact that her quota of the various bodies of men raised by the colony was uniformly lower. In 1646 there were 27 freemen; in 1670, 34; in 1683-4, 40. In 1710, there were 175 heads of families, and allowing that they were one in six or seven, we estimate the number at that time at about 1100. In 1790, it was 1454; in 1800, 1664; in 1810, 2201; in 1820, 2403; in 1830, 2716; and in 1840, 2798.

PATHS, HIGHWAYS, AND BRIDGES.

1634, Oct. 1. The Colony Court appointed Capt. Standish, William Collier, Jonathan Brewster, William Palmer, and Stephen Tracy to lay out highways in Duxburrow, before Nov. 15 of the same year.

1637. A Jury of 12 (four from Duxbury, viz., Love Brewster, Experience Mitchell, Philip Delanoy, Moses Simmons,) were impanneled, "to set forth heigh wayes about Plymouth, Ducksburrow and the Eele River."

The road through Duxbury began at the ferry at Jones River, and thence by *Stephen Tracy's* to the bridge at *John Rogers'*, thence by *Jonathan Brewster's* cowyard, through a valley near the house of *Mr. Prence*, thence by *Christopher Wadsworth's* "whose pallasadoe is to be removned," thence to *Francis Sprague's*, and then fell into the way, that leads "from Morton's hole to Ducksburrow Towne."

From this main path there branched off one, going to the Nook to accommodate *Standish* and *Brewster*, and returning by *William Basset's* and *Francis Sprague's*, through an ancient path, joined again the highway.*

There was also a path from the "Cut," passing between *Basset's* and *Sprague's* to the town.

From *Wadsworth's*, the path led through *Sprague's* and *Basset's* orchards, thence through *John Washburn's* land to *Wm. Palmer's* gate, thence through *Peter Brown's* land to the westward of *Henry Howland's* house, thence through a marsh to *Mr. John Alden's*, thence through a valley by the corner of *Philip Delanoy's* farm to *Edward Bumpasse's*, and thence by *Rowland Leyhorne's* house to Greens harbor.

---

* This was, however, in 1638, made over to these parties, to be kept in repair by them as a private way.

From *Howland's* an upper path was laid out. Note. From the above record the position of the first settlers' habitations can be readily ascertained.

1638. Ordered that the bridge over Jones River be made passable for carts.

Court ordered John Washburn and Joseph Rogers to repair the highways.

1639. Ordered that six from Plymouth and three from Duxbury be appointed to assess the charges of both towns for Jones River bridge.

1644. John Rogers and Joseph Rogers were appointed to lay out roads.

1647. The treasurer (Standish) was ordered to have Jones River bridge repaired. 1650, this bridge was presented as being dangerous for man and beast. 1655, John Howland and Constant Southworth were ordered to agree with workmen to mend the same. 1665, a new bridge was ordered over Jones River.

1650. A way from Jones River through John Rogers' farm to the Massachusetts path was laid out.

1665. A highway, 40 feet wide, laid out through John Holmes' " to the common rode into the bay."

1665. These were "impaneled upon a jury for the laying forth of a footway through the lands of Moses Simons and Samuell Chanler,"—

George Soule, Sen.,
Philip Delano, Sen.,
Experience Mitchell,
Edmund Weston,
Francis West,
Abraham Sampson,

William ———,
Roger Glass,
Joseph Prior,
Samuel Hunt,
John Sprague.

1682. *North River Bridge.* A cart bridge was ordered to be built over the North River, near Barstow's foot bridge, by Scituate, Marshfield and Duxbury; and Duxbury was then freed from any longer repairing Jones River bridge. The cost was for Scituate £10, for Marshfield and Duxbury £5 each; but Mannamoiett was to bear 20s. of Duxbury's part.

1684, Oct. 24. These were a jury to lay out "the rode from Marshfield bounds to Plimoth Rode," and a "hiway from Jones River bridge to North River bridge."

Edw. Southworth,
Isaac Barker,
Francis Barker,
Lt. Hunt,
Elnathan Weston,
John Sprague,

Abraham Sampson, Jr.,
John Russell,
Caleb Sampson,
Benj. Bartlett, Jr.,
Josiah Holmes.

1702, Nov. 30. There were appointed to lay out public roads,—Seth Arnold, Francis Barker and Samuel Bradford.

1715. Road from the Nook was laid out, 30 feet wide, Mar. 26th; and one from the point, 40 feet wide, May 21st.

1722. Road laid out, 30 feet wide, from Asa Delano's, by the Cranberry factory, to the meeting house.

1741. A highway was laid out over South River, at the Saw-mill dam.

1766, March 31st. A road, laid out from the Captain's Nook to the Plymouth Road, was accepted by the Town.

Sept. 22. Voted, to lay out a road from the Plymouth Road to Powder point.

1768. *Road across the Major's pasture.* — May 14, Major Alden may have liberty to place a gate at the highway going into Powder point, if he will allow a cartway into Powder point across his farm. [Two or three years since, this road was accepted by the town, and has become a public highway.]

1798. *Washington Street*, now so called, is the main thoroughfare of the town, and was this year projected, extending from Powder point to the head of the road, coming from the Nook. The first projectors of this road for a long time were its only advocates. They were Seth Sprague, Ezra Weston, Joshua Winsor, and Samuel Delano, and among the number of the most influential citizens of the town. They at their own expense employed an attorney to plead their cause before the Court of Sessions, where he was met by another attorney, who acted in behalf of the town. Their project was nevertheless sanctioned by the Court, and the road was accordingly laid out, and completed in the course of two years. — Soule's Sprague Family Memorial.

1803. *Blue-fish River bridge.* In order to fully accomplish the design of the last mentioned road, it was necessary that a bridge should be built over the Bluefish River; and this was opposed with equal exertions on the part of most of the inhabitants, who argued that, as the river was navigable, the Court had no power to order an erection of a bridge over it. At various meetings, from 1800 to 1803, this question was agitated with much animated discussion, and opposed chiefly on account of its great cost ($3000 at least). To meet this objection a scheme was formed by the projectors, who agreed, privately, to build the bridge and dam conjointly, according to a prepared model. They then petitioned for a town meeting, which was accordingly convened on the second Monday in February, 1803; when, as they expected, the arguments of opposition turned upon the enormous expense. At this juncture, Mr. Sprague moved that the town agree to build the bridge, after the model there exhibited, provided any responsible man would undertake the work for $1500, which motion was carried without any opposition. Thereupon one of them, Joshua Winsor, arose and accepted the offer of the town, rather to its surprise.

On the following day preparations were commenced for the immediate erection of the bridge, by the contractor and his associates. Yet some of the opposition threatened to call another meeting to reconsider their vote; but the work proceeded so rapidly, that before this threat could be executed, it was quite too late to think of retracting.

The work, which was begun in April, was finished on the 3d of July following, to the satisfaction of the Committee of the town (Samuel A. Frazar, Ezra Weston and Isaiah Alden), who had been appointed to oversee and inspect the work of construction.

The next day, being the Fourth of July, was one of uncommon interest to the inhabitants of Duxbury. The bridge was in some measure decorated, and a temporary arch erected over it, on which was perched a broad spread eagle of wood, bore this motto — from Jefferson's inaugural address — "Peace, Friendship, and Commerce with all Nations; entangling Alliances with none." And on the reverse, "Commerce, Agriculture, Fishery." The two military companies of the town, under Captains Dingley and Alden, paraded, and after escorting a large party of ladies and gentlemen to the bridge, they formed in a line on each side, while the procession passed between, and then proceeding a short distance they turned, and recrossing the bridge marched to the hill on the southerly side of the River, where the projectors had prepared a bountiful entertainment. Mr. Sprague presided at the tables, and in the devoration of the sumptuous viands before them, many of the opposition received a check to their feelings of animosity, (if they had any,) and amid the scenes of mirth and rejoicings, many were the thanks expressed for the final completion of that much opposed, yet ably vindicated scheme. The day was remarkably pleasant, and everything that transpired seemed to pass off in happiness, and it is still remembered by the aged yet amongst us, as one of peculiar gratification and enjoyment.

The contractors were losers to some extent by their undertaking; but the ultimate cost of the work to the town was only $400, the mill privilege, created by the dam, having been disposed of for $1100*.— Sprague Memorial.

There is an amusing account of some of the incidents con-

---

* This was bought by Jedediah Holmes, of Kingston, who sold it to Samuel A. Frazar, Reuben Drew, Dea. George Loring and others, and the mill was soon afterwards built. It next passed into Mr. Edward Winslow's hands.

nected with the erection of this bridge, which has once before been in print, yet still will bear it again. The authorship has been attributed by some to Dr. Rufus Hathaway, and by others to Major Judah Alden. One short paragraph is omitted, as it seems "to mar the unity of the subject by irrelevant matters."

"And it came to pass in the days of Cæsar, the King, that he commanded his servant Joshua, saying, get thee up a journey into the land of the Hanoverites, to Benjamin, the Scribe, and say unto him, I, Cæsar, the King, have sent forth my decree, and commanded that the people in the land of Sodom shall no longer be separated from the Westonites, the Drewites, and the Cushmanites, that dwell on the north side of the great river Blue-fish. And also command Benjamin, the Scribe, that he forthwith make out a petition and convey it to the judges and magistrates of our land, commanding that they straightway direct the Sodomites, the Westonites, and all the other Ites, within our borders, to build a bridge over the great river Blue-fish. So the Judges and Magistrates, fearing Cæsar, the King, and Joshua, his servant, commanded that the bridge be built according to Cæsar's decree. But it came to pass that there arose up certain of the tribes of Judah and Levi and of Samuel, and of the Chandlerites, and others most learned in the law, and showed unto the Judges and Magistrates, that Cæsar, the King, had done wickedly, in commanding what was unlawful to be done, and so by the voice of the multitude the decree was set aside. And it came to pass that Cæsar and the Sodomites wrought the minds of the people, and cast such delusions before their eyes, that they had fear before Cæsar, the King, and at length resolved to build the bridge, and connect Cæsar's dominions to the land of Sodom. And now behold Cæsar, the King, has erected an arch fifty cubits high, on that bridge, which the people, in their folly, have built, — and set up an image over on the top of the arch, and commanded all the people from the land of Sodom on the south, the Westonites and all the other tribes in the north to assemble on the fourth day of the seventh month, and bow their heads to the image which the King has set up. And behold the people assembled according to the King's decree, and did as he had commanded."

EARLY SURVEYORS OF HIGHWAYS.

There appear to have been none appointed before 1640, when the bounds of Duxbury were first fixed.
1640. Experience Mitchell, Constant Southworth.
1641. Joseph Bidle, Samuel Nash.

SURVEYORS OF HIGHWAYS.

1642. Edmund Hawes.
1644. John Rogers, William Sherman.
1645. John Maynard, Edmund Hunt.
1646. William Merrick, Moses (?) Truant.
1647. Edward Hall, John Brown.
1648. Francis Sprague, Abraham Sampson.
1649. John Starr, John Washburn.
1650. John Starr, John Washburn.
1651. Thomas Gannet, John Aimes.
1652. Edmund Weston, Thomas Boney.
1654. Joseph Andrews, Robert Barker.
1655. Thurston Clark, Zachariah Soule.
1656. Henry Howland, John Tracy, Thomas Ensign.
1657. Moses Simmons, Francis Sprague.
1658. Experience Mitchell, Francis West.
1659. Jonathan Shaw, Wm. Clark.
1662. Christopher Wadsworth, Moses Simmons.
1663. Mr. Samuel Seabury, Samuel Hunt.
1666. Joseph Wadsworth, Samuel Chandler.
1668. George Partridge, Henry Howland.
1669. John Rogers, Sen., Roger Glass.
1671. John Wadsworth, Samuel West.
1672. Robert Barker, John Soule, Joseph Howland.
1673. John Hudson, Joseph Wadsworth, Josiah Wormall.
1674. John Rogers, Jr., Peter West, Isaac Barker.
1675. John Rogers, Sen., Joseph Wadsworth, Joseph Rogers.
1676. John Rogers, Jr., Thomas Delano.
1677. George Partridge, Peter West, Robt. Barker, Sen.
1678. John Rogers, Abraham Sampson, William Tubbs.
1679. Robt. Barker, Sen., John Tracy, Wrestling Brewster.
1680. John Wadsworth, Peter West, John Hudson.
1681. George Partridge, Joseph Wadsworth, Josiah Holmes.
1682. John Rogers, Edmund Weston, Abraham Peirce.
1685. John Simmons, Joseph Howland, William Tubbs.
1687. Wrestling Brewster, R. Barker, Jr., Elnathan Weston.
1689. Joseph Wadsworth, John Russell, John Simmons.
1690. James Partridge, James Bishop, John Tracy.
1691. Philip Delano, John Boney, James Partridge.
1692. Elnathan Weston, John Russell.
1694. Wrestling Brewster, John Boney, John Soule.

NOTE. Those for 1643, 53, 60, 61, 64, 65, 67, 70, 83, 84, 86, 88, and 94, appear not to have been recorded.

ANCIENT LANDMARKS.

ALLERTON'S HILL. An early mention is made of a hill of this name, which was probably called after Isaac Allerton, one of the first Pilgrims, though I cannot find him mentioned as a resident of Duxbury at any time.

NORTH HILL. This name was given to the eminence which now bears it, by the earliest settlers, in whose vicinity were settled some of the principal men of the town, and around which large grants were made.

CAPTAIN'S HILL. This hill formed a part of an early grant to Captain Standish, who settled near its base, and whose name it still bears. It is situated on a peninsula, which extends in a southeasterly direction, between the bays of Duxbury and Plymouth, and contains about two or three hundred acres of good soil, little inferior to any in the country in fertility. While in other portions of the town the soil is sandy and unproductive, and a considerable part in no state of cultivation, this peninsula is furnished with a deep and fertile soil. The same may be said of the highland on the Gurnet, Saquish and many other similar spots around the bay, where the soil is in immediate proximity to the sea. Clark's Island in some parts possesses a mould, which if equalled, is scarcely surpassed in the county; and while the northern and western sides offer the most desirable qualities for pasturage and grain, its southern and eastern declivities present a perfect garden, abounding with trees, through whose foliage, even during the summer's hottest months, stir the breezes from the sea.*

---

* This Island, called by Hutchinson "one of the best islands in Massachusetts bay," contains 86½ acres of land, and was anciently well covered with a fine growth of trees, (as were also the Gurnet and Saquish,) as appears by various records, wherein are mentioned "the woods thereupon." Morton erroneously describes it as between the Gurnet and Saquish. Of its original forest of red cedar, only three decayed trunks now remain, and having borne the blasts of many a winter, still stand "silent monitors of the past." It is memorable as being the spot, where that devoted Pilgrim band first landed in their voyage of discovery from Cape Cod. Having come under the lee of the island during the night of Friday, December 9th, they landed on the following day, and here kept the Christian Sabbath, while "the dim woods rang to the anthems of the free." Ought not this to cause peculiar attractions hither? Should not a descendant like to witness the scene of his father's rejoicings — rejoicings, as it were, on the threshold of eternity? Think of their situation; — in an unknown harbor, separated from their wives and children, did this band of discoverers prolong the strains of anthems and rejoicing chorus, till the woods reëchoed their praises, and sent their thanksgiving to a propitious Heaven.

It received its name from Clark, the mate of the Mayflower, who, it is said, "first stepped on shore thereon."

In early times salt was made on the Island, and it was also reserved for

The summit of the hill is about 400 yards from the sea, and 180 feet above its level, and when once attained presents a view to him who communes with nature, and who has pondered over the history of the early Pilgrims, is acquainted with their character, and has conceived the purpose of their exile, — to him it presents a spectacle which has in times past, and which, I conceive, must ever cause an impression on his mind, not easily forgotten and scarcely to be eradicated. Full as it is of the most pleasing associations, it calls up in the mind of the beholder those reminiscences, which gladden his heart and arouse his soul into being, and clothe him with all the nobler feelings of mankind, dormant as they may lie within the deep recesses of his heart.

Nor is the loveliness of the scene itself any the less an efficient agent of holy influences, — both cause one to tremble, irresistibly, and to offer praise to his Maker. The circumstances, to be sure, add to the attractions of the spot; but its beauty, its simplicity of grandeur, its busy scenes, and its still silent loneliness give to it a power, whose effects need not be mentioned.

Select, should you visit it, the closing hours of a summer's day, when the burning heat of the declining sun is dispelled by the cooler shades of approaching evening, and ascend to its height. Now as the retiring rays of day form on the heavens above a gorgeous canopy of variegated hues, so on nature's face below, all brightens into richness, and the verdure of her covering softens into mildness; — the shining villages around, and the village spires towering against a background of unfading green, add gladness to the scene. The glassy surface of the bay within, with its gentle ripplings on the shore beneath, — the music of the dashing waves on the beach without, give quiet to the mind and peace within.

Before you, in the distance at the east, appear the white

---

the poor of the town of Plymouth, who obtained their wood and pastured their cattle there. It was early set apart for the pasturage of sheep, whose increase the colonists much strove for, and as early as July 1, 1633, it was ordered, that " no sheep be sold out of the colony, under penalty of forfeiting their due value."

During Philip's war it became an asylum for some of the praying Indians of the colony, and a protection against the attacks of their hostile brothers. In 1675, the Council of War ordered, that the " Namassachusett Indians be speedily removed to Clarkes Iland, and ther to remaine and not to depart from thence without lycence from authoritie upon paine of death."

The island was sold in 1690 to Samuel Lucas, Elkanah Watson, and Geo. Morton. A descendant of Watson now resides there. It is often a resort of parties of pleasure in the summer season from the neighboring towns, who find in the cool and shady retreats on its southeastern slope a place to make merry with dance and song, and an appetite to ease their tables of their delicious viands.

sand hills of Cape Cod, shining beyond the blue expanse, and seeming to encircle by its protecting barrier a spot dear to the heart of every descendant of that Pilgrim band. Still nearer, at your feet and before you, are the pleasant bays of Plymouth, Kingston and Duxbury, enlivened by passing boats, and sheltered from a raging ocean by the beach, crowned at its southern extremity by a light-house, and with the extending arm of Saquish enclosing the Island of the Pilgrims; — turning your eyes to the south, they fall in succession on the promontory of Monamet; on the ancient town of Plymouth, rising beneath, and as if under the protection of the mound beyond, the resting-place of the pilgrim's dead; on the villages of Rocky Nook and of Kingston: — Extending your eye over the extent of forest to the northwest, you see the Blue Hills of Milton, ascending far above the surrounding country; while nearer, at the north, are the villages of Duxbury and Marshfield, scattered over the fields, whose white cottages, shining in the sun, offer a pleasing contrast to the scene. Below you and around you once arose the humble abodes of the Pilgrims. Who can gaze upon the spot which marks the site of the dwelling of Standish, without feelings of emotion? who can but give thanks that that spirit,

> "A spirit fit to start into an empire,
> And look the world to law,"

had been sent amongst them, to be their counsel in peace and their protection in danger? Who can but admire its ready adaptation to a sphere of action so totally different from the school of his youth? Here also arose the dwelling of Brewster, who having followed in his youth in the retinue of kings and princes, preferred a solitary retreat in the western wilds, and there to worship his God in peace. Here too was the abode of Collier, who under every circumstance of danger strove with unceasing toil in the discharge of every duty necessary to the welfare and prosperity of the colony. Here too can be seen the spot whereon was the habitation of Alden, whose prudent counsels and whose rigid justice attained for him a rank in the estimation of the colony, alike an honor to himself and a subject of pride to his descendants.

Turn your vision as you may, and you will feel that you are gazing on a scene of more than ordinary interest, full of the most grateful recollections, and of a nature the most agreeable and pleasing.

> "Scenes must be beautiful, which, daily viewed,
> Please daily, and whose novelty survives
> Long knowledge and the scrutiny of years,—
> Praise justly due to those that I describe."

DUCK HILL, situated in the northeastern part of the town, was called so at a very early date.

THE BAY, comprising the harbors of Plymouth, Kingston, and Duxbury: It is well known that the pilgrims selected the shores of this bay as their settlement, because they found it commodious and "fit for shipping." The writers of "Mourt's Relation"—which has been ascribed to Bradford and Winslow—thus speak of it in 1622. "This harbour is a bay greater than Cape Cod, compassed with goodly lands, and in the bay two fine islands* uninhabited, wherein are nothing but woods, oaks, pine, walnut, beech, sassafras, vines and other trees, which we know not. This bay is a most hopeful place, innumerable store of fowle, and excellent good; and cannot but be fish in their season: Skate, Cod, turbot [i. e. flounder or halibut], and herring, we have tasted of; abundance of muscles, the greatest and best we ever saw; crabs, lobsters in their time infinite. It is fashion like a sickle or fish-hook."

This is a proof of the abundance of forest trees, in the immediate neighborhood of the bay, in early times; and even now the space between the shore and the woodland would not average over a mile in breadth. Of all trees the pine is in the greatest abundance, and chiefly of that species styled *pinus rigida*, or the pitch pine, as it is commonly called. It is stated by Bradford, in his "Typographical Description of Duxbury," (Hist. Coll. II.) that Capt. Samuel Alden, the son of David, and the grandson of the Pilgrim John Alden, remembered the time when the white pine (*pinus strobus*) first began to grow in Duxbury. Capt. Alden died in 1780, æt. 93, and consequently the date of its appearance must have been about 1700. The oak is also found in many places. Maple, birch, ash, cedar, and walnut also grow here. At the present day nearly one half of the territory of the town is covered with forest, and it is said that no town in the county in proportion to its size has larger tracts of woodland. The forests

---

* That there were formerly two islands in this bay, there appears no doubt in my mind. Yet some say, that Brown's Island was always a shoal, as it now is; and that Clark's Island and Saquish must be the two islands intended, supposing, in the case of the latter, that the water once flowed between it and the Gurnet, or that the writers of this Relation were misled by the appearance of Saquish, which at this day has the semblance of an island from the main. But with all deference to these opinions, emanating from the most respectable sources, I cannot but think that Brown's Island was at that time above the water, since we have the fact, that stumps of trees have been seen there by persons now living. Mr. Nathaniel Winsor, who died in 1839, aged 93, often assured his children and others, that he himself had seen the stumps of trees on this shoal. See also Judge Davis' Morton's Memorial, Dr. Young's Chronicles of the Pilgrims, and Richard Soule's Sprague Memorial.

COMMERCE. — WILD FOWL, ETC.

in times past have afforded large quantities of timber for building ships; and a large number of which have been built on its shore; and none have ever stood higher in point of workmanship and finish than the Duxbury ships. The Duxbury mechanics have long been distinguished in this art, and the specimens of their skill have always met with approbation for their fine appearance in the exterior, as well as for their strength and durability. In years past large numbers of ships and barks, as well as of smaller vessels, have been built in Duxbury. In the single year 1837, there were built 11,711 tons. Large numbers have also been owned in Duxbury, and some of the largest ship owners in New England have resided here. The late Mr. Ezra Weston for many years was considered the largest owner in the country, and his sons now living are extensively engaged in the same business. In the year above-mentioned there were owned in Duxbury forty-six vessels engaged in the cod and mackerel fishery. — Appendix III.

The bay has been, from the earliest times, a resort of wild sea fowl of every kind, which has often drawn hither crowds of sportsmen. And as early as 1737, the town, through fear of the total destruction of the game, voted to petition the General Court to regulate the fowling, "because ye wild fowle have almost forsaken ye said bay." In the northern part there are several islands, formed by the various creeks flowing through the marshes in different directions.* These marshes have always been a favorite place for gunners in search of the flocks of marsh birds, with which they abound; though of late years their numbers have greatly decreased. Few now can boast of having secured seventy of a flock at one shot; or that he has by his gun furnished materials for eight featherbeds.

Previous to the Revolution, and during that period, while there was a scarcity of powder, it was frequently manufactured by the town's people themselves, for their own consumption; and private powder mills and magazines were not of uncommon occurrence.

THE BEACH. This narrow neck of land, extending in length about six miles, and varying at different points in width,

---

* The Bay is quite free from rocks, except a few at Powder point, the Nook point, and the northern end of Clark's Island. There is however two rocks of some size, to the westward of the Nook, and lying near the shore, to the eastward of the mouth of Island creek, called *Cripple rocks*. Two others, lying near together in the northern part, and off some distance from Powder point, are known by the name of "*Zachary's rocks*." They are on the very edge of the channel, and are about four or five feet under water at high tide. They probably received their name early from Zachary Soule, the son of the pilgrim George Soule, who lived on Powder point.

forms the harbor of Duxbury. It runs from Marshfield in a southeasterly direction, and is entirely disjointed from the main land by the Cut River canal, as it is called, flowing between. The name of *Salt-house* beach was very early given to it, though now it is more commonly known by the name of Duxbury beach. One of its most remarkable features is the clump of pitch pines, situated about two-thirds of the distance from the Cut to the Gurnet, and known to this day by the name of *High pines*, which name was given to them as early as 1637, or before. At this place the beach is wider than at any other, and they are placed on a slight elevation of land, and nearly surrounded by marshes, with which almost the whole extent of the beach on the inner side is bounded. Another eminence at the northern end is known by the name of "*Rouse's hummock*," which transmits to us the name of John Rouse, an early settler in that vicinity. About twenty-five years ago, the first house on the beach, which was erected by the Humane Society, was burnt down, and in it James Southworth was burnt to death; and a few years after the present one was built.*

Fears have been entertained, in times past, that at some time the sea might force its way through the beach at various places, and to guard against this, there was built, some years ago, with much labor and expense, at many points throughout its whole extent, a kind of sea-wall, placed for the greatest part on the inner side of the beach, and formed by a double line of fences, made by stakes driven in the ground, and sea-weed thrown between. This was accomplished under the direction of L. G. Sampson, Esq., then deputy collector of Plymouth district for the port of Duxbury, and paid for by an appropriation of Congress, amounting to several thousand dollars, and a large number of men were there employed for three or four weeks. At this time an appropriation was made by the town, and the whole extent of the beach purchased, and it is now the town's property.

One of the best methods of preventing the destruction of the beach, is to attend to the preservation of the beach grass. Several times the seed has been sown at different points, and even as early as 1751 the town took measures to prevent the grass being eaten by cattle. At a town meeting this year, on the 20th of May, they voted " to petition the General Court to get an act to prevent neat cattle going upon or feeding on Duxbury beach for the future."

In connection here, it may not be improper to give some account of the promontory, which forms the southern extrem-

---

* For a brief account of the vessels which have been wrecked upon the beach, see Appendix No. II.

ity of the beach, though it belongs politically to the town of Plymouth, as does also another small promontory * connected with this by a beach, which extends in a southwesterly direction into the bay.

The Gurnet contains about twenty-seven acres of good soil. The name is derived from the gurnet-fish, which abounds in great numbers on the coast of Devonshire, England; and in the English channel there are several headlands bearing the name, having taken it probably because of the number of these fishes in their neighborhood; and from one of these, it is probable, the Gurnet of Plymouth received its name, which was very early given to it by the Pilgrims.

This is probably the famous promontory, called by the Northmen, in their discoveries along the coast of the continent in the eleventh century, by the name of *Krossaness*. In the spring of 1004, Thorwald, son of Eric the red, sailing eastward in his large ship from his winter quartèrs at Vineland [Providence], and then northward, passed a remarkable headland [Cape Cod] inclosing a bay; and came to another, but smaller one, on the other side of the bay, covered with wood [Gurnet.] † This spot so charmed Thorwald, that he exclaimed, — "This is a beautiful spot, and here I should like to fix my dwelling." He was soon after wounded in a skirmish with the natives, and perceiving that his wound was mortal, he said to his companions: "I now advise you to prepare for your departure as soon as possible; but me ye shall bring to the promontory, where I thought it good to dwell. It may be that it was a prophetic word, which fell from my mouth, about abiding there for a season. There shall ye bury me, and plant a cross at my head, and another at my feet, and call the place Krossaness in all coming time." This commandment was obeyed.—*Antiquitates Americanæ of the Royal Society of Northern Antiquaries of Copenhagen.*

At the *Gurnet Creek*, in the early days of the colony, bass

---

* This peninsula is known by the name of Saquish, which, says the author of Notes on Plymouth, is an Indian word, and "signifies, doubtless, clams." The name has been variously spelled, as Sagaquab, Sagaquash, Saquaquash, Sasaquish, Sauquish, &c. In early times the town of Plymouth, were "forbade felling trees at Saquish, within 40 feet of the bank." Of its original forest, there were left in 1815, but two solitary trees, standing on the point; one of which stood for several years afterwards. It contains from twelve to fourteen acres of land. On a flat, and a dangerous shoal, which makes off from Saquish point, there was built by the United States, in 1813, a stone pier. It is placed upon a muscle bed, and is about twelve feet square at the bottom, and eighteen feet high, and at high tide six feet above the water.

† By a few it is thought to be point Alderton, (or more properly Allerton,) at the entrance of Boston harbor.

were caught in great abundance, and a point is still called "*Stage point,*" where fishing stages were erected in 1648.

Light houses. An order was passed the legislature of Massachusetts bay, Feb. 17, 1768, authorizing the erection of a light house on the Gurnet, which was to be 30 feet long, 20 feet high, 15 feet wide. It showed two lights, one in each end, with two lamps of four large wicks in each. This was burnt down on the evening of July 2, 1801, and the present ones erected in 1803. They show two steady lights about 70 feet above the level of the sea.

Gurnet Meadows. These meadows anciently belonged to the town of Duxbury, though now they are within the jurisdiction of Plymouth. The following, relating to their disposition by the town, is from the Town records.

1640. " Where as in year [sixteen hundred and] forty the bounds of Duxborrough were set by the Court of New Plymouth, and it was ordered by the s^d Court, that the medow att the gurnit should belong to s^d Duxborrough: and about the year [sixteen hundred and] sixty, the said medow was despossed of by the Town of Duxburrough, as followeth. To Francis West, Edmond Weston, William Clarke, Zachariah Soule, Joseph Alden, John Soule; and ordered Lieuetenant Samuell Nash and Phillip Dilano to lay forth the said medow unto the aboves^d men: which was accordingly dun and bounds made and was recorded in the Towne book: but since that time, the s^d booke being burn'd, their record was lost. But on the 14th day of this instant [May, 1688], the now propriators met to-gether, whose names are as followeth: Samuell Seabury in the Right of Francis West: Edward Southworth in the right of Edmund Weston: Samuell West in the right of William Clarke: Jonathan Alden in the right of Joseph Alden: John Soule in the Right of Zechariah Soule: Joseph Howland in the right of John Soule: And on the said fourteenth day renewed the bounds of s^d medow: which s^d bounds are as followeth;" [here follow the bounds, which are not of enough interest to be inserted here.] In this record there is mention made of a place on the beach " where the *Saltpan* stood," hence it is inferred that salt was once made here, and that works for its production were erected. Also the "crike that makes the Gurnit Island" is named. The Gurnet creek dividing into two channels at its mouth, forms an island of marsh.

BLUE-FISH-RIVER. This stream rises in the eastern part of the town, and flowing north through the meadows, in the form of a brook, it widens and makes what is now called the millpond, and then, contracting itself, it runs into the bay, on the southerly side of Powder point.

It received its name in the earliest infancy of the settlement from the number of blue-fish, which frequented the waters in that vicinity. This fish, known to naturalists by the name of the *temnodon saltator*, is of a species allied to the mackerel; but larger and of a strong and vigorous frame. It was a common fish on the shores of New England; but entirely disappeared from the coast about the year 1763;* but has within a few years reappeared. The bay, which in years past has been in the proper season abundantly supplied with mackerel, which were caught in great numbers, on the appearance of this fish two or three years ago, was wholly left by them; nor have they since appeared there. The fish is of a delicious flavor, and those which have been caught have found a ready market.

Josselyn, an early voyager in thesep arts, thus describes the mode of taking these fish by the natives: "The Bass and Blew fish they take in harbours, and at the mouth of barr'd Rivers, being in their canows, striking them with a fisgig, a kind of dart or staff, to the lower end whereof they fasten a sharp jagged bone (since they make them of iron), with a string fastened to it: as soon as the fish is struck they pull away the staff, leaving the bony head in the fishes body, and fasten the other end of the string to the canow. Thus they will hale after them to shore half a dozen or half a score great fishes."

INDIAN HEAD RIVER was anciently within the bounds of Duxbury, and near it many of the first settlers had extensive grants of land. It is the outlet of Indian head pond, and flowing north empties into the North River, near the angle of the bounds of Hanover, Hanson and Pembroke.

JONES RIVER, which now forms the bounds between Duxbury and Kingston during the last part of its course, received its name from the Captain of the Mayflower. It rises in Jones River Pond in Kingston, and flowing easterly a short distance, it turns to the south, and afterwards to the east, and running throughout the greatest part of its course in that direction, it turns again to the north, and then to the southeast, and finally flows in a northerly direction into the bay.

SOUTH RIVER rises in little Island Creek pond in Duxbury, in the south central part, and, flowing north through Cranberry pond in Duxbury, it afterwards changes its course to northeast through Marshfield, and runs into Massachusetts Bay. *Holly swamp* is mentioned as early as 1638, as the source of the South river; and a large rock is mentioned as being near it and called *Otter rock*.

* This date is given by Bradford, in the New England Chronology. Another species of fish of this name is found on the shores of Cuba, and about the Bahama islands.

ISLAND CREEK. This creek, taking its rise in Island Creek pond, flows in a southerly direction into the bay in the south part of the town, forming in its course, by widening, two smaller ponds, at one of which is now the tack factory of Mr. Samuel Loring.

HERRING BROOK, so called early, rises in Furness pond in Pembroke, and first flows east and then north into the North river.

TUSSOCKS BROOK. In 1714 mention is made of "a creek that leads up to ye place called ye Tussocks." The word tussock or tussuck, now obsolete in English writing, signified a tuft of grass or twigs, which was probably the characteristic herbage of "*ye Tussocks*." The creek, now called as above, rises on the southern borders of Duxbury, and flowing southeast, runs into Stoney brook (which empties into Jones River), forming in its course the bounds, in part, between Duxbury and Kingston.

MILE BROOK rises on the southern edge of Duxbury, and flows southerly into Blackwater pond in Kingston.

PINE BROOK rises in Pembroke, and flowing south forms the southeastern bounds between Duxbury and Pembroke, and running through the northern part of Kingston, empties into Jones River, opposite to Jones River creek.

STONEY BROOK. There were anciently two brooks of this name, one in the northern part of the town (which flowed into Duck hill river, and after the erection of a mill there in 1640, was called *Mill brook*, and is now so called); and the other in the southern part, on the borders of Kingston, and flowed into Jones River.

PHILLIPS BROOK. Vide *Mills*.

BLACK FRIER BROOK. Vide *Mills*.

HOUNDS-DITCH. This brook, which rises in the vicinity of North hill, flows into the Mill pond. It passed through the farm of the pilgrim, John Alden, and is supposed to have been named from some similar stream in the old country.

DUCK HILL RIVER. This is a name given to a stream, which meanders through the marshes in the northeastern part of the town, forming several islands, and flowing by the north of Powder point into the bay.

PINE POINT RIVER flows through the marshes in the northeast of the town, and empties into the bay to the eastward of Pine point.

CUT RIVER. This river, flowing through the lowlands in Marshfield, originally emptied into the ocean, to the north of Rouse's Hummock; but about forty years ago, during a very severe northeast storm, its mouth was barred up by the accumulation of sand, which was soon increased, and in a short time scarcely a vestige of its previous condition remained.

The river now turned its channel through a canal, which had been dug connecting the Cut with the Pine point river, to accommodate sportsmen, and save them the trouble of proceeding around the Gurnet. A few years after it broke out with a new channel, which run out near Branches Island. This last occurred in the fall of 1810, and, in a few days after the water was first discovered oozing through the bank, the channel was sufficiently deep for all purposes for which the former mouth had been used.

The project of cutting the canal, above named, when first proposed, was considerably opposed, and an attempt was made on the part of some persons to fill it up in the night. A bridge was soon after built over it, connecting the beach with the main.

EAGLE NEST. A point and creek of this name are at the "Nook," and were called so by the earliest settlers. In 1639 a wear was ordered to be placed here.

BEAVER POND is mentioned, 1638, as being near the South river.

FRESH LAKE is mentioned, 1638, as being in Duxbury.

JONES RIVER POND is the source of Jones river. It is a large and beautiful sheet of water, and is now included within the bounds of Pembroke, Kingston, and Plympton. It is now named *Silver Lake*, and furnishes a large quantity of ice, which is conveyed in the summer season over a branch road to the Old Colony Railroad, and thence to Boston market.

FURNESS POND in Pembroke.

HOBOMOK * POND in Pembroke.

---

* *Hobomok.* This friend of the English early adopted the Christian religion, and became an inmate of Captain Standish's family, whom he was accustomed to accompany on his expeditions, as a guide and interpreter, and was often of great service to the English, with whom he continued until his death in perfect friendship. It is said that he was a notable *pinese* or chief counsellor of Massasoit; yet he preferred to remain true to the interests of the English, rather than live in the perfect enjoyment of those honors which his high rank in the councils of his nation would secure to him. His attachment to the English was ever manifested, and in all the secret plots of the Indians, he was their steadfast friend and adviser. It is said of him, that during the severe drought in 1623, (which lasted from the third week in May to the middle of July, whereby the English were in great danger of famine on account of the destruction of their crops,) when visited by Mr. Alden, he broke out in language like this: "I am much troubled for the English, for I am afraid they will lose all their corn by the drought, and so they will be all starved; as for the Indians, they can shift better than the English, for they can get fish to help themselves." But when afterwards he met him, after their supplications for rain had been answered by Divine Providence, he said: "Now I see Englishman's God is a good God, for he hath heard you and sent you rain, and that without storms and tempests and thunders, which usually we have with our rain, which breaks down our corn, but yours stands whole and good still; surely your God is a good God." He died in 1642, having served the Colonists for nearly twenty years faithfully and cheerfully.

GREAT SANDY BOTTOM POND }
LITTLE SANDY BOTTOM. POND } in Pembroke.
STETSON POND in the southern part of Pembroke.
OLDHAM POND in Pembroke and Hanson.
MAQUAND POND in Hanson.
INDIAN HEAD POND in Hanson, bordering on Pembroke.

Note. The last nine ponds, though not within the present bounds of Duxbury, were anciently included in its limits.

ISLAND CREEK POND. This fine sheet is the head waters of Island Creek, and is situated in the east central part of the town.

LITTLE ISLAND CREEK POND is the source of the South river, and is situated a short distance northwest of Island Creek pond, and is sometimes called *Round pond.*

CRANBERRY POND. See South river.

MERRICK'S, HAMAR, SOULE'S, BRANT, SKIRT and LONG ISLANDS are in the northeast part of the town, and are composed of salt meadows.

GREAT WOOD ISLAND, mentioned 1637.

POWDER POINT. The first mention I find of this point is in the Col. Rec. 1636 :

"Richard Beare, Maurice [Truant?], George Partridge, John Vobes, & Will Merick were appointed to have five acres of land for each pson together next to the Glade on Powder point." 1637: The Stoney marsh at Powder point is mentioned, and also the "iland and the glade at Pouder poynt."

LONG POINT. This neck of marshy land, extending into the bay, was so called before 1638.

PINE POINT, early so called, extends into the bay in the northern part, between Pine point river and a creek which runs through the marshes to the westward of it.

MUSQUITO HOLE, mentioned 1639.

MORTON'S HOLE was so called as early as 1635, or before. A wear was placed here in 1639. Vide *Settlement.* This place, now so called, is situated to the westward of Captain's Hill, and its vicinity was thought of, as a fit place for uniting the towns of Plymouth and Duxbury in 1636, and building a new town.

CEDAR SWAMP. This swamp was in what was called the "Major's Purchase, near Mattakesett ponds, allias Namasakesett." The ponds thus named are that collection which now are within the bounds of Pembroke and Hanson. The swamp was (14 Oct. 1672) divided into seven lots, of five shares each, which were distributed to proprietors thus :

I. Tho. Prence, Maj. Winslow, Capt. Bradford, Lt. White and Benj. Church.

II. Geo. Partridge, Philip Delano, Mr. Alden, John Soule and Francis West.

III. John Turner, Benj. Bartlett, Francis Walker, Francis Cook and Tho. Dogged.

IV. Nathl. Warren, John Nelson, the Minister, Wm. Pontus and Edward Bumpus.

V. Saml. Fuller, Isaac Howland, Stephen Bryant, Mistress Sarah Warren and Saml. Eedy.

VI. Edward Gray (3 shares), Francis Billington and Andrew Ring.

VII. Capt. Fuller, John Thompson, William Nelson, Isaac Howland and Thomas Burman.

TOWN'S COMMONS.

GRANTS of land were early made to the several towns of the colony, by the Court, to be reserved for their benefit, and were called the "Town's commons." Portions of these were sold at different times by the towns for raising revenues to meet the towns' expenses; while other parts were let out to individuals, also as a means of revenue; and grants made by the towns of other parts, and some remained perfectly free.

1640: The Court ordered a tract of land, on the Duxbury side, extending from Blackwater brook, and thence along back of Island creek pond to "houndsdich," to be reserved for the Town's commons, "to depasture their cattell upon."

1644: The Town requested a grant of land, twelve square miles, in the woods at Jones River.

1661: Granted to the towns of Duxbury and Marshfield, a tract of land lying between Jones River and Indian head river.

1686, *July* 18: "The common medow continewing free from hire & lying free for anny of Duxbury to cute, are Mericks Island, Hamar Island, Soule's Island, Brant Island, Skirt Island, Long Island, & the lower point of Wood neck."

"The town have let out the comon medows for 6*d*. a load, excepting the Islands before mentioned, which are free. The Town have agreed that no man shall cut anny Grase at the comon medows, untill the last Munday in August, 1686, & untill the sun Rise upon that day, and in case anny man cut anny before that time, then he shall forfeit 5 Shillings per load unto the Town's use, unless it be upon the Islands before excepted."—T. Rec'ds.

1687. The common meadows between Gotum and Cut rivers, was leased for seven years, at 13s. per annum (August 12) to John Thomas and Peter West, and (Mar. 14, 1694,) was continued to Peter West and Samuel Delano for seven years longer.

1690. These hired common meadows of the town:

John Thomas, Peter West,	13£.	Francis West, Widow Clarke,	5 £.
John Dillano, John Simmons,	7 £.	Joseph Prior, Samuel Hunt, Philip Delanoy,	4 £.
David Alden, Triphosa West, Lt. Arnold,	8 £.	Samuel Bartlett, Samuel Howland, Joshua Chandler, John Weston, Benjamin Bartlett, John Peterson,	10 £.
Thomas Dillano, Roger Glace, Nathl. Cole, John Michel, Thomas Boney, Jr., Caleb Sampson,	12 £.		
		Abram Sampson, Sen., Abram Sampson, Jr.,	6 £.
Mr. Allix Standish, 1£. 6d.			

"David Alden has paid all his rent for ye common medows."

1698, *May* 28: A tract of land lying between the bounds of Plymouth and Duxbury, and held in common by the towns of Duxbury and Marshfield, was divided between these two towns by John Soule, Isaac Little, Seth Arnold, Samuel Sprague and Robert Barker.

1699, *March* 7: Town chose Abraham Sampson, Benony Delano and Samuel Sprague, "either to act on ye former act made to prevent ye cutting and carrying away coarde wood or any other timber out ye towne, or to make and prosecute such acts as they shall se cause to prevent ye carrying away such timber; ye towne voating to stand by them in ye prosecution of ye same."

June 15: Town ordered a fine to be imposed on those who should cut timber on the commons, unless they carry it to the saw-mills; and further that no wood shall be cut to be carried from the town.

July 17: Appointed Francis Barker, Robert Barker, Joseph Rogers, John Boney, James Bishop and Isaac Barker a committee to prevent the cutting and the carrying off the timber from the town's commons.

1703: Measures were about to be taken by the town for a division of the commons; but was deferred on the remonstrance of the following, May 17th:

Edward Southworth,
Thomas Delano, Sen.,
Philip Leonard,
John Delano,
Stephen Samson,
Caleb Samson,

John Simons,
Elnathan Weston,
Philip Delano, Sen.,
Thomas Boney,
Peter West,
John Glasse,

PROPRIETORS OF COMMONS.

Joseph Chanler, Sen.,
Edmund Chanler,
Nathaniel Cole,
John Weston,
Benj. Delanoe,
Abraham Sampson,
Philip Lathley,
Samuel Hill,
Thomas Fish,
Thomas Southworth,
Samuel Delano,
Josiah Wormwoal,
William Tubbs,
Jonathan Delano,
Joshua Turner,
John Bishop,
Benj. Prior,
Isaac Oldham,
Isaac Peirce, Sen.,
Thomas Delanoe.

1707, *Sept.* 12. Voted to every freeholder and housekeeper twenty acres of the commons, and to those, who had had previous grants, enough more to make up the said twenty acres; and, *June* 5, 1710, it was divided among the freeholders of the town, as follows :†

Robert Barker, Sen.,
Robert Barker, Jr.,
Francis Barker, Lt.,
Isaac Barker,
Francis Barker, Jr.,
Josiah Barker,
Thomas Barker,
Elisha Barker,
James Barker,
Samuel Barker,
Jabez Barker, ... 11
*Philip Delano, deceased,
Philip Delano,
Samuel Delano,
Samuel Delano, 2d.,
Samuel Delano, 3d.,
Jonathan Delano,
Dr. Thomas Delano,
Benony Delano,
Joseph Delano,
John Delano,
Thomas Delano, Jr., . . . 11
Abraham Sampson, Sen.,
Abraham Sampson, Jr.,
Stephen Sampson,
Benjamin Sampson,
John Sampson,
Caleb Sampson,
Ichabod Sampson,
Nathl. Sampson,
David Sampson, ... 9
Benjamin Bartlett, Sen.,
Benj. Bartlett, Jr.,
Ichabod Bartlett,
William Bartlett,
Samuel Bartlett,
Joseph Bartlett,
*Ebenezer Bartlett, ... 7
John Simonson, Sen.,
John Simonson, Jr.,
John Simonson, 3d.,
Benj. Simonson,
Isaac Simonson,
Joseph Simonson,
Joshua Simonson, ... 7
Edmund Chanler,
Samuel Chanler,
John Chanler,
Benj. Chanler,
Joseph Chanler, Sen.,
Joseph Chanler, Jr., ... 6
Abraham Peirce, Sen.,
Abraham Peirce, Jr.,
John Peirce,
Samuel Peirce,
Isaac Peirce,
Thomas Peirce, ... 6
*Mr. John Wadsworth,
Christopher Wadsworth,
Elisha Wadsworth,
Ichabod Wadsworth,
John Wadsworth,
*Joseph Wadsworth, ... 6
William Brewster, Sen.,
William Brewster, Jr.,
Benj. Brewster,
Nathl. Brewster,
Jonathan Brewster, ... 5
Mr. David Alden,
John Alden,
Jonathan Alden,
Benj. Alden,
Samuel Alden, ... 5
Thomas Boney,

† This division was made by F. Barker, S. Bradford, and S. Seabury.

PROPRIETORS OF COMMONS.

Joseph Boney,
Ebenezer Boney,
John Boney,
James Boney, ... 5
Josiah Kein, Sen.,
Josiah Kein, Jr.,
John Kein,
Benj. Kein,
Matthew Kein, ... 5
Benj. Peterson,
John Peterson,
Jonathan Peterson,
Joseph Peterson,
Isaac Peterson, ... 5
Joseph Soule,
Moses Soule,
Joshua Soule,
Aaron Soule,
Josiah Soule, ... 5
Mr. Edw. Southworth,
Constant Southworth,
Benj. Southworth,
John Southworth,
Thomas Southworth, . . . 5
James Bishop,
John Bishop,
Hutson Bishop,
Ebenezer Bishop, ... 4
Samuel Sprague, Sen.,
**Samuel Sprague, Lt.,
**John Sprague,
William Sprague, ... 4
Edward Arnold,
Capt. Seth Arnold,
Benj. Arnold, ... 3
Nathl. Cole, Sen., .
Nathl. Cole, Jr.,
Ephraim Cole, ... 3
Josiah Holmes,
John Holmes,
William Holmes, ... 3
Joseph Rogers,
Timothy Rogers,
Francis Rogers, ... 3
William Tubbs, Sen.,
Joseph Tubbs,
Samuel Tubbs, ... 3
Elnathan Weston,
Samuel Weston,
John Weston, ... 3
Josiah Wormall, Sen.,
Josiah Wormall, Jr.,
Ebenezer Wormall, ... 3
Thomas Hunt,
*Samuel Hunt, dec'd. . . . 2
James Partridge,
John Partridge, ... 2
Isaac Stetson,
Timothy Stetson, ... 2
Caleb Thomas,
James Thomas, ... 2
Samuel West,
Pelatiah West, ... 2
Abraham Booth,
Mr. Samuel Bradford, Lt.,
Lambert Despar,
Nathl. Chamberland,
Thomas Fish,
Samuel Fisher,
John Glass,
Samuel Hill,
Widow Hutson,
Thomas Lambert, Jr.,
Mr. Thomas Loring, Ens.,
Elias Magoon,
John Magvarland,
Joseph Michell,
Isaac Oldham,
Thomas Parris,
Benj. Prior,
Nehemiah Randall,
Mr. John Robinson,
John Saunders,
Mr. Samuel Seabury,
Israel Silvester,
Miles Standish,
Robert Stanford,
Joseph Stockbridge,
Japheth Turner,
George Williamson,
Mr. Peleg Wiswall,
John Russell. . 29 of one each.

Note. Those marked with a ** should be read :—" The proprietors of the farm that [the name] lives on." Those marked with a single * to read " The proprietors of the farm of [the name]."

In has been deemed proper and desirable to insert several lists of a similar character to the foregoing, which, on account of their genealogical importance, ought to be preserved. Nor are they entirely devoid of a general interest, for they serve to show us the ratio which one family bore to another in regard to their numbers at that time. Of the 166 persons abovenamed, there are 58 family names; and of the Barker family, which was then, it will be seen, one of the most numerous in the town, there is now scarcely a representative, and the same can be said of other families mentioned in the list.

1710. *January* 30: Voted, that every proprietor of a lot, with a dwelling thereon, if he had been a townsman ten years, should have 40 acres allotted to him; and those, who have had previous grants, to have enough more to make up the 40 acres. Elnathan Weston, Joseph Peterson, Samuel Chandler, John Simmons, Sen., Stephen Sampson, Joseph Chandler, Sen. and Edmund Chandler petitioned against it. At an adjourned meeting, on *February 1st*, Lt. Samuel Bradford, John Partridge and Joseph Stockbridge were appointed to procure a surveyor to lay it out. At the same meeting a petition was presented from the young men, asking one half a share in the intended division; which was granted to them, notwithstanding the remonstrance of Israel Silvester, Benj. Chandler, Caleb Thomas, Aaron Soule and Thomas Fish, and of Mr. Loring and Benony Delano, who were opposed to the division at all. These commons (salt meadows *) were divided into 33 lots of five shares each, and not until *June* 16, 1712, were they distributed by lot to the proprietors, who were as follows: —

Delano, Samuel, Sen.,	Sampson, Caleb,
" Samuel, 2d.,	" David, ... 8
" Samuel, 3d.,	Simmons, John, Sen.,
* " Philip,	" John, Jr.,
" John,	" Benj.,
" Benoni,	" Joseph,
" Thomas, Sen.,	" Joshua,
" Thomas, Jr.,	" John, deceased,
" Jonathan,	" Benj., ... 7
" Joseph,	*Bartlett, Ebenezer,
" Philip, ... 11	" Benj. Sen.,
Barker, Thomas,	" Benj. Jr.,
" James,	" William,
" Elisha, deceased,	" Samuel,
" Josiah,	" Joseph, ... 6
" Lt. Francis,	Chandler, Samuel,
" Francis, Jr.,	" Edmund,
" Isaac,	" Joseph, Sen.,
" Samuel,	" Joseph, Jr.,
" Robert, ... 9	" John,
Sampson, Stephen,	" Benj., ... 6
" Benj.,	Peirce, Samuel,
" John,	" Abraham, Sen.,
" Nathl.,	" Abraham, Jr.,
" Ichabod,	" Isaac,
" Abraham,	" John,

* This vote was passed at a town meeting, May 16th, 1711: "That all their salt marsh, common meadows, with all their salt and sedge islands and sedge flats that are above the Cove of the beach, so called, should next be laid out."

Peirce, Thomas, ... 6
Wadsworth, Elisha,
* " Joseph, deceased,
" Christopher,
* " John, deceased,
" John,
" Ichabod, ... 6
Alden, David,
" Benj.,
" Samuel,
" John,
" Jonathan, ... 5
Boney, John,
" Joseph,
" James,
" Thomas,
" Ebenezer, ... 5
Brewster, William, Sen.,
" William, Jr.,
" Nathl.,
" Benj.,
" John, ... 5
Kein, Josiah, Sen.,
" Josiah, Jr.,
" Matthew,
" John,
" Benjamin, ... 5
Peterson, John,
" Joseph,
" Benjamin,
" Jonathan,
" Isaac, ... 5
Soule, Josiah,
" Aaron,
" Joshua,
" Moses,
" Joseph, ... 5
Southworth, Edward,
" Thomas,
" Constant,
" Benjamin,
" John, ... 5
Bishop, James,
" Ebenezer,
" Hutson,
" John, ... 4
Arnold, Capt. Seth,
" Edward,
" Benjamin, ... 3
Cole, Nathaniel, Sen.,
" Nathaniel, Jr.,
" Ephraim, ... 3
Holmes, Josiah,
" John,
" William, ... 3

Thomas, Samuel,
" Caleb,
" James, ... 3
Sprague, William,
" Lt. Samuel,
" John, ... 3
Weston, Elnathan,
" John,
" Samuel, ... 3
Wormall, Josiah, Sen.,
" Josiah, Jr.,
" Ebenezer, ... 3
Rogers, Timothy,
" Joseph,
" Francis, ... 3
Hunt, Thomas,
* " Samuel, ... 2
Hutson, Widow,
" Anne, ... 2
Partridge, James,
" John, ... 2
Magoon, James,
" Elias, ... 2
Stetson, Timothy,
" Isaac, ... 2
Tubbs, Samuel,
" Joseph, ... 2
West, Samuel,
" Pelatiah, ... 2
*Wiswall, Ichabod, [dec'd ?]
" Peleg, ... 2
Booth, Abraham,
Bradford, Lt. Samuel,
*Clark, Henry,
Despar, Lambert,
Fish, Thomas,
Fisher, Samuel,
Glass, John,
Hill, Samuel,
Howland, Thomas,
Loring, Thomas,
Magvarland, John,
Oldham, Isaac,
Parris, Thomas,
Prior, Benjamin,
Randall, Nehemiah,
Robinson, John,
Russell, John,
Saunders, John,
Seabury, Samuel,
Silvester, Israel,
Standish, Miles,
Stanford, Robert,
Stockbridge, Joseph,
Williamson, George. . . . 24

Note. Of the 165 persons above named, there are 56 family names. Those marked *, to be read, " the proprietors of the farm of [the name]."

TOWN'S COMMONS.

1712, *Oct.* 6: Town appointed Capt. John Alden, Joseph Stockbridge and John Partridge to assist the surveyors in laying out these lands. Capt. Alden refusing to serve, Capt. Thomas Barker was chosen in his stead.

1713, *Dec.* 11: Lots were drawn in the last division " of upland and swampy" lands in Duxbury and Pembroke, (excepting the Cedar swamps), by 152 proprietors. The Cedar swamps were divided into 34 lots in June, 1714.

1747, *Sept.* 28: At a meeting of the proprietors of Duxbury and Pembroke, of the second division, Edward Arnold, Esq., Capt. Nehemiah Cushing and Joshua Soule were authorized to receive the claims of those who had not had any grants, and make report; which they did Nov. 30. This said meeting adjourned to the 2d Monday in March, when they chose Daniel Lewis, Esq., Mr. Samuel Seabury and Mr. Samuel Weston to take the claims of persons in the Salt meadows, and to see who were qualified to vote at the proprietors' meetings.

1748, *May* 10. The said committee brought in a list, which was recorded.* They then voted to divide the common mea-

---

* The list was as follows:
"John Wadsworth, (4 rights),
Joshua Soul, (12 rts.),
Elisha Wadsworth,
Thomas Boney,*
Joseph Delanoe,
Thomas Loring, dec'd,* (2 rts.),
Gamaliel Bradford, Esq.,
Joseph Freeman,
James Partridge,
Mr. Samuel Seabury,
Christopher Wadsworth, (2 rts.),
Benj. Wadsworth,
Eben'r Samson,
Abraham Samson, (2 rts.),
Benj. Bartlit, (dec'd),*
Wm. Bartlit's (dec'd) heirs,
Philip Delano, (2 rts.),
Thomas Hunt, (1½ rts.),
Thomas Delano, Jr.'s (dec'd) heirs,
Benj. Peterson,
Benj. Prior,
Mr. Peleg Wiswall,
Thomas Prince,
Miles Standish,
Joseph & Joshua Brewster,
William Brewster,
Israel Silvester,
Robert Stanford, (2 rts.),
John Sampson, (3 rts.),
Samuel Sprague,
John Sprague, } (1 rt.),
Abijah Sprague, }
Jonathan Delanoe,
Nathl. Samson,
Josiah Soul,
John Peterson's heirs,
Isaac Peterson's heirs,
Joseph Soul,
Samuel Delanoe's heirs,
Samuel Alden, Jr.,
Jonathan Alden,
Thomas Southworth's heirs,
Joshua Delanoe,
John Southworth, (2 rts.),
Wm. Southworth,
Benj. Southworth,
Moses Simmons,
John Simmons, Jr.'s heirs,
Benj. Simmons,
Isaac Simmons,
Joseph Simmons,
Joshua Simmons,
Samuel Baker,
Samuel Chanler's heirs,
John Chanler,
Benj. Chanler, (2½ rts.),
Joseph Chanler, Sen.'s heirs,
Capt. John Chanler,
Joseph Chanler, Jr.'s heirs,
James Glass,
Moses Soul,
Benj. Alden's heirs, (2 rts.),
Samuel Alden,
Nathl. Brewster,
Nathaniel Cole, Sen.'s, heirs,

dow in this manner, — to divide the 168 shares into three portions, and that some indifferent person should draw lots for each portion; and the same committee, last named, were chosen to perform this division.

1749. Difficulties afterwards arose between the town and the above named proprietors, and at a meeting of the town, June 19, they voted that they would not leave the contentions to be settled by referees. The proprietors then, through their agent, Mr. Joshua Soule, commenced an action before the Court for "trespass and ejectment" in the town's mowing the salt meadows. The action was not brought on at this time; but in January 1750, Mr. Soule was again chosen with full power to sue the town for the damage done them at Rouse's point, to the amount of £200. A summons was soon after served upon the town, by the proper officer, to appear before the In-

---

Jabez Cole,
Ephraim Cole,
Isaac Partridge,
Samuel Weston, (2 rts.),
Samuel Delano, ye 3d's heirs,
Ebenr. Fish,
Caleb Samson,
David Samson,
James Thomas,
Samuel West,
Palitiah West,
Henry Clark, (dec'd),*
John Weston's heirs,
Joseph Boney's heirs,
Josiah Wormal, Jr.'s heirs,
Edward Arnold, Esq., (4 rts.),
James Arnold,
Benj. Prior, Jr.,
Geo. Partridge,
Ebenr. Bartlit,
Joseph Bartlit,
Joseph Stockbridge,
Lt. Francis Barker,*
Josiah Barker's heirs,
Elisha Barker's heirs,
John Boney's heirs,
Timothy Rogers' heirs,
Timothy Stetson,
Morris and Jacob Tubbs, for Joseph Tubbs' right,
Joseph Rogers,*
John Bushop,
James Bishop,*
Nehemiah Randall,
Thomas Lambert, Jr.'s heirs,
Samued Jacobs for Saml. Barker's right,

Hudson Bishop,
Isaac Oldham,
John Russell,
John Mackverland,
Josiah Kein's heirs,
Isaac Kein for Josiah Kein, Jr.'s heirs,
Matthew Kein's heirs,
Benj. Kein's heirs,
Lambert Despar's heirs or assigns,
John Saunders's heirs,
Francis Rogers' heirs,
James Magoon,*
Nathl. Chamberland's heirs,
William Tubbs, Sen.'s, heirs,
Isaac Barker, (2 rts.),
That was Abraham Booth's,*
Josiah for John Kein's right,
Isaac Stetson,
Isaac Tubbs for Tho. Parris' right,
Henry Joseling for James Boney,
Tho. Burton for Abra. Peirce, Jr.,
Isaac Crooker for Isaac Parris,
Thomas Peirce,
Aaron Soul, Jr., (3 rts.),
Isaac Hatch for Josiah Holmes,
David for Elias Magoon,
Robert Barker, Jr.,*
Beriah for Dr. Thomas Delanoe,
Benoni Delanoe,
Eph. Norcut & wife and Mercy Curtis for Ebenr. Boney,
Eben. Wormal's heirs,
Benj. Brewster,
Benj. Bartlett, Jr.'s heirs."

Note. Those marked [*] to be read "the proprietors of the farm of —."

ferior Court at Plymouth in May. This action was continued, though not completed by Mr. Soule, until April 20th, 1752, when the proprietors transferred the power granted him to Messrs. John Sampson and Briggs Alden. The decision of the Court was not however in their favor; but recovered damages from them for the town in the sum of £1. 9. 6. On account of the refusal of the proprietors to remunerate Mr. Soule for his trouble in the prosecution of the above named case, another action was commenced against them at the Plymouth Court; whereupon the Proprietors met and chose an agent to meet the said Soule at Court.

MILLS, DAMS, ETC.

GRIST MILL. 1639 : Previous to this date, the town's people had been obliged to procure their grist from Plymouth, which was very inconvenient, and now began to be much in want of one of their own. Having found two individuals, *Thomas Hilier* and *George Pollard*, who would agree to erect it and sustain it on the following conditions, the town also agreed to be bound to the contract on their part, for securing to them certain privileges. At a meeting of the town, Nov. 7th, Hilier and Pollard agreed " at their owne pper cost and charges to build, frame and set up one sufficient water milne to grind corne on both English and Indian, within the terme of one whole yeare next after the date hereof. As also Stampers to beate Indian corne at, as speedyly as possibly they cann, and to build the said milne and Stampers upon a certaine brooke comonly called or knowne by the name of Stony Brooke." (This brook was afterwards called Mill brook.) The town then agreed : —

I. To allow no other mill to be erected in the town, until they shall not be able to supply the town's wants.

II. To exert their influence in procuring for them the commons, next north of the brook.

II. To allow them £6 pounds to purchase the adjoining lands of John Irish and Henry Wallis.

IV. To grant them other lands, and to permit them to charge a "pottle of corne for grinding every bushell," and to allow them to hold it, themselves and their heirs, forever.

This was signed by William Collier, Jonathan Brewster,

Christopher Wadsworth and Myles Standish in behalf of the town.

1640: They petitioned the Colony Court for liberty to place a mill here, &c., whereupon Mr. Collier, Capt. Standish, Mr. Alden, Mr. Brown, Mr. Winslow and Jonathan Brewster were appointed "to take view of the water course, that should be turned to the milne and make report of it, how prjudiciall it may bee." The above committee soon after reported, "that the same will not be any way prejudiciall to any man;" and then the Court granted unto said Hilier and Pollard, that they "shall have liberty to turne that part of the said streame so viewed into the said milne." At a later period the mill came into the hands of Constant Southworth. In 1746 John Southworth owned it, when he shared it with Dr. Harlow, George Partridge and Joshua Delano.

1767. Liberty was given to Joseph Drew to build a grist mill on Bluefish river.

SAW MILLS. 1701: "Capt. Seth Arnold with some other partner or partners, whom he may take into partnership with him, having an intention to build a Saw-mill on Green's harbour brook, ye said Town did by vote, give free liberty to ye inhabitants of ye said town of Duxborough to cutt and carry off any timber from ye comons of ye said town to ye said saw mill, to keep ye said mill in Imployment."

The only saw mill in the colony for forty years after the settlement at Plymouth, was within the present limits of Pembroke, then Duxbury.

1742. Reuben Peterson owned a saw-mill on Phillip's brook; but the stream being small, he made an agreement (1770, Nov. 23) with Consider Simmons, so that, for 12s. yearly, he might have the stream of the Black-Frier-brook by a ditch, where it runs through the said Simmons' land.

DAMS. 1693, *May* 10: Liberty was given to Robert Barker to build a dam on Pudding brook at the Beaver dam.

1702, *June* 15. Town gave liberty to Ensign Saml. Seabury to make a dam "upon Island creek pond brook, provided that he leaves a sufficient and free passage for ye herrings up and down, and also makes a sufficient cartway over ye said brook."

BOUNTIES, FINES, ETC.

1655: A bounty was early offered by the Colony Court for every wolf and other wild animal, that should be killed; and in the records frequent mention is made of various wolf-traps belonging to the settlers;* and a report of the number of wolves killed was generally made to the Court. This year there was reported one wolf which was killed in Duxbury by an Indian.

1661: The Court ordered that there should be given to every Indian, who should kill a wolf, one half a pound of powder and two pounds of shot or lead.

These animals were sometimes killed near the thickest settled parts of the town, though they generally frequented the woods in the western part in the greatest numbers; and it was not without some difficulty that one of them could be slain; yet they were not unfrequently taken in traps. In 1686, in the town's book of expenses, we find this, — "For a wolfe to an Indian, 7s. 6d.," and many other records of a similar character.

1693: *May* 10. Ordered by the town that "every householder shall kill one crow and six blackbirhds, or twelve blackbirds. Such as kill no crow, between May 1 and July 1 must pay 1s. for Town's use."

1731, *March* 1: "Voted that there should be payd out of ye sd Town's Treasury Twenty Shillings for every wild cat, that may be killed within this town, by any of ye inhabitants thereof, to ye persons that may kill them, viz., Twenty Shillings above what is allowed for killing wild cats of ye province Treasury."

1737, *March* 14: The Town ordered that to any person, who should kill a crow, six pence should be given; and for a crow-bill black bird three pence; and for a bluebird, "of that kind, which usually destroys indian corn," three pence.

1758. *Herring Fishing.* The Town voted "that no herrings shall be caught upon Saturday or the Sabbath day during the present year; nor between sunset and sunrise on other days," and Joseph Russell was appointed to see it obeyed.

1770, *March.* Town voted that herrings may be caught on Saturdays and Mondays between sunrise and sunset.

---

* Collier's "woolftrap" is mentioned as early as 1638; also Dingley's and others.

ORDINARIES.

These puritan taverns could not be kept, according to law, without a license by an express order of the Court. And it has been said, that it was only to the grave and sober that this license was given, and upon them it was enjoined that perfect quiet should be required in their apartments, and that care should be taken that none " drink over much." The rigid justice of the magistrates did not overlook the slightest deviations from propriety, and the records of their proceedings bear ample testimony to the efficiency of their own labors, and those of their not less scrupulous constituents. None escaped the searchings of their suspicious eyes, and both the high and low, on their complaint, were forced to receive justice by the law, and have their names recorded, to be handed to posterity as memorials, perhaps, of their own folly, in that they behaved themselves "in a beastly manner," and acted "unseemly in the sight of God." Nor can the *searching eyes* into musty rolls of the present day complain of this, as regards their own desires, for many, and worthies too, but for their trifling imprudences, have not a record of their being, save in the chronicle of crimes. That men of the highest respectability were selected to retail the "strong water" was certainly the case ; for we find that in 1660, *Mr. Collier*, who was eminently distinguished in the public affairs of the colony, was licensed to sell the beverage to his neighbors in Duxbury; and it can be justly considered that one, who is well known to have been one of the wealthiest among them, would not have selected this as a means of gain, but rather at the instance of the magistrates, who well knew him to be a sober and discreet man, and one who would not be likely to suffer any transgression of their laws. *Constant Southworth*, who is likewise known to have been a man of the highest respectability, and one of the Deputies, was permitted, in 1648, to sell wine in Duxbury.

However, the *first Ordinary* in the town was kept by *Francis Sprague*, who, though he may have manifested an ardent temperament on some occasions,* yet it must be presumed he

---

* He had been previously fined to the amount of £20 for killing a mare of Thomas Hatherly on some provocation, and had recently been arraigned for beating Wm. Holloway, a servant of William Basset. We also find him a transgressor of that law, which the Colonists saw fit to enact for the more perfect security of their lives, that none should sell fire-arms to the Indians. Such Indians, however, as the magistrates knew to be well-disposed and sober, were permitted, by the express order of the Court, to purchase arms for themselves.

was of the sober class. His license was granted, Oct. 1, 1638, "to keepe a victualling on Duxburrow side," and was recalled by the Court in 1666, though for what reason is not stated. In the discharge of his duty, he did not always act in that strict conformity and exactness to the notions of the rulers, which would have removed his name from connections which, at this distant day, seem rather disreputable. He appears to have been somewhat independent in his feelings, and not entirely free from those charges, which in nowise became his situation; and in the same year that he received his license, he was fined to the amount of 40 shillings, for — what it was incumbent on him to admonish — "drinking overmuch." His license was once withdrawn for a short time in 1639; yet continuing "draweing and retayleing wine contrary to the expresse order of the Court," he was fined, and in 1641 was prohibited " to dray any wyne or strong water untill the next gen[er]all [Court], without speciall lycence." The latter part of his life, however, is marked by none of those misdeeds which we find in his earlier days. He was succeded by his son, *John Sprague*, who was licensed in October, 1669. He partook somewhat of the character of his father, and continued as keeper of the ordinary until his death, in 1676.

In 1671, the Court passed a law " for the prevention of great abuse by the excessive drinking of Liquors in ordinaryes," wherein it was required that every keeper should make, to the Court, a report of those, who " doe not attend order, but carry themselves uncivilily, by being importunately desiious of drink, when deneyed, and do not leave the house when required." Any disregard of this order would impose on the keeper a fine of £5. Mr. Samuel Seabury and Francis West were also appointed by the Court " to have inspection of the ordinaries and other suspected places" in Duxbury. This Court also settled the price of rum to be five shillings per gallon, or at retail two pence per gill.

The next license was granted to *Mr. Seabury*, in 1678, " to sell liquors unto such sober minded naighbours, as hee shall thinke meet, soe as hee sell not lesse then the quantie of a gallon att a time to one p'son, and not in smaller quantities by retaile to the occationing of drunkenes."

FIRST SETTLERS.

The first settlers of Duxbury were, many of them, of the highest respectability, and in the colony affairs took prominent and active parts. Of the twenty subscribers to the civil compact, signed in the cabin of the Mayflower, November, 1620, who survived the fatal first winter, these became at some future time inhabitants of Duxbury, — Elder Brewster, Capt. Standish, Mr. Alden, Mr. Howland, Francis Eaton, Peter Brown and George Soule. Most of these were men of high repute among the Pilgrims, and often elevated to the highest offices among them, and in their number appear the names, which we find, with so much honor to themselves, recorded in their civil and ecclesiastical history, and imprinted on their military annals with imperishable fame. The name of Brewster is a token of their purity and religion; and that of Standish a memento of their persevering endurance, their heroism, and their fortitude; while the names of Alden and of Howland have come down to us, as fit memorials of that never-varying justice which has so nobly characterized the lives of their rulers.

Brewster was the very soul of the colony. Striving with the holy design of meliorating the condition of his fellow-men, he voluntarily left the enticing allurements of a life at court, and preferred the enjoyment, with the people of God, of those dearest liberties — the freedom of conscience and the pure worship of their God in peace — even though in a wilderness it might be, to the magnificence and splendor of palaces, and the presence of their haughty inmates.

The accompanying cut is a fac-simile of the Elder's autograph, written somewhat late in life; and the original is believed to be the only signature of his to be found.

Willm Brewster

Standish affords us not only an instance of the nerve of the Pilgrims, but a type of their hearts. It is not only his indomitable spirit and unceasing exertions in the performance of every hazardous duty which was committed to him, but also his openness of heart, his frankness, and sincerity of purpose, which has gained for him that respect from posterity, which is due to the memory of one, whose life was spent in the service of those, who to him owed much for their existence, and for whose security he encountered all the hardships and dangers of a then unexplored region, faced in open conflict, or in the deadly ambush, the cruel attacks of the uncivilized savages, and forced them to a submission to laws of justice and necessity. Nor in the council were his services of scarce less importance; remaining in the office of an assistant, during the whole of his life, and treasurer of the Colony from 1644 to 1649, and once sent to England as their agent. A friend of the Indians in peace, but in war his very name was a terror; not on account of a wanton cruelty, for none have ever attempted to ascribe to him more than a perfect fulfilment of the commands which were given him. His profession was that of a soldier, which he had chosen not merely from inclination, but "being heir apparent to a large estate of lands and livings, surreptitiously detained from him," he was early forced to seek employment for a livelihood. Though of a small stature, "he had an active genius, a sanguine temper and a strong constitution;" and entering into the service of Queen Elizabeth, in aid of the Dutch, he soon proceeded to the Netherlands, the seat of the war, where, on the establishment of peace, he settled, and soon after joined the English refugees at Leyden. On their embarkation for America, he joined the first company, and soon after their arrival was chosen to the command of the first party sent on shore for discovery, consisting of sixteen men, and soon elected to the chief military command, an office of much responsibility. His courage was indisputable. In all his expeditions he wanted but a few men, and the choice of these he claimed for himself. He was always their leader in every hazardous undertaking, and the people, confiding in his bravery and prudence, were ever ready to place themselves under his command, and in the most trying conflicts felt themselves secure. His actions show a forbearance rarely met with in one of his profession; but in the time of decisive action, his courage and perseverance were equal to the boldest resolutions, ever formed upon the impulse of the mind. Perhaps on some occasions he may have shown some slight degree of passion; but then, says Hubbard, seemingly in his defence, "he had been bred a soldier in the Low Countries, and never entered into the school of Christ, or of John the Baptist; or if ever he was there, he had forgotten the first lessons, to offer violence to no man, and to part with the cloak rather than needlessly contend for the coat, though taken away without order. A little chimney is soon fired; so was the Plymouth captain, a man of very small stature, yet of a very hot and angry temper. The fire of his passion soon kindled, and blown up into a flame by hot words, might easily have consumed all, had it not been seasonably quenched."

The account, thus given by Hubbard, has been considered, and rightly too, as graphic, but flippant and unjust. Nor does Hubbard himself invariably give the same tone to his subject; but, evidently in a state of less excitement, he calls him "a gentleman very expert in military service, by whom the people were all willing to be ordered in those concerns. He was likewise (he continues) improved to good acceptance and success in affairs of the greatest moment in the colony; to whose interests he continued firm and steadfast to the last, and always managed his trust with great integrity and faithfulness." In 1623, Standish was sent by the governor, with orders to break up a plot of the Indians, which, it was learned, had been formed to destroy the settlement, and massacre the inhabitants of the English colony at Wessagusset, now Weymouth. On this expedition, the most celebrated one of his life, and which is possibly a fair criterion of his character, he chose but eight men, refusing any more. On arriving at the settlement he found the people scattered, and wholly unconscious of their impending danger. Having quickly assembled them, he informed them of their situation, not, however, without exciting the suspicions of the Indians. Soon after, an Indian bringing the Captain some furs, he treated him "smoothly;" yet the Indian reported, that he "saw by the Captain's eyes, that he was angry in his heart." And at another time, Pecksuot, an Indian warrior of reputed courage, said to Hobomok, Standish's guide and interpreter, and an inmate of his household, that "he understood that the Captain had come to kill him and the rest of the Indians there; but tell him (said he) we know it, but fear him not; neither will we shun him, let him begin when he dares; he shall not take us unawares." And again, a little after, in the presence of Standish, whetting his knife before his face, and boasting of its quality, he said to him — "Though you are a great Captain, yet you are but a little man; and though I be no sachem, yet I am a man of great strength and courage." On the following day, Pecksuot, Wittowamat, and his brother, a youth of eighteen, and another Indian, with Standish and about the same number of his own men, being in a room together, the signal was given by the Captain, and the door instantly closed and fastened. Then seizing Pecksuot, he snatched his knife from his belt, while his men fell upon the others. A short struggle ensued, which ended in the death of Pecksuot by Standish, and that of the other Indians, save the youth, whom they afterwards hung. Hobomok, who stood by, a silent spectator of all that passed, then smilingly exclaimed, — "Yesterday, Pecksuot bragged of his own strength and stature, and told you that though you were a great Captain, yet you were a little man; but to-day I see you are big enough to lay him on the ground."

When Robinson, their pastor at Leyden, heard of this encounter, he wrote to the Church of Plymouth, "to consider the disposition of their captain, who was of a warm temper. He hoped that the Lord had sent him among them for good, if they used him right; but he doubted whether there was not wanting that tenderness of the life of man, made after God's image, which was meet; and he thought it would have been happy if they had converted some before they had killed any." Truly are these words a monument to the character of Robinson, alike honorable and Christianlike. But consider the situation of Standish. Upon his decisive action at this moment, we cannot but feel that depended much, not merely the preservation of the company to whose succor he had come, but the existence, perhaps, of the whole colony. Had they been successful in their designs here, elated by their recent victory, they would have made the settlement of Plymouth the next object for their depredations, and the lives of the whole colony would have fallen victims to their cruel barbarity. This was not distant from the foresight of the Captain. He struck a mighty blow, and by determined action in a time of doubt, dispelled the fears of his followers and sent terror upon the enemy. His action needs no apology. He acted but the part of a brave defender of his country, who feels that upon his own vigorous exertions the defence of the people depends. And, says his biographer, men of his profession will admire his courage, his promptitude and decision in the execution of his orders. No one has ever charged him either with failures in point of obedience, or of wantonly exceeding the limits of his commission. He is called by Prince, one of those heroes of antiquity "who chose to suffer affliction with the people of God; who through faith subdued kingdoms, wrought righteousness, obtained promises, stopped the mouths of lions, waxed valiant in fight, and turned to flight the armies of the aliens."

The following cut is a copy of the signature of the Captain, which is written in rather a bolder style than he generally subscribed himself.

Myles Standish

He settled in Duxbury about 1631, in the southeastern part of the town, on the peninsula, from which arises the hill

known to this day as the Captain's hill. Brewster was also a
settler on this neck, and in the neighborhood of the Captain,
whose house was situated to the southeast of the hill, on a
knoll, near the shore. The sea, it is said traditionally, once
flowed between this and Captain's hill, thus forming a neck,
at the extremity of which was situated his house, which stood
probably about thirty rods from the bank, although now it is
not more than as many yards. The bank here has been continually washing away, and since the beginning of the present
century, thirty feet are known to have gone. And within the
same period, there have been seen, about sixty feet from the
present bank, two stumps of trees, each larger than a barrel.
To the south of the house, where is now a salt flat, not many
years ago were to be seen four acres of good corn, and was
originally covered with a growth of hickory. This is the
fact as given to me by Mr. Kent, who received it from Ezekiel
Soule, Esq., who was informed of it by Mr. Ebenezer Bartlett, who died in 1781, aged 87 years, and who related it from
his own experience.

There is but little doubt, that at the time of the settlement
of Standish here, this whole peninsula, or nearly the whole of
it, was one thick forest. Until a few years ago, there were
standing in another part of the neck, five large sized and
aged white-wood trees, which bore the appellation of "the
Brewster trees," and situated near the Nook point. Primeval
forest trees were also standing at other places until of late
years. The point called "Eagle's Nest," without doubt took
its name from circumstances which the name indicates, as the
trees, a few years ago standing here, continued to be a favorite
place of these birds. The surface of the land in this vicinity
is probably now two or more feet higher than it was two
centuries ago, owing to the vast drifts of sand which have been
here formed.

Standish probably built his house about the time of his first
coming to Duxbury, or about the year 1632. It was occupied
by him until his death in 1656. His son Alexander then succeeded to the estate, who it is said built an addition to it, in
which he kept a store; and in corroboration of this tradition,
it may not be known, that leaden weights have been found in
the remains of this part of the building. A few years ago,
when discoveries were first made here by Mr. Kent, the foundation stones were nearly in their original positions. The ce-
ment employed was evidently ground clam-shells, and the
roof was thatched. The outline of the house is now hardly
distinguishable. We have a tradition that it was burned
down — and this is substantiated by the evident traces of fire
still to be seen — but at what time is not precisely known,

though it has been supposed about the year 1665. About twenty or more years ago Mr. Kent, then pastor of the church in the town, first opened the ground about the site. The first substance discovered was a quantity of barley, perfectly charred, and apparently inwrapped in a blanket. This was found in the east corner of the site, which was thought to be a small cellar. At the chimney in the new part were found the ashes, as perfectly fresh as though the fire had but just been extinguished, and here also was found a portion of an andiron, an iron pot, and other articles. In other parts of the ground there were discovered a buccaneer gun-lock, a sickle, a hammer, a whetstone, a large hinge, a scythe-wedge, portions of stone jugs and other pieces of earthen ware; large quantities of glass, and some beads, some of which show the appearance of the action of great heat; several buckles, and among others a sword-buckle; a brass kettle, a pair of scissors, a small glass phial, chisels and files, parts of pipes, and other articles of household use. There were also found a deer's horn, and a tomahawk of fine workmanship, possibly the veritable instrument of Hobomok. Here I may observe, that numerous implements of Indian manufacture have been ploughed up in various parts of the town, such as stone axes, tomahawks, arrow heads and gouges, generally all of perfect form.*

Some few rods to the southwestward of the house, in a hollow towards the shore, is situated *Standish's Spring*. It has probably never been disturbed since the hero himself, more than two hundred years ago, first laid the stones around. Its water is clear and is with a white sandy bottom, and has never been known to have been dry.

No stone marks the resting-place of his ashes, and we must seek in vain the place where reposes what was mortal of the immortal Standish. He was probably, however, buried on his farm, or perhaps in the old burying-ground in that vicinity at Harden hill. He thus alludes to his burial in his will : —
"My will is, that out of my whole estate my funeral charges to be taken out, and my body to be burried in a decent mannar, and if I die in Duxburrow, my body to be layed as neare as conveniently may be to my two deare daughters, Lora Standish, my daughter, and Mary Standish, my daughter-in-law." There are, a short distance easterly from the site, two stones of considerable size, which are about six feet apart, and were thought to mark, perchance, the grave of some one of the

---

* Many of these curiosities are in the cabinet of the Rev. Benjamin Kent, whose museum, at the close of his labors in Duxbury, contained upwards of four thousand specimens, collected by many years assiduous attention to the subject.

family. A few years ago investigations were made, but without affording any foundation for the supposition.*

The landed possessions of Standish were extensive, and his estate at his death, for the times was considerably large, amounting to £358 7s. His house and farm were valued at £140. Here are given some of the items of the inventory, chiefly for the purpose of showing the condition of the first settlers generally, as regards their domestic and household possessions. Two mares, two colts, one young horse, with equipments, two saddles, one pillion and one bridle. Four oxen, six cows, three heifers, one calf, eight sheep, two rams, one wether, and fourteen swine. Three muskets, four carbines, two small guns, one fowling piece, a sword,† a cutlass and three belts. His furniture: four bedsteads, one settle bed, five feather beds, three bolsters, three pillows, two blankets, one coverlid, four pair of sheets, one pair of fine sheets, and four napkins. One table and table-cloth, another table, one form chair, one common chair and four rugs. Four iron pots, three brass kettles, a frying-pan, a skillet, a kneading-trough, two pails, two trays, one dozen trenchers or wooden plates,

---

* Their peculiar shape, though evidently in their rough state, and the fact that their position to each other was exactly east and west, induced some persons to dig between them, in hopes of making a discovery. Excavations were accordingly made to the depth of eight feet, without, however, any success. In a biographical sketch of the Author, appended to Captain Samuel Delano's Voyages, and written in 1817, it is stated, in speaking of Capt. Standish, "Here he died; and some aged people in the close of the last century pointed out the spot where he was buried."

An antiquarian friend, whose researches in Duxbury commenced about ten years after the writing of the above sketch, and who, as he has informed me, in his conversations with the Octogenarians of that day, always especially inquired relative to the burial-places of the first Pilgrims, tells me, that he could neither find the slightest confirmation of the statement above, in the language of those who were, at the time specified in the account living in their prime; nor moreover in the testimonies of such aged persons as also had manifested in their early days a desire to be informed by their elders on the same point, was there anything in its nature that could in the least degree substantiate the belief.

As to the credit, which that sketch is entitled to in this respect, we cannot, of course, judge, as it is indefinitely chargeable to "A Friend of Capt. Delano."

† His identical sword is said to be in the cabinet of the Pilgrim Society. His coat of mail has been seen by a descendant now living, but at that time was in such a state of decomposition as to crumble into pieces at the touch. He left a library, valued at £10 19s., and among the volumes were "Cesers Comentarys" and "Bariffe's Artillery," and several histories. There is, in the possession of the Massachusetts Historical Society, another sword, which is also said to have belonged to Standish; but the history of the one at Plymouth is said to be established, without a doubt. It was in the possession of his son, Capt. Josiah Standish. See Miss Caulkin's History of Norwich.

one bowl and a churn. Two spinning-wheels, one pair steelyards, a warming-pan, three beer casks and a malt mill; and personal apparel to the value of £10.

Regarding his landed property in England, for the recovery of which, measures have been taken during the last few years, but which was never enjoyed by Standish himself, we find the following clause in his will: " I give unto my son and heir apparent, Alexander Standish, all my lands as heir apparent by lawful descent in Ormistick Bousconge, Wrightington Maudsley Newburrow Cranston and in the isle of Man, and given to mee as right heire by lawful descent, but surreptitiously detained from mee my great grandfather being a second or younger brother from the house of Standish of Standish."

ALDEN. As he was the youngest * of the Pilgrims, who engaged in their government, so did he attain the greatest age, surpassing the allotted length of life on earth, and sustaining to the last that high rank in the councils of the colony, to which he was repeatedly elevated.

While yet very young, he fearlessly joined the followers of Clifton and Robinson, and voluntarily gave himself up to the persecutions and trials of a dissenting church. Suffering in common with his companions the edicts of the Star-chamber, he accompanied them on their pilgrimage to Amsterdam and Leyden, and afterwards formed one of the first company who, arriving on the bleak and inhospitable shores of New England in the dead of winter, laid the foundation of a future republic.

On the landing of the company from the shallop, December 21st, 1620, it is said traditionally, that there was a rivalship between Mr. Alden and a lady,† as to the first landing on New England ground. "No investigation," says Dr. Thacher, "can now decide the claim, be it more or less important to those concerned. The name of John Alden does not occur in the list of those who landed from the shallop on the 11th of December [O. S.], and it is not supposable that a lady would subject herself to such hazard and inconvenience; besides, such an exploit in a female must have been considered as de-

---

* The ages of the principal men of the colony, only, are known. On their arrival in 1620, Carver was probably the oldest; Brewster was 56; Standish 36; Bradford 32; Allerton 31; Howland 28; Winslow 26, and Alden 21. Robinson, the Leyden pastor, was at this time 45 years of age.

† This was Mary Chilton. Among those who came in the Mayflower, were James Chilton (who died Dec. 8, 1621), his wife (who also died during the first winter), and a daughter Mary. She married John Winslow before 1627, and removed to Boston in 1657, where she died in 1679. His daughter Susannah married Robert Latham, and had two children, James and Chilton, and their descendants are in Bridgewater, and those of Mr. Winslow are in Boston. The tradition is in both families. [S. Davis, Esq.

serving particular record at the time. The tradition, which renders the fact questionable, must have reference to the boats which landed the families after the Mayflower arrived in Plymouth harbor. The point of precedence must, however, remain undecided, since the closest investigation discloses no authority for the tradition, nor a shadow of evidence in favor of any individual, as being the first who landed."

We are disposed, however, (says Mr. Davis,) to generalize the anecdote. The first generation doubtless knew who came on shore in the first boats; the second generation related it with less identity; the third and fourth with still less; like the stone thrown into the calm lake, the circles, well defined at first, become fainter as they recede. For the purposes of the arts, however, a female figure, typical of faith, hope and charity, is well adapted." The case, of however great interest to their descendants of the present day may be its decision, is nevertheless doomed to an everlasting uncertainty; and on this account, says Judge Davis, it is not only grateful, but allowable to indulge the imagination, and we expect from the friends of John Alden, that they should give place to the lady.

In the division of the company (Dec. 28, 1620,) into nineteen families, Mr. Alden was assigned a place in the family of Captain Standish, and of his family continued a member until his marriage, which occurred in the early part of 1621. The circumstances connected with it are doubtless well known to my readers, yet still it would be hardly allowable to omit them here. Thus runs the tradition: — "In a very short time after the decease of Mrs. Standish, the Captain was led to suppose, that, if he could procure the hand of the lovely Miss Mullins, the breach in his family would be happily restored. This lady was the daughter of Mr. William Mullins, one of the first comers, and a worthy man. Captain Standish, therefore, according to the manner of his times, sent to ask of the father permission to visit his daughter.* The person chosen by the Captain to perform this delicate embassy, was Mr. Alden, then an inmate of his family, and who, though a Pilgrim, was young and comely. He went, and faithfully communicated the wishes of the Captain. The old gentleman did not object, as he might have done on account of the recency of the Captain's bereavement; but readily gave his consent, stating, however, that the young lady must first be consulted.

---

* This was laid down at a later period, as one of the laws of the colony, when it was ordered, that if any man make a motion of marriage to another man's daughter or maid, without first obtaining leave of her parents or master, he shall be punished by fine, not exceeding five pounds, or corporal punishment, or both, at the discretion of the bench, according to the nature of the offence. Col. Rec.

The damsel having been called into the apartment, Mr. Alden, who is said to have been of a most excellent form, and of a fair and ruddy complexion, arose, and, in a courteous and prepossessing manner, delivered his errand. The young lady listened with respectful attention, and at last, after considerable pause, fixing her eyes on him, replied with perfect naiveté, "Prithee, John, why do you not speak for yourself?" He blushed, and bowed, and took his leave, but with a look which indicated more than his diffidence would permit him otherwise to express. Suffice it to say, however, that he soon renewed his visit, and it was not long before their nuptials were celebrated in ample form.* What report he made to his constituent after the first interview, tradition does not unfold.

It is said that the Captain never forgave his friend Alden to the day of his death. But as he was soon after united to another lady of his choice, we must think that this account of his lasting jealousy is exaggerated. Their long connection in the administration of the government, the intermarriage of their children, and their close communion in the same church, serve to convince us that none other than perfect friendship existed between them; and we are much more inclined to think, that the good humor of the Captain turned upon that circumstance not unfrequently with feelings far otherwise, and that congratulations for his success were extended to his more comely rival.

In 1626 he engaged with Standish, Brewster, Howland and others of the principal men of the colony, to pay their debts, contracted in England, and otherwise to prevent the ruin of the colony by want of credit; and during the following year bargained with the people for a consignment of the trade to them, promising to free them from the payment of the colony's debts.

In 1631 he removed to Duxbury, and settled on the land which had been granted him on the south side of Blue-fish river. He built his house on a rise of land, near Eagle-tree pond,† and the site is still identified to the eastward of the present building, near the dike; and here was his well, which long since having been filled up, it is now with difficulty that its precise

---

* On proceeding to the nuptials, it is said that he covered his bull with a handsome piece of broadcloth, and rode on his back; but on the return he seated his bride upon the animal, and walked by her side, leading the bull by a rope fixed in his nose ring.

† The several oak trees in the region of this pond were formerly a favorite resorting place for eagles, and even to the present day occasionally one is there seen. Mr. Alden, it is said, planted the first orchard. The pear tree, lately standing in full vigor, was probably planted by the pilgrim, though perhaps by Jonathan, his son, and was considered a very old tree ninety years ago.

situation is found. The second house stood a little further to the westward; and the present house, which was erected by his grandson, Col. John Alden, stands still further towards the west, which is now occupied by a descendant of the sixth generation. The farm, which has been in the possession of the family from the first settlement, is one of the best in the town. The original grant to Mr. Alden contained over 169 acres.

In 1633, he was chosen a member of the Board of Assistants to the Governor, and of this body he continued, with few interruptions, to the time of his death. In 1640, however, and for the ten succeeding years, he was not of that number, being most of that time a deputy from Duxbury. In 1666, he was the first on the Board of Assistants; and through the remainder of his life he continued of that rank, and was frequently styled the Deputy Governor, and on him devolved the duty of presiding in the absence of the Governor, and on these occasions he ruled with dignity and perseverance. Holding offices of the highest trust, no important measure was proposed, or any responsible agency ordered, in which he had not a part. He was often one of the council of war, many times an arbitrator; a surveyor of lands for the government as well as for individuals, and on several important occasions was authorized to act as agent or attorney for the colony. He was chosen teasurer in 1656, and held that office for three successive years.

In these times of our ancestors, the honors of a public trust were not so alluring, as their duties and expenses were formidable, and it was perhaps on account of a reluctance of the worthies to accept these public appointments, that the Court was led to pass, at a somewhat earlier period, the following acts : — " January, 1627. It was enacted by the public consent of the freemen of this society of New Plymouth, that if now or hereafter any were elected to the office of Governor, and would not stand to the election, nor hold and execute the office for his year, that then he be amerced in twenty pounds sterling fine; and in case refused to be paid on lawful demand of the ensuing Governor, then to be levied out of the goods and chattels of the said person refusing. It was further ordered and decreed, that if any were elected to the office of Council and refuse to hold the place, that then he be amerced in ten pounds sterling fine; and in case refused to be paid, to be forthwith levied. Also, that in case one and the same person should be elected Governor a second year, having held the place the foregoing, it should be lawful for him to refuse, without any amercement, and the company to proceed to a new election, except they can prevail with him by entreaty." The salary of the magistrates was in the beginning very trifling, and it was not until a late period that any considerable recompense was allowed them. In 1665, it was ordered, that the old magistrates should receive £20 for their services per annum, and the charge of their table be defrayed, and those newly elected to have the charge of their table only; but in 1667, all the Assistants were allowed £50 per annum. Mr. Alden's constant employment in the government, little time being afforded him for attending to his own private affairs, so reduced his estate, that it came under the notice of the Court, who were conscious of his valuable services, and well knew their loss, should he be obliged to resign his labors; and took immediate action, as appears by the following record: "In regard that Mr. Alden is low in his estate, and occationed to spend time att the Courts on the Contreyes occasions, and soe hath done this many yeares; the Court have alowed him a small gratuity the sume of ten pounds to bee payed by the treasurer."—Col. Records.

He was possessed of a sound judgment, and of talents, which though not brilliant, were by no means ordinary and disputable. The writers who mention him, bear ample testimony to his industry, integrity and exemplary piety, and he has been represented as a worthy and useful man, of great humility, and eminent for the sanctity of his life. He was decided, ardent, resolute and persevering, indifferent to danger, a bold and hardy man; stern and austere and unyielding, of exemplary piety and of incorruptible integrity, an iron-nerved puritan, who could hew down forests and live on crumbs.

He was a *puritan*, both in theory and practice; and a professed disciple of Jesus Christ, he lived in accordance with his profession. He was a meek, humble, sincere, pious and faithful follower of the blessed Redeemer, and his end was peace and triumph. The object which in his youthful days he anxiously sought, was fully attained. He came to the howling wilds of America, to enjoy the sweets of religion, pure and undefiled. Like the saints of old, he was willing to endure hardships with the people of God, while he might be instrumental in extending the kingdom of Immanuel, and looking to a better and an eternal state of existence for the reward of grace. He was unmolested in the exercise of the rights of conscience and in the worship of the Most High. In addition to his spiritual blessings, he was crowned with that competence, which is vital to content, with an uncommon length of days, and with a goodly number of children, all of whom delighted in the ordinances of God, and finally left that good name in the world, which is better than precious ointment. He was always a firm supporter of the clergy and the church, and eveything of an innovating nature received his determined opposition.

Though in his earlier days he was possessed of an abundant property, and held a high place among the first settlers in that respect, yet at his death he only left an estate of about £50 sterling. He at one time owned land on the North river in Bridgewater, which he afterwards gave to his son Joseph. He also had land at Taunton. His farm in Duxbury he gave to his son Jonathan before he died. In 1637, he had an addition made to his farm, of a small hill or knoll on the northerly side of the river Blue-fish, " in lue of a pcell of land taken from him (next unto Samuel Nashes land) for publicke use." Old Col. Rec. In 1657, the Court ordered him to look out and obtain land for his sons, and present it to them for their approval. In 1659, he had a grant of some of the commons in Duxbury. In 1661, he purchased a neck of land at Monumet. In the latter part of his life he divided his property among his children, and lived with his son Jonathan.

He died at Duxbury, September 12, 1686, at the advanced age of 87 years. He was, at the time of his death, the last surviving signer * of that original compact of government, signed in the cabin of the Mayflower, at Cape Cod, November, 1620 — the last of the first exiled pilgrims. In his last sickness he was patient and resigned, fully believing that God, who had imparted to him the love of excellence, would perfect the work which he had begun, and would render him completely holy in heaven. — *Alden's Epitaphs, Allen's Biography, Prince's Chronology, Belknap's and Bradford's Biog.*

The following ELEGY, supposed to have been written by the Rev. John Cotton, of Plymouth, though it has before appeared, is still deserving of a record here, not on account of any merit of the style, but for its pure and healthy tone.

> " The staff of bread, and water eke the stay,
> From sinning Judah God will take away
> The prudent counsellor, the honorable,
> Whom grace and holiness make delectable,
> The Judge, the prophet, and the ancient saint ;
> The death of such cause sorrowful complaint.
> The earth and its inhabitants do fall,
> The aged saint bears up its pillars all.
> The hoary head in way of righteousness
> A crown of glory is. Who can express
> Th' abundant blessings by disciples old !
> In every deed they 're more than can be told.

---

* The last surviving *passenger* of the Mayflower, was Mary, daughter of Mr. Isaac Allerton, and wife of Elder Thomas, son of Robert Cushman. She died, aged about 90, in 1699.

The guise 'tis of a wanton generation
To wish the aged soon might quit their station.
Though truth it be, the Lord, our God, does frown,
When aged saints by death do tumble down.
What, though there be not such activity,
Yet in their prayers there's such fervency,
As doth great mercy for a place obtain,
And gracious presence of the Lord maintain.
Though Nature's strength in old age doth decay,
Yet the inward man renew'd his day by day.
The very presence of a Saint in years,
Who lifts his soul to God with pray'rs and tears,
Is a rich blessing unto any place,
Who have that mercy to behold his face.
When sin is ripe and calls for desolation,
God will call home old saints from such a nation.
Let sinners then of th' aged weary be,
God give me grace to mourn most heartily
For death of this dear servant of the Lord,
Whose life God did to us so long afford.
God lent his life to greater length of days,
In which he lived to his Redeemer's praise.
In youthful time he made Moses his choice,
His soul obeying great Jehovah's voice,
Freely forsook the world for sake of God,
In his house with his saints to have abode.
He followed God into this wilderness,
Thereby to all the world he did profess,
Affliction with his Saints a better part,
And more delightful to his holy heart,
Than sinful pleasures, lasting but a season.
Thus said his faith, so saith his carnal reason.
He came one of the first into this land,
And here was kept by God's most gracious hand
Years sixty-seven, which time he did behold,
To poor New England's mercies manifold,
All God's great works, to this his Israel,
From first implanting that to them befell;
Of them he made a serious observation,
And could of them present a large narration.
His walk was holy, humble and sincere,
His heart was filled with Jehovah's fear.
He honored God with much integrity,
God therefore did him truly magnify.
The hearts of saints entirely did him love,
His uprightness so highly did approve,

That whilst to choose they had their liberty,
Within the limits of this Colony,
Their civil leader him they ever chose.
His faithfulness made hearts with him to close.
With all the Governors he did assist;
His name recorded is within the list
Of Plymouth's pillars to his dying day.
His name is precious to eternal ay.
He set his love on God and knew his name,
God therefore gives him everlasting fame.
So good and heavenly was his conversation,
God gave long life, and show'd him his salvation.
   His work now finished upon this earth,
Seeing the death of what he saw the birth,
His gracious Lord from Heaven calls him home,
And saith, my servant, now to Heaven come;
Thou hast done good, been faithful unto me,
Now shalt thou live in bliss eternally.
On dying bed his ails were very great,
Yet verily his heart on God was set.
He bore his griefs with faith and patience,
And did maintain his lively confidence,
Saying to some the work which God begun,
He would preserve to its perfection.
His mouth was full of blessings till his death
To ministers and Christians all; his breath
Was very sweet by many a precious word,
He uttered from the spirit of his Lord.
He lived in Christ, in Jesus now he sleeps,
And his blest soul the Lord in safety keeps.

JOHN ALDEN.   *ANAGRAM.*   END AL ON HI.

Death puts an end to all this world enjoys,
And frees the saint from all that here annoys.
This blessed saint has seen an end of all
Worldly perfections. Now his Lord doth call
Him to ascend from earth to Heaven high,
Where he is blest to all eternity.
Who walks with God as he, shall so be blest,
And evermore in Christ his arms shall rest.
   Lord, spare thy remnant, do not us forsake,
From us do not this holy Spirit take.
Thy cause, thy interest in this land still own,
Thy gracious presence ay let be our crown.
                                           J. C."

His bible, in the cabinet of the Pilgrim Society, bears this imprint: "Imprinted at London by Robert Barker, printer to the King's most excellent Majesty. Anno Dom. 1620. Cum Priuiligio." The text is in the Old English characters.

The autograph of Mr. Alden is exceedingly rare, considering his position in the colony, and the number of times he probably must have written his name in official capacities. His style in his younger days was more open and bolder than when he became further advanced in years.

The signature here given, is from a deed bearing date 1670, which was acknowledged before him, as one of the Assistants.

HOWLAND. The descendants of this pilgrim are numerous, and very respectable. He was a member of Governor Carver's family, whose daughter, Elizabeth, he married. He removed to Duxbury at an early date; but continued in the town for a few years only, having had grants of land in that vicinity, a large tract at Island creek pond, and also two small islands at Green's harbor, viz., Spectacle and Ann islands; and afterwards removed to Plymouth, where the site of his house is identified in Summer street; and then he next removed to Rocky Nook, in Kingston, before 1665, when he petitioned for a way to his house; and there he died, February 22d, 1672, aged 80 years. He was one of the leading men in the colony, and a partaker of their hazardous undertakings, and eminent for his devotions to its interests both in civil and religious matters. He was for many years a deputy from Plymouth, and likewise an Assistant during the greater part of his long and valuable life. In speaking of his death, the Old Colony Records speak of him as "a godly man, and an ancient professor of the ways of Christ; one of the first comers, and proved a useful instrument of good in his place, and was the last male survivor of those who came over in the Mayflower in 1620, and whose place of abode was Plymouth." He was honorably interred at Plymouth, where his remains rested for upwards of a century without a stone, until a few years ago a suitable gravestone was placed over them by his descendant in the fifth generation, Hon. John Howland, President of the Rhode Island Historical Society.

The same may be said in regard to his autograph, as of Mr. Alden's. The following is a copy of the only one, that the author has as yet seen. It was written but a year or two previous to his death, and in his old age, which may account for the error in spelling, which will be noticed.

The following account of a mishap, which befell him on the voyage hither, is found in a fragment of Gov. Bradford's MS. History, recently discovered [New Eng. Hist. Geneal. Reg. II. 187.] : — " In a mighty storm, John Howland, a Passenger, a stout young man, by a keel of ye ship was thrown into ye sea. But it pleased God, He caught hold of ye Topsail Halliards w^c hung overboard and run out y^r length : yet He kept his hold, tho several Fathoms under water, till He was drawn up by ye same Rope to ye surface, & by a Boat Hook & oth^r means got into ye ship : & tho somew^t ill upon it liv'd many years & became a usefull member both in Church & Comon wealth."

FRANCIS EATON, another passenger of the Mayflower, was also one of the first settlers of Duxbury. His autograph is copied from an original in the Colony records.

GEORGE SOULE. This ancestor of a numerous family, was one of Governor Winslow's family on their arrival, and early settled near Eel river; but, in 1637, we find that "a garden place is graunted to Georg Soule on Ducksburrow side by Samuel Nashes to lye to his ground at Powder point," and here he soon settled. Though not a man distinguished in the government of the colony, yet he was of essential service in his town, oftentimes representing it in the Court of Deputies, and holding other offices, to which he could not have been elevated, had he not been a man of integrity and probity.

The children of all the preceding, with the exception of those of Howland and Brown, remained in the town; and of the others, the name of Eaton has now become extinct in the town, and that of Standish also.

Of the twenty-seven heads of families, who arrived in the ship Fortune in 1621, these became at some future time proprietors of land in Duxbury : Robert Hicks, Thomas Prence, Moses Simmons, Philip Delano, Edward Bumpus, William Palmer, Jonathan Brewster, Thomas Morton and William Basset. Simmons and Delano became permanent residents in the town; and here most of their descendants have resided.

SIMMONS, or Moyses Symonson, as he was called, received a grant of forty acres at Duxbury in 1638–9, where he settled, and from him have sprung a numerous posterity.

DELANO. His name was originally spelled *De-la-Noye*, and he is said to have been a French protestant, who joined the church at Leyden. He was aged nineteen years on his arrival; was admitted a freeman January 1st, 1632, and early removed to Duxbury, and settled a little north or northwest of Alden, on the north side of Stoney or Mill brook, below the site of the late tack factory. His farm was confirmed to him in 1637, extending from the marsh at the farther end of the town on the north, to Alden's on the south, and from Bunpus' land on the west, to the sea at the east, comprising about forty acres. He was a man of much respectability, and employed in surveying lands, and was often one of the grand inquest of the colony. — *Vide Geneal. Registers.*

The earliest *physician* of the town was, it is believed, COMFORT STARR, who came from Ashford, Kent, England, to Cambridge in 1633, and then removed to Duxbury, and bought a house of Jona. Brewster, and received a large grant of 120 acres between the North and South Rivers in 1638,— was admitted a freeman in 1639; but finally removed to Boston, where he died January 2, 1659.

The autograph below given, is a copy of his signature to his will.

SAMUEL SEABURY, probably the next in the town, came from Boston and settled in Duxbury before 1660, and was a worthy man, and employed in the business of the town for a number of years. He died in 1681, bequeathing "his surjean bookes and instruments" to his son *Samuel*, who succeeded him as the physician, and was likewise a prominent man in the town, serving as their treasurer and representative, and also a principal member of the church, and an ensign of the militia.

WILLIAM COLLIER. He was one of the merchant adventurers in England, and a wealthy merchant, and quite early came to Plymouth, and soon removed to Duxbury and settled in the southeastern part, near Standish and Brewster. He also had land west of North hill (granted 1635), and a tract called Billingsgate. He was an enterprising man, and engaged much in business, and during most of his life employed in the government of the colony, as Assistant and otherwise. In 1658, "The Court ordered a servant to him, because he can not easily come to public business, being aged and having much private business." He died in 1671 at an advanced age.

WILLIAM MAYCUMBER, a *cooper*, who appears in Duxbury as early as 1638, having had that year a grant of an island of three or four acres north of Powder point, was allowed to settle, "if the comitees of Duxburrow do consent," and in the same year we find liberty granted him "to fetch tymber to make Hoopes of, for vessells for the Colonies use at Clarks Iland & Sagaquash;" and in 1640, he was granted the "wood fitt for coopery growing upon Wood Island, to be used by him so long as he followeth his trade, and forbidding all others to cutt any there, except for the loading of boats and vessels to carry away the hey."

RICHARD CHURCH. This person, a *carpenter*, was at an early date in Duxbury. We find him at Eel river and Plymouth until about 1649, when he appears soon after at Eastham; and then of Charlestown in 1653, when he bought land in Hingham of Thomas Joye of Boston, [Suffolk Deeds] whither he removed, and, it is believed, continued during the remainder of his life. His death occurred at Dedham, Dec. 27th, 1668, though he was buried at Hingham, where his will is dated. — *Hist. Bridgewater.*

RALPH CHAPMAN, a *ship carpenter*, was in Duxbury as early as 1640, when he had a grant of four acres at Stoney brook, and also more to the north towards Green harbor. In 1645 he bought a ferry privilege at New Harbor marshes of Robert Barker, and soon after petitioned the Court to excuse him, "as it would bring him to extreme poverty," which they did, "except on special occasions, as bringing over the magistrates who dwell there."

WILLIAM BASSET, or Bassite, a passenger of the second ship, the Fortune, removed to Duxbury before 1639. He had two in his family on his arrival in 1621. In 1640, he received a large grant of 100 acres at Beaver pond, and was a very large land owner. He left at his death a valuable library. He was one of the early deputies of the town, and a man of some note in the colony.

WILLIAM PABODIE, a man of considerable note in the earlier days of the town, was the son of John Paybody (as his name was spelled). He was much employed in the affairs of the town, and often engaged in the colony government. He was admitted a freeman of the colony in 1650, and frequently was one of the Court of Deputies from Duxbury; and sometimes appeared before the same, as an attorney for individuals, as well as for the town.

William Pabodie

He removed to Little Compton about 1684, where he was selectman and an Associate of the colony. He was also town clerk of Duxbury, and was possessed of considerable landed property.

GEORGE PARTRIDGE. His name is spelled Partrich, Partick, and Patrick. He was one of the most respectable yeomanry of the colony, and came from the county of Kent, England, about 1636, where he was possessed of an estate, which he mentions in his will. In the same year he received a grant at Powder point, and received permission from the Court to settle there, and to build. The next year he was allowed 20 acres at Green harbor path, and in the following year 30 at Island creek, and at the same place, in 1666, a lot of 40 more; and 50 acres at Mile brook, which he sold to Thomas King, Jr., of Scituate, in 1668. He was not admitted a freeman until 1646, and it is not known what relation he was, if any, to Rev. Ralph Partridge. His will, witnessed by Alexander and Josiah Standish, is dated June 26, 1682, and an inventory of his estate (£86 7.) was taken Oct. 10, 1695; so that his death was between these dates. His descendants have not been numerous.

HENRY SAMPSON. This ancestor of a very numerous and respectable family is said to have come over in the Mayflower, and on their arrival, being quite young, was not a signer of their compact. He was admitted a freeman 1637, and early removed to Duxbury, — had a large family, and was allowed in 1667 to look for land for them.

ABRAHAM SAMPSON was of Duxbury in 1640, and lived at Bluefish river; and admitted a freeman in 1654. He is not known to have been any relation to Henry, though he may have been a brother. His conduct was not always in strict accordance with the sentiments of the magistrates, and on several occasions he incurred their censure.

CONSTANT SOUTHWORTH, a son of Mrs. Southworth, (the daughter of Mr. Carpenter,) who came from England in 1623, and had two sons, Constant, and Thomas,* and who soon after married Governor Bradford. Constant was admitted a freeman in 1637, and in 1640 received a grant of 50 acres at North river. He was for many years a Deputy from Duxbury, and often employed more immediately in the government of the colony — having held, from 1659 to 1678 the office of treasurer, often an Assistant, and acting as Commissary-General in Philip's war. He owned land east of North hill, and at Hound's ditch, which he sold to Roger Glass; and in 1657 he bought land at Namasakeeset.

Constant Southworth [signature]

It was narrated traditionally by Mr. Edward Southworth, a direct descendant of Constant, and who died in 1833, aged 86 years, that his house in Duxbury was burned down by the carelessness of his negro, who unintentionally set it on fire with a candle, when he returned home late in the evening; and "that Mr. Southworth was County Registrar, and all the records were burned therein." But it happens that the colony was not divided into counties until some years after Mr. Southworth's death. The tradition may perhaps admit of the interpretation, that he was the town-clerk of Duxbury; and, if so, here must have been destroyed the missing records of the town, and the accident would have happened about 1665. This, however, is wholly conjectural, although it may appear to have far greater affinity to the truth than either of the other

---

* " He was a man eminent for the soundness of his mind and the piety of his heart." He early attracted the attention and won the respect of the people, and on the death of Elder Brewster, was selected to succeed him in that office; but Gov. Bradford, thinking that he would be of greater service in the civil affairs of the colony, the design was abandoned. An Assistant as early as 1652, he continued in that office, with few interruptions, until his death. He was a Commissioner of the United colonies in 1659, and three years after, and in 1664, Governor of the colony's territories at Kennebeck. He married his cousin Elizabeth, daughter of Rev. John Rayner of Plymouth; and their only child, Elizabeth, married Lt. Joseph Howland. He died 8th December, 1669, and his death is thus mentioned in the Colony Records: — " Capt. Thomas Southworth changed this life for a better, being then about the age of fifty-three years; who was a magistrate of this jurisdiction, and otherwise a good benefactor to both Church and Comonwealth; and that which is more than all hath bine named, hee was a very godly man, and soe lived and died full of faith and comfort, being much lamented by all of all sects and condetions of people within our jurisdiction of New Plymouth."

statements. Mr. Southworth, also, was such a man as they would have been most likely to have selected for that office.

ALEXANDER STANDISH, a son of the renowned Captain, was admitted to the freedom of the colony in 1648; and was often the town's deputy at Plymouth, and was one of its first clerks. He inherited the homestead, and also possessed land in the neighborhood of John Alden's, at the Eagle Trees.

He was the chief heir of his father's estate. In his own will appears the following clause: "Also my will is, that whatsoever estate either in New England or in Old, which I have committed unto ye hands of Robert Orchard to recover in England, by letters of attorney from under my hand and seal, and John Rogers of Boston in New England, by a letter of attoney from under my hand and seal, be recovered after my decease, my will is that my wife have her third part, and ye remainder to be divided equally between Thomas Standish, Ichabod Standish, and Desire Standish." He appointed his son Miles, executor of this will, which was dated July 5, 1702, and proved August 10, 1702. His estate amounted to over £600.

CHRISTOPHER WADSWORTH, or, as it is early spelled, "Xxofer Waddesworth." He was one of the earliest settlers, and the first constable of the town, an office, at that time, to which none but the most faithful and honest were elevated. Also a deputy and selectman; and a perusal of the records will at once assure us of his worth and respectability, which his descendants of every generation have well retained; and no family of the town presents a greater array of honored men, — men who have been distinguished in the civil and religious government of their native town, who have held a high rank in the literary institutions of New England, and whose names stand with honor on the muster-rolls of the Revolution.

He had land, in 1638, at Holly swamp; and, in 1655, bought land of John Starr, as also of Job Cole. He dwelt in the southeastern part of the town, in the same vicinity where his descendants reside at the present day.

EDMUND WESTON. This enterprising ancestor of an enterprising family, having served an apprenticeship with John Winslow and Nathaniel Thomas, entered into partnership with John Carew, for planting and farming, in 1639; and in

1640 had a grant of four acres at Stoney brook, and a tract of land towards Green harbor. His descendants have been numerous, and most of them have resided within the town.

For notices of others of the settlers, the reader is referred to the Genealogical Register, at the close of this volume.

The earliest residents were for the most part respectable, and some of them possessed of considerable property. The following list, containing, in part, the names of those in the colony who were taxed by order of the Court, March, 1633, will show the comparative wealth of some of them.

Mr. Wm. Collier,	£2. 5s.	Philip Delano,	18s.
Mr. Edw. Winslow, (M.)	2 5	Francis Weston, (West?)	15
William Basset,	1 7	Christopher Wadsworth,	12
Elder William Brewster,	1 7	George Soule,	9
Mr. Jonathan Brewster,	1 7	Robert Bartlett, (Ply.)	9
Gov. William Bradford,	1 7	Francis Eaton,	9
Richard Church,	1 7	Roger Chandler,	9
Mr. John Alden,	1 4	Samuel Nash,	9
Mr. John Howland,	1 4	Moses Symons,	9
Capt. Standish,	18	Henry Howland,	9
Francis Sprague,	18	Edw. Bumpasse,	9
Experience Mitchell,	18	Samuel Chandler,	9

Their habitations were chiefly *palisadoes*, or fortified cottages, and in some instances the gambrel-roofed houses, generally containing one large room, a bed-chamber and kitchen on the lower floor, with two large and two small chambers above and sometimes an attic above all. The style of building which we sometimes see in ancient houses, that of a high front with the roof behind reaching nearly to the ground, was then frequently employed, though this seems to have been the prevailing style of a somewhat later period. The one-story additions, now so generally adjoined to the main house, were then scarcely known. Barns were very few in number, and their places were supplied by less substantial sheds and other temporary buildings. Their stock of cattle was generally abundant, usually consisting of one or more horses, with oxen, cows, sheep and swine. Several *orchards* were planted at an early date by the settlers.

Some of them owned *slaves*, which was not uncommon, and even to a comparatively late period. Samuel Seabury, who died in 1681, mentions in his will his negro servants, Nimrod, who was to be sold, and Jane, whom he gave to his wife. Other instances can be named.*

SCHOOLS AND EDUCATION.

IN early days, the only schoolmasters were the clergy of the towns, who exercised this office in many instances in addition to the arduous duties of their peculiar avocation. Youths were received into their families to receive a preparation for college, and over the whole body of the younger portion of the inhabitants they extended their care.

In 1663, during the administration of Gov. Prence, who, it is known, was a distinguished patron of learning, the following order was passed the Court : — It is proposed by the Court unto the several townships in this jurisdiction, as a thing that they ought to take into their serious consideration, that some course may be taken, that in every town there may be a school master set up, to train up children in reading and writing. And, in 1670, the "Court did freely give and grant all such profits as might and should accrue annually to the colony, for fishing with net or seines at Cape Cod for mackerel, bass, or herrings, to be improved for and towards a *free school* in some town in this jurisdiction, for the training up of youth in literature for the good and benefit of posterity, provided a beginning be made within one year after said grant." This school was established at Plymouth, and continued until 1677, when it was ordered, "In whatsoever township in this government,

---

* At a later period, Colonel John Alden owned a negro slave, named Hampshire, who was married, April 16th, 1718, to Mary Jones, an Indian woman. Lt. Thomas Loring, who died 1717, left three negroes, valued at £100; and his son Thomas owned a "negro man Bill, alias William Fortune," whom, it appears by the records, he determined (Dec. 1st, 1739) to free "from the yoke of servitude and bondage, for divers good and valuable reasons and causes and considerations," after the 1st day of May, 1752. And in 1759, we find in Chh. Records, "Died Richard Louden's negro girl, about 10 years old."

I have now before me a deed, dated 1741, given by John Cooper, of Plymouth, to Geo. Partridge, of Duxbury, conveying to him "a negro man named Dick, aged about 23 years, of middling stature."

Indians, who had been convicted of certain crimes, were condemned to be sold as slaves in the early times of the colony, as well as those who had been captured in war. A rather unpardonable offence in the opinion of the philanthropists of the present day.

consisting of fifty families or upwards, any meet man shall be obtained to teach a grammar school, such township shall allow at least twelve pounds, to be raised by rate on all the inhabitants of said town, and those that have the more immediate benefit thereof, with what others shall voluntarily give, shall make up the residue necessary to maintain the same, and that the profits arising from the Cape Fishing, heretofore ordered to maintain a grammar school in this colony, be distributed in such towns as have such grammar schools, not exceeding five pounds per ann. to any town, unless the Court treasurer or others appointed to manage that affair see good cause to add thereunto. And further this Court orders, that every such town as consists of seventy families and upwards, and hath not a grammar school therein, shall allow and pay unto the next town, that hath a grammar school, the sum of five pounds, to be levied on the inhabitants by rate, and gathered by the constable of such town by warrant from any magistrate in this jurisdiction." This continued in force for eleven years, during part of the time Duxbury was receiving its share per annum. In 1683, the sum of £8 was granted to the Duxbury school. This school was kept by Mr. Wiswall, the pastor of the church, and continued to be kept by him many years, and under his guidance many young men were fitted for their collegiate course. His powers were well adapted to the duty, and his school, which was well sustained, was carried on with universal satisfaction. Mr. Wiswall died in 1700; but by whom the school was continued we cannot find, nor does there appear any record of a school until *February* 24, 1714, when there is recorded the liberality of Mr. Benjamin Chandler, who "freely gave to ye s^d town liberty to build a school house upon his land neer ye Rhoad for s^d town's use to be set near ye fence, that is ye partition fence between ye s^d Benjamin Chauler and John Glass their lands, and that ye s^d school house might there be settled & kept, with ye privilege, or use of about half an acre of land adjacent so long as ye s^d town shall se cause to keep their s^d school house there."*
And the next year (1715) the town appropriated for a school £30, and appointed Mr. Edward Southworth their agent to procure a schoolmaster for the year, and in their behalf to manage the whole affair, relating to the school. as the law directs. In 1723, £27 pounds were paid to a school master.

---

* The town soon after voted to set the building in the corner of the lot; but through some accident the house was placed in the centre of the lot, whereupon the rhyme was made —

<blockquote>
It is to me a mystery,
It is to me a riddle,
That there should stand, upon any land
A corner in the middle.
</blockquote>

K.

SCHOOLS AND EDUCATION.

In 1734, *January* 16, "at a town meeting ye s^d town by their vote desired & authorized their present Representative, Col. John Alden, to Petition ye Honourable, ye General Court, in their Behalf, for a grant of a Tract of land, ye better to enable them to support a school in s^d Town." A grant was made by the Court, as appears by the following order, passed at a meeting *April* 8 : " Town chose Col. John Alden their agent to procure a Surveyour, & under oath to survey and lay out ye Five Hundred acres of land, granted to ye s^d Town, Feb. ye 15th Anno Dom. 1733-[4], by ye General Court, & to do whatsoever may be Requisite on s^d Town's Behalf, either by himself or his substitute, being any one belonging to ye s^d Town Relating to ye premises." At the same meeting, Philip Delano and James Arnold were appointed to procure a Schoolmaster, and they obtained Jonathan Peterson, Jr.

In 1735 (May 21st) they voted to divide the town into four school districts.
 I. Neighborhood of Powder point.
 II. Neighborhood of Philip Chandler's and Ensign Bradford's.
 III. Neighborhood of Nathaniel Sampson's.
 IV. Neighborhood of Captain's Hill.

And, November 21st, they voted to have two schoolmasters, to serve one half year, one at the north end, and another at the south end of the town.

In 1736, the schoolmaster was allowed a compensation of £20. In 1738, an appropriation of £11½ was made; and during this year John Wadsworth kept for a short time, and also Israel Sylvester for a longer time at 12 shillings per week; and Josiah Thomas eleven weeks for £6 and 12s. The next year (1739) £24 were appropriated to the school, and Joseph Snell was the teacher. In 1741, there were £54 appropriated, and the town was divided into four school districts, to remain so divided for twenty years. In 1742, £54 was the appropriation, and Gamaliel Bradford and Samuel Seabury were authorized to go to the eastward to make some disposal of the land granted to them there by the General Court for the School. In 1743, they voted to sell this land at Souhegan for £750, and in 1747 they disposed of it for that price. This year, and also in 1744, £60 was the school grant, and for the next two years £70. In 1748, Jesse Thomas taught the school; and in 1749 and 1750, Isaac Boles, and for the latter year £100 were granted, and on the next following £60. A Mr. Webb taught the school in 1753, and in 1754 a small appropriation of about £13 was made; and in 1756 £20, and the same in 1578; and this continued to be the annual appropriation until 1778, when it was raised to £80. On the 11th March, 1776, the town " voted to dismiss the Grammar School for six months, beginning at the first of May next; and voted that John Peterson, Judah Delano, Perez Chandler and Calvin Partridge be a committee to draw £20 out of the treasury to pay the common schools for six months, beginning with the first of May next."

Mr. Boles, who kept in Duxbury about 1750, as above, is said to have been a man of learning; but was so continually intoxicated, that he accomplished little good. Mr. Thayer, who afterwards taught here, studied with Mr. Turner, and preached his first sermon in the town. The school was then kept by Mr. George Damon, who had studied also with Mr. Turner, and was afterwards settled in Martha's Vineyard. Mr. Rice then kept in the Point schoolhouse, on the hill above Capt. John Southworth's. John Wadsworth also kept about this time; and then Mr. Francis Winter, afterwards a settled minister in Maine. Mr. Thomas Haven, who studied and occasionally preached here, kept three years. Mr. George Partridge next kept here, and received $8 per month, from 1770 to 1773. Mr. Partridge had, while in college, kept a grammar school in Woburn, and among his pupils were Benjamin Thompson, afterwards Count Rumford, and the late Hon. Loammi Baldwin, nearly his equals in age. Mr. Benjamin Alden began in 1776 to keep school, and kept thirty-three years. He had $7 a month in the beginning, and $14 when he ended. At this period there were four school houses in the town — one at the old meeting-house; the second at Tarkiln village beyond Island creek pond; the third in the northwest quarter; and the fourth called the "Point school." In these Mr. Alden kept three months in the year at each. During this period, Mr. Benjamin Whitman, afterwards Judge Whitman, kept a private school, during his college vacations.

INDIANS.

THERE were probably few, if any Indians in those parts of Duxbury next the bay, at the time of its settlement, as the country for many miles around Plymouth had been depopulated a few years previous to the arrival of the Pilgrims, by a severe and fatal disease.* But a few miles back from the

---

* There is much dispute as regards the time of this pestilence. Gookin places it in 1612 or 1613. It has been generally considered that it was at its greatest extent in 1618. This year, it will be remembered, was the year of the remarkable comet, when the plague was raging in various parts

coast reigned the sachem of Mattakeeset, Chickatabut, *alias* Josiah, who was succeeded by his son Josiah.* A large portion of this tribe became converted to Christianity by the preaching of the various missionaries sent among them, and known by the name of the "praying Indians;" † and on the breaking out of the war with Philip, these Indians were conveyed by the government to Clarks Island, where they might be secure from their hostile brothers. In many places in the colony, the Indians became converted, and were known by the common appellation given above. In 1684, these converts in the colony amounted, it is said, to 1439, (besides boys and girls, who numbered nearly three times as many,) and of these there were at Namasakeeset about forty.

In 1698, there were three or four families of Indians near the Sawmill, (Hist. Coll.) In 1718, Mary Jones, an Indian woman, is named. In 1734, Hacale Jeffery and Betty Tom, both Indians of Plymouth, were married in Duxbury, December 23d. In 1743, Patience, an Indian woman, is named. In " May, 1756, died Amos Jeffery — indian — in ye 17th year of his age, at Fort William Henry; and January 29, 1757, died Hannah Ham — indian — perhaps about 60 years old." [Chh. Rec.] In 1759, J. Peagon, an Indian, served in the old

of the world. Johnson says it was in the summer of the "blazeing starre," which was seen about three hours high above the horizon for the " space of 30 sleeps," and which led the inhabitants " to expect strange things to follow." Some place it as late as 1619; but at any rate, intelligence of its destructive effect had reached England, before James granted the charter of November 3d, 1620, for in it this is given as one of the reasons for granting it. The nature of the disease is also controverted. Some say it was the yellow fever, because Gooken says, he learned from some aged Indians that the bodies of the diseased were all over yellow, both before and after death. Dermer says it was a species of the plague, and others the smallpox. It appears that a French ship had been wrecked on the coast a few years previous, and her crew either were captured or slain. One of the captives afterwards told them, that for their cruelty the Lord would bring upon them destruction, — and in this havoc from the pestilence they recognized the fulfilment of the Frenchman's words. Whole towns were depopulated, and it was estimated that not one inhabitant in twenty remained.

* The father of Chickatabut was Josias Wampatuck; and his grandson, Jeremy, was father of Charles Josiah, the last of the race. Squamaug, brother of Josiah, reigned during the minority of Jeremy.—*Drake.*

† In 1674, there were in the colony 497 of these Indians, of whom 72 could write and 142 could read Indian, and nine could read English. About 100 children had commenced learning, and were not included in this estimate.

Recently, an interesting report has been presented to the Legislature of Massachusetts, by a committee appointed to examine into the state of the Indians in the State, from which it appears there are remains of twelve tribes within the bounds of the State, numbering in all 847, including people of color connected with them; but of these only six or eight are of pure blood.

French war. In 1768, Susy, Indian woman, died, Dec. 31, æt. 33 years. In 1784, Hannah Barnabas, Indian woman, died, July 31st. In 1786, Jan. 2d, Hitty Tom, Indian, died.

It has been estimated, by a learned writer, that on the arrival of the English, there were between thirty and forty thousand Indians in New England, and some fifteen or twenty thousands within forty miles of Plymouth. Comparing this body with the insignificant number of the English, how striking is the imminent hazard, and how remarkable the danger in which they undertook and sustained their settlement. But, says James Otis to Gov. Bernard, in 1767, the Indians had perfect confidence in our fathers, and applied to them in all their difficulties. Nothing has been omitted which justice or humanity required. We glory in their conduct, and boast of it as unexampled! The colonists early enacted laws for the better government of the Indians, and all offences against them by the English were fairly tried; and in the instance, that three Englishmen were hung in 1638, for the murder of one Indian, we can plainly see that the most rigid justice was allowed in their favor. But for their own security they passed a law forbidding the selling of firearms to the Indians; and violations of this were severely punished; not more so, however, than any injury done the Indians. In 1649, Thurston Clark, for letting an Indian have a gun, with powder and shot, was fined. In 1644, Wm. Maycumber, for speaking against the Indians. In 1674, same person, for abusing them on the Lord's day. 1645, Thomas Hayward ordered to pay Wannapooke, a Neipnet Indian, one half bushel of corn for taking venison of his.

A law was also passed, ordering that no lands should be purchased of the natives, without an equivalent recompense; and, previous to the war with Philip, no lands were ever forcibly taken from them.

TOWN OFFICERS.

REPRESENTATIVES.

THESE were more frequently called in early times *Deputies*, and sometimes they were styled *Committee-men*.

1639, *June* 4th. This year the towns first sent Deputies for legislation; and their meeting was on this date. Heretofore, the Governor and Assistants * were the only representatives of the people, and the whole management of the colony was vested in them.†

1639.	Jonathan Brewster, Edmund Chandler.
1640.	William Basset, Christopher Wadsworth.
1641–2.	John Alden, J. Brewster.
1643.	W. Basset, E. Chandler, Tho. Besbeech.
1644.	Capt. Standish, J. Brewster, J. Alden, W. Basset.
1645.	J. Alden, Geo. Soule, W. Basset, E. Chandler.
1646.	J. Alden, G. Soule.
1647.	J. Alden, Constant Southworth.
1648.	J. Alden, W. Basset.
1649.	J. Alden, C. Southworth.
1650–1.	G. Soule, C. Southworth.
1652.	C. Southworth, John Bradford.
1653.	G. Soule, C. Southworth.
1654.	G. Soule, C. Southworth, C. Wadsworth, William Pabodie.
1655–6.	C. Southworth, Wm. Pabodie.
1657.	Wm. Pabodie, John Rogers.
1658–63.	C. Southworth, W. Pabodie.
1664.	C. Southworth.
1665.	C. Southworth, Josiah Standish.
1666–7.	C. Southworth, C. Wadsworth.
1668.	C. Southworth, Josiah Standish.
1669.	C. Southworth.
1670.	W. Pabodie.
1671–82.‡	W. Pabodie, Josiah Standish.
1683–4.	Josiah Standish, John Tracy.
1685.	Josiah Standish, Benj. Bartlett, Sen.

* Of the thirty-three persons, who had been Assistants previous to the annexation to Massachusetts Bay, in 1692, nine were at some time inhabitants of Duxbury: Capt. Standish, Mr. Alden, Mr. Howland, Mr. Collier, Gov. Prence, John Brown, Edmund Freeman, Constant Southworth, and David Alden.

† In the following lists some vacancies will be noticed; but on those years no record of the officers appear to have been made on the town's books.

‡ 1676. Last part of the year, Saml. Seabury.

REPRESENTATIVES.

1686. Francis Barker, J. Tracy.
1687-9. Edw. Southworth, Seth Arnold.
1690. Dea. J. Wadsworth, David Alden.
1691-2. Dea. J. Wadsworth, Edw. Southworth.
1693. Edw. Southworth, Lt. Seth Arnold.
1694. Ens. F. Barker, Dea. J. Wadsworth.
1700. Capt. Seth Arnold.
1701. Lt. F. Barker.
1703. Lt. F. Barker.
1704. Joshua Holmes.
1708. Joshua Holmes.
1709. Samuel Seabury.
1712-3. Capt. John Alden.
1721-2. Capt. J. Alden.
1723-4. Thomas Fish.
1728. Capt. J. Alden.
1731-9. Capt. [styled Col. 1733] J. Alden.
1740. Did not send.
1741-9. Capt. Gamaliel Bradford.
1750. Did not send.
1751-6. Col. G. Bradford.
1757. Did not send.
1758-60. Samuel Seabury.
1761-7. Capt. [Maj. 1762] Briggs Alden.
1768-70. Capt. John Wadsworth.
1771. Did not send.
1772. Capt. J. Wadsworth.
1773. Did not send.
1774-6. George Partridge.
1777. George Partridge, Dea. Peleg Wadsworth.
1778-9. George Partridge.
1780. G. Partridge, John Peterson.*
1781-2. John Peterson.
1783. Capt. Samuel Loring.
1784. Rev. Z. Sanger.
1785. Calvin Partridge.
1786. Did not send.
1787. Rev. Z. Sanger.
1788. Did not send.
1789-90. Gamaliel Bradford.
1791. Did not send.
1792. Gamaliel Bradford.
1793. Did not send.
1794-6. Maj. Judah Alden.
1797. Seth Sprague.

* Last part of the year.

SELECTMEN. 79

1798. Maj. Alden.
1799. Seth Sprague.
1800. Did not send.
1801–5. Capt. Seth Sprague.
1806. Capt. Seth Sprague, Adam Fish.
1807. Capt. Adam Fish.
1808. Capt. Ezekiel Soule.
1809–10. Maj. Alden, Samuel Walker.
1811. Maj. Alden.
1812. Maj. Alden, G. Partridge.
1813. Maj. Alden, Samuel A. Frazar.
1814–5. G. Partridge.
1816. G. Partridge, Samuel A. Frazar.

SELECTMEN.

Selectmen may have been chosen before the first date here given, though no record can be found of them.

1666–7. Christ'r Wadsworth, Josiah Standish, Benj. Bartlett.
1668. C. Wadsworth, Wm. Pabodie, B. Bartlett,
1669–71. C. Wadsworth, Samuel Seabury, B. Bartlett.
1672. Wm. Pabodie, Saml. Seabury, J. Standish.
1673–5. Wm. Pabodie, Samuel Seabury, B. Bartlett.
1677. J. Standish, Samuel Seabury, John Tracy.
1678. J. Wadsworth, Benj. Bartlet, J. Tracy.
1680. S. Seabury, W. Pabodie, J. Tracy.
1681. S. Seabury, B. Bartlett, J. Tracy.
1682–3. J. Standish, B. Bartlett, J. Tracy.
1684. J. Wadsworth, B. Bartlett, J. Tracy.
1685–6. Francis Barker, B. Bartlett, J. Tracy.
1687. Jno. Alden, J. Tracy, Dea. J. Wadsworth.
1688. Jno. Alden, F. Barker, E. Southworth.
1689. Jno. Alden, J. Tracy, Dea. J. Wadsworth.
1690. B. Bartlett, J. Tracy, Dea. J. Wadsworth.
1691. B. Bartlett, J. Tracy, F. Barker.
1692. Jno. Alden, J. Tracy, Wm. Brewster.
1693. David Alden, F. Barker, E. Southworth.
1694. Seth Arnold, F. Barker, J. Tracy.
1695. David Alden, John Partridge, Seth Arnold.
1699. Seth Arnold, F. Barker, Abraham Sampson.
1701. S. Arnold, F. Barker, A. Sampson.
1709. Samuel Bartlett, David Alden, Joseph Stockbridge.
1710. Edw. Southworth, Tho. Parris, Dea. J. Wadsworth.
1714. John Alden, Tho. Loring, Dea. John Wadsworth.
1721. Dea. J. Wadsworth, Joshua Soule, Benj. Delano.
1723. Dea. J. Wadsworth, John Alden, Elisha Wadsworth.

SELECTMEN.

1728. Dea. J. Wadsworth, J. Alden, J. Soule.
1729. Pelatiah West, Edw. Arnold, Wm. Brewster.
1730. Pelatiah West, E. Arnold, J. Alden.
1731. Pelatiah West, Dea. J. Wadsworth, J. Alden.
1732–9. Edw. Arnold, Dea. J. Wadsworth, J. Alden.
1740–4. Gaml. Bradford, Dea. J. Wadsworth, Saml. Weston.
1745. G. Bradford, Saml. Seabury, S. Weston.
1746. G. Bradford, S. Seabury, Dea. J. Wadsworth.
1747–50. G. Bradford, S. Seabury, Saml. Weston.
1751–2. G. Bradford, S. Seabury, Saml. Alden.
1753. Dr. John Wadsworth, Jno. Peterson, Ezra Arnold.
1754–6. G. Bradford, Saml. Seabury, Saml. Alden.
1757. G. Bradford, S. Seabury, Jno. Peterson.
1758–60. Briggs Alden, Wait Wadsworth, Dea. Nathaniel Simmons.
1761–2. Ezra Arnold, W. Wadsworth, Jno. Peterson.
1763–4. B. Alden, W. Wadsworth, Dea. Peleg Wadsworth.
1765. B. Alden, Ezra Arnold, Dr. John Wadsworth.
1766–9. Isaac Partridge, W. Wadsworth, Dea. P. Wadsworth.
1770–1. B. Alden, W. Wadsworth, Dea. P. Wadsworth.
1772–3. Jed. Simmons, W. Wadsworth, Dea. P. Wadsworth.
1774. J. Simmons, W. Wadsworth, Saml. Bradford.
1775. Isaac Partridge, W. Wadsworth, S. Bradford.
1776. Calvin Partridge, W. Wadsworth, Dea. Jas. Southworth.
1777. C. Partridge, W. Wadsworth, Micah Soule.
1778. C. Partridge, B. Alden, Reuben Delano.
1779. C. Partridge, B. Alden, James Freeman.
1780–1. Jno. Peterson, Gideon Harlow, Israel Silvester, Jr.
1783. Jno. Peterson, Elijah Baker, Abel Chandler.
1784. C. Partridge, E. Baker, A. Chandler.
1785. C. Partridge, Levi Loring, A. Chandler.
1786. Jno. Peterson, G. Harlow, Joseph Soule.
1787. C. Partridge, Abel Chandler, Saml. Loring.
1788. G. Bradford, G. Harlow, S. Loring.
1789. G. Bradford, Philip Chandler, S. Loring.
1790. G. Bradford, P. Chandler, John Peterson.
1791–5. G. Bradford, P. Chandler, G. Harlow.
1796. Saml. Loring, P. Chandler, Abel Chandler.
1797–8. S. Loring, P. Chandler, G. Harlow.
1799. Silvanus Sampson, P. Chandler, Ezekiel Soule.
1800. G. Harlow, P. Chandler, E. Soule.
1801. G. Harlow, Dea. Dura Wadsworth, E. Soule.
1803–7. Freeman Loring, Wm. Loring, Jr., E. Soule.
1808. F. Loring, John Winslow, Reuben Delano.
1809–10. Saml. Walker, J. Winslow, R. Delano.
1811. E. Soule, Nathl. Winsor, Jr., Wadsworth Chandler.
1812–3. Saml. Loring, Reuben Delano, Ezra Weston, Jr.

1814–5. Henry Chandler, R. Delano, Levi Loring, Jr.
1816. E. Soule, W. Chandler, Geo. Loring.
1817. E. Soule, W. Chandler, Studley Sampson.

CONSTABLES.

This was an office of high trust and responsibility, and none were elected to it, but men of good standing.

1633. "Christopher Wadsworth chosen Constable for the ward of Duxbury, bounded between Jones River and Greens harbour, and to serve the King in that office for the space of one whole yeare, and to enter upon the place with the Govr elect."

Year	Name	Year	Name
1633–5.	C. Wadsworth.	1667.	Samuel Hunt.
1636–7.	Edmund Chandler.	1668.	Joseph Wadsworth.
1638.	C. Wadsworth.	1669.	Alexander Standish.
1639.	Stephen Tracy.	1670.	John Rogers, Jr.
1640.	Joseph Rogers.	1671.	Benj. Church.
1641.	C. Southworth.	1672.	John Wadsworth.
1642.	Edmund Hawes.	1673.	Mr. Ralph Thacher.
1643–4.	Thomas Boney.	1674.	Samuel West.
1645.	John Tisdell.	1675.	Wm. Brewster.
1646.	George Partridge.	1676.	David Alden.
1647.	Wm. Merritt, [Merrick?]	1677.	Edw. Southworth.
1648.	Thomas Hayward.	1678.	John Simmons.
1649.	Francis Sprague.	1679.	Joseph Chandler.
1651.	John Vobes.	1680.	Wrestling Brewster.
1652.	Wm. Bassett.	1681.	Benj. Bartlett, Jr.
1653.	{ Thomas Heyward, Jr., Abraham Sampson.	1682.	John Partridge.
		1683.	Josiah Holmes.
1654.	{ Stephen Bryant, John Aimes.	1684.	Wm. Vobes.
		1685.	{ Robert Barker, Samuel Bartlett.
1655.	Wm. Clark.		
1656.	Edw. Hunt.	1687.	{ Isaac Barker, Joseph Harlow.
1657.	C. Southworth.		
1658.	John Tracy.	1689.	{ Roger Glass, Francis Barker.
1659.	John Washburn, Jr.		
1660.	Francis West.	1690.	{ Stephen Sampson, John Russell.
1661.	Henry Sampson.		
1662.	Benj. Bartlett.	1691.	{ Thomas Oldham, Thomas Delano.
1663.	John Sprague.		
1664.	Joseph Andrews.	1692.	{ James Partridge, Wm. Tubbs.
1665.	{ Samuel Seabury, Walter Briggs.		
		1693.	{ John Tracy, Samuel Barker.
1666.	{ John Rogers, Richard Dwelly, Wm. Peakes.	1694.	{ John Sprague, James Bishop.

TREASURERS.

The earliest Treasurer of the town was William Brewster, who was succeeded by David Alden in 1701, then by Samuel Seabury; then by Thomas Loring, who held it until his death in 1717; and he was succeeded by Philip Delano, who, in 1758, was followed by Judah Delano, who was succeeded by Maj. G. Bradford, Jr., who resigned to Eliphas Prior in 1777.

TOWN CLERKS.

By the Court it is ordered, "That the Clarke, or some one in every towne do keepe a register of the day and yeare of every marryage, byrth, and buriall & to have 3d apeece for his paynes." — Col. Rec.

The clerks have been, as far as is known —

William Pabodie, 1666–84.
Rodolphus Thacher, 1685–94.
Alexander Standish, 1695–1700.
John Wadsworth, 1701–8.
Samuel Sprague, 1709–10.
John Wadsworth, 1711–50.
Dr. John Wadsworth, 1751–78.
Joseph Freeman, 1779–85.
Benjamin Alden, 1786.

TOWN RECORDS.

It is greatly to be regretted, that the earliest records of Duxbury are lost. We have evidence that they were burned, as the existing records testify. But who was the clerk at that time, and where they were burned, are questions, which probably cannot be answered with any great degree of certainty. As Standish's house was burned about this time, it may be possible that they were destroyed there. The house was then occupied by Alexander Standish, who may have been clerk at the time, as he was many years after. The first entry on the first leaf of the present records was made by Wm. Pabodie, in 1666; but there are entries of a date prior to this about ten or more years, in other parts of the book; and it is a matter of doubt whether they were made at the dates annexed, or copied afterwards into the new book from private records or the Colony records. I allude not to the births, marriages and deaths of Mr. Pabodie's children, prior to that date, which might easily have been entered by him from his own private records, but to other entries, principally deeds, &c., which are entered in different parts of the book. Russell [Guide to Plymouth,] on authority of Lewis Bradford, town clerk of Plympton, favors the supposition that they were burned in Standish's house, Alexander Standish being clerk at the time. Rev. Josiah Moore [Soule's Sprague Memorial,] says, "I am informed, that they [the church records] were burned together with those of the town, at a fire which occurred at Pembroke, where at the time they were deposited." * The earliest existing records consist of a small square parchment-covered book, in which the records are made in very little order, and a larger parchment-covered book; and these bring them down until about the year 1778 of the Revolution. Many of the records of the war were kept on loose sheets of paper, and those of 1781, 2, 3, appear to be missing.

MISCELLANEOUS.

1636, *Oct. 4th.* Mr. Jonathan Brewster and Christopher Wadsworth from Duxbury, with two from Scituate, and four from Plymouth, were appointed to revise the ordinances of the Colony.

Stocks, pound, and whipping-post. 1637: Time was given to the town to provide themselves with a pound and a pair of Stocks, and if they should fail, then "to be fyned by the Court for their defaults." 1640: Francis West, having been censured and set in the stocks at Plymouth for some misdemeanor, was also ordered to make a pair of stocks, to be set up in some convenient place in Duxbury. 1641: The town was presented for not having a pound, and in 1642, there were given them six weeks to provide one, and if they should not in that time then they were to pay £5 fine; and again, in 1650, the town was presented for the same thing; and in 1653 and 1655, for want of pound, stocks and whipping-post.

The *Stocks* were a frame of wood, consisting of two posts, from six to ten feet apart, and connected by a plank; and upon this is let down from above another plank, with openings on the lower edge sufficiently large to receive a man's feet, and by being fastened together the legs of the individual are kept in one position, while his hands are held in the same manner by a third plank above. Being thus confined, and his body supported by a stool, the culprit was doomed to sit,

---

* This is also the account, as Mr. Kent informs me, that he always received from Dr. Allyn, his associate in the ministry, and is perhaps entitled to greater credit, though by no means substantiated. See under C. Southworth, among the "First Settlers."

and to be the laughing-stock of the crowd around, until the term of confinement had expired. The introduction of this machine into England is believed to have been during the thirteenth century. Stocks and whipping-posts were ordinary appendages to a meeting-house until of late years. As late as 1753 we find in the town records this among the town charges: "Joseph Freeman for making stocks, 10 shillings."

1637. Mr. John Howland and Mr. Jno. Brewster were appointed for the town of Duxbury, to attend to the preservation of the beaver trade.

The Court ordered the 500 acres lying between Eel River and the South River to be divided, and Jno. Brewster and Edmund Chandler were chosen on the part of Duxbury "to agree upon an equal course for the division."

1638. Ordered by the Court, "that no more land shal be granted on Duxburrow side untill there be a view taken thereof, that such lands may be graunted as shal be found fitt, not to prjudice the graunts already made to the neighbourhood there."

1639, Nov. 9. A town meeting was held "for making of such lawes and orders as should be thought good and beneficiall." Wears were ordered to be placed at Morton's hole, Bluefish river and Eaglenest.

For the building of the prison at Plymouth, John Barnes and George Bowers were ordered to see the lumber brought, and the Duxbury men "to place it into the leighter."

1641. The Assistants and Deputies had liberty given them to grant land of themselves.

1642. The Town was ordered to give John Rowe satisfaction for the water overflowing his house.

1644. Mr. Collier and "whom he pleaseth wth him," of Duxbury, with the Governor and Mr. Prence of Plymouth, and Mr. Winslow and Mr. Thomas of Marshfield, were chosen to revise the laws.

1646. This is a list of the freemen of Duxbury for this year; those marked with an asterisk are crossed out in the original record on the Colony books. The elections and other business of the Colony were confined to the freemen, who were, on special application, admitted to those rights, church-membership, however, being a necessary qualification. This was a requisite until about 1664, when it began to be discontinued; but was not, however, entirely given up until 1686. A certificate from the pastor of a good moral character, was nevertheless required.

Mr. Wm. Collier,
Mr. John Alden,
Capt. Standish,

Mr. Ralph Partridge,
Jno. Brewster,
*Stephen Tracy,

1659.] MISCELLANEOUS. 85

Wm. Bassett,	Constant Southworth,
*Lt. Wm. Holmes,	John Paybody,
Edmund Chandler,	Wm. Tubbs,
Christopher Wadsworth,	Francis Sprague,
Henry Howland,	Mr. Comfort Starr,
Love Brewster,	*Mr. Wm. Kemp,
Experience Mitchell,	*Job Cole,
Roger Chandler,	*Mr. Thomas Besbeech,
*Joseph Rogers,	George Soule,
Saml. Nash,	*John Tisdall,
Philip Delano,	George Partridge,
Abraham Peirce,	Wm. Brett,
Moyses Symonson,	John Washburn,
Henry Sampson,	Thomas Heyward.

1659. Constant Southworth was sent by Duxbury to conclude with the agents of the other towns, about letting out the trade at Kennebec.

1662. C. Southworth and Benj. Bartlett were appointed for the town, "to take invoice of what liquors, wine, powder and shot" should be brought into the Government.

1668, Nov. 25th. Day of Thanksgiving throughout the Colony.

1670. Freemen of Duxbury —

" Mr. John Aldin,	Mr. John Aldin, Jun'r,
Mr. Constant Southworth,	William Paybody,
*Mr. William Collyare, dec'd,	Edmund Weston,
Mr. John Holmes,	William Clark,
Mr. Christopher Wadsworth,	Robert Barker,
Experience Mitchell,	*John Washburne, Jun'r,
Leift. Samuell Nash,	Abraham Sampson,
Phillip Delano,	Francis West,
Moses Simons,	Benjamine Bartlett,
Henery Sampson,	John Tracye,
*Francis Sprague,	Ensigne Jonathan Aldin,
William Tubbs,	Joseph Wadsworth,
John Rogers, Sen'r,	Mr. Samuell Saberry,
Abraham Peirse, Sen'r,	John Sprague,
Gorg Partrich,	Samuel Hunt,
Gorge Soule, Sen'r,	John Wadsworth,
John Washburne, Sen'r,	Benjamine Church,
Mr. Allexander Standish,	John Rogers, Jun'r,
Mr. Josias Standish,	Rodulphus Thacher."

☞ Those marked * are crossed out on the record.

1671. The selectmen ordered to pay the Indians for damages occasioned by the horses and hogs of the English.

June 13. Day of Public humiliation " in reference unto the sad deplored state of our native contrey."

1672. Saml. Seabury and John Tracy were ordered to prevent the further "transporting of plankes, boards, bolts and barke."

1683. The selectmen were ordered to make provision for the paupers in the town.

1683–4. A list of Freemen of the town presents forty names.

1688. Eighty-four individuals had died in Duxbury up to this date. — *Wadsworth Records.*

1690. John Wadsworth was appointed to view whales, that may be cast ashore in the town.

Rateable estates in Duxbury amount to £1500.

1711, Sept. 4th. Saml. Seabury was chosen to act as the town's attorney at Court; and, Dec. 12th, Capt. Arnold for the same duty.

1712. "Marshfield, Nov. 28 : On Tuesday, the 25th currant, six men going off the Gurnet Beach in a whale boat at Duxberry after a whale, by reason of the Boisterousness of the sea, oversetting the Boat, they were all drowned, viz., William Sprague, Ebenezer Bonney, and Thomas Baker of Duxbury ; Thomas Wright, Job Cole, and Andrew Seaward of Marshfield."— *Boston Newsletter, Dec.* 8, 1712.

1721, Oct. 20th. The town "voted to chuse Trustees to take out of the Treasury ye s^d town's proportion of ye fifty thousand pounds ordered the last year by ye General Court to be emitted, and chose three Trustees, viz., Mr. John Partridge, Capt. John Alden and Mr. John Fish, and ordered that ye s^d money should be hired at five pounds per cent. to such persons as shall give sufficient security for ye same, and that less than ten pounds nor more than tweenty pounds should be hired out to any one particular person." In 1728, (May 16th,) Edward Arnold, Joshua Soule, and Pelatiah West were chosen their Trustees.

1724, Dec. 3d. A whale captured off the beach.

1732. At the launching of a sloop at Bartlett's yard, three and a half gallons of rum were drank.

1765. Dr. Harlow's house burnt at midnight. Abigail his daughter, æt. 13, and Polly Dabney, Mrs. Harlow's daughter, æt. 11, were burnt to death. Mrs. Harlow, a large woman, jumped from the chamber window into the snow without injury. — K.

1770. A dead whale was found a quarter of a mile from the beach, and five sharks were devouring him. One of the sharks was killed, and blubber enough taken out of him to make a full barrel of oil. The whale washed ashore and made 15 barrels.

1772, Feb. 11th. "About one o'clock, P. M. the house of Mr. Richard Louden of Duxborough, inn-holder, took fire. It being considerable advanced before the discovery, though in the day time, there being a large quantity of flax in an upper chamber, where the fire appears to have begun, the weather very dry and windy, the house was consumed with nearly all the contents." — Hist. Coll.

1774, May 16th. "Voted that the Treasurer shall put to suit and prosecute for the time to come any person or all persons, that shall take in any person or families, belonging to any other town, as tenants or mates or friendship, or any straggling persons whatsoever, into their houses or shelters without certifying the Selectmen by a writing from under their hands, of their names and the places where they came from last, and the time they took them in, within the space of twenty days next after they took them in, according to law."

1778. In the months of April, May, June, July and October, about 300 persons were inoculated with the small pox on the islands in the bay, under the treatment of Dr. Winslow of Marshfield, and not one died of the disorder. — Hist. Coll.

1780, May 19th. Very dark, between the hours of 12 and 2, in the day time, and at the same time in the night.

1793. There were living in Duxbury, sixty-three persons over 80 years of age, two of whom were nearly 90, and one male and five females past that age. — Hist. Coll.

In regard to the general health of the town of late years, it may be said, it has been good, and not a larger proportion of deaths have occurred, than in other seaport towns along the coast; and, it is believed, that it would be found that there was not a higher average of deaths, than in most of the inland towns of the State; and the air deriving properties, from its immediate proximity to the sea, is not less conducive to health, than the dryer atmosphere of the interior.

1794, Nov. 3d. The town chose Rev. Dr. Allyn and Benjamin Alden to make surveys for a map of the town.

1797, Nov. 28th. "Dr. Eleazer Harlow's house took fire and was consumed with the effects in it." — Hist. Coll.

1798. An excise was laid upon all carriages for the conveyance of passengers by the U. S. Government. This included chaises, sulkies, chariots, carryalls, etc. The list of individuals owning such, and who were taxed, is preserved. In Halifax there were 3, Hanover 14, Duxbury 16, Kingston 23, Marshfield 26, Scituate 30, and Pembroke 32. Those of Duxbury were Ezra Weston, William Loring, Michael Louden, Mercy Alden, Malicah Delano, John Allyn, Joshua Hall, Nathaniel Winsor, Samuel Chandler, Seth Bradford, Stephen Russell, Jotham Loring, Gamaliel Bradford, Benjamin Freeman, Jonathan Loring and George Partridge.

1801, July 27th. "Voted (by the town) that Major Judah Alden receive communications respecting the villany committed against the Rev. Mr. Allyn, and that he prosecute the same; this Town having been informed that the dwelling house of Rev. Mr. Allyn has been repeatedly broken open and sundries stolen and carried away, and other outrages committed in said house: which conduct is received by the town derogatory to their reputation and honor, and dangerous to the peace and honor of society; especially as it has been committed on the dwelling of their minister. Therefore voted that whoever will detect and bring to legal conviction and punishment, the person or persons concerned in the above audacious villany shall receive the sincere thanks of the town, and a reward of five hundred dollars in money."

This was a time of great excitement in the town. The house of Dr. Allyn was at various times broken open and robbed of household utensils. Other depredations were committed on the premises. Stones were heard at night to strike the roof, and to rattle down the sides of the house, yet no one was to be discovered without, although watches were stationed nightly. On one Sunday, while the family were at church, the house was fired; but it was discovered and extinguished without any great damage being done. So great was the agitation among the people, that some even suspected that the days of witchcraft had returned. Finally a servant girl in Dr. Allyn's employ was suspected, and brought before a court of inquiry; but no evidence was obtained against her, and the matter was dropped.

GENERAL HISTORY.

CIVIL AND MILITARY.

1632. Soon after the settlement of the town, the Court fearing that trouble would arise with the natives, who might take advantage of their dispersed and scattered situation, passed orders for the common safety as follows: — "In regard for our disp^{r}sion so far asunder and the inconveniency that may befall, it is further ordered that every freeman or others inhabitant of this Colony provide for himself and each under him able to beare armes a sufficient musket or other serviciable peece for war wth bandeloroes* and other apurtenenances wth what speede may be. And that for each able p^{r}son aforesaid he be at all times after the last of May next ensueing furnished wth two pounds of powder, and two pounds of bullets, and for each default in himselfe or serv^t to forfeit ten shillings." — Col. Rec.

1635. Lt. William Holmes was appointed to instruct the people of Plymouth and Duxbury in arms; and the next year Capt. Standish was joined to him, and they were to be allowed £20 per annum. And during the year following (1637,) commenced the troubles with the Pequods, which ended in their total subjugation, and nearly total extinction. We find the following in the Colony Records: — "Ordered that the Colony of New Plymouth shall send forth ayd to assist them of Massachusetts Bay and Connectacutt in their warrs against the Pequin Indians, in reveng of the innocent Blood of the English wch the s^d Pequins have barbarously shed, and refuse to give satisfaction for." They then voted to raise 30 men for the land, and seamen enough to man a barque, and chose Lt. Holmes the commander. These offered to serve as volunteers:

Thomas Clark,	John Cook, if his family can be
Richard Church, (Serg't,)	provided for,
George Soule,	Mr. Stephen Hopkins,
Samuel Jenny,	John Heyward,
Constant Southworth,	Thomas Williams,
Mr. Nathl. Thomas, & his man,	Nicholas Presland,
Mr. Goarton,	Thomas Pope,

---

*The *bandoleers* were large leathern belts, worn by ancient musketeers for supporting their arms. It passed over the right shoulder and under the left arm. The name was also given to small cases of leather, suspended from the belt, each containing a charge of powder.

Philip Delanoy
Francis Billington,
Henry Willis
Giles Hopkins,
John Phillips,
Thomas Goarton
Peregrine White,
Caleb Hopkins,
Saml. Nash,
Robt. Mendall,
Henry Sampson,
Thomas Redding,
Love Brewster,
Joseph Robinson, his man,
Edw. Holman,
Wm. Paddy,
John Hearker,
Richd. Clough,
Henry Ewell,
Joseph Biddle,
Wm. Tubbs,
John Barnes,
Geo. Kennerick,
Thomas Holloway,
John Irish,
John Jenkins,
Jacob Cook. — 40.

These would go, "if they be prest," — Mr. Thomas Hill, James Coale, and Thomas Boardman. Mr. John Howland and Mr. Jonathan Brewster of Duxbury were appointed to be joined to the Governor and assistants, and others of the other towns, "to assesse men towards the charges of soldiers," and of the £200 to be paid by the Colony, Plymouth was to pay £100, and *Duxbury* and Scituate £50 each.

1637. "Samuel Chaundler is to be warned to appear at the next Court to answer for shooteing off three guns in the night tyme, as if it were an alarm."

1642. This year, the Indians under Miantinomo of the Narraganset tribe, meditated the extirpation of the English; but their plot was discovered, and the Court ordered and agreed "to pᵣvide forces against them for an offensive and defensive warr;" and the following were appointed on the part of Duxbury a committee for raising the forces, — Capt. Standish, Mr. Alden, Jno. Brewster, Mr. C. Starr, Mr. William Witherell, William Bassett, C. Wadsworth and George Soule. The Court afterwards considered it proper to make further preparations for defence; and a committee, consisting of Mr. Collier, Mr. Winslow, Mr. Hatherly, and Capt. Standish, were sent to Massachusetts Bay to conclude on a junction with them in their present state of affairs; and of this number Winslow and Collier were afterwards authorized to subscribe the articles of Confederation. This union was fully consummated and concluded, and the articles signed at Boston, May 19, 1643, Connecticut and New Hampshire being also included in the compact; and this era of the Confederate union of the Colonies, may be properly looked upon as the grand epoch, when the germ of the present American Republic first appeared in embryo.

Of the forces to be raised, Standish was appointed the Commander; William Palmer, the Lieutenant; Peregrine White, the "aunciemt bearer;" and Mr. Prence was joined to them as counsellor. Of every £25 expense of the war, the proportion of Duxbury was to be £3 10s. And the following were constituted a *council of war:* the Governor, Mr. Winslow, Mr. Prence, Mr. Collier, Mr. Hatherly, Mr. John Brown, Mr. William Thomas, Mr. Edmund Freeman, Mr. William Vassel, Capt. Standish, Mr. Thomas Dimmack, Mr. Anthony Thacher. A sale of moose skins was then ordered to furnish means for procuring powder and lead; and then they passed the following order: "The first Tewsday in July the ma^{trats} meete and eich Towne are to send such men as they shall think fit to joyne wth them in consult about a course to saveguard ourselves from surprisall by an enemie."

1643. It was ordered by the Court, that the towns of Plymouth, Duxbury and Marshfield should be combined into a company or military discipline, and these were appointed officers:—Standish, Capt.; Nathaniel Thomas, Lt.; Nathaniel Souther, Clerk; Matthew Fuller and Samuel Nash, Serg'ts. A constitution was then framed for the company, which was in effect thus,—I: That their exercises begin with a prayer. II: That some one be appointed to preach to them once a year, at the election of their officers; and further that the first sermon be on the 1st of September next. III: That the company shall be composed of none, but "such as are of honest and good report and freemen, not servants, and shall be well approved by the officers and the whole company, or the major part." IV: That every one be subject to the officers' commands. V: That delinquents be punished by the officers, or the company, or the major part. VI: That silence be kept during the exercises, and that every violation be punished. VII: That every absentee, ("except he be sick, or some extraordinary occation, or hand of God upon him,") be obliged to pay a fine of two shillings; and if he should refuse, then to be expelled from the Company. VIII: That every one, appearing without a sword, musket, rest and bandoleers, be fined six shillings for each, and be allowed six months to provide himself with them. IX: That he be expelled from the company, who does not provide himself in that time. X: That but sixteen pikes be allowed in the whole company, viz., eight for Plymouth, six for Duxbury and two for Marshfield. XI: That all officers "be so titled and forever afterwards be so reputed except he obtayne a heigher place." XII: That there be a quarterly assessment of six pence on each member. XIII: That upon the death of any member, "the company upon warning shall come together wth their armes and interr his corps as a souldier and according to his place and quallytye." XIV: That no one be admitted, except he takes the oath of fidelity. XV: "That all postures of pike and muskett, motions, ranks and files, &c., messengers, skirmishes, seiges, batteries, watches, sentinells, &c., bee alwayes pformed according to true millitary discipline." XVI: That applicants, " shal be ppounded one day, received the next day, if they be approved."

Thirty men were ordered to be sent against the Indians; the proportion to be "one in a score;" the number to be required of Plymouth was seven, and of Duxbury and Scituate five each, and of the other towns a lesser number; the share of Duxbury of the £25 to pay expenses, to be £3. The deputies were ordered to make up the number of men as soon as possible; and the Governor, Mr. Winslow, Mr. Prence, Mr. Collier and Capt. Standish were constituted a *council of war*, with power to conduct the management of the campaign; to press men; to demand arms of the towns; to punish offenders; to choose a treasurer or treasurers; to make valuations of arms, and to choose the leader and counsellor of the expedition.

The full equipment of a soldier was ordered to be a musket, (" firelock or matchcock,") a pair of bandoleers, a powder pouch, with bullets, a sword, a belt, a worm, a scourer, a rest and knapsack. His pay " xviii s. p month & dyett & pillage," and his town to provide him with a month's provisions, viz., 30 pounds of biscuits, 12 of pork, 20 of beef, one half bushel of pease or meal. The leader to receive 40s. per month. The towns to bear their share of the loss of arms. A list of the men and their arms to be handed in to the Court, before the 23d of Oct. 1643.

In August, the number of those in each town, between the ages of sixteen and sixty, able to bear arms, was ascertained by the Court, and their names recorded. Those of Duxbury were

Moses Simons,	John Vobes,
Samuel Tompkins,	Wm. Sherman,
James Lindall,	Samuel Nash,
Thomas Oldham,	Abraham Sampson,
Edmund Weston,	George Soule,
Wm. Ford,	Zachary Soule,
Francis West,	Wm. Maycumber,
Francis Godfrey,	Wm. Tubbs,
Solomon Lenner,	Wm. Pabodie,
John Irish,	Wm. Hillier,
Philip Delano,	Experience Mitchell,
Mr. John Alden, Sen.,	Henry Howland,
John Alden, Jr.,	Henry Sampson,
Joseph Alden,	John Brown,
Morris Truant,	Edmund Hunt,

1644.] ALARM ORDERS. — LT. NASH. 93

Wm. Brett,
John Phillips,
Thomas Gannet
Wm. Mullins,
John Tisdall,
Nathl. Chandler,
John Harding,
John Aimes,
Francis Goole,
John Washburn, Sen.,
John Washburn, Jr.,
Philip Washburn,
Wm. Bassett, Sen.,
Wm. Bassett, Jr.,
Francis Sprague,
Wm. Lawrence,
John Willis,
Jno. Brewster,
Wm. Brewster,
Love Brewster,
Constant Southworth,
Capt. Standish,
John Heyward,
John Farneseed,
Thomas Bonney,
Robert Hussey,
Richard Wilson,
Thomas Heyward, Sen.,
Thomas Heyward, Jr.
Thomas Robins,
Arthur Harris,
Edward Hall,
C. Wadsworth,
Wm. Clark,
Mr. Comfort Starr,
John Starr,
Daniel Turner,
Geo. Partridge,
John Maynard,
Stephen Bryant,
John Rogers,
Joseph Rogers,
Joseph Prior,
Benjamin Read,
Abraham Peirce,
Wm. Merrick,
Wm. Hartub,
" Yong " Joseph Brewster,
—— Haden,
Samuel Chandler. — 80.

1644. The Council ordered, that when an alarm is made, and continued in Plymouth, Duxbury, and Marshfield, there shall be twenty men sent from Plymouth, twenty from Duxbury, and ten from Marshfield, to relieve the place where the alarm is continued. And when other places stand in need of help, a beacon to be fired, or a great fire made on the Gallows hill in Plymouth, on the Captain's hill in Duxbury, and on the hill by Mr. Thomas' house in Marshfield. These last regulations, it will be seen hereafter, were followed in the Revolution, and in the war of 1812.

Geo. Pidcock, of Duxbury, "by reason of a cold palsy, that his body is subject unto, is unable to beare armes to exercise wth a piece," and is therefore freed from that duty; but he must, nevertheless, " watch and ward wth such weapons as he can use."

1645. *Samuel Nash* was allowed to be lieutenant of the Duxbury company. Lt. Nash was frequently engaged in the military expeditions of the colony, and an officer in nearly all of them. He was respected by the people, and frequently honored by civil trusts, and held the office of sheriff or chief marshal of the colony, from his appointment in 1652, for more than twenty years. He lived in Duxbury, and, in 1684, "being aged, and not in a capassety to live and keep house of himselfe," he made over his estate to his son-in-law Clark, with whom he lived in his old age.

An expedition was fitted out against the "Narrohiggansats" and their confederates; and Duxbury furnished six men, "wch went wth those that went first," and " were forth xvii dayes." Their names were Samuel Nash (Serg't.), William Brewster, Wm. Clark, John Washburn, Nathl. Chandler, and Edward Hall. They were allowed on their departure one pound of powder, three of bullets, a piece, and one pound of tobacco. The colony allowed Nash £2 10s., and the others £4 5s.; and the town afterwards paid them £6 15s. They all returned on Tuesday, Sept. 2d, and were disbanded on Wednesday. The cost of this expedition to the colony was £70 8s. 6d., and of this Duxbury paid £8 11s.

The *Council of war* of the Colony — Winslow (Pres't.), Prence, Standish, Hatherly, Brown, Alden, and Capt. Wm. Poole, and power to act, was vested in any three of them.

1646. C. Southworth was appointed ensign bearer of the Duxbury company, and held this office until 1653.

1649. Capt. Standish was chosen General officer, and Commissary General over all the Companies in the Colony.

1653. News reached New England of the outbreak of hostilities between England and Holland; and the Court immediately summoned two from each town to meet on the 6th of April, to consult together concerning the best methods of defence in their present state; which was answered by C. Southworth and Lt. Nash on the part of Duxbury. This council ordered, that £50 be raised; a military watch be kept in each town, and that all be obliged to watch: and also recommended to each town to provide a place, whither they might flee for refuge, with their families on any sudden danger: and further ordered, that each town provide themselves with a drum, and pikes; that 20 out of every 80 in each town be constantly armed; that halberds be provided for sergeants; and that a barrel of powder be provided for every fifty men: and also ordered that in the daytime one gun be an alarm, to be answered by any who may hear it; and in the night three guns, or the beat of a drum; that no man should raise an alarm without apparent danger; that one third of every company carry their arms to meeting on the Lord's day, and for neglect of this last a fine of 2s 6d to be paid. The *Colony Council of War* — Bradford, (Pres't,) Prence, Standish, Brown, Hatherly, Alden, Capt. Willet, Capt. Cudworth, and Lt. Southworth; and the same were chosen again in 1654, with the addition of Mr. Collier and John Winslow.

Sixty men were ordered to be raised, and of this number six were to be from Duxbury. The officers were Standish, Capt.; Tho. Southworth, Lt.; and Hezekiah Hoare, Ensign. Two barques were pressed into the service. There were divided among the towns, 5 barrels of powder, 500 pounds of lead, 10 guns, 10 swords, 20 belts and 10 locks. This was for an expedition against the Dutch in New York, and its cost to the Colony was 118£ 15s. In the next year (1654,) still further demonstrations were made against the Dutch; and the council of war ordered that 50 men be raised to meet with Major Robt. Sedgwick and Capt. John Leverett, to accompany them on an intended expedition against the Dutch at "Monhatoes;" and of this number Duxbury was to furnish six men. The officers were Standish, Capt.; Matthew Fuller, Lt.; and Hoare, Ensign. Instructions were given to Standish, dated June 20th, 1654, ordering him to be ready at Plymouth on the 28th of June, and to march on the next day to Manomet, and there to embark on board the bark Adventer, and then form a junction with Sedgwick. This was probably the last expedition in which *Standish* was engaged, and though now far advanced in years, he was still considered the best person upon whom the command could devolve; and he still enjoyed the highest confidence of the people, and in the instructions last named, in speaking of him, they say, "of whose approved fidelitie and abillitie wee have had long experience."

The Commissioners of the United Colonies to send a force of horse and foot against *Ninnegrett*, the Niantick Sachem, and afterwards, if necessary, to send a reinforcement and to make war upon him. Plymouth Colony was to furnish 51 men, and of these Duxbury to find six men with provisions for three days; and of the expense on the Colony (£44 3s) Duxbury paid £3 13s 8d.

Josiah Standish was this year appointed Ensign of the Duxbury Company.

1656. This year occurred the death of *Capt. Standish*, who was at this time the chief commanding officer in the colony. He died Oct. 3d, 1656, ae. 72, "a man full of years and honored by his generation." Secretary Morton in recording his death says, — "He growing very ancient, became sick of the Stone or Strangullion, whereof after his suffering of much dolorous pain, he fell asleep in the Lord, and was honorably buried at Duxbury."

In a copy of the Memorial, in the Library of the Massachusetts Historical Society, and which belonged to Prince, he has written in the margin the following note, from which we determine the day of Standish's death, which is found in no other place recorded. The portions in brackets are gone, and are supplied from conjecture. "In ye List at ye e[nd] of Gou^r Bradford's MSS Folio tis writ y^t Capt. Standish Died Octob. 3, 1655. But his son W^m's Table Book says Oct. 3, 1656, and Capt. Standish being chosen assist[ant] in 1656, shows y^t his death must [have occurred in this last year.]

In this place it may not be improper to give a brief account of the STANDISH FAMILY in England, the particulars of which were not received in time for insertion along with the biographical sketch of the Plymouth hero commenced on p. 48.

Of this stock, of which there is no doubt the Duxbury Captain was a scion, Betham, in his Baronetage of England (II. p. 454) says, — "This family is of good antiquity and note, being denominated from the Lordship of Standish in Lancashire in their possession for many ages. But many of the ancient records and evidences of the family are so worn out by time, and wrote in such strange hands, that no more can be gathered from them, than what follows " — and next is given an outline of the family in the male line, through the first born sons Burke in his "Dormant Baronetages," calls the family one of antiquity and note, and derives the two families of Standishes of Standish and of Duxbury, from the same ancestor. The two sons of Ralph Standish (the son of Thurston de Standish) divided among themselves the estates, and one Jordan is ancestor of the branch of Standish, while the other Hugh is the progenitor of the Standishes of Duxbury. These two families held opposite religious opinions, and became respectively the supporters of the Catholics and Protestants.

The *armorial bearings* of the family have been thus given by Burke, Edmonson, and others, — "Azure, three Standishes argent." Some, however, say "sable" for "azure." And the crest, — "On a wreath, a cock argent, combed and wattled gules;" while another gives, — "An owl argent, beaked and legged or, standing on a rat sable." The baronetcy of Standish was created in 1676 and became extinct in 1812.

Clauses in the wills of Capt. Standish and of Alexander, his son (and it may here be observed that the name of Alexander has been a common one in the English family) show that the Captain was of the family of Standish Hall; and these also have occasioned several attempts on the part of his descendants for the recovery of that property, named in those wills, the portions of which relating to this point have appeared on previous pages. [pp. 55 & 69.]

In the fall of 1846, an association was formed among the descendants of Capt. Standish for the purpose of making investigations, and upwards of $3000 were furnished to their agent, I. W. R. Bromley, Esq., who started on his mission in

November of that year, and returned in October of the following year, without however accomplishing the object of his search. I have been favored with the perusal of some of his correspondence with the Corresponding Secretary of the Association, and some brief minutes which I have gleaned from them may not be uninteresting. The property, to which it was his object to prove the right of Capt. Standish, comprises large tracts of rich farming lands, including several valuable coal mines, and produces a yearly income of £100,000 or more. From a commission, which was found, appointing Standish to a lieutenancy in Her Majesty's forces on the continent, the date of his birth was found, as also from incidents of his life in New England, which have now become a portion of her history, and from other data in the possession of his descendants, which all led to the conclusion that the year 1684 must have been that of his birth. The family seats are situated near the village of Chorley in Lancashire, and the records of this parish were thoroughly investigated from the year 1549 to 1652. And here in connection comes an incident in the researches of Mr. Bromley, which deserves particular attention, and causes the fair conclusion, that Standish was the true and rightful heir to the estates, and that they were truly " surreptitiously detained " from him, and are now enjoyed by those, to whom they do not justly belong. The records were all readily deciphered, with the exception of the years 1584 and 1585, the very dates, about which time Standish is supposed to have been born; and the parchment leaf which contained the registers of the births of these years was wholly illegible, and their appearance was such, that the conclusion was at once established, that it had been done purposely with pumice stone or otherwise, to destroy the legal evidence of the parentage of Standish, and his consequent title to the estates thereabout. The mutilation of these pages is supposed to have been accomplished, when about twenty years before, similar inquiries were made by the family in America. The rector of the parish, when afterwards requested by the investigator to certify that the pages were gone, at once suspected his design of discovering the title to the property, and taking advantage of the rigor of the law, (as he had entered as an antiquarian researcher merely,) compelled him to pay the sum of about £15, or suffer imprisonment.

As it was said that the Captain married his first wife in the Isle of Man, this island was visited with hopes of discovering there his marriage registered, but without success, as no records of a date early enough were to be found. And thus it will be seen that on account of the destruction of all legal proof, the property must forever remain hopelessly irrecoverable.

In addition to the note on page 54, it has been learned that one of the swords of Standish was in the possession of his son, Alexander, and from him descended, through his son and grandson, Ebenezer and Moses, to his great grandson, Capt. John Standish of Plympton, in whose possession it was, when it was borrowed by a military officer of Carver, who wished it to train with, but who never returned it. This is presumed to be the one deposited in the Mass. Hist. Society's Library, concerning which the present librarian can give no account, other than it has been said to have been Standish's sword, and was placed there in the earliest days of the society.

In regard to his coat of mail I have been informed by Mr. Moses Standish of Boston, that he himself has seen it at the house of the above named Capt. John Standish, but then fast going to decay from exposure, though but a few years previous it was in a perfect state. It was a cloth garment, very thickly interwoven with a metallic wire, so as to render it extremely durable, and scarcely penetrable. The suit was complete, including a helmet, and breastplate.

1657. We now come to the commencement of the unhappy persecution of the Quakers. It is neither my object here, nor my inclination to enter into the rise of this people; and neither is it my desire to give a history of the proceedings against them. We cannot but regret the harsh measures which were taken by our ancestors; though in what, we sincerely believe, they thought was in accordance with their duty. Nor is there in the character and actions of the persecuted themselves much wanting to impress upon us, that even they were not what they should be, for their lives certainly bore the semblance of an infatuated zeal. Their persecutions were manifold, both here and elsewhere; but, to the honor of Plymouth Colony, let it be said, says Cotton, that though their provocations were equally great here, yet they were never subjected to those cruel and sanguinary laws which the other Colonies enacted. At first they were punished by the law against heretics in general; but soon after special laws were passed against them; and persons were also prohibited entertaining them, on pain of a fine of £5 or a whipping; and £2 fine was imposed on all who should attend their meetings. Henry Howland of Duxbury was brought before the Court in 1657 for entertaining Quakers at his house, and two years after was disfranchised of the freedom of the Colony on account of his repeated acts in their favor, and still again in 1660, was fined £4 for having two meetings of foreign Quakers at his house. In 1657 Mr. Arthur Howland was likewise presented to the Court for the same proceedings; but refusing to give bonds, was committed and fined £4; and also for resisting the constable on his arrest was fined £5. And again shortly afterwards he presented a paper to the Court concerning the Quakers, full of abuse towards the government, for which he was apprehended, but on consideration of his age and infirmities he was suffered to go with a promise of future good behavior. Zoeth Howland was sentenced in 1657 to sit in the stocks for entertaining Quakers, and saying, "hee would not goe to meeting to hear lyes, and that the Divill could preach as good a sermon as the ministers;" and the next year he and his wife were fined for attending a Quaker meeting. John Howland, a son of the Pilgrim, then residing at Marshfield, was brought before the Court in 1657, for informing the Quakers at a meeting in Marshfield, that a warrant had been issued for them, and that officers were approaching. In 1660 John Soule was fined 10s for being at a Quaker meeting. Some of the families of Duxbury became converted to the tenets of these people, and the Barkers, the Rouses and the Rogerses were principal among them.

A law was afterwards passed, prohibiting any Quaker having the freedom of the Colony, and not allowing him to make an oath in any case; and also that every one should depart the jurisdiction on pain of 20 shillings fine per week. Their books were ordered to be seized, and a fine of £10 to be imposed on any one who should guide them into the Colony. C. Southworth and Marshal Nash were ordered to enforce this. In 1657, one John Copeland was banished because he said that Mr. Alden shook and trembled in his knees, when he was before him. As appears by the following record, the meetings of the Quakers were frequently held in Duxbury: 1660. "Whereas there is a constant monthly meeting of Quakers from Divers places in great numbers, which is very offensive and may prove greatly prejudicial to the government, and as the most constant place for such meetings is at Duxbury, the Court have desired and appointed C. Southworth and W. Pabodie to repair to such meetings, together with the marshal or constable of the town, and to use their best endeavors, by argument and discourse, to convince or hinder them." In 1657, Humphrey Norton, claiming to be a prophet, was ordered to depart the jurisdiction; but he soon returned with John Rouse, and repeated his former most insulting and provoking conduct, and spoke in the presence of the Court unto the Governor in terms like this: "Thy clamorous tongue, I regard no more than the dust under my feet; and thou art like a scolding woman, and thou pratest and deridest me," &c. He was whipped and left the government, and soon after addressed letters to Gov. Prence and Mr. Alden, couched in the most abusive terms. To Prence, he says: "Thou hast bent thy heart to work wickedness, and with thy tongue hast set forth deceit. * * * * * John Alden is to thee like unto a pack horse, whereupon thou layest thy beastly bag. Cursed are all they that have a hand therein; the cry of vengeance will pursue thee day and night." His letter to Mr. Alden was not less scandalous. It was as follows: "John Alden, I have weighed thy waies, and thou art like one fallen from thy first love; a tendernes once I did see in thee and moderation to act like a sober man; which through evill councell and selfe love thou art drawne aside from; if there bee in thee any expectation of mercy doe thou follow the example of Timothy Hatherley;* and withdraw thy body forever appearing att that beastly bench; where the law of God is cast behind youer backes; and from whence God hath withdrawne himselfe untill he have ov^{r}turned it and settled such as shall acte according to his law and contrary to the will of man; alsoe account thou must for that wicked acte in sending forth thy warrant to force away other men's goods for keeping the law of Christ; againe let the cursed purse be cast out of thy house, wherein is held the goods of other men, lest through it a moth enter into thy house, and a mildew upon thy estate; for in keeping of it, and acteing for it, thou art noe other, then a pack horse to Thomas Prence; which of in the councell of God thou stand his p^{r}sent flattery to the, wilbee turned into enmitie and wrath against thee, and then would thou see that thou art sett in the midest of a companie that's like a hedge of vipers, the best of them is not worthy to hew wood in the house of our God. Receive my instruction into thy hart as oyle and depart from amongst them; and thou wilt see that it is beter to live of thyne owne like a poor wise man and att peace with God and his people, then like a selfe conceited fool puffed up with the prid of his hart, because hee hath gotten the name of a Majestrate, as some of them is; in love this is written to disharten thee in time before the evill day overtake thee; lett it bee soe received from thy frind.

HUMPHREY NORTON.

Consider how coruptly thou dealt concerning the paper p^{r}sented to Tho: Prence and thee and others.

Road Iland, this 16$^{th.}$ 4$^{th.}$ mo : 58 :

For John Alden, called Magestrate
    in Plymouth Pattent,
        these deliver."

---

* Mr. Hatherly, it will be remembered, had been left out of the board of assistants, because of his firm opposition to the harsh measures towards the Quakers. And also Capt. Cudworth, Mr. Brown and Mr. Isaac Robinson (son of Rev. John of Leyden,) were removed from the bench; but on the revulsion of public feeling a few years later, these were all restored to their former rights. Capt. Cudworth, in writing to Mr. Brown at London, says: "Mr. Alden has deceived the expectations of many, and indeed lost the affections of such as I judge were his cordial christian friends, who is very active in such ways, as I pray God may not be charged upon him, to be oppressions of a high nature." *Deane's Scituate.*

MILITARY REGULATIONS.

The appearance of the Quakers was at a time, when the colony was in a low and depressed state, both as regards their civil and religious affairs; and sufficient cause was there for the appointment of a *day of humiliation* (Oct. 21st, 1658), to humble their souls before God, and to seek his face, on account of the many manifest signs of his displeasure, as made evident by the prevailing sickness among families, by the unseasonableness of the weather, whereby the crops were endangered, by the appearance of that scourge, the Quakers, and by the prevalence of a spirit of division and disunion in church and civil affairs.

1658. A *council of war* of sixteen were appointed, including Mr. Collier, Mr. Alden and C. Southworth, which ordered that the military company of Duxbury be allowed to exercise and train, when they wish; and of this company Jonathan Alden was appointed ensign. Josiah Winslow was raised to the chief military command, with the title of *Major*. and the following were made members of his council: C. Southworth, Lt. Nash, Lt. Joseph Rogers and Ens. Standish. Thirty shillings were granted to every one of a troop of horse, furnished by each town.

1660. It was ordered, that during any appearance of danger, a military watch be kept in the town in the most convenient place for giving an alarm; that the motions of any vessels that appear on the coast be watched; and that three guns be a signal in the night, and fires be lighted, where the alarm is made.

1667. The *council of war* of the colony at this time were Gov. Prence (Pres't.), Alden, Winslow, Capt. Thomas Southworth, Capt. Wm. Bradford, Hinckley, Anthony Thacher, C. Southworth and Nathl. Bacon. They ordered:— I. That land and sea watches be kept. II. That three guns be an alarm at night, with fires. III. That the troops of each town may be ordered to go out as scouts, and carry intelligence. IV. That each town make return of their number of horse and foot. V. That the soldiers be at the command of their officers. VI. Dutch and French to be considered common enemies. VII. That when any town is in distress, the next town shall send aid to the number of one third or one half of their own men. VIII. That the Indian sachems be advised to employ their men in watching for vessels; and also advised not to venture on board any vessel; and forbid making any false alarm. IX. That no shooting be allowed at pigeons or other game during time of danger. X. That each town provide some place of retreat of their women and children on an alarm, that the "men may with less destraction face an enemie." XI. That the troopers of Plymouth serve as the Governor's body guard. XII. That all above sixty years old, if of competent estates, be required to provide a man. XIII. That whoever should refuse to do duty, when commanded, be fined five shillings. XIV. That the council of each town in time of danger, divide among the inhabitants the arms and ammunition.

The commissioned officers of the town, with Mr. Alden, C. Southworth and Lt. Standish, were to be the council of war for Duxbury. The following orders were imposed on the "*Courts of guard*," to be observed while on duty: I. That there be no quarreling among themselves. II. That there be no correspondence with the enemy. III. That none sleep, or otherwise neglect their duty, or depart at all from their posts. IV. That none disclose the watchword to the enemy. V. That none make a needless alarm, day or night. VI. That on alarm every one fly to his post. VII. That none fly in fight, until a retreat is ordered; or quit a place while it is defensible. VIII. That every private keep his arms clean, and be forbidden to sell them. IX. That none, on pain of death, abuse a sentinel while on duty, but be obliged to obey him. X. That all sentinels carefully attend to their duty.

1671. The Colony council of war consisted of the magistrates, and others joined with them. Messengers were sent to the Saconet Indians, ordering them to bring in their English arms; and then, should they refuse to comply therewith, means were to be taken " to reduce them to reason;" and 100 men were to be sent against them, to start from Plymouth on the 8th of August. Their officers to be Maj. Winslow, Commander; John Freeman, Lt.; C. Southworth, Commissary; Capt. Fuller, Lt. and Surgeon; Wm. Witherell and Elisha Hedge, Sergeants. Forty of the "trustiest Indians" were to accompany them. There were raised 102 men, and Duxbury furnished five. Their pay was, — for the Commander 10*s*. per day; for the Lt. 6*s*.; for the sergeants 4*s*.; for a private (man and horse) 3*s*. The 9th of August was appointed to be observed by the churches of the colony, as a *day of humiliation*, "to seek the favor of God, and his blessing on us on the intended expedition." The council was summoned on the 13th of September, to meet at Plymouth with Philip, to have an interview with him, as it was understood that he meditated hostilities. Philip, however, went to the Massachusetts colony, and made false complaints against Plymouth colony.*

---

* The following original letter I find in Mr. Kent's MS. Collections: It relates to the affairs of this period, and deserves publication. The address is wanting. It was originally in the hands of the Dingley family of Marshfield.

"Swansea: Apri: 1: 1671: much honored sir yours I reseaved this first of April whereby I perseave you desired to know what posture the Indians are in. I doe not finde them to continue in a posture of war as they

1673. The colony council ordered that, when a town shall be in distress, the chief officer of the next town shall send such aid as they may think proper; and that power be given them to press men. Towards the latter part of the year (Dec. 17,) this Court was called together, on an "extraordinary occation," on account of the war with the Dutch. Taking into consideration the repeated demonstrations of hostility on the part of the enemy, their intended invasion of Long Island, their large array of armed vessels, which were very prejudicial, they determined to endeavor to undertake their removal, thinking all this a just ground for war; and notwithstanding the lateness of the season, fearing that the Dutch would have recruits early in the spring, they judged it best to make an immediate attack. Though they considered that they were "apparently overrated" in the proportion of the confederate colonies, they determined to raise their quota, 100 men, if sufficient provisions could be obtained for their voyage and march. Their officers on the expedition were, — Capt. James Cudworth, (pay per day 6s.); Lt. John Gorham, (5s.); Ensign Michael Peirce, (4s.); Sergeants Wm. Witherell, Thomas Harvey, John Witherell and Philip Leonard, (3s. each); Surgeon-General, Matthew Fuller, if the Massachusetts should approve. The pay of a drummer was 2s. 6d., and that of a private 2s. per day. Instructions were given the commander, that he should first summon them to surrender, with a promise of their estates and liberties.

1675. The stifled contentions, which had existed with the Indians for several years, now broke forth in open warfare; and they clearly declared their intention of extirpating the English. The first blood was shed June 24th. The die was now cast, and the English determined on a vigorous prosecution of the war. The United Colonies ordered (Sept. 9th) 1000 men to be raised, and of Plymouth's share (158 men), Duxbury furnished eight (one for the Mount Hope guard). Gov. Winslow was appointed commander-in-chief of the English forces; Major Cudworth commander of the Plymouth troops, and captain of one of the companies, with Serg't Robt. Barker for his Lt.; John Gorham captain of the other company, and Ens. Jno. Sparrow, Lt.; Mr. Hinckley was Com-

---

have beene. I went to Mount hope the last second day one purpos to see there proceedings & was at manie of there houses; but sawe noething as intendings to war, but asking them what was yᵉ reason yᵉ kept together at Mount hope, the[y] answered it was to see Philip's childe buried & did intend to returne home assoune as the child was buried, & I have seene sum returne, but yet the greatest part of them are together, & the[y] give the reason beecause the wind blowd soe agaynst them yᵗ they cannot get home with there canowes, not els, but rest yours to command in what I am able.   HUGH COLE."

missary-General, and Lt. John Brown captain of the Mt. Hope guard, which consisted of 25 men. During times of danger, every one was ordered to go to meeting on the Sabbath armed, with five charges of powder, under penalty of two shillings for the town's use. No one was permitted to shoot a gun, except at an Indian or a wolf, under forfeiture of five shillings. The 14th of October was appointed a day of humiliation throughout the colony, " to humble our soules and seeke and begg the Lords healp in our p^rsent troubles." It was now ordered, that the troops of any town may pursue the attack on the Indians, though without their borders, if a good opportunity offers. The Council of war was next convened at Marshfield, Dec. 8th, when an address was ordered to be sent to the various plantations, exhorting them to express their wonted cheerfulness and courage in engaging in service, assuring them that they would be comfortably provided for, and that those who "cheerfully tender themselves to the expedition, or to presse shalbe looked upon with singular respect."

Lt. Barker was afterwards "degraded from the honor and office of Lieutenant," and fined 15s., because he " broke away from the army, when they were on their march, in a mutinous way, and by his example allured others."

After the march of the above forces, the officers of the town were ordered to exercise one half of their men each day, until further orders. The troops sent against Philip were to assemble at Providence on the 10th of December.

The council was next assembled at Duxbury, Dec. 30th, when 120 more men were ordered to be raised, and of these Duxbury to furnish six; and should any one refuse to go, when he had been pressed, he was to be fined 10s. for the town's use. The Council next met at Marshfield, and in order " to prevent the withdrawing of the inhabitants in this time of publicke callamitie and trouble," every one was forbidden to depart from the town, on pain of forfeiture of his estate. Mr. Alden, C. Southworth, and J. Standish, together with the commissioned officers of the town, were appointed a council of war for Duxbury; and power was given them to establish wards in the day time, and watches in the night; to fix garrisons, send out scouts and have a general supervision of the arms of the town; and to provide their men with "fixed arms and suitable ammunition." The next meeting of the Colony Council was at Plymouth, March 10th, 1676, and at this time power was given to the President of the Council to order the return of the troops, when desirable ; and it was commanded that the order concerning the unnecessary discharging of fire-arms " bee put in reall and vigorous execution." The sum of £1000 was to be raised to pay the soldiers who had served in the expedition, and Duxbury paid her share of £46 11s.

Early in the spring of this year, Capt. Michael Peirce of Scituate was sent against the Narragansets with 50 English, and 20 Indian allies. Near Pawtucket he was met by an overwhelming force of the enemy under Canonacut, and nearly every one of the English fell. This occurred on the Sabbath, March 26. These of Duxbury were slain, — John Sprague, Benjamin Soule, Thomas Hunt and Joshua Fobes; and these of Marshfield, — Thomas Little, Joseph White, Joseph Phillips, John Low, John Brance, John Eams, John Burrows, Samuel Bump and ——— More.

March 29th. The Council ordered "by reason of the near approach of our enemie," that 300 English (sixteen from Duxbury) and 100 Indians should march against them by the 11th of April. All youths in the town under sixteen years of age were required to watch and ward, as they may be judged able by their Commander, and "upon consideration of the late sad and awful hand of God upon Rehoboth," the town was ordered to collect themselves in fewer garrisons of 10 or 12 men each, and especially to guard and defend their mills. April 26th, at Plymouth assembled, the Council determined that in every allowed garrison and fortified place, one-fifth of the men should be constantly armed and in readiness for service. The Town Council were authorized to employ men, "as a scout for the descovery or surprisal of the enemie" in the town and neighborhood; and a fine of £5 was to be imposed, if they did not maintain a standing scout. Twenty-three pounds of bullets were voted to the soldiers of Duxbury.

On the 21st of June, a body of 154 English and 50 Indians marched forth against the enemy. Duxbury sent, of this number, nine men; and of the cost on the Colony for providing them (£164 10s.) she paid £9 10s.

This war was continued for nearly two years with savage fury, when king Philip, driven from swamp to swamp, his family captured, the greater part of his warriors slain, and himself hunted like a beast, was finally killed by Alderman, a friendly Indian of Capt. Church's party, who shot him through the heart, as he was escaping from a swamp, Aug. 12th, 1676. Thus ended the war with the death of Philip of Mount Hope. Philip of Macedon forms not a more conspicuous character in the annals of Greece, than does the Sachem of the Wampanoags in the history of New England. Doubtless he foresaw the unlimited extension of the English possessions, the loss of his own and the extinction of his tribe, and thus determined on a final and, as he might hope, decisive struggle to stay the progress of the white man's sway. After his death the Indians generally submitted, though at the eastward the war was carried on for some years. The loss of the English during the war was about 600 men, 12 or

14 towns and 600 buildings; and many families were entirely bereft of support by the loss of their fathers and brothers. And it was to the generosity of their Irish Christian friends, that New England owed much in their state of distress in the following year. Of this "contribution made by divers christians in Ireland for the releiffe of such as are impoverished, Distressed and in necessitie by the late Indian warr," Duxbury received £2, and Mr. Josiah Standish and William Pabodie were appointed to distribute it. Though the town was in no instance attacked by the enemy, yet many of its inhabitants fell victims abroad to their savage cruelty. The principal actors in this struggle were Gov. Winslow, Maj. Bradford, Capt. Church, Capt. Peirce, and Lt. Jabez Howland.

Capt. Benjamin Church, though by some said to have been son of Joseph Church, who was of Duxbury in 1639, is generally believed to have been born at Plymouth in 1639, and a son of Richard Church, the carpenter. The son was of the same trade. He appears to have come to Duxbury about 1668 or 9, for in the latter year, (May 3d) he had a grant of 30 acres of meadow between Namasakeeset brook, Indian Head river and the great Cedar swamp; and in the next year at a town meeting, May 23d, he requested an addition of five acres, which was granted.* He also owned land at Mill brook, and was probably an inhabitant of the town until about 1680. In 1681 he is called of Punckatcosett. He afterwards settled at Bristol, then at Fall River, and finally at Seconet, and at each of these places he acquired and left a considerable estate. During Philip's war he was a Captain, and commanded the party by which Philip was slain. His military fame at the eastward, while in command of the several expeditions against the Indians in that quarter, and his skill and prudence, as well as courage in conducting them, have earned for him the honor of being possessed of military talents, almost equal to the renowned Myles Standish. On the 17th of January, 1718, then residing at Little Compton, in the morning he visited on horseback his only sister, Mrs. Irish, and returning fell from his horse, and being portly and very heavy, he struck the ground with such violence, as to burst a bloodvessel, which caused his death in about twelve hours; and he was buried with great pomp and parade.

His son Thomas wrote a History of Philip's war and his expeditions at the eastward.

---

* The site of his house was a few years ago identified, by the bricks remaining, between Church's hill and Mr. Peleg Weston's at Duck Hill river.

The autograph of the Colonel, here annexed, was written in 1670, and is in the fairest hand of any the author has met with. His chirography was in general bad.

Benjamin Church

Lt. Jabez Howland was a son of the pilgrim, John Howland. In Church's history is narrated the following anecdote of him. He was one of the first to join Capt. Church on his expedition to Sandwich to secure the alliance of the Sogkonates. Church arrived at Sippican River with only six men, and here, "Mr. Howland began to tire, upon which Mr. Church left him with two men as a reserve at the river, that if he should meet with enemies, and be forced back, they might be ready to assist them in getting over the river." Church having accomplished his design, was returning with some of the Indians, when "having a mind to try what mettle he was made of, imparted his notion to the Indians, and gave them direction how to act their parts. When he came pretty near the place, he and his Englishmen pretendedly fled, firing on their retreat towards the Indians that pursued them. Mr. Howland being upon his guard, hearing the guns, and by and by seeing the motion both of English and Indians, concluding that his friends were distressed, was soon on the full career on horseback to meet them, when he perceived them laughing and mistrusted the truth." He continued in the war during its whole length and was of signal service; and afterwards settled at Bristol, where he was allowed to keep a house of entertainment. He was an officer in the company of that town. His brother *Isaac*, also an officer of the war, settled at Middleboro', kept there an ordinary in 1684 and died 1724. Another brother, *Lt. Joseph*, was also an officer of the war, and lived at Plymouth.

1681. The commissioned officers of the town with three others were constituted a council of war. Samuel Hunt was lieutenant of the company of the town.

1682. The confirmation of their charter privileges and the extension of the same had now engaged the attention of the Government of the Colony for some years, and in view of its establishment, they determined to despatch an agent to the Crown, to solicit and acquire the object of their hopes. The selection of a proper person to represent their views and supplications in the hearing of their King, now seemed desirable, and with great unanimity the Rev. Mr. Wiswall became the object of their choice. Mr. Arnold and Lt.

Morton were next ordered to wait upon the Church and Congregation of Mr. Wiswall at Duxbury, with a letter of entreaty, requesting them to resign for a season the labors of their pastor to the service of their country. This letter is preserved among the Hinckley papers in the Archives of the Massachusetts Historical Society, and is thus addressed:—
"The Generall Court now Assembled at Plimouth to the Brethren of the Church in Duxborrough send wishing the continuance and increase of Grace, and all spirituall Blessings in heavenly places in Jesus Christ o^r Lord." The letter then proceeds, bearing testimony highly creditable to the character of Wiswall, though it is but a reëchoing of that voice of commendation, which was continually proclaiming its praises of the worth of those services among the people of the Colony, which were the labors of him, whose name is still associated with all that is dear to the causes of religion and humanity.

"Brethren, honoured and beloved.

"'The p^{r}sent state of this Colloney, which is much on o^r heart, and we hope on yours also, requiring (as we judge) that we should make o^r Addresse to the King's Majesty in order to the Confirmation and Enlargem^t of o^r priviledges, whereunto we are by him graciously invited & encouraged; we have judged it meet that as a Superaddition to former applications we should addresse ourselves to him by an Agent, and the God of All Wisdome, having (as we hope) of his abundant mercy directed this Court with great unanimity to fix our eyes upon, and make choice of yor Revd Pastour, as a person we esteem well accomplished for that affair: It is our instant request to yourselves in whose hearts we doubt not God hath given him a great interest, that as you have received so great a gift from God, you will now at his Demand Lend him to the Lord for a little season to give up himselfe to a service, wherein not only your own, but the weal of all these churches, and the whole Colloney, together with the Glory of God is highly concerned, in hope that at his hand you shall after a while receive him again with advantage. * * * * * * * Now Brethren, may it please the Lord of his great goodnes to incline yor hearts to deny yourselves thus farr for the publick good; you will therein no doubt bring much honour to God through the Thanksgivings of many, especially if the Lord soe farr delight in us, as to crown the affair with his blessing. * * *
Brethren and friends.
By order of the Generall Court,
NATHANIEL MORTON, Secretary."

This letter bore date at "Plimouth, ffebr 8, 8⅔," and in a postscript was added, — "The time desired you would please to appoint to give meeting to our sd ffriends to receive your answer is on *next fourth* day [February 14th] about ten a clock at your meeting house." A presentation of the facts was also made to the town, and their consideration likewise enjoined upon them.

The assembly was held according to the advice of the Court, and having "sought God by prayer," they with "much agitation and variety of apprehensions, relating to the weighty case," remained until "the day being far spent," when Capt. Standish arose and put the question to vote, and of the thirty-eight persons present — "divers of the inhabitants being absent" — only fifteen, and of these nine were of the Church, voted in the affirmative, while twenty-three dissented, the "Deputy Governor [Mr. Alden] suspending his vote, not acting either way." Most of the "judicious and considerate" of the meeting would have willingly consented to the request of the Court, with the exception of "the worshipfull Mr. Alden, who out of his pious and zealous affection to his pastor and his labors, did dissent, and the Lieutenant, his son." Nevertheless "Mr. Wiswall did fully declare himselfe willing in ye assembly to attend ye work;" but their great objection was that his labors abroad would loosen the ties and bonds of connection, naturally existing between the pastor and his people. Mr. Wiswall however thought otherwise, "assuring them that he was theirs and that if God called him to that work, and spared his life to returne, they might challenge him as their owne."

Mr. Wiswall was afterwards, as it will appear, one of the three appointed agents of the Colonial government, despatched on a similar mission to England in 1690.

1686, May 24th. "The Town was very much dissatisfied with the new laws, espetially respecting the County Courts, and the severyty of the Laws, conserning millitary dissipline and doe therefore give in charge to our Deputys at the General Court absolutely to declare against them."

In 1684, Sir Edmund Andros was sent to New England as a spy, and returning, excited the jealousy of the British Government by collecting false charges against them, and so influenced the high Court of Chancery, that it was decided that the colonies had forfeited their charters, and that henceforth, they should be under the king's control. At this juncture, Andros was commissioned as Governor General and Vice Admiral of New England, New York and the Jersies, and arrived at Boston on the 29th of December, 1686; and like all tyrants began his rule with professions of *high regard for the public welfare.* It was not long, however, before changes occurred. They were unable to brook the petty tyranny of this agent of despotism. The liberty of the press had been restrained; their freedom of conscience infringed, and their cries of oppression sounded for naught. The titles to their land were questioned, and only to be retained by exorbitant fees. Their popular assemblies were forbidden, and the inhabitants of the towns were prevented from joining in meeting, and, lest cries of oppression should reach the throne, all were forbidden to leave the government. Happily his tyranny was of short duration. James having abdicated the throne, (1689) he was succeeded by William and Mary, who were proclaimed in February. A rumor of the landing of William had been received in Boston, but before a confirmation, a most daring revolution was effected by the colonists. The public mind was agitated, and on the morning of the 18th of April, their fury burst upon their oppressors with terrific violence, driving every thing before them, they purged the country of their obnoxious presence. Andros was imprisoned and sent to England.

Measures were immediately taken for restoring their former government, and Gov. Hinckley ordered a council to deliberate concerning the matter. In relation to this, we find in the Town records, the following:—April 30th, "Town mad choice of Benjamen Bartlet, Senr· & Deacon Wadsworth to be their agents (upon the Request of M^r· Thomas Hinkle), and together with the Agents of other Towns to setle a counsell to consider of such things as may [be] expedient for us under the present junture of providence untill our former time of election, which useth to be on the first tewsday in June. 'We, the inhabitants of the town of Duxborough, doe desier that Mr. Hinkle & the rest of the ould magestrates that doe yet survive may be the present counsell according to the former limitation & no other, & father our desier is that all those that have liberty to vote in our Town meetings or the choice of Deputys & others may have liberty to vote in choice of Governer & assistants & if the Countys continew, that all such may have power to chuse their county assistants."

No sooner had the colonies emerged from the troubles above related, than their most strenuous exertions were obliged to be directed in another quarter. A serious outbreak of the Indians had begun in Canada and at the eastward. They had committed depredations on the English, and made other hostile movements against them; and by common consent of the colonies an expedition was fitted out against them, under the command of Capt. Church; and the English and Indians were exhorted to enlist. A sum of £67 10s. was demanded of the towns for fitting it out, and Duxbury was to furnish not less than £2 10s. Duxbury sent two men, each provided with "a well fixt gun, sword, a hatchet, a horne or cartouch-box, suitable amunition & a snapsack." The 28th of August was appointed as a *day of humiliation*. The charge of this expedition on the colony was £750, and on Duxbury £25.

This year Jonathan Alden was elected captain; John Tracy lieutenant; and Francis Barker ensign of the Duxbury company; and this choice was approved by the Court.

Capt. *Jonathan Alden* was the youngest son of the Pilgrim, John Alden, and was born about 1627. He lived on the paternal domain, and was much employed in the civil affairs of the town, and a selectman for several years He was much respected and honored by his townsmen, and inherited the virtues of his father. He was admitted a freeman in 1657, and chosen ensign of the company in 1671, afterwards lieutenant, and then captain, and continued in this capacity until his death, which occurred in February, 1697. He was buried under arms on the 17th, when an Address was delivered at the grave by Rev. Mr. Wiswall, from which these passages are selected. — *Alden's Epitaphs.*

" Neighbours and friends, we are assembled this day in a posture of mourning, to solemnize the funeral of the present deceased, to pay our last tribute of respect to a person well known among us. I need not enlarge upon his character, but, in brief, am bold to say thus much. He stepped over his youth, without the usual stains of vanity. In his riper years he approved himself a good Commonwealth's man; and, which is the crown of all, a sincere Christian, one whose heart was in the house of God, even when his body was barred hence by the restraints of many difficulties, which confined him at home. He could say, in truth, Lord, I have loved the habitation of thy house. He earnestly desired the enlargement of Jerusalem, and inwardly lamented that the ways to Zion did mourn, because so few did flock to her solemn feasts; but is now united to that general assembly, where is no more cause of sorrow on that account.

" As to his quality in our militia, he was a leader, and I dare say rather loved than feared of his company.

" Fellow Soldiers, you are come to lay your leader in the dust, to lodge him in his quiet and solemn repose. You are no more to follow him in the field. No sound of rallying drum, nor shrillest trumpet will awaken him, till the general muster, when the Son of God will cause that trumpet to be blown, whose echoes shall shake the foundations of the heavens and the earth, and raise the dead.

" Fellow Soldiers, you have followed him into the field, appeared in your arms, stood your ground, marched, countermarched, made ready, advanced, fired, and retreated; and all at his command. You have been conformable to his military commands and postures, and it is to your credit. But, let me tell you, this day he has acted one posture before your eyes, and your are all at a stand! No man stirs a foot after him! But the day is hastening, wherein you must all conform to his present posture,— I mean, be laid in the dust."

Mr. Wiswall, after offering various solemn exhortations, with scriptural quotations, concluded his address thus :—

"Fellow Soldiers; Oh! consider how dreadful it will prove, if, after you have with a matchless bravery of spirit acted the part of soldiers on earth, you should in the mean time forget your Christian armor and discipline, and be numbered among those mentioned in Ezek. xxxii. 26, 27, who, having been the terror of the mighty in the land of the living, yet went down to hell with their weapons of war, their iniquities remaining upon their bones! which that you may all escape, follow your deceased leader, as he followed Christ; and then though death may for a short space of time tyrannize over your frail bodies in the grave, yet you shall rise with him in triumph, when the great trumpet shall sound, and appear listed in the muster roll of the Prince of the earth, the Captain of our eternal salvation."

Benjamin Bartlett was chosen Sergeant, and in 1691 Ensign, which latter post was afterwards filled by Samuel Seabury.

1690. The war being still prosecuted by the enemy in Canada, 62 men were sent by water to Albany to join the forces of New York and Albany against the common enemy. Three of these men were from Duxbury. The 31st of April was appointed a day of humiliation. April 2d, several orders were passed for establishing wards and watches, and especially in all seaport towns, &c. A letter was received from Gov. Bradstreet of Massachusetts, stating that more troops were required in the field, and calling upon Plymouth for their quota of men. Thereupon it was agreed to send 150 English and 50 Indians, and Duxbury was called upon for seven men and two stands of arms. Joseph Silvester and John Gorham were chosen captains for the expedition; and £1350 were afterwards raised to pay the troops. The Town council ordered, that one-third of the soldiers attend church armed, on the Sabbath.

The Colonial Government appointed Sir Henry Asherst, Rev. Increase Mather and Rev. Ichabod Wiswall of Duxbury, to apply to the English government for a charter. A meeting was called in Duxbury, in obedience to an act of Court passed Feb. 11th, desiring them to choose an agent, and see how much they could raise "towards the Publique charge, which was thought to be £700 in New England Moneys." We find this record of the meeting:— "Feabruary the 18, 1691-90. The Town of Duxburrough being met together, the majority of the Town by vote did agree to send to England in ord^r to obtaine a charter, by manifesting their willingnes so to doe." They then voted to raise £20 "towards procuring a charter," and chose the "Reverend Mr. Ichabod Wiswald to be their agent, and desier y^t power may be given him to improve whome he sees cause together with himselfe."

It was the intention of the British Government at this time to have annexed Plymouth colony to New York; but, chiefly through the instrumentality of Mr. Mather, this was prevented; and again, say the records, "we were like to be annexed to Boston, but the same [was] hindered [?] by Mr. Wiswall," in hopes of procuring a separate charter. This probably would have been accomplished, could they have found sufficient means (about £500); but, as it was, Plymouth was annexed to Massachusetts by a charter signed October 7th, 1691, and has ever since been under one head with it. In 1691 the Colony Court, considering that they were "not capable to manifest their thankfulness sutable to the obligations that they had," voted 50 guineas to Sir Henry, and 25 apiece to the other agents, Mr. Mather and Mr. Wiswall.

Previous to the sailing of the messenger for England, Gov. Hinckley, in a letter* to Sir Henry Asherst, dated Feb. 4th, 1689[90], says, "Mr. Wiswall, a minister of Duxbury in this colony, and a good man, whom I found at Boston here unexpectedly, bound for England on request of his parish and other friends there to accompany these messengers, can inform you of the state of the Colony." On his arrival in England, Mr. Wiswall returned a letter † to Gov. Hinckley, advising them to prepare and present another address to his Majesty, lest they should be disappointed by neglect of asking in season; for, says he, some taking advantage of your inactivity, have been encouraged to urge our annexation to New York or Massachusetts; and, if you wish to pursue your privileges, "neglect no time *post est occasio calma.*" Petition under the Colony seal, and the King may grant you a patent of protection for the future. "But by the way remember 10 Eccl. 19" — but money answereth all things. After advising them to write to the Earl of Monmouth, and to secure the services of Sir Henry Asherst and Dr. Cook, he concludes,—

"S^r: I am unwilling to come away, *re infecta*, thô I long to be at home as soon as may be. God Almighty direct and protect you and yours, is and shall be the constant prayer of him, who is and remaines, S^r, yours and the Colony's serv^t.

ICHABOD WISEWALLE.

"Dyers Court in Aldermanburg, at ye signe
 of ye golden Angel, London.
 Nov. 10, 1690."

---

* Hinckley MSS. III. 1.   † Idem. III. 27.

As has been before said, through the instumentality of Increase Mather, the project upon which the Government had determined, of annexing Plymouth to New York, was abandoned, and she was finally adjoined in the charter to the colony of Massachusetts; but, says Cotton Mather to Gov. Hinckley,* " when Mr. Wiswal understood it, hee came and told my father, *your colony would all curse him for it*, at wch ye Sollicitor General being extremely moved, presently dash't it out, so that you are now like to be annexed unto ye Government of *N. York*; and," he continues, in relation to Mr. Wiswall, "if you find yourselves plunged thereby into manifold miseries, you have none to thank for it but one of your own." This, however, is but the expression of that secret feeling of animosity, which was manifest in the works and words of Cotton Mather; though perhaps it was a wish to do the best for those whom he represented, that led him to the continuance of those measures which were a source of great annoyance and detriment to the pursuits of Mr. Wiswall, and which caused the occurrence of mutual feelings of dislike.

In a letter† to Gov. Hinckley dated at London, July 6, 1691, Mr. Wiswall thus writes:

" Hono^ble Sir,— I heartily sympathize with you in respect of y^t darke cloud of Providence which hath overspread N: E: and daily entreat ye father of mercie, y^t ye sun of prosperitie may yet once more rise, culminate and scatter ye same to our eternall joy and consolation." And, he continues in a tone of censure, in substance, much blame must be attached to your dilatory action, and " that Plymouth, under its present circumstances, should sit silent so long (may I not say sleep secure) is a great riddle."

When we " consider ye spirit which animated the first planters to venture their all in attempting so great hazards for y^e 'engagement of civell and religious priviledges in that day," and reflect upon other considerations, there is " beget the question, viz., *An sit natura semper sui similis.*"

Appended to this is a postscript in Latin, by Mr. Wiswall, with inferences somewhat derogatory to the character of Cotton Mather.

" Honorande Domine, —
  Si ex animo velis per lumen minimè fallax cognoscere Characterem Domini C : M, (qui inter nos vindicatur patriæ predicatur) consule Dominum Moodum nec non Addingtonum, qui possunt ex pede Herculem metire et delineare.
  Honoris tui Incolumitatisque Plymothensis cupidissimus.
                    I : W :
  Sexto quintilis a partu virginis, 1691."

* Hinckley MSS. III. 33. † Idem. III. 38.

On the 5th of November following, Mr. Wiswall again addressed the governor of the colony,* after the affair had been settled contrary to their hopes and desires; and after giving the particulars of the Charter, and expressing his discontent, he closes with the holy benediction —

"God grant that N. E. may know w^t is the worm which gnawes at the root of our once flourishing gourd. Let Him refine us by his furnace, bring us as gold out of the fire, give us the valley of Ashur for a dore of hope, restore us our vineyard from thence, and make us singe as in the dayes of our youth, when our fathers followed him into this wilderness, and there was no strange God among them. Then was the. High God their refuge, who made them sit down at his feet, and experience that all his saints were in his hand, and that there was the hideing of his power. So prayes he, who is yours and New England's hearty well wisher, servant and fellow-sufferer,
I : W :"

1692. Seth Arnold was chosen lieutenant, and afterwards captain, of the Duxbury company. He was much employed in the public business of the town, and frequently acted as its agent or attorney.

1700–5. About these periods Samuel Bradford and Thomas Loring were lieutenants of the Duxbury company. Lt. *Bradford* is the ancestor of the Bradfords of this town, and held a high station among the inhabitants of that day, as regards integrity and moral worth. Lt. *Loring* is ancestor of the Lorings of the town. He appears to have first purchased land in Duxbury about 1702. He held the highest offices in the town, and some of great responsibility. He was a refined gentleman, much respected by his generation; and possessed of a large estate, which was (chiefly moveable) valued at about £500, exclusive of a large store of provisions, and much landed property, including a farm at Bridgewater.

1713, May 22d. The first notice we find of a *training-field* is under this date, when the town exchanged two or three acres of land with Thomas Prince, for the same quantity near the meeting-house, for a training-field.

1739. This year died Col. JOHN ALDEN, a grandson of the Pilgrim, whose domain he inherited. Col. Alden was a gentleman of a noble mind, of great respectability, affable and courteous in his manner, and of much esteem in society. He was early an officer of the militia, and in 1732 was chosen colonel of the regiment. He was also frequently employed in

---

* This letter, parts of which were published in Hutchinson's History of Massachusetts, second edition, I. p. 365, is among the Hinckley papers, III. 44.

the service of the Province, and despatched on various important missions.

The fac-simile above is of an autograph of his, written in his younger days, about twenty years before his death. A story is told of him, the circumstances of which happened at one time, when the colonel, with two other Duxbury men (Nathaniel Chandler and William Brewster,) accompanying him, went on a visit to Gen. Pepperell, who was then at Saco, Me. The Colonel's visit was of a public nature. Falling into a conversation, the General observed, in a quaint style, that they were three of the most extraordinary men he ever met with. "Brewster," said he, "is famous for telling extraordinary stories, Chandler excels as a singer; but Alden, he is a first rate statesman."—K.

1740. A company was enlisted in the county, to serve in the expedition against the Spanish West Indies, under Admiral Vernon, by Capt. John Winslow, whose original muster-roll on parchment is now before me,* and which I copy. Of the 500 men sent in the expedition by Massachusetts, not more than 50 returned, many having fallen victims to the prevailing tropical fevers. Several Duxbury men will be noticed in their number.

"John Winslow, *Capt.* William Hepburn, *Lieut.*
Joshua Barker, *Lieut.* Samuel Eells, *Ensign.*

Serjants.	*Corporals.*	*Drumers.*
Nathaniel Chandler,	William Reed,	Mark Laveller,
Amos Robens,	Abiah Wadsworth,	Abraham Simmons.
Samuel Jones,	Isaac Bacon,	
Joseph Pryer.	Job Crocker.	

Privates.

Ebenezer Alden,	Jo: Cockennehew,	James Huddleston,
Thomas Byram,	Samuel Douglas,	Jonathan Hill,
Benjamin Burne,	Gideon Daws,	Ezekil Hinkley,
Seth Burge,	Robert Davis,	Abraham Jonas,'
Daniel Coner,	Elisha Delano,	Ebenezer Jackson,
Daniel Cuten,	Joseph Francis,	Josiah Keen,
Jo: Coquish,	Judah George,	Philip May,
Jacob Chipman,	Nathl. Hayford,	John Millar,

---

* Rev. Benjamin Kent's MS. Coll. 126.

1741.]   CAPT. WINSLOW'S ROLL.   117

Alexand[r] McCally,	Timothy Quack,	Peleg Sampson,
Nick Mantomock,	Moses Redding,	George Thresher,
Boney Norcut,	Hezekiah Roben,	Benjamin Tray,
John Nowett,	Moses Ralph,	John Tobe,
Will[m] Norris,	Benjamin Shore,	John Thomas,
John Noaks,	John Sachama,	John White,
Isaac Powers,	Jo: Speer,	Ichabod Wade,
Alexand[r] Perry,	James Samson,	Daniel Weed,
Sam[ll]. Pitcher,	John Smith,	Samuel Woodberry,
Jonathan Peter,	Daniel Simon,	Jo: Weeks,
		Hezekiah Zackary.

Jamaica, June y[e] 4th. 1741. Mustered then in the Third Battallion of his Maj[tys] American Regiment of foot commanded by the Hon[ble] Col[o] William Gooch, the Capt., First and Second Lieut's, one Ensign, four Serjants, four Corporals, two Drumers & fifty-five private men, this muster being for sixty-one days commencing the Twenty fifth of April, & ending the 24th. of June 1741, both days inclusive.

JOHN WINSLOW,
JOSHUA BARKER.

I do hereby certifie that the above were efective in my company from y[e] twenty fifth of April, 1741, to the twenty fifth of June folowing, excepting twenty privet men, that dyed on y[e] days following, viz.—

Peleg Samson,	April 27th.	Ebenezer Jackson,	May 19th.
Seth Burge,	Ditto 27th.	John White,	Ditto 20.
Moses Ralph,	Ditto 29th.	Hezekiah Robins,	Ditto 28.
Joseph Cocknehew,	May 1.	James Samson,	June 2.
Robert Davis,	Ditto 2.	Timothy Quake,	Ditto 2.
Hezakiah Zackari,	Ditto 2.	Daniell Simon,	Ditto 5.
Amos Robens,	Ditto 6.	Benj[n] Tray,	Ditto 10.
Jacob Chipman,	Ditto 8.	Daniel Weed,	Ditto 11.
Abraham Jonas,	Ditto 12.	Joseph Coquish,	Ditto 15.
John Miller,	Ditto 14.	Joseph Pryer,	Ditto 22.

JOHN WINSLOW, *Capt.*

Jamaica, June y[e] 25th 1741."

Ensign Eells died May 9, 1741, and belonged to Hanover.

1759. A company under the command of Capt. John Wadsworth, from Duxbury, joined the English forces in Canada, against the French.

In the Town Records, under date of April 6, 1759, the names of the following persons are given as having served in this company for different periods during the time that it was in the field. The fraction shows what part of the term each man served.

Joseph Chandler,	½	Samuel Winsor,	¼
Enock Freeman,	¼	J. Peagon, (indian),	
Paul Sampson,	¼	John Alden,	½
John Phillips, Jr.,		Israel Silvester, Jr.,	¼
Job Brewster,	½	Ezekiel Chandler,	¼
Blanie Phillips,	½	Robert McLaughlin,	¼
Judah Hunt,	¼	Paul Sampson,	¼
Ichabod Wadsworth,	¼	Perez Chandler,	¼
Thomas Loring,	¼	Israel Delano,	¼
John Roberson,	¼	Sylvanus Prior,	⅜
Zadock Brewster,	¼	Benj. Prior, Jr.,	½
Wm. Sprague,	¼	Samuel Alden, Jr.,	⅛
Joshua Thomas,	¼	Abner Ripley,	¼
James Glass,	¼	Seth Weston,	¼
Levi Delano,	½	Micah Weston,	¼
Benj. Snow,	¼	Benjamin Peterson,	¼

1765. We have now come to a period in the history of New England of striking and peculiar importance. The infringement of the liberties and rights of the Colonies had been continued by the English parliament. The passage of the obnoxious Stamp Act was more than they could endure. Spontaneous in all parts of the province were the protests against it. The towns assembled in meeting, deliberated, and nobly vindicated their rights. Sustained by the example of Boston, they loudly cried for repeal, and their humble voices, reaching the throne, effected their object.

A meeting of the Town was called Oct. 21st, and Major Briggs Alden was placed in the chair. Major Alden then arose, and in his usual dignified manner stated, that the object of the meeting was to see, if the Town "would willingly comply or unite with the late act of Parliament, and rest contented with the stamp act as it now stands with the English empire in America; or else to show their resentments against said act, and to use any measures or means, that they shall think proper to prevent said act being imposed upon us, by giving their representative instructions to stop said act, or to use any other means they shall think proper." He then put the question, and they decided that they *would not comply*. Capt. Wait Wadsworth, Capt. John Wadsworth, Ebenezer Bartlett, Isaac Partridge and Ezra Arnold were then chosen "their Committee to prepare a draught, and to give their reasons why the town would not accept of said act, and to show as far as they were capable of it." The meeting was then adjourned to the 23d of Oct., when the Committee reported the following instructions:

"To Briggs Alden, Esq., Representative of the inhabitants of the Town of Duxbury, in the Great and General Court of the Province of Massachusetts Bay in New England —

"Sir, — Whilst all America is in a ferment, and every patriotic breast is glowing with resentment at the heavy and intolerable burthens imposed upon us, by the late act passed in the Parliament of Great Britain, — We, your constituents, the freeholders and other inhabitants of the ancient and first incorporated town of Duxbury, think it their incumbent duty to inform you of their sentiments upon this important and alarming affair, that you, Sir, may be able in the approaching session of the Great and General Court to act according to their declared mind. We esteem the said Stamp Act to be unconstitutional and subversive of the Rights and Privileges of His Majesty's American Subjects, contrary not only to the Royal Charter granted to our ancestors, and to the Great Charter of British Liberty; but likewise to the grand prerogatives of human nature, and to that Liberty, wherewith our Blessed hath made us free. We likewise think that if this act should take place in the Province in the present distressed condition, we should be involved in inevitable ruin. We do now therefore enjoin and instruct you, that you neither directly nor indirectly be aiding, favoring, countenancing, assisting, or any ways instrumental in promoting the putting the said act in existence; but that you oppose the same with all the eloquence and address you are master of, and that you use your utmost endeavors to vindicate our precious rights and privileges, — those privileges for which our forefathers bled; for which those heroic spirits bid adieu to the tyrannical, to the all-boding names of the Stuarts, traversed the vast Atlantic, and sat down in these then deserts of America; and which, Sir, we their descendants esteem dearer to us than our lives. We likewise enjoin it upon you to oppose in the strongest terms any motion or motions, that may be made in the General Assembly, to make a relation or compensation for the riotous proceedings at Boston."

Thus did the inhabitants of Duxbury plainly and distinctly protest against the unwarrantable proceedings of the mother country. Thus did she proclaim to the world, in full defiance of England's power, that *infringements of her Charter rights were not to be borne.* A repeal of the Stamp Act passed the British Parliament, January 16th, 1766; and on the arrival of the news at Boston, great was the rejoicing. In Duxbury the excitement was of no ordinary nature, and even one half of the town's stock of powder was given away to be used in expressing their unbounded joy for the blessing of a repeal. This was ordered at a meeting on the 31st of March.

Soon after the arrival of the news, it was proposed that there should be a meeting on Captain's hill. Accordingly great numbers assembled, formed themselves into a procession, paraded around the town, and finally marched to the hill, whither they brought six carriage guns and fired a salute. They also carried to the summit effigies of Lords Grenville and Bute, and hung them upon a gallows, which they erected for the occasion. They now selected an orator in the person of Joseph Russell, whose simple wit, and unadorned language, as he addressed himself to the images before him, caused considerable merriment, and his untutored gestures with the exceedingly comic appearance of his figure, caused a forgetfulness of the true solemnity of their rejoicings. Turning to the effigies he began, "Gentlemen, you see now what you've come to. You remember Haman and Mordecai, do ye? You tried to make slaves of them that ought to be free, and you've come to the gallows yourself that built it for us, ye have! Such men as you don't have any fear. And there ye are before the gallows for being so set in your own ways! It would ha' been just upon ye, if they had taken that paper ye sent over to us, and wrapped ye up in it and burnt ye up, it would! But 'twould have been too honorable a death for ye. The gallows was what ye deserved, and there ye are now hanging before us, ye are. You're spited at home and abroad, indeed ye are. Your own kith don't like a traitor, they don't I know." The effigies which had during this time been burning, now fell to the ground, and Russell continued, "There I thought your station was below. I didn't think it was above. If ye'd been now an honest old ditcher as I am, ye'd never come to this, ye would n't."*
The remainder of the day was passed in pleasure, and at

---

* Rev. Benj. Kent's notes. Another story is told of Joe, equally humorous. It happened that there had been a "skimmington fooler," as it was called, in which a man had been ridden on a horse, followed by a crowd of men and boys dressed in the manner of negroes. The person had been cruel to his family. Some of the individuals were afterwards prosecuted by the king's attorney at Plymouth; and, while the trial was going on, Joe was called as a witness. Taking the stand he began to relate several laughable stories, which vexed the attorney, who appealed to Gen. Winslow, the presiding judge, and said, "Is it sufferable that this man should stand here and talk so." The General however who was much amused suffered him to finish his talk. The attorney then asked him, if he could not think of any one, who was engaged in the affair, when Joe turning to the General, said, "Yes I do. May it please your honor 'twas you." "Me!" replied the Judge, "why did you think it was me!" "O!" returned Joe "he was dressed up in a great surplice, and looked very like you, any how he did." The Court now joined heartily in a laugh, and the old General, laying aside the dignity of his office, engaged in it as loudly as any of them.

night each returned home with a strong hope of future happiness for his country.

The flame which had been kindled by James, and which had enwrapped the destinies of Andros, had not died out from the hearts of the people. Before the return of another century, this fire was renewed, and the cries for freedom were no longer to be suppressed. They arose spontaneously from every part; from the humble cottage and the lordly mansion.

"One common right the great and lowly claim." Nor was it in vain, — action, forcible and impetuous, — resistance, powerful and effective, followed on the heels of oppression. Eloquence was not wanting in the language of her people, in support of their cherished wish. Relying on the examples set them in the annals of the past, they saw in the future the consummation of their most ardent aspirations. Their dependence on the parent country they knew and felt. Their attention was turned to the encouragement of their own manufactures. The town of Boston, ever foremost in their struggles for liberty, passed a vote for the support of home manufactures. Other towns soon followed, and among the number Duxbury resolved in concurrence with the orders of Boston. This occurred as early as Dec. 22d, 1762.

1773. Early in this year, the Town of Boston addressed a pamphlet to the inhabitants of Duxbury, on the wrongful subversion of the rights of the Provinces. To take into consideration the contents of this pamphlet, a town meeting was called (March 12th,) and a committee consisting of George Partridge, Capt. Wait Wadsworth, Dea. Peleg Wadsworth, Dr. John Wadsworth, and Bildad Arnold, were appointed "to draw proper resolves or other remonstrances against the invasion of our charter rights and privileges." The meeting was then adjourned to the 29th, when the committee reported the following reply, which was unanimously accepted. It was written, it is said, by the Chairman, Mr. Partridge.

"To the Committee of Correspondence of the Town of Boston, —

GENTLEMEN, — We, the freeholders and other inhabitants of the town of Duxbury, in said Town meeting legally assembled, upon due examination of the contents of a pamphlet from the town of Boston, directed to be laid before us, are truly of the opinion that the rights of the people are therein well stated, and that the list of infringements and violations of the same is just; which gives us the distressing and very alarming apprehensions, that a plan is laid and prosecuted with unrelenting rigor, which will, if thoroughly completed, reduce the colonies, and this province in particular, to a state of vassalage and desperation. It would give us uneasiness, Gentlemen, should you imagine from our so long neglecting an answer, that we are in any degree careless, idle spectators of the calamities and oppression under which we groan. We inherit the very spot of soil, cultivated by some of the first comers to New England, and though we pretend not that we inherit their virtues also in perfection; yet hope we possess at least some remains of that Christian and heroic virtue and manly sense of liberty, in the exercise of which, they in the very face of danger emigrated from their native land to this then howling wilderness, to escape the iron yoke of oppression, and to transmit to posterity that fair, that amiable inheritance — Liberty, civil and sacred. And give us leave to add that we esteem it not only detracting from the virtue of their design; but an affront to their natural understanding, should we adopt the sentiments lately expressed to the public, viz, — that our worthy ancestors, when they first took possession of this country, when they necessarily lost a voice in the British legislature, consented, at least tacitly, to be subject to the unlimited control and jurisdiction of that very government, the merciless oppression of which was intolerable by them, even when they had a voice in that legislature. We glory in a legal, loyal subjection to our sovereign; but when we see the right to dispose of our property claimed and actually exercised by a legislature a thousand leagues off, and in which we have no voice; and ships and troops poured in upon us to support the growing, or rather overgrown power of crown officers in exercising that same power; the power of our Vice Admiralty courts enlarged beyond due bounds; our principal fortress, built and maintained by us for our defence against a foreign enemy, taken out of our hands, as though we were not worthy to be trusted, and committed into the hands of the standing army; our Governor forbid signing any bill of our Assembly, subjecting a certain number of crown officers to pay any proportion of the charge of the government they live under; our Governor's usual dependence on the people unnaturally and unconstitutionally cut off; the Judges of our Superior Courts, on whose determination life and property so much depend, made to the great danger of the people solely dependent on the crown; and many things of a like nature take place — shall it then be deemed disloyalty and even faction to complain? By no means: we esteem it a virtue and a duty, which people of every rank owe to themselves and posterity, to use their utmost exertions in all reasonable ways, so far as their influence may extend, to oppose tyranny in all its forms, and to extricate themselves from every dangerous and oppressive innovation. And it gives us the greatest pleasure to see so much unity of sentiment in the several towns of this province, and trust there is and will soon appear that unanimity in the several colonies on the continent; and we look upon ourselves peculiarly obliged to the town of Boston for their care and vigilance in this day of darkness and danger, and shall be ever ready to co-operate with them, and our other brethren through the Province, in all reasonable and constitutional measures, for the vindication of our wounded Liberties, and the restoration of the same to their former estate. Imploring the divine benediction on our honest endeavors to maintain and promote constitutional liberties in our land, and hoping to see the time when liberty shall again flourish here, and harmony and concord betwixt Great Britain and the Colonies be restored and confirmed."

1773. This year the first minute company in the town was raised. Previous to this the towns people were in the habit of frequently assembling for military exercise, and were usually drilled by Maj. Judah Alden. The officers of the company now raised were as follows. Ichabod Alden, captain; Andrew Sampson, lieutenant, and Judah Alden, ensign. Among the other individuals, who composed the company, the following are remembered.

Samuel Loring,
Peter Bradford,
John Hanks,
Daniel Loring, } Serg'ts.

Joshua Cushing,
James Shaw, } Corporals.
John Drew, drummer,
Amherst Alden, fifer.

Privates.

Saml. Alden,
Thomas Chandler,
Saml. Chandler,
Thomas Dawes,
Nathl. Delano,
Luther Delano,
Berzilla Delano,
Thomas Delano,
Seraiah Glass,
Peleg Gullifer,
John Glass,
John Oldham,
John Osyer,
Kimball Ripley,

Thaddeus Ripley,
John Southworth,
Joshua Sprague,
Thomas Sprague,
Saml. Sprague,
Uriah Sprague,
Wm. Sampson,
Ichabod Sampson,
Joseph Wadsworth.
Chas. Thomas,
Prince Thomas,
Consider Thomas,
Wait Wadsworth,
Seneca Wadsworth,

Some time after this a regiment of minute men was formed out of Plymouth County, and Theophilus Cotton of Plymouth was chosen colonel; Ichabod Alden of Duxbury, lt.-colonel; and Ebenezer Sprout of Middleboro', major.

Mr. George Partridge was now chosen commander of the company.

The officers of the two companies of militia at this time were, of the first — Capt. Levi Loring, Lt. Bildad Arnold, Ens. Benjamin Freeman; of the second — Capt. Calvin Partridge, Lt. Elijah Baker, Ens. Adam Fish. The next officers were, of the first — Capt. Samuel Loring, Lt. Benjamin Freeman, Ens. Nathaniel Sprague; of the second — Capt. Elijah Baker, Lt. Nathan Sampson, Ens. Cornelius Delano. Capt. Baker was next promoted to a Major.

Another body of men was organized about this time, consisting of all the men over 50 years of age, who were styled the "alarm list," and were under the same officers as the militia. Sentries were also stationed at different points in time of danger, and at Captain's Hill.

1774. These were appointed a Committee of Correspondence, (May 30th): Capt. W. Wadsworth, Dea. P. Wadsworth, Geo. Partridge, Capt. Samuel Bradford and Micah Soule, to unite with the Committee in general for the Province. They also chose (Sept. 19th) Geo. Partridge, Capt. W. Wadsworth, and Dea. P. Wadsworth, a Committee, to join the County Committee, in order to act upon the political affairs of the Province.

On the 6th of July, the justices of Plymouth county addressed a letter to General Gage, and after congratulating him on his appointment to the office of Governor-General, and his safe arrival, continue in substance as follows: — "We consider you a person in whom are centred all the qualifications necessary for the discharge of that important trust; and though sensible that the endeavors of your predecessors were met with bad success, yet we think that your Excellency has power to check every disorder, and to secure for us our constitutional privileges. We have seen with serious concern the influences of those persons calling themselves *Committees of Correspondence*, and against these and their abettors we promise our incessant aid." To this Gen. Gage returned an answer, dated July 12th, assuring them that he would "take every step in his power to secure to them the peaceable enjoyment of all their constitutional privileges, and to give that free course to the laws, on which every State depends for its support, and without which no government can subsist." Among the signers of the address of Plymouth, were Major Briggs Alden and Capt. Gamaliel Bradford of Duxbury. These, however, afterwards at a town meeting (Sept. 19th,) made each a public recantation, and craved the forgiveness of the town. Their declarations were nearly as follows: — "The Address to Thomas Gage, Esq., Captain General and Governor, &c., of the Massachusetts Bay in New England, of the General Sessions of the Peace, and Justices of the Inferior Court of Common Pleas for the county of Plymouth, published in Draper's & Byles' papers [Boston Newsletter] of the 14th of July, 1774, I acknowledge I voted for. For which I am sorry from my heart and humbly ask the forgiveness of the town of Duxbury and all the inhabitants of the Province; and I likewise promise and declare upon the true faith of a Christian, that I will not take a commission, nor act upon any under this new plan of government, if offered to me."

Beside Maj. Alden and Capt. Bradford, the following Justices also subscribed the above Address: Thomas Foster, Joseph Josselyn, Abijah White, Edward Winslow, Pelham Winslow and Gideon Bradford.

The political affairs of the province were now fast drawing to a crisis. On the arrival of Gen. Gage, this year, the General Court assembled at Boston, of which Mr. Partridge was a member from Duxbury. This was soon adjourned to Salem. Here they met, and a secret caucus was proposed, and many of the leading whigs accordingly met in the night, a short distance from the town. Mr. Partridge was present, and took, with others of those noble spirits, those decisive and determined positions, which could not be mistaken, and which much conduced to the completion of that efficient organization of opposition, which was then in embryo. We have the words of Mr. Partridge relative to the occasion of this conclave, — "Gen. Gage (said he) had come over with his troops and proclamations, to frighten us rebels into submission! We soon had his mandate, dissolving the Court, and directing us to meet at Salem, in order, as he said, to 'remove us from the baneful influences — the baneful influences of Boston!' So we met there. And in a short time one began to ask another, 'What can we do? the worst must come to the worst!' 'Why, we will have a caucus and see what can be done.' Then, when we met a member in whose eye we saw one true to the cause, we touched him on the shoulder — 'Be silent — meet with us to-night — at such an hour — in such a place — and *bring your man*.' All were prompt to the hour. The meeting was full. Order was called. 'Shall we submit to Great Britain, and make the best terms in our power, or shall we resist her encroachments to the point of the sword?' — There was a pause. We looked at each other; and the unanimous answer was given, 'We *will* resist her encroachments to the point of the sword!' Now came the question —'What shall be done? The gulf is passed!' 'We will have a Congress at Concord. We will send letters to all the colonies, and urge them to send delegates to meet at Philadelphia. We will have committees of safety. We will take care of our arms. We will go to our homes, and wake every one that sleeps.'" [Rev. Benj. Kent's Address.]

A provincial congress was convened at Salem on the 7th of October; but adjourned on the same day. It was again convened at Concord, on Tuesday the 11th. A meeting of the town was held (Oct. 3d,) and Geo. Partridge was chosen to attend in their behalf at the adjourned meeting of the congress, with these instructions: "To Mr. George Partridge,—As it is unlikely, in the present situation of our public affairs, that the House of Representatives should sit to do business, we instruct and require you to join with the intended Provincial Congress to be holden at Concord, in order to deliberate and determine on the most wise and prudent measures to be adopted for the true interest, happiness and freedom of the Province."

Previous to this, a congress of Plymouth county had been held on the 26th of September, at Plympton, when it adjourned on the next day to the Plymouth court-house, when a committee reported some resolves; and of this number Mr. Partridge of Duxbury was one. The congress at Concord adjourned on the 15th; again assembled at Cambridge on the 17th, and adjourned on the 29th; it met again at Cambridge on the 23d of November, and dissolved on the 10th of December.

1775. The town chose (Jan. 16th) Mr. George Partridge to attend as their representative to the Second Provincial Congress at Cambridge on the 1st of February; and also voted £32 8s. 4d. in aid of the same. This congress adjourned on the 16th; met again at Concord on the 22d of March, adjourned on the 15th of April; again met at Concord, on the 22d, and adjourned the same day; then at Watertown on the 24th, and finally dissolved on the 29th of May.*

At the same meeting, (Jan. 16th,) these were appointed a *Committee of Inspection*, to see the resolves of the Provincial Congress duly executed: Capt. Saml. Bradford, Joshua Hall, Maj. Gamalial Bradford, Jr., Dea. Perez Loring, Capt. Benja. Wadsworth, Jacob Weston, and Peleg Wadsworth. The town afterwards (Jan. 30th) voted to procure thirty fire-arms with bayonets, for the use of the town; and Geo. Partridge, Ichabod Alden and Wm. Thomas were appointed to obtain them, and £60 were furnished them. A meeting had been called previously, to see "if ye town will provide proper fire-arms and all other warlike instruments, and amunition suitable for to defend ye town and country as need may require."

Some time before the open rupture of hostilities, Gen. Gage, at the solicitation of the tories, had stationed at Marshfield a body of the British troops, the *Queen's Guards*, for their pro-

---

* Mr. Partridge was, this year, a member of the General Court from Duxbury, and was one of the Committee ordered to wait upon General Washington, on his arrival.

tection. An address, dated at Pembroke Feb. 7th, 1775, was sent to Gen. Gage by the selectmen of Plymouth, Kingston, Duxbury, Pembroke, Hanson and Scituate, protesting against placing an armed force among them in time of peace, assuring him that there was no truth in the statements of those of Marshfield and Scituate, who declared that this was necessary to protect them from the exasperated fury of the whigs. They declared that no plan of attack had been formed, and begged that his Excellency would examine the case, before he complied. On the 15th of the same month, the Massachusetts Provincial Congress voted that these six towns are highly approved of in finding out the malicious designs of their enemies in requesting Gen. Gage to station there a body of troops. They recommended them to continue "steadily to persevere in the same line of conduct, which has in this instance so justly entitled them to the esteem of their fellow-countrymen; and to keep a watchful eye upon the behavior of those who are aiming at the destruction of our liberties." Gen. Gage, however, thought fit to comply. The following letter, from a tory in Marshfield, to a gentleman in Boston, gives some of the circumstances of the case; which must be read, however, as a loyalist's account. It is dated Jan. 24th, 1775.

"Two hundred of the principal inhabitants of this loyal town, insulted and intimidated by the licentious spirit, that unhappily has been prevalent among the lower ranks of people in the Massachusetts Government, having applied to the Governor for a detachment of his Majesty's troops to assist in preserving the peace, and to check the insupportable insolence of the disaffected and turbulent, were happily relieved by the appearance of Capt. Balfour's party, consisting of one hundred soldiers, who were joyfully received by the Loyalists. Upon their arrival, the valor of the minute men was called forth by Adams' crew; they were accordingly mustered, and to the unspeakable confusion of the enemies of our happy constitution, no more than twelve persons presented themselves to bear arms against the Lord's annointed. It was necessary that some apology should be made for the scanty appearance of their volunteers; and they colored it over with a declaration, that, 'had the party sent to Marshfield consisted of half a dozen battalions, it might have been worth their attention to meet and engage them; but a day would come when the courage of their minute host would be able to clear the country of all their enemies, howsoever formidable in numbers.' The King's troops are very comfortably accommodated, and preserve the most exact discipline; and now every faithful subject to his King dare fully utter his thoughts, drink his tea, and kill his sheep as profusely as he pleases."

The following letter, from a *loyalist* of Boston to a gentleman of New York, also relates to the affair, and is dated Jan. 26th, 1775.

"About a week ago one hundred and fifty of the principal inhabitants of Marshfield entered into Gen. Ruggles' association against the Liberty Plan. When this was known at Plymouth, the faction there threatened to come down in a body and make them recant, or drive them off their farms. On this the Marshfield association sent an express to Gen. Gage to acquaint him of their situation and determination, and begged support. This was readily granted, and a captain and three subalterns and a hundred private men were immediately detached on board two small vessels to Marshfield, where they landed very quietly last Monday; and, when last accounts came, there was no appearance of the Plymouth rebels.

The detachment carried with them 300 stands of arms for the use of gentlemen of Marshfield; one hundred and fifty more having joined the association on advice of the Plymouth threatenings; the whole three hundred have solemnly engaged themselves to turn out in case of attack.

That the liberty rebels of this town [of Boston] might save their own credit, and that of their adherents in Plymouth, and that they might have something to say for not opposing the detachment, they, on first hearing where the soldiers were going, wisely sent off an express to their confederates, begging them to desist from doing what they really had no mind to do."

In speaking of this case Gen. Gage in a letter to the Earl of Richmond said: "It is the first instance of application to Government for assistance, which the faction has ever tried to persuade the people they would never obtain; but be left to themselves."

The town of Marshfield, in town meeting assembled on the 20th of Feb. 1775, voted not to adhere to Congress; and also to make addresses to Gen. Gage, and Admiral Graves. Dr. Winslow was moderator of the meeting, and framed the addresses. Their original answers are now before me.* Gen. Gage's is as follows:

"To the Loyal Inhabitants of the Town of Marshfield.

Gentlemen, — I return you my most hearty thanks for your address, and am to assure you, that I feel great satisfaction in having contributed to the safety and protection of a people so eminent for their Loyalty to their King, and affection to their country at a time, when Treason and Rebellion is making

---

* Rev. B. Kent's MS. Coll. 210, 211.

such hasty strides to overturn our most excellent constitution and spread Ruin and Desolation thro' the Province.

I doubt not that your duty to your God, your King and country will excite you to persevere in the Glorious Cause in which you are engaged, and that your laudable example will animate others with the like Loyal and Patriotic Spirit.

Tho. Gage."

Admiral Graves replied as follows:

"To the Inhabitants of the Town of Marshfield.

Gentlemen, — The warmth with which you declare your principles of Loyalty to your Sovereign and his Constitutional Government cannot fail of being grateful to the mind of every lover of his country: and it is much to be wished that the uniform propriety of your conduct will extend its influence to the removal of those groundless jealousies, which have unhappily warped the affections of too many of your countrymen from the parent state, and which are now tending to raise violent commotions, and involve in Ruin and Destruction this unfortunate Province.

The approbation you are pleased to express of His Majesty's appointment at this critical juncture to the command of his American fleet, is flattering; and you may be assured that my countenance and support shall never be wanting to protect the Friends of British Government and reduce to order and submission, those who would endeavor to destroy that Peace and Harmony, which is the end of good Legislation to produce. Saml. Graves."

A protest was circulated against the proceedings of the above meeting and received 64 signatures.

This detachment was under the command of Capt. Balfour, and consisted of one hundred men with two field pieces. The presence of these troops caused but little uneasiness to the inhabitants, as they were under good discipline, and used no improper conduct towards them. They frequently visited Duxbury in various numbers; and one Sabbath surrounded the meeting house, during the services, and amused themselves in looking in at the windows, somewhat to the discomposure of the more timid within. Toward the close of March, Capt. Balfour devised a project of attacking Plymouth, and accordingly a conference was had at the house of Edward Winslow, Esq., and in the discussion of the question Capt. B. enquired of John Watson, Esq., "Will they fight?" "Yes, like devils," was the cheerful assurance of Mr. Watson, and upon further consideration the plan was abandoned.

Immediately after the news arrived of the bloodshed at Lexington, Col. Cotton with his regiment formed for an attack on Balfour's party. On the 20th Col. Cotton and Maj. Sprout met in Duxbury, at Col. Briggs Alden's for consultation. Maj. Judah Alden, who was in Rhode Island when the news came of the fight, had just returned, having ridden all day on horseback, and soon after learning the circumstances of the case, he met Cato, a negro who had been sent by Capt. Balfour to ascertain the numbers of the men who were marching against him. Maj. Alden suspecting his design, told him to tell Balfour, they were coming in a host after him, and dismissed him. Col. Cotton again returned to Plymouth; and, about 7 o'clock, on the morning of the 21st, marched for Marshfield with a portion of his regiment, consisting of the Plymouth company under Capt. Mayhew, the Kingston under Capt. Peleg Wadsworth, and the Duxbury under Capt. Geo. Partridge. They proceeded to Col. Anthony Thomas', about a mile N. W. of Capt. John Thomas', where were Balfour's troops. At this juncture Col. Cotton and Lt. Col. Alden held a long conference, as to the course to be taken. At noon there were assembled about 500 men, including the crews of many fishing vessels in the harbor. In the afternoon Capt. Clapp's company from Rochester and Capt. Harlow's from Plympton arrived. Capt. Peleg Wadsworth was greatly dissatisfied with the delay, and moved forward his company until within a short distance of the enemy, and then halted as his numbers were too small to venture an attack. About 3 o'clock, P. M., two sloops hove in sight and anchored off the Brant rock. Balfour then conveyed his company through the Cut river in boats, and reaching the sloops soon sailed for Boston, leaving however several sentinels behind to watch the movements of the Americans, who also set guards for the night. The British watch finally left and in going to their boats, they passed one of the American sentry posts, where were stationed Blanie Phillips, and Jacob Dingley, both of Duxbury. Dingley was seized, and conveyed to their boat, when they concluded to release him. Phillips escaped, fired his gun, and gave an alarm, which roused the country for many miles around. Balfour, it is reported, said that if he had been attacked, he should have surrendered without a gun. In their hurry to escape they left much of their camp equipage behind. He fought with his company at Bunker Hill, and, as he afterwards told an inhabitant of Duxbury, whom he recognized in New York, he left the field with but five men following him, upon which he had entered with as fine a company as was in His Majesty's service.

On the 1st of May, four companies of the Regiment were ordered to Plymouth. The company from Duxbury was now commanded by Samuel Bradford, whose officers were the same as had been previously. These were stationed at Plymouth until the 1st of Sept. as a guard. During this time a detachment of twelve men under Maj. Judah Alden performed guard duty at Captain's Hill. In August, Col. Davis, the quartermaster, came from Roxbury with orders for the regiment to embark in whaleboats, and proceed to Sandwich to receive 100 barrels of flour, which had been brought from New York, and conveyed across the isthmus. Twenty boats were immediately despatched under the care of Capt. Sylvanus Drew, and the command of the expedition was given to Capt. Samuel Bradford. Converting their blankets into sails they reached Sandwich about one o'clock, having been five hours on their passage. In passing the bar they had to encounter a strong wind, in which some of the boats were swamped, though none of the men were lost. Having loaded their boats with the flour, they started on the next day, and landed it safe about five o'clock in the afternoon on Cohasset beach, and it was conveyed by land to Roxbury. On the 26th of June preceding, the committee of correspondence of Plymouth, those of Duxbury and Kingston joining in the prayer, sent a memorial to the Provincial Congress, expressing their regret that they had made a determination to move to Roxbury a portion of Col. Cotton's Regiment. "We know," said they, "that Admiral Graves has said we were a rebellious people, and because we have built a fort, it would not be long before he would blow the town about our ears;" and we now request that the troops may be permitted to remain, or else the town will be left.

On the 1st of Sept. Col. Cotton moved his regiment to Roxbury, which formed a part of the detachment ordered to throw up entrenchments on Dorchester heights, March 4th, 1776. The officers of the regiment at this time were — Theophilus Cotton, Col.; Ichabod Alden, Lt. Col.; William Thomas, Surgeon; John Thomas, Surgeon's mate; John Cotton, Jr., Quarter-master; Joshua Thomas, Adjutant.

Captains.	Lieutenants.	Ensigns.
Tho. Matthew,	Nathl. Lewis,	Benj. Warner,
Earl Clapp,	Isaac Pope,	Chas. Church,
John Bradford,	Jesse Sturtevant,	Tho. Sampson,
John Brigham,	Edw. Sparrow,	Nehemiah Cobb,
Joshua Benson,	Wm. Thompson,	James Smith,
Isaac Wood,	Abiel Townshend,	Foxwell Thomas,
Peleg Wadsworth,	Seth Drew,	Joseph Sampson,
Amos Wade,	Archelaus Cole,	Lemuel Wood,
Saml. Bradford,	Andrew Sampson,	Judah Alden,
Edw. Hammond.	Timothy Ruggles.	Nathan Sears.

On the removal of the Americans to New York in 1776, several others of Duxbury joined Capt. Bradford's company,

and proceeded on with the regiment. Among others were
Isaac and Nathl. Delano, and Consider and Oliver Glass.
The company remained in New York about a year, when
Capt. Bradford resigned his commission, and came home with
a great part of his company, many of whom soon again
enlisted. Commissions were now granted to Joseph Wadsworth, Adam Fish, and Judah Alden, all of Duxbury, to be
Captains. Each of these immediately raised their companies,
and had many Duxbury men under their command. In the
summer of 1777, Capt. Wadsworth having raised a company
in Duxbury, marched to Boston, to proceed to join the army
of Gen. Gates.

Col. Cotton's second in command, *Lt. Col. Ichabod Alden*
of Duxbury, had not, previous to the commencement of hostilities, seen any military service, except that he had been for a
short time an officer of the militia. He inherited much of
the fortitude and independence of his ancestors. His feelings
were in perfect unison with the whigs, and he denounced the
provoking usurpation of their rights as tyrannous and not to
be borne, and was among the foremost to resort to means of
violence for the protection of those privileges bequeathed to
him from his ancestors, and to whose memory he owed it to
preserve them for posterity. He thought, that

"To fight
In a *just* cause and for our country's glory,
Is the best office of the best of men;
And to decline, when these motives urge,
Is infamy beneath a coward's baseness."

He was soon after promoted to the rank of Colonel, and
after the capture of Burgoyne, at Saratoga (Oct. 17th, 1777),
was stationed with a regiment of the continental army at a
place called Cherry Valley, sixty miles west from Albany, for
the defence of the frontiers. In consequence of its exposed
situation a fortification had been erected here, during the
preceding spring, by order of Lafayette, and its command
was at once solicited by Col. Gansevoort, with the regiment
which had so greatly distinguished itself in the preceding
year in the defence of Fort Schuyler. It was nevertheless
given to Col. Alden, under whose superintendence it had been
built, who soon after arrived with his regiment. We have
now to relate his sad and mournful end, while in command
of this post. He was attacked by surprise by the enemy
under Capt. Walter N. Butler, a royalist, and Brant, a noted
Indian Mohawk Chief, with about 700 loyalists and Indians.
Col. Alden with a large portion of his officers and men fell
victims to their savage cruelty. He had received due notice

of this preconcerted plan of the tories and Indians, for on the 8th of November he received a despatch from Fort Schuyler, conveying the intelligence, which had been received there by an Oneida Indian, who reported that he had learned it from one of the Onondagas, who had been present at a great meeting of the Indians and tories at Tioga, at which this determination had been formed. Col. Alden discredited it, and for good reasons perhaps, as a mere idle Indian rumor, yet he took precautions, but refused the inhabitants of the village permission to deposit their valuables in the fort, (from whence they had been removed, not anticipating farther hostilities before spring,) giving as a reason that it would only be a temptation for his soldiers to plunder; and at the same time assured them, that he would use all diligence against surprise, and by means of vigilant scouts be at all times prepared to warn them of approaching danger. Accordingly scouts were sent out on the 9th, and proceeding down the Susquehannah, as it were in the very face of the enemy, they kindled a fire in the evening, and by the side of which very foolishly laid themselves down to sleep. The result might have been foreseen, for they were prisoners when they awoke.

Had they followed the dictates of prudence, the scenes to follow would probably have never occurred, and the charges of imprudence, now sometimes so unjustly imposed on the vigilant colonel, would have missed their record on the page of the historian. In the mean time the enemy, drawn thither by the light of the fire, soon surrounded them, and, having extorted all necessary information, moved forward on the 10th, encamping, however, for that night on the top of a hill thickly covered with evergreens, about a mile southwest of the fort and village of Cherry Valley. There was a light fall of snow in the night, but it turned to rain in the morning, with a thick and cloudy atmosphere. The officers of the garrisons were accustomed to lodge about among the families near the fort, and from the assurances of their colonel the apprehensions of the people were so much allayed, that they thought themselves reposing in perfect security. Col. Alden, with Stacia, his lieutenant-colonel, lodged with Mr. Robert Wells, a gentleman of great respectability. The enemy having ascertained the localities of the officers, approached the unsuspecting village in the greatest security, veiled by the haze which hung in the atmosphere. An alarm was however given before the enemy had actually arrived at the village, by the firing of an Indian upon a settler upon the outskirts, who was riding thither on horseback. He was wounded, but nevertheless pushed forward, and gave instant information to the colonel, who still disbelieved the approach of an enemy in force, supposing the shot to have proceeded from a straggler.

He was soon convinced of his error, for, before the guards could be called in, the Indians were upon him. Unfortunately for the inhabitants, Butler, with his rangers, had halted just before entering the village, to examine their arms, the rain having damaged their powder. During this pause the Indians sprang forward, and the Senecas, being at that time the most ferocious of the six nations, were in the van. The house of Mr. Wells was instantly surrounded by the warriors of that tribe, and several tories of no less ferocity, who rushed in and massacred the whole family. Col. Alden himself escaped from the house, but was pursued down a hill by an Indian, who repeatedly demanded of him to surrender. This he refused to do, turning upon his pursuer, and repeatedly snapping his pistol at him, but without effect. The Indian ultimately hurled his tomahawk with unerring aim, and, springing forward, seized in an instant his scalp. Thus in the outset fell the commander, who unfortunately was but little accustomed to Indian warfare; and had he been as prudent as he was brave, might have averted the tragic scenes of that hapless day.*— *W. S. Stone's Life of Brant.*

Although some blame should be attached to the incredulity of Col. Alden, yet it must be recollected that many rumors of a like nature (though to be sure not always in the form of a despatch) were constantly reaching his ears, and all proving to be equally false and without foundation. And, perhaps, still further it may be urged in his favor, that the extreme lateness of the season would have seemed almost a guaranty, that no attack would be attempted, even upon the outermost posts of the frontier. Yet there are some who view his course more harshly, and consider him guilty of a "most criminal neglect of duty."

As an officer, Col. Alden was brave and persevering; as a gentleman, he was accomplished and agreeable; and in all his relations of life, he formed around him lasting and steadfast friends, and in his intercourse with others was honorable and just; and his untimely death could not but be lamented by all who knew him.

His widow in Duxbury received official tidings of the event, as she was proceeding toward Boston in her chaise; though none of his effects ever reached her.

1775. The town appointed (April 26th) Capt. Joshua Hall, Ezra Weston and Ichabod Alden a committee to pur-

---

* Lieut. Col. Stacia was taken prisoner, and most of the guard at Mr. Wells' house were captured or slain. Thirty-two of the inhabitants, mostly women and children, fell victims, while the garrison in the fort remained secure. — *Stone.*

chase a cargo of corn in a vessel at Duck hill, and store it for time of need.*

A third provincial congress was convened at Watertown on the 31st of May, and dissolved on the 19th of July. This congress, June 29th, "Resolved, that thirteen thousand coats be provided as soon as may be, and one thereof given to each non-commissioned officer and soldier in the Massachusetts forces, agreeable to the resolves of Congress on the 23d of April last; and in order to facilitate their being procured," provisions were made for the several towns to furnish a certain number of the 13,000. Plymouth county was to provide 1054; Essex, Worcester, Middlesex, Hampshire and Suffolk alone furnishing none. The towns of Plymouth furnished in this proportion: Bridgewater 188, Middleboro' 160, Scituate 125, Plymouth 100, Rochester 86, Pembroke 66, Plympton 56, Marshfield 54, Abington 46, *Duxbury* 44, Kingston 38, Hanover 37, Wareham 30, and Halifax 24. A resolve was afterwards passed, advising the inhabitants to kill no more sheep, except in cases of necessity.

These were chosen (July 10) a *Committee of Safety*: Ezra Arnold, Levi Loring, Joshua Stanford, Dea. Southworth, Capt. Hall, and Isaac Partridge; and afterwards (Aug. 7th,) it was voted not to use powder, except to shoot destructive vermin.

1776. *Liberty or Death!* was now the prevailing sentiment of the land. The flag of freedom flying from the Liberty-poles throughout the province, bore this far-famed motto to the skies, and its holy influences upon all the assemblies of the people were exerted. "*We leave the affair relating to independency to the Continental Congress, to* STAND OR FALL WITH THEM," was the emphatic declaration of the town (May 23d), who were willing and ready to place in the hands of the chosen of the people the destinies of their lives and fortunes. To stand by them in prosperity, or to fall with them in adversity, was a duty, which they alike owed to the memory of those, of whose happiest boons they were the grateful recipients; which they owed to each other, and which they owed to posterity.

The *Committee of Correspondence* for this year (chosen May 11th,) were G. Partridge, Isaac Partridge, E. Arnold, Peleg Wadsworth, James Southworth, Perez Loring, Levi Loring, Gaml. Bradford, Jr., Bildad Arnold, Eliphas Prior, Judah Delano, Joshua Stanford and Reuben Delano.

Mr. Partridge was also this year the town's representative. He was appointed one of a committee of three of the General

---

* During the operation of the Boston Port Bill, supplies were sent to the suffering inhabitants of that town by many of the towns throughout the province. Duxbury forwarded (March 13th) twenty-one cords of wood, and (March 27th) the sum of £4 5s. 8d.

Court, to visit the Commander-in-chief at New York, and obtain his advice concerning the term of enlistment, and the amount of bounty of the Massachusetts quota of troops. They had been instructed by the Massachusetts General Court to raise the men for one year; but on their arrival at New York, Gen. Washington requested Mr. Partridge to proceed to the National Congress, then sitting at Philadelphia. There he was advised to propose first to Washington a compliance with this instruction; but if the Commander-in-chief should disapprove of it, to propose the enlistment of men for three years, or during the war. When Mr. Partridge returned, he mentioned first the Massachusetts instructions to Washington, who, raising his eyes to heaven, and clasping his hands, exclaimed, — "My God! Sir, are you going to give me an army to last but one year? I cannot consent to be commander-in-chief of such any army." Mr. Partridge then advanced the second proposition, and the men were raised for that period. — *Rev. Benj. Kent's Address.*

Early in the spring of this year, 700 bushels of corn, from a Virginian vessel, were purchased, to store it for time of need, at an expense of £99 3s. 4d. Other expenses attending it, made it amount to £106 13s. 9d.

Late in the year (Oct. 7) a meeting of the town was called, and it was decided, that it was not expedient for the General Court to form a new constitution or plan of government; but "to go on in the same method as is usual, or as heretofore they have done." However, early in the next year (May 14th, 1777), they instructed their representatives "to act upon a new plan of government."

A *fort* was, early in this year, built at the *Gurnet* by the towns of Plymouth, Kingston and Duxbury. On the part of Duxbury, Isaac Partridge and Dea. Peleg Wadsworth were chosen (Feb. 20th,) their agents in the work of erection. No attack, it is believed, was made on this during the war. A few shots, however, were exchanged with the British frigate Niger, Capt. Talbot; and at this time one of the balls from the frigate pierced the light-house; and the vessel grounded on Brown's Island shoal, but soon got off.

A *beacon* was also erected on *Captain's hill*, and in the night time in any danger of attack by the enemy, tar barrels were fired, which called the neighboring towns to assistance.

The Gurnet fort mounted three 12-pounders, one 6-pounder, and two 9-pounders. The garrison consisted of about 60 men, nearly one half of whom were from Duxbury. The first officers were Capt. Wm. Weston of Plymouth, Lt. A. Sampson, and Ens. Nathl. Carver. These were succeeded by Capt. Andrew Sampson of Duxbury, Dea. Smith and Ebenezer Barker, both of Pembroke were Lt. and Ens.; and afterward Capt. Stephen Churchill, whose second in command was Lt. John Washburn.

Early in this year an incident occurred, which caused considerable confusion in the country around. The valiant Capt. Manly with a number of valuable prizes approached the harbor, and entering it anchored off Saquish point. It was supposed at the time that it was a British fleet, come to burn the towns around the bay. A beacon was immediately fired on Saquish, which was soon followed by another at Captain's hill, and at Monk's hill in Kingston, and at Plymouth. Troops came pouring in from the neighboring towns, and the companies of Duxbury assembled under arms at Captain's hill; but soon after the facts of the case were known, and the crowd dispersed.

This was a time of general fear along the coast by those who were expecting the execution of the threats of Admiral Graves. Sentinels were constantly posted, and they attended divine service on the Sabbath, with their arms.

In General Sullivan's campaign in Rhode Island, nearly the whole body of militia in the county were ordered to his aid. The two companies of Duxbury marched under the command of Capt. Calvin Partridge, and were gone about two months. Arriving at Little Compton, they were placed under the immediate command of Gen. Peleg Wadsworth, who had charge of the militia, then assembled to the number of about 2000 men. On one occasion, while Gen. Sullivan was skirmishing with the British at some distance, Gen. Wadsworth by his command drew up his militia in a body and formed them ready for an attack, whenever orders came for advancing. While thus arrayed, he was informed that they would probably be soon ordered forward. Gen. Wadsworth then for a short time harangued his men, and prepared them for the onset; but as no orders came they saw no fighting on that day. This occurred late in the summer of 1777.

During the absence of the men, the harvesting was done by the matrons of the town, who divided themselves into two companies, the one commanded by Miss Rachel Sampson, and the other by Mrs. William Thomas, and met by turns at the different farms, and gathered the crops; there being none but the old men remaining in the town.

1777. The following were chosen (March 17) a *committee of correspondence and safety:* Deacons Wadsworth, Southworth and Loring, Capt's Hall and Arnold, Ezra Arnold, Eliphas Prior, Reuben Delano, Judah Delano, Joshua Stanford, and Perez Chandler. There were but few towns in the province, who did not number among their inhabitants some of the supporters of the British Government, who were induced to act the part, more from fear, than from a sincere belief in their duty of loyalty; though doubtless there were some of the latter class. Few towns were destitute of a *tory house*, where these bondmen of British tyranny were wont to congregate, either in secret or openly. In Duxbury (and to its honor may it be said,) there was not a single tory! None dared to profess themselves the friends of British tyranny.

Liberty-pole recantations in Duxbury were not numerous, as there were none to recant. However the tories of other towns did not altogether escape their strict regimen, which they judged perhaps conformable to the duties of perfect patriots. An attempt was made to seize upon Nathaniel Phillips, one of the principal loyalists of Marshfield; but he contrived to escape their vigilance. At one time Dr. Stockbridge, Paul White, and Elisha Ford, three of the leading tories in Marshfield, were seized and carted under the liberty pole in Duxbury, and forced to sign recantations. The liberty pole was placed on the hill near Col. Bradford's and stood several years after the war. However it appears from the records that (May 14th, 1777) the town appointed John Sampson with instructions "to procure all evidence that he could get against all the enemies of the State, and to make report thereof to proper authorities."

Marshfield was the centre of toryism in this quarter. A large number was also collected at Sandwich. There were some at Plymouth, Halifax and Taunton, and a few in Bridgewater; and these seemed to constitute nearly the whole tory legion in the Old Colony. The *associated loyalists* at Marshfield numbered about 300 persons. Among the principal characters of this body may be mentioned nearly every member of the ancient Winslow family, and the residence of Dr. Isaac Winslow was one of the chief places of their meeting; yet he alone of the family was permitted to remain on his estate during the war. He died here in 1819, æt. 81, having lived a life of usefulness in his profession. Another member of this association, Nathaniel Ray Thomas, bore the odious office of mandamus counsellor. He embarked for Halifax on the evacuation of Boston by the British army in 1776, where he died in 1791. He is called in McFingal,

"That Marshfield blunderer, Nat. Ray Thomas."

In the month of July in the year 1774, about seven hundred persons from different parts of the county assembled in Marshfield, and marched to the dwelling of Mr. Thomas, to endeavor to compel him to resign his commission of mandamus counsellor. Arriving here they were told that he had gone to Boston; however they searched his house, and put the family under oath, administered by a justice of Pembroke, who was present, and they solemnly declared that he was absent.

Another, Abijah White, who had been the representative of the town in the General Court, and a government man of great zeal, but of little discretion, carried to Boston the celebrated Marshfield resolves, censuring the whigs, and caused them to be published, which drew upon him their wrath, and he sunk under the burden of general ridicule. He was obliged to flee to the protection of the British in Boston, to escape the fury of the whigs, and here in remuneration for his services, the English General appointed him superintendent of a turnip field, which had been planted (where now is the Boston Latin School,) by the troops to furnish themselves with vegetables for the sick, the town at that time being deprived of all intercourse with the country without. This proved scarcely consistent with the dignity of the Marshfield loyalist. In McFingal, in recounting one of his exploits, it says,—

> "Abijah White, when sent,
> Our Marshfield friends to represent,
> Himself while dread array involves,
> Commissions, pistols, swords, resolves,
> In awful pomp descending down,
> Bore terror on the faction town."

He was of the party of tories and marines, captured by Maj. Tupper at the light house in Boston harbor, and was wounded in the encounter. Isaac Joice, Seth Bryant, Caleb and Melzar Carver, Israel Tilden, Thomas Decrow and Joseph Phillips were likewise odious to the friends of liberty, and were proscribed and banished in 1778. The mob sometimes acted with indiscretion, though it is not known that the town on any occasion forced upon these enemies of their liberties any unwarrantable punishments. Some, it is true, were compelled to sign recantations of sentiments under the liberty pole. The following account is given* of the treat-

---

* *Lorenzo Sabine's American Loyalists.* Of the colonies, says the same authority, New York was undeniably the loyalists' strong hold, and contained more of them than any other colony in all America. Massachusetts furnished 67,907 whig soldiers between the years 1775 and 1783, while New York supplied but 17,781. In adjusting the war balances after the peace, Massachusetts had overpaid her share in the sum of $1,248,801 of silver money; but New York was deficient in the large amount of $2,074,846. New Hampshire, though almost a wilderness, furnished 12,496 troops for the continental ranks, or quite three quarters of the number enlisted in the *Empire State.*

One more fact may serve to throw a still stronger light, to illuminate more brightly the *nearly unanimous* whig principles of the OLD BAY STATE. Virginia, whose established quota was the next highest and within four thousand of that of Massachusetts, failed to comply therewith in the

ment of a Halifax tory, at the hands of some of the furious whigs. One Jesse Dunbar by name, having bought some fat cattle of a mandamus counsellor in 1774, drove them to Plymouth for sale. The whigs soon learned with whom he had presumed to deal, and after he had slaughtered, skinned and hung up one of the beasts, commenced punishing him for the offence. His tormentors, it appears, put the dead ox in a cart and fixed Dunbar in his belly, carted him four miles and required him to pay one dollar for the ride. He was then delivered over to a Kingston mob, who carted him four other miles and exacted another dollar. A Duxbury mob then took him and after beating him in the face with the creature's tripe, and, endeavoring to cover his person with it, carried him to counsellor Thomas' house, and compelled him to pay a further sum of money. Flinging his beef into the road, they now left him to recover and return as he could. When he was received from the Kingston mob, he was put into a cart belonging to Mr. William Arnold. By the command of Capt. Wait Wadsworth, he was first allowed to walk by the cart; but while some of the boys, who were collected in great numbers, were dancing around him, he tripped some of them up with his feet, which so irritated the people, that they placed him again in the cart with renewed violence; and soon again transferred him to another ox cart, which carried him and finally tipped him out in front of the counsellor's door.

The town chose (Nov. 24th) Bezaleel Alden, Nathan Chandler and Joseph Soule a committee " to fulfil the resolves of the Court, relating to the soldiers in the Continental army."

1778. Early in this year (Jan. 15th), the town assembled, and voted to instruct their representatives to comply with the resolves of the Continental Congress, and to keep a confederate union with the United States, to be entered upon for the good of the whole. Dea. Loring, Capt. Arnold, and Mr. Partridge were appointed to draw up instructions, which they reported as follows : — " To George Partridge and Dea. Peleg Wadsworth, Representatives ; — You are directed to act and to do in the matter, relating to a compliance of a perpetual union and confederate commerce with the United States, as you shall judge most meet for the advantage of this and the other United States, for the good of the whole relative to the matter."

These were appointed (April 6th) a *committee of inspection and safety*, — Wrestling Alden, James Freeman, Jr., Judah Delano, John Sampson and Dea. Loring.

number of about 22,000 men : while Massachusetts overrun over 15,000 men. Thus Massachutetts, though required by Congress to furnish only 4,000 more men, raised over 37,000 more !

At the above-named meeting in January, Jacob Weston was authorized by the town " to procure one hundred pounds in lawful money, to buy s^d money's worth in arms and ammunition for ye town's store." It was afterwards voted, that the selectmen dispose of the arms, thus procured, by lot; but this vote was rescinded at the next meeting, and it was ordered that they be apprized, and that the selectmen retain them until further orders.

At a meeting, March 23d, the town "voted to grant the petition of Capt. Arnold and Lt. Hall, for establishing the several votes passed in the first company of militia in Duxbury, for raising soldiers for the Continental and State service, agreeable to said petition."

At a very large meeting of the town, on the 1st of June, called to consider the expediency of the country's adopting a new plan of government, it was nearly unanimously decided in the negative (103 noes and 3 ayes). Assessors were chosen to raise money for the militia companies; Col. Alden, Benj. Alden and Judah Delano for the north; and Joseph Freeman, Jr., Capt. Andrew Sampson and Saml. Chandler for the south. Capt. Bildad Arnold was chosen to attend the convention to be held at Concord in October next.

The Board of War delivered (Nov. 28th,) "to Capt. Sylvanus Drew, 19 firearms for the town of Duxburough at £6."

1779. The town voted (May 17th) that their representative, Mr. Partridge, be instructed, that if the major part of the State be for a change of government, he should vote for a committee for that purpose. The vote was then taken as regards a new constitution, which was decided in the negative by a majority of 21 votes (neg. 30, aff. 7). They then requested Capt. Hall, Lt. Elijah Baker, Capt. Calvin Partridge, Lt. Saml. Chandler and Ezra Weston, to engage three soldiers for the Continental army, and four for ———. *Voted*, that a tax be levied to pay the soldiers' polls, which were 3s. 6d. on the hundred.

At a meeting, Aug. 16th, they chose " Col. Briggs Alden and Mr. Eliphas Prior to attend the county convention to be held at Mr. Caleb Loring's, the 24th day of this instant August."

1780. This year exhibited greater activity on the part of the inhabitants, to bring the struggle for freedom at an end. They appear to have entered upon the year with more determination and greater fortitude. The war, which had now been raging for nearly five years, demanded their most strenuous exertions to bring it at once to a speedy and honorable close. Discouragement and discontent became to be manifested among the troops. Their families at home beggared, themselves receiving but poor pay and a scanty subsistence, they turned from the ranks in despair. To retain them in the service was of the greatest moment to the country. To do this, large sums of money must be raised by taxation, and measures were undertaken throughout the provinces to raise the requisite amount. With high expectations of a future acknowledged independence, or at least with the consciousness of doing all in their power to secure this blessing for posterity, many of the towns immediately came forward to the assistance of their common country. Early in the opening of this year, (Feb. 8th,) this town assembled, to take into consideration means for procuring the necessary sum which would be required of them to discharge the debts already contracted by the war, and to furnish money for the removal of the same. Most of those who had enlisted for the term of nine months, had received no remuneration. After some discussion, it was voted to raise £5000 for the payment of these.

Dea. James Southworth, Capt. Bildad Arnold and Eliphas Prior were appointed (Mar. 7th,) the *committee of correspondence* for the ensuing year. The form of government was, at a meeting held on the 22d of May, presented to the town for their approval or rejection. It was duly considered; and, on taking the question, the vote stood 44 for it, with five dissenting voices.

The terms of service of the troops were now fast expiring, and recruits were wanted to supply their places. The town took all necessary measures to supply her quota of men in the coming campaign. It was not however until somewhat late in the season, that a company could be gathered. They assembled on the 19th of June, but without transacting any business, save voting to unite in the forming of the company, they adjourned to the next day, and met at the house of Wrestling Alden. Eighteen men were now selected, who were required to provide one man each. The meeting then adjourned to the meeting-house, where the following votes for raising more money were next passed. First, to raise £800 by a tax on the polls and estates of the town, to pay the soldiers raised pursuant to the three resolves of the General Court, for reënforcing the Continental army. Second, to raise £10,000 to pay the nine months' men, last in the army. At an adjourned meeting, it was voted that the above committee of eighteen be empowered to engage the men "at 20 hard dollars a month, including the State's bounty, which the town is to have the benefit of, or 20 bushels of corn, or 15 bushels of rye, or other produce at this same rate." A vote was also passed "to indemnify the officers in case there is a fine amerced on them." On the 3d of July the town again assembled, when it was ascertained that this committee, with the exception of six, had procured each a man to serve for six months. Six others were now added to the committee, to exert their influence in procuring the residue. The company was called together by their officers, ready for the departure on the 10th instant.

Now came another demand for 22 militia men, to serve three months; and they agreed to raise these at their own expense; and a committee, corresponding to the number required, were authorized to procure each a man, and to agree with him. At this time the town determined, that those who shall pay the tax levied for paying the three and six months men *in silver*, shall be exempted from paying more for said purpose. It will be observed, that the currency was required to be *hard;* for at this time the paper currency had so much depreciated, that one dollar in silver would purchase nearly an hundred in paper.

A call was also made on the town by the State, for her quota of beef, which was 6190 pounds, and a tax was voted to be levied to procure funds for purchasing the same, estimating the beef at $4 per pound, which would make the amount $24,760. Eliphas Prior was afterwards (Oct. 3d) appointed to purchase it, and to hire a sum equal to the amount, if he could; and to deliver the beef to a person authorized to receive it, by the General Court. The treasurer was also told to issue notes, payable in six months, to any person who would sell the beef or lend the money.

The following men, of Duxbury, at this period served three months in Baron Stuben's infantry:—Isaac Delano, Joshua Brewster, Consider Glass, Oliver Delano, and James Weston.

1781. The *Committee of Correspondence, Inspection and Safety* of last year, were reappointed for the present year.

The town met on the 1st of January, and determined to raise 14 more men to serve for three years; and a committee of the same number were appointed to procure each a man. The militia officers were requested to assist in the levy; and, at an adjourned meeting (Jan. 5th), a new plan was agreed upon, by dividing the town into classes, and requiring each class to provide one man, agreeing with him as they may think best. Assembling again on the 29th, no further steps were taken, except they passed a vote, stimulating the inhabitants to renewed action. Afterwards (April) they voted to pay the twenty men, who were to march to Tiverton, three shillings per day, including the State's pay. A committee was also appointed to settle accounts with those before chosen to settle with the three, six, and nine months men. This committee consisted of Col. B. Alden, Bezaleel Alden and John Peterson.

In July three men were enlisted in the west part of the town to serve in the Rhode Island campaign for five months. Some farther resolves were made at a meeting on the 9th of

this month, in relation to the three months men. They voted
to allow them £6 per month, exclusive of the State's pay;
and voted to raise for this purpose £36; and also agreed to
indemnify the officers if they did not draft the men.

In this place it may be well to give some account of the
part the inhabitants of Duxbury took in the maritime affairs
of this period.

In the early part of the war, a fishing schooner, belonging
to Elijah Sampson of Duxbury, was taken and burnt by the
enemy, off the beach within sight of the town. She was
commanded by Capt. Lewis Drew, and manned by Ezra
Howard, Joseph Delano, Zebdiel Delano, Abiathar Alden,
and Zadock Bradford. They were taken to New York and
put on board the Jersey prison ship, where they all died
excepting Alden and Bradford, who returned home.

The English forty-gunship Chatham took the schooner
Olive, belonging to Capt. Nathaniel Winsor, by whom she
was at that time commanded, and manned by Wm. Winsor,
Thomas Sampson and Lot Hunt. They were finally released
on parole with the loss of their mainsail, which the enemy
retained.

Shortly after the above, Samuel Chandler's schooner Polly
Johnson, commanded by Capt. John Winsor, and manned by
Consider Glass, Thomas Chandler, Asa Tour, and James
Weston, was taken by the English thirty-two gunship Perseverance. The enemy put on board the schooner several of
their crew, who started on a cruise for the purpose of ascertaining her sailing qualities. They however returned on the
next day, and, putting on board her original crew with the
crew of another prize, which they had taken, belonging to
Cape Ann, released them on parole, giving to the two crews
the schooner, which they afterwards returned to the rightful
owner.

Capt. Eden Wadsworth, George Cushman, and Joshua
Brewster served in the public armed vessels. In the summer
of 1779, Freeman Loring, Studley Sampson, Amasa Delano,
and Joseph Bestow joined the crew of the privateer Mars, an
armed vessel of 22 guns, fitted out at Boston by Mr. David
Sears and commanded by Capt. Ash. James Tour and
William Ripley served aboard the Alliance frigate.

Messrs. Warren Weston, Abel Sampson, Bisbee Chandler,
Howard Chandler, and Samuel Delano were with Capt.
Simeon Sampson in a brig, when he was taken by the English
ship Rainbow. Abel Sampson died in the Halifax prison.
The Rainbow was soon after nearly lost in a fog in the vicinity of Cape Sable; but was finally rescued from her perilous
situation by the skill of a Marblehead captain who was a

prisoner on board, and who thus obtained his liberty, which was granted to him as a recompense for his services.

In the year 1781, a small vessel, called a "*Shaving Mill,*" was built and equipped at Kingston, to proceed along the coast to the Penobscot, and there to plunder and seize the British stores. She was a long craft, had three lateen sails and fourteen oars. She sailed from Captain's hill under the command of Capt. Joseph Wadsworth, whose lieutenant was Daniel Loring, and was absent on her cruise about three weeks.

1782. On the 1st of August an order came from the Hon. Henry Gardner for the town to furnish the sum of £222¼ for three men in the State service, in accordance with the resolve of the State, March, 1782.

1783. The blessing of peace at last came upon the States, and with it, too, the consummation of their most ardent aspirations. Liberty and independence had been acquired, though through rivers of blood and plains of desolation. As to the founders of New England we owe the blessing of religious liberty; so to the heroes of the revolution must we look, as the source of our civil independence. Both the choicest favors in the gift of Providence. Temporary has been the admiration bestowed on the mightiest exploits; but lasting as the soil upon which they trod, must be the love and veneration ever to be manifested for the memory of those who first acquired and handed to posterity, the richest of Heaven's blessings, CIVIL AND RELIGIOUS LIBERTY. They acted from principles, — principles, which made them look rather to the future, than the past, rather to the acquirement of liberty and prosperity for their children, than to the augmentation of their own personal happiness. They strove for the establishment of those institutions now so endeared to our hearts, and so beneficial to our security. They strove in unity, — unity of purpose and of deed, and may their example ever be before us, and may it prompt us to a regard for the union of our States, and may our dying ejaculations be in anticipation of an eternal concord, peaceful and happy. They bequeathed to us the choicest boons. It is to the character of the primitive settlers of New England, that we are indebted for our system of general education, now so justly the subject of our own pride, and the object of universal admiration; and their children, drinking in the spirit which actuated their fathers in the performance of those deeds, still and ever will uphold that native energy and inborn perseverance, which has made New England what she is, her sons the models of uprightness, alike distinguished for integrity and probity, and the possessors of that enterprising spirit, which has caused the world to be encircled by her numbers, and every sea whitened with her sails.

But few of the participators in that struggle are now left amongst us. In 1840, there were in the town nineteen survivors, who received pensions from the government, but since then many of them have died.* Their names were Joseph Kinney, aged 85 years, Howland Sampson 85, Andrew Sampson 91, Thomas Chandler 87, Samuel Gardner 76, Howard Chandler 81, James Weston 79, Oliver Delano 81, Reuben Dawes 95, Nathaniel Hodges 78, Isaiah Alden 81, Abner Sampson 88, Levi Weston 83, Judah Alden 89, Uriah Sprague 92, Seth Sprague 80, Joshua Brewster 77, Jeptha Delano 81, and Edward Arnold 92. The aggregate age of these was 1603 years; the average age 84 $^{7\text{-}19}$. There were four over 90; eleven between 80 and 90; and four between 70 and 80. At the same date there were thirteen widows receiving pensions, whose husbands had served in the war. Their aggregate age was 1025 years, and the average 78 $^{11\text{-}13}$ years. Of all the towns in Plymouth county, no other, except Middleboro', had a larger or so large a number.

* Under the first pension law, there were 22 pensioners in Duxbury. It has been estimated that there were about sixty individuals from Duxbury actively engaged through the revolution in the army and navy. The following is an imperfect list of those men belonging to Duxbury, who were either killed in action or died in the army during the war : of Capt. S. Bradford's company, Elisha Sampson, Asa Hunt, and Thomas Sprague, at the battle of White Plains. Col. Ichabod Alden at Cherry Valley, and of his regiment in the retreat from Ticonderoga to Albany, Carpus White, and also James Wright and Nathaniel Weston, who died by disease. Joshua Sprague, a sergeant under Capt. Bradford, died at New York, Aug. 20, 1776 æt 25. Ira Bradford served on board a privateer and was killed in a fight on Long Island Sound. Samuel Alden received a mortal wound in the Penobscot expedition.

BIOGRAPHICAL SKETCHES

OF THE

MEN OF THE REVOLUTION.

Col. Briggs Alden. He was quite young elected an officer of the militia, and in 1762 elevated to the office of Major, and in 1776 received the rank of Colonel. During the war he continued in firm opposition to the proceedings of the English government, and his exertions in support of the measures of the Continental Congress were untiring, truly believing that in that the fate of the country could be safely intrusted. At most of the meetings of the town during his long and active life, he presided, and his customary stately and dignified mien secured for him the respect of the people, for whose interests he toiled much, and whose services were by them duly appreciated. It is true, he was in the commencement of the troubles with England, opposed to the proceedings of the provincials, and an esteemed friend of Gov. Hutchinson. When however the English Parliament asserted their right to tax the colonies in every case without their consent, he was convinced of their unjust purpose, and felt true indignation at their course, declared that they ought to be resisted, expressed himself prepared to fight them, and came out a warm and decided whig.

He was an active member of the church, for many years a justice of the peace, and much interested in the cause of education. In person he was portly and of great size, weighing about 220 pounds; dignified in his manner, and of lofty bearing.

The portrait of Col. Alden, which accompanies this work, is copied from a miniature likeness, taken by the late Dr. Rufus Hathaway, but a few years previous to the Colonel's death, and is said by his grandchildren, in whose possession the original now is, to have been a striking likeness.

Having faithfully served his generation he departed this life on the 4th of Oct. 1796, aged 74 years. His son *Samuel* served in the Penobscot expedition under Gen. Lovell, where he received a wound from which he afterwards died, Nov. 1778, aged 27.

Major Judah Alden, son of Col. Briggs Alden, served during the first years of the war in Col. Bailey's regiment as a Captain, and was a brave and valiant officer; and likewise an officer of the minute company in the town, and in the capacity of clerk of which he commenced his military career. As an officer, Major Alden was skilful and prudent. He was an intimate and confidential friend of Washington, and of whom he always spoke with freedom; yet nothing ever escaped him but in praise. In the use of arms he was dexterous, and his fine manly form manifesting great physical strength, eminently qualified him for the profession he led in early life; but which he chose from a conscientious regard for duty, and though of a disposition much averse to the bloody consequences of war, he pursued it for his country's good, and regardless of his own private happiness, he spent the vigor of his days, amid the turmoil of the camp, and the confusion and din of strife, to secure for his children an everlasting freedom. Living to an extreme old age and enjoying it in comparative health, preserving his erectness of figure until within a few years of his death, he died in the full possession of his intellectual powers, on the 12th of March, 1845, aged 94.

While at Roxbury in 1776, he accompanied Col. Learned into Boston with a flag of truce, immediately after the news came of the defeat of Montgomery at Quebec. As they approached the British out-sentries, a British Colonel, with half a dozen subordinate officers, met them. They inquired the news from Quebec, and were very freely informed. Their interview was about one half of an hour. Maj. Alden inquired of the Colonel, why they did not come out and make the troops at Roxbury a visit. "Ah!" replied he, "we should have to think of that some time first." About this time a party of the British landed and took possession of one of the islands near Quincy. Gen. Thomas determined to dislodge them, and sent Col. Tupper with Maj. Alden and others, and a party of men in the Plymouth whale boats. The English, however, left the island before they arrived there, and were too far to the eastward for pursuit, and the party then returned safe. Maj. Alden was for several years preceding his death President of the Massachusetts Society of Cincinnati, of which he was an active and devoted member. He was also a member of the Pilgrim Society.

CAPT. BILDAD ARNOLD. He was early one of the minute men of the town, and commanded a company of its militia. He also had command of a company in Col. Thomas Lathrop's regiment, and continued in the war during a greater part of its continuance.

HON. GAMALIEL BRADFORD. He was a son of Lieutenant Samuel Bradford of Duxbury, and a great-grandson of Hon. William, the second Governor of Plymouth colony. He shared largely in all the duties of the public offices of the town, and was always selected to bear the responsibilities of its important agencies. He was a friend of education, and did much towards the maintenance and improvement of the public schools. He for several years represented his town in the legislature, and during the trying period from 1764 to 1770, was a member of the executive council. He was for many years a justice of the peace, and judge of the county court. He also held command of the company of militia in his native town; and about 1750, was raised to the rank of major, and afterwards promoted to the command of the regiment, with the rank of colonel. In his declining days he witnessed with patriotic ardor the uprising of the Sons of Freedom; and though his heart was with them, he was unable by active exertion to assist in the crowning glories of true-born freemen. He died in Duxbury on the 24th of April, 1778, having nearly reached his seventy-fourth year.

Col. GAMALIEL BRADFORD, a son of the subject of the preceding sketch. Like his father, he was a man of eminence and worth in his town, serving it in various capacities, and intrusted with its highest honors. During the period of 1756-8, he was in command of a company of militia, and on the commencement of hostilities at the beginning of the Revolution, he held the rank of major. He was one of the magistrates of the county, and formed one of the number who presented an address to Gen. Gage, for which act he afterwards asked the forgiveness of the town and signed a recantation of sentiments. His future career, however, was entirely free from any disaffection to freedom. Soon after the commencement of the war, in 1776, he was appointed to the command of one of the continental regiments, and in this capacity he served until the close of hostilities. He was likewise a colonel of the militia, and also for some years the representative of the town. He died in Duxbury, Jan. 9th, 1807, aged 76 years. He was father of Captains Gamaliel, Daniel, and Gershom, and of the Hon. Alden Bradford, late Secretary of the Commonwealth.

CAPT. GAMALIEL BRADFORD, a son of Col. Bradford, the subject of the preceding notice. He was born at Duxbury on the 4th of November, 1763, and received his early education under the tuition and care of the Hon. George Partridge. On the eve of the birth of American freedom, when at the youthful age of thirteen, he accompanied his father to the American camp, and ever after, amid the confusion and turmoil of the scenes of war and in the din and strife of conflict, he remained true and steadfast in his country's cause, until he witnessed her possession of acknowledged independence. In 1779, he received the rank of ensign, and in the following year was promoted to the station of a lieutenant. After the establishment of peace, his active and energetic nature led him to the decision upon a life at sea as a means of his livelihood. In 1784, he performed his first voyage to France. While remaining and travelling on the continent, he gave his attention to the study of the modern European languages. Of the French he acquired a thorough and accurate knowledge, and spoke it with ease and fluency. Of the Spanish, Italian and Latin he also acquired considerable knowledge. His letters to his friends at this period evince his literary attainments, and his account of his ascent of Mount Vesuvius, and description of the entrance of Napoleon into Venice, are fine examples of epistolary literature.

In 1798, at the time of the difficulties with France, he was offered the command of the Boston frigate by President Adams, but he declined the appointment.

In 1799, while in command of a merchant ship of 400 tons, he was attacked in the Mediterranean by four French privateers, and made a successful resistance. And again, in the following year, while on the coast of Spain, he was assailed by two large French armed vessels, and in the engagement which ensued he received a wound in his thigh, which rendered amputation necessary.

Now for a short time he engaged in commercial pursuits at home; but soon after, though laboring under such great disadvantages, he again assumed the duties of a commander at sea, and thus continued until the year 1808, when he returned once more to mercantile engagements on the land, and finally in 1813, received the appointment of Warden of the State's Prison. He died March 7th, 1824, aged 61.— See a Memoir in Mass. Hist. Coll. 3d ser. I. 202.

CAPT. SYLVANUS DREW. In the beginning of the Revolution he had command of a small schooner, the Lady Washington, and a number of whale-boats, which were employed as cruisers in Boston harbor. On one occasion, the schooner was chased by a British frigate, when, running into shoal water, out of the reach of the enemy's guns, boats were sent by the frigate to board her; but they were repulsed, and driven off with great loss, and the schooner escaped unharmed.

CAPT. SAMUEL LORING. Soon after the commencement of hostilities, he joined the company raised in the town, and was chosen their lieutenant. With his companions in arms he served in the memorable campaigns of 1776 and 1777 in the Jerseys. But by the many exposures and hardships of the camp, his constitution was weakened and his health impaired.

Suffering from an attack of a fever, he was obliged to return home, as were many others of his company. He was then shortly after chosen to the command of the company of militia in his native town, and in the possession of this office he continued until somewhat late in life. He was at one time of Capt. James Lincoln's company, Col. Cotton's regiment. After the war, he was appointed by the government one of the assessors for levying a land tax in Plymouth county, and performed the duty with that integrity which was conspicuous in his more private concerns. His brother, *Judah Loring*, also served in the ranks in the early part of the war. Another brother, *Daniel Loring*, was in the army, and accompanied the expedition to Rhode Island in 1775, — was at the escape of Putnam at Horseneck, and at the surrender of Cornwallis at Yorktown, October, 1781. *Seth Loring*, also brother of the preceding, was clerk of the Duxbury company in 1776, and at a later period an officer in one of the Boston companies, and at the time of his death he was secretary of the Massachusetts Board of War, under Gen. Heath. The records of the Board, much of which are in the elegant hand-writing of Mr. Loring, are in the State archives. He was in Boston during the siege, and suffered, in common with others, the privations to which they were subjected. He was bred a merchant in the counting-room of Samuel Partridge, and was a large dealer in teas. At the early age of twenty-four, and in the midst of his usefulness he died, at Boston, Sept. 10th, 1779. He held a high standing in society, and was a true gentleman in feelings and deportment, and his early death was greatly lamented by a large circle of friends and relatives, and of which honorable mention is made in the public prints of the day.

Col. Jotham Loring was a native of Hingham, though a resident of Duxbury in his latter years. He served in the Old French War, as a private, under the command of Col. Benjamin Lincoln, and was at Fort William Henry when it was taken by Gen. Montcalm, in 1757. On the commencement of hostilities in 1775, he was one of the committee of Hingham, chosen to have inspection of the militia, and shortly after received a captain's commission in the regiment of Col. Greaton in Roxbury; and in June we find him a major in Col. Heath's regiment, and soon after fighting in the ranks of aspiring freemen on the heights of Bunker's Hill. At the time of the landing of the British at Nantasket, Maj. Loring, with Maj. Vose and others, succeeded in escaping with about a thousand bushels of barley, which they had cut. They then proceeded to the light-house at the entrance of the harbor, burned it, and captured three boats of the British, who were out on a fishing excursion from Boston, and succeeded in effecting their escape, bringing off with them three casks of oil and fifty pounds of powder. They also burned a barn and some hay on the Brewsters. Although this was done amid an almost incessant fire from the British men-of-war and tenders lying in the harbor, yet they escaped, having only two men slightly wounded. Col. Loring was also present in the assault on Danbury, and in the affair his horse was shot from under him. — *MS. Records of the Loring Family.*

COL. CALVIN PARTRIDGE. Soon after the commencement of the war, he was chosen to the command of one of the militia companies of the town; and in the Rhode Island expedition he had command of the forces sent by Duxbury. He was afterwards elevated to the rank of colonel of the regiment, and was a man of usefulness in his town. The character of Col. Partridge was such, that he secured by its nature of joviality and jocoseness, and by his agreeableness of manners, the regard of his cotemporaries.

HON. GEORGE PARTRIDGE. He was born on the 8th of February, 1740, of reputable parents. His mother was a daughter of Dea. Foster of Plymouth, and his father was the grandson of one of the first settlers of Duxbury, who bore the name of his descendant, and who ranked high among the most respectable yeomanry of the period, and whose family connections bespeak him to have been a man of substance.

The subject of this sketch pursued his early studies under the care of the Rev. Charles Turner, and doubtless partook something of the ardent patriotism of that worthy divine. Having traversed the course of study preparatory to entering upon a collegiate course, he joined the University at Cambridge, where he graduated in 1762. He was next engaged as an instructor of youth in Kingston, and afterwards this was relinquished for the study of divinity, which had always been his cherished purpose. He was, however, soon afflicted with a disease which blasted his prospects as a public speaker. He now again turned his attention to the education of youth, and in this capacity was employed from 1770 until 1773, when he emerged more openly into public view, by the grounds he took in that troubled and momentous period. His services during this time were valuable, as will be seen in connection with the history of the town. His name stands conspicuous on the annals of the State, and the records in her archives bear ample testimony to his character and his services.

His patriotism was sincere, yet ardent and zealous. He strove for a purpose, — for a purpose, whose only object was the political independence and advancement of his countrymen. His zeal was rational; it was no blind conductor of the will; it was not that zeal which, as Johnson has expressed it, is an eagerness to subvert, with little care what shall be established — but it was considerate and prudent.

In 1777, he succeeded Gen. Warren as sheriff of Plymouth county, and held the office with little interruption until 1812.

In 1781, he was a delegate to Congress under the old Confederation, and at his death was the last surviving member, with the exception of the venerable Charles Carroll of Maryland. He remained there constantly until the close of the Revolution, and was on several important committees, and was at Annapolis when the news came that our Independence was acknowledged, and was present in 1783, when Washington delivered up his commission — a scene, as he often described it, of the most thrilling interest. In 1784, he was again a delegate to Congress; in 1788, once again a representative, and in 1790 was again chosen for another term of two years. In 1792, he was one of the electors of the President and Vice President, and afterwards a member of the State Legislature.

In his latter days he lived a life of usefulness in his native town, and finally died on the morning of the 7th of July, 1828, at the advanced age of 88 years, universally beloved as a Christian, a friend and pillar of the Church, a supporter of the cause of education, and esteemed as an example of patriotism and morality. His memory is still perpetuated by his own endowment of a seminary of learning, which shall transmit to future generations the name of a devoted friend of learning, and a Christian philanthropist.

DR. JOHN WADSWORTH. He had served in the Canada war as an officer, and on the commencement of the Revolution was a Captain of the militia. His opposition to the tyrannical power of Great Britain was firm and steady; and he used his utmost endeavors to instigate his fellow-townsmen in that path, which he truly believed led to their own happiness and to the acquirement of their liberty. During the stifled contentions between the colonies and the mother country, which preceded the open outbreaks of hostilities, he was a member of the legislative assembly of the province, and his exertions in the cause of freedom were manifest and open. His actions and words breathed that same spirit of independence which characterized the declarations of the town on several occasions, and in the formation of which he so largely contributed.

In his private character, Dr. Wadsworth was eccentric, and the manner of his life was characteristic and amusing. In his speech he was rapid and witty. He was a man of strong passions and prejudices, and when excited was as invincible by remonstrance as he was immovable in his opinions. It is related of him that when a mere boy, he once accompanied his father, Dea. Wadsworth, on a trip to Boston by water. On the passage he discoursed considerable with his father on logic, and finally his conversation tended to the point "that it was best for us in this world to let all things take their own course." Shortly afterwards the vessel was accidentally set on fire in the cabin, and John immediately went to work with all haste to extinguish it. "Ah, John!" said his father, "stop! It is best to let all things in this world have their own course." "True," replied John, "if you can't help it." His father, who was a very pious deacon, confessed that he had seen one instance, where terrible language did good. The Doctor, being with him bound out of Boston harbor in a sloop, they run afoul a British frigate. They made no effort to clear him until the Doctor opened upon them a battery of profaneness so tremendous, that they stood aghast and soon pushed him clear. They were about to cut his jib stays, but forbore in awe of him. The Doctor was remarkable for the neatness of his farm, and the fine order in which he kept his fences. It so happened that his next neighbor's fences were continually out of repair. Meeting with her one morning he assailed her with his volcanic battery. Being members of the same church she applied to Mr. Turner for redress, who called upon the Doctor on the next day, and in vain tried to expostulate. He listened for some time; but at last interrupted and said, "Parson, it's of no use, it isn't, that woman wont keep her fences in repair. I wish her ribs were a gridiron to roast her soul upon!" "Good morning, Doctor," said Mr. Turner and left him.

Dr. Wadsworth prided himself much on possessing the art of prophecy, and was frequently consulted by the credulous concerning stolen property, absent friends, and coming events. It is still reported that he conjured with wonderful accuracy, and individual instances are often related. He always denied that his power was superhuman; but affirmed that it was capable of being learned and as simple as any operation in arithmetic, and that all errors in his foretelling were occasioned by mistakes in his calculations.

As a physician, Dr. Wadsworth was self taught, and of considerable eminence in his profession. He was a man of energy and activity, and retained his physical powers until late in life. His talents were by no means disputable. He died in 1799, at the advanced age of 92 years.

His son JOHN WADSWORTH, a gentleman of excellent talents, having completed a collegiate course, graduated at H. C. in 1762, and was considered a good scholar. He was engaged in Duxbury during a few following years as an instructor of youth, and as a teacher he was surpassed by few. He had a taste for metaphysical and logical discussions, and gave much of his time to the study of treaties on those subjects. He had a discriminating mind, and was indeed thought by some of his friends to be unprofitably critical in the distinctions he urged or proposed. He intended to have been a lawyer; but was however chosen a tutor in Harvard University in 1770, and had the reputation of an able logician, and his superior power in metaphysical discussions was universally acknowledged.* This office he held during his life and was from 1774, as he was the eldest tutor, *ex officio* a member of the corporation. He was distinguished more for fine talents, than for extensive erudition. No tutor was ever better adapted for the branch of instruction which fell to his share. As an acute logician, he made accurate distinctions, was fluent in speech and copious in ideas. He could make the worse appear the better reason, which from love of disputation he frequently did; or defend truth in the most lively and ingenuous manner. He was as fond of politics.

He was in Duxbury at the time of the first difficulties with England, and strongly favored the loyalists. This was however not much to the surprise of his friends, who clearly understood the motives which actuated him in the preference he had given. It was in fact no other than a love of argument which moved him. All others around him were urgently favoring the opposite side, and he gloried in the prospects of discussions and bandied disputations. With Mr. Turner he had been previously on terms of great intimacy, and used frequently to accompany him in his walks. Turner, who was an ardent whig, now took his walk unaccompanied. A friend one day meeting him asked him the reason. "Why,"

---

* In the various branches of science he was also a close student, and to the subject of electricity he was particularly partial. It is said of him that soon after Dr. Franklin had made his discoveries, and declared them, he undertook to construct an electric machine. His father, the Doctor, who was rather incredulous, laughed at him considerably and spurned the idea. John not in the least daunted still continued his work, and finally finished it. Having satisfied himself of the efficacy of the instrument, he determined that the Doctor should suffer for his incredulity. The old gentleman consented, still disbelieving, and did as John commanded, who gave him so severe a shock as nearly to prostrate him, when rising up in considerable heat, he exclaimed, "You rascal you, do you mean to kill your father?" He confessed himself convinced, and seldom after dared to be skeptical. — Rev. B. K.'s notes.

replied he, "that John Wadsworth is a turn-coat, and I'll have no more to say to him now." Thus in several instances he sacrificed to his love of argument friendship of years standing. At one time during the absence of Mr. Turner from town, he thought it would be a good time for him to preach, and urged it hard upon Dea. Wadsworth, who absolutely refused him, knowing him to be a tory, and thinking it probable that he wished to give the people a blast from the desk.

His tory principles would have lost for him the tutorship but for the attachment of his pupils and the exertions of his friends, who urged in his favor his remarkable faculty of communicating his ideas, so necessary in an instructor. It was likewise suggested that his political errors were more in appearance, than reality. His fondness for talking had led him to express himself imprudently on some occasions, yet it was no more in his heart, than in his power to injure the commonwealth. Nevertheless he was retained by a vote of only one majority. He fell a victim to the small pox, July 12th, 1777. He had long before anticipated death by this disorder. Having declined inoculation through fear of the result, he was much alarmed when he learned that he had taken it. He was greatly lamented by the students, for the older ones could appreciate his talents and learning, and the younger ones regarded him with affection for his mild and courteous deportment. "He was a man of eminent talents, of clear conceptions, a perspicacious reasoner, fluent in speech, and above all mild in the exercise of authority. In the midst of his usefulness he was snatched from the University by a fatal disease. The bosoms of the students were filled with consternation. 'What honors shall we pay to the memory of so beloved a tutor?' They address the government of the College, — 'Do not by appointing one of your own body, deprive us of the melancholy pleasure of pronouncing his panegyric. Let one of our number be the organ of the rest and speak the grateful sentiments of our hearts.' The request was granted, and Mr. Minot was selected to deliver the funeral oration. With what pathos and eloquence he performed the duty, his cotemporaries will remember. They never can forget his impassioned tones, the deep sorrow which clouded his own brow, and the grief which filled the hearts of all his hearers."

Thus says the eulogist of Judge Minot, in speaking of the character of Mr. Wadsworth, in its influences upon him as his pupil.

In 1808, there was erected in the old burying ground at Cambridge, a monument to his memory "by a few contemporary friends, who loved and honored his character, and several pupils who enjoyed at the University the benefit of his instruction." It bears the following epitaph.

>Huic tumulo mandantur exuviæ
>JOHANNIS WADSWORTH, A. M.
>Duxburgiæ nati
>Collegii Harvardini Alumni,
>Cujus
>Septem per annos
>fideliter utilissimèque
>Tutoris officium præstitit
>et modo aptissimo, facillimo, gratissimoque
>optimis præceptis ac institutis
>Juvenum animos imbuit
>moresque ipsorum amicè ac sedulò curavit.
>Hujus temporis tres per annos et ultra
>Senatus Academici Socii munera peritè explevit.
>Ingenio sagaci et acutissimo
>Literis Scientiisque penitus instructo,
>etiam facilitate mira Sententias impertiendi,
>Omnium observantiam sese attraxit.
>Amicitia ingenua atque constanti,
>et consuetudinis suavitate facetiisque,
>Amor ac deliciæ fuit amicorum.
>Inter alias virtutes
>Pietas erga Parentes et affectio Fraterna
>præcipue fuerunt insignes.
>Viri tam boni ac utilis omnibusque cari,
>in Ætatem senectam spes vitam prodüxerat.
>Ah spes inanis!
>Variolis (illo generi humani flagello) correptus,
>Animam efflavit
>Die Julii 12mo Anno Salutis MDCCLXXVII
>Ætatisque suæ XXXVII.

DEA. PELEG WADSWORTH was a brother of the Doctor, though quite a different man; yet was also a great wit. In his language his style was characteristically quaint and fanciful, often indulging in expressions which struck the stranger's ear not only as singular, but also as wonderfully significant. At the time when the modern innovation of singing the psalm in church, without first reading it line by line, began to be established, many were opposed to it, and were strongly in favor of continuing in the old method. Some, it is said, even left the church, shocked at the idea of the impending extinction of that time-honored practice. One individual, in particular, frequently went out. This same person shortly after having purchased of the Deacon a barrel of cider, which had begun to work, was assisted by him in placing it upon his wagon, and was about leaving, when the deacon called out to him, in a tone of admonition, "Have a care, have a care, neighbor Delano, this cider may sing before you get home, without reading." The cut was irresistible, and Mr. Delano henceforth gave up his prejudices.

GEN. PELEG WADSWORTH was a son of Dea. Peleg Wadsworth. He graduated at Harvard College in 1769, and it was the intention of his father that he should be educated in the ministry. However, he unknown to him opened a private school in Plymouth. At the same time Gen. Alexander Scammel, famous in the Revolutionary annals, was likewise teaching there. They had been very intimate friends throughout their college course. Gen. W. afterwards kept a store in Duxbury, and soon after removed it to Kingston. In 1775 when minute companies were formed and manual exercise arrested general attention, he devoted much of his time in the instruction of young men in the use of firearms, and instilling into the minds of youth a true sense and value of Liberty and Freedom. He had at this time the command of a company of minute men in Kingston; and immediately after the battle of Lexington, joined Col. Cotton's regiment. In September he joined the army at Roxbury, and was employed as an engineer; but afterwards as Gen. Ward's aid-de-camp. In 1776 he was appointed Captain in Col. Bailey's regiment. In 1777 he received the appointment from the State, of Brigadier General, and had command over the whole district of Maine. In the spring of 1778, while he was in Boston, General Lovell was appointed to command an expedition against the possessions of the British on the Penobscot; and Gen. W. was chosen second in command. Capt. Saltonstall was charged with a fleet to coöperate with them. They landed and made an attack; but failed of complete success. At this time Samuel Alden of Duxbury was mortally wounded. A British fleet now hove in sight, and their ships were run up the river, and set on fire; and soon after they marched off their men through the forests. Gen. W., in 1780, had the command of a detachment of State troops at Camden, Me., and here he was assaulted and captured by a host of the enemy, and in the affair was wounded in the arm. He was at first treated with great humanity; but soon confined in prison, to await his removal to England to be tried as a *rebel of consequence.* He however escaped from his confinement. After the war he was a very successful merchant in Portland, and built the splendid mansion, since occupied by his son-in-law, Stephen Longfellow, Esq. He took as pay for his services from the State 7000 acres of land on the Saco river, which was then valued at the rate of 12½ cents per acre. He afterwards removed and settled on this tract, and was considered the patriarch of the settlement. Here he built him a house, and passed his old age, and died in 1829, aged 80. He was for eight years, while he resided in Portland, a member of Congress. Gen. W. was very energetic in his nature, and quick and rapid in his motions, and of restless activity. Mr. Ward of Boston, who was fellow aid-de-camp with him in Roxbury, used to say of him, "It makes no difference what you do with Peleg Wadsworth. If he were a porter, he would have the office respectable."*

His son ALEXANDER SCAMMEL WADSWORTH, was second lieutenant on board the Constitution, when she captured the Guerriere. The citizens of Portland, his native place, in testimony of their high sense of the brave and important part he acted on that memorable occasion, presented him with an elegant sword, decorated with appropriate devices. *Alden's epitaphs.* Another son, *Henry Wadsworth*, became a lieutenant in the navy, and fought under Com. Preble at the seige of Tripoli. He was one of that devoted band of thirteen, who conducted the attack, and, says Com. Preble, "determined rather to suffer death and the destruction of the enemy, than captivity and torturing slavery." And by the resolves of Congress he was esteemed "an honor to his country and an example to all excellent youth." He was buried at Portland, and his monument bears this inscription: In memory of Henry Wadsworth, Lieutenant in the United States Navy, who fell before the walls of Tripoli on the evening of the 4th of September, 1804, in the 20th year of his age, by the explosion of a fire ship which he with others gallantly conducted against the enemy.

> My country calls,
> This world adieu,
> I have one life,
> This life I give for you. — *Alden's Epi.*

---

* Hist. Plymouth, Dwight's Travels, Thacher's Military Journal, and B. Kent's notes.

ANNALS SUBSEQUENT TO THE REVOLUTION.

1788. The town chose Geo. Partridge delegate to the Convention to be holden at Boston on the second Wednesday in January.

1795. At a meeting, called to consider the question of revising the Constitution, it was decided that it was not expedient, all the votes (47) being against it.

1808. The *Embargo Act* of Congress fell upon the inhabitants of this town like a thunderbolt. They were solely dependent on the sea for support, and the interruption of their business, occasioned by the enforcement of this act, soon brought them to a deplorable situation. Assembled in town meeting, they resolved to petition, and accordingly a memorial was sent to the President, dated Sept. 5th, 1808. Therein they stated, that they were chiefly dependent on the sea for support; and the sterility of their soil was such, that means for their subsistence could not be raised.. That the fishermen, who could before but hardly support their families, were now wholly dependent on the fish caught previously, which still remained unsold, and that they had no means to support their households. That there was a large quantity of fish in the town, which must perish if liberty is not given to export them. They represented their inability to enter into manufactures, and want of skilful men to instruct them, and of money to purchase materials, and of buildings necessary for carrying it on, and their reluctance to have their sons and daughters engage in that unhealthy employment, and be reduced to the state of that class in the old country. They granted, that without doubt the legislators thought it for the good and happiness of the country; but the embargo, when not felt in Europe, brought injury and ruin upon themselves. They also thought, that as large an armed force would be required to prevent the citizens from exporting their perishing commodities, as would serve to protect their commerce against any foreign power; that merchants and seamen, heretofore exemplary, would acquire habits of evading the laws and cheating the revenues of the country; that the prostration of our commerce would afford other nations the opportunity of building up flourishing trades, and turn its channels into new kingdoms, which it might be impossible to prevent. To this President Jefferson returned an answer, stating, that the embargo could not be raised, consistent with the good of the country, until a repeal of the obnoxious edicts of Europe.

At one time fears were entertained by the authorities of the custom-house at Plymouth, that an attempt would be made to run the embargo, on the part of some vessels in Duxbury; and accordingly an armed sloop was stationed in the bay to prevent any violation of the Government orders. Nevertheless, taking advantage of a thick and foggy night, a schooner, laden with fish, and belonging to Mr. Samuel A. Frazar, succeeded in an attempt to escape, and on the next morning was not to be seen. She was commanded by Capt. Asa Hewitt, and it is supposed went to the West Indies, where she was disposed of.

1812. WAR WITH GREAT BRITAIN. As New England was distant from the principal scenes of the war, her towns suffered not much from the immediate incursions of the enemy, — their sufferings being chiefly occasioned by the interruption of business and the scarcity of foreign commodities. Her fishermen suffered most from the numerous disguised vessels of the enemy, which often cruised along her coasts.

Most of the townsmen, as were a majority of the State, were decidedly opposed to the war and the measures of the administration, and favored the principles of the Federal party. Soon after the declaration of war by the Government (June 18th), the friends of peace in this county determined to hold a meeting for deliberation; and the 29th of July was appointed as the day. On the 27th the town assembled, and chose Capt. Samuel Loring, Reuben Delano, Ezra Weston, Judah Alden, and Capt. Abner Dingley to attend; and at the same meeting this delegation was authorized to circulate a memorial for peace, — to obtain as many signers as they could, and to print it in the Boston papers. Capt. *Loring*, at the head of this delegation, though now far advanced in years, was a firm opposer of the war. Having in his younger days assisted in the establishment of that liberty too precious to be hazarded, he now looked upon the preparations for war with no feigned feeling of regret. Major *Alden* was also strongly in favor of the Federalists, and one of the most influential on their side, as were most of the older inhabitants of the town, who had seen the victories and defeats of one war, and naturally shunned another, though, in time of danger from their country's foe, they were ever ready to act and fight for their country's good. They would oppose the war in the beginning; but when once entered upon, it was in accordance with their honor and patriotism to repel all hostile aggressions.

Preparations were afterwards made for the defence of the town. Many of the larger vessels in the harbor were drawn up the river to prevent their falling into the hands of the enemy. There were at one time two ships, one brig, and six schooners here secured. At the entrance of the river two small forts were built. For the fortification of these a commit-

tee of safety was chosen to devise ways and means. Mr. Seth
Sprague, one of the number, was directed to make application
to the Board of war, then sitting at Boston, for cannon and
ammunition. In reply to their applications, General Cobb, a
member of the Board, remarked, that it would be idle to listen
to it; for, he alleged, the inhabitants would not know how
to use cannon and ammunition if they had them. Governor
Brooks thought differently, and influenced the Board to comply; and accordingly a quantity of powder and balls, and two
field pieces were granted.* Three other field pieces were provided by the custom-house at Plymouth, and others were procured by the inhabitants.† The upper fort mounted three six-
pounders, and the lower two twelve-pounders. Cannon were
also placed at other places along the shore, where it was expected the enemy might land. There were two on the wharf
of Mr. Sampson, and one near Mr. Lot Hunt's. These were
manned in the night-time by a company of *Sea-Fencibles*,
formed among the inhabitants for the defence of the coast,
consisting of between thirty and forty men. They were commanded by Capt. Gershom Bradford. Thomas Winsor was
first lieutenant, Capt. Thomas Herrick the second, and Wm.
Sampson, clerk. There was a company of militia stationed
at the barracks, amounting to nearly ninety men, from the
neighboring towns, and commanded by Capt. John Alden.

The entrance to the harbor was guarded by the fort at the
Gurnet, which mounted six or eight cannon, some of them
forty-two pounders, and was manned by a detachment of State
troops, consisting of about thirty men, under the command of
Capt. Pope of Salem, and afterwards of Lt. Simmons of Scituate. Alarm-boats constantly plied in time of danger between
Plymouth beach and Saquish. One was furnished by Plymouth, and another by Duxbury. This was manned by the
row-guard, who served six at a time, under the command of
Capt. Zenas Winsor. Instructions were given them to fire a
gun on the approach of any of the enemy's barges, which was
to be answered by the cannon at the batteries and along the
shore, and a lighted tar-barrel at Captain's Hill, and similar
demonstrations in Plymouth and Kingston.

Notwithstanding their vigorous preparations for the defence
of the town, it was proposed by some members of the Committee of safety, while they were making out an official report,
to recommend that a messenger be sent to the British ships

---

* Soule's Sprague Memorial.

† The owners of the shipping, Messrs. Reuben and Charles Drew, Nathaniel and Joshua Winsor, Ezra Weston, Job and Levi Sampson, at an
expense of $140, purchased two nine-pounders, and also two casks of
powder, containing each one hundred weight.

cruising between the capes, with the assurance of the neutrality of the inhabitants. These measures were favored by the majority, and the vote was about to be taken, when Mr. Seth Sprague, one of the number, arose, and most strenuously opposed it; stating that it was cowardly and treasonable, and inconsistent with their previous means of defence; but still the motion prevailed, and the report was made to the inhabitants legally assembled. Before this town meeting Mr. Sprague again protested, but yet the report was accepted. However, at a later stage of the meeting, Capt. John Alden, in a few remarks, so influenced the meeting, that the vote was reconsidered and the motion rejected. But still a message of this kind was sent by some persons, though unauthorized and unknown to the greater part of the inhabitants, to the commander of the British ship, as the reply of the latter is still preserved.

"His Britannic Majesty's Ship Leander,
10th August, 1814.

"To the Selectmen and the Committee of Safety
of the Town of Duxbury:

GENTLEMEN: I am to acknowledge your letter of the 9th instant. I can easily understand the motives which have induced your addressing me; and, much as I deplore this war, and deeply as I feel for the distresses of innocent individuals, a sense of public duty will always compel me to follow up the utmost extent of my instructions. But in the belief that your town has neither the means nor intention of carrying on offensive war, I shall, as far as lies in my power, endeavor to respect it accordingly. The schooner you require, [i. e. the Despatch, see following,] shall therefore be returned as soon as opportunity permits, and that [as soon as] I have obtained the sanction of Captain Ragget, which I shall urge by every honest means in my power. But I must again remark, in addition to the observations contained in a letter to the magistrates of Plymouth, which you allude to, that nothing but neutrality *the most perfect* will induce me either to respect your fishing craft, or the town itself. It is not in the character of Englishmen to act harshly towards the unoffending, — though in a state of war, — unless provoked to a system of retaliation. And thus far (though not authorized) I am sure I only speak the sentiments of my superior officers. Be therefore tranquil! carry on war only to defend your homes, and do not permit your fishermen to assist directly or indirectly,— as any deviation will be marked some day or other!

The fishermen who took possession of the Rover did wrong; but not more so than those who towed in the barge sunk off the battery near Plymouth. Had they left her to her fate, no mischief would have perhaps ever threatened the fishermen of Plymouth; but, as it is, until that barge is returned, it must be supposed that the fishermen of Plymouth are authorized by their Government to intrigue in war.

I have the honor to be, Gentlemen,
Your most Obedient Servant,
GEORGE R. COLLIER,
Captain H. B. M. S. Leander.

" P. S. — As there are some American armed boats *disguised as fishermen*, is is necessary that *every* fishing boat should be examined; and unless they bring to when fired at, they will be punished accordingly."

[The allusion to the Rover and the barge will be explained in the sequel, pp. 166–7. — *Sprague Memorial.*]

Gen. Dearborn, of Boston, was immediately informed of this, and orders were despatched to the fort at the Gurnet to allow no boat of the enemy to pass that point, if it could be prevented. Shortly after, a boat from the British vessel appeared with a white flag, and the officer desired permission to visit the town. He was told to make his communication, if he had any, to the commander of the fort; and if he proceeded further he would be fired upon; when, taking the hint, he quietly returned to the ship.

During 1814, there were three of the enemy's ships cruising between the capes. They were, the flag-ship Spencer; the La Hogue, Capt. Ragget, and the Leander, Capt. Collier. These were a source of great annoyance to the various fishing and other small craft of the bay, and especially to boats running along the shore with commodities from New York, which had been transported across the isthmus, as it was unsafe to proceed around the cape, owing to the enemy's vessels. They were also in constant danger of capture by the many boats and barges of the English, many of which were disguised crafts taken from the Americans. At times, one or more of the British frigates were seen off Duxbury beach, and their presence was the cause of greater vigilance on the part of the inhabitants, who feared an attack from the numerous barges of the enemy, who would attempt to burn their shipping.

This year the town records, which heretofore have been destitute of every thing relating to the war, show that the town voted (June 13th), that the committee of safety appoint sentinels and posts of alarm. In the autumn (Oct. 8th) they determined that if the exempt militia form themselves into a company, those who are unable to furnish themselves, be provided from the equipments in the town's possession. The militia were to be furnished with provisions, if called out of town on camp duty. They also agreed to continue preparations for defence.*

Though no indication was made on the part of the enemy of attacking the town; yet an incident occurred from which we may judge that they would not quietly have submitted to the invasion of their soil and the devastation of their property. One clear moonlight evening it was agreed upon among the members of the *row guard* to execute a scheme for testing the courage of the people. They accordingly gave the usual signal for the approach of the enemy, which was immediately answered, as they had expected, when they returned with all haste to the town. The report spread like electricity from house to house, the forts were instantly manned, all assumed the attitude of defence, and their cannon pointed in the direction of the looked for enemy. The militia were paraded on the hill by the barracks, and countermarched in the streets. A body of about thirty men with Captain Seth Sprague at their head, were despatched to reconnoitre the shores, and sentries were immediately stationed at the posts. The inhabitants of the neighboring towns came pouring in to their assistance; while the women and children were conveyed to places of security. A few minutes of silence prevailed, all were endeavoring to espy the awaited foe, but the clear beams of the moon as they fell on the smooth and unruffled surface of the harbor, and the glowing light of the beacon towering to the sky, disclosed to their extended visions naught but the silent waves, untouched by hostile keels! †

In the summer of this year (July 23d, 1814,) while two of the enemy's barges were chasing a small boat, loaded with flour and bound for Boston, the American ran under the guns of the Gurnet fort, where the men landed. At this time the barges were fired upon by the fort, and the second shot, aimed by the commander himself, though at a distance of nearly

---

* Mar. 11, 1816. Voted to make up the first detachment of soldiers' pay, including State's pay, $14 per month. — Town Rec.

† This trick of the *guard* was suspected by some on the same night, though it has never yet been fairly acknowledged. The officers of the two companies of militia at this time were of the South — John Alden, Capt. ; Prince Bradford, First Lt. ; and Martin Sampson, Second Lt. : of the North — John Partridge, Capt. ; Eleazer Harlow, First Lt. ; and Daniel Weston, Second Lt. These belonged to the coast division of Gen. Wm. Gooding, consisting of four brigades.

The previous officers of the militia companies since the Revolution, had been — of the first (after Capt. S. Loring,) Capt. Samuel Delano, and Lt's Joshua Brewster and Eliphalet Waterman ; Capt. Seth Sprague was the next commanding officer, who was succeeded by Capt. Alden, whose officers at first were Lt. Wm. Freeman and Lt. James Weston — of the second, (after Capt. Baker,) were Captains Nathan Sampson, Ichabod Sampson, Abner Dingley, and John Partridge, as above.

three miles, struck one of them, wounding some of the men. The boat immediately filled, and the crew were taken up by the other barge, which then returned to the ship then lying off the beach. A small English flag, which they recovered from the sunken barge, was afterwards displayed at the fort in token of victory. In revenge for this Capt. Epworth of the Nymphe frigate burnt and sunk a Plymouth schooner of 25 tons. An inhabitant of Duxbury, having occasion a short time afterwards to visit the enemy's frigate La Hogue, Capt. Ragget, while speaking of this affair, the Captain praised in high terms the courage and skill of the troops at the battery, and did not blame their firing; but coming to the fact that one or more shots were fired after the men were in the water, he gave vent to his rage in a characteristic manner, accompanied by no ordinary imprecations, threatening vengeance upon them. However the Englishman's threats were never executed.*

The following are some of the fishing and other crafts, belonging to Duxbury, which were captured by the enemy during the war. — The schooner *Cherub*, owned by Joshua Winsor, and manned by John Winsor, George Winsor, (son of Joshua,) and James Chandler, who were taken by the La Hogue. — The schooner *Ospra*, owned by Ahira Wadsworth, was captured by the Leander, and her crew, (Stephen Churchill, James Woodward and a small boy) were retained for a short time as prisoners. — The sloop *Lady Jane*, owned by Perez H. Sampson, James Soule and Richard Soule, was sailing in the bay on a pleasure excursion, with a party, when an enemy's barge suddenly appeared and gave chase. The sloop was run aground on Plymouth flats, and the company escaped. The barge coming up endeavored to float her; but seeing the beach thronging with men, they retreated.

* An eye witness to the scene testifies, that a third shot was fired; but at the other barge which came to rescue the men of the first. Soon after the sails, water casks, &c. of the barge were picked up by the schooner Despatch of Duxbury, and carried into port. The barge was raised and towed into Plymouth on the afternoon of the same day. These affairs were the cause of a special deputation to the authorities at Plymouth on the part of the English commander, who sent a barge with a white flag to the town. The officer had an interview with Gen. Gooding, who agreed to return the barge, which gave ample satisfaction to the officer, whom they dismissed, having filled his barge with a large quantity of fresh provisions. When returning from Plymouth, they were met by a boat having on board Mr. David Turner and others of Duxbury, who held a short conversation with the British officer, who showed much feeling in regard to the outrageous conduct, as he alleged, of the commander of the fort, expressing himself in strong terms, and declaring that he should be delivered to the exasperated fury of his men, should he be taken at any time. The officer of the fort, when informed of this shortly after, replied with perfect coolness, that "he would be a hard one to catch."

— The schooner *Despatch*, owned by Nathaniel Winsor, Jr., Eliphalet Waterman and David Turner, and manned by Samuel Hunt, Noah Simmons, Joseph Prior and George Winsor (son of James,) sailed from Duxbury about the 15th of July, 1814, and was captured at night on the following day by a barge from the Leander, and the prize sloop Rover, from the La Hogue, sailing in company. A transfer of their crews was made, those of the Despatch being placed in charge of the Rover, and ordered to follow the former. This they did for some time, using drags however to impede her progress; but night coming on, they ventured to make their escape, and putting about for the Gurnet, they reached the harbor in safety, and the Rover was afterwards claimed by her rightful owners. The Despatch was then recovered by a series of cunning devices on the part of a single individual. After her capture, as above, she continued to cruise in the bay, and when near the Gurnet took a boat which was manned by Captains Matthew H. Mayo and Winslow L. Knowles,* whom they conveyed on board the flag ship Spencer, where they were kept three days, when they made an offer of $300 to ransom themselves and boat. Knowles was permitted to go to Boston, where he was advised by his friends and a certain naval officer to give up the scheme. After seven days Mayo was placed on board the Despatch as pilot, with three British officers and twenty men, with a brass four-pounder and other warlike implements. They were ordered to cruise in the bay; but after two days they experienced a severe north-wester, and were advised by Mayo to make a harbor under Billingsgate point. To make the schooner sail faster a portion of the ballast was thrown overboard, and Mayo hinted that it would be well to throw over more to make comfortable sleeping quarters. Being thus lightened, the schooner, as Mayo had expected, would not bear a sufficient press of canvass to reach the proposed harbor. Afterwards when ordered to anchor, he took occasion, while letting the anchor go, and just as the cook had called all hands below for dinner, to cut the cable nearly off with his knife. This

---

* These men belonged to Eastham, and had been to Boston with a load of rye, and having sold their cargo, and purchased articles for their own and other families, and exchanged their boat for a larger one were now returning home. The Despatch lie at anchor and apparently fishing and showing five men on deck. Suddenly a cannon was fired and the shot struck within fifty feet of the boat; but keeping on their course another was fired, which skipped over them, when they hove to, and were boarded and taken as in the text. Previously, however, Mayo had secretly thrown overboard his valuable spyglass to prevent its falling into the enemy's hands. *Rev. Enoch Pratt's Hist. of Eastham, Orleans and Welfleet,* 1845, from which the facts of the text are derived, as also from *Soule's Sprague Memorial.*

done, he followed the rest to the repast. In a few moments the schooner was observed to be rolling and tossing about, and some of the crew rushing on deck cried out, "She's adrift!" Mayo pretended to be much alarmed and exclaimed "Pay out!" But it proved in vain, for the anchor itself was gone. He then hauled in the cable, carefully rubbing the end, that no mark of a knife might be seen. He next advised them to make a harbor to the leeward ten miles distant. The place selected was about three-fourths of a mile from his own door at Eastham, where he ran her ashore on the flats. The officers now began to suspect him; but he only assured them that they were on the outer bar and would soon beat over, and advised the men to go below that they might not be suspected by the people on the shore, who were fast gathering; and giving them a gimlet they tapped a cask of New England rum and soon became intoxicated. As the tide ebbed the schooner heeled, when the officers finding themselves deceived, ordered their men on deck for resistance; when Mayo, throwing overboard the arms on deck, threatened to shoot any who should attempt his life. He had previously picked the lock of the first officer's writing desk, and secured a brace of brass pistols and secreted them under his jacket. Going on shore the authorities were notified of his circumstances, and the militia ordered out, and they took possession of the vessel and men, who were marched to Mr. Thomas Crosby's tavern, and placed under guard for the night; but they were removed on the next morning to a barn, and then permitted to escape to the ship. The commander of the station demanded of Eastham the sum of $1200 in specie, and if not paid in twenty-four hours, he threatened to destroy the town, which was then paid. The owners of the schooner afterwards obtained her of the Government officer, who claimed her for the United States.* — The schooner *Thomas Hardy*, belonging to Mr. S. A. Frazar, was captured in the early part of the war, and her crew were soon released. — A small boat, the *Liberty*, owned and commanded by Capt. Joshua Brewster, was taken by the Leander, and soon after Capt. Brewster was allowed to return in his own boat, under pretence of obtaining a ransom, and thus effected his escape. — A sloop called the *Christopher Columbus*, owned by Joshua Winsor, and commanded by Capt. John Winsor, while near the shore of Scituate, discovered an enemy's barge in full pursuit of them, from the harbor of Scituate, where they had been to fire the shipping. They then abandoned the sloop in

---

* The Despatch, as were other of the enemy's prizes, was often seen off the Gurnet in disguise, with chairs hanging over her quarter, as if transporting merchandize along the coast.

a boat and made for the shore, when the British boarded her, and having fired her in her cabin, left her. The crew now again took possession and having extinguished the fire, proceeded on their cruise. — The schooner *Maria*, owned by Nathaniel Winsor, Sen., and under the command of Capt. Joseph Fish of Duxbury, was taken, and carried into Halifax, and the crew afterwards returned home safe. Capt. Fish afterward performed three voyages in privateer David Porter, a large schooner of two hundred and six tons, and mounting eight guns, with one long 24-pounder. These of Duxbury also accompanied him in different cruises, — Capt. Charles Soule, prize master and boarding officer; Capt. Geo. Soule, prize master; Asa Weston, prize master and quarter master; Capt. Otis Baker; Nathaniel Holmes; Eden Wadsworth, and a brother of Capt. Fish. The David Porter was a fine sailing vessel, and owned in Boston. On the second cruise, proceeding from Fairhaven in the month of August, 1813, they soon fell in with, and captured, an English brig, and on the next day, they took a valuable prize, a large English ship, laden with hides and tallow; and soon after a British brig, with an American captain, and first officer, bound for Halifax, from Liverpool, having on board the rigging and anchors for a frigate building on the Lakes, and mounting herself four guns, which were thrown overboard. On the next day, they fell in with the English privateer schooner Pictou, and gave chase; but, however, soon perceiving that they were gaining upon the enemy, they put about, as they were not in a proper state for an engagement, their guns being so blocked up with the captured commodities, that it would have been almost impossible to have worked them, and having accomplished their object in frightening her away, they shaped their course in another direction. One prize, a schooner which they captured, was afterwards lost by the artful designs of two English boys, who were on board. Soon after her capture, they transferred the English crew, with the exception of these two boys, on board their own vessel, and putting on board a prize master with six or eight men, they ordered him to make for the nearest port. Some wine, which was on board, having been too freely indulged in by the officers and crew, watching an opportunity, when the captain was prostrate upon the deck in an intoxicated state, and the remainder of the men, with the exception of the man at the helm, were carousing in the forecastle, they suddenly locked them down, and one seizing a handspike, threatened the life of the other man if he attempted any resistance, while the other bound the captain, hand and foot. And thus having taken the vessel, they carried her unharmed into Halifax. Capt. Fish after having taken five prizes in fifteen days, three of whom arrived safe in port, entered the harbor of Boston. Proceeding from this port on his third cruise, he shaped his course for the rock of Lisbon, and there fell in with and captured an English brig, bound for Trieste, and which was originally an American privateer. The English crew were taken out, and Capt. George Soule and a prize crew were put on board, and after a passage of seventy days, Capt. Soule made the American continent; but unfortunately at this time, an English seventy-four hove in sight and took them. She was however afterwards recovered according to the treaty, for she happened to be re-taken after the declaration of peace; yet this was not accomplished without considerable expense. From the coast of Portugal, Capt. Fish went to South America, and after cruising with little success for some time, finally returned to New York, after the settlement of peace. Capt. Fish was an officer of great abilities, and his enterprizes were conducted with prudence and skill. He was afterwards lost at sea, and as he never was heard of, his vessel probably foundered.

The receipt of the news of the establishment of peace, which arrived late in an evening in February, was the occasion of much joy on the part of the inhabitants, and early on the following morning a salute was fired from the fort; and soon after a company of about seventy persons walked to the Gurnet on the ice, and spending here three or four hours in amusement, performing feats of agility and otherwise entertaining themselves, returned in a body. On the next day salutes were fired again at the forts, at the Gurnet battery and at Plymouth.

HISTORY

OF THE

CHURCH OF DUXBURY.

FORMATION.

THE CHURCH OF DUXBURY was gathered about 1632, though they had not a settled pastor until some years after. Before this period, self-preservation dictated the policy which forbade the "erection of cottages remote from prompt protection;" and we find the principal settlers of the suburbs of Duxbury town-dwellers (of Plymouth) in winter, that "they better repair to the worship of God." *

"In the year 1632, a number of the brethren inhabiting on the other side of the bay, at a place since called Duxborough, growing weary of attending the worship of God at such distance, asked and were granted a dismission; and soon after, being embodied into a church, they procured the Rev. Mr. Partridge (a gracious man of great abilities,) to be their pastor." Thus Duxbury appears to have been the second church in Plymouth colony. Previous to the settlement of their pastor, Elder Brewster, of the Plymouth church, who resided in Duxbury, assisted in the services.

REV. RALPH PARTRIDGE was the first minister, who was settled over the church in Duxbury in 1637. He had previously been a clergyman of the church of England, and had arrived at Boston on the 17th of November, 1636. The vessel in which he came had had a very boisterous passage, and was short of provisions.

---

* Their removal to Plymouth in the autumn was not required, however, a year or two after. Still, great precautions were necessary to insure their perfect security from the depredations of the savages; and in 1634, we find that in the south-eastern part of the town, where Standish, Brewster, Pabodie, and others resided, a palisade was ordered to be erected beyond Eagle-nest creek. Among other considerations which prompted its erection, doubtless was the defence which it would afford their cattle, and preserve them from the depredations of the Indians, to which they were greatly exposed. Their stocks were now considerably increased, and even as early as 1632, the Court had deemed it necessary to require that they should be confined in fenced pastures, and in 1638, it was considered desirable that an annual fair should be held at Duxbury, for the improvement of their cattle, and for the show of various commodities.

He soon came to Duxbury, at the invitation of the church, and was admitted a freeman on the 6th of March, 1637-8. In the same year he received a grant of forty acres to the southeast of North Hill, and also about this time bought land of William Basset and Francis Sprague in the southeastern part of the town; and in 1639 bought a house * of William Latham.

It would seem by the following record, in 1637, that the character of the settlers which were pouring into the newly established town did not agree in all respects with the feelings of the founders. " Upon peticon p^rferred to us by Mr. Partrich on behalf of the Church and neighbourhood of that side, wherein they shewed the danger of the disolution of their church estate, except the Court would bee pleased to consider their necessyty, and help them therein. That seeing the church of Plymouth now called home their members who held much lands on that side, and they being but few, and the lands there were desposed in a great part to servants and other yeong men, from whom they could expect little help, they humbly requested that such lands, as were yet ungranted betwixt the North and South rivers might be reserved for farms to such fitt men, as they should approve of, and might be fitt and helpfull unto them. It was therefore granted unto them by the

---

* This was a two-story gambrel-roofed building, somewhat superior to the common habitations of the settlers. On the lower floor was the parlor, an ordinary room, carpeted however, and furnished in a manner which might be considered luxurious. Here in the centre was a round table ; and another, though of less pretensions, was placed against the wall. In the fire-place were the andirons and tongs, and against the wall hung a looking glass. In the corner was his staff and cane. Here was also kept the silver plate, and on the table was placed " his silver beer cup," which was retained in the family of his daughter Mary, as a family heir-loom. Three high chairs, and one wooden one, with two cushions, completed the furniture of the room. Adjoining this was his study ; in the midst was a small table, and a desk, before which was placed a cushioned stool. Two bookcases were placed against the wall, one called his Latin case, wherein were arranged his library of about four hundred volumes. An old safe stood in the corner, and various kinds of personal apparel were scattered around the room. Next to this was another but smaller room, and on this floor was also the kitchen. In the cellar below were nine beer casks, affording, no doubt, abundance of the beverage to his visiting parishioners. In the second story was the parlor chamber, furnished with a valanced bed, and a cupboard of drawers, with a cloth upon it. The kitchen chamber had likewise a bed. On each side of these was a small leanto chamber, having in them two beds, and one truckle bed. And above all was the attic. Near the house was his orchard, and a cow-house. His stock of cattle was four oxen, one bull, seven cows, two yearlings, two calves, two ewes, and two swine ; with also six hens and five chickens ; and a cart, plough, &c., constituted his farming implements. These items are given to show the state of the earliest inhabitants in their domestic situation. The above was the condition of the estate of Mr. Partridge at his death, as appears from the inventory. He died possessed of about 150 acres of land.

Court, that not any of those lands should be granted, but such as these foure, viz., Mr. William Collyer, Mr. Ralph Partrich, Jonathan Brewster and Willm. Basset should approve of as fitt for their societie." They feared, it seems, the dissolution of their church for want of support; the motley throng which would assemble there, if left entirely open and free, would not be able or willing to contribute to their aid; and they thus wished for measures to insure to them a congregation of men, which would be a benefit to the town.

1638. A. Sampson was presented to the Court, "for striking and abusing John Washburn the younger in the meetinghouse on the Lord's day."

1641. There were eight churches in Plymouth colony, eight in Connecticut, and twenty-three or four in Massachusetts Bay.

1650. Edward Hunt fined for shooting deer on the Sabbath. Abraham Peirce, for idleness and neglecting public worship.

1651. Nathaniel Basset and Jo: Prior were fined twenty shillings each, for disturbing the church; and at the next town meeting or training-day each to be bound to a post for two hours in some public place, with a paper on their heads, with their crime written thereon in capital letters.

1652. James Lindall, at his death, left to the church one cow and one calf. George Russell was fined for not attending church at Namasakeeset in the liberties of Duxbury.

1658. The church suffered a sad bereavement in the death of their beloved pastor, which occurred in the present year. And here it seems best to follow the words of Secretary Morton, who, in recording his death in his Memorial, thus mentions him:

" Mr. Ralph Partridge died in a good old Age, having for the space of fourty years dispensed the Word of God with very little impediment by sickness. His pious and blameless life became very advantageous to his Doctrine; he was much honored and loved by all that conversed with him. He was of a sound and solid judgement in the main Truths of Jesus Christ, and very able in his Disputation to defend them; he was very singular in this, that notwithstanding the paucity and poverty of his Flock, he continued in his Work amongst them to the end of his life. He went to his grave in peace, *as a Shock of Corn fully ripe*, and was honorably buried at Duxbury.

" In whose Remembrance, one who was a true Admirer of his worth, presented these at his Funerall:

" Not Rage, but Age; not Age, but God's decree,
Did call me hence my Saviour Christ to see

And to embrace, and from his hand receive
My Crown of Glory : Oh who would not leave
A flattering World, nay Friends, or what's most dear,
The Saints' Communion that's enjoyed here,
At once to have God, Christ, Saints, Angels, all,
To make compleat, and sum our Joyes totall?
Now I behold God's Glory face to face ;
Now I sit down with Christ, who've run my race ;
Now I sing praise to God, and to the Lamb ;
Now I Companion to the Angels am ;
Now I behold with greatest joy my Sons
And Daughters all ; I mean Converted ones,
Which I was instrumentall in my place
To bring to God, but all of his Free Grace.
How am I changed ! that of late was weak,
Above the force of Satan now to break ?
How am I changed ! Son of Sorrow late,
But now triumphing in my heavenly state.
How was I vex'd with pains, with griefs molested !
How in a moment am I now Invested
With Royal Robes, with Crowns, with Diadems,
With God's Eternall loves ? Such precious Gems,
He hath in Store for them his Saints that are ;
For such indeed he counts his Jewels rare.
Oh Brethren, Sisters, Neighbours, Country, Friends,
I'me now above you : Hark to them God sends,
As yet surviving in their worthy Charge,
Whose work it is God's Vineyard to enlarge.
God and my Conscience, your Experience knows,
Whiles I was with you, I was one of those,
That labour'd faithfully God's Vineyard in,
Sowing his Seed, and plucking up of Sin.
Now is the Harvest to my self indeed ;
The Lord grant a supply of one to feed
Your Souls with heavenly food, and one to lead
In wayes of God, untill his Courts do tread.
Next to God's love, my Flock, love one another,
And next to Christ, preserve love to thy brother.
Let ever precious be in your esteem
God's holy Word, and such as slight it, deem
Of Serpents brood : whatever they pretend,
By no means to such Blasphemies attend.
Decline all wanderings, lest from all you stray ;
If stept aside, return in this your day :
Keep close to God, so he that is Most High
Shall you preserve as Apple of his Eye,

And give you peace, on Earth Tranquillity,
Mansions in Heaven to Eternity;
Where we that Death doth for a time now sever,
Shall meet, Embrace, and shall not part forever.

"R un is his Race,
A nd his work done;
L eft Earthly place,
P artridge is gone.
H e's with the Father and the Son.

P ure joyes and constant do attend,
A ll that so live, such is their End.
R eturn he shall with Christ agen,
T o Judge both just and Sinful men.
R ais'd is this Bird of Paradise:
I oy heaven entred breaks the ice.
D eath under foot he trodden hath;
G race is to Glory Straitest Path,
E ver Enjoyes Love free from wrath."

His ministry was peaceful and happy. No jars served to disturb the quiet of the church, and his gentleness of spirit and meekness of heart brought upon him the affection of his people, and secured for him that name, which has been handed to posterity as a token of holiness. The fanciful Mather in his Magnalia in giving the life of Mr. Partridge, thus wrote:—

"When David was driven from his Friends into the Wilderness he made this Pathetical Representation of his Condition. '*Twas as when one doth hunt a Partridge in the Mountains.*' Among the many worthy persons who were persecuted into an *American* Wilderness for their Fidelity to the Ecclesiastical Kingdom of our true *David*, there was one that bore the *Name*, as well as the *State* of an *hunted Partridge*. What befel him, was, a *Bede* saith of what was done by *Fœlix*, *Juxta nominis sui sacramentum*.

"This was *Mr. Ralph Partridge*, who for no Fault, but the *Delicacy* of his good Spirit, being distress'd by the Ecclesiastical *Setters*, had no Defence, neither of *Beak*, nor *Claw*, but a *Flight* over the Ocean.

"The Place where he took covert, was the Colony of *Plymouth*, and the Town of *Duxbury* in that Colony.

"This *Partridge* had not only the Innocence of the *Dove*, conspicuous in his blameless and pious Life, which made him very acceptable in his Conversation; but also the Loftiness of an *Eagle*, in the great Soar of his intellectual Abilities. There are some Interpreters, who understanding *Church Officers* by the *living Creatures*, in the Fourth Chapter of the *Apocalypse*, will have the *Teacher* to be intended by the *Eagle* there, for his quick Insight into remote and hidden things. The Church of *Duxbury* had such an *Eagle* in their Partridge, when they enjoy'd such a *Teacher*."

Mr. Mather then continues to speak of his connection with the Cambridge Synod of 1647, at which Mr. Partridge was the only delegate from Plymouth Colony, but whether he went at the instance of his church is not known.

"By the same token, when the *Platform* of *Church Discipline* was to be compos'd, the *Synod* at *Cambridge* appointed three persons to draw up each of them, *A Model of Church-Government, according to the Word of God*, unto the end, that out of those, the Synod might form what should be most agreeable; which three persons were Mr. *Cotton*, and Mr. *Mather*, and Mr. Partridge. So that in the opinion of that Reverend Assembly, this person did not come far behind this first three, for some of his accomplishments.

"After he had been *Forty Years* a faithful and painful *Preacher* of the Gospel, rarely, if ever, in all that while interrupted in his works, by any Bodily Sickness, he dy'd in a good Old Age about the Year 1658."

In conclusion Mr. Mather presents a striking illustration of the character of Mr. Partridge, truly expressive of his lowliness and humility of spirit.

"There was one singular instance of a *weaned Spirit*, whereby he signalized himself unto the Churches of God. That was this: there was a time when most of the ministers in the Colony of *Plymouth*, left the Colony, upon the Discouragement which the want of a *competent maintenance* among the needy and froward inhabitants gave unto them. Nevertheless Mr. Partridge was, notwithstanding the *Paucity* and *Poverty* of his Congregation, so affraid of being any thing that look'd like *a Bird wandering from his Nest*, that he remained with his poor People, till he *took wing* to become a *Bird of Paradise*, along with the winged *Seraphim* of Heaven. EPITAPHIUM. AVOLAVIT!"

Mr. Partridge was probably interred in the first burial place of the town, which was a knoll in the south eastern part at Harden Hill, as it is called. If any stones were ever placed here they have since been destroyed by the ravages of time or otherwise, as none at the present day exist. Probably, however, none were erected, in hopes of concealing from the Indians their loss by death, and consequent weakness; or in the earliest periods the difficulty of procuring stones from

England was so great, that few, if any, could have been placed here.

This was probably used as a place of sepulture for about sixty years, and here were, doubtless, buried most of the founders of the town and church. Here, probably, rest the remains of Standish, Alden, Collier, Partridge and others, whose memory we delight to cherish, but whose graves must forever remain unknown.

We have the most positive evidence that there was a burying ground here. Some years ago, while a sloop was building in this vicinity, there were found by the workmen, the bones of a female and an infant buried together. About the close of the last century a small sloop grounded on the marsh near by in a severe gale, and a party of workmen proceeded to get her off. While here, they discovered in the bank lately washed by the sea, the appearance of a coffin, and on closer examination they perceived the nails, though all were in a very decayed state. On the shore beneath there were found three skulls and several bones, apparently of the thigh. The teeth in one were perfect, and in one there were two. On one there was some light sandy hair. The bank here has washed away some twenty feet within fifty years. Some, however, incline to the belief that this was an Indian yard, but the fact that it was near the first church, and other considerations influence me to believe that it was an English burial place. There were fifty or seventy years ago, traditional reports, that there was a burying ground a short distance to the West of the Methodist Episcopal Church, and Esq. Sprague, when plowing, used always on that account to leave undisturbed this portion. Maj. Alden was accustomed to observe that he believed John Alden, the Pilgrim, was buried here, and that this was the first burying ground, and the one at Harden Hill cliff was an Indian one. However, there is no positive evidence on this point either way.

Mr. Partridge preached in a very small building in the south eastern part of the town, near the water, and tradition now marks its site. This building probably stood for about 70 years, and in it preached the first three pastors of the church. It is a matter of much regret, that we have not the records of the early state of the church, which would no doubt throw much light on the subject, and be of peculiar interest. Of the first one hundred years of the existence of the church, we have no authentic records; and all the information respecting the progress and history of it during this period is derived from other and various sources.

Mr. Partridge's will bears date Sept. 20th, 1655; and was proved May 4th, 1658. His wife was Patience ———, who survived him. He mentions in the will his daughter *Eliz-*

abeth, who married Thomas Thacher,* May 11th, 1643, and died June 2d, 1664. To this daughter he gave all his landed property, both in Old and New England, and after her decease to her second son Ralph Thacher, who was living on the estate in Duxbury as late as 1681; but afterwards was settled over the church at Martha's Vineyard, in 1697. His daughter *Mary* married John Marshall† in England. His will also names his sister Elizabeth Tidge, and his man servant Joseph Prior, and maid servant Anna Rainer.

Rev. John Holmes succeeded in the ministry. He had a peaceful and happy settlement, and was, it would appear, respected by his people. As a preacher he was sincere, but mild and gentle, and though, says tradition, he caused not deep impressions, yet he is said to have been endeared to his flock by the meekness and lowliness of his soul.

1661. Zoeth Howland fined 10 shillings for breaking the Sabbath.

1664. There is a deed, bearing date, Sept. 9th, 1643, conveying to Thomas Bird of Scituate, one half of a fifty acre

---

* He was son of Rev. Peter of Old Sarum, England, and was born May 1st, 1620, arrived at Boston, June 4th, 1635, ordained at Weymouth, Jan. 2d, 1645, and at Boston was installed first pastor of the Old South Church, Feb. 16th, 1670, and died Oct. 16th, 1678, æt. 58. His children were Thomas, died at Boston, April 2d, 1686 : Ralph, mentioned in the text; and Peter, who was born July 18th, 1651, H. C. 1671, ordained at Milton, June 1st, 1681, was married thrice, had nine children, and died 27th Dec., 1727, æt. 77 years. *Farmer.* He had also a daughter Patience, who married William Kemp of Duxbury. Of the mother of these, Cotton Mather says — "She was a person of the most amiable temper, one Pious and Prudent, and every way worthy of the man to whom she became a Glory."

† Concerning this marriage in the Suffolk deeds, we find the following, (an abstract.) " Sybil Marshall of Lenham, county of Kent, widow, and John Marshall of Lenham, Grocer, sonne and heir apparent of the said Sybil Marshall, to Ralph Partrich of Sutton near Dover, county of Kent, Clark, & Gervase Partrich, citizen and cordwainer of London. In consideration of a marriage between the said John Marshall and Mary Partrich, one of the daughters of the said Ralph Partrich. Several parcels of Land and Buildings in Rinnarton alias Renardington in the county of Kent, England, as a jointure for the said Mary in case she shall survive the said John Marshall. Nov. 29th, 1631. Recorded Jan. 4th, 1660." Then follows, bearing the same dates, " John Marshall to Ralph Partrich, £200 Bond, respecting the marriage described in the above writing." In Mr. R. P.'s will he mentions Mary's two sons, John and Robert. The latter married Mary Barnes in 1660, and had John and Robert (born 15th Aug., 1663).

lot at "Mattacheessita," which was given by Daniel Hicks. This afterwards became the property of the church, as appears from the following record, and was afterwards delivered to Mr. Holmes, as is recorded, July 10th, 1666: "On the fourth day of October, 1664, Anthony Dodson, & Ann, the wife of Thomas Bird of Scituate, late deceased, appeared in Court and certified that this deed and ye land therein expressed was freely given by the said Thomas Bird unto the church of Duxburrow: Pr. me Nathaniel Morton, Clarke of the Court for ye Jurisdiction of New Plymouth."

1666. Edward Land, John Cooper & John Simmons were fined 10 shillings each, "for prophane and abusive carriages each towards other on Lord's day at the meeting house."

1666. Mr. Samuel Seabury was summoned before the Court to answer to the charge, that "hee hath busied himselfe to scandalise and defame the minnestry of Duxbury." He gave the Court no satisfaction, and was exhorted and reproved, and admonished to desist from such action in future, and was then released with the assurance, however, that on its repetition, he must expect to be again questioned.

1667. Nathaniel Soule was brought before the Court for abusing Mr. Holmes, "by many false scandulous and approbuouse speeches," and was sentenced to make a public acknowledgment, to pay a fine of £20 and to sit in the stocks at the pleasure of the Court, which last was revoked at the urgent request of Mr. Holmes. He confessed that he was guilty of "wickedly speaking and with a high hand contumeliously villifying and scandulizing Mr. John Holmes, and," said he, "that this my wickedness in soe speaking of soe godly a man is greatly agravated in that it hath a tendency to the hinderence of the efficacye of that great and honorable worke of the preaching of the Gospell, unto which he is called."

1669. "It is enacted that any person or persons that shall be found smoking of tobacco on the Lord's day, going to or coming from the meetings, within two miles of the meeting house, shall pay 12 pence for every such default for the Colony's use."

1675. This year died *Mr. Holmes*,* on the 24th of December. His ministry though not remarkably long was productive of much good. He was buried in the old burying ground. He married 11th Dec., 1661, Mary, da. of John Wood,†

---

* It is said that he came from England. I have not ascertained that he belonged to any of the families of Holmes in the Geneal. Registers.

† "*John Wood, sen.*, m. Sarah, and his ch'd were John, Mar. 4th, 1650; Nathaniel, Isaac, 27th Feb., 1653, Mary m. Rev. Mr. H., Sarah m. Fallowell, Abigail m. Leonard, Mercy, Elizabeth, and Hannah."

John Atwood, perhaps father of the preceding, was of Plymouth early, *alias* Atwood of Plymouth. She survived him and became the third wife of Major William Bradford.

Rev. Ichabod Wiswall was next settled the pastor of the church in 1676. He was born about 1638, and, it has been said, came from England while a youth. Some have made him the son of one of the three of this name, who early settled in Dorchester: John, Thomas, and Enoch. But I think it more probable that he was not. There was an Ichabod Wiswall, who was in the colony in 1667, when his name and that of Remember Wiswall (perhaps his wife), are attached to an instrument on record in the colony books. Mr. Ichabod Wisewall, of Mass. took the oath of fidelity, 1674. He m. Priscilla Pabodie Sept. 2d, 167–, and had ch'd — *Mary* (or Mercy,) Oct. 4th, 1680, m. John Wadsworth Jan. 25, 1704; *Hannah*, Feb. 22d, 1681, m. Rev. John Robinson, Mr. W.'s successor; *Peleg*, Feb. 5th, 1683, grad. H. C. 1702, head master of the North free grammar-school of Boston from 1719 to his death, Sept. 2d, 1767, æt. 84; *Perez*, Nov. 22d, 1686; *Deborah*, m. Samuel Seabury, Oct. 21st, 1717; *Priscilla*, m. Gershom Bradford, 1716. His will bears date May 25th, 1700, and makes his wife his chief heir. The witnesses were Alexander Standish, John and Samuel Sprague, and John Wadsworth. Inventory of his estate, taken August 9, 1700: whole amount was £351 15s. including money and clothing, £170, books £60, plate £15; horse, cattle, sheep, swine, &c., £21 10s., and six bee-hives.

His oldest son *Peleg*, of Boston, named above, m. Elizabeth ——, and had Elizabeth, 4th Nov. 1720; Daniel, 13th Feb. 1722; Priscilla, 17th Dec. 1725; John, 15th April, 1731.

Mr. Wiswall had been at Harvard College three years, but did not graduate. He was a man of energy and piety; and under his ministry the prospects of the church were bright, and the highest prosperity was secured to his people. He was assisted in the affairs of the church by Dea. *John Wadsworth*, an humble and pious man, whose highest aim was for the wel-

---

owned a house in town valued at £150, and the Plain Dealing Estate (£162,) and other property amounting to £125. His wife Ann, died June 1st, 1654. He died late in 1643. His will names "his little kinsman Wm. Crowe," and his brother Lee and his wife, and their ch'd Ann and Mary. *Stephen*, (perhaps his son,) Plymouth, had Hannah Oct. 14, 1649. *Henry*, Plymouth, had Jonathan, Jan. 1, 1650, and Sarah, who m. John Nelson, 28 Nov., 1667. A *Mary* Wood b. at Sandwich, Mar. 29, 1649. *Abigail* m. Jonathan Pratt, 2 Nov, 1664.

fare of the church. His equal in age, he joined his exertions with those of the pastor, and continually strove in the performance of the duties allotted. His death occurred a few months previous to Mr. Wiswall's; and it appears by the records, he "deceased May ye 15th, Anno Dom. 1700, very early in ye morning before ye dawning of ye day, being about sixty-two yeares of age." It is worthy of remark, that the descendants of this gentleman for four generations have held the same office in the church — all worthy men. In these times of our fathers, it would not seem, it appears, inconsistent with the dignity of the deacon's office, to be engaged sometimes in more servile occupations; for we frequently find Dea. Wadsworth mentioned as receiving pay for sweeping the meeting-house. In the public business of the town, as well as in the civil government of the colony, Dea. Wadsworth was employed, and for several years represented his town in the General Court.

The salary of the minister at this date was small, (about £50,) and he was chiefly dependent on the liberality of a few for his support; for there were some who refused to pay their just share of the contribution necessary for his maintenance. And it was with a sensibility peculiar to himself, that soon after he had recovered from a severe attack of sickness at this time, that he addressed a letter * to Gov. Hinckley, containing serious considerations in regard to the sufficiency of the support of ministers and their families. It was, said he, a mournful reflection, when I thought what would be the condition of my family after my death. "It was no small exercise in my sickness," he continues, "to think y^t when my eyes were closed by death, their eyes would be forcibly kept open by streames of teares, in part because they must be turned out of dores, and could chalenge no habitation."

"Therefore, Sr. for as much as you are *in utrumque paratus*, viz., have conversed with both law and gospell, which direct professors, but especialy preachers of divine truth, howe they should walke with God and man, especialy with their owne flesh and bone, I humbly crave your serious consideration and resolution of a few queries."

He then proceeds to institute a set of inquiries; in the first place suggesting for reflection the meaning of the text, to be found in the first epistle of Timothy, v. 8. Secondly, he asks, whether God has not provided for the support of the ministry; and, thirdly, whether He has delegated power to any people to call a pastor to their service without providing a suitable maintenance for him. Fourthly, he inquires, whether the civil authorities should not be "a nurseling father," according

---

* Hinckley MSS. II. 12 — a fragment.

to Isaiah xlix. 23; and lastly, he asks, "whether my case, all circumstances considered, can be paraleled in the coloney."

And, in continuance, he proceeds:

"Sr, probably you may looke on it as ominous, if not prodigious, that I salute you with a script of this nature; and therefore, that you may not wander in uncertaine conjectures concerning ye nature of ye present phenomenon, be pleased to consider that ye mature and grey-headed observation of ye Roman orator (non nobis solum nati sumus) hath a weighty and abiding impresse on my spirit." I plead for all (he continues in substance), not for myself alone, but for all the ministers of the colony. Like the man of ages, who planted a young tree by the roadside, and inscribed it with the motto, POSTERITATI, I keep the emblem of futurity before me, and strive to acquire that competence, that shall provide for my widow and orphans for a time, that security and prosperity which I may know in my dying moments will preserve them from trouble and danger. Having thus proceeded with language of emotion, he concludes with the divine benediction;—

"The Father of Lightes cloathe you with a spirit of wisedom and resolution to understand, project and effect w^t may be acceptable to Him through Christ Jesus, that in this Coloney there may be no extinguishing, but a lasting progressive continuance of the brightness of that Lamp ordained for the Anointed. So prayes he, who is,

Sr, your humble servant,
ICHABOD WISEWALLE.

Duxbury: 6 :: 9 :: 85."

The town, however, at a meeting, Sept. 10th, 1687, voted to raise his salary, provided he does not charge "those debtor that pay their proportions, for the neglect of those that refuse or neglect to pay their dews, p'vided that the town doe adres themselves to authority for the obtaining of the whole."*
This was not passed, however, without some opposition, and at the same meeting several townsmen remonstrated against it. They were John Soule, Isaac Barker, Robert Barker, Joseph Howland, James Bishop, Abraham Sampson, Jr., and Josiah Holmes. In the following year Mr. Wiswall received a grant of Bump's meadow. Grants of land were commonly made to the ministry, or to the individual holding at the time the office of pastor, either to be left to his disposal with a right to sell, or only to enjoy the improvement thereof.

In 1694, we find the first mention of a parsonage, when a committee was appointed to give Mr. W. a deed of "the

---

* About this time a petition was addressed to his excellency, "in order to get in Mr. Wiswall's erariges for the work of the ministry among us."

towne house," and "the land he now lives on." At this time the town granted him "halfe yᵉ meadow called Rouse's meadow, yᵗ belonged to yᵉ ministry, to him and his heirs forever, and yᵉ use of yᵗ whole his lifetime." The house above named was built by the Rev. John Holmes, on land which he purchased of John Sprague, and was situated West of the road, "leading from the meeting house into the Noock, or Capt. Standish's point," containing about five or eight acres. The house was afterwards sold by Major William Bradford, who married the widow of Mr. Holmes, to the town. At the same time they gave him one half of Bump's meadow, and the old pasture, bounded N. E. by the before mentioned house lot; N. W. by Mr. Ralph Thacher's homestead; S. W. by Morton's hole marsh; and S. E. by Thomas Boney's. The town also appointed Mr. John Wadsworth, and Capt. Jonathan Alden to give him a deed; but they dying without doing it, the town, May 7th, 1700, chose Samuel Seabury and John Sprague, then agents to do it. Mr. Wiswall at this time acquitted the town of all arrears from 1678 to the end of 1694, and also quitclaimed all former grants. The original deed, bearing date May 20th, 1700, is now before me, signed by the agents, and witnessed by Alexander Standish and John Wadsworth; and acknowledged before Major William Bradford.

Mr. Wiswall died in Duxbury, July 23d, 1700, aged 62 years, much lamented by his people, among whom he had been as a friend, an adviser, and instructor. He was a gentleman of piety and learning, and was of much use in the Colony, sometimes serving in civil capacities, and for many years was an instructor of youth.

He was buried in Duxbury, in the second burying yard, and his monument bears this inscription. — "HERE LYETH BURIED Yᴱ BODY OF Yᴱ REVEREND Mᴿ· ICHABOD WISWALL, DECᴰ JULY Yᴱ 23, ANNO 1700, IN THE 63ᴰ YEAR OF HIS AGE." This stone, the oldest in the yard, is still perfectly legible; and free from moss — emblematic of the good man's purity, whose remains lie buried beneath. How long before 1700, this yard was first used is not known. Its original bounds were somewhat smaller than the present; for in 1734, the town (April 8th,) voted to exchange a small lot of land with Benjamin Prior, for a lot of his, "which lyeth joining the burying ground for the enlargement of said burying ground." The second church stood at the easterly end of this yard, where its site is now identified, and was probably erected in the latter part of Mr. W.'s ministry, though from the following record it would seem not until somewhat later. "Reckoned with yᵉ town agents Feb'y yᵉ 25th, anno 1707. Then rec'd of said agents the sum of one hundred and eighty pounds in full for building ye meeting house in Duxbury. I say rec'd by me Samuel Sprague." This building was not torn down until June 7th, 1785.

It is related of him, that while in England with Mr. Mather, in 1691, endeavoring to obtain a distinct charter for the Colony, and strenuously striving to prevent the union with New York or Massachusetts; but being as strongly opposed and baffled by the endeavors of Mr. Mather, that some feelings of animosity arose between them, and a paper warfare ensued. Plymouth was, however, joined to Massachusetts, and Mr. Mather, after their return home used to taunt him with his defeat, familiarly calling him *the little weazel*. Mather writing home from England, after Wiswall had lost his cherished project, says, he hopes the "old *weazel* will be content in his den." He was, as one who observed in after years the influences of his ministry has said, nearly a faultless man, very high in the estimation of the whole Plymouth Colony for his talents, piety and incorruptible integrity. A sound preacher, though not remarkable for popular eloquence.*
He wrote much, and some of his compositions are highly creditable to him. His style was plain, though forcible and effective. A poem of his, written on the Comet of 1680, and published in London, is preserved among the papers of the Historical Society.

Mr. Wiswall is said to have been famous as an astrologer, and to have predicted the death of one of his children, which happened while he was in England.

Rev. John Robinson † was next settled as pastor in 1702. He graduated at H. C. in 1695, and for a few years, possibly, preached at Newcastle, Pennsylvania. At a meeting of the town, Sept. 2d, 1700, it was "voted to call Mr. John Robinson to ye work of ye ministry here; they also voted to give

---

* Rev. Benjamin Kent's notes.

† He was born at Dorchester, April 17th, 1675, and was son of James Robinson, who m. Mary Alcock, July 27th, 1664, and died 1694, and whose other children were Thomas, April 15th, 1668, Samuel, Sept. 14th, 1670, James, 1665, Mary, Mar. 17th, 1673, and Ebenezer, July 5th, 1682. Mr. R. m. Hannah, dau. of his predecessor, Mr. Wiswall. Their children were *Mary*, Feb. 23d, 1706 ; *Hannah*, Nov. 2d, 1708, m. Nathaniel Thomas, Esq., Sept. 1st, 1729, (he was the father of Hannah, who m. Col. John Thomas, and their children were Col. John Thomas, and the wife of Rev. Z. Willis of Kingston ;) *Alethea*, May 26th, 1710, m. Mr. Ripley of Abington ; *Elizabeth*, Sept. 28th, 1712, m. Rev. Jacob Eliot of Lebanon, Ct., May 4th, 1732; *John*, April 16th, 1715, removed to Wilkes-

£60 a year annually towards his maintainance in ye aforesaide worke, one halfe silver money, and ye other halfe, corn or provisions at ye common price; they allso made choice of Mr. Seth Arnold, Mr. Edward Southworth, Mr. Samuel Seabury, and Mr. William Brewster as their agents to acquaint Mr. Robinson with their proceedings herein, and allso to discourse with him concerning his acceptance thereof in order to his settlement amongst us in ye aforesaid worke of ye ministry." He accepted and was settled Nov. 13th, 1702.

The ministry of Mr. Robinson was long, and in the beginning comparatively quiet, yet there were some in the town who continually opposed him, and delighted in thwarting his plans, especially in the latter part of his ministry, when troubles of a pecuniary nature disturbed the quiet of the church.

1714. The town gave leave to John Chandler, Ichabod Bartlett, Philip Delano, Nathaniel Brewster, Pelatiah West, Constant Southworth, Jonathan Alden, John Simmons, Jr., and Benony Delano, "to build a seat in s^d town's meeting house adjoining ye front gallerie." At the same meeting (Feb. 24th,) "Y^e said town also gave to their agents formerly chosen by s^d town to pew s^d meeting house round, &c., Lt. Saml. Bradford, Mr. Thomas Loring, Mr. Saml. Seabury, Mr. John Partridge, and Capt. John Alden ye front or free seat in ye uppermost or second gallerie in ye north west end of ye s^d meeting house, whereupon ye s^d agents gave to ye s^d towne their right to ye two hindermost seats in s^d gallerie."

1722. Mr. Robinson was called to mourn the death of his wife, and his oldest child, Mary; and her sad end was no less an affliction to her bereaved husband, than a great loss to an affectionate circle of friends and relations. Having determined on a visit to Boston, she had taken passage on board of a coaster, together with her daughter, and Mr. Fish, a young gentleman of Duxbury, and were all drowned by the upsetting of the vessel in a sudden tempest off Nantasket beach, Sept. 22. She was in her 42d year, and the daughter in her 17th, and Mr. Fish was a member of Harvard College. The remains

---

barre, Penn., where he left posterity; *Ichabod* removed to Lebanon, Ct., was a merchant, and father of Joseph, John, and Rev. William, who was b. at Lebanon, Aug. 15th, 1754, and died Aug. 15th, 1825, æt. 71, was minister of Southington, and m. Naomi Wolcott, who died April 16th, 1782, æt. 28; *Faith*, 1718, m. Gov. Jonathan Trumbull of Ct., Dec. 9th, 1735, and died at Lebanon, 1780, æt. 62, and he died Aug. 9th, 1785, æt. 75, and had ch'd, Joseph, who died 1778, æt. 42, and Gov. Jonathan, who was b. Mar. 26th, 1740, and died Aug. 7th, 1809, æt. 69 years. Mr. Trumbull became acquainted with her while on a visit to Duxbury on business.

of the daughter were recovered and interred at Duxbury, where a stone was erected with a suitable inscription. Those of the mother were found six weeks after by the natives, at Race Point, Cape Cod, and identified by papers preserved in her stays, and a golden necklace, which the swelling of her neck had concealed, and which is now in the possession of her descendants. A gold ring which she wore, was probably plundered by the natives, who had cut off her swelled finger to obtain it. She was buried at the Cape, where a monument marks her grave with an inscription by her husband, closing with this quotation from Psalms, — "Thus he bringeth them to their desired Haven." An elegy was written on her death, and addressed to her husband, by Rev. Mr. Pitcher of Scituate, and which is more precious on account of its purity of sentiment, than for any intrinsic merit of the style. She is called, —

> " One of the Gowned tribe and Family,
> Of bright descent and Worthy Pedegree;
> A charming daughter in our Israel,
> In ventuous acts and Deeds seen to excell:
> As Mother, Mistriss, Neighbour, Wife, most rare;
> Should I exceed to say beyond compare?
> Call her the Phœnix, yet you cannot lye,
> Whether it be in prose or poetry.
> For Meekness, Piety, and Patience;
> Rare Modesty, Unwearied Diligence;
> For Gracious Temper, Prudent Conduct too,
> How few of the fair sex could her outdo." *

1723. This year occurred the death of Dea. *Wm. Brewster*, on the 3d of November, aged nearly 78 years, having served in the office of Deacon for many years. He was a son of Love Brewster, and grandson of the Elder of Plymouth, — a worthy man, who was often employed to good advantage in the civil affairs of the town.

1731. Dr. Benony Delano was appointed (March 12th) to get the meeting-house repaired. And again, (Sept. 8th,) Dr. Delano, Wm. Brewster and Thomas Loring were appointed for the same purpose.

1736. The town chose (Aug. 9th,) Nathaniel Sampson, Thomas Phillips, George Partridge, and Isaac Simmons, Jr., " to take care and order the children in town, and restrain them from any unbecoming carriage, making disturbance in

---

* Deane's Scituate.

meeting-time, or between the services." Mr. Robinson's salary this year was £120.

1737. The unhappy circumstances, which finally led to the dismission of Mr. Robinson, arose for the most part from disputes in regard to the sufficiency of his salary. His stated allowance in the beginning, as appears from the town records, bearing date May 19th, 1701, was £60 a year, as long as he continued in the ministry, which was to be raised by selling the common lands of the town. The same year the town voted to purchase a convenient place for a parsonage for the use of the ministry; and a committee, consisting of Mr. Edward Arnold, Mr. Edward Southworth, and Ensign Samuel Seabury, were appointed to make the purchase. He had also considerable grants of land made to him at various times, to meet his continual demand for increase of salary, in order, as he expressed it, that he might live *in the body*.*

The first notice we can find concerning the difficulties that ensued, is in the town's books, when, at a meeting held 14th March, 1737, "the town chose Edward Arnold, Col. John Alden, Mr. Joshua Soule, Samuel Weston, and John Wadsworth a committee to treat with Mr. Robinson concerning the making up of his salary, about which there is an action depending at the next Superior court." This action, we believe, was never brought on. On the 2d of June, a meeting of the church was held, and "then ye Rev. Mr. Robinson their Pastor declared, that if ye town & church would give him a dismission from his pastoral office from among them, that he would accept of it." On the 3d of August the town agreed "to accept of ye above s^d Mr. Robinson's above s^d proposals." At this meeting there was much diversity of opinion, and a number of the most influential townsmen entered a protest against the controversy. Samuel Alden, Joshua Soule, Philip Delano, Philip Chandler, John Wadsworth and Samuel Chandler were the signers of this remonstrance. They finally, after much contention, appointed a committee to try to make an agree-

---

* *Rev. Benja. Kent's Notes.* On one of these occasions, when he petitioned the town for this purpose, he was addressed by one of his most active, if not influential parishioners, who doubtless thought that he had a sufficiency. "Well! Parson Robinson," said he, "what do you want now? You know we have raised your salary once, and besides that we have given you the improvement of Hammer Island, and upwards of thirty acres upland in Weechertown! Isn't that enough?" "Ah! yes," replied Robinson, in his not unusual, and truly characteristic manner, "Hammer Island! and I've mowed it too this year, and I don't want a better fence around my cornfield than one windrow of the fodder it cuts! My yearlings will come up to it, and smell of it, yes, smell of it, *and run and roar!* Weechertown! Thirty acres in Weechertown! Why, if you were to mow it with a razor, and rake it with a fine tooth comb, you wouldn't get enough from it to winter a grasshopper!"

ment with Mr. Robinson. Nothing more appears to have been done until December 5th, when it was voted to pay the difference between Mr. Robinson and the town, and also the present year's salary, if he would leave the ministry." These proceedings were sent to Mr. Robinson, who returned the following answer:—

"Duxb. Decem^r· 5, 1737, in answare to ye above vote, I promise to comply therewith, if ye town will make my salary for ye currant year £170, and ye which forthwith payed & ye church will give me a dismission. JOHN ROBINSON."

The meeting then voted to pay him £412 6s. 12d., and the present year's salary. They also desired him to preach on the next Sabbath as formerly. On the 16th of December the following protest of some of the town's people was presented, the original of which, in Mr. Kent's MS. Coll., is now before me.

"We ye subscribers, inhabitants of ye town of Duxborough, being sensible of the Troubles and Contentions in ye s^d town by reason of a party that are not willing to pay our minister, viz., ye Revnd M^r· John Robinson, so much in value as our engagement was to him as to his yearly salary, when he first setled among us, nor to comply with ye judgement of Court relating thereto, nor any other ways to agree with him about ye same; but still are going on in their Contentions, which have occasioned great charge upon ye s^d town, & is likely to occasion more, if speedy care be not taken to prevent, We therefore whose names are hereunto written do hereby declare our aversness to ye maintaining ye s^d Contentions & do protest against paying any further charge which may be brought on ye s^d town by such contentions, & do declare our willingness to comply with ye judgement of Court relating to ye above s^d salary, & to pay our parts of what yet remains due concerning ye same, that so our s^d Minister may be well supported & encouraged to continue in the work of ye Ministry among us." Signed by Joseph Soule, Isaac Peterson, Ebenezer Sampson, Moses Simons, Pelatiah West, Philip Delano, Joshua Soule, John Simons (his mark), Amasa Turner, John Sprague, Jr., Thos. Southworth, Nathaniel Fish, and Joshua Cushman.

Either neglected payment on the part of the town or new difficulties of a similar nature renewed the contention; and at a meeting, July 5th, 1738, a communication was received from Mr. Robinson, stating "that he did not look upon himself as ye minister of Duxborrough; but that he was dismissed by a result of an ecclesiastical council, and said that he would be no hinderance to them in procuring another minister." I can find no account of the council referred to. On the 7th of the next month, a committee was chosen to make up accounts with Mr. Robinson, "*from the beginning of the world to the present day.*" These few words convey better than any sentiments of mine, the feelings of the people towards their pastor. Another meeting was held on the 25th of Sept., but adjourned to the third of October, when it was "voted that they would not have any thing to do with' ye Rev^nd Mr. Robinson as their ecclesiastical minister or pastor in s^d town; and further that ye s^d town will not pay the s^d Mr. Robinson any salary ever since he left off ye work of the ministry and preaching ye Gospel in s^d town, declaring solemnly that he was not ye minister of Duxburough, and that ye s^d town might proceed to get another minister to supply ye pulpit, he would be nothing against it; and then ye s^d town voted that they would joyn with the church in procuring an ecclesiastical council to dismiss Mr. Robinson from his pastoral office in ye s^d town." The meeting then adjourned to the 19th, when this vote was passed and recorded, — " Voted, that ther meting hous shuld be shut up so that no parson shuld open ye same so that Mr. John Robrson of Duxborrough may not get into s^d meting hous to preach anay more, without orders from the town."

The precise date of Mr. Robinson's dismission is not given; but in the town records under date of Nov. 11th, 1738, it is stated that Mr. Robinson acquitted the town of all charges.

"Received of the town agents £412 10*s.* 6*d.* by judgement of the Court of Assize, in April, 1737.

Nov. 11th, 1738. JOHN ROBINSON."

Mr. Robinson afterwards removed to Lebanon, Ct., the residence of the Elder Gov. Trumbull, who had married his daughter, where he died of diabetes, Nov. 14th, 1745, æt. 74 years.

As a preacher* he was sound in his discourse, and earnest and sententious in his arguments; but painful oftentimes in character. He was remarkable for his occasional sermons and texts; and the occurrence of great events or remarkable phenomena afforded him a theme to his liking, which he would treat in a manner truly as eccentric as characteristic. He seldom exchanged, and always appeared in the pulpit in a short jacket, and in consequence of this, as of his name, he went familiarly by the name of *master Jack*. It is said, that he never wore an outside garment.

He lived in a two story house on a rising knoll, a little northeast of the present residence of Capt. Richardson. He had for a near neighbor one Josiah Wormall, with whom he

---

* The remaining account of Mr. Robinson is derived chiefly from Mr. Kent's notes.

lived in perpetual turmoil and conflict, and whom he very kindly denominated "*All worm*" or "*Wormwood*," as the circumstances of the case required. This Christian of the Old School usually went to church in a leathern apron, smoking his pipe until he reached the meeting-house door. On one occasion, having deposited his pipe in the pocket of his coat, before he had extinguished the fire within, he walked deliberately up the broad aisle with becoming solemnity, and leaning on a gigantic staff, and having taken a seat directly before the pastor in the "old men's long seats," he fixed through his shaggy eyebrows his searching gaze upon the preacher. It was however but for a moment, for springing suddenly from his seat with a stare of consternation, and seizing the skirt of his coat all on fire, he rushed from the house. "There," cried Mr. Robinson with imperturbable gravity, "there, brethren, neighbor Wormall comes smoking into the house, and he goes smoking out!" And at another time, as this Christian brother sat looking up from his place, mimicking in miniature his gestures, and pouting occasionally at what he deemed heretical doctrines, Mr. Robinson came to a sudden and solemn pause, looked down upon his auditor and audience, and said,—"Brethren, I 've done! If you will follow me to my house I will preach. But I cannot and will not preach here, while that man sits grinning at me!" He instantly left the pulpit; but was followed by Pelatiah West, another particular friend, who gave him on the door step the anxious assurance, — "Why, Parson Robinson, I would not have left the meeting-house, if the devil had been there!" "Neither would I," was the ready response. On another occasion, Pelatiah West, a member of the society, wrote the following original lines, and handed them to one of the deacons at church, to be read and sung line by line, as was then the custom, and which was written with direct reference to some previously expressed sentiment of Mr. Robinson.

> " He that does bring the fattest pig,
> And eke the goose most weighty,
> He is the independent Big,
> And eke the saint most mighty.
>
> " But he that does withhold his hand,
> And eke shut up his purse,
> The Lord shall drive him from the land,
> And eke lay on his curse! "

Not less peculiar are his farewell words, which he is said to have addressed to the town on his departure, savoring of that independence and eccentricity of character, which was always manifested by him. "Neighbors, I am going never to return, and I shake the dust from my feet as an everlasting testimony against ye, vipers as ye are."

An anecdote is related of him concerning an earthquake, which happened during his ministry. Being visited shortly after its occurrence by one of his society, he appeared in great distress, and upon inquiry he answered, "Neighbor A., there has just been, you know, an earthquake, and I must preach about it. But I don't know what to do. I 've no book that says a word about earthquakes." He preached, however, on the next Sabbath, and two such sermons, it is said, were never delivered.

Another story is related which particularly illustrates a peculiar trait of his character. One of his church once calling upon him, he appeared in a mood of unusual meditation, and in answer to his interrogatories replied with an air of confidence, "This morning I got up and went without doors, and saw a hawk in the sky, a large hawk, and," said he, turning to his friend with a look of assurance, "that dog sat upon his tail." Robinson followed this story by another, equally marvellous, apparently. The individual expressed his astonishment, and even dared to state his disbelief. "Ah!" replied Robinson, "No one can believe any thing here without it is miraculously wrought before them." "Surely," returned the other, "one must be in a great delusion to believe a lie," and the matter after little further disputation was dropped. Shortly after, Robinson was called upon before the church to explain in regard to the strange stories which he had related; when, rising, he replied with an air of extreme indifference, "Disbelieve it if you please, but I know that dog sat upon his tail." "Upon the hawk's tail?" asked some one. "No," replied Robinson with considerable feeling, "upon his own tail of course."

Rev. Samuel Veazie* was the next settled minister of the church. We find by the Town Records that the town (Aug.

---

* Mr. Veazie was born Jan. 8th, 1711, and was a descendant of Robert of Braintree, William and Alice were of Braintree, and had Alice, May 4th, 1659; Samuel and Mary of the same place had Mary, June 17th, 1687, and Samuel, July 19th, 1689.

Mr. Veazie grad. at H. C. in 1736; m. Deborah Sampson, Aug. 6th, 1742, and had a son, John, born in July, and died Aug. 3d, 1745, and a second John. He lived at the Nook, and built and occupied the house, where resided the late Andrew Sampson.

Church Records. With his ministry commence the extant records of the church, and it is said that the earlier ones were burnt at a house in Pembroke.

7th, 1738,) voted to give him an invitation to become their pastor, and appointed Dea. Alden to treat with him. Still later this call was renewed, (March 9th, 1739,) and Col. Alden, Wm. Brewster, and John Chandler were then chosen and empowered to make an agreement with him about settling among them. The Town offered as an inducement, the sum of £400, and an annual salary of £50. In 1741, however, we find among the appropriations of the Town, for the minister £150. He was ordained Oct. 31st, 1739. The services were a prayer by the Rev. Jno. Parker of Plympton; a sermon by the Rev. John Shaw of Bridgewater; the charge by Rev. John Auger of the same place; the R. H. of Fellowship by the Rev. Shearjashub Bourn of Scituate.

1739, Sept. 8th. In the midst of his usefulness in the church and society, died Dea. Jedediah Southworth, aged 37 years.

1740, May 27th. Mrs. Catharine White presented to the church a large damask table cloth. At a meeting on the 25th of June, they chose a committee "to return their grateful thanks for the generous gift."

1741, April 14th. Died Dea. Benjamin Alden, who was a carpenter by trade, and was drowned near the Gurnet. The church voted to receive none at the communion, who were not in charity with their church at home, and that it was a grievance for any church to do otherwise.

1743. This year may be considered the date of the first serious outbreak between the church and its pastor. Some of the church in the beginning were opposed to the settlement of Mr. Veazie, and continued throughout his ministry much dissatisfied with his labors. Some even left the church, and joined themselves to others. His ministry, like his predecessor's, in the latter part was turbulent and inauspicious, and he was finally obliged from want of a support, to ask a dismission. During the first part of his ministry he was a moderate Calvinist. The part he afterwards took in the religious controversies of the times, however, served to heighten the animosity, which had previously exhibited itself. But it was his fortune to live at a time in the history of New England, when religion was most generally observed, the period of the *Great Revival*. Whitfield was then itinerating through the country, stirring the people to reform. His adherents, the *New Lights*, rapidly increased; so that between the years 1740 and 1750, about thirty congregations of *Separatists* were formed. On the contrary the Old Lights considered the zeal of their opponents as mere wild fire, and very pernicious to the well being of the community, and strove to suppress it. Of this latter class were most of the inhabitants of Duxbury. Nevertheless, Whitfield visited, converted, and made Mr. Veazie a complete fire brand or new light; and (says Mr. Kent,) if it never so happened to any one else, he was evidently made a worse man by his conversion. He was rendered morose, dogmatic, and furious, whipping his own children with the utmost severity for the least freedom on the Sabbath, which he kept formally but strictly from sunrise to midnight. In Duxbury most of the influential men of the town adhered strongly to the old doctrines, and against these Mr. Veazie waged a fierce and bitter warfare; but he could neither persuade nor drive them to embrace his new doctrines or bear with his dogmatisms.* Among the firmest in the opposition was Capt. Samuel Alden, who sincerely believed that more evil than good must arise from these exciting addresses to the fears and passions of the common people.† Mr. Veazie at first boasted that a majority were in favor of the new doctrines. His conduct had long been objectionable to many of his parishioners, and frequent altercations occurred between them. There is extant a paper written about this period, of which the following is a copy. ‡

"We the Subscribers Look upon the Reverend Mr. Veazie's Doctrines many of them to be Erroneous. Sometime ago he Preached concerning Assurance and in his discourse he delivered these words, that dreadful false opinion, that a man may have true grace and not know it. Yea, I say, that dreadful soul damning principle, that a man may be converted and not know it. No greater delusion or stratagem the devil hath not to delude souls into Hell than that. Another time he was preaching from the 10th chapter of Romans at the 13th, 14th and part of the 15th verse, he said in that Sermon, the reason why God's judgment was turned away from the Ninevites was because they lived nigh a place, as it were a channel where God's blessings were wont to flow, and not because

---

* Rev. Benjamin Kent's notes.

† Capt. Alden was a grandson of the pilgrim, and a pious man, ever cheerful, through the christian hope he had attained; and was remarkable for his strength of mind, soundness of judgment, and exemplary deportment through life. He was a friend of education, and took an interest in the intellectual improvement of the mind, as he deemed that essential for the reception of divine truth. He lived until he was impatient to depart, and enter a happier state, though he suffered but little from bodily infirmities. He lived to see a new country peopled with three millions of white men, successfully opposing the ungenerous usurpation and tyranny of the parent empire, where his grandfather saw nothing but a savage wilderness. Had the pilgrims been told that their grandchildren would see this astonishing population, establishing national liberty and independence, they would have thought it a thing utterly improbable, if not totally impossible. —Alden's Epitaphs, Bradford's and Eliot's Biog., and Alden's Centennial Sermon.

‡ Rev. B. Kent's MS. Coll. 129.

they humbled themselves and returned from their evil ways. He likewise declared in the pulpit, that there was not a promise in the whole word of God for a man in a state of Nature, and since has declared to the contrary.

"His *conversation*, we think, is also unbecoming. His saying a person in a state of nature is half a beast, and half a devil, and afterwards denying that he ever said so, or ever thought so. And denying that ever he acknowledged to any, that he had preached false doctrines. Further, his asserting that it was a sin for a man in a state of nature to pray.

"And sometime in July, 1742, Mr. Veazie being at Mr. Nathaniel Samson's, he undertook to examine his wife, what she built upon for salvation, and she told him not upon his works nor her own, and he said what then; she told him she hoped it was her desire to build upon Christ, that rock; and he said that will not do. Then she said unto him, you are my teacher, tell me what will do; and he said die for your brother; and she told him if you will not teach me better I will go to my Bible, and he said unto her, The Bible, the Bible; and he told her, that all the world had been in jest with God until now, and now they were got in earnest. And we asked him what was become of our fathers, and good Christians as we had reason to call them, and he said they are gone to Hell! And he told us that a man in a state of nature had as good sit down upon the floor, and curse and swear, as to go to prayer; and he told us that he would go on in this way for all the men upon Earth or devils in Hell! About the same time Mr. Veazie said at Mr. Joshua Soul's house to his daughter Mercy and one or more of his family in the hearing of his wife, that Christ now standeth with his arms open to receive them, therefore come now this minute, this moment, for without you are cursed damned creatures or devils. The woman saith devils, the daughter she is not sure which. And sometime last March, Mr. Veazie being at Mr. Benjamin Loring's in company with several, asked Mr. Freeman the reason of his not coming to the sacrament; he told him he had many reasons for it, and that he intended to take a convenient opportunity and talk with him; but after other talk he told Mr. Veazie he would give him one reason why he did not come to meeting, and that was, he heard he had preached false doctrine. Mr. Veazie said he had preached the Arminian Scheme, and did not know it, and that he had preached up justification by works, and that he was resolute in the Arminian Scheme, one point of which insisted on would sink all down to Hell. Mr. Veazie was asked why he did not make a public recantation of those doctrines; he said he preached contrary to them now, and that was sufficient, and further said he did intend to make a Public recantation upon a certain day; but it happened there were many Marshfield people, and so omitted it. The beginning of last August Mr. Veazie and Mr. Torrey, our school-master, were talking concerning mirth, and he told Mr. Torrey he showed himself to be just such a person as he always took him to be, and afterwards denied it. And further he told him he wished he never had come into town. Mr. Torrey asked him what provocation he had given him for any such wish. Mr. Veazie said, because he justified singing and dancing. Afterwards he told Torrey he took him to be a person destitute of grace, or he believed he had not one spark of saving grace. Mr. Torrey told Mr. Veazie he admired very much at his talk, and asked him whether he knew that his life was scandalous. The answer he gave Mr. Torrey was, he sung and danced, or justified singing and dancing.

"At another time Mr. Veazie told Mr. Torrey, the reason why he did not join with the people on Sabbath-day noons in reading and prayer in the meeting-house, was because he had no communion with God in prayer. Mr. Torrey told him he did not know that, or it was more than he knew. Mr. Veazie's talk being so censorious and uncharitable without any provocation, especially to one who came into the town to serve it, we think it unsufferable and not to be borne with. Furthermore, when Mr. Veazie was reading Mr. Alden's reasons, that he gave into the Church, why he absented himself from the table of the Lord, he did not read it as it was written, but made an alteration that very much altered the sense. And also we remain very much dissatisfied about our brother Alden's suspension, and think the Church has been irregular in their proceedings with him.

Duxborough, September the 20th 1743.

JOSEPH FREEMAN,   JOSHUA SOULE,
PHILIP CHANDLER,   SAMUEL ALDEN."

1744–5, Mar. 18th. At a meeting of the town on this date, they "voted to choose some persons to take care of their meeting house to keep out of it itinerant preachers." Rev. Joseph Croswell, an itinerant "New Light," frequently preached during the excitement, from house to house.*

1746. In the summer of this year, an ecclesiastical council was convened, to which Mr. Veazie addressed the following note:

"The occasion of this, viz., things being so circumstanced with us that I am very uncomfortable, and not able in any good measure to discharge my ministry, having received of my people for salary since the year 1743, if I mistake not, but about £91 4s. 8d. old tenor. There being also a great sepa-

---

* About this period the church on the other hand voted, that their minister might ask whomever he pleased into his pulpit.

ration from our church and ministry, and appearing no disposition to return, or probability of any accommodation, I therefore desire the judgment of this venerable council whether it be not advisable for me to ask a dismission from my pastoral office." After the decision of this council, Mr. Veazie sent this communication to the town :

"By advice of this council I propose to the town as a condition of my leaving them, that they pay me my salary to the time of my separation from them, according to what they voted me in the year 1744, i. e. £170 per annum, and if they are not willing to do this, that we refer the case of my salary to five men, mutually chosen by us, and we oblige ourselves to be set down by this award. I likewise desire the town to discourse with a committee of the council about my house and land here, to see whether I may not have some security with regard to my little interest in this place.

"Hull, Nov. 11th, 1746."

1747. In Dec. of this year the subject was referred to the Justices of the Court of General Sessions at Plymouth, and Gamaliel Bradford and Capt. Samuel Alden were chosen on the part of the town to answer to the complaint. This Court advised Mr. Veazie and the town agents, to call an ecclesiastical council, and at a meeting of the town, Jan. 25th, 1748, "after several times reading the advice" of the justices, and "considerable debate thereon," it was voted to receive it, and also to "axcept those Gent., nominated by Mr. Veazie and ye town agents, viz., ye Rev. Mr. Eells of Scituate, ye Rev. Mr. Bass of Hanover, ye Rev. Mr. Auger of Bridgewater, and Elijah Cushing, and Thomas Foster, Esqrs, to come and advise and assist in ye affairs." This council assembled, and the following petition signed by forty of his parishioners, was laid before them.

"To the Reverend Council here met. Revd and Hond Sirs,

We having laid before you the ground of our uneasiness with our Reverend Minister, who seemed to us erroneous in his preaching, unchristian and unbecoming in his conduct, we pray you to resolve this case for us, which very much troubles and perplexes our consciences — whether a man that betrays such weakness of understanding (as we call it,) in the doctrine of the Gospel, such unsoundness of speech, if not gross errors in his preaching and conversation (all this for divers years past to this day,) be one that we ought to be easy under and submit ourselves unto as our pastor and spiritual guide, and may with safety intrust our souls and the souls of our children to his ministerial instruction and care."*

* Mr. Kent's MS. Coll.

The affair seemed not to be settled here; but was again to be referred to the Court. At a meeting of the town, May 12th, 1748, after some consultation, Mr. Miles Standish was sent to Mr. Veazie, to make an agreement, if he could, as the case was depending at the Court to be holden the next week. Mr. Veazie then appeared in town meeting, and declared that he was willing to have a compromise. Messrs. Gamaliel Bradford, Samuel Alden, and Samuel Seabury were then chosen to meet him, and were also directed that if they could not agree, to answer him in Court. In the July following, Mr. Veazie sent the following note to the church, asking his dismission.

"To the Church of Christ in Dux:

Though I would gladly and willingly serve you and yours in the work of the ministry with all the strength and grace that God should afford to me, yet for the want of a support and merely for the want hereof, I am obliged to, and now do ask a dismission of this Church from my pastoral office and charge, which I have taken of this church and congregation.
Pastor of the Church   SAMUEL VEAZIE.
in Duxborough: July 5: 1748."

This request was considered on the same day, and of the twenty-one members present, a majority of nine voted not to grant it.

On one of the occasions, when Mr. Veazie entered a lawsuit for the recovery of his salary, he placed his case in the hands of the elder Otis, while the town rested their cause in the ability of the younger Otis, his son. The trial came on, and the latter rested his defence on the ground, "that the charter and laws mentioned, that every town should support a faithful, pious and learned minister, neither of which as he would be able to show from MS. sermons of the plaintiff in his possession, could he possibly be." Mr. Otis then read from these sermons, and commented upon their spirit, doctrines, grammar, and orthography, with so much skill and severity, that he gained for the time his case.*

1749. The disputes still continued between them, though frequent measures were taken for some final settlement. Sept. 14th, the town appointed Capt. Samuel Alden, Samuel Seabury, and John Sampson to settle the difficulties. A meeting was held with Mr. Veazie, but without success.

1750, April 18th. A council of four churches, — that of Hanover, the first of Plymouth, that of Halifax, and the first of Marshfield, met at Mr. Veazie's house in Duxbury. "After

---

* Mr. Kent's Notes.

prayer for direction, and hearing what the pastor and church had to say, this council came to the following conclusion. That they think it advisable that this church give the Rev. Mr. Veazie a dismission from his pastoral relation to them, attended with suitable recommendation, that some way may be made for his usefulness in the ministry elsewhere. Persuant to this advice the church upon Mr. Veazie's request gave him a dismission as follows: *

"The church of Christ in Duxborough, having for some years set under the ministry of the Rev. Mr. Samuel Veazie, and he now applying to us for a dismission from his pastoral relation to us, we in answer to his request say: that Divine Providence having permitted an unhappy controversy to arise some years ago, relating to our said pastor, which still subsists, though we have used many means, which we judged most suitable, to put an end to it, and to regain our dissatisfied brethren, particularly that of an ecclesiastical council mutually chosen, the result whereof our Rev. Pastor unreservedly complied with, we (though with great reluctance,) for the sake of our pastor's comfort and serviceableness, judge it convenient (in consequence of the advice of an ecclesiastical council, convened at our and our pastor's call,) to give our said pastor a dismission from his pastoral relation and office over us. And accordingly we now dismiss him, and freely recommend him to the work of the ministry, where Providence may open a door for his re-settlement, trusting that by the soundness of his doctrine, and by the holiness of life he will approve himself a workman, that need not be ashamed, and praying that he may be an instrument of turning many to righteousness, who may be his crown of joy and rejoicing in the day of Christ.

Signed by   PHILIP DELANO, JAMES ARNOLD, EZEKIEL SOULE, } In the name and by the vote of the chh.

"The church having thus dismissed the Rev^{ud} Mr. Veazie, the council do declare that they look upon this as a regular and valid dismission, and do heartily join with the church in recommending Mr. Veazie to the work of the Gospel ministry, hoping that Divine Providence will open a door for his serviceableness in that work in some part of Christ's vineyard. Finally this council declare their hearty sympathy with this church, under their present broken circumstances, and would earnestly beseech and advise them, together with their breth-

---

* The originals of the two following papers (on one sheet) are in Mr. Kent's MS. Col., 152. The first in Mr. Soule's, and the second in Mr. Cotton's hand.

ren of the congregation, to humble themselves before God for what has been amiss in them in this time of division and temptation; and we would particularly take notice, that we think this town very FAULTY in wholly withholding from their minister his temporal support for several years, and also in suffering the House of God to lye waste, which we take to be a great contempt of the Divine Majesty, and beg leave to express our earnest wish, that every man would lay his hand upon his heart and solemnly inquire, *what have I done?* And we would entreat them all for the future to pursue those measures, that tend to peace, so far as is consistent with truth and holiness, and particularly to endeavor to unite in settling a pious and orthodox minister in this place, as soon as conveniently may be, withal praying that the great shepherd of the sheep would undertake for this flock, and heal the divisions subsisting in the town, and give them another pastor after his own heart, that may prove a lasting blessing to them and theirs. And now, Brethren, we recommend you to God and to the word of his grace, who is able to build you up, and give you an inheritance among them that are sanctified. *Amen.*

ISRAEL THOMAS,	BENJAMIN BASS, Mod^r,
JOHN ATWOOD,	NATHANIEL LEONARD,
EBENEZER FULLER,	JNO. COTTON,
SAMUEL SKIFFE,	SAML. HILL."

He was afterwards presented with letters of recommendation to the church of Hull, over which he was settled April 12th, 1753, and here he died in 1797, at the advanced age of 86 years.

There are extant* several drafts and addresses, written in these contentious times; but without dates, so that it is difficult to place them under their proper year. It appears there was an address framed for His Excellency, stating the sad condition of the church and town; that nothing could be procured to pay the minister, who has had nothing but by particular men for several years; that a vote to pay him was passed in the negative by five or six majority; that "several big men" persuade the lesser, that Mr. Veazie can never get his salary at law, if they do not pay him; that after two years non-payment, Mr. Veazie was persuaded to bring it before the Quarter Sessions, and procured Mr. Kent, a lawyer of Boston, but the action was withdrawn; that several councils had been held between the minister and one man, all of which were decided in the minister's favor; that notwith-

---

* Mr. Kent's MS. Coll. 122, 137, 199.

standing he has so many hot headed fellows, who come to meeting on all occasions, and so many neglect, that the case is brought to this pass; that we have spent as much in law as would support a minister for a year, and that many are willing to pay the minister, but not to be at an expense of keeping him from his just dues. In conclusion they desired His Excellency's advice, that they might be set at peace, and be able to build a new meeting house, or repair the old, which they affirm to be a shame to the town. Another paper is a note, addressed thus: "To the Rev^d Mr. Veazie, a number of your aggrieved people make our complaint, and request as follows." This was because he had not complied with the advice of an ecclesiastical council, which sat here "last summer," and has since given us offence; 1st, because he asserted that a true saint is merely omnipotent; 2d, because he said that unbelief was the only soul damning sin, and that sin against the Holy Ghost was not a sin under the Gospel; 3d, in declaring that conversion was but the return of the soul to itself; 4th, that the devil has not a greater stratagem to delude souls to hell, than waiting God's time, &c. Thus going on and giving nine reasons in the substance of the paper of Sep. 20th, 1743, they conclude, asking for redress or an ecclesiastical council.

Another paper, a draft of an address of the adherents of Mr. Veazie, of which this is an abstract:

"Although we have had divisions, yet we have reason to say with the Psalmist, the Lord reigneth. Although we were much divided in our thoughts, what would be most for the glory of God, and for the peace of this place; and were almost broken up, (which was a great joy to our enemies, who have been a long time striving to molest our peaceable worship,) we were brought to such a pass, that we may well say, that our feet had well nigh slipped, and had we not had God's help, we had despaired of ever again having a reconciled church here. The door our minister was to be thrust out of, appears now to be nearly shut, and that it may be shut quite, we the subscribers do think well of him, and desire to overlook his faults, and that he would forgive ours. We forgive our brethren, and may they forgive us. We are fully resolved not to part with our minister without other grounds, than merely to satisfy the Spirit, which has arisen among us. We resolve that our minister have an honorable support, and as soon as can be a suitable house of worship. We pray that the difference among us may not prevent any from joining our church. We do not think that our bad case would be made better by dismissing our pastor, and pray that we may all seek peace in doing justice to our Minister and one another."

In his farewell sermon, Mr. Veazie used these words: — "Brethren, (said he) I shall probably not come to you again in this place until I come in the clouds!" which occasioned the remark of one of his elder hearers as he was leaving the house, who said to a particular friend, "Why, the creature does not expect to come again *until it rains toads!*" *

1749, March 15th. Ezekiel Soule was chosen Deacon of the Church; he removed to Woolwich in 1766.

1750. Dea. John Wadsworth "deceased, May ye 3d, Anno Domini, 1750, between ten and eleven a clock at night, being seventy-eight years, one month and twenty-one days old."— He was clerk of the town until his death, and for many years a selectman. A virtuous and honorable man.†

1750. The town voted to raise £400 for the ministry.

May 7th. The church "think it proper to have a day of fasting and prayer under their present broken circumstances."

May 14th. It was voted to build a new meeting-house, and three gentlemen of the neighboring towns were chosen to select the site; but it was afterwards agreed to enlarge the old one.

July 25th. Gaml. Bradford, Geo. Partridge and Saml. Seabusy were chosen to join the church committee to choose a preacher as a candidate for the winter.

1751. Voted by the town £500 for the ministry.

1752. Appropriation for the ministry £53 6s. 8d.

The question of building a new church was again agitated; but in 1754, the old one was repaired at an expense of £176, and fifteen new pews were built and sold, £20 13s. 4d. being the highest price paid for one.

1753. The church and town (Sept. 3d) united in extending to Mr. Jonathan Vinal an invitation to become their pastor, which he, in a communication dated Oct. 13th, declined. The church, April 18th, (confirmed by the town May 27th,) voted to call Mr. Cornelius Jones, who also declined.

---

* Rev. Benj. Kent's MS. Notes; where is related another anecdote. Mr. Veazie was frequently visited by Gideon Soule, a crazy person, whom he generally put in the attic to lodge, where he spent the night in boisterous preaching. On coming down one morning, Mr. Veazie said to him in a passion, "Gideon, I wont have it. You must not disturb me so over my head with your eternal preaching! I cannot sleep a wink all night for your bawling and clatter!" "Preaching, Brother Veazie," returned Gideon, "You can't sleep a wink all night for my preaching! Well, I can sleep soundly all day in spite of yours."

† Dea. Wadsworth acquired, and lost, in different ways, a large estate. In the time of his prosperity, he bought and paid for Lindall's Row, a lane leading from Merchants' Row to the north of Long wharf in Boston. He afterwards lost this, with his money also, as another person appeared with a better title than the one who sold it.—B. K.

Rev. Charles Turner,* a graduate at Harvard College, of the class of 1752, was the next settled minister. An invitation was extended to him by a vote of the church, Nov. 14th, 1754, which was concurred in by the town, Dec. 16th, and Samuel Alden and James Arnold were chosen to wait upon him and ask his acceptance. He complied, and was ordained July 23d, 1755. The services at his ordination were a prayer by the Rev. Jacob Bacon of Plymouth; a sermon from Eph. v. 8, by Rev. William Rand of Kingston; the charge by Rev. Ebenezer Gay of Hingham, and the right hand of fellowship by Rev. Thomas Smith of Pembroke. A large concourse of people was assembled, and scarcely more than half could get within the church. The sermon by Mr. Rand was published.

1755, Aug. 7th. "Voted, that ye sacrament of ye Lord's Supper should be administered seven times in a year;" also, "Voted, that when persons should desire to join with the church in full communion, previous to their admission into i, their knowledge, &c., should be inquired into by ye pastor, with two or more of the brethren, unless the persons choose rather to make relations."

1755, August 21st. Peleg Wadsworth, son of Dea. John Wadsworth, was chosen a deacon, which office he held for thirty-five years, until 1790; serving for a part of the time as the treasurer of the church also.

1755, Sept. 25th, died Dea. James Arnold, æt. 56 years, who held that office fourteen years, having been chosen after the death of Dea. Alden, June 24th, 1741.

1760. The town chose a committee to take care of the wretched boys on the Lord's day.

1762, Sept. 25th. Dea. Samuel Seabury died, aged 70, having for many years held the office; though not, at the same

---

* He was born September 3d, 1732, and was a descendant of Humphrey Turner, an early settler of Scituate. This *Humphrey*, a tanner, married Lydia Gainer, and died in 1673. His children were Thomas, John, Joseph, young son John, Daniel, Nathaniel, Mary Parker, and Lydia Doughty. *Thomas* married Sarah, da. of Thomas Hyland, in 1652, and had several children, one of whom, *Charles*, was born 1664, and married Mercy, da. of Samuel Curtis, and was the father of *Charles*, who married Eunice, da. of John James, and *he* was the father of Rev. Charles, born as above. He married Mary, da. of Rev. Mr. Rand of Kingston, and had children,— I. *Hon. Charles Turner*, June 20th, 1760, member of Congress, and master of Marine hospital at Chelsea, who married Hannah, da. of Col. John Jacob, and was the father of Theodore, and Samuel A. Turner, Esq., (who m. Lydia Turner); II. *Eunice*, June 9th, 1758; III. *William*, April 8, 1762; IV. *John*, July 7, 1763; V. *Mary*, June 5, 1764, died June 26, 1769; VI. *Persis*, April 19, 1768, died July 5, 1769; VII. *Mary*, Nov. 27, 1770. — *Deane's Scituate; Duxbury Records*. Mr. Turner's annual salary was £73 6s. 8d.

time, exempt from the civil duties of the town, being employed frequently in the town offices, and representing it in the General Court.

1770. Voted, "to desire Dea. Peleg Wadsworth to purchase a silver tankard for the church as soon as he can conveniently."

1772, March 16th. They voted to build a new meetinghouse, if a place could be agreed upon. And two years later, (March 16th, 1774) they passed a vote to place it on Joshua Cushman's land; which vote was reconsidered, and the old site preferred. Nothing, however, was done.

1775. The ministry of Mr. Turner was particularly happy, and by far more productive of good than either of his predecessors since the days of Mr. Wiswall. During his settlement one hundred and thirty-one were admitted into the church. Nothing happened to sever the ties of friendship and break the bonds of happiness between the pastor and his flock. Possessed of eloquence and judgment, and with fine powers of communicating his thoughts to others, he was met on the Sabbath day by a concourse of his people, who listened attentively to his teachings. And finally, when the limit he had assigned to his ministry in the town had expired, it became necessary, as also on account of continued ill health and bodily infirmities, for him to ask a dismission. This was granted (April 10th), though with reluctance, feeling that they should be deprived of an instrument of the greatest good among them. It was concurred in by the town on the same day. In a letter of recommendation to the second church in Scituate, they thus speak of "their late worthy and beloved pastor:" — "We lament that the righteous Governor of the world has in his Holy Providence deprived us of the ministerial labors of a man, so universally esteemed by us as a friend, a minister, and a Christian, and with whom we have lived in peace and happiness for this almost twenty years. But while we deplore our important loss, we heartily wish him the restoration of health, that he may yet be extensively useful in the world, and largely contribute to the happiness of mankind, in such a way as God in his wisdom shall see fit."

Mr. Turner then returned to his father's house in Scituate. As he was the most popular man in the district at the time, when a convention was called to act upon and offer to the people the Federal Constitution, he was chosen one of its number. He was at first decidedly opposed to it, thinking it not liberal enough, and, as he had previously expressed himself in Duxbury, determined to resist it step by step. He was however convinced of his error by Theophilus Parsons and others, and declared in the assembly just before the final question was given, his determination to vote in the affirmative, and his reasons for it. This came rather unexpectedly on the ears of the opposite side, and one of their number, Dr. Matthew Spring, a member from Watertown, immediately rose and exclaimed, "*Help, Lord, for the godly man ceaseth!*" He was also a member of the convention which formed the State constitution, and several years a State senator. He was appointed chaplain of the castle in Boston harbor, and for three years preached there to the convicts. After his establishment in 1790, he was met by Judge Parsons, who esteemed him very highly, and who congratulated him on his appointment. "Why do you so?" asked Mr. Turner. "Because," replied the judge, "your hearers are *convicted* already, and you will have nothing to do but to *convert* them." Another anecdote is related of him. On one occasion on leaving the chapel, he passed the famous Stephen Burroughs, who had been compelled for some misdemeanor, "to ride the wooden horse." Mr. Turner observing him, said, "Why, Burroughs, what are you doing here?" "I am running, sir, the christian race, steadfast and immoveable," was the quick reply of Burroughs.* Mr. Turner afterwards settled in the town of Turner, Maine, where he died in 1813, at the advanced age of 81. In his private and public life, virtue and integrity, firmness and decision, equality of feelings, mildness of disposition, and a bland and courteous deportment, secured for him the affections of those with whom he was associated; and the happy influences of his holy deeds of benevolence, of purity and of religion, still breathe upon the mind of the present generation, exerted by a kind remembrance in the hearts of their elders, who were the partakers of his toils, and the recipients of his goodness. Going from their midst, he carried with him the good wishes of all who knew him. In his character, Mr. Turner was thoughtful and contemplative,† and his life a continual series of thoughts and meditations. His mind was studious, and his heart eager for the discharge of every duty which became him as a Christian, and a man. He was, as one of his people called him, a man with whom you could not differ, a peace maker, and yet a man of few words.

During the interim between the dismission of Mr. Turner and the settlement of another minister, invitations were given

---

* Rev. Benjamin Kent's notes.

* Mr. Kent tells the following anecdote. It happened that a short time after his return to his father's house, as one morning his father entered his room, he said "Father, I have been contemplating." "Yes, Charles," said his father interrupting, "you are always contemplating; but I wish you would go to work and *do* something."

by a vote of the church, July 23d, 1775, (concurred in by the town, Aug. 7th,) to Mr. John Shaw; and by another, Nov. 7th, (by the town Dec. 25th,) to Mr. Samuel Henshaw, to settle in the ministry; but both of these gentlemen refused.

REV. ZEDEKIAH SANGER,* a graduate of H. C. of the class of 1771, was the next settled pastor of the church. The church voted to invite him to become their pastor on the 8th of Feb., 1776, which was concurred in by the town (May 11th,) and Mr. Sanger returned the following acceptance on the 19th of the last month:—

"Honored Fathers and Brethren—

Not long since you were pleased to give me an invitation to settle with you in the work of the Gospel ministry. And that being a matter of great importance, I have taken it into my most serious and deliberate consideration, and have been seeking direction of God, the father of lights and the fountain of wisdom. And as God often makes use of instruments to communicate his mind, and as in his word he has told us, that in the multitude of counsellors, there is safety, I have taken the advice of my Revnd Fathers in the ministry, and my relatives, and am now determined, and do accept of your friendly invitation.

And now under a conviction of my insufficiency for this great work, I entreat your earnest prayers to Almighty God for me, that I may have grace and wisdom given me, faithfully to discharge the duties of this arduous station.

I sympathize with you under that afflictive dispensation of Providence, which has deprived you of the skillful and faithful labors of your late worthy pastor in the meridian of his

---

* He was born at Sherburne, Oct. 4th, 1748, and was descended from *Richard Sanger*, a blacksmith, who removed from Sudbury to Watertown, where he died, Aug. 20th, 1691. His wife was Mary, and his son *Richard*, (b. Feb. 22d, 1667,) m. Elizabeth Morse, and his son *Richard*, (b. Nov. 4th, 1706,) m. Deborah Rider, Feb. 19th, 1730, and died 1786, having had ten children, the eighth of whom was the minister of Duxbury.

MR. SANGER m. Irene Freeman, 1771, and their children were *Richard*, 1778, H. C. 1800, m. Sally Tisdall of Taunton, 1807; *Deborah*, 1779, m. John Ames, Jr., 1799; *Joseph*, 1781, m. Hannah, da. of Dr. Marcy, 1812; *Caroline*, 1782, m. Rev. Samuel Clark, 1810; *Zedekiah*, 1784; *Samuel F.*, 1788, m. Susan, da. of Caleb Alden; *Olive*, m. George Moore of Burlington, 1815; *Ralph*, H. C. 1808, m. Charlotte, da. of Ezra Kingman, Esq., 1817, and settled in the ministry at Dover; *Sarah;* and *Eliza.*—*Barry's Hist. Framingham,* 387—*Hist. Bridgewater*—*Dux. Records.*

life and the height of his usefulness; and I sincerely join my supplications with yours to the Throne of Grace, that his life may be continued, that he may be recovered from his weakness, and be restored to a confirmed state of health, and to his former usefulness, and be an eminent blessing to the world, in that department of life in which Providence shall place him.

And though I am sensible of my unfitness to stand in the place of my honored predecessor, yet notwithstanding my great deficiency, I beseech you not to cease in your prayers for me, that I may in some measure be enriched with those amiable graces and shining accomplishments, which appeared in his public and private life; and that by deriving grace and wisdom from the head of the church, in whom are hid all the treasures of wisdom and knowledge, I may deliver unto every one his portion in due season, and by the divine blessing attending my labors may be made instrumental in bringing many sons and daughters amongst you into the fold of Christ, the great shepherd and bishop of souls, and the cause of the Redeemer. And though you may find many imperfections in me and my services, yet I hope you will never have any just occasion to say or think, but that your best interest lies nearest my heart.

I conclude by wishing that you may be directed by wisdom from above in all your future proceedings, and that the spirit of *Unity*, *Love* and *Peace* may be with you, and the divine blessing rest upon us all. I subscribe myself your friend and humble servant, ZEDEKIAH SANGER."

He was ordained July 3d, 1776. The services were a prayer by Rev. Mr. Smith of Pembroke; a sermon by Rev. Elijah Brown of Sherburn, from Malachi ii, 7; the charge by Rev. William Rand of Kingston; and the right hand of fellowship by Rev. Gad Hitchcock of Pembroke. They concluded with a prayer by the Rev. William Shaw of Marshfield.

Mr. Sanger's first sermon was from the text in Lev. xxv, 10, " And ye shall hallow the fiftieth year, and proclaim liberty throughout all the land unto all the inhabitants thereof," having reference to the Declaration of Independence, which had but just been proclaimed.

1780, Oct. 13th. " Voted that the psalms should be sung without being read line by line by the great majority."

1784, Feb. 2d. The town passed a vote to build a new meeting-house, which was erected the same year, midway between the North and South boundaries of the town. The building was raised Aug. 12th, 1784, and on the 18th June, 1785, it was first occupied for worship. This stood nearly sixty years, when it was torn down to give place to the present edifice on the same site. The burying ground adjoining, was first used in 1787.

1786, April 3d. The church held a meeting when Mr. Sanger asked a dismission. The consideration of the request, however, was deferred until the 6th of the month, which was Thanksgiving day. After the services they took it into serious and deliberate consideration, and "on account of his infirmities in his eyes, which rendered him unable to pursue his studies, and the improbability of his being able to discharge the duties of the ministerial office in future," a dismission was granted him. It was nevertheless desired that he should be the moderator of the church, until it should become into a more settled state. On the 10th of the same month, the town concurred. Mr. Sanger's salary was £80 per annum.

Mr. Sanger was afterwards settled over the church in South Bridgewater, Dec. 17th, 1788, as colleague to the Rev. John Shaw, and here he died, Nov. 17th, 1820, aged 73. He died, says Judge Mitchell, "after a life of usefulness and great activity. He was a scholar and learned divine. His house was a seminary in which he prepared young men for college and instructed young students in divinity. He was also preceptor of the academy, and enjoyed in a high degree the affection and respect of his people."

Previous to his removal to Bridgewater, he engaged in navigation in Duxbury; but was very unsuccessful, two of his vessels having been destroyed by lightning.

1787, April 9th. The town extended an invitation to Mr. Jacob Haven to become their pastor, and he refused.

1788, May 7th. To Mr. Alden Bradford, who refused.

REV. JOHN ALLYN * was the next settled pastor. The town voted to call him to the ministry, Sept. 1st, 1788. He accepted on the 12th of October, and was ordained on the 3d of De-

* He was born at Barnstable, Mass., March 21st, 1767. Deane (Hist. Scituate) conjectures that he was descended from *John Allen*, who was of Plymouth 1633, Scituate 1646, and died 1661, whose wife was Ann, and whose children were Capt. John of Scituate, in 1698, and a daughter Jeane, who married John Marshall.

Dr. Allyn pursued the preparatory studies for admission to college under the care of the Rev Mr. Hilliard of Barnstable. He entered Harvard College in 1781, and took the degree of A. B. in 1785, and that of A. M. in 1788. Shortly before his graduation he was seized with a severe and violent sickness, which prevented him from appearing in the part assigned him at

cember. The sermon was by the Rev. Samuel West of North Bridgewater, (2 Tim. ii. 15); charge by Rev. Dr. Hitchcock of Pembroke; right hand of fellowship by Rev. David Barnes of Scituate. These performances were printed.

1790, April 5th. Voted, that the Sacred Scriptures should be read in the meeting-house every Lord's day by the minister.

1804. The church library was commenced.

1825, December. Dr. Allyn asks a colleague. See under Rev. Benj. Kent.

1833, July 19th. Died, Dr. Allyn, in his 67th year. His death occurred on Friday, and he was buried on Monday, in the tomb of the Hon. George Partridge. Several obituary notices of his death appeared in the newspapers at the time. The following sketch is chiefly an abstract from a memoir by his son-in-law, Rev. Convers Francis, which was published in the Mass. Hist. Society's Collections, of which association he was a member.

The ministry of Dr. Allyn was long, and for the most part happy. He discharged his duties with uniform fidelity and ability. He was the personal friend as well as the spiritual guide of his people — heartily devoted to their temporal and eternal welfare; judicious, but fearless in rebuking sin; wise and faithful in the administration of the interests of religion. He was the benefactor of the poor, the comforter of the distressed, the counsellor of all. His professional reputation was such as to secure his rank among the first clergymen in the commonwealth. His opinion was valued, and his aid sought in those ways, which implied that his judgment was regarded with respectful confidence. After the settlement of his colleague, he seldom engaged in any public service, as his strength and spirits were constantly declining. It will be conceded by all who knew Dr. Allyn, that in the general cast of his mind there was much striking originality. He was seldom content to express his thoughts as other men, and exhibited all his ideas in such relations, as to give them the interest of novelty. He manifested a strong disposition to avoid the beaten track of thought, and thereby often expressed him-

---

Commencement. In his eighteenth year he left the college. During his academic course he was distinguished by persevering industry, and by a development of talent, which gave him a high rank among the members of his class. Returning to Barnstable, he was engaged some time in instruction. Then determining to devote himself to the ministry, he studied theology under the direction of the Rev. Dr. Samuel West of Dartmouth. — 3 *Mass. Hist. Coll.* V. 245. Dr. Allyn married Abigail Bradford. His children were *Rufus Bradford*, March 27th, 1793, grad. at H. C. 1810 ; *John*, June 24th, 1794, died March 7th, 1824, unmarried, grad. at H. C. 1814 ; *Abigail Bradford*, Jan. 13th, 1796, married the Rev. Convers Francis, of Watertown ; *Augusta*, Aug. 18th, 1800, died unmarried ; *James*, Oct. 30th, 1801.

self in a manner which might frequently admit of misconstruction. A man who unites with such a disposition an incautious frankness of conversation, is very liable to be mistaken, and this was the case with Dr. Allyn; but those, who were familiar with him, recognized in these very expressions his far-reaching wisdom, and were struck with the felicitous novelty with which they were arrayed. His imagination was rich, but peculiar, though by no means poetical; it was the homely, yet playful one of strong common sense. He had none of that patience of investigation, which arrives at results through a long process; but delighted to wander from topic to topic, as they were suggested by resemblances and relations.

His conversation also possessed a peculiar zest, which few of those who had the pleasure of listening to it, will ever forget, and hardly can the deep impressions caused by it be eradicated. His benevolence was proverbial, and he gave his charities almost to a fault. If ever a man lived free from the debasing influences of selfishness, it was Dr. Allyn, and none in doing good took more delight. His piety was sincere, rational and constant. Few men had more of the reality of religion, and less of its trappings, which are sometimes mistaken for its essence. If there are those, who thought that he might justly be charged with speaking lightly of sacred subjects, they must remember that his views were expressed upon the appendages and speculations which men have connected with religion, and by no means upon its solemn truths.

His sermons were not distinguished for popular eloquence; but were adapted to be useful in the most effectual manner. In his illustrations of the scriptures, he was always pertinent and impressive. In his religious opinions he was independent of all denominations, and no one was ever less shackled in his belief; though he always expressed a great dislike of religious controversy. As a scholar he stood high. In early life he directed his attention to the perusal of books; but latterly he most delighted in the observation of man and nature.

Thus was Dr. Allyn in the days of the full power of his intellectual endowments. The latter part of his life was darkened by disease, suffering and decay, when a premature feebleness came upon him. He was gradually reduced to bodily helplessness and mental prostration, by the effects of a paralysis.

His published writings are not many. In the summer of 1807, he was employed on a mission to Maine, for propagating the gospel among the Indians. He was elected a member of the Mass. Hist. Soc. in 1799; of the American Academy of Arts and Sciences in 1808; and received the degree of Doctor of Divinity from Harvard College in 1813.

REV. BENJAMIN KENT was ordained as colleague to Dr. Allyn, on the 7th of June, 1826. After a short, but trying and very laborious ministry, he was obliged to ask his dismission, which was granted on the 7th of June, 1833.

The time has not yet come, when it would be becoming to speak of his faithful labors, among a people, who by him were much beloved, and from whose midst he was separated not without deep sorrow.

To the unwearied labors of Mr. Kent, the town owed much for the establishment at that time of a High school, which chiefly through his instrumentality was commenced, and by his exertions a sum sufficiently large was raised for its maintenance, and teachers, eminently qualified for the duties of instructors, were procured. It was first under the charge of Mr. George Putnam, now the Reverend Doctor P. of Roxbury, who was succeeded by Mr. William Augustus Stearns, who has since been settled as pastor of the church at Cambridgeport.

REV. JOSIAH MOORE, the next pastor, was settled over the church in 1834, over the affairs of which he still continues to preside.

GENEALOGICAL REGISTERS.

The following Registers have been prepared, not without much labor; yet they are presented with a consciousness of their great and many imperfections. However, it is hoped that no considerable and important omissions have occurred, especially among the earliest settlers and inhabitants of the town; though among the families of later times many deficiences may happen. It has been my endeavor to give the families previous to about 1780 in as perfect a state as the records and other documents within my reach would allow. It will be seen, that some families I have continued to the year 1800, and some even far later; especially those concerning which my knowledge of the later generations was more complete.

It is to be hoped, that some one of all the various families which are registered here, will consider the importance of continuing to a greater length the genealogy of his family, and bring it to a higher state of completion; and should the slender accounts which I have gathered, be deemed suitable foundations of other memorials, and more extended biographies, the object of my toil will have been accomplished.

Perhaps a word may be necessary concerning the plan. The progenitor of a family is placed first, and (except in cases where there are more than one ancestor of the name,) is numbered 1; as is also one of the progenitors (when there are more than one,) so marked; while the other receives the next highest number after that of the last family of the descendants of the first progenitor. Immediately following the name of the father of a family, the brackets enclose the letters "s. of —" (i. e. "the son of,") followed by a figure referring to the family so numbered, where among the children of that family will be found the father's name, followed again by a figure in brackets referring forward to the original number. If a date follows *immediately* a name, it is that of the birth of that individual.

The principal sources of my information have been the town and church records, the colony and probate records, and among printed works, Judge Mitchell's Bridgewater, and Deane's Scituate. Numerous other sources and authorities will be enumerated in their respective places. In tracing the branches of a family, frequently it has been carried into the neighboring towns, and in such cases the town is carefully noted. It is owing to the formation of several towns out of the original limits of Duxbury, that a family may now be noted as residents of another town, whose ancestors, though dwelling on the same estate, were given as inhabitants of Duxbury.

A list of abbreviations, such as are used in the following pages, is here appended. Some others may perhaps occur, but they are such as will be readily understood.

Dux.	Duxbury.	a.	about.
M.	Marshfield.	b.	born.
K.	Kingston.	d.	died.
Pem.	Pembroke.	da.	daughter.
Bridgew.	Bridgewater.	B.	brother.
Scit.	Scituate.	m.	married.
G. H.	Green Harbor.	unm.	unmarried.
S. R.	South River.	s.	son.
N. R.	North River.	ad.	admitted a freeman.
chd.	children.	s. p.	sine proles, (without issue.)
prob.	probably.		
prop.	proprietor.	Chh.	Church.
asst.	assistant.	Chh. Rec.	Church records.
bk.	brook.	Col. Rec.	Colony records.
bap.	baptized.	T. Rec.	Town records.
Dep.	Deputy.	Prob. Rec.	Probate records.
Rep.	Representative.	H. C.	Harvard College.

J. W.

Boston, 1849.

ALDEN.

1. Hon. John,* b. 1599, Plymouth, m. Priscilla Mullins, removed to Dux., and d. Sept. 12th, 1686, æt. 87. He had ch'd — *John*, 1622 (2); *Joseph*, 1624 (3); *Elizabeth*, 1625, m. Wm. Pabodie; *David*, (4); *Jonathan*, 1627 (5); *Sarah*, m. Alexander Standish; *Ruth* m. John Bass of Braintree, Feb. 13, 1657; *Mary* m. Thomas Delano.

2. Capt. John, (s. of 1,) Dux; ad. 1648; removed to Boston about Dec. 1659, and lived in the west part of the town at Alden's lane, now so called. He had command at different times of several of the Massachusetts armed vessels, and often visited the coast at the eastward, where the few English settlers were much exposed to the attacks of the French and Indians. He accompanied Major Church in his first expedition in 1689 in the Mary sloop. In this as well as in all the other expeditions, he was of essential service to the forces, as he was well acquainted with the coast, and possessed of considerable skill in naval tactics. His brave and resolute spirit and his open heart gained for him the esteem of all. He again joined the second expedition to the eastward, and also in the fourth, in 1696, commanded the Brigantine Endeavor. He continued until late in life in command of the public vessels. In 1696 he went with a reinforcement to Col. Church in the Massachusetts transport, accompanied by Col. Hawthorn of Salem, and in the account of this expedition,

---

* From what part of England he came, we have not been able to ascertain. A very few of the name appear to have been in England. In the London Directory of 1840 none appear. In Germany, on the continent, the name is more common. One has been a graduate of Cambridge, England. A Mr. Alden, of Bedford county, a scholar of St. John's College, suffered the tyrannical Bartholomew act. The name of Robert Alden appears among the names of the merchant adventurers of Plymouth, 1626.

Arms. Guillim (Desplay of Heraldry) gives the following coat. "He beareth gules, three crescents within a border engrailed ermine by the name of Alden. This coat was assigned 8th Sept. 1607, by Wm. Camden, clarencieux, to John Alden of the Middle Temple." Alden's Epitaphs, iii. Burke and Edmonson give the same arms, placing a *bezant* between the crescents, and add a crest—" Out of a ducal coronet per pale gules and sable a demi lion or." This (add they) is borne by the Aldens of Hertfordshire and the Temple, London, and granted 1607. The following is also given as borne by the Aldens — " Or, a bat's wing gules, surmounted by another azure," with a " crest, out of a coronet argent two wings as in the arms." Edmonson (vol. i. p. 78) gives also—" Alden or Aldon, Gules a mullet argent between two crescents ermine, within a bordure engrailed of the second."

given by Church he is called "old Mr. Alden," being at this time over seventy years of age. He did not probably afterwards engage actively in the campaigns. He d. Mar. 14th, 1702, æt. 80, and his will is dated Feb. 17th, preceding. He makes his sons John and William his executors, and it is witnessed by Thomas Savage, Chas. Chauncey, and Edward Turfrey. His estate amounted to £2059 11s. 7d.; including a wooden house £400, a brick house, (bought of Samuel Jackson,) £270, and debts due the estate, "most of which are desperate," £1259. He m. Elizabeth ———, and had *Mary* Dec. 17th, 1659; m. 2d, Elizabeth Everill (widow of Abiel Everill, who d. Apr. 1st, 1660, and she was da. of Maj. Wm. Phillips of Saco); and by her, had *John*, Nov. 20, 1660; *Elizabeth*, May 9, 1662, d. July 14, 1662; *John*, Mar. 12, 1663 (6); *William*, Mar. 16, 1664, d. young; *Elizabeth*, Apr. 9, 1665, m. a Walley, m. 2d, (before Aug. 4, 1704) a Williard; *William*, Mar. 5, 1666, d. young; *Zachariah*, Mar. 8, 1667, d. young; *William*, Sept. 10, 1669 (7); *Nathaniel*, a. 1670 (8); *Zachariah*, Feb. 18, 1673 (9); *Nathan*, Oct. 17, 1677; *Sarah*, Sep. 27, 1681.

3. JOSEPH, (s. of 1,) Dux.; ad. 1657; removed to Bridgew.; inherited land there, and at Middleboro'; m. Mary Simmons. His will is dated Dec. 14, 1696, and his estate amounted to £76. His chd. were Isaac, Joseph, John — For a full and extended account of their descendants, see Thayer's Family Memorial, Alden's Epitaphs, and Judge Mitchell's Bridgewater.

4. DAVID, (s. of 1,) Dux.; was much employed in the public business of the town, one of its selectmen, its deputy, and likewise an assistant in the Government. He was likewise a prominent member of the church, said to have been one of its deacons, and a man of the highest respectability. He received a grant of 40 acres in 1679, west of South river. He m. Mary Southworth. He had *Benjamin* (10); *Samuel* (11); *Alice* m. Judah Paddock, and d. æt. 93.

5. CAPT. JONATHAN, (s. of 1,) Dux.; inherited the homestead; d. Feb., 1697, leaving an estate of £309. He m. Abigail Hallett,* Dec. 10, 1672. She d. Aug. 17, 1725, æt.

---

* This name on the Dux. Records appears to be *Ralat*, as it has been frequently copied; but the following abstract from the will of Andrew Hallett of Yarmouth, shows that it was intended for Halat, that is, Hallett. His will is dated June 4, 1684, and mentions his wife Ann, who survived him, and sons John (who was b. Dec. 11, 1650,) and Jonathan (who was b. 20 Nov., 1647,) and daughters Mehetable, *Abigail* the wife of Jonathan Alden, and Ruhamath, who m. Mr. Bourn (and had Timothy, Hannah, Eleazer, Hezekiah and John). Mr. Hallett's estate amounted to £1180, including £909 in real estate.

81, and was buried in the old burying ground, where her stone now stands. His children were *Andrew* (12); *Jonathan* (13); *John* 1680 (14); and *Benjamin* (15).

6. JOHN, (s. of 2,) Boston. At the time of the Salem witchcraft, he was sent for by the magistrates of that town upon the accusation of several poor distracted and possessed creatures or witches. Upon his examination, these wretches began their juggling tricks, falling down and crying out, and staring in the faces of the people in an impudent manner. The magistrates demanded of them several times, who it was of all the people in the room, that afflicted them; one of the accusers pointed several times at one Capt. Hill; but said nothing, until a man standing behind her to hold her up, stooped down to her ear, when she immediately called out, "Alden, Alden afflicted her." Being asked if she had ever seen Alden, she replied No; but, said she, the man told her so. All were then ordered into the street, and a ring was made; when she cried out — "There stands Alden, a bold fellow, with his hat on, sells powder and shot to the Indians," &c. Capt. Alden was then committed to custody, and his sword taken from him, for it was with this, they said, he afflicted them. He was next ordered before the magistrates at the meeting-house and placed on a chair, to the open view of all the assembly. The accusers again cried out, that Alden pinched them, while he stood on the chair, and one of the magistrates bade the marshal hold open his hands that he might not touch them. Mr. Gidney, one of the justices, bid Capt. Alden confess and give glory to God. Capt. Alden replied that he hoped he should always give glory to God, but never would gratify the devil. He next asked, why they thought he should come to that village to afflict persons that he had never seen before, and appealed to all, and particularly challenged Mr. Gidney to produce a charge against his character. Mr. Gidney replied, that he had known him for many years, and had been to sea with him, and always believed him to be an honest man; but now he saw cause to alter his opinion. He then asked Gidney what reason could be given why his looking upon him did not strike him down as well as his miserable accusers; but no reason could be given. He assured Gidney, that a lying spirit was in his accusers, and that there was not a word of truth in all they said of him. Capt. Alden was however committed to prison, May 31st, 1692, where he remained fifteen weeks, when having been prevailed upon by his friends, he made his escape, and absented himself until the people recovered the use of their reason. He chose Duxbury as the place of his concealment, and here he remained at the house of one of his relatives, where he arrived late in the evening after his escape, and

saluted them with the cheerful assurance that "he was come from the devil, and the devil was after him." He m. Elizabeth, who d. Nov. 26, 1719, æt. 50; m. 2d, Susanna; he d. Feb. 1, 1729-30, æt. 67. He had chd. *Elizabeth*, Nov. 7, 1687; *Hannah*, Nov. 20, 1688; *John*, Sep. 20, 1690 (16); *Mary*, Dec. 15, 1691; *Catharine*, Aug. 19. 1697, d. Oct. 31, 1702; *Gillam* and *Ann*, (twins,) July 7, 1699. An Anna Alden m. Henry Burchsted of Lynn, 20 May, 1728; *Nathaniel*, July 6, 1700; *Thomas*, b. & d. Aug. 13, 1701; *Catharine*, Sep. 17, 1704; *Thomas*, Mar. 1, 1707; *William*, May 9, 1710, d. Dec. 27, 1714.

7. CAPT. WILLIAM, (s. of 2,) Boston; a sea captain; in 1708, commanded the ship Content; and he frequently performed voyages to Newfoundland, Nova Scotia, and the eastern coast, as well as to Barbadoes and the West Indies. He m. Mary Drewry, May 21, 1691; she was b. July 10, 1672, and d. Feb. 11, 1727, æt. 56; he d. Feb. 10, 1728, æt. 60. He had chd.—*Mary*, Feb. 10, 1693, d. Oct. 22, 1702; *Elizabeth*, Mar. 10, 1695; *William*, July 23, 1697; *Lydia*, Dec. 22, 1701; *Mary*, June 12, 1706; *Drewry*, May 12, 1708; *John*, Jan. 22, 1711.

8. NATHANIEL, (s. of 2,) Boston; d. a. 1702, leaving an estate of £86; m. Hepzibah Mountjoy, Oct. 1, 1691; she m. 2d, John Mortemore, June 8, 1703. He had *Mary*, Aug. 20, 1692; *Nathaniel*, Aug. 6, 1694 (19); *Elizabeth; Hepzibah*, m. Nathaniel Hayward, April 28, 1718; *Philip*, Dec. 31, 1698.

9. ZACHARIAH, (s. of 2,) Boston; H. C. 1692; m. Mary Viall, 1700, Jan. 13; d. 1709; had *Zachariah*, Oct. 11, 1701, (20.)

NOTE. *Mary*, m. Joseph Brightman, 3 Oct., 1714; *Elizabeth*, m. Thomas Batterby, 26 July, 1720. Boston Records.

10. BENJAMIN, (s. of 4,) Dux.; m. Hannah, who died Jan. 8, 1763, æt. 74⅓ years; had *Mary*, Jan. 1, 1710, m. Dr. John Wadsworth, Dec. 31, 1734; *Sarah*, April 5, 1712; *Elizabeth*, Sept. 12, 1714, d. July 9, 1771, æt. 56, of apoplexy; *David*, Feb. 14, 1717, removed to Maine; *Ichabod*, Oct. 5, 1719; *Bezaleel*, May 15, 1722 (21); *Wrestling*, Oct. 11, 1724 (22); *Abiathar*, July 29, 1731 (23).

11. CAPT. SAMUEL, (s. of 4,) Dux.; m. Sarah Sprague Feb. 26, 1728; he d. Feb. 24, 1781, æt. 92 yrs. 2 mos. and 3 days; she died March 28, 1773, æt. 71 years; had *Rebecca*, Jan. 4, 1730, m. Capt. Thomas Frazier Nov. 27, 1760; *Sarah*, Dec. 2, 1731, m. Col. Gamaliel Bradford; *John*, March 30, 1734, d. at Crown Point, 1761, æt. 27; *Alethea*, Sept. 5, 1735, m. Wm. Loring Jan. 8, 1767 (her name on the records is Alice);

ALDEN. 217

Samuel, Aug. 13, 1737 (24); *Ichabod*, Aug. 11, 1739 (25); *Abigail*, m. Rev. Francis Winter Oct. 27, 1768.

12. ANDREW, (s. of 5,) Dux.; removed to Lebanon, Ct.; m. Lydia Stanford Feb. 4, 1714; had *Jabin* Nov. 19, 1714; *John* July 23, 1716 (26); *Prince*, Oct. 28, 1718 (27); *Andrew*, June 20, 1721 (28); *Walter*, m. widow Irene Blackmore; *Lydia*, m. Seth Alden; *William* (29).

13. JONATHAN, (s. of 5,) Dux.; removed to Lebanon, Ct.; m. Elizabeth, widow of Anthony Waterman of M.; had *Josiah*; *Seth*, 1721, m. Lydia Alden; *Anthony*, 1720; *Austin*, 1729, March 25, settled in Gorham, near Portland, Me., and was a deacon of the chh. His chd. were Humphrey, 1763, alive 1839, and other sons and da's. in Me. — Humphrey Austin, son of Humphrey and Mary Alden, was b. 26 Sept. 1794, at Boston.—Boston records.

14. COL. JOHN, (s. of 5,) Dux.; inherited the old domain. He d. July 24, 1739, æt. 59; m. Hannah Briggs 1709, who d. Feb. 8, 1740, in her 55th year. She was a da. of Capt. John Briggs, whose wife was most probably Deborah Hawke, and his father was Walter of Scituate, whose wife was Frances. His chd. were *John*, Oct. 7, 1710, d. Oct. 15, 1712; *Samuel*, Nov. 7, 1712 (30); *Capt. Judah*, Aug. 10, 1714, was bred to the sea, and died, while in command of a merchantman, on his passage to Scotland, having shortly before married Miss Row of Boston; *Anna*, June 14, 1716 (family record), and, "June ye 2nd anno 1716," (town records,) m. Benja. Loring Feb. 8, 1739; *Deborah*, May 16, 1721, d. Oct. 2, 1730; *Briggs*, June 8, 1723 (31); *Abigail*, Feb. 27, 1727, m. Col. Anthony Thomas of M., and had Maj. Briggs, Waterman, and Judah.

15. DEA. BENJAMIN, (s. of 5,) Dux.; a carpenter, m. Hannah; — "Dea. Benjamin Alden deceased and was drowned [near the Gurnet,] April ye 14th—anno domini—1741. The widow Hannah Alden, his wife, deceased Jan'ry ye 8, 1763." Town records.

16. JOHN, (s. of 6,) Boston; removed to Needham; m. Anna Braine May 1, 1718; m. 2d Thankful Parker, Nov. 26, 1728, had *John*, Nov. 29, 1719, d. young; *Anna*, Jan. 29, 1722; *Benjamin*, Sept. 18, 1724; *Jemima*, Mar. 9, 1730, d. young; *John*, Oct. 9, 1731, settled in Vermont; *Alice*, July 12, 1733, m. Jona. Capron of Attleboro'; *Henry*, Nov. 27, 1734, of Needham; *Dea. Silas*, Oct. 23, 1736 (see the Family Memorial); *Samuel*, 1743 (see ditto); *Moses*, d. young; *Moses*; *Thomas*, of Middlebury, Vt.; *Thankful*; and *Mary*, m. Samuel Paine of Roxbury.

17. HENRY, (s. of —,) Dedham; d. Feb. 18, 1730; m. Deborah; had *William*, Aug. 14, 1709, m. Ruth and had

Mary, who died May 29, 1744 — Ruth, the w. d. Dec. 17, 1766.

18. THOMAS, (s. of —,) Boston; m. Jane; had *Thomas*, 10 June, 1725; *William*, 26 Oct., 1727; *John*, 30 Oct., 1729.

19. NATHANIEL, (s. of 8,) Boston; m. Mary and had *Elizabeth*, Aug. 3, 1730; *Nathaniel*, 1731, d. Feb. 25, 1746; *Hannah*, June 3, 1735.

20. ZACHARIAH, (s. of 9,) Boston; m. Jemima and had *Mary*, Mar. 8, 1725; m. 2d, Lydia Crane of Milton, Nov. 17, 1728, and had *Lydia*, June 3, 1730; *Zachariah*, July 20, 1731; *Mary*, July 6, 1733.

21. BEZALEEL, (s. of 10,) Dux.; m. Lydia Bartlett, Dec. 22, 1748, and d. Feb. 9, 1799, æt. 76; she d. Mar. 24, 1810, æt. 84; had *Benjamin*, a faithful and efficient school master for many years, clerk of the town, was never m. and d. Jan. 8, 1835, æt. 85; *Lydia*, 1755, d. unm., Nov. 1812, æt. 60; *Isaiah*, Nov. 26, 1758, (32).

22. WRESTLING, (s. of 10,) Dux; m. Elizabeth ———, who d. Mar. 24, 1807, æt. 81; he d. Sep. 4, 1813, æt. nearly 89; had *Michael*, Feb. 9, 1749, d. unm., Nov. 19, 1841, æt. 91; *Bartlett*, Mar. 22, 1750; *Wrestling*, June 14, 1751; *a son*, Jan. 24, 1753; *Priscilla*, 1756, d. unm.; *Sarah*, 1758; *Patmos*, 1759, d. unm., April 14, 1836, æt. 77; *Elizabeth*, 1761, d. unm., Mar. 25, 1836, æt. 74; *Abiathar*, 1763; *Sabra*, 1764, d. unm., Jan. 1, 1842, æt. 77; *Mary*, 1767, d. unm.; *Hannah*, 1769, m. John Sampson, Nov. 28, 1791.

23. DR. ABIATHAR, (s. of 10,) a physician of uncommon metaphysical talents; removed to Saco, Me. Sabine (Am. Loyalist,) states concerning him, that he was one of the two tories of Saco and Biddeford at the beginning of the Revolution. At one time an armed whig party took him, placed him on his knees on a large cask, and with their guns presented to his body, told him to recant his opinions or suffer instant death. He signed the required confession and was released. Subsequently he removed to Scarborough in the same State.

24. SAMUEL, (s. of 11,) Dux.; m. Abigail Sylvester, July 21, 1774; he d. Feb. 29, 1799; she d. Sep. 11, 1806; had *Samuel*, June 12, 1778, d. young; *Abigail*, m. Ebenezer Waterman; *Lucy*, m. Michael Soule; *Nancy*, unm.

25. COL. ICHABOD, (s. of 11,) Dux.; he was kl'd at Cherry Valley. He m. Mary Wakefield, who afterwards m. Col. Calvin Partridge. Chd. — *John*, Nov. 25, 1774, (33); *Rebecca Partridge*, Aug. 7, 1777, m. Constant, son of Miles Sampson.

26. JOHN, (s. of 12,) Ct.; m. Elizabeth Ripley, and had

Parthema, m. Woodbridge Little, Esq.; *Violetta*, m. Isaac Fitch; *John; Judah*, a captain of the Rev. army; *Gen. Roger*, of Pennsylvania; *Elizabeth*.

27. PRINCE, (s. of 12,) Ct.; m. Mary Fitch, had Mary; Mason Fitch; Abigail; Sarah; Lydia; Andrew.

28. ANDREW, (s. of 12,) m. Rebecca Stanford, and had *Fear*.

29. WILLIAM, (s. of 13,) m. a Metcalf; and had Eunice; William; Jabin; Sarah; Lydia; Andrew.

30. CAPT. SAMUEL, (s. of 14,) Dux.; he was bred a sailor, and soon rose to the command of a merchant ship; and finally settled in England, at Bristol, as a merchant, and corresponding with Samuel Partridge of Boston, Mass. He m. in Eng. Edith, but died without issue, in 1744, æt. 32. He bequeathed the homestead which he had inherited to his brother Col. Briggs Alden. He also left about £10,000 in personal property, the interest of which his widow was to have during her life, and after her it was to go to his sisters Mrs. Loring and Mrs. Thomas, and his brother Col. Alden. This property was in the charge of guardians, who leased it to Carolinian merchants, and scarcely £800 was ever recovered.

31. COL. BRIGGS, (s. of 14,) Dux.; resided at the family mansion; he married Mercy Wadsworth Nov. 19, 1741, and she d. May 20, 1812, æt. 87⅔ years; he d. Oct. 4, 1796, æt. 74; he had *Hannah*, Oct. 24, 1743, m. Capt. John Gray of Boston Jan. 6, 1767, and d. 1790, æt. 47; *John*, Jan. 24, 1745, who was "drowned on his passage, Novem^r ye 17th 1766, as he was coming from Casco bay to Duxborough, in ye 23^d year of his age;" *Deborah*, Aug. 7, 1748, d. 1792, m. Caleb Coffin, of Nantucket, Feb. 12, 1767, m. 2d Isaac Belknap of Newburgh, N. Y., and by her first husband had Caleb, Hannah, Fanny, and by her second had Briggs, Lydia, Judah, m. Betsy, widow of Seth Winsor, and Deborah, who m. Seth Brooks, now of E. Boston; *Maj. Judah*, Oct. 31, 1750 (34); *Samuel*, July 1, 1751, d. Nov. 1778, æt. 27; *Nathaniel*, May 30, 1752, m. Rebecca Ripley, 1783, and settled in Maine; *Edith*, Jan. 3, 1754, never m.; d. Jan. 7, 1815, æt. 51; *Abigail*, July 7, 1755, m. Hon. Bezaleel Hayward of Bridgewater, Nov. 1784, he d. at Plymouth June 4, 1830, æt. 78; *Amherst*, July 22, 1759, never m.; d. Dec. 20, 1804, æt. 46 years.

32. ISAIAH, (s. of 21,) Dux.; m. Mercy Weston, Jan. 1, 1787, who was b. June 29, 1767; had *Ichabod*, Nov. 4, 1788, m. Abigail Delano; *Isaiah*, Dec. 17, 1789, of Scituate Harbor, m. Mercy Vinal, da. of Lemuel, the son of Israel, the son of Israel; *Mercy*, July 4, 1792; *Benjamin*, March 22, 1794, m.

Martha Sampson, da. of Bradford, and had Rebecca, 1833; *Martha*, Feb. 22, 1796; *Ruth*, Nov. 14, 1799; *Peleg*, June 6, 1806; *James*, April 20, 1808, a hatter in Boston.

33. Capt. John, (s. of 25,) Dux.; m. Anna ———, and had *Deborah*, Jan. 30, 1802, d. May 16, 1804; *Ichabod*, Mar. 30, 1806; *Samuel*, April 21, 1808; *Deborah*, June 5, 1815.

34. Maj. Judah, (s. of 31,) Dux.; inherited the estate; m. Wealthea Wadsworth, who d. Mar. 3, 1841, æt. 81 years, and he d. March 12, 1845, æt. 94 years. He had chd.— *Lucia*, Dec. 5, 1780, m. Capt. Sylvanus Smith; *John*, Nov. 22, 1784 (35); *Briggs*, Oct. 8, 1786 (36); *Mercy*, Sept. 24, 1788, m. Capt. Henry R. Packard, who d. at sea, August 1834, æt. 50, and she died March 18, 1840, æt. 53, and they had Marcia, who m. Capt. Robert Welch, and Hannah James, the young poetess, who was born April 15, 1815, and d. Aug. 10, 1831, æt. 16; *Judah*, Aug. 11, 1790, d. Dec. 15, 1792; *Wealthea*, Aug. 13. 1792, m. William James of Scituate; *Hannah*, Jan. 4, 1795, d. April 25, 1804; *Judah*, June 9, 1797, d. April 20, 1804; *Mary Ann*, March 12, 1801; and *Samuel*, Jan. 24, 1803, a physician of Bridgewater.

35. John, (s. of 34,) Dux.; inherited the family domain; m. Mary Winsor, and had *Mary*, Oct. 28, 1811, m. Daniel Sampson, m. 2d Capt. David Cushman; *John*, April 14, 1813, m. a Brewster; *Henry*, Nov. 3, 1815, m. Sarah Ann Woodward.

36. Briggs, (s. of 34,) Dux.; m. Hannah, sister of William James; he d. Jan. 4, 1840, æt. 54; had *Judah*, July 22, 1820, d. Aug. 18, 1823; *William James*, Apr. 22, 1822, m. a Woodward; *Lucia P.*, April 20, 1824; *Judah*, Aug. 24, 1825, m. Julia Whitney, Nov. 1848, *Samuel*, April 28, 1827; *Amherst*, May 15, 1832.

Note. *Rebecca* is mentioned in the Col. Rec. 1661, as of marriageable age; *Elizabeth*, m. John Seabury Dec. 9, 1697; *Anna*, m. Josiah Snell Dec. 2, 1699. Mitchell says she was da. of a Zachariah Alden. *Priscilla*, m. Samuel Cheesbrook, Jan. 1699; *Sarah*, b. 1722, d. March 29, 1773, æt. nearly 51; *Alice*, m. Oliver Seabury May 7, 1760.

AMES.

1. John, (s. of Richard of Burton, Somersetshire, England,) it is said, "came out of England for stealing a calf;" Dux. 1643; removed to Bridgew.; m. Elizabeth Hayward Oct. 20, 1645, and d. s. p. 1698, leaving a large estate to his B.'s heirs.

2. William, (B. of 1,) Dux.; removed to Bridgewater; has numerous descendants, including the orator, Fisher Ames, for whom see Mitchell's Hist.

ANDREWS.

Joseph, Dux., 1654 — *Abigail*, 1647, m. John Wadsworth, July, 1667; *Stephen*, Dux., 1734, owned land at the beach.

ARMSTRONG.

GREGORY, Dux., 1638, permitted to dwell in Dux. "with the leave of the committees of that place;" d. at Plymouth, Nov. 5, 1650; m. Eleanor, widow of John Billington.

ARDDATON.

THOMAS, Dux., had *Ruby* Aug. 14, 1759; *Thomas*, March 2, 1763.

ARNOLD.

1. REV. SAMUEL, M., minister of the chh.; will dated Aug. 19, 1693, bequeaths to Mr. Rowland Cotton "his great Latten Book, called Augustine Marloret, being an exposition of the New Testament;" his library was valued at £7½; d. Sep. 1, 1693; m. Elizabeth; and had *Seth* (2); *Rev. Samuel*, ord. at Rochester, 1684, and d. before 1717; *Elizabeth*, m. Abram Holmes.

2. CAPT. SETH, (s. of 1,) Dux.; had *Edward*, Mar. 20, 1680 (3); *Penelope*, April 21, 1682; *Desire*, m. Ichabod Bartlett of M., Nov. 14, 1709; *Benjamin* (4); *Dea. James*, 1699 (5); and perhaps *Elizabeth*, who m. Anthony Waterman, and 2d, Jona. Alden in 1718.

3. EDWARD, (s. of 2,) Dux.; a justice of the peace; m. Mary Brewster, Oct. 8, 1706, had *Ezra*, July 30, 1707 (6); *William*, May 6, d. May 26, 1718.

4. BENJAMIN, (s. of 2,) Dux.; m. Hannah Bartlett, Mar. 8, 1714; had *Samuel*, Feb. 1, 1716.

5. DEA. JAMES, (s. of 2,) Dux.; m. Joanna Sprague, Oct. 19, 1735, who d. May 19, 1766, æt. nearly 51; he d. Sep. 25, 1755, æt. 56; had *Bildad*, Nov. 20, 1735 (7); *Luther*, Sep. 1737; *James*, Sep. 23, 1740, d. Sep. 9, 1742; *James*, 1745; *Benjamin*, 1751, d. Jan. 18, 1776, in the camp at Roxbury.

6. EZRA, (s. of 3,) Dux.; m. Rebecca Sprague, July 27, 1732; she d. Oct. 25, 1805, æt. 95; he d. Feb. 18, 1780, æt. 72; had *Seth*, June 12, 1733, d. Mar. 14, 1819, æt. 85; *Gamaliel*, Aug. 8, 1735, "about 6 of yᵉ clock in yᵉ morn-

ing;" *Rebecca*, a. 1642, d. Dec. 23, 1763; *Edward*, 1749, m. Susanna, who d. April 17, 1811, æt. 66; he d. Aug. 1, 1843, æt. 93, and had Oaks, Galen, Ezra, Jedediah, and Rebecca; *William*, 1750, d. Aug. 13, 1836, æt. 86.

7. CAPT. BILDAD, (s. of 5,) Dux.; m. Mercy Seabury, Nov. 26, 1766, and had *Bildad*, May 19, 1776, d. April 25, 1780; *William*, d. 1780.

NOTE. Several early settlers of the name were in Rhode Island; *Edward* of Boston, d. 8 Aug., 1657; *John*, Cambridge, Boston, 1660; *Thomas*, Watertown, had Ichabod and Richard, 1642; *William*, Hingham, 1635.

BAKER.

1. SAMUEL, (perh. s. of Rev. Nicholas of Scituate,) M., m. 1656, Eleanor, da. of Kenelm Winslow; m. 2d, 1677, Patience Simmons; he d. 1699; had *Kenelm*, 1657 (2); *Lydia*, 1659; *Elizabeth*, 1661; *Mary*, 1662; *Alice*, 1663; *Ellen*, 1665; *Samuel*, [by 2d w.,] in. Sarah Snow, 1699.

2. KENELM, (s. of 1,) M.; m. Sarah Bradford; had *Kenelm*, m. Patience Doten of M., at Dux., Jan. 22, 1719; and *Samuel* (3).

3. SAMUEL, (s. of 2,) Dux.; m. Hannah Ford; had *Eleanor*, Sep. 21, 1727; *Hannah*, Feb. 25, 1729; *Bethiah*, March 11, 1733, m. Henry Perry, Dec. 25, 1760; *Huldah*, June 23, 1734; *Samuel*, Feb. 26, 1735, drowned at the eastward, May, 1759; *James*, Jan. 4, 1737; *Thomas*, Jan. 24, 1739; *Charles*, April 26, 1741; *Elijah*, July 1, 1744 (4); *Abigail*, Sep. 24, 1746, m. Israel Perry, Oct. 15, 1769; *Sarah*, Oct. 5, 1741.

4. CAPT. ELIJAH, (s. of 3,) Dux.; m. Mary Whitemore; had *Anna W.*, Apr. 29, 1778; *Elijah*, Oct. 8, 1782, m. Betsy Fish, and had Elijah, (m. Augusta Winsor,) Lysander, Thomas, Elizabeth, Augusta, Amanda, Francis H., Marcia and Mary; *Jabez W.*, June 7, 1786; *George*, Nov. 14, 1787, m. Rebecca Snell, 1816; *Daniel*, July 2, 1790.

5. EDWARD D. (s. of —) Dux., m. Olive; m. 2d Sarah; he died May 24, 1824; had *Sylvanus W.*, 1792; *Otis*, 1794, a sea captain; *Edward D.*, 1796, m. Lucy Turner; *Lucy W.*, 1799; *George; Almira*, m. Joseph Brewster; *Barker C.; John; William; James; Sarah; Mary E.*, 1824.

6. THOMAS, (s. of —,) Dux.; drowned Nov. 25, 1712.

NOTE. Francis, early of Yarmouth, had Samuel, 1648, and Daniel, 1650. Two *Samuels* were in Barnstable in the 17th century, and also a *John* there in 1696.

BARKER.

1. ROBERT, Dux.; "Jan. 20, 1632. Robt. Barker, serv^t· of John Thorp, complayned of his M^r· for want of clothes. The complaint being found to be just, it was ordered, that Thorp should either foorthwith apparell him, or else make over his time to some other that was able to provide for him." He was subsequently bound to Wm. Palmer, as a carpenter apprentice, and his time expired April 1, 1637. — Col. Records. He was ad. 1654. In 1648, he bought the house and land of John Ferniside for 45 shillings; in 1665, he bought of E. Hall land at Namasakeeset Bk., and of C. Southworth 4 acres, and of John Willis 50 acres, and of E. Hunt at the Bay path; and of S. Leonard at Bluefish, which he sold to A. Sampson. His will is dated Feb. 18, 1689, and he d. between this and the taking of the inventory of his estate (£142 1s. 11d.) March 15, 1692. He kept a ferry at New Harbor, which he sold to R. Chapman. His chd. were *Robert* (2); *Francis* (3); *Isaac* (4); *Rebecca*, m. Wm. Snow; *Abigail* m. a Rogers.

2. LT. ROBERT, (s. of 1,) Dux.; owned land, 1684, at Pudding bk.; "medo" at Robinson's ck.; and at North river "over against a place commonly called Palmer's landing place." He appears of Scituate in 1698-9; but however of Dux. again, and in 1701, sixteen acres adjoining his farm were given him. He m. Alice; m. 2d, Hannah; had *Abigail*, Aug. 24, 1682; *James*, Jan. 1, 1683, Dux., d. 1718; *Caleb*, May 24, 1685 (5); *Deborah*, Dec. 7, 1686; *Susannah*, Dec, 20, 1689; *Robert*, July 5, 1693; *Alice*, June 3, 1695; *Lydia*, Sep. 5, 1697, m. Ebenezer Stetson, 1728; and by 2d wife, *Isaac*, b. at Scit., Mar. 15, 1699, of Pembroke; *Mary*, May 13, 1701; *Margaret*, Apr. 18, 1704.

3. LT. FRANCIS, (s. of 1,) Dux.; m. Mary Lincoln, Jan. 5, 1674; had *Joshua*, Nov. 16, 1676; *Elizabeth*, Oct. 31, 1677; *Josiah*, Sep. 21, 1679, Dux. 1710; *Ruth*, Jan. 31, 1682; *Francis*, Oct. 18, 1682.

4. ISAAC, (s. of 1,) Dux.; left an estate of £130; m. Judith Prence, 28 Dec., 1665; had *Rebecca; Lydia; Judith; Martha;* a da.; *Francis; Samuel*, Dux., 1693; *Isaac* (6); *Jabez; Robert*.

5. CALEB, (s. of 2.) He m. Anna, who d. at Pownalboro', Me., May, 1769, æt. 80; he d. 1772; of the Society of Friends; had *Robert*, May 27, 1712; *John*, Aug. 15, 1714; *Elizabeth*, Mar. 17, 1717, d. 1724; *Caleb*, Oct. 29, 1719; d. Sep. 23, 1742, at Red Rrook, E. Jersey; *Joshua*, Feb. 22, 1721, d. 1724; *Gideon*, Dec. 22, 1723; *Joshua*, July 26, 1726; *Charles*, Aug. 5, 1729; *Anna*, Feb. 14, 1730, d. 1732. — Friend's records.

6. ISAAC, (s. of 4,) Dux.; m. Elizabeth; she d. Aug. 18, 1774; he d. "7 d. of 5 mo., 1754;" had *Mary*, Aug. 1, 1708; *Silvester*, 1710; *Peleg*, 1712; *Prince*, 1716, m. Abigail, da. of Benj. and Deborah Keen, and she d. Sep. 2, 1790, and he d. Jan. 27, 1784, and had Abigail, who d. Jan. 7 1789; *Elizabeth* and *Lydia*. — Friend's records.

7. ROBERT, (s. of —,) m. Hannah; had *Ann*, Sep. 21, 1739, and *Thomas*, Apr. 29, 1738. — Friend's records.

8. JOHN, (s. of —,) m. Grace; had John and Carr. — Idem.

10. JOHN, (B. of 1,) by trade a bricklayer; 1638, kept a ferry at Jones river; and was fined (1638,) "for drawing blood upon Henry Blaque" 20 shillings; resided in Dux.; next of M., and bought a ferry privilege of Jona. Brewster, at a place now called Little's bridge, and was drowned there, Dec. 14, 1652, leaving an estate of £113. He m. 1632, Anna, da. of John Williams, senr. of Scit.; had *John* (11); *Anna; Deborah; Mary*. — Deane's Scit. and Col. Rec.

11. JOHN, ESQ., (s. of 10,) Barnstable; Scituate, 1683; Sergeant in Philip's war and freed (1680) from bearing arms "on account of sore wounds received." A justice of the peace and a lawyer; m. Desire Annable, Jan. 18, 1676, she d. 1705; m. 2d, Hannah, da. of Thomas Loring of Hingham, and widow of Rev. Jeremiah Cushing; had *John*, May 4, 1678; *Desire*, Sep. 22, 1680; *Anna*, Aug. 26, 1682, d. 22 Nov. 1682; *Anna*, Nov. 1, 1683; *Williams; Samuel, Esq.*, 1684, m. Hannah Cushing of Scituate, and had Samuel, 1707, Ignatius, Ezekiel, 1714, Hannah and Deborah (the 3d w. of Shearjashub Bourn in 1750). — Deane's Scit. and N. E. Hist. and Geneal. Reg., II.

NOTE. *Thomas* and *Elisha* were of Dux. in 1710, Elisha d. or removed before 1712. *John* and *Maria* Cushman, both of Plymouth, were m. at Dux., Dec. 10, 1732 — Francis of Concord, 1646, has descendants in that vicinity: Richard is ancestor of the Andover family. Nicholas, a carpenter, of Boston, in 1655; Edward of Boston, in 1650, had Thomas 1657; James, of Rowley, in 1640.

BARSTOW.

JOSEPH, Dux.; m. Lydia Soule, 1786, and had Joseph 1787, (m. Nancy Wadsworth), and Samuel, 1791. She d. in 1812, æt. 44.

NOTE. William, of Scit. d. 1668, his w. was Anna, and his estate £53; Mercy Bestow of Pem. m. Joshua Thomas, 1747; Jacob Bestow m. Desire Brattles, March 13, 1760; James Bastow, of Dux. 1780.

BARTIN.

JOHN, Dux.; m. Abigail, who d. Nov. 6, 1807, æt. 54; he d. Dec. 20, 1835; had *George W.*, 1785; *John D.*, 1788; *Jedediah*, 1789; *Anderson*, 1793, d. 1796; *Matthew*, 1795.

BARTLETT.

1. ROBERT, b. in England 1603; arrived 1623 at Plymouth; m. 1628, Mary, da. of Richard Warren, a Mayflower pilgrim, and d. 1676, æt. 73, and his w. survived a few years. Chd. *Benjamin* (2); *Joseph*, 1638 (3); *Mary*, m. Richard Foster Sept. 10, 1651, m. 2d Jona. Morey July 8, 1659; *Rebecca*, m. William Harlow 20th Dec. 1649; *Sarah*, m. Samuel Rider of Yarmouth, Dec. 23, 1656; *Elizabeth*, m. Anthony Sprague of Hingham, Dec. 20, 1661, d. Feb. 7, 1712; he d. Sept. 3, 1719, æt. 84; *Mercy*, March 10, 1650, m. John Ivey of Boston, Dec. 25, 1668; *Lydia*, June 8, 1647, m. Jas. Barnaby, m. 2d John Nelson of Middleboro'.

2. BENJAMIN, (s. of 1,) Dux.; ad. 1654; m. Sarah Brewster, 1656; m. 2d Cecilia, 1678, who d. a. 1691; he d. 1691, leaving a farm valued at £140, and other property amounting to £250. His will gives his Indian servants, Robin and wife, 20 shillings apiece. Chd. — *Benjamin* (4); *Samuel* (5); *Ichabod* (6); *Ebenezer* (7); *Rebecca*, m. William Bradford, 1679; *Sarah*, m. Robert Bartlett, 1687.

3. JOSEPH, (s. of 1,) of Pond's Parish, Plymouth. For his descendants see Mitchell's History of Bridgewater.

4. BENJAMIN, (s. of 2,) Dux.; lived at North hill; inherited his father's farm, and lands at Rochester, and a double portion of his property; m. Ruth Pabodie, Sep., 1672; had *Robert*, Dec. 6, 1679; *Benjamin*; *Mercy*, m. John Turner of Scituate, Aug. 5, 1714; *Priscilla*, Jan., 1697, m. John Sampson, Dec. 31, 1718; *Deborah*, m. Josiah Thomas of M., Dec. 19, 1723; *Ruth*, m. John Murdock, Jr.; *Abigail*, 1703, m. Hon. Gamaliel Bradford, 1728; *Rebecca*, m. John Bradford; *Sarah*, m. Israel Bradford.

5. SAMUEL, (s. of 2,) Dux.; a mariner; Dux., 1710, but d. or removed before 1713; m. Hannah Pabodie, Aug. 2, 1683; had *Benjamin*, May 4, 1684; *Joseph*, Apr. 22, 1686 (8); *Samuel*, 1691, an officer at Louisburg, had Samuel (called "Quaker Sam") who had Capt. Joseph, Amasa, Anselm, and others; *Ichabod*; *Judah*; *William* of Dux. — Hist. Bridgew. Perhaps also *Hannah*, who m. Benjamin Arnold, 1714.

6. ICHABOD, (s. of 2,) Dux., 1710; of M. previously; inherited land in Middleboro', m. Elizabeth, da. of Joseph Waterman, 1699, she d. Oct. 1708; m. 2d, Desire Arnold, Nov. 14, 1709.

7. EBENEZER, (s. of 2,) Dux.; inherited land at Little Compton; d. prob. before 1712; m. Hannah; had *Ebenezer*, 1694 (9).

8. JOSEPH, (s. of 5.) Dux.; m. Lydia, who d. Apr. 6, 1739; he d. Jan. 9, 1764, æt. 77; had *Isaiah*, Mar. 24, 1716; *Patience*, July 27, 1718, m. Jethro Sprague, Dec. 12, 1738; *Hannah*, Mar. 27, 1721, d. July 11 or 12, 1739; *Lydia*, Aug. 30, 1725, m. Bezaleel Alden, 1740.

9. EBENEZER, (s. of 7,) Dux.; m. Jerusha Sampson, Oct. 8, 1730; she d. Jan. 2, 1778, æt. 73; he d. Oct. 24, 1781, æt. 87; had *Nathaniel*, Jan. 31, 1723 (10); *Jerusha*, Jan. 9, 1732, m. James Robinson, and their da. Jerusha Bartlett, m. Wait Wadsworth, 1774; and perhaps *Lydia*, who m. Lemuel Delano, 1741.

10. NATHANIEL, (s. of 9,) Dux.; m. Zenobe Wadsworth, June 10, 1742; had *Zenobe*, Apr. 2, 1743; *Nathaniel*, Mar. 30, 1745; *Mary*, Aug. 9, 1746; *Elizabeth*, Dec. 3, 1749.

11. JOSEPH, (styled Jr., son of —,) Dux.; m. Dorothy Wadsworth, Dec. 25, 1729; had *Amie*, Mar. 11, 1735; d. July 22, 1735; *Ichabod*, Aug. 1, 1736, d. Sep. 8, 1736; *Joseph*. Mar. 26, 1740; *Dorothy*, Apr. 21, 1743; and on the chh. records *Bathsheba*, bap. 1740; *Uriah*, bap. 1743; *Elizabeth*, bap. 1747.

12. BENJAMIN, (s. of —,) Dux.; had *Mary*, bap. 1747, and *Sarah*, bap. 1757.

NOTE. Mrs. *Hannah*, m. Thomas Delano, 1692; *Sarah*, m. Cornelius Drew, 1729; *Rebecca*, m. Chs. Ryder of Plymouth, Oct. 8, 1741; *Seth*, m. Charity Cullifer, Feb. 27, 1736; *Seth*, m. Martha Bourn, Nov. 23, 1737; *Nathaniel*, m. Abiah Delano, Dec. 16, 1725, of Dux.; *Robert*, of Plymouth, m Hopestill Seabury, Oct. 15, 1772; *Sarah*, 1732, d. 1813, æt. 81; and *John*, m. Sarah Seabury, Mar. 19, 1770.

NOTE. The Bartletts of Newbury are a distinct family.

BASSET.

WILLIAM Bassite. He d. 1667. He m. Elizabeth Tilden (?); had *William; Nathaniel*, of Dux.; *Joseph; Sarah*, m. Peregrine White, and d. 1711; *Elizabeth*, m. Thomas Burgess, 8th Nov. 1648; *Jane;* and *Ruth*, m. John Sprague 1655, and m. 2d a Thomas. — Hist. Bridgewater.

NOTE. James of K. and Bethia Phillips were m. at Dux. Oct. 14, 1773.

BATES.

Joshua, of Dux., came from Hanover; m. Irene Delano; had *Amasa D.*, April 13, 1792; *Betsy*, Oct. 31, 1794, m. a Patten; *Nancy D.*, Feb. 29, 1798, m. Samuel Soule; *Seth*, March 26, 1801; *Hannah Clark*, Oct. 19, 1803.

NOTE. *Caleb*, of Pembroke m. Novice Thomas, 1782, and had Caleb.

BEARE.

Richard, Dux., 1636, had land granted to him at Powder point, and was allowed to build there, giving bonds of £50 for good behavior, as he was somewhat of a refractory character. In 1636, he was in the stocks for contempt of court. In 1637-8, had granted him 20 acres at G. H. path. He sold, in 1642, for £18, his house and land south of Mill brook to F. West, and removed to M. In 1659 he was disfranchised.

BIDDLE.

Joseph, Dux., 1635, July, bought land at Island creek, of Isaac Robinson; 1640, fined 20s. "for suffering men to drinke drunken at his house;" but of M. in 1643. Name also spelt Bidle.

BISBEE.

The name was originally spelled Besbeech, Besbidge, and later Bisbee and Bisby.

1. Thomas, came from Sandwich, Eng., with six chd. and three servants; of Scit. 1634, and deacon of the chh. there; ad. Jan. 2d, 1637-8; Dux. 1638, when he bought Wm. Palmer's house, and then of M. He had *Elisha* (2); *Alice*, m. John Bourn July 18, 1645.

2. Elisha, (s. of 1,) a cooper; in 1644 kept a ferry where now is Union bridge, and his house was on the west side and was a tavern. His estate amounted to £84. — Hist. Scituate. He had *Hopestill*, 1645, m. Sarah, who survived and m. a Lincoln. He d. Nov. 12, 1695; *John*, 1647 (3); *Mary*, 1648, m. Jacob Beals; *Elisha*, 1654, d. 1715; *Hannah*, 1656, m. Thomas Brooks, 1687.

3. John, (s. of 2,) M.; m. Joanna Brooks, Sept. 13, 1687; had *Martha*, Oct. 13, 1688; *John*, Sept. 15, 1690; *Elijah*, Jan. 29, 1692; *Mary*, March 28, 1693; *Moses*, Oct. 20, 1695; *Elisha*, May 3, 1698.

4. AARON, (s. of —,) Dux.; m. Sarah Soule, Nov. 26, 1747; had *Joanna; Abigail; Studley,* a. 1756, d. 1771; *Thomas,* a. 1760, d. 1761.

NOTE. *Abigail,* m. Andrew Sampson, 1748; *Deborah,* m. Abner Sampson, 1756; *Silvia,* m. Thomas Chandler, 1749; *Isaac,* m. Abigail Howland, 1781; *Alice,* m. William Kendar, 1788; *Oliver,* m. Huldah Simmons, 1791; *Elisha,* m. Mary Pattengell, 1779; *Martha,* m. Jona. Turner, 1667.

BISHOP.

1. RICHARD Bushup, lived with Love Brewster, 1638, m. Alice Clark, Dec. 5, 1644; she was convicted of the murder of her own child, and was hung 1648. He is called of "Pascattaway in Artercull or New Jersey," when he sold to Capt. Church his property in the colony.

2. JAMES, Dux., owned land at Indian Head river in 1679, alive in 1710. His chd. were perhaps the following: *Ebenezer,* Dux., m. Amy Stetson Nov. 20, 1710; *Abigail,* m. James Boney, 1695; *John,* Dux. 1710; *Hudson,* Dux. 1710, Scit. 1711, Dux. 1712.

NOTE. *Tabitha* m. Jedediah Soule 1741; *Nathaniel,* of Boston, 1634, Ipswich, his w. Alice, had Joseph 1642, Benjamin, John, and Samuel — Mr. John Bushop, an ancient freeman of Taunton.

BLUSH.

ABRAHAM, Dux., bought land at Eagle nest, of Richard Moore in 1637; and sold it, 1638, to John Willis.

BONNEY.

The name is generally spelled on the records Boney.

THOMAS, Dux., a shoemaker; 1640, had land N. W. of North hill, and thirty acres at Namasakeeset; d. a. 1693; m. Dorcas Sampson; m. 2d Mary, who survived him; had *Thomas,* inherited his father's land in Dux., m. Sarah Studley, July 18, 1695.

NOTE. The following were perhaps chd. of Thomas — *Mary,* m. John Mitchell, Dec. 14, 1675; *Joseph,* Dux., 1710; *Ebenezer,* Dux., 1710, drowned, 1712; *John,* Dux., 1691—1710; *James,* m. Abigail Bishop, 1695, of Dux., 1710; *William,* had land at Namasakeeset, 1694, d. or removed before 1710 — The following is from the town records, "1691, Town did agree that Goodman Boney should have a paire of shoes bought with part of the rent dew for the comon meadows"—*Mercy*, m. Nathl. Delano, 1714; and *Elizabeth*, of Pem., m. Saml. Delano, 1719.

BOOTH.

ABRAHAM, (prob. son of John of Scituate, and b. 1673); of Dux., 1710, and this year received a grant.

BOSWORTH.

BENJAMIN, (s. of widow Abigail of Boston, who m. James Soule of Dux., 1773,) b. June 20, 1767, m. Mercy Prior, who was b. Apr. 22, 1767, and had *Abigail*, 1791; *Benjamin*, 1793; *Hiram*, 1795; *Sally*, 1797, d. 1799; *Mercy*, 1799, m. Capt. Eden Wadsworth; *Betsy*, 1801, and *Mary*.

NOTE. *Mary*, m. Warren Weston, 1767—The *widow Abigail*, above named, was a da. of Joshua Seaver, and born Jan. 4, 1744, and her husband, Benjamin of Boston, was born Jan., 1743. They were m. Aug. 17, 1766, and he died Nov. 15, 1769, and she d. Aug. 26, 1832, æt. 88. *Records*. A *Benjamin* was early in Hingham, and had Edward, 1659, Bridget, 1660, Hannah, 1668, and perhaps others. —*Hobart's Journal*.

BOURN.

1. THOMAS, b. 1601; M.; d. May 11, 1684, æt. 83; m. Martha, and had *John* (2); *Martha*, m. John Bradford, m. 2d, Lt. Thomas Tracy, and d. 1689; *Elizabeth*, m. Robt. Waterman, 1638; *Margaret*, m. Josiah Winslow, a. 1636; *Anne*, m. Rev. Nehemiah Smith, Jan. 21, 1639–40; and *Lydia*, m. Nathl. Tilden.

2. JOHN, (s. of 1,) M.; but of Dux., 1665, when he lived on land belonging to Wm. Pabodie; of M. in 1681, when he was authorized to solemnize marriages, and d. a. 1685; m. Alice Bisbee, who d. May, 1686; had *Elizabeth*, 1646; *Thomas*, 1647 (3); *Alice*, 1649; *Anna*, 1651; *Martha*, 1653; *Sarah*, 1663.

3. THOMAS, (s. of 2,) M.; had land in Dux., 1701; m. Elizabeth Rouse, Apr. 16, 1681; had *George*, May 29, 1690 (4).

4. GEORGE, (s. of 3,) Dux.; m. Elizabeth Chandler, May 21, 1713; had *Elizabeth*, Feb. 9, 1714; *Martha*, Dec. 23, 1716, m. Seth Bartlett, 1737; *Sarah*, Oct. 5, 1718; *Benjamin*, July 21, 1721; *Alice*, Aug. 26, 1724.

NOTE. *Hannah*, m. William Wilson of Scit., Nov. 28, 1739. — *Richard*, (B. of Henry, who was ad. 1737-8, and of Scit. 1637, and Barnstable, 1639,) Lynn, removed to Sandwich 1637, a teacher of Marshpee Indians, m. Ruth, d. a. 1682, and had Job, (m. Ruhamath and had Timothy, Eleazer, Hezekiah and others), Shearjashub, Elisha, who m. Patience Skiffe, 26 Oct., 1675 — *Ezra* was b. at Sandwich, 12 May, 1648.

BOWERS.

GEORGE, Dux., 1637–8, owned land in Dux.; and was presented "for leaving no passage for man or beast neither by the sea side, nor for cattle through his ground." Perhaps the one of Cambridge, 1644.

BOWMAN.

MR. NATHANIEL, of Dux., in 1636. Vide Edmund Chandler.

BRADFORD.

Gov. WILLIAM, b. in Austerfield, Eng., and d. May 9, 1657, æt. 68. For an account of Gov. B., see Belknap's Biog. He m. in Eng., Dorothy May, who was drowned in C. C. harbor, Dec. 7, 1620; m. 2d, Mrs. Alice Southworth, Aug. 14, 1623, and da. of Mr. Carpenter.* She d. Mar. 26, 1670, æt. 80; he had by Dorothy, *John*, b. in England (2); *William*, June 17, 1624 (by 2d w.,) (3); and *Mercy*, 1630, (m. Benjamin Vermage, Dec. 21, 1648) and *Joseph*, 1630, (gemini,) who m. Jael Hobart, da. of Rev. Peter of Hingham, May 25, 1664, he d. July 10, 1715, æt. 84, she d. 1730, æt. 88, lived at Jones river, and were licensed by the Court. in 1678 to sell liquors, and had Joseph, Apr. 18, 1665, and Elisha, who m. Bathsheba Le-Brocke, Sep. 7, 1718, and had 15 chd.

2. JOHN, (s. of 1,) Dux., 1645–52; M., 1653; removed to Norwich, Ct., where he d. s. p. 1678; m. Martha Bourn, who m. 2d, Lt. Thomas Tracy, and d. 1689.

3. MAJ. WILLIAM, (s. of 1,) of Plymouth; an asst.; Dep. Gov.; one of Sir Ed. Andros's council, 1687; chief military officer of the colony. He d. Feb. 20, 1703, æt. 79. His will

---

* "1667: Mary Carpenter (sister of Mrs. Alice Bradford, the wife of Governor Bradford) a member of the church at Duxbury, died at Plymouth, March 19-20, being newly entered into the 91st year of her age. She was a goodly old maid never married." — Ply. Chh. Rec. It is also supposed that Priscilla, wife of Wm. Wright, and Bridget, wife of Dr. Saml. Fuller, were sisters of Mrs. Bradford.

bears date Jan. 29, 1703. His wife Alice, da. of Thomas Richards of Weymouth, d. Dec. 12, 1671. His second wife was a widow Wiswall. His third was Mary, widow of Rev. John Holmes of Dux., and she d. June 6, 1714–15. His will gives to David, his house after his mother's decease; to John, the land he then lived on, and also "my father's manuscript, viz., a narrative of the beginning of New Plymouth;" * to Thomas, land in Norwich (which was his uncle John's); to Joseph, land at Norwich; to Samuel, his right of commons in Dux.; to Israel, Ephraim, David and Hezekiah, his estate, enjoining upon them to sell it to none that do not bear the name of Bradford, and be not descended from him; to Israel, a house; to David, a silver bowl, "not to be alienated from the family of the Bradford's;" to Hezekiah, a gold ring; to Samuel, his Latin books, "to encourage him in bringing one of his sons to learning, which said bookes it is my will, that they shall by him be given to his said son, whom he shall so bring up."

His chd. were, *Maj. John*, Feb. 20, 1653, d. Dec. 8, 1736, m. 1674, Mercy (da. of Joseph) Warren, who was b. Sept. 23, 1653, and d. 1748, and had John 1675, m. Rebecca Bartlett; Alice, 1677, m. Ens. Edmund Mitchell, 1708, m. 2d Joshua Hersey; Abigail, 1679, m. Gideon Sampson, Mercy, 1681, m. Jona. Freeman 1708, m. 2d Lt. Isaac Cushman; Lt. Samuel, 1683, had a family, Priscilla, m. Seth Chipman, and William, 1688, m. Hannah, da. of Dea. John Foster, who m. 2d Geo. Partridge of Dux.; *William*, March 11, 1655, d. 1687, m. Rebecca Bartlett, 1679, had William, Alice, 1680, m. William Barnes, and Sarah, 1683, m. Jona. Barnes, and d. 1720; *Thomas*, of Norwich; *Samuel* (4); *Alice*, m. Maj. James Fitch of Norwich; *Hannah*, m. Joshua (s. of John, s. of Wm.) Ripley, Nov. 28, 1682; *Mercy*, m. a Steel of Hartford; *Melatiah*, m. John Steel of Hartford; *Mary*, m. William Hunt of Weymouth; *Sarah*, m. Kenelm Baker; *Joseph*, (by 2d wife,) of Norwich; *Israel*, (by 3d w.) m. Sarah Bartlett; *David*, m. Elizabeth Finney, 1714, and d. 1730; *Ephraim*, of K.; and *Hezekiah*, of K.

4. SAMUEL, (s. of 3,) Dux., b. 1668, d. April 11, 1714, æt. 46; had a grant adjoining his house lot, 1713; m. Hannah

---

* This history of Gov. B. was destroyed by the British at the siege of Boston, with other papers in the belfry of the Old South church in Boston. Gov. B. in his will makes this mention of other works of his, which have been published in the Hist. Coll. of Mass. To T. Prence, Capt. Willet, and Capt. T. Southworth, he says — "I comend to youer wisdome some small bookes written by my owne hand to bee improved as you shall see meet. In speciall I comend to you a little booke with a blacke cover wherein there is a word to Plymouth, a word to Boston, and a word to New England with sundry useful verses."

Rogers, July, 1689, a da., says Mitchell, of Gamaliel Rogers. Their chd. were, *Hannah*, Feb. 14, 1689, m. June 16, 1709, Nathaniel Gilbert of Taunton; *Gershom*, Dec. 21, 1691, of K., m. Priscilla Wiswall, Oct. 23, 1716; *Perez*, Dec. 28, 1694, H. C. 1713, d. at Attleboro' June 19, 1746, æt. 52; *Elizabeth*, Dec. 15, 1696; *Jerusha*, March 10, 1699, m. Rev. Ebenezer Gay Nov. 3, 1719; *Wealthea*, May 15, 1702; *Gamaliel*, May 18, 1704 (5).

5. Hon. Gamaliel, (s. of 4). He resided in Duxbury. He m. Abigail Bradford, Aug. 30, 1728; she d. Aug. 30, 1776; he d. Apr. 24, 1778, æt. nearly 74 years. Chd.— *Abigail*, Sep. 24, 1728, m. Wait Wadsworth; *Samuel*, Jan. 2, 1730 (6); *Gamaliel*, Sep. 2, 1731 (7); *Seth*, Sep. 14, 1733 (8); *Capt. Pabodie*, Mar. 8, 1735, d. at K., Sep. 5, 1782; *Deborah*, Aug. 17, 1738, d. Aug. 1, 1739; *Hannah*, July 20, 1740, m. Robt. Stanford, Nov. 13, 1774; *Andrew*, June 2, 1745, H. C. 1771, m. a Turner; *Peter*, June 2, 1745 (9); *Ruth*, July 5, 1743, m. Elijah Sampson, Sep. 3, 1761.

6. Capt. Samuel, (s. of 5,) Dux.; m. Grace; he d. Feb. 27, 1777; had *Deborah*, Dec. 11, 1750; *Samuel*, Mar. 27, 1752 (10); *Lydia*, Apr. 6, 1754, d. May 7, 1768; *William*, Nov. 25, 1755; *Wealthea*, Nov. 15, 1757, m. Isaac Drew; *Lyman*, Oct. 1, 1760, d. at New York, 1776; *Grace*, Apr. 6, 1765, d. 1847; *Elihu*, bap. 1765; *George*, Nov. 20, 1767; *Isaiah*, Nov. 25, 1769, m. Joanna Dingley.

7. Col. Gamaliel, (s. of 5,) Dux.; he m. Sarah Alden, Mar. 10, 1757; he d. Jan. 9, 1807. Chd.— *Perez*, Nov. 14, 1758, m. Judith Cooper, who d. June 13, 1792, had Samuel Cooper, who d. at sea, and Judith Cooper, who m. a Huntington; *Sophia*, Nov. 16, 1761; *Gamaliel*, Nov. 4, 1763 (11); *Alden*, Nov. 19, 1765 (12); *Daniel*, Dec. 27, 1771 (13); *Sarah*, Feb. 24, 1768, m. Wm. Hinckley; *Jerusha*, Jan. 30, 1770, m. Ezra Weston; *Gershom*, Feb. 3, 1774 (14).

8. Capt. Seth, (s. of 5,) Dux.; m. Lydia Southworth, Feb. 7, 1760; had *Isaac*, of Maine; *Lydia*, m. Dea. Dura Wadsworth; *Abigail* and *Hannah*, (gemini); *Seth*; *Susan* and *Sarah*, (gemini), Susan m. Joseph Brewster; Sarah m. Ezra Cushman; *John*, d. at sea; *James*; *Southworth*, d. at sea; and *Joel*, who d. at N. Y., 1776.

9. Peter, (s. of 5,) Dux.; m. Abigail Loring, Jan. 18, 1770; had *Judith*, Apr., 1770; *Priscilla*, Jan., 1773, m. Wm. Rand; *Alexander*, Dec., 1776, d. s. p.; and *Nathaniel*.

10. Samuel, (s. of 6,) Dux.; m. Lydia Bradford, 1783; he d. Apr. 10, 1816, æt. 64; had *Prince*, Dec. 19, 1783, m. Harriet Churchill, who was b. Oct. 4, 1791, and had Gershom, 1816, Perez, 1818, d. 1821, Harriet, 1821, Otis, 1823, Hannah

B., 1825, Lydia, 1827, and Susan, 1832; *Samuel*, Mar. 6, 1786, m. Anne Sampson, da. of Tho., who was b. Sep. 4, 1789, and had Lucy T., Lydia A., and Samuel B.

11. Capt. Gamaliel, (s. of 7,) Dux., but removed to Boston. He m. Elizabeth Hinckley, and d. Mar. 7, 1824, æt. 60; had chd. — *Dr. Gamaliel*, Nov. 17, 1795, H. C. 1814, a physician, in 1833 chosen Superintendent of Mass. General Hospital, and d. Oct. 22, 1839, æt. 44, he m. Mar., 1821, Sophia, da. of Col. Nathan Rice. See a memoir in 3d Mass. Hist. Coll. IX. 75; chd. — *Sarah; Margaret; George Partridge*, H. C. 1825.

12. Hon. Alden, (s. of 7,) Boston, H. C. 1786; he studied theology and was ord. in the ministry at Pownalboro', Me., Nov. 14, 1793. He obtained some celebrity as a historian and biographer, and was the author of many useful and valuable works. He was afterwards appointed Secretary of the State of Massachusetts. He m. Margaret Stevenson, Sep. 24, 1795, who was a da. of Tho. and Isabel Stevenson. Chd. — *Margaret Boies*, May 28, 1796, m. Wm. H. Elliot; *William John Alden*, Nov. 19, 1797, H. C. 1816; *Lucy Ann*, Sep. 14, 1800, m. Henry Dwight; *Thomas Gamaliel*, Dec. 13, 1802, H. C. 1822; *Duncan*, Aug. 15, 1804, m. Eliza Jaques, June 11, 1841, grad. H. C. 1824; *Isabella Thomas*, Apr. 25, 1806; *Sarah*, Apr. 29, 1808; *John Robinson*, Sep. 1813, d. while in H. C., Oct. 24, 1828.

13. Capt. Daniel, (s. of 7,) Dux.; removed to Keene, N. H.; m. Sarah Drew; had *Emily; Sarah*, m. Amherst A. Frazar; *Wealthea*, m. in Illinois; *Daniel*, m. Mrs. Caroline Wadsworth Hunt; *Mary; Jerusha W.*, who d. Feb. 10, 1809, æt. 2 yrs.; and *Frances*, m. Thomas Frazar.

14. Capt. Gershom, (s. of 7,) Dux.; m. Sarah Hinckley, and d. Aug. 8. 1844; had *Maria W.*, 1804, m. Rev. Claudius Bradford of Bridgewater; *Lucia A.*, 1807; *Elizabeth H.*, 1809; and *Charlotte*, 1813.

Note. Widow *Wealthea*, d. Apr. 27, 1783, æt. 41; *David* of K., m. widow Betty Thomas, Feb. 16, 1779; *Perez*, m. Lucy Rand, 1782.

15. Eliphalet, (s. of —,) came to Dux. from Plymouth; m. Hannah Prince Aug. 8, 1751, she d. July 11, 1756, æt. 26; m. Hannah Oldham Feb. 9, 1758; had *Hannah*, May 31, 1752, m. Benjamin Freeman, 1774; *Lydia*, Jan. 28, 1754, m. Samuel Bradford, 1783; *Lucy*, Nov. 9, 1758, m. Zachariah Sylvester; *Abigail*, Dec. 26, 1759, m. Bisbee Chandler; *William*, Nov. 17, 1761, m. Lucy, da. of John Sampson, and had Mary, who m. James Soule; *Zadock*, Aug. 11, 1765, a sea-captain, m. Lucy Gray, and had Zadock 1798, d. 1833, m. a Peterson; Nancy, 1800; George, 1801; Lucy G., 1803; Caroline, 1805, m. Joshua Cushing; Charles, 1806, d. 1831;

Lewis E., 1809, and James, 1812; *Deborah*, Dec. 26, 1767, m. Capt. Freeman Loring; *Mary*, 1774; and *Eunice*, m. Uriah Wadsworth, 1789, and d. Aug. 1795.

BRETT.

WILLIAM, Dux., 1640, had land at Namasakeeset and at North hill, at Hounds ditch; sold his lands to C. Southworth, Wm. Pabodie, and John Rogers. He removed to Bridgew. and d. 1681; m. Margaret; had William, Elihu, Nathaniel, Alice, Lydia, and Hannah. See Mitchell's Bridgewater.

BREWSTER.

1. ELDER WILLIAM, b. 1560, grad. at Cambridge Coll. Eng.; afterwards the confidential friend of William Davison, Queen Elizabeth's ambassador to Scotland; then joining the Independent Chh., he entertained their meetings at his house; fled with them to Amsterdam and Leyden; was appointed their elder; sailed with the minority in 1620, and, arriving at Plymouth, " with the most submissive patience bore the novel and trying hardships to which his old age was subjected, lived abstemiously, and after having been in his youth the companion of ministers of state, the representative of his sovereign, familiar with the magnificence of courts, and the possessor of a fortune, sufficient not only for the comforts but for the elegancies of life, this humble puritan labored steadily with his own hands in the field for daily subsistence. Yet he possessed that happy electricity of mind, which could accommodate itself with cheerfulness to all circumstances, destitute of meat, of fish and bread, over his simple meal of clams, would he return thanks to the Lord, that he could suck of the abundance of the seas, and of treasures hid in the sand." — Ply. Chh. Rec. He enjoyed a healthy old age, and was sick but one day, when he died, April 16, 1644. His wife d. before 1627. He left a library of over 300 volumes (valued at £43), of which 64 were in the classic languages. His whole estate was £150.* He early removed to Dux., and settled in the

---

* Elder Brewster's estate occupied the south eastern part of the Nook, adjoining the farm of Capt. Standish. Some years ago, on a piece of land, which was originally included in the limits of his farm, was found a small silver spoon bearing the initials " J. B." Elder Brewster, it is said traditionally, planted here the first apple tree in New England. In the time of the Revolution the original tree was gone; but there had sprung up from its roots another, which was then of large size, and known as the " Brewster tree."

neighborhood of Capt. Standish, and his house was afterwards occupied by his son Love. At his death, his estate was divided among his two sons, who met after his funeral at Gov. Bradford's in Plymouth, and in the presence of the Governor, Mr. Prence, Mr. Winslow, and Capt. Standish, determined mutually on the division. Chd. — *Patience*, b. in Eng., arrived in 1623, m. Gov. Prence, 1624, and d. 1634; *Fear*, b. in Eng., arrived 1623, m. 1626 Mr. Isaac Allerton, and d. 1633; *Love*, b. in Eng. (2); *Wrestling*, b. in Eng., d. before his father; *Jonathan* (3).

2. LOVE, (s. of 1,) Ply.; ad. 1636; early removed to Dux. and settled with his father by the bay side, and afterwards sold the estate to Saml. Eaton. His servant, Thos. Graunger, was hung for a capital crime, 1642. His will is dated Oct. 1, 1650; his w. Sarah Collier, he m. March 15, 1634; she afterwards m. a [John?] Parks, (Col. Rec. VI. 1679); had *Nathaniel*, owned land about the old tarpits, and d. 1676; *William* (4); *Wrestling* (5); *Sarah*, m. Benjamin Bartlett, 1656.

3. JONATHAN (s. of 1). He came to Dux. a. 1632. He was frequently the town's deputy, and one of the principal men in the formation of its settlement, and in the establishment of its church; he sometimes practised before the Court as an attorney, and is also styled gentleman. He received grants of land in Dux., and likewise kept a ferry, (employing Peter Meacock in its management,) at New Harbor marshes, and was presented to the Court in 1639 for neglecting it, and in 1641 sold it. In 1638 he sold his house to Dr. Comfort Starr. He went to New London, Ct., and from that place, it seems by the following letter addressed to the widow of his brother Love, he contemplated a return to England.

"LOVEING AND KIND SISTER, I thanke you for youer letter I received, being glad to heare of youer well doeing in youer affliction of Widdowhood; the Lord will make up youer losses and healp you to bee thankfull for raiseing youer good brother to bee instead of an huband to you. In my judgement I would advise you to marry one whom you could love. I would to God I were nearer you, I should doe something for you; but I fear I shall the next year goe further from you, for I with my whole family resolve for old England, and then I shalbee able to doe very little for you and youers, whom I love and respect, being glad to hear of youer daughters improvement, both in Sperituall and temporall thinges; the Lord bestow his further blessing upon her and the rest of youers: I doe heer by this give unto her all my interest in the pcells of Land, which was left by my father, lying near Plymouth, to her and her heires for ever; I pray you remember my Love and Respects to the Capt. and his wife and children with the

rest of my frinds with you, to whom I cannot write; excuse me to them all; those with my best love Remembered to you and youers; I pray to the Lord to blesse you and keep you in all youer ways in his feare. Amen, and doe rest
Your unfeigned brother,
JONATHAN BREWSTER.
"MOHEKEN, this 1 of September, 1656."

He m. Lucretia, and had *William*, who was in the Indian wars in 1645; *Mary*, m. John Turner of Scit. Nov. 12, 1645; *Jonathan*, 1627; and *Benjamin*, who removed from Dux. after 1648, to Norwich, then to New London, where he m. Anna Dart 1659, and had Anna Sept. 1662, Jonathan 1664, Daniel 1667, William 1669, and Benjamin 1673.

4. DEA. WILLIAM, (s. of 2,) Dux.; d. Nov. 3, 1723, æt. nearly 78; m. Lydia Partridge, Jan. 2, 1672, she d. Feb. 2, 1742; had *Sarah*, April 25, 1674, m. Caleb Stetson 1705; *Nathaniel*, Nov. 8, 1676 (6); *Joseph*, March 17, 1694 (7); *William* (8); and, according to Mitchell, a *Benjamin*.

5. WRESTLING, (s. of 2,) Dux.; a carpenter; d. Jan. 1, 1697, leaving an estate of £330. "13 Decemb. 1689, the Town did engage to Wrestling Brewster, that if he in curtesy did take Nathaniell Cole into his house, they would secure him from being burthened with keeping of him said Cole."—Town Rec. He m. Mary, who is prob. the Mary who m. John Partridge 1700. He had *Jonathan*, m. Mary Partridge May 6, 1710, went to Windham, Ct. after 1725, she was alive 1733; *Wrestling* — prob. the one "of Plymouth," who m. July 12, 1722, Hannah Thomas — a deacon of K., had Wrestling 1724; d. at K. Feb. 8, 1810, æt. 86, Thomas, Isaac, Elisha, and Mary; *John* (9); *Mary*; *Sarah*; *Abigail*; *Elizabeth* and *Hannah*.

6. NATHANIEL, (s. of 4,) Dux.; m. Mary Dwelley of Scit. Dec. 24, 1705, who died July 29, 1764, æt. 80; had *Samuel* and *Mercy* (gemini) April 5, 1708; *Ruth*, Dec. 9, 1711, m. Joseph Morgan of Preston, Ct.; May 8, 1735; *William*, Feb. 14, 1715, m. Priscilla Sampson Cotte, Jan. 1, 1747, and had Daniel a. 1746, Nathaniel a. 1748, and Stephen a. 1750; *Joseph*, July 3, 1718 (10).

7 JOSEPH, (s. of 4,) Dux.; m. Elizabeth, who d. April 1786, æt. 82; he d. April 20, 1767; had *Lemuel*, bap. 1740; *Eunice*, m. Timothy Walker 1758; *Truelove*, 1737 — "January 18, 1757, Truelove Brewster fell through the ice, attempting to come over Oakman's ferry, and was drowned."—Chh. Rec.

8. WILLIAM, (s. of 4,) Dux., m. Hopestill Wadsworth, May 20, 1708; had *Olive*, July 16, 1708; *Ichabod*, Jan, 15, 1711, m. Lydia Brewster of Pembroke, June 3, 1735; *Elisha*, Oct.

29, 1715; *Seth,* Dec. 20, 1720; *Lot,* Mar. 25, 1724; *Huldah,* Feb. 20, 1726, m. John Goold* of Hull, June 13, 1745, she d. Apr. 27, 1750.

9. JOHN, (s. of 5,) Dux.; had *Joseph,* and *Job,* who served in the old French war.

10. JOSEPH, (s. of 6,) Dux., and Attleboro'; m. Jedidah, who d. Mar. 26, 1794, æt. 72; he d. Sep. 3, 1791, æt. 73; had *Zadock,* bap. 1742, had Cyrus, Dec. 7, 1772, m. Ruth Sampson, Apr. 5, 1798, and who had Zadock, Darius, and Sarah; *Mary,* m. Silas Freeman, 1763; *Joseph,* m. Deborah Hunt, Apr. 13, 1773; *Ruth; Nathaniel,* bap. 1755; *Truelove,* bap. 1760.

11. NATHAN, (s. of —,) b. 1723, Dux., m. Hannah, who d. June 4, 1776; he d. Nov. 1807, æt. 84; had *Anne,* bap. 1756.

12. JOSHUA, (s. of —,) Dux.; m. Lydia Weston, who d. Oct. 22, 1841; had *Daniel W.,* 1788; *Job E.,* 1791; *Mary B.,* 1793; *William N.,* 1796; *Betsy E.,* 1799; *Sarah C.,* 1801; *Warren W.; Priscilla; Harriet.*

13. JOSHUA, (s. of —,) Dux.; had *Deborah* 1787; *Rachel* 1790; *Selah* 1792; *Nathan* 1796; *Hannah* 1798; *Joshua* 1801; *Ruth,* 1803.

NOTE. *Joshua,* 1698, d. Mar. 27, 1776, æt. 78; *Rachel,* 1727, d. Apr. 26, 1757; *Deborah,* 1704, d. Sep. 1, 1769, æt. 65; *Mercy,* m. Edward Arnold, 1706; *Sarah,* m. Joseph Wright of Plympton; *Jane,* m. Asa Weston, 1777; *Elizabeth,* m. Saml. Walker, 1784; *Nathan,* m. Diadema Dawes, 1784; Joseph, drowned while returning from the Gurnet, 1807. — " Young Joseph Brewster " bore arms in Dux., 1643.

BRIGGS.

WALTER, Scit., 1651. See Deane's Hist.; in 1665, on the Col. recds. he is given as one of the constables of Dux. I doubt whether he ever lived in Dux., and think that the brace which joins his name with the constables of Dux., should not have included him, who belonged most probably to those of Scituate next written. He m. Mary, who was living 1658, m. 2d, Frances, who survived. Chd. — *John,* m. Deborah Hawke, prob. the da. of Matthew† of Hingham, and had

---

* His chd. were John, 1746, d. 1746; Huldah, 1747, m. Samuel Loring, 1783; Hopestill, 1748, d. 1749. The mother was buried in Duxbury. A Robert Goold of Hull, m. Judith ——, 1666. — *C. J. F. B. from Goold. Fam. Geneal.*

† Matthew Hawke came from Cambridge, Eng., and d. at Hingham, Dec. 7th, 1684, and his wife Margaret, died Mar. 18, 1684. His children were Elizabeth, bap. July 1639, d. Nov. 25, 1713; Sarah, bap. Aug. 1,

Hannah, 1684, m. Col. John Alden of Dux.; Deborah, 1685, and Capt. John; Lt. James; Cornelius; and Hannah, who m. Saml. Winslow.

NOTE. Elizabeth, m. Ebenezer Wormall, 1717. Clement, arrived 1621, of Weymouth, had Thomas, June 14, 1633; Jonathan, June 14, 1635; David, Aug. 23, 1640; Clement, Jan. 1, 1642, and others.

BROWN.

1. JOHN, ad. 1635; Dux.; had land at Is. ck., 1636; asst. and commissioner of the United Colonies; d. near Rehoboth. His wife Dorothy, d. Jan. 27, 1673, æt. 90. He had *James* of Swanzey, who m. Lydia Howland; and perhaps *Capt. John*, who m. Anne, and had Anne, 19 Sep., 1673, John, 1675.

2. PETER, came in the Mayflower, Dux., 1637, m. Martha, had Mary alive, 1627.

3. AMOS, (from Boston,) Dux.; m. Rhoda Winsor, Jan. 1, 1784; had *John*, Feb. 17, 1784, a merchant of Boston, perished on board the Lexington steamer in Long Is. Sound; m. Cornelia Little, and had John, Cornelia and Dephina; *Rhoda*, who was the second wife of Henry Gooding; *Betsy*, the first wife of Henry Gooding; *Nancy*, m. Charles Prior; *Charles; Adriana.*

NOTE. Hannah, d. at Dux., Oct. 10, 1763, æt. 17 — *Joseph* of Swanzey, m. Hannah Fitch, 1680, and had Joseph, and Hannah (gemini), 21 Nov., 1681. James, Jr. of Swanzey, had Margaret, 28 June, 1682. *Andia*, (Swanzey,) m. Hezekiah Willet, Jan. 7, 1675 — William of Plymouth, m. Mary Murdock, July 16, 1649, and had Mary, 14 May, 1650, George, Jan. 16, 1651, William, Apr. 1, 1654, Samuel, Mar. 1655–6. Priscilla, m. Wm. Allin at Sandwich, Mar. 21, 1649.

BRYANT.

1. STEPHEN, a planter, 1643 able to bear arms in Dux.; ad. 1654; 1650, bought 100 acres of meadow land North of Pine Point; m. Abigail, da. of John and Alice Shaw, and lived at Plymouth; had *John*, Apr. 7, 1650; *Mary*, 1654; *Stephen*,

1641, m. John Cushing, 1657, d. 1679, æt. 38; Bethiah, bap. Jan., 1644, m. Benj. Stetson, Aug. 15, 1665; Mary, bap. Aug. 1646, m. Benj. Loring, 1670, d. at Hull, 1714; James, bap. May 27, 1649, m Sarah Jacob, July 9, 1678; *Deborah*, bap. Mar. 22, 1652, vide text; Hannah, born July 22, 1655, m. Peter Cushing, and d. Apr. 4, 1737. An Elizabeth Hawke, m. Stephen Lincoln, Feb. 1660. — *Hobart's Journal.*

Feb. 2, 1657, m. Mehetable, both alive 1691 (a Stephen, styled "of ye Major's purchase," m. in Dux., Sarah Magoon, Nov. 23, 1710); Sarah, Nov. 28, 1659; *Lydia*, 23 Oct., 1662; *Elizabeth*, Oct. 17, 1665.

NOTE. *John*, m. Elizabeth Witherell, Dec. 22, 1651. *John*, m. Abigail Bryant, 23 Nov., 1665. Col. Rec. — *John* of Scit., m. Mary, (da. of Geo. Lewis of Barnstable,) Nov. 4, 1643, who d. July 2, 1655, and had John, 17 Aug., 1644, Hannah, 25 Jan., 1645, Sarah, 29 Sep., 1648, Mary, 24, Feb, 1649, d. 28 Apr., 1652, Martha, 26 Feb., 1651, Samuel, 6 Feb., 1653. Col. Rec.

2. JOSHUA, (s. of —,) Dux.; b. Oct. 8, 1781, m. Princess, who was b. May 29, 1778, and had a family.

BUMPUS.

The name was originally spelled Bompasse; but now Bumpus or Bump.

1. EDWARD, arrived at Plymouth, Nov. 10, 1621; of Dux. before 1634; bought land of Wm. Palmer, at Eagle Nest creek, built a house and "palisado" there, and sold it, 1634, to John Washburn; next of M., before 1640; and lived at Duck hill in 1684, within M. bounds. Chd. — *Edward; John*, had Mary 1671, John 1673, Samuel 1676, James 1678, and this family were of Middleboro' and Rochester; *Jacob* 1644, of Scit., m. widow Elizabeth Blackmore, 1677, and had Benj. 1678, Jacob 1680; and perhaps *Joseph*, who had Lydia, 2 Aug., 1669, Wybra, 15 May, 1672; and *Philip*, who was alive 1677; and *Thomas* of Barnstable, 1679, for whose chd., see N. E Hist. Geneal. Reg. II.

NOTE. Thomas, m. Rebecca Robinson at Boston, Dec. 19, 1711.

BURGESS.

1. THOMAS, Dux., 1637 lived near Wm. Basset; and 1638, sold his house and land to Nicholas Robbins, and next of Sandwich, when he m. Elizabeth Basset, 8 Nov., 1648.

2. JACOB, Dux., m. Sarah Glass, 1779, d. Jan. 12, 1827; had Patience 1780, James 1784, Jacob 1785, Charles 1788, Spencer 1791, Consider 1793, Sarah 1795, Alden 1799, Nathl. A. 1803.

NOTE. *Jacob*, m. Mary Hunt, Apr. 27, 1704; *Nathl.*, m. Ruth Chandler, Dec. 19, 1748; *Patience*, m. Malachi Delano, 1770; *Lucia*, m. Benj. Pierce, May 11, 1775; *William*, m. Lucy Sampson, 1783, and had Abner, 1785. Town Records — Francis, Boston, 1655. Roger, m. Sarah, and had Samuel, Nov. 17, 1660. Boston Records.

BURNE.

1. WILLIAM, Dux., 1638, when he was presented to the Court for disorderly living. A Richard Burne was of Lynn, and removed to Sandwich, 1637.

BURTON.

1. THOMAS, Dux., m. Alice Wadsworth, May 10, 1722, and removed to Pembroke a. 1753.

NOTE. *Stephen*, was of Swanzey, 1683, and of Bristol, 1690. Col. Rec.

BUTLER.

1. THOMAS, Dux., 1637; Sandwich, 1640; Dux. again 1657, when he took the oath of fidelity.

CARVER.

1. ROBERT. In 1638, had a grant of 20 acres at G. H. river; and a garden place at Stony bk. in Dux.; ad. 1644; and d. 1680, æt. 86; is called a "sawyer;" had *John*, m. Millicent Ford, and d. at M., 1679, æt. 42, had 8 chd. of whom John, removed from M., m. Mary Barnes, and had Dea. Josiah, who d. at Plymouth, 1751, æt. 63; *William*, d. at M., Oct. 2, 1760, æt. 102. A short time previous to his death, he with his son, grandson and great grandson, were all to work together in the field, and a great-great-grandson was in the house at the same time. — Belknap.

NOTE. A Robert was in Boston, 1668. Joshua d. at M., æt. 90.

2. JOHN, Dux., 1640, when a meadstead was granted him there. A Ruth m. Beriah Delano, 1772.

NOTE. *Gov. John*, arrived 1620; first governor of the Colony, a deacon of the chh. in Holland; came over with a family of eight persons, viz., himself and wife, John Howland and wife (who was Carver's da.), one or more chd., (one of whom, Jasper, d. Dec. 6, 1620), and perhaps Henry Sampson and Humility Cooper. See Belknap's Biography. He d. April, 1620, and his wife five or six weeks after.

CARY.

JOHN Carew (as the name is early spelled) came from Somersetshire, Eng., at the age of 25, and settled in Dux. about 1637, when he had a grant of ten acres; but removed to Bridgewater; m. Elizabeth, da. of Francis Godfrey, June, 1644; he d. Nov. 2; 1681; she d. 1680; had at Dux. *John,* 1645, *Francis* 1647, *Elizabeth* 1649, and at Braintree *James* 1652; and at Bridgew. eight others. See Hist. Bridgew.

CHAMBERLAIN.

1. NATHANIEL, Dux., owned land a. 1710 near James Bonney's. His name is written Chamberlane and Chamberland. Perhaps the one of Scit. who came prob. from Hull, and had Freedom 1697, Eunice 1698, and Joseph 1699.

NOTE. Nathaniel of Pem. had Abigail and Joanna.

CHANDLER.

The name is early spelled Chaundler, and later Chanler, but now Chandler.

1. EDMUND, of Dux. 1633, owned land near R. Hicks, which he sold, 1634, to John Rogers, and also land to Isaac Robinson. In 1636, he had granted to him "fourty acres of land lying on the east side of Moyses Symonson, where Morris formerly began to cleare for Mr. Bowman;" which was afterwards made void, and 60 other acres granted. He had an apprentice, John Edwards, in 1638. Of Scit. in 1650. He d. 1662, (will dated May 3, 1662,) leaving an estate of £38. He owned land at Barbadoes, which he gave to his das. *Sarah, Anna,* and *Mary.* He had another da. *Ruth;* and sons, *Benjamin* (2), *Samuel* (3), *Joseph* (4).

2. BENJAMIN, (s. of 1,) Scit.; m. Elizabeth, da. of Cornet John Buck; d. 1691, leaving an estate of £130; had *Benjamin* 1672, *Martha* 1673, *Samuel* 30th Nov. 1674, *John* 1675, *Mary* 1678.

3. SAMUEL, (s. of 1,) Dux.; had a grant, 1665, of 60 acres, "with condetion that he shall not sell it except to a townsman;" d. a. 1683, leaving an estate of £25.

4. JOSEPH, (s. of 1,) Dux.; perh. of Sandwich 1661; however of Duxbury in 1684; had *John* (5), *Joseph* (6), and perhaps *Edmund* of Dux. 1710, and *Benjamin* 1684, who d. March 26, 1771, æt. 87.

5. JOHN, (s. of 4,) Dux. "June 2, 1687. The town did give unto Joseph Chandler's son John, who by God's providence has lost his hand, 50 acres of land lying on the easterly side of the South river, and northerly side of the place called the Rockes, provided that his father shall have liberty to sell or otherwise improve said lands for the benefit of the aforesaid child." — Town Rec. He m. Sarah Weston (b. 1668), March 4, 1708, and she d. April 13, 1764, æt. 75½, and he d. April 7, 1759, æt. 82½.

6. JOSEPH, (s. of 4,) Dux., m. Martha Hunt, Feb. 12, 1701; had *Philip*, July 21, 1702 (9); *Mary*, Aug. 3, 1704; *Joshua*, July 7, 1706 (10); *Zachariah*, July 26, 1708; *Edmund*, April 9, 1710; *Ebenezer*, Sept. 8, 1712 (11); *Sarah*, Oct. 25, 1714, m. Moses Soule, 1729; *Martha*, Nov. 23, 1716, (m. Thomas Weston, 1767?); *Jonathan*, Feb. 18, 1718 (12); *Judah*, Aug. 13, 1720.

7. SAMUEL, (perhaps s. of 3,) Dux.; m. Margaret; had *Martha*, Sept. 22, 1719; *Abigail*, July 1, 1721, m. David Delano, 1740; *Samuel*, Oct. 3, 1723; *Thomas*, April 30, 1725 (8).

8. THOMAS, (s. of 7,) Dux.; m. Silvia Bisbee Aug. 24, 1749, m. 2d Rhoda Blackmore May 6, 1762; had *Thomas*; *Lt. Samuel*, m. Rebecca Johnson, who d. July 6, 1775, m. 2d Mary Johnson of K. March 18, 1779, and had Rebecca, m. Joshua Soule; Olive, m. Samuel Winsor, m. 2d Samuel Bryant; Mary, m. Clark Winsor; Lydia; Deborah, m. James Weston; Abigail m. (2d w.) James Weston; Samuel m. Nancy Winsor; and Sophia; *Bisbee*, June 1, 1755, m. Abigail Bradford, had Lucy, 1787, Bisbee 1789, Abigail 1790, Deborah 1794, Bradford 1799; by 2d w. *Luther*, 1766, d. 1775; *Stephen*, June 9, 1768, m. Mary, who was b. May 11, 1772; *Howard*, m. Peggy, who d. May 19, 1844, and he d. March 11, 1844, and had Luther 1794, Joseph 1795, Thomas 1797, Howard 1800, Seth D. 1803, and Jane 1809; *Aaron*, m. Silvia Delano, and was lost at sea, had Pelham July 22, 1795, and Nancy Aug. 17, 1799; *William*; *Abigail*, m. Thomas Phillips 1771; *Silvia*; *Jemima*; *Sarah*, and *Lydia* m. Zenas Delano 1789.

9. PHILIP, (s. of 6,) Dux.; m. Rebecca Phillips Dec. 16, 1725, who d. Jan. 1782, æt. 78; he d. Nov. 15, 1764, æt. 62; had *Nathan*, Oct. 28, 1726 (13); *Betty*, Oct. 21, 1728; *Perez*, July 10, 1730 (14); *Esther* and *Martha* (gemini) May 31, 1732; *Peleg*, April 27, 1735, removed to New Gloucester a. 1764; *Philip*, Oct. 24, 1738, m. Christianna, had Adah Jan. 13, 1765, m. Wm. Brewster, Molly March 6, 1767, m. Wadsworth Chandler, Charles m. Anna Peterson, George removed to Maine, Christian m. Sylvanus Prior, Mercy and Orisone; *Asa*, March 1, 1743, m. Martha Delano June 30, 1763, had Asa, Jesse Oct. 19, 1776, m. Abigail (who was b. Oct. 17,

1783), Peleg m. Mercy Darling 1791, m. 2d Clarissa, and d. Feb. 24, 1825 (and had Peggy Oct. 11, 1791, Levi April 7, 1794, Rebecca Jan. 16, 1799, Betsey July 16, 1802, Mercy, April 8, 1805, Peleg July 24, 1807, John July 24, 1807, Polly Soule, Sept. 5, 1810, Lydia D. Sept. 4, 1813, and by 2d w. Merrick Jan. 28, 1818, Edward Aug. 20, 1822, and Betsy D. April 2, 1825); *Mary*, Sept. 25, 1744; *Elijah*, Jan. 4, 1747.

10. JOSHUA, (s. of 6,) Dux.; m. Mary Waste Nov. 27, 1728; he d. May 1, 1782, æt. a. 76; she d. April 28, 1794; had *Joseph*, Sept. 27, 1729, served in the Canada Expedition, d. on the return, had Esther, Susanna and Joseph; *Ezekiel*, Sept. 4, 1733, m. Mary, and had Hannah Soule Oct. 20, 1764, d. 1780, Sarah Sept. 6, 1770, d. 1780, Charles June 9, 1771, Joshua 1758, Mary 1760, m. Oliver Delano 1783, Eunice 1775, d. 1780; *Sarah*, Oct. 9, 1735, m. Noah Allen Nov. 18, 1762.

11. EBENEZER, (s. of 6,) Dux.; had *Simeon*, 1744, d. April 17, 1767; *Judah*, d. April 24, 1772; *Nathaniel*, d. June 14, 1773; *Zilpha*; *Anna*; *Sceva*, m. Edith Sampson, who d. June 2, 1796.

12. JONATHAN, (s. of 6,) Dux.; m. Rebecca Packard Nov. 27, 1751; had *John*, d. young; *John*; *Nathaniel*, m. Ruth Fish of M. 1782; *Ichabod*; *Reuben*; *Avire*, and *Hannah*.

13. NATHAN, (s. of 9,) Dux.; m. Ruth, who d. Aug. 26, 1767, æt. 42, m. 2d Esther Glass Feb. 20, 1770; had *Ephraim*, *Lucy*, *Celah* May 21, 1754, d. May 21, 1773, *Hannah*, *Ruth*, *Deborah*, and by 2d w. *Joseph* and *Ira*.

14. PEREZ, (s. of 9,) Dux.; m. Rhoda Wadsworth, Dec. 11, 1755; had *Betty*, June 13, 1758, m. Joseph Darling, 1780; *Philip*, Apr. 12, 1761, lost at sea, m. Sally Loring; *Perez*, Dec. 28, 1764, m. Rebecca (Stetson?), who was b. Oct. 4, 1768, and d. March 19, 1800, m. 2d, Ruth, who was b. at Pembroke, Apr. 25, 1774, and had Stetson, Nov. 30, 1791, Harvy, Mar. 24, 1793, Rebecca, Nov. 21, 1794, Rhoda W., Mar. 25, 1798, Ruth, Mar. 6, 1800, Lydia, (by 2d w.) May 2, 1801, Nancy, May 23, 1802, Isaac, June 5, 1803, Benjamin, July 27, 1804, Perez, Aug. 7, 1805, Philip, Nov. 30, 1806, Ebenezer, Mar. 11, 1808, James, May 6, 1809, Judith, July 6, 1812, Sally, Feb. 23, 1814; *Dr. Seth*, Feb. 22, 1767, removed to Maine; *Wadsworth*, 1769, m. Molly Chandler, and had Elbridge, Wadsworth, and others; *Rhoda*, 1772, d. 1791; *Wealthea*, 1774; *Acenith*, 1778; *Daniel*, Nov. 15, 1778, m. Joanna, 1800, m. 2d, Alice, 1807.

15. NATHANIEL, (s. of —,) Dux.; d. in the expedition against the Spanish W. I., 1741; m. Zeruiah Sprague, Mar. 19, 1724, who d. Oct. 10, 1778, æt. 73; had seven das., of whom *Mercy*, m. Peleg Sprague, 1746, m. 2d, Phineas Sprague, m. 3d, Ichabod Simmons.

16. CAPT. JOHN, (s. of —,) b. 1696, of Dux., d. Apr. 21, 1764, æt. 67½, had *John*, 1721, d. June 23, 1780, m. Sarah Weston, Nov. 4, 1743, who d. Feb. 10, 1773, æt. a. 51, and had Rebecca, Candice, Elizabeth, m. John Oldham, 1779, and Abel m. Sarah Weston, 1783.

17. ROGER, ad. 1637, of Dux., at one time, d. before 1665, when mention is made in Col. Rec. of his "three daughters." Probably *Roger* was a son, of Concord 1658, m. Mary Simmons 1671, d. 1717, she d. 1728. See Hist. Concord.

18. NATHANIEL, of Dux. 1643, able to bear arms.

NOTE. *Lydia*, m. Richard Higgins, Nov. 27, 1634. Col. Rec. *Esther*, m. John Glass, 1705; *Mary*, m. Ambrose Dawes, 1714: *Joseph*, 3d m. Elizabeth Delano, Sep. 8, 1720; *Elizabeth*, m. Pelatiah West, 1722; *Keturah*, m. Nathl. Sampson, 1703; *Ruth*, m. Nathl. Burgess, 1748; *Ruby*, m. Wm. Weston, 1760; *Lydia*, m. Abraham Evesor, Jan. 11, 1763; *Elizabeth*, 1736, d. Nov. 22, 1766, æt. 30. — Town Rec. — *Thomas*, of M. was father of Captains James and Henry (who m. Susanna Delano, 1790,) of Duxbury.

CHAPMAN.

1. RALPH, Dux. 1640; was a ship carpenter by trade, and latterly lived in M. He d. a. 1671. He m. Lydia Wills, Nov. 23, 1642. Chd. — *Lydia*, d. Nov. 26, 1649; *Ralph*, 20 June, d. 29 July, 1653; *Mary*, last of Oct. 1643, m. William Troop of Barnstable, 14 May, 1666; *Sarah*, 15 May, 1645, m. William Norcut; *Isaac*, 4 Aug., 1647 (2); *Ralph*, whose son was John (3).

2. ISAAC, (s. of 1,) Barnstable, m. Rebecca Leonard, 2d Sep., 1678. Chd. — *Lezaia*, 15 Dec., 1679; *John*, 12 May, 1681; *Hannah*, 26 Dec., 1682, d. 6 July, 1689; *James*, 5 Aug., 1685; *Abigail*, 11 July, 1687; *Hannah*, 10 April, 1690; *Isaac*, 29 Dec., 1692; *Ralph*, 19 Jan., 1695; *Rebecca*, 20 June, 1697. — N. E. H. & G. Reg. III. 84.

3. JOHN, (s. of Ralph, s. of 1,) M., removed to Newport, Rhode Island, returned and at Pembroke, "deceased 3d day of the 1st mo., 1811, and from the most accurate accounts which can be had in the matter, was one hundred and four years, two months and some days old." He retained to a remarkable degree his health and vigor to the last. About two years previous to his death, he rode on horseback a distance of nine miles to visit his great grand daughter, that he might hold on his knees her two children, his descendants in the fifth generation. Going into the yard he split a log of wood, mounted without assistance, and returned home. He m. Sarah, da. of Abraham and Abigail Booth, June, 1730.

Chd. — *Abigail*, m. Ignatius Sherman, d. Dec. 1, 1821, æt. 88; *Abraham*; *Ralph*, m. Prudence Coleman, and his da. Prudence, m. Saml. Loring of Dux.; *Deliverance*, June 4, 1736, m. Wing Rogers, 1764, d. 1766; *Sarah*, Sep. 5, 1738, m. John Rogers, 1759; *John*, Apr. 5, 1741; *Mary*, Jan. 2, 1743, m. Joseph Rogers, 1786; *William*, Nov. 6, 1745. — *Miss Thomas' Communication*.

NOTE. *John*, ad. 1634; *Jacob*, Boston, 1642; *Richard*, Braintree, m. Mary, and was kld. by the Indians, and had Susan 1647, Hope 1654, Mary 1659, and Richard 1662. *Dea. Samuel*, Westfield, 1660; *Robert* of Conn. — *Farmer & Boston Rec.* "1639, Nov., Old Chapman died." *Hobart's Journal*.

CHURCH.

1. RICHARD, b. 1608, arrived 1630, admitted a freeman, Oct. 4, 1632, (see p. 66), m. Elizabeth, da. of Richard Warren, a. 1636, who d. at Hingham, Mar. 4, 1670. He was a sergeant in the Pequod war. He had chd. — *Elizabeth*, m. Caleb Hobart at Hingham, Jan. 20, 1657, and d. 1659; *Benjamin*, b. at Plymouth, 1639 (2); *Richard*, d. young; *Nathaniel*, Hingham and Little Compton, m. Sarah Barstow, and d. before 1700. — See Hist. Bridgewater; *Joseph*, see idem; *Caleb*, see idem; *Abigail*, b. June 22, 1747, m. Samuel Thaxter, 1666, and d. Dec., 1667; *Deborah*, Jan. 27, 1657, m. John Irish, Jr.

2. COL. BENJAMIN, the distinguished hero of the Indian wars, having served with honor in the war with Philip, was commissioned by the Governors of Plymouth, Massachusetts and Maine, in Sep., 1689, to be commander of the forces to be sent against the Indians at the eastward, and here engaged in five campaigns, and finally returned home to his farm at Little Compton in 1705, where he died in 1718, as appears from his grave stone, which is inscribed as follows —

Here lyeth Interred the Body
of the Honourable
COL. BENJAMIN CHURCH, ESQ.,
who Departed this life January
the 17th, 1717–8, in ye 78 year of
his Age.

See page 106. He m. Alice Southworth, Dec. 26, 1667, and she d. Mar. 5, 1718–9, in her 73d year. Their chd. were *Thomas*, 1674 (3); *Constant*, May 12, 1676, a captain under his father; *Benjamin*, d. a bachelor; *Edward*, a captain under his father, was father of Dea. Benjamin of Hollis street church in Boston, who was the father of Dr. Benjamin, the traitor of the Revolution, who married in England, and has posterity in this country; *Charles* had a numerous issue; *Elizabeth*, Mar. 26, 1684, m. Mr. Rothbotham; and *Nathaniel*, July 1, 1686, and d. Feb. 29, 1687.

It may here be mentioned that the house of Col. Church at Bristol, was standing a year or two since, if not now, and then bore visible proof of its age.

3. Thomas, (s. of 2,) Little Compton, m. 1st, Sarah Hayman, Feb. 21, 1698, m. 2d, Editha Woodman, da. of John and Hannah, Apr. 16, 1712. She was born Sep. 7, 1685, and d. June 3, 1718; m. 3d, Sarah ———, who d. Apr. 22, 1768, æt. 73 years. He d. Mar. 12, 1746, æt. 72; he had chd., by 1st wife — *Sarah*, Jan. 15, 1700, d. Aug. 29, 1701; by 2d w. —*Elizabeth*, Jan. 10, 1713; *Hannah*, Sep. 23, 1714; *Priscilla*, Jan. 16, 1717, d. Mar. 15, 1744; *Thomas*, d. young; and perhaps *Sarah*; by 3d wife— *Thomas*, d. young; *Sarah*, May 15, 1721, m. Saml. Bailey, Apr. 29, 1742; *Thomas*, d. young; *Benjamin*, d. young; *Mary*, Jan. 2, 1725, m. Aaron Wilbor, Mar. 31, 1748; *Hon. Thomas*, Sep. 1, 1727, m. Ruth Bailey, Jan. 31, 1748, she was da. of Wm. and Dorothy, and was b. Aug. 3, 1727, and d. Jan. 31, 1771; he m. 2d, Mary, da. of Wm. and Anne Richmond, Sep. 10, 1772, who was b. Dec. 26, 1735. His chd. were 17 in number, and his da. Mercy, b. Mar. 3, 1756, m. Dea. Sylvester Brownell, and d. Mar. 31, 1837, and they were parents of Bishop Brownell of Conn.; *Benjamin*, d. æt. 17; *Mercy*, Sep. 18, 1734, m. Perez Richmond, Feb. 3, 1754.

Note. Hannah Church, bap. Aug. 8, 1647. Charles, killed by the overturning of his cart, Oct. 30, 1659. Mary, died at Duxbury, Apr. 30, 1662. — *Hobart's Journal.*

CLARK.

1. Thurston, Plymouth 1634, Dux. afterwards. He came to his death on the night of Dec. 6, 1661, by exposure to the cold, while returning from Plymouth. Estate £97 12s. 6d. He m. Faith. Chd. *Thurston* and *Harry*. From some cause these two were unable to take care of themselves, and the town was ordered, 1682, to do it; in 1690, as, say the records, "by reason of their age, indiscretion and weakness of understanding," they cannot provide for themselves, the Court appointed certain individuals to have the management of their estates, which were sufficient for them; *Faith*, m. Edward Dotey, who had Edward (d. a. 1690), John, Isaac, 8 Feb., 1647, Joseph, 30 Apr., 1651.

2. Thomas, supposed mate of the Mayflower, arrived 1623, m. Susanna, da. of widow Mary Ring, before 1631, and d. Mar. 24, 1697, æt. 97. He m. 2d prob., widow Alice Nichols

of Boston, 1664, da. of Richard Hallet. Chd.—*William* (3); *James*, m. Abigail Lathrop, Oct. 7, 1657; *Nathaniel*, the secretary; *Andrew*; *Susanna*, m. Barnabas Lathrop, 13 Nov., 1658.

3. WILLIAM, (s. of 2,) Dux., 1643; prob. of Bridgewater 1645; will dated Jan. 3, 1687, d. same year. He m. Martha Nash. He bequeathed to her his land and orchard; to his "pretending relation," Wm. Clark of Plymouth, 18*d*; to Wm. Conney, whom he brought up, his house. His estate £50, as per inventory May 9, 1687.

4. JOHN, (gd. s. of Thomas 2,) Barnstable, m. Mary Benjamin, 16 Aug, 1695; d. at Plymouth, 1712. Chd. *John*, 16 Nov. 1697; *Joseph*, father of Isaac, who went to Hardwich; *James*.

5. ELIAS, Dux. Chd. *Melinda*; *Silvia*; *James*; *Mary*; *Barnabas*; *Elbridge G.*; *John S.*, born from 1794 to 1815.

NOTE. *George*, m. Alice Martin, 22 Jan., 1638. Col. Rec.—*Abigail*, m. Dr. Harlow, Sep. 11, 1745.—*Sarah*, m. John Southworth of M., 9 Nov., 1748.

COE.

1. JOHN COE, Dux., m. Sarah Pabodie, Nov. 10, 1681. Chd. *Lydia*, Feb. 26, 1682; *Sarah*, Feb. 25, 1685.

NOTE. *Matthew*, Portsmouth, 1640; *Robert*, ad. 1634, Conn., removed to Long Island.

COLE.

1 JOB, Dux., removed to Eastham, ad. 1639; m. Rebecca Collier, May 15, 1634. Chd. *John* (2); *Job* (3); *Rebecca*; *Daniel* (4).

2. JOHN (s. of 1). His will mentions "Master Collyer's men," Edward, Joseph, Arthur, Ralph and John. Perhaps the Lt. John Cole, who died at Eastham, 1667, whose son John, m. Ruth Snow, 10 Dec., 1666, and had Ruth and John and six others.

3. JOB (s. of 1). Chd. *Rebecca*, 26 Aug., 1654; *Daniel*.

4. DANIEL (s. of 1). Town Clerk of Eastham. Chd. *Israel*, 8 Jan. 1653; *Mary*, 10 Mar., 1658.

5. JAMES, Plymouth, innkeeper, 1638. His children were *James*, m. Mary Tilson, 23 Dec., 1652, and had Mary, 3 Dec., 1653, who m. John Lathrop, 3 Jan., 1671.

6. HUGH. Plymouth, removed to Swanzey, m. Mary Foxwell, Jan. 8, 1654, and had chd. *James*, Nov. 8, (3) 1655;

Hugh, March 15, (8) 1658; *John*, May 16, (15) 1660; *Martha*, Apr. 14, (16) 1662; *Anna*, Oct. 14, 1664; *Ruth*, Jan. 17, (8) 1666; *Joseph*, May 15, 1668.

NOTE. The days of the month are recorded differently in two separate places as above.

7. NATHANIEL, Dux., 1679, had 26 acres granted him east of S. R.; m. Sarah ———, and was alive in 1710. Chd. *Rebecca*, Sep. 21, 1680; *Mary*, Nov. 13, 1682; *Nathaniel*, Oct. 11, 1685, m. Abigail West, Aug. 4, 1714; *Ephraim*, June 14, 1688 (8).

8. EPHRAIM, (s. of 7,) Dux., removed to North Yarmouth, 1753; m. Susanna Waste, March 2, 1724, and had chd. *Job*, Mar. 20, 1725; *Noah*, Mar. 26, 1727; *Rebecca*, Nov. 28, 1729; *Ebenezer*, Oct. 28, 1732; *Ruth*, May 5, 1735; *Eunice*, Feb. 12, 1740.

9. JABEZ, m. Grace Keen, Aug. 23, 1744, had *West*, 1745, and removed to Pembroke about 1750.

NOTE. *John* Cole m. Elizabeth Ryder, 21 Nov., 1667. Col. Rec.— *Sarah*, m. John Delano, July 2, 1718; *Samuel*, d. at Dux., 1756, Dec. 4, æt. 59; *James*, Scituate, 1653, had perhaps Ambrose, also of Scituate. Hist. Scituate; *George*, Lynn, removed to Sandwich, and d. 1653; *Samuel*, Boston, arrived 1630, kept a house of entertainment, a confectioner or comfit maker, m. Margaret Greene, d. 1667, had a da. Mary, who m. Edmund Jackson, cordwainer; *Isaac*, Charlestown 1640, d. June 10, 1674, had Abraham, 1636, and Jacob, 1641; *Richard*, Hampton, 1643. *Suffolk Deeds*.

COLLIER.

1. MR. WILLIAM, Dux., vide *first settlers*. He d. a. 1671; m. Jane ——— (?); chd. *Surah*, m. Love Brewster, May 15, 1634, m. 2d, ——— Parks, and d. 1650; *Elizabeth*, m. C. Southworth, Nov. 2, 1637; *Rebecca*, m. Job Cole, May 15, 1634; *Mary*, became the 2d w. of Gov. Prence, Apr. 1, 1635.

COOPER.

1. JOHN. Dux., 1666. Vide chh. history.

CORVANNEL.

1. WILLIAM, Dux., yeoman, 1637, fined for breaking into Robert Paddock's house (1638) and taking from a chest 13s. 8d.

CULLIFER.

Name also spelled GULLIVER. *Henry*, m. Mary Trasie, Jan. 27, 1712; *Charity*, m. Seth Bartlett, Feb. 27, 1736; *Thomas*, m. Keturah Sampson, Oct. 26, 1743, and d. at the eastward, Sep. 8, 1762, æt. 42 years; *John*, m. Betty Delano, Aug. 31, 1769; *Peleg*, m. Ruby Sampson, Dec. 15, 1774, had two sons, one Peleg m. a da. of Jephthah Delano, and the other removed to Maine; *John Cullifer*, a mariner, was in Boston 1656.

CURTIS.

Elisha m. Amy West, May 17, 1705; *David*, of Hanover, m. Bethiah Sprague, Dec. 14, 1732; *Sylvanus*, of Plymouth, m. Dorothy Delano, Nov. 26, 1734, had Hannah 1739 and Sylvanus, b. at Dux., who served in Capt. Sturtevant's company in 1755, and d. in the West Indies 1766, æt. 26; *Simeon*, of Scituate, m. Acenith Sprague April 20, 1742; *Elijah*, m. Abigail Soule 1756, and had Zynthia Bartlett and Capt. Elijah; *Hannah* m. Zebdiel Weston Feb. 22, 1769; *Jesse*, m. Hannah Phillips July 28, 1774.

CUSHING.

Joshua, Dux. 1711. *Joshua* m. Mary Freeman, Sept. 27, 1763, and had children — Nathaniel, Joshua, and Benjamin — *Joshua* (s. of Josh. and Mary) m. Joanna Prior and had chd.; Joshua m. Caroline Bradford (and had Joshua, George, and Thomas B.); Joanna m. Capt. M. Waterman; Nancy; Sally m. George Peterson, m. 2d Mr. Atkins of Provincetown; Jane m. Peleg Cook of Dux.; and Mary. — *Jairus*, d. at sea, æt. 26, Jan. 1765; *Mary*, d. July 4, 1769, æt. 25; *Bethiah*, m. Benjamin Peterson 1758; *Nathaniel*, and Jemima Ford, both of M., m. April 16, 1747; *Lydia*, m. Isaac Simmons Oct. 24, 1732.

CUSHMAN.

1. JOSHUA (perhaps s. of Thomas of Dux. in 1701,) had chd. *Joseph* (2); *Joshua* (3); *Mary*, m. Joshua Soule, Jr. Feb. 14, 1765; *Ezra; Paul; Apollos*, bap. 1744; *Cephas*, 1746; *Soule*, 1748.

2. JOSEPH, (s. of 1,) Dux., m. Elizabeth ———, had chd. *George*, Jan. 5, 1759; *Hannah*, Nov. 8, 1761; *David*, 1767,

d. young; *David; Joseph Soule; Abigail; Lydia Soule; Sarah; Elizabeth.*

3. JOSHUA, (s. of 1,) Dux., m. Mercy Wadsworth Nov. 17, 1763. Chd. *Joshua,* Aug. 14, 1764, d. Nov. 12, 1776; *John Wadsworth,* Aug. 29, 1766, lost at sea; *Mary,* Aug. 15, 1768; *Capt. Ezra,* Oct. 24, 1770, m. Sarah Bradford, and had Julius Bradford, Sept. 1801, d. Nov. 8, 1804, Sarah, who m. William Bradford; *Mercy,* March 25, 1774, m. Mr. Owen of Portland; *Charlemagne,* June 30, 1776, m. Miss Owen of Portland, where he settled.

4. GEORGE, (s. of 2,) lived at Powder point, had chd. *Anna,* 1788; *George,* 1791, m. Saba Ripley; *Abigail,* 1793, m. Dura Wadsworth; *Hannah; Betsy,* 1798; *Joseph,* 1800; *Briggs,* 1807.

5. DAVID, (s. of 2,) Dux., had chd. *Capt. David,* m. Mary Alden, widow of Daniel Sampson; *Elisha.*

NOTE. *Allerton* of Plympton m. Alethea Soule, Jan. 30, 1735; *Marcia* of Plymouth m. John Barker, Dec. 10, 1732; *Joshua* of Lebanon, Conn., m. Mary Soule, Jan. 2, 1733.

Widow Mary *Casement* d. Aug. 25, 1735, "about ye middle of ye forenoon."

Job *Crooker's* wife, Elizabeth, d. 1789.

DAMMON.

Israel m. Zeruiah Wattles, March 8, 1769, had Mason and Irene; *Thomas* had Ezekiel, who d. 1778, æt. 6 years; *Gamaliel* m. Huldah Delano, 1780, who d. Dec. 18, 1781; *Samuel,* d. Dec. 1795.

DARLING.

SAMUEL, (s. of Samuel, who d. May 31, 1790, æt. 55,) Dux., m. Priscilla ——. Chd. *Lydia* 1774; *Mary; Mercy C.,* d. June 1, 1792; *Hannah* 1784; *Betsey* 1786; *Samuel* 1789; *Abigail* 1791; *John* 1793; *Joseph* 1796; *Weston* 1798; *Peter* 1801.

NOTE. *Joseph* m. Betty Chandler, 1780 — *John,* Braintree, 1660-90.

DAVIS.

Dolor, Dux. 1640, had land N. W. of North hill; and same year 50 acres at Namasakeeset. Removed to Barnstable.

DAVY.

John, (planter,) owned 100 acres north of Pine point, which he sold 1650. There was a *John*, ad. 1637, Mass. Colony; *George*, Wiscasset, 1666; *Daniel*, Kittery, 1652; *Humphrey*, ad. 1665, Boston, asst., merchant.

DAWES.

1. Ambrose, Dux., m. 1st Mehitable ———; m. 2d Mary Chandler, July 8, 1714. She d. Feb. 1, 1768, æt. 89. Chd. *Priscilla*, Sep. 13, 1712; *Ebenezer* (2) and *Thankful* (twins) April 16, 1715; *Gideon*, Sep. 26, 1718.

2. Ebenezer, (s. of 1,) Dux.; m. Mary ———, and had chd. *Ambrose*, July 21, 1740, m. Deborah, had Nancy April 22, 1764; Huldah Jan. 18, 1766; Rispah June 23, 1767; Reuel April 22, 1769; *Diana*, Oct. 30, 1741; *Gideon*, Feb. 7, 1743, m. Sarah Phillips Dec. 26, 1771, d. in the camp at Roxbury, March 26, 1776; *Thomas*, m. Rebecca Phillips July 31, 1771; *Ebenezer*, 1750, m. Priscilla, d. at Kingston May 2, 1822, æt. 72, and she d. Dec. 13, 1838, æt. 86 years. Their son Abraham m. Deborah, and is the father of Capt. Allen, Capt. Josephus, James H., and Harriet; *Reuel*, 1744, d. at sea Nov. 18, 1767, æt. 23 years.

Note. *William*, bricklayer, Boston, ad. 1646, d. 24 March, 1703, æt. 86, had Ambrose, at Braintree, July 25, 1642, William, at Boston, 1655, and Robert 1656. *Diadema* m. Nathan Brewster 1784.

DELANO.

1. Philip, (vide *first settlers*,) b. 1602; ad. Jan. 1, 1632; m. Dec. 19, 1634, Hester Dewesbury; m. 2d Mary, widow of James Glass, in 1657; d. a. 1681, æt. 79 years, leaving an estate of £50. They had chd. *Philip* (2); *Thomas* (3); *John* (4); *Jane; Rebecca; Samuel* (5); *Mary*, m. Jonathan Dunham 29 Nov. 1655; she d. and he m. Mary Cobb 16 Oct. 1657; *Jonathan* (6); *Hester*.

2. Philip, (s. of 1,) Dux. Chd. *Philip* 1678 (7).

3. Thomas, (s. of 1,) Dux., m. Mary, da. of John Alden, before 1667; m. 2d, widow Hannah Bartlett, Oct. 24, 1699; had *Thomas*, who lived in the southeast part of the town.

4. John, (s. of 1,) Dux., was alive 1690. Lived on the north side of the path, which led from the Mill to South river.

5. SAMUEL, (s. of 1,) Dux., m. Elizabeth, da. of Alexander Standish. In 1686, he was allowed to settle on land north of G. H. bk.

6. JONATHAN (s. of 1,) removed to Dartmouth, where he was selectman and lieutenant. Had *Jabez*, who m. Mercy Delano of Dux. Feb. 8, 1710.

7. PHILIP, (s. of 2,) Dux., a prominent member of the Chh.; m. Elizabeth ——, who d. Nov. 7, 1756, æt. 75. He d. May 24, 1761, æt. 83¼. Chd. *Mary*, Oct. 27, 1717, m. John Hanks Jan. 16, 1735; *Elizabeth*, Nov. 12, 1719; *Malachi*, Sept. 20, 1721; *Judah*, Aug. 16, 1724 (8); *Abigail*, Sept. 30, 1725, m. Abisha Soule May 14, 1741.

8. JUDAH, (s. of 7,) Dux., m. Lydia ——. He d. May 1816, æt. 92. Chd. *Alpheus*, bap. 1744, m. Margaret Sides, 1770, had Nathan 1771; *Saluma*, bap. 1746; *Malachi*, bap. 1748, m. Patience Burgess 1770, who d. 1776, m. 2d Sybil Delano, 1778, and had Jabez 1772, Asa 1773, Nathaniel 1774, and Nathan; *Judah*, bap. 1752; *Noami; Jephthah*, Oct. 29, 1754, m. Rebecca, who was b. Oct. 25, 1764. He d. Dec. 23, 1843, and had Salomi 1785; Martha 1786, Abigail 1787, Joanna S. 1789, d. 1792, Asa C. 1791, d. 1792, Joanna S. 1796, Asa C. 1799, Rebecca M. 1801, Henry S. 1803, Jephthah 1806; *Priscilla*, bap. 1756; *Philip*, bap. 1761, m. Mary Fuller 1783; *Tirzah*, bap. 1765; *Eunice*, bap. 1768.

9. JONATHAN, (s. of —,) Dux. He was b. 1676, m. Hannah Doten Jan. 12, 1699. He d. Jan. 6, 1765, æt. 89. She d. April 12, 1764, aged 87⅔ years. Chd. *John*, Oct. 11, 1699, m. Sarah Cole July 2, 1718. The widow Sarah d. Feb. 19, 1764, æt. 70; *Jonathan*, Nov. 3, 1701; *Nathan*, Oct. 26, 1703; *Amasa*, Nov. 15, 1705, d. May 14, 1706; *Ruth*, May 25, 1707; *Amasiah*, Aug. 7, 1709 (10); *Hannah*. Dec. 28, 1711; *Dorothy*, April 3, 1714, d. Dec. 10, 1714; *Dorothy*, Oct. 14, 1715, m. Sylvanus Curtis of Plymouth, Nov. 26, 1734; *Ebenezer*, March 29, 1717 (11); *David*, June 3, 1720, m. Abigail Chandler May 28, 1740, and d. in the army at the westward, of small pox, 1760.

10. AMASIAH, (s. of 9,) Dux.; m. Ruth Sampson Jan. 8, 1730. He d. Aug. 5, 1790. Chd. *Zenas*, 1741, killed by the Indians at the westward 1760; *Cornelius*, 1742, m. Sarah Peterson June 24, 1762, who d. 1816. Their chd. were George, Zenas m. Lydia Chandler 1789, and Sylvia, who m. Aaron Chandler; *Jemima*, 1745, m. Benja. Gooding, of Pembroke, Oct. 11, 1764; *Thomas*, 1748, m. Azaba Wormall Dec. 23, 1762; *Silvia*, 1750; *Ezekiel; Hannah; Ruth*, 1753; *Barzilla*, 1756, m. Elizabeth Delano 1779.

11. EBENEZER, (s. of 9,) Dux., familiarly styled "old king Eben," m. Lydia Wormall May 16, 1745, she d. Sept. 4, 1756;

m. 2d Deborah Delano Dec. 29, 1757; he d. March 23, 1794. Chd. *Nathaniel*, m. Deborah Sprague March 3, 1774, had Nathaniel, the father of Nathaniel, Alden, Luther, John, and others; *Luther* m. Irene Sampson Jan. 20, 1774; *Bernice* m. John Glass May 30, 1773.

12. EBENEZER, (s. of —,) Dux., m. Martha Simmons, Dec. 29, 1699. She afterwards m. Samuel West, June 20, 1709. Chd. *Joshua*, Oct. 30, 1700 (13); *Thankful*, June 8, 1702; *Abia*, Aug. 17, 1704, m. Nathaniel Bartlett, Dec. 16, 1725.

13. JOSHUA, (s. of 12,) Dux., m. Hopestill Peterson. Chd. *Lydia*, July 12, 1723; *Rhoda*, Feb. 28, 1731, m. Samuel Winsor, Feb. 18, 1746; *Silvia*, Jan. 22, 1733; *Hopestill*, (son,) June 19, 1735; *Beza*, (da.) Nov. 24, 1737; *Martha*, Sep. 21, 1739, m. Asa Chandler, June 30, 1763; *Wealthea*, Dec. 7, 1741; *Joshua*, Sep. 30, 1744; *Thankful*, d. Jan. 13, 1749.

14. SAMUEL, (s. of —,) Dux., m. Elizabeth Boney of Pembroke, May 1, 1719; she d. Mar. 17, 1777. Chd. *Ruth*, Feb. 25, 1720; *Elisha*, May 25, 1722; *Prince*, Apr. 26, 1725; *Ichabod*, Apr. 28, 1728, m. Huldah, and d. May 8, 1778, had a son Samuel, who d. 1778, æt. 18 years. Huldah Delano m. Gaml. Dammon, 1780; *Betty*, June 30, 1730, m. Ephraim Waterman, "late of Kingston, now resident in Dux.," June 4, 1746; *Abigail*, Nov. 12, 1734.

15. BERIAH, (s. of —,) Dux., m. Naomi, and had chd. *Ichabod*, June 7, 1735, m. Huldah Sampson, Feb. 15, 1759; *William*, May 31, 1737; *Sylvanus*, June 15, 1739, m. 1st, Azuba, who d. Jan. 17, 1764, æt. 21½ years, m. 2d, Huldah Woodcock, Dec. 3, 1764; *Lemuel*, Sep. 24, 1741, m. Rachel Gurnet of Abington, Nov. 11, 1768, and removed to Hanover; *Elizabeth*, May 28, 1743. (Betty Delano m. John Cullifer 1769); *Benjamin*, 1745.

16. BENJAMIN, (s. of —,) Pembroke, removed to Scituate 1770, a ship builder for 40 years; m. Mary, da. of Wm. Brooks 1774, had chd. *William*, 1775, d. 1814, m. Sarah Hart, had 3 sons and 4 das.; *Mary*, 1776, m. widower Rev. Elijah Leonard of M.; *Sarah*, 1782, m. Samuel Foster.

17. BERIAH, (s. of —,) Dux., m. Ruth Carver, Apr. 11, 1772, had *Ichabod*, June 7, 1773; and *Beriah*, June 25, 1775.

18. REUBEN, (s. of —,) Dux.; m. Deborah ———. He d. 1797. Their chd. *Elizabeth*, Sep. 10, 1755, m. Barzilla Delano, 1779; *Rebecca*, Sep. 25, 1727; *Reuben*, June 26, 1761, m. Luna ———, who was born Feb. 18, 1766, and had Elijah 1792, Anna 1795, Cynthia 1797, and Celia 1802; *Deborah*, July 25, 1765, m. Peter Winsor, Oct. 1783; *Sarah*, Feb. 18, 1771; *Beri*, Oct. 9, 1772.

19. LEMUEL, (b. 1712; s. of —,) Dux.; m. Lydia Bartlett, July 9, 1741, and d. Sep. 6, 1778, æt. 66, nearly. Chd. *Esther*, m. Ezra Howard, Dec. 17, 1772; *Lydia*, never m.; *Rebecca*, m. Joseph Peterson, Apr. 21, 1773; *Jerusha ; Ichabod* removed to Maine; *Hannah*, m. Joshua Winslow, Dec. 3, 1772; *Mary*, unm.

20. ICHABOD, (s. of —,) Dux., m. Lydia. and had chd. *Huldah*, Sep. 17, 1788; *Betsy*, Mar. 23, 1790; *Lydia*, Nov. 3, 1791; *Rebecca*, June 9, 1793; *Olive*, July 2, 1795; *Sophia*, Aug. 7, 1797; *Samuel*, Oct. 22, 1798; *Nancy*, May 16, 1800; *Mary*, June 3, 1801.

21. CAPT. SAMUEL, (s. of —,) Dux., b. 1739, d. Nov. 6, 1814, æt. 75; m. Abigail Drew, Apr. 5, 1762; she d. Sep. 25, 1811, æt. 69, nearly. Their chd. were *Capt. Amasa* Delano, Feb. 21, 1763; *Samuel*, m. Lucy Winsor, and had Franklin, Olive T., Alexander, Lucy W., Samuel, Almira, Henry T., Benj. F., Nancy and Winslow; *William*, m. Fanny Sampson, and was lost at sea, and two sons with him; *Alexander*, 1780; *Irene*, May 6, 1765, m. Joshua Bates; *Betsy*, m. 1st Mr. Moody, m. 2d Mr. Thaxter; *Abigail*, Sep. 28, 1771, m. Winslow Thomas; *Elizabeth Turner*, Nov. 25, 1778; *Nancy*, m. Dea. George Loring.

22. ISAAC. (s. of —,) Dux.; m. Elizabeth White Ripley, Aug. 26, 1782; chd. *Lucy*, July 4, 1784, m. Saml. Loring; *Elizabeth*, 1788, m. John Partridge; *Dorcas*, 1790; *Benjamin*, 1794, d. in Dartmoor prison, 1814; *Hannah*, 1796, m. George Winsor; *Sally*, 1799; *Nancy*, 1801, m. Mr. Drew of K.; *Judith*, 1803; *Isaac*, 1805; *James*, 1808.

23. JOSEPH, (s. of —,) Dux., m. Hannah ———, who d. Jan. 16, 1763, æt. 73; he d. May 22, 1770, æt. 84¾ years. He was the father of *Elijah*, who d. Jan. 1, 1739.

24. DANIEL, (s. of —,) Dux. His chd. *Levi*, 1741, d. in the army at the westward, of small pox, 1760; *Martha*, 1743; *Zispah*, 1745; *Jonathan*, 1748, m. Ruth Delano, Sep. 14, 1774.

NOTE. *Hasadiah*, b. 1691, d. Dec. 9, 1770; *Mary*, b. 1692, d. May 7, 1771; *Jane*, 1685, d. Apr. 7, 1765; the selectmen were ordered "to take care of her and improve her estate;" *Lydia*, m. Josiah Soule, 1704; *Mercy*, m. Jabez Delano, 1710; *Mercy*, m. Wm. Spooner of Dartmouth, Nov. 25, 1713; widow *Mary*, d. Jan. 4, 1781, æt. 72½, b. 1709; *Nathaniel*, m. Mercy Boney, Oct. 24, 1714; *Hannah*, m. Eleazer Harlow, Oct. 6, 1715; *Rebecca*, m. Benj. Southworth, 1715; *Priscilla*, m. Benj. Simmons, 1715 d. "in ye night," Feb. 7, 1746; *Elizabeth*, m. Joseph Chandler 3d, 1720; *Israel*, b. 1720, d. Sep. 4, 1765, æt. 44 years 11 months; *Mary*, b. 1732, d. May 12, 1783, æt. 60; *John, Jr.*, m. Ruth Prior, Jan. 30, 1724; *Rebecca*, m. Amasa Turner, May 2, 1727; *Sarah*, m. Joshua Simmons, 1728; *Ju-*

dith, b. 1728, d. May 6, 1773, æt. 45 ; *Mercy*, m. John Prior, 1735 ; *Lydia*, m. Ichabod Wormall, 1736 ; *widow Delano*, alias *Curtis*, had Mary and Nathl., bap. 1741 ; *Abigail*, 1756, d. 1771 ; *Jesse*, d. "in ye army at ye westward," Aug. 8, 1758 , *Elijah*, b. 1756, d. Jan. 8, 1785, æt. 29 ; *Joseph, Jr.*, had Mary, 1764 ; *Isaac*, d. 1777 ; *Salome*, m. Joshua Winslow, 1780 ; *Nathan*, Sep. 8, 1780, m. Mercy, who was b. Sep. 10, 1781 ; *Ichabod*, m. widow Delano, 1780 ; *Oliver*, m. Mary Chandler, 1783 ; *John*, May 5, 1789, m. Sally, who was b. Oct. 4, 1785 ; *Dr. Benony*, d. Apr. 5, 1738 ; two *Samuels* are mentioned 1710.

DESPARD.

LAMBERT, Dux., 1701. "The town gave their consent to Mr. Despar to purchase about fourteen acres of land within this township of an Indian named Jeremiah." In the town as late as 1712.

DEVELL.

WILLIAM, desired land in Duxbury, 1640.

DINGLEY.

1. JOHN, Lynn, Sandwich, 1637, Marshfield, ad. 1644, had chd. *Jacob* (2) ; *Mary*, m. Josiah Standish ; *Hannah*, m. J. Kein.

2. JACOB, M. d. 1691, m. Elizabeth, had *John* (3), and *Joseph*.

3. JOHN, M. d. 1690, m. Sarah Porter, had *Jacob* (4).

4. JACOB, Dux., d. Dec. 24, 1772, æt. 69, m. Mary ——, and had chd. *Abner*, Jan. 21, 1732 (5) ; *Mary*, Nov. 10, 1735, m. Simeon Cook Jan. 1, 1756 ; *Sarah*, April 11, 1742 ; *Abigail*, May 5, 1745 ; *Jacob* (6).

5. ABNER, Dux., m. Ruth ——, had *Amasa*, Feb. 15, 1760 ; *Abner*, July 23, 1761 ; *Nathaniel Barker*, June 19, 1764.

6. JACOB, m. Susanna, who d. March 17, 1782, æt. 48, had chd. *Elkanah*, Nov. 9, 1754 ; *Levi*, Oct. 18, 1756 (7) ; *Desire*, Feb. 7, 1758, m. Mr. Bisbee ; *Susanna*, April 26, 1764, m. Capt. Bailey Young of M. 1782 ; *Jacob*, Nov. 1, 1767 ; *Ezra*, Aug. 5, 1770 ; *John*, June 6, 1773.

7. LEVI, Dux., m. Hannah Peterson, 1778, had *Spencer*, April 14, 1779.

8. JOSEPH, (s. of —,) m. Hannah, and had *Joseph*, June 29, 1793 ; *Hannah*, Nov. 9, 1794 ; *Esther*, Oct. 14, 1796.

DREW.

1. JOHN, a Welshman, and ship-carpenter, arrived at Plymouth 1660, had five sons, of whom three settled in Plymouth and two in Duxbury — so says an authority; but I find no mention of a Drew in Dux. previous to Samuel, No. 3. He had a da. *Elizabeth*, 5 Feb. 1673. His son *Samuel* d. 21 May, 1678; "going on board of a shallopp, finding there a bottle of liquor and drinking too much of it, that as he went to gett out of the boate, he fell from the boate into the water and sand" and was drowned.

2. SAMUEL, prob. gd. s. of John No. 1, m. Lydia.

3. SAMUEL, (s. of William, who was b. in Dux., but lived and died in K.) Dux.; b. Aug. 1713. He m. Anna, da. of Richard and Katuen White of Plymouth, Dec. 28, 1736. She was b. March 1716, and d. May 27, 1745, æt. 29. He m. 2d Faith Peterson, Oct. 22, 1746; he d. in 1800, æt. 89. Chd. *Joseph*, who m. a da. of Dea. Thomas of M.; *Sylvanus* (4); *Perez* (5); *Isaac*, 1748 (6); *Consider* (7); *Lewis*, bap. 1758; *Sarah*, m. Dea. James Southworth, 1762; *Abigail*, m. Capt. Samuel Delano 1762; *Lucy*, bap. 1740; *Eunice*, bap. 1741; *Lydia*, bap. 1742; *Ann*, bap. 1750, m. Joseph Wadsworth, 1773.

4. SYLVANUS, (s. of 3,) Dux., m. Mercy Clark, and had chd. *Charles*, Nov. 3, 1765, who had Betsy 1795, m. John Frazar, m. 2d Capt. Winthrop Babbage; Clark, 1797, m. Catharine Wadsworth; Sylvanus, 1799, m. Miss Nickerson; Sally, 1800, m. Briggs Thomas; Hannah, 1801, m. George Winslow; Charles, 1803, m. Hannah Thomas; George, and Lucy died young — *Reuben*, Dec. 27, 1766, m. Sally Loring, m. 2d Temperance Brooks of Scituate, who d. Nov. 8, 1838. They had Mary 1793, Reuben 1795, and Joseph 1797; and by 2d w., William 1806, m. Mary Basset, Henry 1808, Temperance 1810, George 1812, John B. 1817, m. Frances James Winsor 1848, Edward 1814, Alfred 1821 — *Clark*, April 3, 1769, m. Eliza Bosworth 1792 — *Sally*, m. Daniel Bradford — *Hannah* m. Dea. George Loring 1802, he d. July 1819 — *Wealthea*, m. Dea. G. Loring 1820 — *Lucy* — *Joshua*, killed accidentally Dec. 11, 1790 — *Zilpha*, m. Capt. Jonathan Smith.

5. PEREZ, (s. of 3,) m. Zilpha Wadsworth Feb. 6, 1772, who d. Jan. 3, 1778.

6. ISAAC, (s. of 3,) Dux.; m. Wealthea Bradford, Oct. 1, 1781, and had *Timothy*, m. Miss Thompson of Bridgewater; *Lazarus*; *Wealthea*; *Capt. Joshua*, m. Merinda Wadsworth; and *John*. A da. m. Dr. Snow of Boston, and six others.

7. CONSIDER, (s. of 3,) Dux.; bap. 1745, m. Jane; and had *Ellis*, Jan. 15, 1769; and *Lucia*, June 16, 1771.

NOTE. *Cornelius* of K. m. Sarah Bartlett, Feb. 27, 1729; *Perez* of K. m. Abigail Soule, Sept. 3, 1730, who d. Oct. 23, 1767, aged 51½; he d. Nov. 12, 1774, æt. 70, had Lemuel and John; *Hannah*, m. Benjamin Switzer 1757.*

DWELLEY.

RICHARD, of Dux., early m. Eamie Glass, m. 2d Elizabeth Simmons. He was also of Hingham, and had chd. there in 1660. *Mary*, (Scituate) m. Nathaniel Brewster, 1705.

Jeremiah *Dillingham*, Dux., 1758; his w. d. Oct. 10, 1779, æt. 82 — Princee *Dillingham* (Pemb.) m. Nehemiah Peterson Dec. 13, 1764 — Joseph *Dace*, Dux., 1800, m. Lydia (b. June 13, 1773), had Susanna and Hannah C.

EATON.

1. FRANCIS, arrived in 1620; a carpenter; removed to Dux. His 1st w. d. before 1627, and he next m. Christian Penn, and d. in 1636 or 7. He had *Samuel* (2); *Benjamin*, of Dux. 1648, of Plym. 1650; m. Sarah; had William, who d. before 1691; perhaps *Rachel*, who m. Joseph Ramsden March 2, 1645.

2. SAMUEL, (s. of 1,) Dux., bound himself an apprentice to John Cook in 1636 for seven years. He bought land of Love Brewster, and sold it in 1663 to Josiah Standish; removed to Middleboro', and d. intestate a. 1684. He m. Martha Billington 10 Jan. 1660. A Samuel m. Elizabeth, da. of Rev. Saml. Fuller.

ENSIGN.

THOMAS, Dux. 1656. A Thomas Ensign had land in Scituate, 1640, m. Eliz. Wilder, 1638, and d. 1663. His son John was killed at Pawtucket in 1676.—Hist. Scit. Hannah Ensign was bap. at Hingham July 6, 1640.—Hobart's Journal.

---

* *Drew*. From Boston Records. Mr. Robert m. Jemima, had Elizabeth July 22, 1660; John, Oct. 17, 1663. Richard and Mary had Mary Oct. 14, 1679, Elizabeth July 23, 1682, and John July 21, 1689. Samuel and Ann had Ann April 26, 1691.—B. Rec.

John Drew bap. at Hingham April 1641.—Hobart's Journal.

EVERSOR.

ABRAHAM, Dux. m. Lydia Chandler Jan. 11, 1763, and had *Abraham* and *Lydia.*

FERNISIDE.

JOHN, Dux., owned house and land, sold it to R. Barker, 1648, m. Elizabeth Starr, and both d. in Boston. Was in Dux. in 1643; name spelled "Farnyseede;" had at Boston, *Mary*, May 8, 1646; *Hannah*, May 8, 1650; *Lydia*, Apr. 3, 1653; *Elizabeth*, 26 Oct., 1658, and *Ruth*, 20 Aug., 1661.

FISH.

THOMAS, Dux., chd. *Thomas*, May 22, 1700; *Ebenezer*, Dec. 13, 1703, d. Mar. 23, 1791, had Abel 1740, Lydia 1742, m. Jeptho Taylor, 1771; *Joseph*, Jan. 28, 1706; *Lydia*, Mar. 24, 1708, m. Eliakim Willis of Dartmouth, July 20, 1738; *Samuel*, Oct. 18, 1710, m. Elizabeth Randall of Scituate, Mar. 1, 1733; *Nathaniel*, Apr. 11, 1713.

NOTE. *John*, Lynn, Sandwich, m. Cecelia, d. 1663, had Jonathan (who had Nathaniel, 18 Dec., 1650,) and Samuel. *Nathaniel*, had John at Sandwich, 13 Apr., 1651; *Nathaniel*, b. at Sandwich, 27 Nov., 1648; *Ruth*, m. Nathl. Chandler, 1782; *Huldah*, m. Ezekiel Sprague, 1785.

FISHER.

SAMUEL, Dux., 1710, m. Deborah, had *Rebecca*, Aug. 25, 1717; *Samuel*, Nov. 12, 1722.

FOBES.

Spelled *Vobes*, early.

JOHN, Dux., 1636, land at Powder point; 1637 at G. H. path; Bridgewater, m. Constant, sister of Ex. Mitchell; she after his death (which occurred 1661,) m. John Briggs, 1662. Chd. *John*, d. at Sandwich, 1661; *Dea. Edward* (Vide Mitchell's Hist.); *Mary; Caleb*, Norwich; *William*, Dux., Little Compton, m. Elizabeth Southworth; *Joshua*, kld. at Pawtucket, 1676; and *Elizabeth.*

FORD.

1. WILLIAM, Dux., 1643, a miller, b. 1594, lived near Gavelly beach in M., before 1640, d. 1676, æt. 82; m. Ann; sold land in Dux., 1661, to F. West. Chd. *Dea. William*, m. 1658, Sarah Dingley, and had John 1659, Mercy, 1662, m. Samuel Thomas, Josiah 1664; *Michael*, m. Abigail Snow, 1667, m. Bethiah Hatch 1683, had a large family, one of whom, Thomas (1685) had Amos (1714), who m. Lillys, who d. at Dux., Sep. 29, 1756, æt. 41½; a second wife of Amos d. Dec. 18, 1781. [Hist. Scituate.] — *Millicent*, m. John Carver; *Margaret*.

2. WIDOW FOORD, came in the Fortune 1621, with *William* (No. 1 ?), *Martha*, and *John*.

3. ANDREW, Weymouth, ad. 1654, had *Nathaniel* 1658, *Ebenezer* 1660, *Silence* 1661, *Prudence* 1663. His wife was Eleanor.

NOTE. *John*, d. at M., 1693, his w. was Hannah; *Bathsheba*, (M.) m. Eben Sherman, May 4, 1730; *Jemima*, m. Nathaniel Cushing, both of M., Apr. 16, 1747; *Othniel*, m. widow Mary Barnes, Jan. 10, 1758; *Hannah*, m. Nathaniel Rogers, (M.) 1781; *Nathaniel*, m. Lydia Simmons, 1783; *Lydia*, (b. Feb. 2, 1783,) m. Tho. W. Peterson; *Joshua T.*, (b. June 29, 1766,) m. Deborah ——, (who was b. May 10, 1765,) m. 2d, Abigail, and had Oakman, Benjamin, Elisha, George, Celia, Elizabeth and Ruth. — Dux. Rec.

FRAZAR.

1. CAPT. THOMAS,* Dux., m. Rebecca Alden, Nov. 27, 1760, who d. July 21, 1818, æt. 88. He d. Nov. 18, 1782, æt. 47¾. Chd. *Samuel Alden*, 1766 (2); *Rebecca*, 1769, d. Nov. 7, 1840, æt. 71, and in her will left $500 to the Pilgrim Society. "Warm in her friendship, and of a generous heart, the tears of the poor are her eulogy."

2. SAMUEL A., (s. of 1,) Dux., m. Abigail Drew, 1791, d. Aug. 28, 1838, æt. 72. A funeral discourse delivered at his burial by Rev. J. Moore, was published. Chd. *Thomas*, 1793, d. June 24, 1807; *John*, 1794, m. Betsy Drew, d. Mar. 3,

---

* His name is spelled on the records *Frasher*; on his grave stone *Frazier*; but by his descendants *Frazar*. He is said to have been of Scotch origin. The name Fraser or Frazier is of French derivation, and derived from the French *fraise*, signifying a strawberry, hence the well known heraldic object of the family is explained. The French word was probably derived from the fragrance of the fruit, as was the Latin *fragaria*. Chamber's Encyc.

1822, had Elizabeth; *Abigail,* 1796, m. Nathaniel Weston; *Mercy C.,* 1798, unm; *Samuel A.,* 1800, m. Maria Winsor; *George,* 1801, m. Ann Little, who d. July 28, 1842, æt. 37; *Amherst Alden,* 1804, m. Sarah D. Bradford, merchant of Boston; *Rebecca Alden,* 1808, m. Rev. William Augustus Stearns of Cambridgeport, Mass., Dec. 14, 1831; *Sarah D.,* 1810, m. Mr. Mansfield of Braintree; *Thomas,* 1812, m. Frances Bradford.

NOTE. *John,* Dux., 1733, when he was chosen petty juror; perhaps the one of M., who m. Anne Fullerton, Nov, 12, 1729, and had John, May 1, 1731. A *John* of M. had John, 20 Dec., 1761, and Thomas, 22 June, 1764; *John* drowned off Nantasket, Feb., 1782. Dux. Rec.— Daniel Frazier m. Hannah Hatton, Nov. 7, 1733; James m. Mary Rankin, July 3, 1733; Elizabeth Frazer m. Edward Carpenter, Oct. 21, 1714.—Boston Records.

FREEMAN.

1. MR. EDMUND, Lynn, 1632, Dux., Sandwich, 1637, d. a. 1682, leaving an estate of £180. Had chd. *Edmund,* m. Rebecca Prence, 1646; *John,* (2) m. Mary Prence, Feb. 14, 1649; *Alice,* m. 1639, Dea. William Paddy, m. 2d, Samuel Wensley; a. da. m. Edward Perry; *Elizabeth,* m. Mr. Ellis (the father of Mathias).

2. JOHN (s. of 1,) Eastham had *John,* 2 Feb., 1650, d. young; *John,* Dec. 1651; *Thomas,* Sep. 1653; *Edmund,* June 1657; *Mercy,* July, 1659; *Prence,* 3 Feb. 1665; *Nathaniel,* 20 Mar. 1669.

3. SAMUEL, Watertown, 1630, returned to England. His widow m. Gov. Prence. His chd. were *Henry,* d. 1672, had James of Boston; *Dea. Samuel,* 1638, d. 1700, m. Mercy Southworth, and had Samuel (m. Elizabeth Sparrow, had Judge Enoch), Constant, 31 Mar. 1669, Edward, Aphia, d. young, Elizabeth, Mercy, m. Mr. Cole, Alice m. Mr. Merrick, and Aphia, Jan. 1, 1666.

NOTE. *Henry* was of Watertown, 1648.

4. JOSEPH, (s. of —,) Dux., m. Miss Tobey. He d. June 6, 1790, æt. nearly 92. Chd. *Benjamin,* m. Hannah Bradford, Nov. 13, 1774, and had Bradford (who had Hannah, m. Capt. Benj. Winsor, Eunice, m. Mr. Washburn, Joseph, Elizabeth, Sally and others), Eunice m. Capt. Phineas Sprague, and Nancy, who is unm.; *Enoch* June 1, 1737, m. Abigail Weston, Dec. 20, 1764. She was b. Mar. 26, 1739, and d. Aug. 7, 1812; they had Abigail, Oct. 6, 1765, m. Amasa Sturtevant; Enoch, July 28, 1767; William, May 25, 1769, m. Wealthea Sampson, (who was b. Apr. 22, 1773, they had

William, Enoch, Sally, Wealthea, Martin, Deborah and Abigail;) Lydia, July 29, 1771, m. Nathl. Soule; Daniel, Nov. 14, 1773; Sally, Nov. 25, 1775, m. Dea. Martin Sampson; Weston, Feb. 6, 1777; and Mary, Dec. 29, 1779, m. James Loring. — *Edmund*, bap. 1740, m. Lucia Arnold, Apr. 9, 1771, and had Abijah, Feb. 4, 1772, m. a Chandler; Edmund, Feb. 19, 1773, d. at sea; Lucia, Nov. 21, 1774; Arnold, May 15, 1777; and Acenith m. Joseph Simmons. — *Joseph*, lived S. of Is. Ck. Bk. had Irene, m. Rev. Z. Sanger; Olive m. James Shaw, Apr. 1, 1772; Sarah, m. Ira Wadsworth, 1783; Samuel; Chandler. — *Sarah*, m. Dea. Perez Loring. — *Lydia*, unm. — *Mary*, m. Joshua Cushing, Sep. 27, 1763.

5. SILAS, (s. of —,) Dux., m. Mary Brewster, Dec. 8, 1763, had *Brewster*, 1765.

6. EMANUEL, (a Portuguese,) m. Lucia, and had *Alice* Nov. 1, 1769, and *Joseph*, May 13, 1775, m. Althea Joice, (b. 1774) and had James 1799, Henry, John and several das.

FROST.

ISAAC, Dux., m. Anna Wadsworth, who d. April 26, 1843; had chd. *Samuel*, 1797, d. 1821, *Judith, William, Elizabeth, Charles, Nancy, Anna, Abigail.*

FULLER.

1. ABIEL, Dux., m. Sarah ———, who d. April 27, 1737. They had chd. *Sarah*, April 11, 1737, d. young; *Gamaliel*, 1745; *Sarah*, 1747; *Anice*, 1749.

NOTE. *James* came from Dartmouth a. 1740, a blacksmith, soon removed to Plymouth; had Hannah, bap. 1741; Capt. *Zephaniah*, m. Polly Loring Dec. 11, 1781, and had Sarah; Dr. *Jabez*, m. Lucy Loring, Aug. 1781; *Mary*, m. Philip Delano 1783.

GANNET.

THOMAS, (B. of Matthew of Scit.) Dux., 1642, removed to Bridgew, and d. 1655. Widow Sarah survived him.—*Deane's Scit. and Mitchell's Bridgew.*

GARDNER.

JOHN, Dux. 1640, owned land north of the Mill, towards G.H.

GLASS.

1. JAMES, (s. of —,) Dux., apprenticed to Hy. Coggen, 1639, and then to Mr. Kempton; m. Mary Pontus Oct. 31, 1645. He came to his death Sept. 3, 1652; "it being very stormy weather, riding att the Gurnetnose in a boate," he was forced by stress of weather on shore back of the beach, and was knocked from off the "fore cuddey," into the surge and was drowned. His w. m. P. Delano. Chd. *Hannah*, 2 June, 1647, d. 15 June, 1648; *Wybra*, 9 Aug. 1649; *Hannah*, 24 Dec. 1651; *Mary*.

2. ROGER, (s. of —,) Dux.; was put out to John Crocker; but because he treated him barbarously, he was transferred to John Whetcome in 1639; m. Mary ——; d. in 1691 or 1692; estate £90; lived at Hounds ditch, also owned land east of North hill; and had chd. *Elizabeth ; James*, d. in Canada Expedition, 1690; *Eamie*, m. R. Dwelley; *Mary ; John*, m. 1st ——, m. 2d Esther Chandler, Feb. 14, 1705.

3. JAMES, (perhaps s. of John, s. of Roger 2,) Dux.; d. Oct. 17, 1759, æt. 50 years. Chd. *John*, 1739 (4); *James*, Jan. 16, 1740, m. Lucy Burgess, and had James (May 18, 1792), m. Silvia Soule, and d. Aug. 20, 1827, and Nancy 1796; *Serajah* bap. 1744 (5); *Ezekiel* 1747; *Jonathan* 1750, d. 1756; *Mary; Nathaniel* 1755, d. 1756; *Sarah* 1758, m. Jacob Burgess Mar. 25, 1779, and *Consider* 1766.

4. JOHN, (s. of 3,) Dux., m. Bernice Delano May 30, 1773, d. 1829, æt. 89; had *Ezekiel*, Sept. 10, 1775, m. Miss Thomas of M., served in the flying artillery in Canada in 1812, had Ezekiel, John, and Daniel; *Jonathan*, Sept. 23, 1776, m. Desire Chandler, (who was b. Nov. 22, 1778,) and had Levi, Seth, Jonathan and others; *Levi; Lydia ; Mary*.

5. SERAJAH, (s. of 3,) Dux.; m. Hannah Oldham Dec. 26, 1771; had *Hannah ; Nathaniel*, m. Sarah Ripley, (who d. June, 1826), had Nathaniel 1799, Sarah 1803, Lucy 1805, Daniel B. 1808, killed at sea 1839, Charles B. 1810, d. June 1815; *Amasa*, m. Desire Weston; *Mary*, m. William Read, who came from North Carolina; *Arispah*, m. William Henry ; *Wealthea*, m. Spencer Burgess.

NOTE. *Amy* m. Richard Willis, 1639; *Esther* m. Nathan Chandler, 1770.—*Col. & Dux. Rec. Richard*, of Mass., took oath of fidelity 1674.[*]

---

[*] *Glass.* From the Boston Records. James m. Elizabeth, and had William Jan. 11, 1687; Robert, Sept. 19, 1692; Elizabeth, Nov. 6, 1695. John m. Martha Temple, April 1, 1703, had Martha Jan. 3, 1704. Mary m. John Lattany Sept. 22, 1715.

GODFREY.

FRANCIS, Dux., 1638, had land at G. H. brook; bore arms 1643.

GOOLE.

FRANCIS, Dux., 1643, a planter, lived near Jones River.

GORHAM.

RALPH "Goarame," Dux., 1637, lived near P. Delano. His son *John* was of Marshfield 1643, m. Desire Howland Nov. 6, 1644, lived at Plymouth, M., Yarmouth and Barnstable, and d. of a fever while in command of a company in Philip's war, at Swansey, Feb. 5, 1676. She d. 13 October, 1683. Chd. Desire (at Ply.) 1644, Temperance (at M.), 1646, Elizabeth 1648, James, 28 April, 1650, John, 20 Feb. 1651, Joseph (at Yarmouth) 10 Feb. 1653, Jabez (at Barnstable) 3 Aug. 1656, wounded in Philip's war, Mercy 1658, Lydia 1661. [N. E. Hist. & Geneal. Reg. II. 67.

HADEN. [HAYDEN?]

One of this name bore arms in Duxbury 1643.

HALES.

A *George* early asked a grant of land in Duxbury, which was given him; but he not settling upon it, it was granted to another.

HALL.

1. EDWARD, Dux., 1638, permitted to build in Dux.; 1637, ten acres at G. H. path; 1638, sold his house to Wm. Witherell; 1641, he appears of Taunton; 1642, had a house at Hounds ditch; 1645, prop. of Bridgew.; 1652, left the colony a debtor.

An Edward Hall sold, 1665, land in Duxbury. An Edward was at Cambridge 1636, ad. 1638 (perhaps s. of John of Lynn), and d. 1669, leaving w. Sarah, and Joseph, Ephraim, and several daughters. An Edward of Braintree m. Hester, and had John 1651, and Hester Oct. 23, 1654.

2. GEORGE, Dux., 1637, owned land at G. H. path.
3. CAPT. JOSHUA, (s. of —,) Dux., m. Alethea Soule, Sept. 30, 1762; had *Joshua*, Oct. 26, 1769, who had Joshua 1794, Harriet I. 1796, Henry 1798, d. 1804, and Catharine 1811; *Daniel*, March 27, 1772, had Daniel 1799; *Lot*, July 14, 1774, m. Ursula Chandler, he d. July 25, 1840, she d. April 4, 1838, had Alethea 1797, Lot 1804, Nancy, Martin, Lucy, Jane, Laura; *David*, May 10, 1777.

NOTE. *Sarah* (K.,) m. Joseph Sampson, May 6, 1747; *Ashehel* m. Abigail Barnes, 1771.

John, Yarmouth, 1655, had Samuel; *Samuel*, Taunton, had Samuel Dec. 1664, John Oct. 1666, Nicholas Oct. 1670, Mary Oct. 1672, Ebenezer March 1677, Sarah March 1679, George Jan. 1680. *John*, Taunton, m. Hannah Penniman 4th Feb. 1679, had John June 1672, Joseph April 1674, James Dec. 1675, Benjamin Dec. 1677. *Nathaniel*, " a maimed souldier in the late indian warr," 1684, allowed £5 per annum.

HANBURY.

MR. WILLIAM, Dux., 1639, bought John Brown's house near Jones River; was living there in 1643.

HANDMER.

JOHN, Dux., 1640, had land north of the Mill towards G. H.

HANKS.

JOHN, Dux., m. Mary Delano, Jan. 16, 1735; had *Chloe; John*, m. Abigail Sampson March 25, 1773; and *Nathaniel*.

HARDING.

JOHN, Dux., 1643, perhaps the one of Mass. Bay, and ad. 1640. For descendants see Mitchell's Bridgew.

HARLOW.

1. SERG'T WILLIAM, Lynn, 1637, Sandwich, Plymouth; m. 1st, 1649, Rebecca Bartlett; m. 2d, July 15, 1658, Mary Faunce, who d. 4 Oct. 1664; m. 3d, Mary Shelly 25 Jan.

1665, who survived him. Chd. *William*, b. and d. Oct. 1650; *Samuel*, 27 Jan. 1652; *Rebecca*, 12 June, 1655; *William*, 2 June, 1657; *Mary*, 19 May, 1659; *Repentance*, 22 Nov. 1660; *John*, 19 Oct. 1662; *Nathaniel*, 30 Sept. 1664; *Hannah*, 28 Oct. 1666; *Bathsheba*, 21 April, 1667; *Joanna*, 24 Mar. 1669; *Mehetabel*, 4 Oct. 1672; *Judith*, 2 Aug. 1676.

2. JOSEPH, (s. of —,) Dux., 1687, constable.

3. ELEAZER, (s. of —,) Dux., m. Hannah Delano Oct. 6, 1715, had *Eleazer* (4).

4. DR. ELEAZER, (s. of 3,) Dux., m. Abigail Thomas, of M. March 1739; she d. Nov. 24, 1743; m. 2d Abigail Clark of Plymouth Sept. 11, 1745; and m. 3d widow Dabney of Boston, and had chd. *Arunah*; *Gideon* (5); *Thomas*; *Asaph*; *Abigail*; and *William*, d. young.

5. GIDEON, (s. of 4,) Dux., had chd. *Eleazer*, Nov. 4, 1784; m. Alethea Thomas of M., had Judah 1811, Briggs 1815, Alden, Thomas, Henry, the two latter d. young; *Gideon*, m. Olive Thomas of M., had Thomas, Hannah, Lydia, Mary, Henry, Gideon, and others; *Lydia*, d. young— (for the descendants of the remaining three sons, see Ward's Shrewsbury) —*Arunah*, Shrewsbury, m. 1799, Sarah Bannister; *Dea. Thomas*, Shrewsbury, m. 1798, Thankful Bannister; *Abner*, Shrewsbury, m. 1st Persis B. Oakman of M., who d. 1814, March 14, æt. 36; m. 2d Sarah McFarland of Worcester, who d. 1847, æt. 67.

HARMON.

JOHN, Dux., 1657, took oath of fidelity.

HARRIS (or HARRISON).

1. ARTHUR, Dux., 1640, had land in Dux. woods given him, "due for his service," also at the Mill Brook; removed to Bridgew.; ad. 1668; removed to Boston, and d. there 1673; m. Martha ——. (For descendants see Mitchell's Bridgew.)

2. SAMUEL Harris, Dux., had *John*, bap. 1756.

HARTUB.

WILLIAM, Dux., 1643, was able to bear arms.

HATCH.

SAMUEL, Dux. 1684, lived near M. line.

HATHAWAY.

1. ARTHUR "Hadaway," M. 1643, m. Sarah Cook 20 Nov. 1652, had *John*, 17 Sept. 1653, and *Sarah*, 28 Feb. 1655. — There was a John in Barnstable, of Taunton, 1689, had a son John, may have been a B. of Arthur.

2. DR. RUFUS, Dux., m. Judith Winsor; he d. Oct. 13, 1822, had chd. *Mary*, Feb. 7, 1796, m. Lewis McLaughlin; *Joshua W.*, Dec. 14, 1798, m. Prudence McLaughlin; *Silvia Church*, Feb. 1, 1801, m. Andrew Stetson; *Deborah*, April 20, 1802, m. Mr. Latham, and she d. Oct. 16, 1831; *Isaac W.*, April 16, 1804; *Juliet*, Aug. 11, 1806, m. Jairus Magoon, his 2d w.; *Maria*, Jan. 23, 1809, m. Jairus Magoon, she d. Oct. 18, 1833; *Rufus*, Sept. 25, 1812; *Nancy P.*, Aug. 21, 1815; *Thomas D.*, May 13, 1818; *John*, Dec. 24, 1821, m. Miss Faunce.

HAWES.

EDMUND, Dux., 1637, had ten acres at G. H. path; m. Lucy; yeoman; removed to M., sold his land there to Thos. Bourn; removed to Yarmouth before 1649.

HAYWARD.

THOMAS, Dux., before 1638, ad. 1646, prop. of Bridgew. 1645; 1640 in Dux., had a grant of land northwest of North hill, and also at Namasakeeset; sold his land to Wm. Pabodie 1669; removed to Bridgew. d. 1681; m. Martha ——; had a large family, for whose descendants see Mitchell's Bridgew.

HEWITT.

JOSEPH, Dux., m. Abigail —— 1796, and had *Nancy*, *Elizabeth*, and *Joseph*.

NOTE. John Hewet of M. m. Martha (who d. 1691, mentioning in her will sister Anne, and niece Anne Turner and son Winter). She was da. of Christopher Winter, and had chd. — Solomon, Christopher, Bridget, Elizabeth, Mercy, and Lydia.

HICKS.

MR. ROBERT, arrived 1621, Dux. before 1634, removed to Scituate, d. before 1662. He m. 1st, Elizabeth, m. 2d, Margaret; had *Samuel*, m. Lydia Doan, 1645, Plymouth, removed to Nauset, had Dorcas, 14 Feb., 1651; Margaret, 9 Mar., 1654; *Ephraim* m. Elizabeth Howland, 13 Sep., 1649, he d. Dec. 12, 1649, she then m. John Dickarson, 10 July, 1651; *Lydia; Phebe.*

NOTE. Daniel Hicks m. Elizabeth Hanmore, Sep., 1657 — Sarah m. Joseph Churchill 3 June, 1672. — Col. Rec.

HILLIER.

WILLIAM, Dux., carpenter, first miller in 1639; in 1640 had a grant of 40 acres "on the milne brook."

HILL.

SAMUEL, Dux., m. Phebe Leonard, Nov. 6, 1694, had chd. *Abigail*, May 26, 1697; *Philip*, Aug. 8, 1699; *Samuel*, June 25, 1701, m. Hannah Turner, Nov. 1, 1722, had Joseph, July 31, 1723, and Hannah, June 7, 1725; *Richard*, Feb. 3, 1703; *Ebenezer*, Dec. 6, 1705; *Ephraim*, Dec. 13, 1707; *Joseph*, (d. July, 1711,) and *Lydia*, (twins,) b. 25 Aug., 1710.

HOLMES.

1. LT. WILLIAM, Plymouth, ad. 1634; a commander in Pequod war, a major in Mass. forces; had land in Dux. 1638, which he sold to Mr. Howland; d. 1649, leaving no children.

2. WILLIAM, Scituate, removed to M., settled on North river before 1662, d. 1690, m. Elizabeth, who d. 1693, had chd. *Abraham*, 1641, m. 2d, Abigail Nichols of Hingham, 1695; *Israel*, 1642, m. Desire Sherman, and was drowned with Joseph Trewant in Plymouth harbor, Feb. 24, 1684; *Isaac*, 1644; *Sarah*, 1646; *Rebecca*, 1648; *Josiah*, 1650; *Mary*, 1655; *Elizabeth*, 1661. An Abraham Holmes m. Elizabeth, da. of Rev. Samuel Arnold of M., and had chd. Elizabeth, Isaac, Rose, Bathsheba, who m. Samuel Dogget. Was this Abraham the one b. 1641, and was Elizabeth his 1st wife?

3. MR. JOHN, Dux., had (1665,) a large grant at Robinson's ck., and in 1672 a small one in Dux.; m. Patience Faunce, 20 Nov., 1661, and d. a. 1697, had *John*, 22 Mar. 1662; *Richard; Patience; Mehetable; Sarah; George; Nathaniel; Ebenezer; Thomas; Joseph; Desire* m. John Churchill before 1695.

A John Holmes was of Plymouth, ad. 1634, and messenger of the General Court.

4. JOSIAH, (s. of —,) Dux., m. Hannah Sampson, Mar. 20, 1665; had *Hannah*, Oct. 11, 1667; *Darbous*, Aug. 4, 1669; *Josiah*, Aug. 13, 1672; *Mary*, Nov. 5, 1674; *John*, May 28, 1678, m. Joanna Sprague; *William*, Jan. 18, 1679.

5. SAMUEL, M., m. Mary, and d. 1690. A Samuel was in Rehoboth, and had a son Samuel, 6 Sep., 1674. A Samuel in Dux., had Consider, who was b. 1702, and d. Sep. 28, 1770.

6. BARTLETT, of Manomet ponds, Plymouth, was the father of the following who settled in Dux. — *Bartlett*, m. Sarah Winsor, 1796, who d. Nov. 1807, æt. 30, and had William, 1797, Melzar, 1799, and Lucy, 1801 — *Nathaniel*, m. Anne Prior; *John; Calvin*, m. a da. of Reuben Peterson; *Naoman; Sarah*, m. Jabez Prior of Dux.

7. NATHANIEL, Dux., m. Hannah Weston, 1795. He d. at Labrador. He had Lucy, George, Thomas, Charles, Sarah and Samuel.

NOTE. "*Miss Sara*" d. at Plymouth, Aug. 18, 1650; *Nathaniel*, m. Mercy Faunce, 29 Dec., 1667; *Experience* of Dartmouth, m. Hannah Sampson of Rochester, Dec. 13, 1737; *George*, Dux., 1740; *Urany*, m. Ichabod Simmons, 1783; *widow Rebecca* of K., m. Rev. Wm. Rand, Feb. 11, 1779.

HOUSE.

AMOS, Dux., m. Sarah Ripley, Jan 11, 1748. He d. of small pox, Dec., 1762; she d. Sep. 7, 1790, had *Mary, Lot, Irene, Mary, Lucinda, Sarah, Thankful*.

NOTE. *Caleb* m. Elizabeth Randall, July 12, 1759; *Samuel* of Scituate, d. Sep. 12, 1681, leaving Samuel and Elizabeth.— In Boston, *William* m. Mary before 1660.

HOWARD.

1. JOHN and JAMES, (brothers) are said to have come to N. E. with Standish; were of Dux.; James went to Bermuda, and John to W. Bridgew. Vide Mitchell's Bridgew.

2. EZRA, Dux., m. Esther Delano, Dec. 17, 1772; he d. Nov. 25, 1781, æt. 31; had *Ezra*, Aug. 1, 1773; *Parmelia*, Feb. 27, 1776; *Daniel*, Mar. 16, 1778.

3. A WIDOW HOWARD had a da. *Leonice* bap. in Dux., 1757.

HOWLAND.

1. Hon. JOHN HOWLAND, arrived 1620, Plymouth, removed to Dux. (Vide first settlers.) He m. Gov. Carver's da. Elizabeth. She d. 1687, æt. 81. His chd. *John* (2); *Jabez*, m. Bethiah Thacher, and settled after the conquest of Mt. Hope at Bristol, had Jabez, Nov. 15, 1669; John, Jan. 15, 1672, d. same month, Bethiah, June 3, 1674, Josiah, Aug. 6, 1676, John, July 26, 1679; *Isaac*, m. Elizabeth, da. of Geo. Vaughan, and settled at Middleboro'; *Joseph*, Plymouth, m. Elizabeth Southworth, Dec. 7, 1664; *Desire*, m. John Gorham; *Hope*, m. John Chipman of Barnstable, had large family; *Elizabeth*, m. E. Hicks, 1649, m. 2d, July 10, 1651, John Dickarson; *Lydia*, m. James Brown of Swansey; *Ruth*, m. Thomas Cushman of Plymouth, Nov. 7, 1664.

2. JOHN, (s. of 1,) M., removed to Barnstable, where he was ensign, lieutenant, and selectman, and authorized to retail cider of his making; m. Mary Lee Oct. 26, 1651. [She was da. of Mistress Mary Lee, who d. Oct. 1681, having lived for the last eight years of her life with her son-in-law Howland. John Atwood's will, 1643, names brother and sister Lee, with their chd. Anne and Mary.] Their chd. were *Elizabeth*, May 17, 1655, m. John Bursley Dec. 1673; *Isaac*, 25 Nov. 1659, m. Ann Taylor Dec. 27, 1686; *Hannah*, 15 May, 1661, m. Jonathan Crocker 20 May, 1686; *Mercy*, 21 Jan. 1663; *Lydia*, 9 Jan. 1665, m. Joseph Jenkins; *Experience*, 28 July, 1668; *Anne*, 9 Sept. 1670, m. Joseph Crocker, 18 Sept. 1691; *Shobal*, 30 Sept. 1672, m. Mercy Blossom, 1700; *John*, 31 Dec. 1674 (3).—N. E. Hist. Geneal. Reg.

3. JOHN, (s. of 2,) Barnstable, m. 1st —— ——; m. 2d Mary Crocker. The oldest child by the 2d m. was *John*, Feb. 13, 1720. This son John graduated at H. C. 1741, and was ordained at Carver 1746. "This exemplary pastor, of humble desires, of primitive simplicity of manners, of cheerful and of hospitable disposition, after having lived to see his parish become a town, and surviving that era fourteen years, died, Nov. 4, 1804, in his 84th year." He m. a da. of Rev. Daniel Lewis of Pembroke. Four sons and three daughters survived him. One son, John, a promising young man, educated a merchant at Plymouth, d. in the West Indies early in the Revolution. One of the das., Anna, m. Rev. Ezra Weld, of Braintree, and d. July 10, 1774, æt. 31; another da. m. Noah Thomas. One of his sons, Daniel, lived in Pembroke, m. Thankful Morse of Falmouth. She d. Sept. 21, 1828, æt. 76, and was da. of Theodore, who d. 1795, æt. over 80. This *Daniel* d. Dec. 19, 1824, æt. 76, and was the father of Capt.

John, who was b. Nov. 23, 1780, and m. Nancy Winsor; Daniel, who was lost at sea; Josiah, who m. Eunice Salmon; Lucia, who m. Mr. Cushman of Plympton; Betsey, who m. Mr. Folger of Nantucket; Cynthia, who m. Mr. Chaddock of Nantucket; and Susan, who m. Mr. Bartlett of Bridgewater. The chd. of *Capt. John* (s. of Daniel,) of Dux., were Ann Thomas, Feb. 12, 1809, m. Nathl. Winsor, April, 1829; John, March 30, 1812, killed by lightning at sea, Sept. 20, 1832; Cordelia Maria, Dec. 16, 1813; Lucian Lorenzo, July 25, 1819, m. Eliza Newell, da. of Mr. Jonas Smith of Barre, June 4, 1846, who d. Nov. 1847, leaving one son, Lucian Herbert, who was b. March 8, 1847; Jerome, d. young; Jerome F., Feb. 23, 1827, m. Harriet, da. of James Fowle, Esq. of Boston, and has one da., Ella Fessenden.

4. HENRY, Dux., 1633; lived by the bay side, near Love Brewster; "one of the substantial landholders and freemen;" prop. of Bridgew. 1645, m. Mary, who d. June 16, 1674; he d. 1670.

5. ARTHUR, M., 1643; m. Margaret; owned land near Thos. Chillingworth; 1669, considering his age and low condition, the Court freed him from paying the minister's fee; her will, dated Jan. 1683, mentions grandson (son-in-law, say Col. Rec.) John Walker. Their chd. were *Arthur* (6), and *Deborah*, who m. John Smith, Jr. of Plymouth, Jan. 4, 1648 (and had Hazadiah 1649, John 1651, Josiah 1652, Eleazer 1654, and Hezekiah 1655).

6. ARTHUR, (s. of 5,) M.; 1660, fined £5 for making proposals to Elizabeth, da. of Gov. Prence, contrary to their parents' mind and will; and in 1667, he promised not to make any further offers to her. They were, however, m.; and had *Ebenezer, Thomas* of Dux., and *Arthur*.

From him came Robert Howland, who m. Margaret Sprague July 5, 1733, and had Prince, who m. Abigail Wadsworth in 1779, lived in Dux., and had Eden, Peleg B., and Alice.

7. ZOETH, Dux. and M. before 1657. He m. ——— ———.

8. SAMUEL, Dux.; 1662, for carrying, on the Lord's day, a grist from mill, fined 10s. or be whipt; 1662, he was charged with "discharging of a fowling peece on the body of William Howse" of Sandwich, while gunning at the "high pyne on Salthouse beach." A verdict was given by the jury, "not guilty of willfull murder, yett we find that the said House received his deadly wound by Samuel Howland's gun goeing off, as it lay on his shoulder." He appears in Dux. in 1690–2. A Samuel Howland was selectman of Freetown 1690.

9. JOHN, (perhaps s. of 4,) m. Mary Walker, Jan. 29, 1685, at Dux.

10. JOSEPH, Dux. 1679; m. 1683, Rebecca, da. of John Hussey of New Hampshire, who survived him, and m. Samuel Collins of Lime, Aug. 6, 1695. He d. June 15, 1695. His estate £500, including a negro servant, lands (£224) at Little Compton and Duxbury. Chd. *Jedediah*, 1685, Little Compton; *Patience*, 1687; *Lydia*, 1689.

11. PEREZ, Dux., m. Deborah, who d. 1790; m. 2d, Ruth Delano, 1791, had *Rouse*, Feb. 15, 1793; *John*, Oct. 15, 1794; *Benjamin*, Sep. 10, 1796.

NOTE. *Rebecca* m. Samuel Thomas, (both of M.,) Feb. 15, 1727; *Saba* m. Capt. Andrew Sampson, Jan. 3, 1779; *Benjamin* (of Pembroke) m. Experience Edgarton of Halifax, Feb. 10, 1743; *Ruth* m. Luke Stetson, June 10, 1762, she d. 1764; *Alice* m. Beriah Sampson, May 6, 1756; *Abigail* m. Isaac Bisbee, Sep. 5, 1781. Dux. Rec. *Nathaniel* m. Abigail Lane, 22 Nov., 1739; *Richard* m. Mercy Mousall, Sep. 29, 1720. Boston Records.

HUDSON.

JOHN, Dux., d. a. 1683. His will (Nov. 20, 1683,) witnessed by Thomas and Elizabeth Palmer. His wife, Ann Rogers, survived, and to her he bequeathed, " provided she keep herself a widow," his house, tillage land, &c. His chd. were *Hannah* m. Japheth Turner; *Rhoda* m. —— Palmer; *Elizabeth* m. —— Vicory; *Abigail* m. a Stetson.

HUNT.

1. EDMUND, Cambridge, 1634; Dux., 1637; prop. of Bridgew., 1645.

2. EDWARD, Dux., owned land at Hounds ditch, d. a. 1655. An Edward, perhaps his son, sold land in Dux., 1665, to R. Barker.

3. SAMUEL, of Dux., 1663 — 1690.

4. THOMAS, of Dux., kld. at Pawtucket, 1676.

5. THOMAS, of Dux., m. Honor Stetson, Jan. 15, 1708; she d. Aug. 22, 1739.

6. THOMAS, of Dux., m. Geen Weston, Apr. 28, 1748. He d. Nov. 6, 1806. Chd. *Anne* m. William Winsor, July 23, 1775; *Acenith* m. Samuel Winsor; *Abigail* m. Ichabod Kent, 1771; *Melzar* d. young; *Thomas*, Oct. 3, 1761, m. Susanna Fuller of K., who was b. May 30, 1761, and he d. June 7, 1840, and had Elizabeth, 1781, Capt. Samuel, 1784, (m. Deb-

orah Kent and had Hiram, Allen M., Edward G., Hannah G., and d. Dec. 26, 1823,) John, 1786, Susanna, 1788, Melzar, 1791, Lucy, 1793, Anna, 1796, Lewis, 1799, d. 1807, and Barker, 1802 (m. Lucy Louden).

7. JOHN, (s. of—,) Dux., m. Esther, who d. June 18, 1743; m. 2d, Deborah Soule, May 1, 1746, had *Judah* (8); *John* m. Mary Simmons, Apr. 24, 1764; *Mary* (1st w.); *Samuel*, d. at Liverpool, 1771; *Lot* m. Mary Sampson, Mar. 4, 1773, had Sarah, Nov. 28, 1773, Samuel, Sep. 22, 1775, Asa, Mar. 21, 1778, Ziba, July 26, 1780, Jane, Mar. 6, 1784, Lot, Apr. 15, 1789, d. at sea; *Deborah* m. Joseph Brewster, 1773; *Asa*, d. 1776, at N. Y.

8. JUDAH, (s. of 7,) Dux., m. 1st, Betsy Oldham, Dec. 18, 1764, who d. June 11, 1774, æt. 32; m. 2d, Deborah Weston, Aug. 21, 1776. He d. Apr. 18, 1826, æt. 89. Chd. *Esther*, Sep. 21, 1765; *Judah*, drowned 1771, æt. 3; *Seth*, July 22, 1778, m. Huldah Wadsworth; *Elizabeth*, 1780, m. Nathaniel Delano.

NOTE. *Martha* m. Joseph Chandler, Jr., 1701; *Mary* m. Jacob Burgess, Apr. 27, 1704; *Anne* m. Ichabod Wadsworth, 1736; *Asa* m. Sarah Partridge, Dec. 2, 1736; *Abigail* m. Hezekiah Ripley, Dec. 3, 1739; *Lydia* m. Wm. Ripley, 1756; *Lucy* m. Jona. Peterson, Apr. 23, 1771; *Judah* d. Aug. 26, 1776. Dux. Rec.

Christian m. Richard More, Oct. 20, 1636; *Hannah* m. Daniel White, 1674; *Lt. Peter*, Rehoboth, 1650, had Daniel, Sep. 15, 1673; *Enoch*, Weymouth, had Sarah, July 4, 1640; *Enoch*, Rehoboth, m. Mary Paine, 29 Oct., 1678, had Enos, Jan., 1679, Mary, Sep., 1679, Elizabeth, Oct., 1682; *John*, Swansey, had Peter, Feb., 1679; *Samuel* (æt. 17 in 1657,) and *John* were brothers. Col. Rec.; *Ephraim*, Ct., 1642, Weymouth, 1655, m. Ebbet, a rep. and Capt., and had William, 1655 and Enoch, 1657; *John*, Boston, 1676, butcher, m. Martha; *John* m. Ruth Quincy at Hingham, Oct., 1686; *Thomas* m. Elizabeth, had Jabez, June 11, 1654, and John, Apr. 11, 1656; Thomas m. Hannah Paine, Feb. 15, 1694; Thomas m. Susanna Saxton, June 21, 1694; Samuel m. Mary Langdon, Apr. 24, 1712. — Boston records.

HUSSEY.

ROBERT, Dux., bore arms 1643.

IRISH.

1. JOHN, Dux., 1640, had a "meadstead" granted him, and the next year land at Stoney brook; prop. of Bridgew., a

roper, m. Elizabeth, went to Little Compton, d. 1677; had *John*, Dux., m. a sister of Col. Church; *Elias* m. Dorothy Witherell, 26 Aug., 1674, went to Taunton. A John was in Middleboro', 1671.

2. GEORGE, Dux., early.

JACKSON.

1. SAMUEL m. Elizabeth, had *Rebecca*, Oct. 29, 1727, and *Mercy*, Mar. 5, 1733.

2. DR. RANSOM, had *Hannah*, a. 1740, and *John*, a. 1743. Dr. J. removed from Plympton to Dux., a. 1740, and bought an interest in a forge on the South river, and lived near by.

JOICE.

ASA, b. July 2, 1766, m. Lucy Ann Southworth, who was b. June 25, 1772, had *William, John, Lucy, Peter, Stephen* had Wealthea, 1795, and Hannah, 1798, *Abigail, Deborah, Alethea* and *Hannah*.

NOTE. John Joice, Lynn, removed to Sandwich, 1637, Yarmouth, d. a. 1666. Walter was of M., before 1668.

KEIN (KEAN OR KEEN).

JOSIAH, Dux., 1665, m. Hannah Dingley, had chd. *Josiah* m. Lydia, and had Benjamin, July 26, 1682, Josiah, Sep. 27, 1683, Abigail, Apr. 7, 1685, Nathaniel, Nov. 11, 1692; and perh. *John*, alive 1710; *Matthew*, alive 1710; *Hannah* m. Isaac Oldham, Nov. 21, 1695.

NOTE. *Samuel* m. Ruth Sprague, Apr. 18, 1719; *Sarah* m. Timothy Rogers, Apr. 6, 1710; *Grace* m. Jabez Cole, 1744; *Diana* m. Noah Simmons, 1771; *Lemuel*, Dux., a. 1750, removed to Pembroke, Bridgew. Vide Hist. Bridgew.; *Alice* d. Oct. 1, 1771; *William* (Bristol), m. Celano Wadsworth, 1784.

KEMP.

WILLIAM, Dux., m. Elizabeth; inventory taken Sep. 23, 1641; estate £150; 1640, had land at Beaver pond, S. river, and Namasakeeset. He had a son *William*, who m. Patience Thacher(?); was of Dux.; his da. Patience m. Samuel Seabury.

KIDBYE.

JOHN, Dux., 1640, land at Namasakeeset, mentioned 1665.

KNIGHT.

WALTER, Dux., 1638, requested land in Duxbury. A carpenter.

LAMBERT.

THOMAS, JR., Dux., 1710; no other mention of him.

NOTE. *Thomas* Lambert, Sen., Barnstable, 1639, d. 1663, m. Joyce; had Jemima, m. Joseph Benjamin, 10 June 1661, Thomas, Caleb, Barnard (ensign of Barnstable Co.), Jedediah, 20 Sept. 1640, Benjamin, 26 Aug. 1642, Joshua, and Margaret, who m. Edward Coleman. — *Bernard*, Barnstable, b. 1607, had Martha 1640, and Jabez 1642.—Col. Rec. *John*, Hingham, Scituate, 1693 — *Thomas*, Scituate — *Thomas*, of Boston, m. Mary, had Thomas, Nov. 6, 1659, Susanna, Feb. 28, 1662.—Boston Rec.

LAND.

EDWARD, Dux., 1666. See Church History.

LATHAM.

1. WILLIAM, yeoman, Plymouth 1623, Dux., 1637, sold his house to Rev. Mr. Partridge, 1639, M. 1643, his house burnt 1648. Cary Latham was perhaps his brother.

2. ROBERT, (perhaps s. of 1,) M. 1643; Cambridge; convicted of abusing his servant, John Walker, so that he d. Jan. 5, 1654, æt. 14; m. Susanna, da. of John Winslow; for descendants see Hist. Bridgew.

LATHLEY.

PHILIP, Dux., 1694, alive 1703. *Anne* of M. m. John Rouse of Little Compton, June 29, 1720.

LATHROP.

MARK, Dux., removed to Bridgew., d. 1686; had Elizabeth,

m. Samuel Packard; Mark d. in Canada Expedition, Samuel, and Edward, who. d. 1696, s. p. Vide Bridgew. Hist.

NOTE. *Rev. John*, Scituate, Barnstable, d. Nov. 8, 1653, had Thomas, Barnstable; Samuel, Ct.; Joseph, Barnstable; Benjamin, Charlestown; John, m. Mary Cole 3 Jan. 1671; Barnabas, 1635, d. 1715, æt. 79, m. Susannah Clark, 13 Nov. 1658; Jane; Barbara. Who was Abigail, who m. James Clark, 7 Oct. 1657?

LAWRENCE.

WILLIAM, Dux., 1643, able to bear arms; m. a da. of Francis Sprague.

LAZELL.

JOHN, Hingham. 1647, m. Elizabeth, da. of Stephen Gates, Nov. 29, 1649, d. 1695; of Bridgew.; had *John*, bap. Sept. 8, 1650; *Thomas*, bap. Sept. 19, 1652, Dux., m. Mary Allen, April 26, 1685, removed to Plympton, Falmouth and Windham, Ct.; and *others*, for whom see *Mitchell's Hist.*, *Hobart's Journal*.

Joshua, Dux., 1709, was son of Joshua (bap. May 6, 1655) who was a son of the first John. A John Lazell d. at Hingham May 14, 1665.—*Hobart's Journ.*

Abigail m. Barnabas Hatch June 7, 1728.

LEONARD.

1. SOLOMON, Dux., 1637, spelled "Lenner;" had land at Bluefish; d. 1686; m. Mary; had *Samuel* (of Worcester perhaps); *John, Jacob, Isaac, Solomon* (for descendants of these see Mitchell); *Mary*, m. John Pollard 24 Dec. 1673.

2. PHILIP, M. 1678, a nailer, Dux., m. Lydia, who d. Nov. 13, 1707; he d. July 3, 1708; had *Phebe*, m. Saml. Hill, 1694.

NOTE. *James, Jr.*, Taunton, m. 2d —— Caliphar, of Milton, 29 Oct. 1675; had Eunice 1668, Prudence 1669, James 1677, Lydia 1679, and Stephen 1680—*Joseph*, had Mary 1680—*Benjamin*, m. Sarah Thrasher 15 Jan. 1678, had Sarah 1680, and Benjamin 1683—*Thomas*, m. Mary Watson 21 Aug. 1662.—Col. Rec.

LEURICH.

WILLIAM, 1637, "houselott of Mr. Willm. Leurich, now layed forth for him" in Dux.—Old Col. Deeds.

LEYHORNE. (LEIGHORN.)

ROWLAND, Dux., 1636, land granted him.

JAMES, Dux.; March 4, 1638-9, "is hyred to serve Francis Sprague for a yeare for vi £ x*s*. and two pounds of tobacco, his tyme began the first of Februar last past."—Col. Rec.

LINDALL.

JAMES, Dux., 1640, a garden place was granted him in Dux. on Mill brook; m. Mary ——; both d. a. 1652; had *Timothy*, b. in Dux. 1641; ad. 1678, removed to Salem, representative; d. Jan. 6, 1699; m. Mary Verren, had nine chd., of whom Timothy, H. C. 1695, was Representative, Speaker of the House, Judge of Common Pleas, and d. 1760, æt. 83, — and *Abigail*.

NOTE. James of Boston m. Susanna, had Elizabeth July 16, 1680, and James May 28, 1684.

LORING.

1. DEA. THOMAS, arrived from Axminster, Devonshire, Eng.; of Hingham, 1635; ad. 1636, m. Jane Newton; had chd. *Thomas* (2), *Benjamin, Josiah* and *John.*

2. THOMAS, (s. of 1,) b. in Eng., 1629; ad. 1673; settled at Hull, m. Hannah, da. of Nicholas Jacob, Dec. 13, 1657, who survived him, and m. Capt. Stephen French, and d. Oct. 20, 1720; had *Hannah*, Aug. 9, 1664, m. Rev. Jeremiah Cushing, m. 2d, John Barker; *Thomas* (3); *Deborah*, Mar. 15, 1668, m. Hon. John Cushing; *David*, 1671, Barnstable; *Caleb*, 1674, m. a da. of Edward Gray, Plympton; *Abigail* d. 1679.

3. LT. THOMAS, (s. of 2,) b. Mar. 15, 1668, bought land in Dux., 1702; held offices of responsibility in the town; m. Deborah, da. of Hon. John Cushing, Apr. 19, 1699, at Boston, who d. Nov. 30, 1755, æt. 78; he d. Dec. 5, 1717; had *Thomas* (4); *Joshua*, 1701 (5); *Nathaniel* (6); *Benjamin* (7); *Hannah; Deborah*, m Sylvester Richmond, Esq., Feb. 18, 1727.

4. THOMAS (s. of 3,) Dux., m. Mary Southworth, Feb. 3, 1724; had *Thomas*, Apr. 12, 1725, m. Zilpha, da. of Capt. Robert Bradford; *Simeon; Levi* (8); *Perez*, Aug. 26, 1729 (9); *Joshua*, Feb. 5, 1735, d. Feb. 3, 1754; *Deborah*, Mar. 31, 1738.

5. JOSHUA, (s. of 3,) Dux., was never m.; d. Oct. 28, 1781, æt. 80; was buried in the old grave yard, and his stone bears these lines.

> "O death thou'st conquered me,
> And by thee I am slain;
> But Jesus Christ has conquered thee;
> And I shall rise again."

By his will he left the sum of £13 6s. 8d. to the church.

6. NATHANIEL, (s. of 3,) Dux., m. Priscilla Bailey, 1736; had *William* (10); *Nathaniel* (11); *Priscilla*, m. D. Baker; *Hannah*; *Abigail*.

7. BENJAMIN, (s. of 3,) Dux. He was bred a farmer, and passed a life of quiet happiness in his chosen pursuit. He was esteemed for his sound judgment, and respected for his uprightness and integrity, — a man of remarkable piety. He early joined the church in his native town. He built the house in which his grandson, the late Samuel Loring lived, and to which, says the tradition, he carried his wife on a pillion behind him, and then after partaking of a frugal meal, reading the Scriptures and returning thanks, retired for the night. His family devotions he never omitted until a short time previous to his death, which occurred from consumption, "1781, March ye 1st, three quarters after 8 in ye morning in the 73d year of his age;" and at his funeral a mourner pronounced a eulogy; which, though brief, was all that could be desired — repeating the passage of Scripture, Woe unto him that every one speaks well of, he added — This man's, my friends, this man's woe was never taken away. He m. Anna Alden, Feb. 8, 1739. She was a kind mother, and endeared to her children, who always spoke of her with affection. Among the excellent qualities of her character, the benevolent nature of her heart was perhaps the most marked. Those memorable words which she was accustomed to repeat, are still vivid in the imagination of her grand children — Give to him that asketh; and from him that would borrow turn not away. She d. July 1, 1804, æt. 89. Their chd. were *Mary*, Mar. 31, 1739, d. Jan. 5, 1740; *Benjamin*, Mar. 31, 1742, d. Aug. 8, 1745; *Sarah*, Feb. 14, 1744, d. Aug. 11, 1745; *Benjamin*, Nov. 25, 1745, d. Nov. 11, 1752; *Samuel*, May 1, 1747 (12); *Judah*, June 5, 1749 (13); *Daniel*, Jan. 8, 1751 (14); *John*, Sep. 27, 1752, d. Oct. 27, 1753; *Seth*, Feb. 7, 1755 (15); *Lucy*, Apr. 23, 1758, d. Nov. 8, 1847, æt. 89, m. Dr. Jabez Fuller of Medfield, Aug., 1781, and he d. Apr. 12, 1813, æt. 59, and his son, Dr. Seth, d. Sep. 4, 1807, æt. 25.

8. LT. LEVI, (s. of 4,) Dux., m. (when 60 years old,) Alethea, widow of Joshua Hall; and she d. June 5, 1823, æt. 81.

9. DEA. PEREZ, (s. of 4,) Dux., m. Sarah Freeman, (da. of Joseph,) Feb. 23, 1758, and she d. Aug. 26, 1806; he d. 1827, æt. 98; had *Mary*, Dec. 26, 1758, m. Zephaniah Fuller, Dec. 11, 1781; *Braddock*, Aug. 21, 1760, m. Mary Matthews, 1783; *Freeman*, July 25, 1762 (16); *Deborah*, Oct. 22, 1764; *Barak*, Apr. 4, 1766, d. in West Indies; *Belinda*, Mar. 6, 1768, m. Rev. Calvin Lincoln of Fitchburg; *Sarah*, Mar. 4, 1770, m. Reuben Drew, Feb., 1793; *Perez*, Mar. 10, 1772, d. in West Indies; *Persis; Levi*, Feb. 13, 1775 (17).

10. WILLIAM, (s. of 6,) Dux., m. Alethea Alden, Jan. 8, 1767, who d. Apr., 1820, æt. 76; he d. Oct. 18, 1815; a justice of the peace; had *William*, May 9, 1768 (18); *George*, Feb. 2, 1770 (19); *Ichabod*, Apr. 14, 1774, d. in W. I.; *Joshua*, Dec. 5, 1774 (20); *Samuel*, Nov. 3, 1775 (21); *Alden*, 1780 (22); *Sophia*, 1783, m. Elisha Tilden of M.; *Clarissa*, 1785, m. Abner Stetson; *Bailey*, Dec. 10, 1786 (23).

11. NATHANIEL, (s. of 6,) Pembroke, m. Miss Baker; had *Deborah*, m. Mr. Barstow; *Sarah*, m. Charles Little, m. 2d, Dea. White; *Nathaniel*, m. Catherine Smith Thomas, and had Nathaniel; *Baker; Seneca; Emily* m. Mr. Barstow.

12. SAMUEL, (s. of 7,) Dux., m. Prudence Chapman, Dec. 25, 1777, who d. Mar., 1829; he d. Oct. 16, 1816, æt. 79; had *Anna*, Nov., 1778, d. Oct. 25, 1779; *Hannah*, May 16, 1780, m. Nathl. Winsor, Dec. 9, 1800; *Benjamin*, Jan. 9, 1784, d. July 2, 1788; *Prudence*, Aug. 11, 1789, m. Capt. Richard Soule; *Lucy*, Sep. 8, 1790, was the 2d w. of Capt. R. Soule; *Samuel*, July 17, 1798 (24).

13. JUDAH, (s. of 7,) Dux., a house carpenter; went to Broad Bay, Me., carried on there the salt business; returned to Dux.; never m.; d. Oct. 4, 1832, æt. 83.

14. DANIEL, (s. of 7,) Dux.; Braintree; m. Mary Thayer of Braintree, 1779; had *James*, June 18, 1780 (25); *Mary; Judah* (26); *Barnabas Thayer*, 1790, d. s. p.; *Nathaniel W.*, m. Joan Bowditch, Braintree; *Esther; Anna*.

15. SETH, (s. of 7,) Boston, d. Sept. 10, 1779, æt. 24.

16. FREEMAN, (s. of 9,) m. Deborah Bradford Oct. 25, 1791; of Dux.; d. Nov. 7, 1820, æt. 58; had *Belinda*, Dec. 22, 1793; *Freeman*, April 25, 1796, m. Ann Sprague, settled at Medina, Ohio; *Seth*, Jan. 11, 1799; *Deborah*, Oct. 4, 1800, m. Mr. Gilson; *Barak*, Dec. 28, 1802; *Rufus*, June 18, 1804; *Eliza*, May 1, 1806; *Caroline*, Nov. 18, 1807; *Cynthia*, July 23, 1809.

17. LEVI, (s. of 9,) Dux.; deacon of Chh.; m. 1st Joanna Josselyn of Pembroke, who d. April 10, 1805; m. 2d Sarah Brooks, who d. April 10, 1828; m. 3d Joanna, who d. April 10, 1845; had *Sarah*, Feb. 19, 1804, m. Lewis Ripley of K.;

Levi Edwin, Jan. 28, 1812, d. Nov. 15, 1835; *Sarah Brooks,* Aug. 20, 1813; *Perez,* Feb. 17, 1817, m. a da. of Asa Chandler.

18. WILLIAM, (s. of 10,) Dux.; m. Judith Little, 1794; had *William Little,* June 15, 1796, H. C. 1820, Springfield, m. Lucy W. Smith of Hanover, d. 1840, had Lucy W. 1822, Benja. W. 1824, Maria F. 1826, Bailey 1828, Eliza 1834, Sophia B. 1836; *Judith,* Oct. 1, 1801, m. Geo. B. Standish; *Emiline,* Jan. 8, 1806, m. Alfred Rogers; *Bailey Hall,* June 3, 1809.

19. DEA. GEORGE, (s. of 10,) Dux.; fell from a load of hay, July 12, 1847, and, striking his head, broke a blood-vessel and expired immediately; m. Nancy Delano, Nov. 24, 1796, who d. Sept. 22, 1797, æt. nearly 22; m. Hannah Drew Jan. 31, 1802, who d. July 25, 1819; m. Wealthea Drew 1820; had *Charles,* Dec. 3, 1802; *Zilpha D.,* Nov. 15, 1804, m. Capt. Nath. Thomas Aug. 28, 1825; *George,* Nov. 30, 1806, d. at sea May 16, 1830; *Capt. Bailey,* May 3, 1813, m. Mary Basset, who d. May 28, 1848; *Clarissa,* Oct. 14, 1810, m. Chas. Jas. Fox Binney, Esq.; *Frederic W.,* Jan. 12, 1816, d. June 27, 1842; *John Smith,* Feb. 4, 1823; *Omar,* Oct. 13, 1825.

20. JOSHUA, (s. of 10,) Dux., m. Hannah Dingley 1810; had *Joshua* 1812; *Thomas D.,* m. Adeline Sherburn 1847; *Winslow; George W.; Anna P.,* m. Asa Sherman; *Alethea Alden,* m. James Hunt 1829; *Sarah D.; Sophia B.; Hannah; Elizabeth.*

21. SAMUEL, (s. of 10,) Dux., m. Lucy Delano; had *Abigail Soule,* Dec. 1, 1805, m. Peleg Barker Nov. 7, 1847; *Ichabod A.,* Feb. 17, 1807; *Samuel,* May 21, 1809; *Lucy,* July 7, 1812; *Laura Anne,* Feb. 19, 1815, m. Samuel Loring; *Benjamin D.,* May 16, 1817; *Isaac D.,* Aug. 18, 1820.

22. ALDEN, (s. of 10,) m. Lucinda Muggs; had Lucinda 1809, m. George Bailey; Laura 1811; Elisha 1813; William 1815; Hannah D. 1819; John Alden 1821; Elizabeth 1823; Sophia 1825; Gustavus 1828; Barnard 1831; Emily 1833.

23. REV. BAILEY, (s. of 10,) grad. Brown Univ. 1807, studied with Dr. Allyn; ord. at Andover Sept. 19, 1810, resigned March 1, 1849, on account of ill health; m. 1816, Sarah Pickman, only da. of Isaac Osgood, Esq. of Andover; had *George Bailey,* 1807, H. C. 1838, appointed, 1842, surgeon U. S. Hospital; *Isaac Osgood,* 1819, m. Ellen Maria, da. of Hon. D. P. King, Dec. 1, 1847, who d. March 4, 1849; *Gayton P.,* 1822, of Ware; *John Alden,* 1824, counsellor at law.

24. SAMUEL, (s. of 12,) Dux., m. Mercy Sprague Oct. 6, 1819, who d. Oct. 1847. Chd. *Samuel,* Oct. 6, 1820, m. Laura Loring; *Harrison,* Oct. 25, 1822, m. Eliza H. Tobey, who

d. 1848; *Seth Loring Sprague*, Aug. 23, 1824, grad. Middletown College, Ct., physician, Boston; *Julia Norris*, Aug. 6, 1826, m. Nathan Brewster; *Ann*, Nov. 25, 1828, d. Nov. 26, 1846; *Martha*, Nov. 23, 1831; *Emily*, Jan. 27, 1834, d. Nov. 1846; *Prudence C.*, May 20, 1837, d. 1839; *Charles Carrol*, Jan. 2, 1840; *Abbott*, Feb. 15, 1844.

25. JAMES, (s. of 14,) Dux., m. Mary Freeman, who d. Nov. 9, 1816; m. Ruth, widow of Nathaniel Delano, and she d. Feb. 10, 1830; had *Daniel*, Feb. 8, 1807, m. Hannah Norris of Gardiner, Me.; *Judah*, April 15, 1809; *Barnabas Thayer*, Nov. 8, 1811, m. Frances E. Porter of Boston; *James Thayer*, July 1, 1816; *Mary*; *Frances*, Dec. 29, 1827.

26. JUDAH, (s. of 14,) Braintree, m. Elizabeth Nash; had *Samuel Clark*; *Judah Alden*, m. Martha V. Edson, 1847; *Anna Alden*; and *Mary*.

27. COL. JOTHAM. (He was a son of Thomas Loring and Sarah Hearsey of Hingham, and grandson of Elder John, of Hull, who m. Jane, da. of Samuel Baker, and who was son of John, of Hull, whose father was Dea. Thomas, No. 1.) Hingham, removed to Dux.; m. Mary Richmond, who d. Nov. 14, 1776, æt. 43; m. 2d in Dux., Luna, widow of Benja. Wadsworth, and she d. June 20, 1815; he d. Sept. 28, 1820. He had *Sarah*, May 8, 1769, m. Philip Chandler Nov. 3, 1792; *Sylvester Richmond*, June 15, 1775, d. Nov. 18, 1796; *Jotham*, June 12, 1772, d. 1776; *Polly*, 1776, m. Ezra Leavitt 1806; by 2d w., *Wadsworth*, Oct. 9, 1786, m. Lucy Sampson, who was b. Nov. 17, 1787, and d. June 27, 1837, had Wadsworth Sept. 7, 1809, Mary R. Sept. 13, 1812, d. July 21, 1839, Edward T. Nov. 27, 1814.

NOTE. I am much indebted to a MS. account of the Loring family, by Mr. James S. Loring of Boston.

LOUDEN.

Abner m. Mercy, who afterwards m. Robert Keen of Bristol, 1780. He d. Jan. 2, 1766, æt. 40, had Josiah, Feb. 9, 1774; Mercy, July 3, 1776.

Sylvanus, (b. Feb. 30, 1768,) m. 1790, Elizabeth, who was b. Nov. 9, 1770, and d. Aug. 1, 1840, and had Betsy, 1792, Eunice, 1794, Joanna, 1796, Huldah, 1799, Lydia, 1801, and Mary, 1804.

Richard, Dux., about the middle of the last century.

Nathaniel, Dux., removed to Bridgewater, m. Experience Pratt, 1762. Vide Mitchell.

Bethiah m. Jona. Crooker, Jr. of Pembroke, Jan. 14, 1743; *Michael* m. Eunice Prior, Nov. 25, 1760; *Ruth* m. Bezaleel

Merrick of Rochester, 1760; *Michael* m. Martha, 1796, and had a family.

MAGOON.

Early McGoun, now Magoon and Magoun.

1. JAMES, Dux., m. Sarah, had *James*, Mar. 25, 1697.
2. ELIAS, Dux., m. Hannah, had *David*, Nov. 1, 1703, m. Rachel Soule, Sep. 26, 1728; *Mary*, Mar. 24, 1705; *Elias*, Oct. 9, 1707.

NOTE. Elias, the elder, may have been the son of John of Scituate, in 1666, who had John, 1668, Elias, 1673, and Isaac, 1675 — *Hist. Scit.* This was probably the John "Makoon" of Cambridge, in 1663. A John "Maggone" was m. at Hingham, 1662, and had a da. 1663, and a son, James, June 25, 1666. — *Hobart's Journal.* Sarah m. Stephen Bryant, Nov. 23, 1710. — *Dux. Records.*

MAYCUMBER.

1. WILLIAM, Dux., 1638. See *first settlers.* M., 1667; a William of Dartmouth, 1684.
2. JOHN, Taunton, carpenter, 1644; a John of Taunton, had Thomas, Apr. 30, 1679, William, Jan. 31, 1683. A Sarah of M., m. Wm. Briggs of Taunton, 6 Nov., 1666.

MAYNARD.

JOHN, Dux., 1643, and after.

McFARLAND.

1. JOHN, Dux., spelled Magvarland, had *John*, Feb. 11, 1706 (2); *Hannah*, June 8, 1709.
2. JOHN, (s. of 1,) Dux., m. Martha, had *Robert*, removed to Pembroke, and *Sarah* (3).
3. SARAH, (da. of 2,) was b. 1739, and for an account of her, see The Sprague Family Memorial.

McLAUGHLIN.

JOHN, K., d. Sep. 14, 1772, æt. 77½; had *John*, m. Jedidah Sampson, July 7, 1763; *Jenny* m. Samuel Sampson, Aug. 22,

1769; *Daniel*, Dux., m. Acenith Stetson, 1779, had Acenith m. Joseph Ford, Mary m. Benj. Prior, Sophia m. Levi Sampson, Prudence m. Joshua Hathaway, Bartlett, Simeon, and Lucy; *Joseph* had Capt. John, who m. Parmelia, removed to Shrewsbury, d. Nov. 17, 1831, æt. 42 (see Ward's Shrewsbury); *Margaret*, d. July 31, 1776, æt. 27.

NOTE. Mr. Robert, d. at K., Sep. 26, 1825, æt. 85; Capt. Robert d. at K., Dec. 28, 1836, æt. 66.

MENDALL.

ROBERT, Dux., 1639, sold house and land to John Phillips. A *John* was of M., 1677.

MENDAME.

ROBERT, Dux., 1639, m. Mary.

MENDLOWE.

MARK, Dux., 1640, presented for drawing eelpots on the Lord's day, but it was shown to have been done "of necesytie meerly."

MERRICK.

WILLIAM, Dux., 1636, allowed 5 acres next the glade at Powder point; 1637, 20 acres at G. H., 1645, prob. of Bridgewater. A William Merritt (Merrick?) was constable, 1647.

NOTE. *William*, Eastham, had William, Sep. 1643, m. Abigail Hopkins, 23 May, 1667, (had Rebecca 1668, and William 1670,) Stephen, May 1646, m. Mercy Bangs, 28 Dec., 1670, Rebecca 1648, Mary 1650, Ruth 1652, Sarah 1654 and John, Jan. 15, 1656.— *Col. Records.* John Merrick d. at Hingham, July 2, 1647. *Hobart's Journal.*

MITCHELL.

EXPERIENCE, arrived 1623, Plymouth, Dux., 1645, Bridgewater, d. 1689, æt. 90, m. Jane Cook, m. 2d, Mary; had *Thomas; Jacob*, Dartmouth, d. 1675; *John*, Dux., m. Mary Boney, Dec. 14, 1675, who d. May 13, 1677, m. 2d, Mary Lathrop, Jan. 14, 1679, who d. Feb. 13, 1680, m. Mary Prior, May 24, 1682, sold his house in Dux., to Geo. Williamson, had Mary, Feb. 28, 1682, Hannah, Feb. 13, 1683, Joseph, Mar. 23, 1684, Dux., 1710, Elizabeth, Mar. 25, 1685, Elizabeth, May 29, 1686, John, Jan. 13, 1689, Sarah, May 9, 1690, Esther, Jan. 22, 1692; *Edward* m. Alice Bradford, Hingham, sold land in Dux., at Bluefish to Samuel Sprague; *Elizabeth* m. John Washburn, 1645; *Sarah* m. John Hayward; *Mary* m. James Shaw, 1652, d. 1679; *Hannah* m. Joseph Hayward. — For an extended account of this family, see Mitchell's valuable history.

MOORE.

1. RICHARD, Dux., yeoman, lived near Wm. Brewster, sold (1637) his land at Eagle nest.
2. GEORGE, was of Edw. Dotey's family, 1630, Plymouth, 1637; kept ferry at Jones' River, was allowed to charge a penny; Scituate, 1642; d. 1677, "by a fainting fit, or a sudden stoppinge of his breath."

MORREY (MOREY).

GEORGE, Dux., 1640, was granted land for a house in Dux., near North hill, and d. same year.

MORTON.

1. NATHANIEL, Dux., 1638, had land at "long poynt" meadow.
2. THOMAS, Dux., 1639, had land at Mosquito hole.

MULLINS.

WILLIAM, arrived 1620, with wife and three others, (one a da. m. John Alden,) he d. Feb. 21, 1621. *William*, perhaps his son, is mentioned in connection with land in 1637, Dux., 1640, had 10 acres at G. H. path; alive 1662, and styled one of "the first borne children of this Gov'ment." A *William Mullings* m. Ann Bell, widow, at Boston, May 7, 1656. *Joanna* m. John Laughton, 21 Sep., 1659, at Boston.*

* We find also these on the Boston Records.—John Mullings m. Ann Bowden, Feb. 17, 1708; Thomas Mullings m. Hannah Bullard, Feb. 10, 1708.

MYNOR.

JOHN, Dux., early, took oath of fidelity.

NASH.

LT. SAMUEL, Dux., b. 1602, was sheriff of the colony for many years, appointed 1652; a Rep.; prob. of Bridgew.; lived in his old age with his son-in-law, Clark; had *Martha* m. Wm. Clark; ——— m. Abraham Sampson;—His will names his grand daughters Elizabeth Delano and Mary Howland.

NOTE. *James* m. Sarah Simmons, Dux.; *James*, Weymouth, 1655, had Jacob, James, Joseph of Scituate; *John*, Boston, cooper, 1656; *James*, shoemaker, Boston, 1651; *Robert*, butcher, Charlestown, 1642, and d. Sep. 3, 1661, and had Elizabeth, who m. John Conney, June 4, 1654. *Joshua* and Elizabeth at Boston, had Elizabeth, 17 Feb., 1661, Sarah, Feb. 20, 1663, Joseph, Feb. 14, 1671. *John* and Rebecca at Boston, had Mary, 26 Nov., 1667, John, 9 Mar., 1671. *Timothy* m. Mary Foster, Apr. 2, 1694, and had Rebecca, 1695.

NEAL.

JOHN, Dux., m. Sarah Wadsworth, Feb. 3, 1774, had John, Aug. 6. 1775; Charlotte, Aug. 25, 1778; Barker, Feb. 12, 1792; Parmenia, Jan. 12, 1785.

NOTE. *John*, above, was probably the son (b. 1744,) of Job Neal, (and Sarah Barker), the son of Joseph, who went from Provincetown to Scituate, 1700. Deane's Scituate.

NELSON.

SAMUEL, appears in Dux. 1740. Abiel m. Benj. Prince 1717.

NORCUT.

EPHRAIM, Dux., m. Elizabeth, had *John*, April 6, 1732.

NOTE. *William*, d. 1693; m. Sarah, had Ralph, the heir, William (who had John), John, Thomas, Isaac, Ephraim, Ebenezer, Lydia, Anne, Sarah, Patience, Experience. His will calls Ralph Chapman his brother-in-law.

OLDHAM.

1. THOMAS, Dux. 1643, cooper, Scit., 1650, m. Mary Witherell Nov. 20, 1656; d. 1711; had *Mary*, Aug. 20, 1658; *Thomas*, 30 Oct. 1660, m. Mercy, da. of Robert Sprout, 1683, had Mercy m. Andrew Newcome 1708, Desire m. Samuel Tilden 1717, Joshua and Mary (twins) 1684; *Sarah ; Hannah ; Grace ; Isaac*, m. Hannah Kein Nov. 21, 1695, of Dux.; *Ruth ; Elizabeth ; Lydia*, 1679.

2. JOHN, Dux., m. Elizabeth Chandler 1779, d. June 19, 1832, æt. 78; had *Elizabeth*, Jan. 6, 1780; *John*, March 1, 1782, removed to Pembroke; *Chandler*, June 28, 1784; *Thomas*, April 25, 1786; *Anna*, March 15, 1789; *Hannah*, Feb. 14, 1792; *Sally*, June 17, 1794.

3. PELEG, (B. of 2,) Dux., m. Anna Simmons, Nov. 29, 1764, had Josiah, Caleb, Mercy and Anna.

NOTE. *Sarah* m. Samuel Sprague 1741. *Bethiah* (sister of 2 and 3,) m. Micah Weston 1761. *Hannah* (sister of 2 and 3,) m. Serajah Glass 1771. *Betty* m. Judah Hunt 1764. *Oliver* d. in Canada Expedition, Oct. 1759. *Hannah* m. Eliphalet Bradford 1758.

OSBORN.

CHRISTOPHER, Dux., 1638, presented to the Colony Court for being disorderly.

NOTE. John, of Weymouth 1657, had Ephraim.

PABODIE.

The name is also spelled Paybody, though the family at the present day spell it Pabodie, which also was the usual spelling of the signatures of William of Dux., though sometimes he spelt it Paibody.

1. JOHN, 1637, had 10 acres at Bluefish; ad. Jan. 2, 1637-8; prop. of Bridgew. 1645; will dated July 15, 1649; d. a. 1666; m. Isabel, who survived him; had *Thomas ; Francis ; William* (2); *Anice*, m. John Rouse.

2. WILLIAM, (s. of 1,) Dux., b. 1620; was "a man much employed in public affairs and of much respectability;" m. Elizabeth Alden Dec. 26, 1644, and d. Dec. 13, 1707, æt. 87. The following account of her death is from the Boston Newsletter, June 17, 1717: — "Little Compton, 31 May. This morning died here, Mrs. Elizabeth Paybody, late wife of Mr.

William Paybody, in the 93 year of her age. She was a daughter of John Alden, Esq. and Priscilla his wife, daughter of Mr. William Mullins. This John Alden and Priscilla Mullins were married at Plymouth in New England, where their daughter Elizabeth was born. She was exemplarily virtuous and pious, and her memory is blessed. She has left a numerous posterity. Her grand-daughter Bradford is a grandmother." Mr. Pabodie lived in Dux., east of Eagle nest creek, and near Brewster and Standish; had *John*, Oct. 4, 1645, d. Nov. 17, 1669, æt. 24; the verdict of a jury was, " that hee ryding on the road, his horse carryed him underneath the bow of a young tree and violently forceing his head into the body thereof brake his skull;" *Elizabeth*, April 24, 1647, m. John Rogers 1666; *Mary*, Aug. 7, 1648, m. Edw. Southworth 1669; *Mercy*, Jan. 2, 1649, m. John Simmons 1671; *Martha*, Feb. 24, 1650, m. Samuel Seabury 1677; *Priscilla*, Nov. 16, 1650, d. young; *Priscilla*, Jan. 15, 1653, m. Rev. Ichabod Wiswall; *Sarah*, Aug. 7, 1656, m. John Coe 1680; *Ruth*, June 27, 1658, m. Benj. Bartlett, Jr. 1672; *Rebecca*, Oct. 16, 1660, m. prob. Wm. Southworth; *Hannah*, Oct. 15, 1662, m. Samuel Bartlett 1683; *William*, Nov. 24, 1664, removed to Little Compton and m. Judith, who d. July 20, 1714; m. 2d Ruth, who d. Dec. 14, 1717, and he d. Sept. 17, 1744; and *Lydia*, April 3, 1667.

PADDOCK.

1. ROBERT, Dux., 1638, a smith; m. Mary; d. July 25, 1650, at Plymouth; had *Robert; Susanna*, m. John Eedy, Nov. 6, 1665, d. March 14, 1670; *Zachariah*, 20 March, 1636; *Mary*, 10 March, 1638; *Alice*, 7 March, 1640, m. Zachariah Eedy 7 March, 1663; *John*, 1 April, 1643, Swansey, m. Anna Jones (?) 21 Dec. 1673. His son-in-law *William Palmer* was b. 27 June, 1634.

NOTE. *Zachariah* (prob. father of 1), it is said, came-over in the Mayflower, at that time a minor. *Mary* m. Thomas Roberts 24 March, 1650, at Plymouth.

PALMER.

LT. WILLIAM, Dux. 1632, ad. Jan. 1, 1634, owned land at Eagle nest; 1638, sold his house in Dux. to Thos. Besbeech; 1643, Yarmouth; a " nayler."

PARRIS.

THOMAS came from London to Long Island 1683, removed to Newbury 1685, Pembroke 1697, of Dux. 1710. He was son of Rev. John of Ugborough, Eng., who was son of Thomas, a merchant of London. His chd. were *Thomas*, May 8, 1701, at Pembroke, m. Hannah Gannet 1724, d. 1786, and for whose children see Deane's Scituate, and Mitchell's Bridgew.

John Parris m. Mary Judd, at Braintree, 30 Aug. 1663.—Elizabeth, da. of Tho. and Elizabeth, b. at Boston 10 July, 1693.—Boston Rec.

PARTRIDGE.

1. GEORGE, Dux., yeoman, 1636, (see *first settlers*); m. Sarah Tracy Nov. 1638, d. about 1695; had *John*, Nov. 29, 1657 (2); *Lydia*, m. Dea. Wm. Brewster 1672, and d. Feb. 3, 1743; *Ruth*, m. Rodolphus Thacher Jan. 1, 1669; *Triephosa*, m. Samuel West, Sept. 26, 1668; *Mercy*; *Sarah*, 1639, m. Dea. Samuel Allen of Bridgew.; *James* (3).

2. JOHN, (s. of 1,) Dux., inherited lands in Middleborough; m. Hannah Seabury Dec. 24, 1684; m. 2d Mary Brewster May 23, 1700; had *Sarah*, Sept. 21, 1685, d. Nov. 18, 1685; *Samuel*, March 10, 1687; *George*, Aug. 17, 1690 (4); *Mary*, May 2, 1693, m. Jona. Brewster Mar. 6, 1710; *John*, Dec. 27, 1697; *Benjamin*, March 5, 1701; *Isaac*, March 2, 1705 (5).

3. JAMES, (s. of 1,) inherited his father's lands in Dux.; m. Mary Stetson of Scituate, April 24, 1712, who d. æt. 50, Sept. 27, 1727, "about nine of ye clock in ye evening." He d. Jan. 20, 1744.

4. GEORGE, (s. of 2,) Dux., inherited his estate from his father; m. Hannah, da. of the first Dea. Foster of Plymouth and widow of William Bradford, who d. Dec. 17, 1778, æt. 84; he d. Jan. 24, 1768, æt. 78; had *George*, Feb. 8, 1740 (6); *Hannah*, m. Nov. 23, 1758, Bartholomew Richardson, the father of Capt. Geo. P. Richardson, who lives on the estate of his uncle George Partridge, in Dux.; and *Samuel*, (7).

5. ISAAC, (s. of 2,) Dux., lives on the homestead; m. Grace Sylvester March 10, 1730, who d. April 2, 1768, æt. 61, he d. Jan. 26, 1794; had *Ruth*, May 23, 1730, d. Jan. 15, 1756, æt. 24; *John*, May 28, 1732, d. Sept. 14, 1755, æt. 23½; *Lucretia*, May 2, 1735, never m.; *Calvin*, May 29, 1739 (8).

6. HON. GEORGE PARTRIDGE (s. of 4). He d. on the morning of July 7th, 1828, in the 89th year of his age. See p. 152. An address was delivered at his funeral by Rev. Mr. Kent,

which was published, and from which I have frequently extracted.

7. CAPT. SAMUEL (s. of 4). He resided in Boston, where he was a merchant successfully engaged in business. He was twice married. His second wife was Miss Hubbard. His da. *Rebecca* m. Benj. Barker of Pembroke, who removed to Scit.

8. COL. CALVIN, (s. of 5,) Dux., m. Mary, widow of Col. Ichabod Alden, Oct. 24, 1779. He d. Nov. 27, 1815; had *John*, Nov. 22, 1781, m. Elizabeth Delano of M., who was b. Sept. 30, 1788, and had Elizabeth, Lucretia, Ruth, Mary and John; *Ralph*, Nov. 13, 1783, m. Hannah Sprague, had Almeda 1815, m. Wm. Ellison, Ralph 1816, d. at sea 1836, Wealthea L. 1821, m. Capt. Ebenezer Howes, George Leroy 1829; *Mary*, Dec. 10, 1786, m. Nathl. Soule, Jr.; *Rebecca*, m. Constant Sampson; *Ruth ; Hannah*, Dec. 12, 1792; *Ichabod Alden*, May 1, 1798.

NOTE. *Mehetable* m. John Soule 1730; *Sarah* m. Asa Hunt 1736.*

PEAKES.

WILLIAM, Dux., constable, 1666.

PEIRCE.

1. ABRAHAM, Plymouth, 1627, Dux., 1643, prop. of Bridgew. 1645, d. before 1673, had *Abraham* (2); *Isaac* (3); *Rebecca*, m. —— Wills; *Mary*, m. —— Baker; *Alice*, m. —— Baker.

2. ABRAHAM, (s. of 1,) Dux., had land in Dux.; had *Abraham*, who removed to Pembroke, and m. Abigail Peterson, Sept. 25, 1729, and *Hannah*, April 1706.

---

* There was a family of Partridge early in Medfield, but it is not known what connection, if any, existed between them and the Duxbury branch. I glean the following from the Boston records: *William*, of Medfield, m. Sarah Peirce, Nov. 23, 1654, and she d. May 16, 1656, m. 2d Sarah Colburne, Nov. 19, 1656, and had Eleazer, May 13, 1656, Nathaniel, Nov. 3, 1660, John, Feb. 13, 1662, Elisha, Feb. 27, 1665. *John*, of Medfield, m. Magdalen Bullard, Dec. 18, 1655, had John Sept. 21, 1656, Hannah April 15, 1658, Deborah Aug. 16, 1662, and Eleazer Feb 20, 1664.—Boston Rec. Priscilla m. Joseph Plympton Aug. 22, 1699. Elizabeth m. Wm. Caswell May 10, 1716; Elizabeth m. Joseph Ellis 12 Dec. 1716. William m. Rachel Goss Nov. 15, 1711. Magdalen, of Medway, m. David Daniels 11 Feb. 1724. Stephen, of Medway, m. Mary Maccane April 7, 1737. Deborah m. Zach. Barbar 24 Dec. 1717. Sarah m. Joseph Marsh Feb. 24, 1717. Lydia, of Medfield, m. Nathl. Smith 24 June, 1717. Margery, of Medfield, m. Thomas Mason April 23, 1653.—Boston Rec.

3. ISAAC, (s. of 1,) Dux., 1684, alive 1710; owned land west of Namasakeeset brook.

4. SAMUEL, m. Mary Saunders, Jan. 18, 1703, Dux. 1710, removed to Gloucester. JOHN and THOMAS were also in Dux. 1710.

5. BENJAMIN, Dux., m. Lucia Burgess, May 11, 1775, had *John*, who was drowned; *Benjamin*, who lived at Saquish.

6. JOSEPH, Dux., d. Jan. 5, 1796, m. Olive, had *Joseph*, July 25, 1774; *Luther*, May 9, 1776; *Calvin*, July 26, 1778; *Seth*, March 7, 1786.

NOTE. Abigail m. Lemuel Simmons 1770; Joseph d. Jan. 1, 1813, æt. 82.

PETERSON.

1. JOHN, Dux., d. 1690, m. Mary Soule.

2. JOSEPH, (B. of 1,) Dux., had *Jonathan* (3); *Benjamin*, 1670 (4); *David*, Oct. 1, 1676, d. Sep. 30, 1760, æt. 84, nearly; *Isaac* (5); *John*, Dux., 1710.

3. JONATHAN, (s. of 2,) Dux., m. Lydia Thacher, who d. May 26, 1756, æt. 77¼; had *John*, Aug. 22, 1701; *Hopestill*, Jan. 20, 1703, m. Joshua Delano; *Jonathan*, Sep. 20, 1706 (6); *Reuben*, Apr. 8, 1710 (7).

4. BENJAMIN, (s. of 2,) Dux., m. Hannah Wadsworth, Feb. 9, 1698, who d. the "night following the 6th day of February, anno, 1733." He d. Feb. 11, 1760, æt. 90½ years; had *Jacob*, Feb. 22, 1711 (8).

5. ISAAC, (s. of 2,) Dux., m. Mary Hobart, da. of Daniel. She was b. 1689, and d. Mar. 22, 1763, æt. 74; had *Priscilla*, m. Eliphas Weston.

6. JONATHAN, (s. of 3,) Dux., d. May 5, 1765, æt. 58; had *John* (14); *Jonathan* (16); *Laurania* m. Charles Rider of Plymouth, Apr. 20, 1773; and committed suicide, Mar. 9, 1791; *David*, a. 1757; *Turner*, a. 1760.

7. REUBEN, (s. of 3,) Dux., m. Rebecca Simmons, July 6, 1732, who d. Jan. 25, 1764, æt. 50; had *Elijah* (9); *Mary*, d. æt. 38, June 25, 1772; *Nehemiah* (10); *Abigail* m. Zenas Thomas, Feb. 14, 1765; *Sarah* m. Cornelius Delano, 1762; *Lydia*, a. 1742; *Thaddeus* (11); *Luther* m. Priscilla Cushman, 1789; *Reuben* (12).

8. JACOB, (s. of 4,) Dux., m. Mary, who d. Oct. 20, 1777, æt. 60. He d. Jan. 27, 1784, had *Benjamin*, Mar. 4, 1739, who m. Bethiah Cushing, June 22, 1758, and had Sarah, Apr. 16, 1759; Hannah, Jan. 2, 1761, m. Levi Dingley, 1778;

Benjamin, July 10, 1763 (13); Bethia m. Joseph Prior, Apr. 18, 1769.

9. ELIJAH, (s. of 7,) Dux., m. Abigail Whittemore of M., Oct. 24, 1765, and had *Whittemore,* Apr. 13, 1784, m. Jerusha, who was b. Oct., 1791, and *Joel,* who was twice m.

10. NEHEMIAH, (s. of 7,) Dux., m. Princee Dillingham, Dec. 13, 1764; had *Nehemiah,* removed to Me.; *Lydia; Mary* m. Stephen Churchill; *Princee* m. Joshua Bryant; *Elisha,* drowned; *Ezias,* Dec. 12, 1782, m. Lydia, who was b. Apr. 26, 1779.

11. THADDEUS, (s. of 7,) Dux., m. Anne Wadsworth; he d. July 27, 1825, æt. 82; had *Selah,* Feb. 22, 1771; *Luke,* 1773; *Frederic,* Dec. 25, 1775; *Anne,* Jan. 30, 1780; *Ichabod Wadsworth,* May 14, 1782; *Rebecca,* July 22, 1784; *Mary,* Aug. 23, 1787; *Sophia,* Aug. 16, 1790.

12. REUBEN, (s. of 7,) Dux., m. Abigail, who d. Jan. 13, 1842; had *Samuel G.,* 1779; *Ichabod,* 1781, d. 1805; *Abigail,* 1783; *Thomas,* 1786; *Charles,* 1788; *Reuben,* 1791; *Clark,* 1793; *Sarah,* 1797; *Lucy,* 1799.

13. BENJAMIN, (s. of Benj., s. of 8,) Dux., m. Sarah Prior, 1783; had *Henry,* Oct. 30, 1783, d. at Guadaloupe, May 19, 1799; *Allen,* Nov. 17, 1785; *Hannah,* Apr. 4, 1788; *Louis,* July 25, 1790; *Benjamin,* Nov. 20, 1793; *Africa,* Oct. 12, 1796; *Sarah,* Oct. 11, 1800.

14. JOHN, (s. of 6,) Dux., m. Sarah Hewitt of M., Sep. 20, 1765; removed to Me.; had *John,* lost at sea; *Levi; Charles* b. at Me.; *Hewett* b. at Me.; *Sarah* b. at Me., m. Robert Bosworth.

15. JONATHAN, (s. of 6,) Dux., lived at Mill Brook, m. Lucy Hunt, 1771; had *Lewis,* m. Sarah Fuller of K., lost at sea; *George* m. Sarah Prior; *Wealthea* m. a Robinson; *Olive.*

16. JOSEPH, (s. of ?) Dux., m. Rebecca Delano, Apr. 4, 1773; had *Daniel,* Oct. 9, 1775, m. Bethia Weston, and had Daniel, 1803, Hannah, 1806, Amanthis, 1807, Jerusha, 1809, George, 1812, m. Hannah Prior, Martha m. William Prior; *Betsy* m. Joseph Wadsworth.

17. JOSHUA, (s. of ?) Dux., m. Silvia Soule, Feb. 1780, had *Joshua* 1786, *James* 1792, and *Mehetable.*

NOTE. *Rebecca* m. John Weston, 1717; *Mercy* m. Joseph Weston, 1721; *Abigail* m. A. Peirce, 1729; *Rebecca* m. Bethuel Packard, 1783; *Mary* m. Zadock Weston, 1767; *Alice* m. Aaron Soule, 1727; *Packard* d. May 10, 1843, æt. 56; *Thomas W.,* Mar. 24, 1766, m. Lydia Ford; *Benjamin,* lost at sea, Jan., 1765, æt. 26; *Faith* m. Samuel Drew, 1746; *Mary* d. Apr. 3, 1763, æt. 75; *Sarah* m. Timothy Williamson, 1767; *Susanna* m. Gershom Ewell, Jr., 1767.

PHILLIPS.

1. JOHN, 1639, Dux., 1640, had a garden place on Stoney brook, and land towards G. H.; was b. 1602; lived also in M., m. 1st in England; m. 2d, widow Faith Doten, Mar. 14, 1667; he d. 1677,* and she survived; had *John* (2); *Samuel* who had chd.; *Benjamin*, M., 1685, had s. John; *Mary*, of whom her father says in his will, that "by reason of ye weakness of her reason and understanding, she is incapable to maintain and provide for herself."

2. JOHN, (s. of 1,) Dux. and M., m. 2d, Grace Holloway, 1654, and d. July 31, 1658; † had *Hannah*, 1654; *Grace*, 1654; *Joseph*, 1656; *Benjamin*, 1658, m. Sarah Thomas, 1681, and had John, 1682, m. Patience Stevens, 1710, Joseph 1685, Benjamin 1687, Thomas 1691, Jeremiah 1697, Isaac 1702.

3. THOMAS, (s. of?) Dux., d. Dec. 17, 1759, æt. 81, m. Rebecca, who d. Mar. 4, 1761, æt. 80; had *John*, 1707, d. 1791, Mar. 16, æt. 84, m. Mary, who d. Mar. 21, 1791, æt. 82; *Samuel*, 1709, d. Nov. 26, 1734; *Rebecca* m. Philip Chandler, 1725; *Thomas* (4); *Blanie* (5).

* His first wife died June 23, 1666, as appears from a letter by the Rev. Samuel Arnold of Marshfield, to the Rev. Mr. Mather of Boston, in 1683, wherein the circumstances are thus related:—"We being sorely distressed with drought, had on the fourth day of the week made our address to the Most High God, by humble fasting and prayer. The drought continued until the last day of the said week, on which day it pleased God to answer us by terrible things in righteousness, who was yet the God of our Salvation; for about the middle of the day thare arose in the North the most dismal black cloud, I think that ever I saw." It came up, and was very dark, and there was much thunder and lightning. There were at the house of John Phillips, fourteen persons. "Instantly a terrible clap of thunder fell upon the house and rent the chimney, and split the door in many places, and struck most of the persons, if not all." Three were "mortally struck with God's arrows, that they never breathed more." They were the wife of Mr. Phillips, and his son, aged about ten years, and one William Shertly, "who had a little child in his arms, which was wonderfully preserved." This Shertly had just before been burnt out of his own house, and with his family was at this time "a present sojourner" at said Phillips'. A dog also, which was under a table behind two small children, was killed, while they were preserved. — *Mather MSS.*

† The manner of his death was as follows:—Being at work in the meadow, making hay, a tempest suddenly arose, and he immediately started for the nearest house. Having entered, he sat down in a chair between the door and the chimney, when the lightning struck the chimney, and descending, passed out the door, knocking him lifeless upon the ground. Persons who were within three feet of him escaped unharmed. — *Deposition of Capt. Nathaniel Thomas, among the Mather MSS.*

4. THOMAS, (s. of 3,) Dux., m. Jedidah, who d. Jan. 8, 1741; he d. Nov. 11, 1778, æt. 73; had *Mary*, Jan. 29, 1731; *Rebecca*, May 18, 1732, m. Thomas Dawes, July 31, 1771; *Abigail*, Apr. 1, 1733; *Thomas* (6).

5. BLANIE, (s. of 3,) Dux., m. Christian Wadsworth, May 23, 1733; had *Samuel*, May 9, 1734, d. young; *Blanie*, July 3, 1736 (7); *Samuel*, May 2, 1738, d. Sep. 18, 1756, of a fever; *Christian*, Apr. 7, 1740; *Mercy*, Mar. 10, 1742, d. Sep. 16, 1744; *Mercy*, Oct. 6, 1744; *Seth*, a. 1750; *Lot*, a. 1755; *Betty*, a. 1757.

6. THOMAS, (s. of 4,) Dux., m. Abigail Chandler, 1771; had Abigail B., 1774, Rebecca, Luther, Mary, Chandler, and Silvia.

7. BLANIE, (s. of 5,) Dux., m. Mary, who d. July 20, 1773; æt. 35; he removed to Fitchburg, a. 1789; had *Olive*, Jan. 24, 1763, m. 1782, Robert Sampson; *Eunice*, Sep. 29, 1764, d. young; *Samuel*, Aug. 5, 1766; *Eunice*, June 30, 1768; *Mary*, Nov. 8, 1769; *Huldah*, Dec. 5, 1771.

NOTE. *Nathaniel* m. Joan White, both of M., Jan. 16, 1635; Dea. *Elisha* m. Mary Wadsworth, July 1, 1756; *Susanna* m. Abner Russell, Dec. 24, 1764; *Amos* m. Priscilla Seabury, Dec. 24, 1778; *Asa* m. Clynthia Southworth, Oct. 5, 1769; *Sarah* m. Gideon Dawes, 1771; *Bethiah* m. James Basset of K., Oct. 14, 1773; *Hannah* m. Jesse Curtis, July 28, 1774; *Benjamin* m. Olive, and had Joseph, Nov. 13, 1797. — Dux. Rec.

John m. Ann Torrey, 1677; *Richard* Weymouth, 1673; *William*, Boston, vintner, 1655; *Jeremiah* d. at M., 1666; *Thomas*, Yarmouth, 1657; *William*, Taunton, d. a. 1654, m. Elizabeth, and had James; *James*, Taunton, had James, Jan. 1, 1661, Nathaniel, Mar. 25, 1664, Sarah, Mar. 17, 1667, William, Aug. 21, 1769; *Samuel* m. widow Cobb, May 15, 1676, and had Mehetable, Jan. 9, 1676. — Col. Rec.

PIDCOCK.

GEORGE, Dux., 1644, a tailor. A George Pidcoke was a householder of Scituate before 1640, m. Sarah Richards in the same year, and was living, 1670. — Hist. Scituate.

POLLARD.

GEORGE, 1639, Dux., miller, 1640, land North of Mill brook; came from Stokeslere, England; yeoman; had an elder brother, John Pollard, "of Belchamp, St. Paule, Essex, England," who in 1671, after his brother's death, made application for the share of his brother in the mill; but C. Southworth, who now owned the other half, refused to give it up on account of the trouble he had had with it, and was sustained by the Court.

A John Pollard, had John, 20 Mar., 1675. — *Col. Rec.*

PONTUS.

WILLIAM, d. at Plymouth Feb. 9, 1652, had *Mary*, m. Jas. Glass, m. 2d P. Delano; *Hannah*, m. James Churchill.*
A William was in Namasakeesett, 1663.

PRENCE.

Gov. THOMAS, b. 1600, arrived 1621; Governor of the Colony, Plymouth, removed to Dux. 1635; Eastham 1644; m. 1st, 1624, Patience Brewster, she d. 1634; m. 2d, 1635, Mary Collier; m. 3d, Mary, widow of Samuel Freeman, 1662; and, d. April 8, 1673, æt. 73; his w. survived—of Plymouth 1658. Had *Thomas*, went to England, m. there, d. young, leaving Susanna, who is called in 1677, of "Catheren Gate, near the Tower, London, singlewoman;" *Elizabeth*, m. Arthur Howland, Jr.; *Mercy*, m. Feb. 14, 1649, John Freeman; *Rebecca*, m. Edmund Freeman, Jr. 1646; *Hannah*, m. Nath. Mayo 13 Feb. 1649 (and had Thomas, Nathaniel, Sàmuel, Hannah, and Theophilus), m. 2d, Jona. Sparrow; *Jane*, m. Mark Snow 9 Jan. 1660; *Judith*, m. Isaac Barker 28 Dec. 1665; m. Wm. Tubbs 1691; *Mary*, m. John Tracy of Dux.; *Sarah*, m. Jeremiah Howes 1650.

PRINCE.

1. BENJAMIN (see note below), Dux., m. Abiel Nelson April 1, 1717; removed to North Yarmouth, Me., and ad. to the Chh. there a. 1730; he d. Dec. 1, 1737, æt. 44, and she d. 15 Sept. 1744; and they had,—*Benjamin*, April 14, 1718, m. Rebecca Fisher at N. Yarmouth, m. 2d, Hannah —— a. 1742, and she d. March 8, 1796; *Paul*, March 14, 1720, m. Hannah Cushing at N. Yar., and d. Nov. 25, 1809, æt. 90, and she d. Feb. 6, 1814, æt. 92; *Sylvanus*, Sept. 17, 1722, m. Elizabeth Johnson, and d. Sept. 18, 1790, æt. 68, and she d. April 7,

---

* *John Churchill*, who d. Jan. 1, 1662, had Hannah 12 Nov. 1649; Eleazer, 20 April, 1652 (who had Hannah 23 Aug. 1676, and Joan 25 Nov. 1678); and Mary, Aug. 1, 1654. *Joseph* Churchill m. Sarah Hicks 1672, and had John 22 July, 1678. *John* m. Desire Holmes before 1695.—Col. Records.

1800, æt. 71 years; *Sarah,* April 8, 1725, and *John,* May 20, 1727.

2. THOMAS, b. 1695, shipwright, Dux.; bought a farm of Samuel Sprague; m. Judith Fox, Nov. 25, 1729; had *Hannah,* Oct. 22, 1730, m. Eliphalet Bradford 1751; *Judith,* m. Eden Thomas 1757.

NOTE. *Thomas,* Dux., 1713, exchanged land; *Thomas* m. Lydia, and returned to K. 1755; *John, Jr.* was of Namasakeeset 1669.—JOHN b. 1610, (s. of Rev. John of East Strafford, Eng.) Nantasket 1638, Hull 1644, d. there Aug. 6, 1676, æt. 66, had *John* 1638, d. 1690; *Elizabeth,* 1640; *Joseph,* 1642, m. Joanna Morton Dec. 7, 1670; *Martha* 1645; *Job* 1647; *Mary* 1648; *Samuel,* 1650 (father of Rev. Thomas, the chronologist). Vide Mitchell's Hist. *Sarah* 1651; *Benjamin* 1652; *Isaac* 1654, m. Mary Turner 1683; *Deborah* 1656, m. Wm. King; *Thomas,* bap. Aug. 3, 1658, Scituate, m. Ruth Thomas (who next m. Israel Sylvester of Dux.), and had Thomas, July 10, 1686, Benjamin 1693 (probably No. 1), Job 1695.—History Scituate. Mary Prince m. Joseph Joye Aug. 29, 1667.—Hobart's Journal.

PRIOR.

1. THOMAS came from England, Scituate 1634, and d. 1639; had *Samuel, Thomas, Elizabeth, Mary,* all in Eng. in 1639; *Joseph* (2); *John* (3); *Daniel,* m. Mary.

2. JOSEPH, (s. of 1,) b. 1623, Dux. 1643; lived with John Rogers of Dux. in 1644, then not quite 21 years old; 1672, had a grant of land; m. Hannah; inventory of estate taken Feb. 12, 1690.

3. JOHN, (s. of 1,) removed to Dux.; m. there Eleanor Childs Aug. 1695.

4. BENJAMIN, (s. of –,) Dux., m. Bethiah Pratt Dec. 9, 1697, who d. Dec. 25, 1756, æt. 77; had *Benjamin,* Oct. 30, 1699 (5); *Abigail* Sept. 9, 1701; *Ruth,* Aug. 4, 1704, m. John Delano, Jr. 1724; *Joshua,* Aug. 1, 1709; *John,* March 21, 1712 (6).

5. BENJAMIN, (s. of 4,) Dux., tanner; m. Deborah Weston Nov. 7, 1723, who d. Dec. 7, 1775, æt. 73; he d. Dec. 3, 1766, æt. 67; had *Rebecca,* Feb. 14, 1725; *Jabez,* April 16, 1727, d. Oct. 3, 1757, æt. 30; *Lois,* Jan. 25, 1729, d. Sept. 18, 1812, æt. 84; *Eunice,* Feb. 25, 1731, d. Sept. 2, 1734; *Eliphas,* Sept. 11, 1733 (7); *Sylvanus,* June 13, 1735, d. June 28, 1738; *Eunice,* Dec. 15, 1736, m. Michael Louden 1760; *Sylvanus,* Feb. 3, 1739, d. at Martinique Oct. 6, 1762; *Benjamin,* Oct. 23, 1740 (8); *Ezra,* a. 1743, d. Oct. 15, 1756; *Joseph,* a. 1745 (9).

6. JOHN, (s. of 4,) Dux., m. Mercy Delano Oct. 14, 1735; had *Hannah*, Aug. 10, 1736; *Nathaniel*, Oct. 31, 1739; *Ruth*, April 11, 1742; *John*, Nov. 5, 1744, m. Lydia Osyer April 13, 1767, had Susanna July 7, 1768; *Elias*, Dec. 21, 1747.

7. ELIPHAS, (s. of 5,) Dux.; m. Hannah, da. of Josiah Howard, who d. May 31, 1776; had *Sylvanus*, Aug. 3, 1764 (10); *Sarah*, m. Benj. Prior 1783; *Hannah*.

8. BENJAMIN, (s. of 5,) Dux., m. Sarah Soule Jan. 1765; had *Jabez*, Dec. 23, 1765; *Joanna*, March 22, 1766, m. Joshua Cushing; *Mercy*, April 22, 1767, m. Benj. Bosworth; *Anne*, Oct. 21, 1770, m. Nathl. Holmes; *Jabez*, April 26, 1772, m. Abigail, who d. Nov. 2, 1799; *Matthew*, April 2, 1774; *Sarah*, m. George Peterson; *Benjamin*, m. Mary Mc Laughlin, who d. Nov. 22, 1832.

9. JOSEPH, (s. of 5,) Dux., m. Bethia Peterson April 18, 1769, had *Mary*, March 15, 1770; *Joseph*, Aug. 27, 1771; *Ezra*, Nov. 16, 1773; *William*, Feb. 22, 1776; *Melzar; Deborah*.

10. SYLVANUS, (s. of 7,) Dux., m. Christian Chandler Jan. 31, 1793, who was b. Feb. 20, 1770; had *Eliphas* Feb. 13, 1794; *Charles* Feb. 11, 1796; *Lucy Chandler*, Nov. 23, 1801; *Sylvanus*, Jan. 1, 1805; *George C.*, Feb. 6, 1807; *Henry*, Oct. 16, 1808; *Hannah*, March 22, 1811; *Allen*, Oct. 5, 1813.

11. JOHN, (s. of 2,) Dux., East Bridgewater, m. Bethia Allen, d. 1742. Vide Mitchell.

12. JAMES, (s. of —,) Dux., m. Abigail, had *Joanna*, d. Jan. 20, 1757; *Deborah*, m. Ebenezer Thompson of Halifax, 1781; *Abigail*.

RANDALL.

1. NEHEMIAH, Dux. 1710. He was probably the s. (b. 1688) of Job, of Scituate, who was the son of Joseph, the son of William, who was of Rhode Island 1636, M. 1637, Scituate 1640.—Vide Deane's Scituate. An Elizabeth m. Caleb House July 12, 1759; and another of the same name m. Saml. Fish 1732. Job, of Dux., d. in Canada Expedition, Nov. 1759.

2. THOMAS, Dux., had Thomas 1786, Washburn 1789, d. 1799, Luther 1792, John 1795, Asksah 1797, Betsy 1799, James 1803, Mary 1805, Sarah 1807, and Rufus 1810.

READ.

BENJAMIN, Dux., 1643, able to bear arms.

RHENOLDS (REYNOLDS).

WILLIAM, Dux., 1636, in Feb. had a grant of land in Dux., and soon after the Government allowed him to build. 1637–8, presented to the Court for being "drunk at Mr. Hopkins his house, that he lay under the table vomiting in a beastly manner, and was taken up between two." He m. Alice Kitson, 30 Aug., 1638.

John (and Ann,) Reynolds, Weymouth, 1660.

RICHARDS.

WILLIAM, Dux., had Rispah, bap. Apr., 1740. Mercy m. Jona. Weston, May 8, 1728.

RICHARDSON.

1. DR. EDMUND, Dux., d. May 30, 1761, æt. 29, of "of plurisy." He was a native of Woburn, and was there buried.

2. BARTHOLOMEW, m. Hannah Partridge, 1758, and was the father of Capt. Geo. P. Richardson of Dux.

RIPLEY.

1. CAPT. HEZEKIAH, Dux., m. Abigail Hunt, Dec. 3, 1739; removed to K., 1759; had *Rufus* a. 1741; *Spenser* a. 1746; *Olive* a. 1749; *Sabin; Hezekiah*, 1751, d. at K., Oct. 18, 1841, æt. 90, had Rufus, 1787, who d. at sea, Nov. 10, 1810, æt. 23.

2. ABNER, (s. of ?) m. Abigail Robbins, Mar. 14, 1746, who d. Dec. 12, 1773, æt. 55.

3. WILLIAM, (s. of ?) Dux., m. Lydia Hunt, 1758, who d. Dec. 23, 1774; he was cast away on Duxbury beach, and perished, Nov. 17, 1766, æt. 32; had *Rebecca*, Sep. 5, 1760, m. Nathaniel Alden, 1783; *Piram*, Nov. 22, 1762; *William*, July 10, 1764; *Pelham*, 1766.

4. KIMBALL, (s. of ?) Dux., m. Sarah Sprague, Jan. 24, 1771; she d. Mar. 28, 178-, æt. 39; had Daniel, Kimball, and Sarah.

NOTE. *Sarah* m. Amos Howes, Jan. 11, 1748; *Sarah* m. Consider Thomas, Mar. 10, 1774; *Joshua* had Alice bap. 1756; *Abigail* m. Gideon Wing, 1767; *Elizabeth W.* m. Isaac Delano, 1782. — *Dux. Rec.* A *Joshua* Ripley b. at Hingham, Nov. 9, 1658, d. May 18, 1739. — *Hobart's Journal.*

ROBBINS.

1. NICHOLAS, Dux., 1638, bought Thomas Burgess' house; 1640, land at North hill, and at Namasakeeset; a shoe maker; m. Ann; had *John*, who was of Dux., 1661, afterwards of Bridgewater, became helpless, m. Jehosabeth Jourdaine, 14 Dec., 1665, had Jeduthan 1667, for whose descendants, see Mitchell's Hist; *Mary ; Hannah ; Catherine.*

2. THOMAS, Dux., 1643, able to bear arms.

NOTE. *William*, Hingham, m. Susanna Lane, 1665, and was perhaps son of Richard of Hingham, Cambridge, and Boston.—*Abigail* m. Abner Ripley, 1746.

ROBERTS.

THOMAS, Dux., 1640, had land with George Morrey.

ROBINSON.

1. ISAAC, (s. of the Leyden pastor, Rev. John) Plymouth; Dux., before 1635 bought land at Is. ck. of Edmund Chandler, sold it to Thomas Bidle; Scituate, 1636; Barnstable, 1639; m. a sister of Elder Faunce; d. æt. 93. *Deane's Scit.*

NOTE. *George* (Swanzey,) m. Elizabeth Gaille, Nov., 1680, had John, 1681; *Samuel* (s. of Geo. Jr.,) b. Nov., 1679.

2. JOHN "Roberson;" Dux.; m. Elizabeth; had *Betty*, Sep. 16, 1754; *Martha*, Mar. 29, 1756; *John*, Mar. 1, 1768; *Isaac*, Sep. 6, 1760; *Robert*, Nov. 22, 1762; *Nancy*, Apr. 30, 1775.

ROGERS.

1. JOHN, 1634, bought land in Dux., of Edmund Chandler, for £12; will dated, Feb. 1, 1660; m. Frances; had *John* (2); *Joseph ; Timothy*, M., 1681, freed from bearing arms, being lame; *Ann*, m. John Hudson; *Mary ; Abigail.*

NOTE. One of the daughters m. George Russell.

2. JOHN, (s. of 1,) Dux., d. a. 1696; m. Elizabeth Pabodie, Nov. 1666; had *Hannah*, Nov. 16, 1668; *John*, Sep. 22, 1670; *Ruth*, Apr. 18, 1675; *Sarah*, May 4, 1677; *Elizabeth.*

3. JOHN, M.; by his will gives to gd.-son John Tisdell, for the use of his mother Anne Tenney, land in Middleboro'; had *Elizabeth* m. a Williams; *John ; Abigail* m. a Rich-

mond, and had Joseph and Edward; *Hannah* m. John Tisdell, Jr., 23 Nov., 1664, she is called of Dux.

4. JOHN, (Deane conjectures he was a descendant of the Springfield martyr,) Scituate, 1644, Mitchell says he was in Dux.; m. Ann Churchman, Apr. 16, 1639; he d. Feb. 11, 1661, at Weymouth; had *Lydia*, Mar. 27, 1642; *John* (5); *Thomas*, M., had Samuel, who went to E. Bridgewater; *Samuel*, M.

5. JOHN, (s. of 4,) Scit., m. Rhoda, da. of Thomas King, Oct. 8, 1656; a quaker; had *John* of M., had Alice 1682, Daniel, Elizabeth, Thomas, Hannah, Joshua, Mary, Caleb 1718; *Abigail* m. Timothy White, 1678; *Mary* m. John Rouse, 1659; *Lydia* m. Joseph White, Sep. 19, 1660; *Hannah* m. Samuel Pratt, Sep. 19, 1660. Deane's Scituate.

6. JOSEPH; a Lt.; Sandwich; had *Sarah*, b. and d. 1633; *Joseph*, 19 July, 1635, m. Susanna Deane, Apr. 4, 1660, d. Dec. 25, 1660, because John Hawes "gave him a most deadly fall;" had Joseph (who had Thomas); *Thomas*, 29 Mar., 1638; *Elizabeth*, 29 Sep., 1639, m. Jona. Higgins, 9 Jan., 1660; *John*, 3 Apr., 1642; *Mary*, 22 Sep., 1644; *James*, 18 Oct., 1648, m. Mary Paine, 11 Jan., 1670 (?); *Hannah*, 8 Aug., 1652.

7. JOSEPH, kept a ferry at Jones River, where he lived, and was allowed by the Court to charge a penny for transportation. A *Joseph* was of Namasakeeset 1663, when he was ordered to leave the colony for a crime. *Joseph, Jr.*, d. at Eastham, Jan. 27, 1660. *Joseph*, Dux. 1643. *Joseph*, 1640, had 50 acres at North river. *Joseph*, Dux. 1689-1710.

NOTE. *Timothy* m. Sarah Kein April 6, 1710; *Francis*, Dux. 1710; *Elizabeth*, of Abington m. Thomas Terrill Sept. 13, 1720; *Nathaniel*, of M. m. Hannah Ford July 23, 1781; *John, Jr.* of M. m. Hannah Sprague Dec. 11, 1700.—T. Records. *Lt. Rogers* d. at Eastham 1678, leaving Thomas. *Symon*, tanner, Boston, m. 1st Mary, who d. Aug. 1, 1640, m. 2d Susan, had Nathaniel, Feb. 14, 1642, Lydia Dec. 1, 1645, Symon 28 April, 1654, Gamaliel March 26, 1657, Joseph July 29, 1662.—Boston Records.*

ROSE.

1. JOHN, M.; he "was overcome by the violence of the weather, Feb. 13, 1676, while gunning on the beach." The

* We also find on the Boston records—At Weymouth John Rogers m. Mary Bates Feb. 8, 1663; Susanna, da. of Joseph and Elizabeth Rogers, was b. Dec. 4, 1688. Jane, da. of Gamaliel and Mercy, was born Jan. 3, 1688. These two were probably sons of Symon.

"ruens of Rose ould house" are frequently mentioned in Dux. records, as being near Mill brook.

2. THOMAS, (B. of 1,) Scituate, 1660, had John, killed at Rehoboth; *Thomas*, m. Lydia Turner; *Gideon*. See Deane's History.

NOTE. *Joseph*, M., 1657. *Robert* and *John* were of Conn. early.

ROUSE.

1. JOHN, M., and Dux. 1640; m. Anice Pabodie; his will is dated 1682; her will gives Samuel Cornish her servant, a "gun, sword and belt, wch he useth," and her bible to Anna; had *John*; *Simon*, inherited land in Dux., Saconet 1681, kept a house of entertainment for strangers; *Mary* m. a Price; *Anna* m. a Holmes; *Elizabeth* m. Thos. Bourn April 10, 1681.

2. JOHN, (s. of —,) Scituate; M. 1640; a quaker; had *John* 1643; *George* 1648.

NOTE. A John m. Mary Rogers 1659. A John had a grant of land at Namasakeeset in 1665. A John, of Little Compton, m. Anne Lathley, of M., June 29, 1720.*

ROWE.

JOHN, Dux., early, took oath of fidelity.

RUSSELL.

1. GEORGE, Hingham 1636, Scituate 1646, m. 2d widow Jane James Feb. 14, 1640; had *George* (2), and *Samuel*, (who m. Mary, and was killed at Rehoboth,) by 1st w.; by 2d w. *Mary*, bap. April 1, 1641; *Elizabeth*, bap. Feb. 1643; *Martha*, bap. Oct. 9, 1645.—Hobart's Journal.

2. GEORGE, (s. of 1,) Dux., 1652; M. 1657; m. a Rogers; d. 1675; had *George*, who in 1684 had land at Robinson's creek; and *John*, who had the same.

3. NATHANIEL, Dux. 1657.

4. JOHN, Dux., m. Esther Mayes Jan. 21, 1702, had *Samuel*, Aug. 31, 1703, d. March, 1782; *George*, Aug. 26, 1704; *Elizabeth*, Dec. 21, 1705; *Anne* and *Solomon* (twins) March 1, 1709.

---

* *Rouse*. William m. Sarah, and had Mary 29 Dec. 1676, m. Erasmus Harrison Jan. 3, 1694,—and William, May 25, 1678, m. Lydia Bell Nov. 15, 1705 (and had Joseph 14 July, 1706, and William 8 Nov. 1707.)—Boston Records. Jonathan m. Martha Waters Dec. 15, 1710. Alexander m. Elizabeth Goff April 6, 1713.—Idem.

5. JOSEPH, Dux., m. Abigail Wadsworth Dec. 31, 1740; she d. July 2, 1770; he d. Feb. 12, 1791, æt. 79; had *Silvina*, Dec. 21, 1745, d. Aug. 4, 1764; *Abner*, May 28, 1744, m. Susanna Phillips Dec. 24, 1764; *Abigail*, June 13, 1749, m. Malachi Waterman March 30, 1772; *Saba*, Jan. 9, 1754.

SAMPSON.

The name on the early records is generally spelt *Samson*.

1. HENRY, arrived 1620, Dux., m. Ann Plummer Feb. 6, 1635–6; he d. Dec. 24, 1684; had *Stephen* (2); *John*, inherited land in Dartmouth; *James*, settled in Dartmouth; *Caleb* (3); *Elizabeth* m. Robert Sprout; *Hannah* m. Josiah Holmes 1665; ―――― m. John Hammond; *Mary* m. John Summers, (Mitchell says Simmons); *Dorcas* m. Thomas Boney.

2. STEPHEN, (s. of 1,) inherited land at Dartmouth; m. Elizabeth, lived in Dux.; d. 1714; had *Benjamin, Cornelius, Hannah, Mary, Elizabeth, John*, Aug. 17, 1688 (4), *Dorcas Abigail*.

3. CALEB, (s. of 1,) m. Mercy, da. of Alexander Standish; had *Rachel* Dec. 5, m. Moses Simmons March 26, 1718; *Lora* m. Benj. Simmons Jan. 3, 1706.

4. JOHN, (s. of 2,) Dux., m. Priscilla Bartlett, Dec. 31, 1718, who d. July 2, 1758, æt. nearly 61; had *Susanna*, Aug. 30, 1720; *Zilpah*, Feb. 27, 1722, d. July 1796, æt. 74; *John* (d. Sept. 11, 1724) and *Priscilla* (gemini) May 21, 1724; *Elizabeth*, Feb. 1726; *John*, Aug. 8, 1727 (5); *Elisha*, April 6, 1730, d. at New York 1776; *Sylvanus*, March 13, 1732, d. in East Indies 1758; *Elijah*, June 7, 1734 (6).

5. JOHN, (s. of 4,) Dux., m. Rebecca Brewster, who d. Aug. 6, 1759, æt. 25; m. 2d, Abigail Stetson; had *Lucy*, who d. June 5, 1759, æt. 4; *Lucy* m. Wm. Bradford; *Celia*, who d. Jan. 8, 1842; *Dolly; Rebecca; Andrew; Sylvanus*(7); *Lewis; Cynthia*, who d. Feb. 17, 1844, æt. 68.

6. ELIJAH, (s. of 4,) Dux.; m. Ruth Bradford, Sep. 3, 1761; m. Hannah; he d. Mar. 16, 1805; had *Elijah* m. Hannah Sprague, 1784; *Stephen*, Sep. 23, 1768, m. Christianna Lewis, Dec. 12, 1802, who was b. Apr. 11, 1774; *Bradford*, Nov. 11, 1772; *Martin*, Oct. 10, 1783, m. Sarah Freeman; *Thomas*, Feb. 27, 1786, m. Mary Thomas, who was b. Apr. 25, 1791; *Bartlett; Zophar; Priscilla* m. William Soule, 1784; *Abigail; Elizabeth; Deborah; Wealthea; Dorcas; Ruth*, Apr. 24, 1767, m. Cyrus Brewster.

7. SYLVANUS, (s. of 5,) Dux., m. Silvia Church Weston, who d. 1836; had *Silvia Church*, Dec. 3, 1788, d. 1789;

Church, Nov., 1790, d. 1793; *Salumith Weston*, Nov. 25, 1793, m. Otis Soule; *Ezra Weston*, Dec. 1, 1797, m. Celenah Wadsworth; *Elizabeth*, Oct. 13, 1802; *Silvia Church*, Oct. 21, 1804, m. John Owen; *Sylvanus*, Oct. 12, 1807, m. Mary Chapman Soule.

8. ABRAHAM, (perhaps B. of No. 1,) Dux., 1638; ad. 1654; had land at Blue fish; alive 1686; m. a da. of Saml. Nash; m. 2d, ——— ———; had *Abraham* (9); *Isaac* (10); *Samuel* (11); and *George*, 1655 (12).

9. ABRAHAM, (s. of 8,) Dux., m. Lorah Standish; had *Abraham*, 1686 (13); *Miles*, 1690 (14); *Ebenezer* (15); *Rebecca*; *Sarah* m. Joseph Sampson of Dartmouth, May 6, 1719(?); *Grace*, d. Jan. 2, 1786, æt. 85.

10. ISAAC, (s. of 8,) m. Lydia, da. of Alexander Standish; he d. 1726; had *Isaac*, 1688, m. Sarah; *Jonathan*, 1690, m. Joanna; *Josiah*, 1692, d. 1731; *Lydia*, 1694; *Ephraim*, 1698, m. Abigail; *Peleg*, 1700, m. Mary Ring, had Mercy, 1731, and Capt. Simeon, 1736, who was a naval commander of the Revolution, and who m. Deborah Cushing, 1759, who d. 1830, æt. 90, and he d. 1789 [see Hist. Plymouth]; *Priscilla*, 1702, m. Jabez Fuller; *Barnabas*, 1705, m. Experience.

11. SAMUEL, (s. of 8,) Dux., kld. in Phillips' war; m. Esther, who after the death of her husband was granted £5 per year for two years; had *Samuel*, and *Ichabod*.

12. GEORGE, (s. of 8,) Plympton; m. Elizabeth, a. 1678, who d. May 27, 1727, æt. 70; he d. July 26, 1739, æt. 84; had *Joseph*, July 14, 1679; *Abigail*, Jan. 22, 1681; *Judith*, Mar. 3, 1683; *Ruth*, Dec. 22, 1684; *Benjamin*, Sep. 19, 1686; *Martha*, Oct. 25, 1689; *George*, Mar. 10, 1691 (16); *Elizabeth*, Dec. 22, 1692; *William*, July 8, 1693; *Seth*, Dec. 22, 1697.

13. ABRAHAM, (s. of 9,) Dux.; m. Penelope; he d. Nov. 16, 1775, æt. 89; sold his farm to Joshua Soule, 1729, for £400; *Ruth*, July 2, 1713, m. Amasa Delano, Jan. 8, 1730; *Hannah*, Nov. 4, 1715; *Rebecca*, Oct. 26, 1718, m. Nathl. Blackmore of Dartmouth, May 22, 1740; *James*, Feb. 19, 1720; *Abraham*, July 31, 1721; *Stephen*, Oct. 23, 1722; *Henry*, Aug. 4, 1724, m. Joanna Sampson, May 11, 1749.

14. MILES, (s. of 9,) Dux., m. Sarah Studley, Apr. 28, 1713, who d. Nov. 2, 1782, æt. 93; he d. Nov. 26, 1784, æt. 92; had *Andrew*, Sep. 28, 1714 (17); *Alice*, Feb. 21, 1717, m. Robert Sampson, Dec. 19, 1734; *Joseph*, Nov. 16, 1719, (18); *Sarah*, Mar. 25, 1723; *Deborah*, June 12, 1726, m. Amos Sampson, Oct. 19, 1744; *Beriah*, Nov. 1, 1728, m. Alse Howland, May 6, 1756; *Miles*, May 13, 1731 (19); *Judah*, Aug., 1735.

15. EBENEZER, (s. of 9,) Dux., m. Zeruiah Soule April 23, 1728, who d. Dec. 21, 1782, æt. 77; he d. Nov. 25, 1778, æt. 82; had *Eunice; Abigail*, m. John Hanks March 25, 1773; *Nathan; Hannah.*

16. GEORGE, (s. of 12,) Dux., Plympton, m. Hannah Soule of Dux. Dec. 10, 1718; he d. Feb. 6, 1774, æt. 83; she d. Sept. 22, 1776, æt. 79; had *Gideon*, Oct. 15, 1719; *Sarah*, April 29, 1721; *Deborah*, March 1, 1725; *Zabdiel*, April 26, 1727 (20); *Hannah*, Oct. 15, 1730; *George*, Jan. 20, 1733, d. Feb. 1733; *Rebecca*, Jan. 27, 1735; *Elizabeth*, June 19, 1737.

17. ANDREW, (s. of 14,) Dux., m. Sarah, who d. Oct. 14, 1746; m. 2d Abigail Bisbee Feb. 1, 1745; he d. Sep. 6, 1776, æt. nearly 72; had *Samuel*, m. Aug. 22, 1769, Jenny Mc Laughlin; *Jedidah*, m. John McLaughlin July 7, 1763; *Andrew*, [2d w.] m. Saba Howard Feb. 3, 1779; he d. April 21, 1842, æt. 93, had Saba Oct. 6, 1789, who m. John Brown; *William, Abigail.*

18. JOSEPH, (s. of 14,) Dux.; m. Sarah Hull of K. May 6, 1747; had *Abel*, d. at Halifax, Nov. 23, 1777; *Isaiah*, m. Betsy Sampson 1782; *Kenelm*, 1761; *Sarah*, 1762; *Cela*, 1764; *Sylvanus*, 1667; *Mercy*, 1771; *Daniel*, 1774.

19. MILES, (s. of 14,) Dux., m. Deborah; had *Ichabod* Feb. 5, 1753, who had Ichabod (who m. Elizabeth Thomas, and had Ichabod 1828, Elizabeth T. 1830), Nathan (who m. Waity Wadsworth), Spencer and Charles (who m. Mary Woodworth) —*Ruby*, Feb. 25, 1757, m. Peleg Cullifer Dec. 15, 1774; *Acenith*, Oct. 18, 1758; *Betty*, June 21, 1760, m. Isaiah Sampson 1782 (?); *Ahira*, June 15, 1762.

20. ZABDIEL (s. of 16,) Plympton, m. Abigail Cushman Dec. 31, 1747, who d. May 4, 1751, æt. 23, m. 2d Abia Whitmarsh Aug. 27, 1752, who d. Dec. 26, 1800, æt. 76; he was killed at Haerlem battle, Sept. 16, 1776, æt. 49; had *Sarah*, June 2, 1749, m. Wm. Bent; *Zabdiel*, July 6, 1754, d. June 25, 1776; *George*, Sept. 3, 1755; *William*, Feb. 3, 1757; *Abigail*, July 11, 1758, m. Gideon Bradford; *Gideon*, March 15, 1760 (21); *Hannah*, March 3, 1762, m. Richard Cooper; *Abia*, Feb. 15, 1764, d. young; *Philemon*, March 6, 1766, m. Fanny Drew of Halifax; and *Issachar*, June 12, 1768.

21. GIDEON, (s. of 20,) Plympton; m. Lydia Ripley June 29, 1780, who was b. Oct. 1, 1759; he d. Sept. 22, 1839, æt. 79; she d. Sept. 23, 1846, æt. 86; had *Abiah*, May 29, 1781; *Lucy*, Dec. 28, 1783, m. Joseph Mitchell 1806; *Sally*, Dec. 4, 1785, d. 1819; *Gideon*, d. young; *Lydia*, Sept. 3, 1790, m. Joseph Winsor Oct. 11, 1810; *Gideon*, d. young; *Abigail*, April 6, 1793, m. Capt. Ebenezer Fuller 1817; *Deborah*, Aug. 19,

1795, m. Capt. Richard Cooper, Jr. 1817; *John*, Sept. 28, 1798, m. Hannah Wright 1828, m. 2d C. S. Parker 1835, m. 3d P. E. Parker 1841; *Nancy*, April 16, 1800, d. 1819; *William Henry*, Aug. 20, 1802, of Dux., m. Sarah Sprague of Dux., and had Oscar H., Eugene, Leonice, Lucy Sprague.

22. NATHANIEL, (s. of —,) Dux.. m. Keturah Chandler Jan. 19, 1703, who d. Jan. 14, 1771, æt. 88⅓ yrs.; had *Noah*, Jan. 24, 1705; *Perez*, Oct. 21, 1706; *Fear*, Nov. 16, 1708, m. Benjamin Simmons, 1731; *Robert*, April 2, 1712 (23); *Nathaniel*, Feb. 22, 1716; *Keturah*, Jan. 14, 1719, m. Thomas Cullifer 1743; *Anna*, Mar. 1, 1723; *Abner*, July 3, 1726 (24).

23. ROBERT, (s. of 22,) Dux., m. Alice Sampson, Dec. 19, 1734; he d. June 12, 1775, æt. 63; had *Robert*, m. Olive Phillips 1782; *Levi*, 1751, d. in the army Sept. 13, 1778, æt. 27; *Consider; Noah* (25).

24. ABNER, (s. of 22,) Dux., m. Sarah; m. 2d Deborah Bisbee April 20, 1756; had *Mary*, March 22, 1750, m. Lot Hunt Macrh 4, 1773; *Abner*, April 10, 1752, m. Ruth Burgess 1781; *Sarah*, May 13, 1757, m. James Weston 1785; *Isaac*, March 21, 1760; *Deborah*, Oct. 18, 1761, m. Hon. Seth Sprague; *Lucia*, Feb. 6, 1763; *Luna*, March 29, 1765; *Nathaniel*, April 25, 1767, m. Hannah, who d. April 19, 1846, æt. 75, he d. Aug. 23, 1813, æt. 46; *Aaron*, Sept. 20, 1769; *Wealthea*, April 22, 1773, m. William Freeman, and d. April 14, 1847.

25. NOAH, (s. of 23,) Dux., m. Abigail; had *Beulah*, Sept. 28, 1780, and *Levi* July 21, 1783, who m. Sophia Mc Laughlin, and who had Augustus Aug. 24, 1806, m. Sally Brewster, Erastus Aug. 28, 1808, m. Elizabeth Winsor (and had Erastus, b. July 19, 1832, and Agnes), Noah, Nov. 16, 1810; Daniel Nov. 22, 1812 (m. Mary Alden), Simeon, Feb. 20, 1815, m. Caroline Sampson, lives in Illinois, Alexander 1817, m. Hannah Weston, George 1819, Lucy 1821, m. Edmund Gifford, who resides in Illinois, Charles Eddy 1826, and Frederic 1828.

26. JOSHUA, (s. of —,) Dux., m. Mary ——, who d. Nov. 11, 1780, æt. 87; he d. Aug. 4, 1741; had *Amos*, Nov. 6, 1725 (27); *Anthony*, April 16, 1728 (28); *Sarah*, Oct. 5, 1741; *Huldah*, June 23, 1734, m. Ichabod Delano 1759.

27. AMOS, (s. of 26,) Dux., m. Deborah Sampson Oct. 19, 1744; he d. Dec. 1795; had *Joshua; Elijah; Amos; Studley* April 27, 1759 (29); *Lauraina; Lydia*, April 6, 1747, m. Uriah Sprague 1796, and d. Sept. 1, 1842.

28. ANTHONY, (s. of 26,) Dux., had *Nathaniel* 1751; *Oliver; Anna; Keturah; Lucy*, d. young; *Thomas*.

29. STUDLEY, (s. of 27,) Dux., m. Abigail Prior, Nov. 16, 1780, who was b. July 20, 1753, and d. Feb. 23, 1824, æt. 70;

m. 2d Peleg Churchill's widow, and he d. May 9, 1835; had *Jabez P.*, 1781, d. 1782; *Deborah* 1783; *Studley* May 10, 1784, drowned Oct. 10, 1819; *Gaius*, June 26, 1785, m. Mary Sampson, removed to Boston, d. July 9, 1842, had Gaius (who m. Sarah Harvey), George (who m. Isabella Soule), Mary m. Mr. Frothingham, Marcia, and Louisa; *Abigail*, Sept. 24, 1787, m. Noah Simmons; *Alfred*, Sept. 1791, m. Wealthea Joyce, and has Alfred, George F., Studley, Catherine P., Olive R., Maria F., Mary F.; *Deborah*, Sept. 26, 1793, m. Stephen Churchill, m. 2d Capt. Samuel Hunt; and *Joanna*, who d. young.

30. CALEB, (s. of —,) Dux., m. Rebecca Stanford Jan. 30, 1729, had *Martin*, bap. 1741.

31. PAUL, (s. of —,) Dux., had *Sylvia* a. 1754; *Olive; Martin*, d. Sept. 4, 1760; *Luther* (32), *Caleb, Martha, Esther* a. 1766.

32. LUTHER, (s. of 31,) Dux.; m. Abigail, had *David* Jan. 26, 1784; *Harriet* June 19, 1785; *Charlotte* June 12, 1787; *Silvia* March 19, 1790; *Rozelle* June 9, 1792.

33. CAPT. CHAPIN, (s. of —,) Dux., m. Betty; he d. in W. Indies Sept. 1, 1773; had *Elizabeth* June 10, 1762, m. Wm. Weston 1781; *Chapin*, Aug. 14, 1764; *Job*, Sept. 19, 1766, m. Betsy Winsor, and had Henry Briggs (who m. Nancy Turner), Betsy (who m. Thomas Power, Esq. of Boston), William (who m. Caroline Sprague), and Judith; *Judith* Dec. 10, 1768; *Briggs* May 20, 1772, d. unm.

34. PEREZ, (s. of —,) Dux.; m. Mary, had *Arunah*, Oct. 5, 1762; *Stephen*, Feb. 27, 1765.

35. GIDEON, (s. of —,) Dux.; had *Abigail*, b. 1773, d. 1781; *Hepzibah*, 1775.

36. JOHN, JR., (s. of —,) Dux.; m. Hannah; had *Sarah Alden*, Sep. 12, 1792; *Anne Green*, June, and d. Sep., 1795.

NOTE. David, Dux., 1710, d. May 10, 1772, æt. 85; Jerusha m. Ebenezer Bartlett, 1710; Elizabeth m. Jona. Thayer of Mendon, Feb. 21, 1723; Hannah m. Robert Tyler of Mendon, Dec. 13, 1721; Hannah of Rochester, m. Experience Holmes, Dec. 13, 1737; Joanna m. Henry Sampson, 1749; Sarah, b. 1729, d. 1759, Dec. 2; Rachel 1730, d. Apr. 20, 1789; Keturah, widow, d. Feb. 18, 1791, æt. 70; Deborah m. Rev. S. Veazie, 1742; Irene m. Luther Delano, Jr., 1774; Edith m. Seva Chandler, 1782; Lucy m. Wm. Burgess, 1783; Mrs. Hannah d. Dec. 10, 1843, æt. 75; *Dux. Rec.* Hugh and Mary of Boston, had Hugh, Sep. 13, 1690. Edward and Lettice of Boston, had Edward, Nov. 22, 1715. Alexander of Boston, m. Rebecca, and had Elizabeth 1728, Alexander 1729, and John 1731. *Boston Rec.*

SAUNDERS.

JOHN, Dux., 1710, m. Elizabeth, widow of Thomas Wright, and had *Edward*.

NOTE. *Mary* of Dux., m. Samuel Peirce, Jan. 18, 1703; *Henry* d. at Sandwich, 1685, leaving 2 sons; *Martin* and *John* were of Braintree, 1657.

SEABURY.

1. JOHN, Boston, d. before 1662; m. Grace, had *John*, went to Barbadoes; *Samuel*, Dec. 10, 1640 (2); and some daughters.
2. SAMUEL, (s. of 1,) removed to Dux.; a physician;—We find the following memorandum in Suffolk Deeds, vol. III: "Samuel Seaberry, sonne of the late John Seaberry of Boston (now living in Duxbury), this 10th of April, 1662, entered his claim to a certain house and parcel of land heretofore belonging to his father, now belonging to his brother John Seaberry of Barbadoes and himself, the said house and land being in possession of one Nathaniel Fryer, who detains it from them under a pretence of a purchase from Alexander Adams, and he from John Milom, the land being about half an acre more or lesse, and bounded with the land formerly Isaac Grosse, northwest, Walter Merry on the southeast and southwest, and the bay northeast, which claim he resolves to prosecute, &c." His name is spelled variously, Sebury, Saberry, Saberrey (to his will), Sabery, &c. He owned land at Is. Ck., North river, the Gurnet. and at the brick-kilns. He m. Patience Kemp, Nov. 9, 1660, at Weymouth; she d. Oct. 29, 1676; m. 2d, Martha Pabodie, Apr. 4, 1677; he d. Aug. 5, 1681. His will gives to his son Samuel his landed property in Dux.; to son Joseph, "those great silver buttons, which I usually weare;" to son John my birding piece and musket; "I will that my negro servant Nimrod (valued at £27) be disposed off either by hier or sale in order to the bringing up of my children, especially the three youngest now borne." The "Seabury house" stood where Wait Wadsworth's now stands, and was a large old fashioned building, very high in front, but with the roof nearly reaching to the ground behind. He had *Elizabeth*, Sep. 16, 1661, who probably removed from the town, as in her mother's will, she has given her a negro girl Jane, and a cow, "if she returns;" *Sarah*, Aug. 18, 1663, who also removed; *Samuel*, Apr. 20, 1666 (3); *Hannah*, July 7, 1668; *John*, Nov. 7, 1670, d. Mar. 18, 1672; *Grace* and *Patience* (gemini), Mar. 1, 1673, G. d. Mar. 16, 1673, P. d. Mar. 17, 1673;

Joseph, June 8, 1678; *Martha*, Sep. 23, 1679; *John*, m. Elizabeth Alden, Dec. 9, 1697; and a *posthumous child*.

3. SAMUEL, (s. of 2,) Dux.; m. Mrs. Abigail Allen, Dec. 13, 1688; had *Benjamin*, Sep. 24, 1689; *Patience*, Apr. 11, 1691, d. Feb. 3, 1699; *Samuel*, Oct. 24, 1692 (4); *three* sons and *one* da., each b. and d. same month; *Barnabas*, Jan. 29, 1700, m. Mary, m. 2d, ———, settled in E. Bridgewater, soon removed, had Rebecca 1723; *two* das. each b. and d. same day; *Abigail*, Mar. 7, 1705, m. David Seabury, "now resident in Duxborough," Jan. 3, 1727; *Patience*, Aug. 10, 1710.

4. DEA. SAMUEL, (s. of 3,) Dux.; m. Deborah Wiswall, Oct. 21, 1717, who d. Apr. 22, 1776, æt. 84; he d. Sep. 25, 1762; had *Sarah*, July 21, 1718; *Hannah*, June 26, 1720, m. Benj. Clap of Scituate, Sep. 6, 1764; *Hopestill*, May 31, 1722, m. Robert Bartlett of Plymouth, Oct. 15, 1772; *Faith*, Oct. 12, 1724; *Paul*, Nov. 26, 1728, m. Ruth Thomas, Mar. 31, 1757, had Deborah, who d. 1764, æt. 5; *Oliver*, Dec. 26, 1730, m. Alice Alden, May 7, 1760, and had Samuel, Alice, and Abigail; *Wiswall*, Apr. 6, 1733, d. Sep. 20, 1768; *Deborah*, Apr. 13, 1727; *Mercy*, Nov. 10, 1735, m. Capt. Bildad Arnold, 1766.

NOTE. Sarah m. John Bartlett, 1770; *Stephen* who d. Dec. 14, 1775, æt. 71, had son Paul ;—Of what family was Rev. *Samuel* of Groton and New London? Was he father of Samuel, D. D., b. 1728, grad. Y. C., 1751, first bishop of the Episcopal Chh. in U. S.?—See American Loyalists, and Alden's Epitaphs.

SHAW.

1. EDWARD, Dux., 1637; ad. 1637; presented for "feloniously takeing certaine money from the person of William Cornelly," and was sentenced to be "severely whipt, and burnt in the shoulder wth a hot iron, wch was accordingly executed upon him." Col. Rec.

2. JONATHAN, Dux., 1659; m. Phebe Watson, Jan. 22, 1656.

3. CAPT. JAMES, Dux., m. Olive Freeman, Apr. 1, 1772; had *James*, Sep. 12, 1772; Olive, Feb. 16, 1774; *Caroline*, June 7, 1776; *Joseph*, Oct. 1, 1777; *Samuel*, June 7, 1779; and *Sarah*, Feb. 12, 1781.

NOTE. *John* and Alice ("6th Mar., 1654, d. Alice, wife of John Shaw." Col. Rec.), of Weymouth, had Elizabeth, Abraham, Mary, Nicholas and Joseph ; *James* m. Mary Mitchell, 24 Dec., 1652, had James, 6 Dec., 1654 ; *John*, Rehoboth, had Anne, Mar. 15, 1682.—Col. Rec.

SHAWSON.

GEORGE, Dux., 1638, sold land to Thomas Heyward, and before 1640, removed to Sandwich.

SHERMAN.

WILLIAM, Dux., 1637-8, had a grant of a garden place at Powder point, "if it can there be had;" and in 1640 "a 'meadstead' about the Stoney brooke," and land towards G. H.; m. Desire Doten; he "fell destracted" in Philip's war; she had £20 relief granted to her at that time; and next m. Israel Holmes, and then Alexander Standish. John and Peleg were of Dartmouth in 1684.

SIMMONS.

1. MOSES, arrived 1621; Dux., 1638; had *Thomas* (2) and *Moses* (3).

2. THOMAS, (s. of 1,) servant of Saml. Fuller; perhaps of Braintree, 1640; Scituate, 1647; had *Moses*, d. a. 1675, m. Patience, (Qu.: Is this the Patience who became the 2d wife of Samuel Baker of M.?) and had Moses 1660, d. in Canada expedition, John 1667, Sarah 1670, Aaron 1672, Job 1674, Patience 1676; *Aaron* m. Mary Woodworth 1677, and had Moses 1680 (had a family), Rebecca 1679, Mary 1683, Elizabeth 1686, Ebenezer 1689, (see *Deane's*) Lydia 1693.

Qu.: What Moses m. a da. of Wm. Barstow of Scituate?

3. MOSES, (s. of 1,) Dux.; d. 1689; m. Sarah; had *John* (4); *Aaron* (5); *Mary* m. Joseph Alden; *Elizabeth* was the 2d w. of Richard Dwelley, 1690; *Sarah* m. James Nash of Dux. — A "Moses Symons" was bap. at Hingham, Jan. 19, 1662. *Hobart's Journal.*

4. JOHN, (s. of 3,) Dux.; m. Mercy Pabodie, Nov. 16, 1669; had land granted him, 1686; had *John*, Feb. 22, 1670, m. Experience Picknel, Apr. 19, 1703; *William*, Sep. 24, 1672; Isaac, Jan. 28, 1674 (6); *Martha*, Nov. 1677, m. Ebenezer Delano, 1699.

5. AARON, (s. of 3,) Dux. Perhaps the following were his chd. — *John* (7): *Benjamin* m. Sarah Sampson, Jan. 3, 1706, m. 2d, Priscilla Delano, July 7, 1715, and she d. "in ye night," Feb. 7, 1746; *Joseph*, 1683, m. Mary Weston, Feb. 8, 1709, he d. May 20, 1761, æt. 78; *Joshua* 1688, m. Sarah Delano,

Apr. 4, 1728(?), and he d. Jan. 15, 1774, æt. 85¾; *Rebecca* m. Constant Southworth, Feb. 10, 1715.

6. ISAAC, (s. of 4,) Dux.; 1699, had a grant at Simmons' meadow; had *Isaac*, 1701 (8).

7. JOHN, (perhaps s. of 5,) Dux.; m. Susanna Tracy, Nov. 4, 1715; she d. Sep. 12, 1756, æt. 82; had *John*. Aug. 22, 1716, d. Dec. 10, 1770; *Ruth*, Apr. 26, 1719; *Joel*, Feb. 5, 1723; *Leah*, Sep. 7. 1728.

8. ISAAC, (s. of 6,) Dux.; m. Lydia Cushing, Oct. 24, 1722, m. 2d, probably Elizabeth Samms, May 11, 1737; he d. Aug. 30, 1767, æt. 66; had *Consider*, Apr. 30, 1734, m. Mehetable Soule, Feb. 25, 1763, and had *Jona*. Soule, Lydia, Lucy, and Lydia Soule; *Martha*, Feb. 20, 1736; *Martha*, Mar. 13, 1746.

9. BENJAMIN, (perhaps s. of Benj. s. of 5,) Dux.; m. Fear Sampson, Oct. 26, 1731; she d. Apr. 13, 1772, æt. 63; had *Persis; Micha; Elizabeth; Keturah; Lucy* a. 1741.

10. ICHABOD, (s. of ?) Dux.; m. Lydia ———; m. 2d, widow Mercy Sprague, 1781; had *Consider*, Sep. 27, 1744; *Noah*, Apr. 2, 1745 (11); *Lemuel*, Feb. 22, 1749 (12); *Abigail*, May 24, 1753; *Nathaniel*, Apr. 3, 1757 (13); *Ichabod*, Mar. 25, 1761, m. Urania Holmes, 1783.

11. NOAH, (s. of 10,) Dux.; m. Silvia Southworth, July 2, 1769; m. 2d, Diana Kein, Sep. 19, 1771; had *Peleg S.; Wealthea; Charles* m. Lydia, had Joshua W., Alden, James, Peleg, Henry and two das.; *Nathan; Daniel*.

12. LEMUEL (s. of 10,) Dux.; m. Abigail Peirce, Mar. 15, 1770; had *Anderson*, 1776, d. 1779; *Mary; Beulah; Lydia; George*.

13. NATHANIEL, (s. of 10,) Dux.; m. Lydia Sprague, Dec., 1780; had *Barthena* 1781; *Sarah* 1784; *Anna* 1786; *Nathaniel* 1788; *Rebecca* 1791; *Alethea* 1793; *Lydia* 1795; *Lucy* and *Nancy* (d. 1801,) (gemini) 1798; *Ichabod* 1801; *Mary* 1804; *Joshua S.* 1807.

14. AARON, (s. of ?) Dux.; m. Sarah; had *Mary*, Sep. 22, 1755; *Abraham; Jesse*, Sep. 19, 1760, m. Lucy, and had Weston 1783, Ruby 1786, Martin 1788, Sally 1791, Aaron 1797, Lyman 1807.

15. MOSES, (s. of ?) b. 1691, d. June 21, 1761, æt. 70⅔; had *Dorothy* m. Jacob Weston, Dec. 25, 1755; *Lemuel* bap. 1743; *Abigail* bap. 1745.

16. DEA. NATHANIEL, (s. of ?) Dux.; m. Mercy Simmons, Jan. 12, 1739; had *Mary*, m. John Hunt, Jr., 1764; *Zebediah; Sarah; Dorothy; Stephen;* and *Rachel*.

17. THOMAS, (s. of ?) Dux.; m. Bethia Sprague, Feb. 8, 1769; had Joshua, who d. young.

NOTE. *Rebecca* m. Reuben Peterson, 1732; *Priscilla* 1710, d. Mar. 5, 1768, æt. 58; *Mary* 1689, d. Jan. 23, 1759, æt. 70; *Artemas* 1735, d. Oct. 20, 1760, æt. 25; *Zachariah*, s. of widow Deborah, bap. 1741, d. of small pox in the army at the West, 1760; *Ahiel* m. Deborah, who d. Oct. 1, 1762, æt. 24; *Achsah* b. 1751, d. 1769; *Anna* m. Peleg Oldham, 1764; *Cyrus* m. Hannah Cook, Oct. 2, 1766; *Susanna* m. John Pratt of Hingham, Jan. 11, 1774; *Lydia* m. Nathl. Ford, 1783; *John* had Susanna bap. 1777; *Content* d. 1784; *Ruth* 1725, burnt to death, 1790; *Lewis* Apr. 21, 1783, m. Lucy (who was b. Apr. 25, 1786); *Seth* Nov. 15, 1769, m. Abgail (who was b. Aug. 1, 1773), and had Seth, Abigail, and Hiram. — *Dux. Rec.* — *John* of Boston, m. Mary, had Joseph, Aug. 31, 1663; *James* m. Rebecca Gibson, Oct. 1, 1719; *Benjamin* m. Margaret Gibson, Sep. 19, 1720. Boston Records.

SMITH.

1. JOSEPH, Dux., m. Lucia Wadsworth Aug. 20, 1771.

2. BENJAMIN, Dux., m. Sarah; had *Mary*, Aug. 5, 1776; *Sarah*, Jan. 16, 1778; *Jacob*, March 11, 1780, m. Betsy Sprague, m. 2d Persis, da. of Robert Cushman; *Patience*, Feb. 17, 1782, m. Martin Sampson; *Benjamin*, May 25, 1784; *Lucy*, July 5, 1786; *Judith*, April 6, 1789; *John*, Jan. 4, 1792; *Hannah*, March 7, 1794; *Polly*, May 11, 1797; *William*, June 25, 1799, of Bridgew.

3. CAPT. JONATHAN, b. Oct. 29, 1780, m. Zilpah Drew, who was b. July 7, 1779; he d. May 6, 1843; had *Capt. Sidney*, who d. at sea; *Sylvanus, Wealthea, Zilpah,* and *Jonathan*.

SNOW.

1. WILLIAM, came from England, an apprentice to Richard Derby 1637, and was b. 1624; settled in Dux. early, but removed to W. Bridgew.; d. a. 1708, æt. 84; m. Rebecca Barker; had William, James, Joseph, Benjamin, Mary, Lydia, Hannah and Rebecca. Vide *Mitchell's Hist.*

2. BENJAMIN, JR., (s. of —,) Dux., m. Mercy Wadsworth Sept. 17, 1756; had Jemima 1758, d. 1781; Benjamin 1763.

NOTE. *Anthony*, Plymouth 1638, felt maker, M., m. Abigail, had Josiah, (who m. Rebecca, d. a. 1692, had eight das.), Lydia, Sarah, Alice, Abigail (d. before 1685) m. Michael Ford — *Mark*, m. Ann Cook, da. of Josiah, 18 Jan. 1654, Eastham, she d. 24 July, 1656, m. 2d Jane Prince, 1660, had Anna July 7, 1656, and Thomas Aug. 6, 1668 — *Jabez*, Eastham, m. Elizabeth ——. *Sarah* m. Wm. Walker Feb. 15, 1654.

SOULE.

The name is early spelt Sole, Soal, Soul; and Soule seems to be of late adoption.

1. GEORGE, arrived 1620; 1623 had a grant of one acre, and next a lot "at the watering place," which he sold to R. Hicks 1639; lived north of Eel River bridge 1638, relinquished his land there to Constant and Thomas Southworth, and removed to Dux., and settled at Powder point; prop. of Bridgew. 1645; sold his right to Nicolas Byram; m. Mary Becket, or Bucket, who d. 1677; he d. 1680, very aged; had *John*, 1632 (2); *George*, inherited half of his father's lands at Dartmouth; *Benjamin*, killed at Pawtucket March 26, 1676; *Zachariah*, b. before 1627, ad. 1653, m. Margaret, lived at Powder point, d. a. 1663; *Nathaniel*, Dux., inherited land in Dartmouth; *Elizabeth*, m. Francis Walker of Middleboro'; *Susanna*; *Mary*, placed to Jno. Winslow 1652 for 7 years, married before 1672 John Peterson.

2. JOHN, (s. of 1,) Dux., m. Esther, who d. Sept. 12, 1733, æt. 95; he d. 1707, æt. 75; he was made the chief heir of his father, viz. "And for as much as my eldest son John Soule and his family hath in my extreme old age and weakness bin tender and careful of mee and very healpfull to mee; and is likely for to be while it shall please God to continew my life heer, therefore I give and bequeath unto my said son John Soule all the remainder of my housing and lands whatsoever," &c.—*Geo. Soule's Will.* He had *John*, perhaps the one who d. at Dux. 1734; *Joseph*, July 31, 1679 (3); *Joshua*, Oct. 12, 1681 (4); *Josiah*, 1682 (5); *Benjamin*, m. Sarah Standish, one of the first settlers of Plympton, had Hannah, who m. Geo. Sampson; *a da.* m. Edmund Weston; *a da.* m. Adam Wright.

3. JOSEPH, (s. of 2,) Dux., m. Mary; he d. July 11, 1763; had *Mary*, Dec. 18, 1711; *Alethea*, Jan. 9, 1714, m. Allerton Cushman of Plympton Jan. 30, 1735; *Lydia*, March 9, 1715; *Hannah*, March 6, 1717; *Rebecca*, May 3, 1722.

4. JOSHUA, (s. of 2,) Dux., m. Joanna Studley; he d. May 29, 1767, æt. 85; had *Zeruiah*, Nov. 2, 1705, m. Ebenezer Sampson 1728; *John*, March 4, 1709 (9); *Ezekiel*, Feb. 17, 1711, m. Hannah Delano Jan. 4, 1733; *Joshua*, May 30, 1713 (10); *Abigail*, April 30, 1716, m. Perez Drew of K., Sept. 3, 1730; *Joanna*, April 18, 1719; *Sarah*, July 25, 1728, m. Aaron Bisbee, Nov. 26, 1747; *Joseph*, March 15, 1722 (11); *Nathan*, July 12, 1725 (12); and prob. *Lydia*, who m. a Simmons.

5. JOSIAH, (s. of 2,) Dux., m. Lydia Delano May 25, 1704, who d. Nov. 24, 1763, æt. 83; he d. June 25, 1764, æt. 82;

had *Jonathan*, June 23, 1705, d. April 4, 1776; *Mary*, Dec. 5, 1706, m. Joshua Cushman of Lebanon, Ct., Jan. 2, 1733; *Abisha*, Nov. 25, 1708 (13); *Micah*, April 12, 1711 (14); *Nathaniel*, Nov. 4, 1714 (15); *Lydia*, Oct. 2, 1719.

6. ZACHARIAH, (perhaps s. of Zachariah, s. of 1,) Dux., d. in the Canada Expedition, 1690; had early a large grant in Dux., which was confirmed to his brother John in 1690.

7. MOSES, (s. of —,) Dux., a householder, and had, 1707, an addition to his land granted. *Moses*, probably his son, m. Sarah Chandler Jan. 15, 1729.

8. AARON, (s. of —,) Dux.; had a grant 1693, and in 1699 "a small tract of land ate ye South end off his lott iff he and they (appointed to lay it out) can agree," and having paid 40 shillings, 15 acres were accordingly laid out. *Aaron* (perhaps his son; though styled of Pembroke,) m. Alice Peterson, May 5, 1727. An Aaron d. at Pembroke, 1783, had John, Leonice, who m. a Brewster, Huldah, who m. Thomas Church, and three other das. *Hist. Bridgewater.*

9. JOHN, (s. of 4,) Dux.; m. Mehetable Partridge, Aug. 5, 1730; he had *Lydia*, May 6, 1733; *Samuel*, July 6, 1734 (16).

10. JOSHUA, (s. of 4,) Dux.; m. Mary Cushman, Feb. 14, 1765; had *Luther*, Dec. 21, 1765, d. May 21, 1771; *Alethea* 1769, d. 1771, May 20; and *Joseph*.

11. JOSEPH, (s. of 4,) Dux.; m. Mercy Fullerton,* 1742; had *Sarah*, m. Benj. Prior, Jan., 1765; *Olive*, bap. Sep. 2, 1750, m. Nathaniel Winsor; *Ezekiel* (17); *Silvina*, 1754, d. May 16, 1771; *Joanna* m. Lot Stetson, May 8, 1777; *William* (18); *Ruby* m. Eden Wadsworth; *Joseph* (19); *James* 1746 (20).

12. NATHAN, (s. of 4,) Dux.; inherited the W. part of his father's farm; m. Sarah; had *Thomas*, July 8, and d. Sep. 24, 1748; *Levi*, Sep. 9, 1749; *Simeon*, Dec. 16, 1751 (21); *William*, May 15, 1754, d. Jan. 15, 1755; *Anna*, Oct. 11, 1762; *Sarah*.

13. ABISHA, (s. of 5,) Dux.; m. Abigail Delano, May 14, 1741; he d. Jan. 4, 1778, æt. 70; had *Alethea* bap. 1743; m. Capt. Daniel Hall, m. 2d, Levi Loring; *Esther* d. young; *John* bap. 1747, went to Maine; *Esther* bap. 1750; *Lydia* bap. 1752; *Abigail*; *Dewsbury* bap. 1761, m. Seneca Wads-

---

* She was the da. of John Fullerton of M., who m. Ruth Sampson, in 1720, and whose chd. were Mercy, Nov. 11, 1721, m. as above, Mary, 10 Sep., 1723, William, 24 Dec., 1726, Ann, 26 July, 1728, Alethea, 1732, m. Ebenezer Joyce in 1754. A John Fullerton m. Rebecca Delano of Dux., 1746. — *Marshfield Records.*

worth; *Mary* bap. 1763, d. unm.; *Nathaniel* bap. 1767 (22); *Abisha* bap. 1770.

14. MICAH, (s. of 5,) Dux.; m. Mercy Southworth, May 30, 1740, she d. 1797; he d. Nov. 4, 1778, æt. 67; had *Aphela* a. 1740; *Josiah* a. 1742 (23); *Constant S.* a. 1744, "insane, drowned in a brook, July 10, 1790;" *Rebecca* a. 1750, d. Oct. 14, 1778; *Asa* a. 1752, m. Olive Southworth, Apr. 15, 1773; *Esther* a. 1753; *Lydia* a. 1756, d. Oct. 19, 1778.

15. NATHANIEL, (s. of 5,) Dux.; m. (when 60 years old) Abigail Tolman of Scituate, Apr. 27, 1775; she d. July 9, 1834; had *Nathaniel*, July 28, 1777, m. Polly Partridge, and had Nathaniel, Calvin P., Jane, and Polly; *Lydia* m. Andrew Sampson; *Mary; Alethea.*

16. SAMUEL, (s. of 9,) Dux.; m. Mehetabel White, Oct. 1, 1756; he d. Jan. 19, 1768, at Carolina; (a widow Mehetabel m. Ichabod Weston, 1769;) had *Abigail*, May 20, 1757; *Silvia*, May 20, 1759, m. Joshua Peterson, Feb., 1780; *Alice*, May 3, 1763, m. Josiah Soule, 1782; *Lydia*, July 23, 1766.

17. EZEKIEL, (s. of 11,) Dux.; m. Clynthia Wadsworth, 1777; he d. Nov. 3, 1843, æt. 92; had *Marshall*, Apr. 24, 1778, unm.; *Capt. George*, Dec. 4, 1779, m. Ruth Sprague, who d. Mar. 25, 1836; and he d. at St. Thomas, W. I., Feb. 11, 1820, and had George, 1807, d. 1812, Laura, 1811, d. 1813, George Marshall, 1813 (m. Lucy Ford), Laura Ann, 1816 (m. Paul Wing 2d, of Sandwich), James 1818, Nicolas Brown 1820, d. 1842; *Capt. Charles*, Apr. 22, 1782, m. Mercy Sprague, who d. Dec. 17, 1840, and had Isabella 1811, (m. George Sampson,) Caroline 1811, (m. George Holmes,) Harvy 1812, (m. Lydia Peirce,) Elizabeth 1814, d. 1837, Charles 1819, (of Boston, m. Prudence Soule, and has a da. Isabella,) Otis 1823, Edwin A. 1825, Susan A. 1825, m. Walter Bartlett, Marcellus 1827, Peleg S. 1831, d. 1832, Mercy S. 1835; *Harvey*, May 29, 1785; *Capt. Otis*, Feb. 11, 1787, m. Salumith Sampson, d. 1821, and had Salumith, Mary Townsend (who m. J. A. Sampson); *Clynthia*, Apr. 20, 1791, d. unm., Aug. 4, 1846.

18. WILLIAM, (s. of 11,) Dux.; m. Priscilla, da. of Elijah Sampson, 1784; had *Lucy; Elijah; William; Samuel* m. Nancy Bates; *Stephen* m. a Peirce, had Lydia, who m. Eden Sampson.

19. JOSEPH, (s. of 11,) Dux.; he was the father of Bishop Joseph Soule.

20. JAMES, (s. of 11,) Dux.; m. Abigail, widow of B. Bosworth (see under Bosworth,) Jan. 17, 1773. He d. Aug. 29, 1794, æt. 48. Their chd. *Sally*, July 7, 1774, d. Sep. 12, 1775; *Joseph*, Dec. 27, 1775, d. Aug. 27, 1778; *Joshua*, Dec.

19, 1777, d. Sep. 17, 1803; *Joseph*, Jan. 2, 1780, d. Jan. 5, 1806; *Abigail*, Sep. 20, 1784, m. Asa Hunt; *James*, Sep. 20, 1784, m. Mary Bradford, who was b. Sep. 7, 1789, and had James O. 1821, Justus 1823, Lucy B. 1823, and Henry M. 1825; *Capt. Richard*, Nov. 7, 1786, m. Prudence Loring, June 24, 1810, who d. Dec. 15, 1823, m. 2d, Lucy Loring, Nov. 24, 1824, and had Richard, June 8, 1812, (m. Harriet Winsor, and has Charles Carroll, Ella and Richard,) Mary Chapman, Oct. 27, 1814, (m. Sylvanus Sampson, Jr.,) Elizabeth Seaver, Apr. 6, 1818, (m. Isaac Sweetzer, Esq.,) Prudence Loring, Mar. 10, 1823, (m. Charles Soule, Jr.,) and by his 2d w., Horace Homer, Sep. 13, 1827, Helen Maria, Oct. 20, 1829, d. Jan. 20, 1834, and Charles Carroll, June 26, 1832, d. May 17, 1837.

21. SIMEON, (s. of 12,) Dux.; m. Jane Weston, Dec. 29, 1776; m. 2d, Acenith Brewster, who was b. Mar. 8, 1778; he d. Dec. 21, 1831; had *Mary*, Dec. 14, 1777; *Sarah*, Aug. 19, 1779, d. Sep. 14, 1800; *Nathan*, Jan. 18, 1781, m. Bethiah Freeman, and had Zeruiah, Lot (m. Elizabeth Brooks) and George; *Silvina*, June 21, 1784; *Thomas*, July 24, 1786; *Susanna*, Sep. 1, 1788, d. Sep. 13, 1790; *Simeon*, Oct. 2, 1790; *Jane*, Sep. 23, 1794, d. Oct. 21, 1796; *Alethea*, July 4, 1797; *Henry*, Mar. 2, 1800; *Charles*, May 18, 1806.

22. NATHANIEL, (s. of 13,) Dux., m. Lydia Freeman; had *Daniel*, Oct. 14, 1796; *Lydia F.*, 1798, m. Capt. Martin Waterman; *Hannah, Abigail, Nathaniel, Mary, Capt. Freeman, John*, and *Enoch*.

23. JOSIAH, (s. of 14,) m. Alice Soule 1782, he d. Aug. 12, 1806; had *Micah*, who m. Lucy Alden, had Micah, m. Sarah Wadsworth, Sarah and Lucy; *Asa; Samuel*, May 11, 1786.

24. DEA. EZEKIEL, (s. of 4,) Dux., m. Hannah Delano Jan. 4, 1733; she d. Sept. 25, 1768, æt. 50; removed to Woolwich; had *William* a. 1738; *Lucy* a. 1740; *Lydia, Amasa, Hannah, John, Deborah*.

NOTE. *James*, Middleboro', 1690, find £5 for refusing to go in the Canada expedition.— *Rachel* m. David Magoon, 1728; *Jedediah* m. Tabitha Bishop, Nov. 4, 1741; *Deborah* m. John Hunt, 1746; *Alethea* m. Joshua Hall, 1732; *Abigail* m. Elijah Curtis, 1756; *John* m. Patience Wadsworth, Jan. 11, 1759; *Nepheta* m. Consider Simmons, 1763; Miss *Ruth* d. Mar. 17, 1777; *Rebecca* m. Gideon Sampson, 1784.— *Dux. Rec. Ann* da. of *John* and Ruth Soule, b. Mar. 10, 1687, at Boston.

NOTE. The progenitor of this family, George, was a member of Gov. Winslow's family, and it is not known whence he came. The name of SOLE is an ancient English name, (and we find the name so spelled in the Col. and town records,) and Guillim gives this armorial bearing of the family. — "He beareth argent, a chevron gules between three sole fishes hauriant proper in a bordure engrailed sable"—and adds, "This coat belongs to the family of Soles in Brabanne in the county of Cambridge, according to the bearer's name, and it is very common for persons having their names from any kind of animals or vegetables to bear the like in their coat armour. Such sort of bearings the French call arms parlant, speaking coats, because they plainly declare the name of their owner." — *Guillim's Banner displayed.* Burke (*General Armory*) gives the same, except "gules" for "sable," and adds that they are borne by the Soles of Bobbing place, Kent. Arms by the *Soles* of London (granted 1591) — "Gules a tower or. Crest, out of a mural coronet or, a demi lion sable, langue'd and armed or." Another — "*Sole.* Sable an inescutcheon within an orle of owls argent." — *Burke's Armory.*

SOUTHWORTH.

1. CONSTANT, (s. of Constant,) b. 1615, came to New England in 1628,* an early settler of Duxbury; m. Elizabeth Collier Nov. 2, 1637, and d. March 10, 1679; leaving an estate of £360—among the items was an Indian boy £10; had *Edward*, b. at Plymouth (2); *Lt. Nathaniel*, b. at Plymouth 1648, m. Desire, da. of Edward Gray, Jan. 10, 1672, who was b. Nov. 6, 1651,—he d. Jan. 14, 1711, and she d. Dec. 4, 1690; their chd. were, Constant of Tiverton, b. Aug. 12, 1674, and d. before 1706; Mary, April 3, 1676, m. Joseph Rider 1707; Capt. Ichabod, March 1678, of Middleboro', m. Esther, and d. Sept. 20, 1757; Elizabeth, m. James Sproat; Capt. Nathaniel, May 1684, m. Jael Howland, and he d. April 8, 1757, and she d. Nov. 1743, or 1745; Edward, of Middleboro' 1788, m. Bridget Bosworth at Hull, June 25, 1711, and d. April 26, 1749, æt. 60 years; *Mercy*, m. Samuel Freeman May 12, 1658; *Alice*, 1646, d. March 5, 1719, æt. 72, m. Col. Benj. Church 1667; *Mary*, m. David Alden; *Elizabeth*, m. William Fobes. The following is from her father's will: "Item, I will and bequeath unto my daughter E. S. my next best bed and furniture, with my wife's best bed, provided shee doe not marry William Fobbes; but if shee doe then to have five shillings;" *Priscilla; William* (3).

2. EDWARD, (s. of 1,) Dux.,a deputy; often employed by the town in running ranges and settling bounds; had grants of land 1674, 1685 at Mill bk., and in 1689. He inherited the homestead and mill. He m. Nov. 16, 1669, Mary Pabodie; had *Elizabeth*, Nov. 1672, m. Saml. Weston March 4, 1716; *Thomas*, 1676 (4); *Benjamin*, 1680, m. Rebecca Delano

---

* Among the accounts of the Plymouth Company, published in the Mass. Hist. Coll., we find the following item; "1628, Paid for Constant Souther's passage and diet 11 weeks at 4*s.* 8*d.*—£3. 11. 4."

Aug. 4, 1715, he d. May 12, 1756, æt. 75; she d. Sept. 6, 1774, æt. 90; *Constant*, m. Rebecca Simmons Feb. 10, 1715, and d. a. 1731; *John*, 1687, d. Aug. 10, 1751, æt. 64; *Mercy*, m. Micah Soule 1740; *Priscilla*, 1693, d. June 7, 1671, æt. 68.

3. WILLIAM, (s. of 1,) Dux.; removed to Little Compton and Tiverton, m. a. 1680 Rebecca [Pabodie, probably], who d. at L. C. Dec. 3, 1702, æt. 42, and he d. June 25, 1719, æt. 59; had *Benjamin*, April 18, 1681, m. Elizabeth 1701, m. 2d Alice Church 1717, m. 3d Susanna Blackmore 1722; *Joseph*, Feb. 1, 1683, m. Mary Blake 1710, d. 1739; *Edward*, Nov. 23, 1684, m. Mary Fobes 1708, m. 2d Elizabeth Palmer 1716; *Elizabeth*, Sept. 23, 1686; *Alice*, July 14, 1688; *Samuel*, Dec. 26, 1690; *Nathaniel*, Oct. 31, 1692; *Thomas*, Dec. 13, 1694; *Stephen*, March 31, 1696, m. Lydia Warren 1715; by a 2d wife—*Gideon*, March 21, 1707, m. Priscilla Pabodie 1727, m. 2d Mary Wilbor 1728; and *Andrew*, Dec. 12, 1709.

4. THOMAS, (s. of 2,) Dux., m. Sarah ———; he d. Sep. 9, 1743, æt. 67; had *Jedediah*, April 13, 1702 (5); *Mary*, Sept. 18, 1703, m. Thomas Loring Feb. 3, 1724.

6. DEA. JEDEDIAH, (s. of 4), Dux., removed to North Yarm. Me. 1730, returned to Dux. 1735; m. Hannah ———; he d. Sept. 8, 1739; had *Sarah*, Oct. 8, 1729; *Susanna*, July 27, 1731, m. prob. Dr. John Bartlett of N. Yarmouth, who removed to Lebanon before 1760; *Dea. John*, Oct. 22, 1733, of N. Yarmouth, d. May 17, 1814, m. Joanna Mitchell, who d. Oct. 28, 1798; *James*, Nov. 17, 1735 (7); *Lydia*, Oct. 11, 1738, m. Seth Bradford 1760.

The following, on a catalogue of the members of the First Church in N. Yarmouth (published 1848), were probably the children of Dea. John, — *Mary*, m. Jonathan Bradford of N. Yar., removed to Minot in 1799; *Joanna*, m. Nathl. Scales of N. Yar., and removed to Freeport in 1814; *Lucy*, m. Asa Lewis, and d. March 25, 1798, æt. 31 yrs.; *Loraina*, m. Wm. Wyman, and d. Jan. 22, 1817, æt. 48; *John*, d. May 12, 1790, æt. 25; *Sarah*, m. Paul Prince, and removed to Cumberland 1795; and *L*———, who m. John D. Blanchard, and d. April 22, 1844, æt. 72.

6. WILLIAM. (perhaps s. of Constant and Rebecca,) Dux.; m. perhaps Betty, da. of Saml. Fullerton, and had *Reumah* a. 1742, m. Jasper Southworth May 5, 1763, and he d. 1828, æt. 86; *Edward*, 1747, d. 1833, æt. 86, m. Mercy Thomas Jan. 18, 1769; *John*, 1753, d. 1827, æt. 73; *Nathaniel*, 1757, m. Deborah Hatch of Pembroke 1782; *William*, 1759, d. June 16, 1759; *Alice*, 1764, m. Jacob Weston 1784.

7. JAMES, (s. of 4,) Dux., m. Sarah Drew Nov. 28, 1762; he d. Oct. 8, 1811; had *Jedediah*, Aug. 23, 1764, m. Betsy Thomas; *Abigail*, June 7, 1769; *Capt. Thomas*, July 13,

1771, removed to Scituate, d. at New Orleans 1819, father of Nathan, artist, of Boston; *John,* May 19, 1773; *Hannah,* July 22, 1776; *Nathan,* June 6, 1778, d. at sea; *Sarah,* Mar. 31, 1780; *James,* April 3, 1782, and was burnt in the beach house.

[SOUTHWORTH PEDIGREE.

The following pedigree was procured by Horatio G. Somerby, Esq. from the Herald's College, London, for Nathan Southworth, Esq., artist, of Boston, and with the permission of the last-named gentleman I copy it. In its details, as regards intermarriages, etc., it is uncommonly full, much more so than most of so early a date.

SIR GILBERT SOUTHWORTH, = Elizabeth, da. and sole heir of
of Southworth Hall in Nicholas Dayes of Salmsburye
the county of Lancaster, Knt. in Lancashire.

SIR JOHN SOUTHWORTH, = Elizabeth, da. of John Haughton
of Southworth, Knt. of Lancashire.

SIR THOS: SOUTHWORTH, = Jane, da. of John Boath,
of Southworth. of Barton, Esq.

RICHARD SOUTHWORTH, = Elizabeth, da. of Edw. Mollineaux,
of Salmsburie, Esq. of Segton in Lancashire, Esq.

SIR CHRISTOPHER SOUTHWORTH, = Isabel, da. of John Dutton,
of Southworth. of County Chester.

SIR JOHN SOUTHWORTH. = Ellen, da. of Richard Langton,
of Salmsburie, Knt. of Newton Walton, Lanc.

Sir Thomas, CHRISTOPHER SOUTHWORTH = Richard,
the heir, m. Margery, (2d son.) (3d son), d. s. p.
da. of Tho. Butler,
of Warrington,
Lanc.

RICHARD SOUTHWORTH = Jane, da. of Edw. Lloyd, John,
London, Merchant. of Shropshire. d. s. p.

Henry = Elizabeth, THOMAS SOUTHWORTH, = Jane,
of Somerset- da. of John Pell- Recorder of Wells, da. of
shire, living in sant, of London, in Somersetshire. Nicholas
1623. Merchant.   Mynne, of
  Norfolk.

CONSTANT SOUTHWORTH = Alice Carpenter, who afterwards
 m. Gov. Bradford, of Plymouth
 Colony, New England.

THOMAS, = Elizabeth Reyner. CONSTANT = Elizabeth Collier,
of New Eng. (See pp. 68-9.) Nov. 2, 1637.]
(See p. 68.)

8. THOMAS, (s. of —,) Dux., m. Anna; had *William*, Feb. 18, 1763; *Content*, Aug. 20, 1764; *Lydia*, Nov. 8, 1766; *Hannah*, Jan. 9, 1769, d. young; *Elizabeth*, April 24, 1773; *Anne*, Dec. 23, 1774; *Hannah*, May 24, 1776.

NOTE. *Hannah* (of M.) m. Hezekiah Herrington (of M.), March 1, 1739; *Silvia* m. Noah Simmons 1769; *Clynthia* m. Asa Phillips, 1769; *Olive* m. Asa Soule 1773; *John* of M. m. Sarah Clark of Duxbury Nov. 9, 1748; *Abigail*, 1742, d. Sept. 19, 1768, æt. 26; *Rebecca* 1694, d. March 16, 1771, æt. 77; *James* m. Elizabeth, had Joseph 1797, Betsy 1798, Charlotte, Hiram, Thomas, Jairus.—*Dux. Rec. Constant* Southworth drowned himself July 1790.—*J. D.'s Jour.*

SPRAGUE.

1. FRANCIS, arrived 1623; ad. June 17, 1637; removed to Dux. about 1632, and settled in the southeastern part of the town, near the Nook, so called, and in that vicinity "about his owne ground," and "at the Eagle," he was allowed in early years to mow; in 1640, had land at North river; prop. of Bridgew. 1645; was alive 1666; had *John* (2); *Anna; Mary; Mercy*, m. Wm. Tubbs 1637; one of the das. m Robt. Lawrence.

2. JOHN, (s. of 1,) Dux.; but first resided at M.; joined Michael Peirce's company in Philip's war, and was killed at Pawtucket March 26, 1676; m. Ruth Basset 1655, who afterwards m. a Thomas; had *John* (3); *William* (4); *Samuel* (5); *Eliza; Ruth*, Feb. 12, 1659; *Desire; Dorcas*, m. Joseph Hatch Jan. 10, 1710.

3. JOHN, (s. of 2,) Dux., m. 1st Lydia; removed to Lebanon, Ct., and m. 2d Mary Babcock; had *Ephraim* March 15, 1685; *Benjamin*, July 15, 1686, — for his chd. see Soule's Sprague Memorial; by 2d w. he had *Ebenezer* and others at Lebanon, for whom see idem.

4. WILLIAM, (s. of 2,) Dux., m. Grace, prob. da. of the first Dea. Wadsworth; drowned Nov. 25, 1712; had *Ruth*, Feb. 22, 1702, m. Samuel Kein April 19, 1719; *Zeruiah*, Dec. 10, 1704, m. Nath. Chandler 1724; *Terah*, Feb. 17, 1712; *Jethro*, Nov. 30, 1709, m. Patience Bartlett Dec. 12, 1738, she d. Mar. 1741, m. 2d Bethia Sprague, removed and settled on the Kennebec after 1760, had Silvina Oct. 8, 1739, and William Nov. 19, 1740.

5. SAMUEL, (s. of 2,) Dux.; carpenter; m. Ruth Alden Nov. 29, 1694; m. 2d Elizabeth (says Mitchell), and removed to Rochester, and d. there 1723; had *Noah*, Jan. 18, 1696; *Elizabeth*, July 4, 1699; *Nathaniel*, Jan. 10, 1702; *Samuel*, June

23, 1704; *Mary*, Dec. 20, 1706, d. April 19, 1708; *Priscilla*, March 18, 1709, and *Ephraim* (according to Mitchell).

NOTE. There arrived at Salem, 1629, three brothers, Ralph, Richard, and William Sprague, who removed to Charlestown. They were sons of Edward of Upway, Dorset county, England, who d. 1614, leaving widow Christian and six chd. William was 21 years of age when he arrived, and removed in 1636 to Hingham, m. Millicent Eames 1635, and d. Oct. 26, 1675, æt. 66; she d. Feb. 8, 1696; they had Anthony 1635, John 1638, Samuel 1640 (6), Elizabeth 1641, Perses 1643, Joanna 1644, Jonathan 1648, William 1650, Mary 1652, and Hannah 1655.—See Hosea Sprague's Account of Hingham Spragues, and Soule's Memorial.

6. SAMUEL, (s. of William,) removed to M. before 1644; selectman, representative and colony secretary; d. 1710; m. Rebecca; m. 2d Sarah da. of Thomas Chillingworth; had *Samuel* 1674 (7); *John* (8); *Nathan*, M., m. Margaret, and had James (the father of Capt. Jonathan), and perhaps Margaret of M., who m. Robt. Howland 1733; *James*, m. Hannah Black, and had James, m. Sarah Jackson, and Hannah, m. Barnabas Ford; *Sarah*, m. Joseph Holmes; *Mary*, m. Nathl. Williamson; *Joanna*, m. John Holmes; *Hannah*, m. John Rogers, Jr. of M. Dec. 11, 1700.

7. SAMUEL, (s. of 6,) removed to Dux. a. 1710; m. Bethia Thomas, who d. Oct. 1, 1761, æt. 79¾; he d. Feb. 15, 1764, æt. 90; had *Phineas*, 1714 (9); *Samuel* (10); *Sarah*, m. Samuel Alden Feb. 26, 1728; *Bethia*, m. 1st a Cushing (says Soule. A Bethia Sprague m. David Curtis of Hanover Dec. 14, 1732), m. 2d Jethro Sprague.

8. JOHN, (s. of 6,) Dux.; m. Love, had *John*, perhaps the one who m. widow Deborah Simmons, Dec. 5, 1744, and the one who d. Sept. 1784; *Abigail;* *Peleg* (11); *Joanna*, m. Jas. Arnold Feb. 19, 1735; *Rebecca*, m. Ezra Arnold July 27, 1732.

9. PHINEAS, (s. of 7,) Dux., m. Mercy, widow of Peleg Sprague, d. Jan. 20, 1776, æt. 62; had *Peleg*, bap. 1758; *Seth*, July 4, 1760 (12); *Mercy*, m. John Chandler; *Ruth*, m. John Burgess of Plymouth, and d. 1845.

10. SAMUEL, (s. of 7,) Dux., m. Sarah Oldham July 8, 1742; he d. March 26, 1766; had *Uriah* June 11, 1743 (13).

11. PELEG, (s. of 8,) Dux., m. Mercy Chandler, Feb. 18, 1746, d. a. 1754; had *Nathaniel*, m. Hannah, removed to Me. and had Caroline Feb. 2, 1771, Peleg, Nathaniel, William, Sarah, Hannah and Mercy; *John*, removed to Weymouth, and then to Maine; *Peleg*, 1751, d. May 6, 1756.

12. HON. SETH, (s. of 9,) Dux. When a mere youth, he engaged in the war of the Revolution, and continued in the

service of his country until the summer of 1778. He next engaged in the occupation of fishing, and pursued this calling with but little interruption until the year 1790, when he invested his small capital in trade, and entering by degrees into navigation, having acquired a moderate competence, he withdrew from active business pursuits, and devoted his attention to the more grateful labor of husbandry.

Mr. Sprague quite young entered upon the public duties of the town, and continued through the prime of his life a frequent recipient of public trusts. He was for forty years a justice of the peace and of the quorum, and for twenty years — sometimes in the senate and at others in the house—a member of the Massachusetts legislature, and also twice a member of the Electoral college, which determines the choice of President and Vice President of the United States.

He was the leader of the friends of the administration in Duxbury at the time of the war of 1812, and to him in justice it should be said, much credit is due for his strenuous opposition to all measures of neutrality, which some of the inhabitants would have urged upon the town.

In the moral and religious reforms of the age, Mr. Sprague took a great interest, and manifested a truly commendable zeal. In the cause of temperance he was an early laborer, and presided at the first temperance meeting ever held in Duxbury, and also over the first held in the county. With the Abolitionists he has always been in sympathy, and an officer of several of their societies.

Mr. Sprague died in Duxbury, July 8, 1847, four days after the occurrence of his eighty-seventh birth-day, and after an illness of about five weeks.—*Memorial of the Sprague Family.*

He m. Deborah Sampson March, 1779, who d. Nov. 21, 1844. They had Capt. *Phineas*, Nov. 2, 1779, m. Eunice Freeman, m. 2d Hannah Brown, and had one da. Hannah B. who m. Edw. Silas Tobey, Esq. ; m. 3d Betsy, widow of Silas Tobey; *William*, Dec. 28, 1780, m. Patience Rogers, who d. Nov. 18, 1833, æt. 48, m. 2d widow Priscilla (Barker) Peirce, and he d. Oct. 17, 1840, and had Susan, m. Charles Copeland; Charity m. James Gooding; Almira m. Samuel Gilbert of Boston; William; Harriet m. Edward Winsor; Eliza m. Henry Tolman; Seth d. at sea in 1843; Julia, and Francis; *Deborah*, Aug. 19, 1782, m. Ahira Wadsworth; *Wealthea*, June 2, 1784, m. Thomas Winsor; *Ruth*, Dec. 4, 1785, m. George Soule; *Hon. Seth*, Nov. 21, 1787, m. Wealthea, da. of Isaac Little; *Mercy*, Dec. 25, 1789, m. Charles Soule; *Zeruiah*, Sept. 5, 1791, m. Perez Thomas, and d. April 2, 1829; *Hon. Peleg*, April 27, 1793, Rep. and Senator from Maine, and now Judge of the U. S. Dist. Court for the Mass. District. Chd. Charles, d. unm., Seth m. a da. of Wm. Lawrence, Esq. of Boston,

Sarah, and Francis; *Caroline*, Oct. 6, 1795, m. Wm. Sampson; *Hannah*, Sept. 26, 1797, m. Ralph Partridge; *Judith*, April 25, 1799, m. Hon. G. B. Weston; *Nancy*, April 23, 1801, m. Samuel Loring; *Lucy*, Aug. 2, 1803, m. Rev. Robert W. Cushman, she d. Nov. 9, 1841; *Sarah*, Sept. 20, 1805, m. Wm. Henry Sampson.

13. URIAH, (s. of 10,) Dux., m. Lydia Sampson, who d. Sep. 1, 1842; he d. Feb. 1, 1842, æt. 99; had *Eden*, Apr. 12, 1770, m. Sarah Hinckley; *Alethea*, April 10, 1772; *Lydia*, Apr. 17, 1776, d. Oct. 12, 1843; *Luranna*, May 18, 1780, m. Weston Freeman Feb. 10, 1802; *Joshua*, May 17, 1783, d. at sea, Feb. 9, 1807; *Betsy*, Aug. 28, 1788, m. Jacob Smith May 26, 1803, she d. May 11, 1814.

14. EZEKIEL, (s. of —,) came from M.; m. Huldah Fish 1785; she d. April 5, 1835, æt. 76; had *Peleg*, Dec. 27, 1787; *John*, Sept. 7, 1790; *Ezekiel*, Dec. 8, 1792, m. Susan.

NOTE. See the Memorial of the Sprague family, by Richard Soule, Jr. *Acenith* m. Simeon Curtis of Scituate, April 20, 1742; *Abijah*, 1710, d. 31 June, 1772; *Sarah* m. Kimball Ripley 1771; *Lydia*, March 21, 1761, m. Nathaniel Simmons 1780; *Thomas*, 1756, d. at New York July 31, 1776; *Joshua*, 1751, d. at New York Aug. 20, 1776; *Bethia* m. Thomas Simmons 1769; *Deborah* m. Nathl. Delano 1774; *Mary* m. William Hilton of Bristol 1782; *Hannah* m. Elijah Sampson, Jr. 1782.

SPROUT.

ROBERT, Scituate 1660, Namasakeeset 1668, had meadow in Dux. 1634, d. 1712 at Middleton; m. Elizabeth Sampson; had *Mercy*, 1661, m. Thomas Oldham 1683; *Elizabeth* 1664; *Mary* 1666; *Robert* 1669, d. in Canada expedition June 1690; *Anna* 1671, m. a Richmond; *James* 1673; *Ebenezer* 1676; *Hannah* 1680.—Deane's Scituate.

STANDISH.

1. CAPT. MYLES, b. at Lancashire, a. 1584, [see *First Settlers*]; owned the greater part of the "Nook," and also possessed land at Namasakeeset, where he sold thirty-five acres to R. Barker, Sen., by deed, Dec. 10, 1651; m. Rose, who d. Jan. 29, 1621; m. 2d. Barbara, who probably came over in the second ship, 1621, and she survived him; he d. Oct. 3, 1656, æt. 72; had *Alexander* (2); *Miles* (3); *Josiah* (4); *Charles*, d. young; *Lora*, d. before her father; *John*, d. young.

2. ALEXANDER, (s. of 1,) Dux., m. Sarah Alden, m. 2d Desire Holmes, widow of Israel; she d. 1723; he d. 1702; had *Miles*

(5); *Ebenezer* 1672 (6); *Sarah*, m. Abraham Sampson; *Lydia*, m. Isaac Sampson; *Mercy*, m. Caleb Sampson; *Sarah* m. Benja. Soule; *Elizabeth*, m. Samuel Delano; by 2d wife: *Thomas* 1687 (7); *Ichabod*, m. 1719, Phebe Pring, d. 1772; had Mary, Phebe, and Desire, who m. David Hatch; *Desire*, b. in M. 1689, m. a Weston; and probably *David*, who was killed in Dux. by the fall of a tree in 1689.

3. MILES, (s. of 1,) removed to Boston, living 1662, d. s. p. before 1665, m. Sarah, da. of John Winslow, 19 July, 1660 (who afterwards m. 1665, Tobias Paine, and Richard Middlecott, and d. 1726).

4. CAPT. JOSIAH, (s. of 1,) Dux., ad. 1655; removed to East Bridgewater, and was Lieut. of the company there; returned to Dux., and bought, 1663, of Samuel Eaton his estate of 43 acres, including an orchard, for £20; and was selectman, deputy and captain; returned to Norwich, Ct. 1686, bought land at Preston, Ct. of John Parks 1687; m. Mary, da. of John Dingley 1654, who d. same year; m. 2d Sarah, da. of Samuel Allen of Braintree; and had *Miles*, m. Dec. 5, 1700, Mehetabel Adams; *Josiah; Samuel* (8); *Israel* m. Feb. 8, 1704, Elizabeth Richards; *Mary; Lois; Mehetabel; Martha* and *Mercy*.

5. MILES, (s. of 2,) Dux., inherited the homestead, and died there Sept. 15, 1739; m. Experience [Sherman or Holmes], who by his will, dated Aug. 31, received half the income; and to his son he gave the farm of 120 acres; she d. March 31, 1744, and was probably the last of the name at the Captain's Hill; had *Sarah*, April 15, 1704, m. Abner Weston March 2, 1730; *Patience*, Aug. 16, 1707, m. Caleb Jenny of Dartmouth April 6, 1738; *Priscilla*, April 1, 1710, m. Elisha Bisbee (?); *Miles*, March 11, 1714 (9); *Penelope*, April 13, 1717, d. Nov. 11, 1739.

6. EBENEZER, (s. of 2,) he d. 1734; had *Ebenezer*, m. 1739 a Churchill, and d. 1748; *Zachariah* (10), *Moses* 1689 (11), *Hannah; Zeruiah* m. Zebedee Tomson of Halifax 1745; *Sarah* m. Josiah Cushman 1749; *Mercy* 1716, m. 1736 Ebenezer Lobdell; m. 2d Benj. Weston, d. 1794.

7. THOMAS. (s. of 2,) M.; removed to Pembroke, m. Mary; had *David*, m. Jan. 24, 1746, Hannah Magoun, d. 1793, had David, and Lemuel, who was b. 1746, d. 1824, æt. 74, m. Rachel Jackson of Bath, where he settled and had David and Lemuel; *Amos; Thomas*, Jan. 23, 1725, m. Martha Bisbee Feb. 10, 1748, d. June 18, 1759, at Fort Miller, had Thomas, who d. 1780; *Mary*, Jan. 21, 1733; *William*, June 24, 1737; *Betty*, Sept. 6, 1739.

8. SAMUEL, (s. of 4,) Dux., Preston, Ct.; m. June 1, 1710, Deborah Gates; had *Deborah*, Dec. 27, 1711, d. 1805, unm.;

Samuel, Dec. 1, 1713, had Samuel; *Lois*, Jan. 9, 1715; *Abigail*, Feb. 9, 1717, m. Rufus Rood; *Sarah*, Feb. 1719, d. 1745 unm.; *Israel*, March 1, 1722, m. Content Ellis, m. 2d Dorcas Bellows; *Thomas*, May 19, 1724, Williamstown, Mass., m. widow Sarah Williams, [Hubbard's MS.]

9. MILES, (s. of 5,) Dux., inherited the homestead; sold it, July 3, 1763, to Samuel and Sylvanus Drew, who sold it to Wait Wadsworth, who sold it to John, the father of George Faunce; removed to South Bridgew., and 1765, bought a farm at Titicut [Guide to Plymouth]; d. 1765, æt. 80; m. Mehetabel Robbins of Plymouth Dec. 17, 1738; had *Miles*, m. Naomi, da. of Daniel Keith, removed to Pennsylvania, and had a son Miles; *Penelope*, bap. June 27, 1741, m. Nathaniel Cobb, Jr. 1763; *Lydia*, bap. May 1, 1743; *Experience*, bap. Sept. 24, 1744, m. Simeon Ames 1765; *Hannah*, April 27, 1746, m. Daniel Fobes 1769; *Sarah*, May 22, 1748; *Priscilla*, bap. 1755.

10. ZACHARIAH, (s. of 6,) South Bridgew., d. 1780; had *Ebenezer, Hannah; Sarah*, m. Josiah Cushman, Jr. 1749; *Abigail*, m. Samuel Wright 1752; *Peleg, Zachariah*. — History of Bridgew.

11. MOSES, (s. of 6,) Plympton, m. Rachel; d. 1769, æt. 80; had *Moses*, (the father of Moses, whose son is Moses of Boston); Capt. *John*, d. at Plympton 1787; *Aaron, Rachel, Rebecca* m. 1751 Zachariah Weston.

STANFORD.

ROBERT, Scituate 1670; M. 1685; Dux. 1710; m. Fear; he was probably father of ROBERT, who was b. 1693, and d. in Dux. May 26, 1774, æt. 81; and the last-named had probably *Robert*, who was b. 1744, and d. April 19, 1752, and a second *Robert*, who m. Hannah Bradford Nov. 13, 1774, and *Joshua*, who had Robert, bap. 1760, Joshua, Rebecca, Hannah, Samuel B., and Frederic who d. young.

NOTE. *Rebecca* m. Mary Sampson 1729; *Lydia* m. Andrew Alden 1714. Dux. Rec. *Robert* m. Mary Parsons Jan. 16, 1700. *Grace* m. Robert Rowles Oct. 28, 1706.—Boston Rec.

STARR.

1. COMFORT came from Ashford, Kent, Eng. to Cambridge; removed to Dux., then to Boston, and d. there Jan. 2, 1659; he m. Elizabeth, who d. at Boston June 25, 1658, aged 63. The following account of his family is gathered chiefly from

his will; but for a further account of his descendants, see Hinman's Connecticut Genealogies. He had chd. *Thomas*, Dux. 1639; Scituate 1644, a surgeon, d. before his father, as did also his wife, had Comfort 1644, and Elizabeth 1646; he next removed to Yarmouth, and had there Benjamin Feb. 6, 1648, Jehoshaphat Jan. 12, 1649; *John*, sole executor of his father's will, Dux., 1643, Bridgew. 1645, sold land in Dux. 1655.—A John and Martha, at Boston, had Comfort Feb. 4, 1661, John Dec. 7, 1664, Benjamin, Aug. 19, 1667; *Comfort*, H. C. 1647, minister (says Farmer) of Carlisle, Cumberland, Eng., and Lewis, Sussex, and d. 1711.—A Comfort and Mary Starr, at Boston, had Joseph March 7, 1663, and Mary Jan. 18, 1671. The will of the first Comfort also names a Samuel Starr, and five daughters of his da. —— *Maynard*, who was deceased; his grandson, Simon Eire, whose parents were dead, and who received a bequest from his grandfather to " to help him to learning;" his da. *Elizabeth*, w. of John Ferniside; his da. *Hannah*, who was in England; his brother-in-law John Morley, and Faithful Rouse. This will bears date April 22, 1659.

From the Boston Records — Eleazer (a cooper) m. Mary, and had Margaret Nov. 16, 1663; Eleazer and Martha, had Abigail Nov. 26, 1681, Joseph Aug. 26, 1687, Benjamin March 7, 1691–2.

STETSON.

For a full and perfect account of this family see *J.S.Barry's Memoir of the family.* The progenitor was *Cornet Robert*, of Scituate 1634, d. 1702, æt. 90, and had seven sons and two das. The following are found on the Dux. Records: *Caleb*, m. Sarah Brewster March 4, 1705; *Elisha*, m. Abigail Brewster Oct. 28, 1707; *Honor*, m. Thomas Hunt 1708; *Amy*, m. Ebenezer Bishop 1710; *Isaac* and *Timothy* in Dux. 1710; *Mary*, of Scituate, m. James Partridge 1712; *Ebenezer*, of Scituate, m. Lydia Barker of S. 1728; *Lot*, m. Joanna Soule May 8, 1777; *Acenith*, m. Daniel McLaughlin 1779.

STOCKBRIDGE.

JOSEPH, Dux. 1672, (the son of Charles and Abigail, b. before 1638, and d. 1683, the s. of Charles, s. of John of Scituate 1638,) lived near Indian head river, m. Margaret Turner, and d. 1772, æt. 100 years; had *Joseph*, who m. Ann Turner, and had David, who m. Deborah, da. of Judge John Cushing, and who had David, Esq. of Hanover.—Deane's Scituate.

SWITZER.

BENJAMIN, m. Hannah Drew March 17, 1757, had *Betty* and *Abigail*.

SYLVESTER.

1. RICHARD, Weymouth 1633, Scituate 1642; M., d. a. 1663; m. Naomy Torrey, who complained to the Court that her husband left her but a small share of his property (£245); had *Lydia*, Dec. 8, 1633, m. Nathl. Rawlins Sep. 4, 1652, who had Elizabeth 1653, and Ruth 1655; *John*, March 14, 1634, had Sarah 1671, John, Joseph, Samuel and Lydia; *Peter* 1637, shot himself 1642; *Joseph*, April 12, 1638, a captain under Col. Church, d. in Canada Expedition; m. Mary; his estate £416; had Joseph 1664, who had land at Hugh's Cross, Mary 1667, Anna 1669, Benjamin 1672, Amos 1676, David 1682; *Dinah* April 2, 1642; *Elizabeth*, Jan. 23, 1643, m. John Lowell of Boston 24 Jan. 1658; *Richard*, 1648, Milton 1678, m. Hannah Leonard; *Naomy*, 1649, was J. Lowell's 2d wife 1666; *Israel*, 1651 (2); *Hester*, 1653; *Benjamin*, 1656, M., m. Lydia Standlake 1684, and had Benjamin and Joseph.

2. ISRAEL, (s. of 1,) had *Israel*, 1674 (3); *Silence*, 1677; *Richard*, 1679, had Nehemiah and Seth; *Lois*, 1680; *Martha*, 1682; *Mary*, 1683; *Elisha*, 1685; *Peter*, 1687, m. Mary Torrey 1712, Leicester; *Zebulon*, 1689, had Elisha and Israel 1717, d. 1812, æt. 95; *Bathsheba*, 1692; and *Deborah* 1696.

3. ISRAEL, (s. of 2,) Dux., m. Ruth, widow of Thomas Prince; had *Ruth*, June 26, 1701; *Israel*, May 5, 1705 (4); *Grace*, Nov. 1706, m. Isaac Partridge 1730.

4. ISRAEL, (s. of 3,) Dux., m. Abigail, da. of Josiah Snell, 1734; he d. 1785, she d. July 22, 1775, æt. 72; had *Joseph*, July 6, 1735 (5); *Israel*, Nov. 1, 1737, d. of hydrophobia, Nov. 23, 1810; *Seth*, Aug. 30, 1840, d. Dec. 11, 1756; *Josiah*, May 14, 1742, d. Sept. 13, 1768; *Zachariah*, Feb. 24, 1745 (6); *Abigail*, April 17, 1747, m. Samuel Alden 1774.

5. JOSEPH, (s. of 4,) Dux., removed to N. Bridgew. 1769; m. Lucy, da. of Ephraim Sampson; had *Seth*, Feb. 12, 1762; *Joseph* and *Benjamin* (gemini), March 9, 1764; for chd. of J. see Hist. Bridgew.; *Josiah*, Nov. 15, 1768, Tiverton; *Lucy*, 1772; *Ephraim*, 1774.

6. ZACHARIAH, (s. of 4,) Dux., m. Mehetabel, da. of Zachariah Carey; had *Mehetabel*, Jan. 31, 1773, m. Zachariah Snell; *Daniel*, March 30, 1775; *Zachariah*, April 20, 1778, m. Lucy Bradford; *Susanna*, July 4, 1781; *Hannah*, 1789.

NOTE. *Nathaniel*, of Scituate, m. at Dux. Silvina Sprague Dec. 6, 1760. Vide Deane's Scituate and Mitchell's Bridgew.

THACHER.

1. RALPH, (s. of Rev. Thomas, of Boston, and gd. s. of Rev. R. Partridge of Dux.; queme vide,) Dux. as late as 1681; in 1679 had a grant at South river.
2. RODOLPHUS, Dux., town clerk; m. Ruth Partridge Jan. 1, 1669; had *Thomas*, Oct. 9, 1670, Dux. 1697; *Elizabeth*, March 1, 1672; *Anna*, Nov. 26, 1673; *Ruth*, Nov. 1, 1675; *Rodolphus*, Jan. 9, 1677; *Lydia*, Jan. 24, 1679, m. Jona. Peterson; *Mary*, March 8, 1682; *Anna*, March 30, 1684; *Peter*, Aug. 17, 1686.
3. JAMES, Dux. 1688.

THOMAS.

1. WILLIAM, M., a Welchman, arrived 1630; d. Aug. 1651, æt. 77; his estate amounted to £375; he had *Nathaniel*, who inherited the estate, had Mary, Elizabeth and Timothy, and served in Philip's war.
2. JOHN, (s. of —,) Dux.; owned land, 1686, N. W. of the path from M., near "Dingley's wolfe trap;" was in Dux. as late as 1691, and probably d. that year.
3. CALEB, (s. of —,) Dux.; 1710 had a share in the commons.
4. JOHN, (s. of —,) Dux., m. Mary; had *Mary*, Sept. 27, 1693; *James*, Feb. 10, 1696 (5); *Hannah*, Aug. 30, 1698, m. Wrestling Brewster 1722; *John*, Nov. 4, 1700; *Ebenezer*, Sept. 30, 1703; *Ezekiel*, Sept. 29, 1706.
5. CAPT. JAMES, (s. of 4,) Dux., m. Deborah; he d. Jan. 16, 1751; had *Abiah*, March 25, 1720; *Deborah*, May 7, 1722; *James*, Feb. 1, 1726; *Jesse*, Sept. 10, 1728.
6. JOSIAH, (s. of —,) Dux., m. Deborah Bartlett Dec. 19, 1723; had *William*, Nov. 1, 1724; *Joshua*, Sept. 9, 1726, m. Mercy Bestow (of Pem.) Dec. 1, 1747, he d. May 20, 1812, æt. 85; *Peleg*, Nov. 25, 1728; *Adam*, March 31, 1731; *Deborah*, Aug. 2, 1734; *Ruth*, June 13, 1736, m. Paul Seabury 1757; *Benjamin*, Nov. 21, 1737, m. Abigail, who d. Oct. 26, 1769, æt. 26, he d. Jan. 8, 1776; *Consider*, a. 1709, m. Sarah Ripley March 3, 1774.
7. WINSLOW, (s. of —,) Dux., m. Abigail Delano; had *Nehemiah*, Jan. 12, 1793; *Nathaniel*, Sept. 20, 1794; *Charles*, June 3, 1796; *Briggs*, Feb. 14, 1798; *Abigail*, March 10, 1800; *Nancy D.*, Feb. 11, 1802; *Lucy*, Dec. 26, 1804; *William D.*, Jan. 7, 1806.

NOTE. Abigail (M.) m. Eleazer Harlow 1739; Anna (M.) m. Nathl.

Oales of Boston Dec. 26, 1747; *Edward* m. Judith Prince May 23, 1757; *Zenas* (M.) m. Abigail Peterson Feb. 14, 1765; *Mercy* m. Edward Southworth 1769; *Peleg* m. Mary Jones of Charlestown Nov. 21, 1775; *Deborah* m. John Osyer March 2, 1775; *Sarah G.* m. George Winslow 1781; *Novice* m. Caleb Bates 1782.

THORP.

JOHN, Dux. 1633, a carpenter, his wife was Alice.

TISDELL.

JOHN, Dux., 1637, had a grant of ten acres at G. H. path; had land at Hounds ditch, and Namasakeeset, which he sold to Wm. Brett 1657; removed to Taunton, where he was selectman; he was murdered by the Indians 27th June, 1675; his wife Sarah d. Dec. 1676; had *John*, who m. Hannah Rogers Nov. 23, 1664, and had Abigail July 15, 1667, John Aug. 10, 1669, Anna Jan. 27, 1672, and Remember July 8, 1675; *James, Joshua, Joseph.*

TOMPKINS.

SAMUEL, Dux., 1640, had four acres at Stoney Brook, and land towards G. H.; m. Lettice Foster of Scituate 1639; removed to East Bridgew.; had a brother John.

TOWER.

ELISHA, Dux., m. Mary, who d. June 6, 1795; had *Asaph, Elizabeth* 1757, d. 1759, *Lydia, James* 1766.

TRACY.

STEPHEN, Plymouth 1623; Dux. 1639; returned to England before 1654, for in the Col. Rec. is recorded a disposition of his property in New England, dated at London 20th March, 1654-5, and empowering John Winslow to perform it. He calls himself of St. Yarmouth, Eng., and says he has five chd. living in New Eng.; they were *Ens. John*, of Duxbury, had the estate in Dux., held many offices in the town; m. Jane Prence, m. 2d Deborah, who survived him, and he d. a. 1701; *Lt. Thomas*, of M., removed to Norwich, Ct., a. 1660; *Ruth, Mary*, and *another.*

NOTE. *Mary* m. Henry Cullifer Jan. 27, 1712; *Susanna* m. John Simmons 1715.

TRUANT.

Morris or Maurice, Dux. 1643, ad. 1658, also of M.

TUBBS.

William, Dux., ad. Jan. 2, 1637–8, m. Mercy Sprague Nov. 9, 1637; in 1664 he published a protest at the Court, "disowning all debts that she shall make him this time forward." She afterwards went to R. I., and the Court granted him a divorce July 1668; m. 2d Dorothy, whom he mentions in his will dated Feb. 20, 1677; had *William*, who had grants of land in Dux. at various times in 1670, at Namasakeeset 1684 and in 1686, upon condition that he bear his share of the Church and town charges; m. Judith, widow of Isaac Barker 1691; *Samuel*, Dux. 1710; *Joseph*, Dux. 1710; *Benjamin, Bethia.*

Note. *Deborah* m. Elisha Doten, Jr. of Plymouth, March 6, 1729; *Joseph* (of Pembroke) m. Eunice Wadsworth June 20, 1773.

TURNER.

1. David, Dux. 1643, able to bear arms.
2. George, Dux. 1660.
3. Japheth, Dux., m. Hannah Hudson, who survived him, he d. 1690; had *Ann*, Aug. 18, 1679; *Joshua*, April 9, 1681, Dux. 1703; *Japheth*, Jan. 4, 1682, Dux.; *Ruth*, March 19, 1685.

Note. *Hannah* m. Samuel Hill, Jr. 1722; *Amasa* m. Rebecca Delano March 2, 1727, sold his homestead to Joshua Soule 1739; *John*, Dux. 1728–33; *Elizabeth* m. Robert Wells 1784.

Joseph *Treeble* and Anna Jones, both of Plymouth, were m. in Duxbury Dec. 19, 1729. Silence *Trouest*, Dux. 1747. —*Chh. Rec.*

USSEL.

George, Dux., m. Molly, who d. July 20, 1757, æt. 40; m. 2d Mercy Osyer Nov. 3, 1757; he d. July 31, 1784; had a da. *Molly*, who d. Feb. 22, 1756 O. S., æt. 18 years, of consumption.

VINCENT.

Mr. John, Dux. 1637, had land near Wm. Basset; ad. 1637; Sandwich 1640. A Henry was of Sandwich in 1657.

WADSWORTH.

1. Christopher,* Dux.; bought land of John Starr and Job Cole; m. Grace; his will is dated July 21, 1677, and his estate amounted to £70; her will is dated Jan. 13, 1687; had *Joseph* (2); *John*, 1638 (3); *Samuel* (4); *Mary*, m. an Andrews.

2. Joseph, (s. of 1,) Dux.; m. Abigail Waite; ad. 1655; his will is dated March 22, 1689, in which he names "his dear and loving wife Mary," who was probably a second wife. —estate £158; had *Elisha* (5); *Samuel* and *Joseph* inherited lands in Dux. and Bridgew.; *Mehetabel, Ruth, Bethia*.

3. Dea. John, (s. of 1,) Dux., inherited land in Dux.; m. Abigail Andrews July 25, 1667; he "deceased May the 15th, Anno Dom. 1700 very early in y̆e morning before y̆e dawning of y̆e day, being about sixty-two yeares of age," and his will is dated April 23, preceding; "she deceased about midnight, betwixt y̆e 24th and 25 days of November, anno Domini 1723, being about 76 years of age;" had chd. *Mary*, Sept. 18, 1668; *Abigail*, Oct. 25, 1670; *John*, March 12, 1671 (6); *Christopher*, March 15, 1685 (7); *Ichabod*, March 1687 (8); *Isaac*, Dux. 1724, inherited land in Middleboro'; *Lydia; Sarah*, non comp. men.; *Grace*, m. prob. Wm. Sprague; *Hopestill*, m. Wm. Brewster May 20, 1708; *Mercy*.

4. Capt. Samuel, (s. of 1,) Dux., removed to Milton, where he bought land of Robert Babcock, 1672–3. A captain in Philip's war, he was sent to the relief of Sudbury with thirty-two men; but marching in the night, he fell into ambuscade, and was slain, with most of his men; this occurred three miles from Sudbury, on the 18th of April 1676, (say Hubbard, and Hobart's Journal; but on the 21st, say Gookin, and Judge Sewall). He left an estate of £1,248, including a farm at Milton of 300 acres. He m. Abigail, who survived 1687; and had chd. *Christopher*, who d. at Milton 1687; *Ebenezer*

---

* It is not known whence he came. The family of Wadsworth is a Yorkshire family, and of some antiquity. Burke gives this armorial bearing of the Yorkshire Wadsworths : " Gules three fleurs de lis stalked and slipped or." He also adds this crest to the same arms — " On a globe of the world, winged proper an eagle rising or."—General Armory.

(23); *Joseph* (24); *John* (25); *Timothy* (26); *Benjamin* (27); *Abigail*, not of age in 1687.

5. ELISHA, (s. of 2,) Dux., inherited most of the lands of his father, and a boat "in building;" m. Elizabeth Wiswall, who d. Jan. 25, 1741; had *Elizabeth* March 6, 1695; *Alice* April 15, 1697, m. Thomas Burton May 10, 1722; *Anne* April 14, 1700; *Abiah* June 4, 1703; *Patience* Aug. 20, 1706, m. Saml. Gray of K. Dec. 7, 1727; *Fear* Aug. 19, 1709; *Wait* Oct. 23, 1714 (9).

6. DEA. JOHN, (s. of 3,) Dux.; m. Mercy Wiswall June 25, 1704, she d. "upon ye 12th day of November Anno Domini 1716, about ten or eleven of ye clock in ye forenoon, being æt. thirty and six years one month and eight dayes;" he m. 2d at Boston, widow Mary Verdie of B. April 4, 1718; she d. (gravestone) July 20, 1742, æt. 58, but (according to records) June 22, "about an hour before the sun rising;" he "deceased May ye 3d Anno Domini 1750, Between Ten or Eleven a clock at night, Being Seventy Eight years one month and Twentyone Days old;" he had chd. *John* May 24, 1706 (10); *Uriah* July 5, 1708, d. at "two o'clock in ye morning," April 29, 1784; *Dorothy* June 25, 1710, m. Joseph Bartlett Dec. 25, 1729; *Ichabod* May 3, 1712 (11); *Peleg* Aug. 29, 1715 (12); *Mary* July 19, 1721, m. Dea. Elisha Phillips July 1, 1756.

7. CHRISTOPHER, (s. of 3,) Dux., m. Mehetabel Wormall Feb. 19, 1713; inherited land in Middleboro', d. before 1748; had *Christian* Feb. 5, 1715, m. Blanie Phillips Mar. 23, 1733; *Abigail* Feb. 17, 1718, m. Joseph Russell Dec. 31, 1740; *Christopher* Jan. 12, 1721 (13); *Zenobe* April 24, 1723, m. Nathl. Bartlett 1742.

8. ICHABOD, (s. of 3,) Dux.; m. Margaret Marshall Feb. 10, 1720, who afterwards m. Samuel Forster, and d. 1773; he d. Aug. 1, 1746; had *Joseph* Dec. 4, 1720, d. March 20, 1721; *Sarah* Feb. 20, 1722; *Mercy* Sept. 7, 1724, m. Col. Briggs Alden 1741; *Daniel* Sept. 28, 1726, d. Sept 12, 1730; *Eunice* Nov. 27, 1727, m. Joshua Tubbs of Pembroke June 20, 1773; *Hannah* Dec. 6, 1732; *Benjamin* Dec. 1, 1735 (14); *Lydia* Oct. 18, 1736.

9. CAPT. WAIT, (s. of 5,) Dux., a lieutenant, and chosen captain 1766; m. Abigail Bradford; had *Abigail* June 3, 1749, d. young; *Joseph* July 7, 1750, m. Anne Drew Feb. 1773; *Ahira* Nov. 1, 1751; *Seneca* April 9, 1753 (15); *Wait* Oct. 7, 1754 (16); *Clynthia* March 25, 1756, m. Ezekiel Soule 1777; *Robert* Sept. 26, 1757, d. April 25, 1760; *Eden* May 12, 1759 (17); *Beulah* June 8, 1762, m. Arthur Howland of M.; *Celanah* Dec. 9, 1763, m. Wm. Keen of Bristol 1784; *Elisha* June 15, 1765; *Zenith* Oct. 5, 1766 (18); *Abigail* Oct. 25, 1768; *Wiswall*, bap. 1768.

10. DR. JOHN, (s. of 6,) Dux.; m. Mary Alden Dec. 31, 1734; she d. April 4, 1789, æt. 78; he d. March 26, 1799, æt. 92; had *Mercy* Dec. 28, 1736, m. Joshua Cushman 1763; *John* Nov. 14, 1739 (see page 155); *Salumith* Mar. 10, 1742, m. Ezra Weston 1770; *Sarah* Dec. 23, 1744, m. John Neal Feb. 3, 1774.

11. ICHABOD, (s. of 6,) Dux., m. Anne Hunt Nov. 25, 1736; he d. April 21, 1771; she d. Aug. 9, 1773, æt. 59; had *Rhoda* Aug. 20, 1737; *Luna* Nov. 2, 1739, m. Capt. Benja. Wadsworth 1759; *Luke* Dec. 27, 1743, removed to M.; *Alpheus* Oct. 2, 1744; *Selah* Jan. 25, 1746, d. Dec. 24, 1754; *Anna* bap. 1748, m. Thaddeus Peterson.

12. DEA. PELEG, (s. of 6,) Dux., m. Susanna ———; had *Zilpha* June 21, 1742, d. March 23, 1744; *Cephas* Aug. 12, 1743, of K.; *Jeptha* April 5, 1745, d. May 2, 1745; *Zilpah* April 8, 1746, m. Perez Drew Feb. 6, 1772; *Peleg* April 25, 1748 (19); *Uriah* March 13, 1751, m. Eunice Bradford 1789 she d. Aug. 1795, and had Gamaliel 28 May 1793; *Ira*, bap. 1757 (20); *Wealthea*, bap. 1759, m. Maj. Alden 1780; *Dura*, bap. 1763 (21); *Lucy*.

13. CHRISTOPHER, (s. of 7,) Dux.; had *Prince* bap. 1744; *Eunice* bap. 1746; *Sarah* bap. 1747; and *Ephraim* bap. 1749.

14. CAPT. BENJAMIN, (s. of 8,) Dux.; m. Luna Wadsworth, Jan. 1, 1759; he d. Feb. 23, 1782; (she m. 2d, Col. Jotham Loring, 1785,) "eleven children buried by him;" had *Hannah*, Apr. 13, 1760, d. June 23, 1771, æt. 11; *Ichabod*, Jan. 13, 1762, d. July 11, 1780, æt. 18; *Daniel*, Jan. 27, 1764; *Marshall*, Feb. 20, 1766, d. June 25, 1771, æt. 5; *Frederic*, Nov. 28, 1767, d. June 21, 1771, æt. 3; *Selah*, July 30, 1769, d. June 25, 1771, æt. 2; *Sophia*; *Anne*, and others.

15. SENECA, (s. of 9,) Dux.; m. Dewesbury Soule, Jan. 5, 1777; had *Ahira*, Apr. 4, 1777, m. Deborah Sprague, who d. Oct. 30, 1813, m. 2d, Olive Wadsworth, May 20, 1822, had Celenah, 1801, m. Ezra W. Sampson, Catherine, 1802, m. Clark Drew, m. 2d, F. G. Ford, Merinda, 1805, m. Capt. Joshua Drew, Alexander, 1808, m. Beulah Holmes, Deborah 1813, Harriet 1822, Henry 1829, Horace 1830, Helen 1833, Hamilton 1837, and Harrison 1842; *Betsy Wiswall*, Dec. 17, 1778; *Lucy*, Sep. 24, 1780, m. 1801, Seth Stetson; *John*, Jan. 20, 1782, removed to Hingham; *Daniel*, Dec. 18, 1784; *Celanah*, Oct. 18, 1786, d. Mar. 9, 1790; *Sophia*, Feb. 18, 1791; *Charlotte*, Dec. 20, 1793.

16. WAIT, (s. of 9,) Dux.; m. Jerusha Bartlett Robinson, May 14, 1794; m. 2d, Priscilla Stetson Weston, widow of John; he d. Mar. 11, 1840; had *Robert*, July 3, 1774; *Matil-*

da, July 23, 1776, m. Jas. Chandler; *Silvia*, July 28, 1781, m. Ziba Hunt; *Lucinda*, Sep. 6, 1785, m. Zenas Winsor; *Jerusha*, May 25, 1789, m. Zenas Faunce; *James*, Feb. 14, 1792; *Waity*, Nov. 4, 1797, m. Nathan Sampson; *Caroline*, Mar. 15, 1802, m. Allen Hunt, m. 2d, David Bradford; *Lewis L.*, Jan. 23, 1804; *Jane*, Feb. 23, 1809.

17. EDEN, (s. of 9,) Dux.; m. Ruby Soule, who d. Apr. 6, 1816; he was drowned, Apr. 30, 1818; had *Eden* and *Zenith*, (gemini) May 15, 1793, Eden m. Mercy Bosworth, and Zenith d. at sea; *Nancy*, m. Mr. Barstow; *Beulah*, m. Chas. Winsor.

18. ZENITH, (s. of 9,) Dux.; m. Mahala Winsor; he d. July 10, 1832; had *Olive*, 1797; *Rufus*, 1799; *John*, 1801, d. 1822; *Daniel*, 1803; *Alden*, 1805; *Mahala*, 1807, m. Mr. Thompson, m. 2d, Mr. Tho. Blasland of South Boston; *Harvey*, 1811; *Lawrence*, 1813.

19. GEN. PELEG, (s. of 12,) Dux., Plymouth, Portland, Me.; m. Elizabeth Bartlett of Plymouth, and had *Charles Lee*, *Zilpha*, *Henry*, and *Alexander Scammel*. General W. d. at Hiram, Me., Nov., 1829, æt. 80 years.

20. IRA, (s. of 12,) Dux.; m. Sarah Freeman, 1783, who d. Jan. 18, 1836; he d. Dec. 28, 1826; had *Sarah*, June 29, 1784; *Ira*, Oct. 26, 1789, Cambridgeport; *Joseph F.*, Nov. 12, 1792.

21. DEA. DURA, (s. of 12,) Dux.; m. Lydia Bradford; removed to Maine; had *Dura*, 1788, m. Mercy Taylor, who d. 1814, m. 2d, Abigail Cushman, and had by the first wife a da. Mercy, and by second, Henry, who m. Abby Winsor, Lucy, Abigail, Gamaliel, Dura, Elizabeth, Briggs, and William; *Peleg*, 1791; *Seth*, 1792; *John*, 1794; *Hannah*, 1796, m. Stephen Churchill Bradford; *Susanna*, 1797; *Zilpha*, 1800; *Lydia*, 1802; *Uriah*, 1808.

22. JOSEPH, (s. of —,) Dux.; had *Huldah*, Aug. 4, 1783, m. Seth Hunt; *Abigail B.*, Jan. 24, 1796.

23. DEA. EBENEZER, (s. of 4,) Milton, m. Mary, who survived him; he d. a. 1717, leaving an estate of £860; had *Samuel*; *Recompence* (28); *George*, 1699, m. Hannah Pitcher of Milton, 17 June, 1720; *Mary*.

24. JOSEPH, (s. of 4,) Boston; m. Hannah; had *Joseph* 25 Jan. 1697, d. young; *Hannah* May, 1699; *Abigail* July 27, 1701; *Joseph* 30 April, 1706.—A Joseph m. Elizabeth Savage Oct. 8, 1716.—Boston Rec.

Hon. Joseph Wadsworth died at Boston 20 Nov. 1750.

25. JOHN, (s. of 4,) Milton; he m. Elizabeth; he d. a. 1733, leaving a large estate of £7,082; had *John*; *Benjamin*; *Joseph*; *Ebenezer* 1717; *Samuel* 1719; *Elizabeth* m. a Tolman;

Ruth m. a Parret; *Grace* m. a Dean; *Abigail, Margaret, Hannah.*

26. TIMOTHY, (s. of 4,) Boston; member of the Ancient and Hon. Art. Comp.; a gunsmith; removed to Newport, R. I.; m. Susanna, and had *Recompence* 19 March, 1688; appointed Master of the North Free Grammar School, in Boston, 1713; *Susanna* 29 Oct. 1687, m. Edward Langdon 2d Dec. 1718; *Timothy* 3 Nov. 1692.

27. REV. BENJAMIN, (s. of 4,) b. 1669; grad. H. C. 1690; ordained over the First Church in Boston Sept. 8, 1696, and dismissed June 16, 1725, and inaugurated President of Harvard College in July, 1725. Vide Quincy's Hist. Harv. Coll., and Eliot's Biog. Eliot says of him: "His mind was rather strong than brilliant; as a preacher, he was rather grave than animated. He delivered his sermons without notes; and his memory was so tenacious that, on all occasions, he could quote any chapter or verse of the Bible, without recurring to the pages." It is said of him, that he devoted one-tenth of his income to charitable purposes. He died, March 16, 1737, "lamented with more than ordinary demonstrations of sorrow." His wife Ruth d. Feb. 17, 1744-5, in her 73d year.

28. RECOMPENCE, (s. of 23,) Milton, m. Sarah, d. a. 1729; left an estate of £1325; had *Sarah*, who d. before 1729; *Mary* 1717; *David* 1720; *Jonathan* 1722.

NOTE. *Hannah* m. Benj. Peterson 1698; *Mercy* m. Benja. Snow 1756; *Lenity* m. Henry Seaver of K. Feb. 7, 1765; *Lucia* m. Joseph Smith 20 Aug. 1771; *Abigail* m. Prince Howland 1779.

WALKER.

SAMUEL, Dux., m. Elizabeth Brewster 1784, who d. July 29, 1787, æt. 28; m. 2d Judith 1790, and had Benjamin, Elizabeth, Judith, Kendall, Cynthia, and Samuel.

NOTE. *Mary* m. John Howland 1685; *Timothy* m. Eunice Brewster 22 Nov. 1758. John at M. d. 1663, leaving wife Lydia. *William*, at Eastham, had William b. Aug. 2, 1659.

WALLIS.

HENRY, had land at Stoney brook, Dux.; but d. before 1641.

WANTON.

EDWARD, appears to have owned land in Dux. 1694, though he probably resided in Scituate at the time. It is said he came from London to Boston before 1658, and to Scituate 1661, and d. Oct. 11, 1716, æt. 85. He was a ship carpenter. See Deane's Scituate, p. 371.

WASHBURN.

1. JOHN, Dux. early, purchased a farm of Edward Bumpus beyond Eagle Nest creek; had *John* (2); *Philip*, received a farm from his father in Dux.; sold it to Saml. Seabury 1679, and a part to Thomas Lazell in 1684; his brother John in his will directs his son John to take of "his uncle Philip."

2. JOHN, (s. of 1,) Dux., a tailor; m. Elizabeth Mitchell 1645; ad. 1654; sold his land in Dux.; had John, Samuel, Joseph, Thomas, Jonathan, Benjamin, James, Mary, Elizabeth, Sarah, and Jane. For further account, see Mitchell's Bridgewater.

WATERMAN.

1. ROBERT, Plymouth, Dux., M., (had a brother Thomas of Roxbury, who d. 1670, leaving Thomas, who had Robert, b. 1680); he m. Elizabeth Bourn Dec. 11, 1638, and d. a. 1651; had *John* 1642, who m. Ann Sturtevant Dec. 7, 1665, and had Samuel 16 Oct. 1666, and Elizabeth 15 Jan. 1668; *Thomas* 1644; *Joseph; Robert* m. Susanna Lincoln Oct. 1, 1675.

2. EPHRAIM, "late of Kingston, now resident in Duxbury," m. Betty Delano June 4, 1746.

An *Ephraim* of Dux. (perhaps a son) had Lucy Oct. 15, 1786; Betsy Aug. 18, 1790; Samuel Aug. 31, 1792; Elisha Aug. 18, 1794, and Jerusha July, 1797.

Malachi m. Abigail Russell Mar. 30, 1772, and may have had a son. An *Oliver* b. 1753, d. July 2, 1756.

3. ELIPHALET, (came from Halifax) Dux.; m. Sylvina Winsor, and had *Martin* Oct. 1, 1792, m. Joanna Cushing, m. 2d Lydia Soule; had by his first w. Joanna (who m. Capt. Jona. Nickerson), Martin Thomas, Joseph Langdon, Lauretta, and Lucius; *Betsy*, July 12, 1796, m. Wm. V. Kent, Esq., who d. at Boston Aug. 10, 1849; *Thomas Waterman Herrick*, Oct. 9, 1806, m. Emily Winsor.

WATSON.

JOHN, Dux.; had Elizabeth R. 1795; Sally 1797, Lucia, Daniel, Eunice and Nancy.

WEST.

1. FRANCIS, Dux.; m. Margery Reeves Feb. 27, 1639; M. 1641; returned to Dux.; ad. 1655; bought land at Mill brook 1642, also in 1661, and in 1670 received a grant; he d. Jan. 2, 1692, leaving a small estate; had *Samuel* 1643 (2), *Peter* (3); *Pelatiah* went to Conn.; *Richard*.

2. SAMUEL, (s. of 1,) Dux.; m. Triephosa Partridge, Sep. 26, 1668; she d. Nov. 1, 1701; he d. May 8, 1689, æt. 46; had *Francis*, Nov. 13, 1669; *Jeuen* (son), Sep. 8, 1671, d. Dec. 29, 1671; *Samuel*, Dec. 23, 1672 (4); *Pelatiah*, Mar. 8, 1674, m. Elizabeth Chandler, July 12, 1722, and d. Dec. 7, 1756, æt. 83, nearly; *Ebenezer*, July 22, 1676; *John*, Mar. 6, 1679; *Abigail*, Sep. 26, 1682, m. Nathl. Cole, 1714.

3. PETER, (s. of 1,) Dux.; 1680, had a grant West of South river; m. Patience; had *Mary*, Oct. 3, 1675; *Margery*, Mar. 12, 1678; *Ester*, Sep. 20, 1680; *Anne*, Feb. 16, 1682, m. Elisha Curtis, May 17, 1705; *Lydia*, Feb. 11, 1680; *William*, May 4, 1683; *Mary*, Dec. 7, 1685; *Benjamin*, July 7, 1688; *Elisha*, Mar. 2, 1693; *Samuel*, Apr. 4, 1697.

4. SAMUEL, (s. of 2,) Dux.; m. Martha Delano, June 20, 1709; removed to Pembroke, 1749; had *Amos*, May 29, 1710; *Nathan*, Aug. 18, 1711; *Sarah*, Nov. 8, 1712; *Moses*, Mar. 4, 1716.

NOTE. *Twiford* West in 1635 was apprenticed to Gov. Winslow for 7 years, and was of M., 1643; *Nathaniel*, a stranger from R. I., returning to Providence, fell through the ice and was drowned, 1658; *John* of Swansey, m. Mehetabel, and had William, 11 Sep., 1683. — *Col. Rec.*

WESTON.

1. EDMUND, Dux.; m. a Soule (?); had *Elnathan* (2); *Samuel; John*, Dux., 1661, had a grant 1694 and 1796.

2. ELNATHAN, (s. of 1,) Dux.; m. Jane; she d. May 13, 1735; he d. Apr. 23, 1729.

3. SAMUEL, (s. of —,) Dux.; m. Elizabeth Southworth; had *Samuel*, Mar. 5, 1718; *Zebdiel*, Jan. 22, 1720, d. Oct. 12, 1739; *Mary*, July 18, 1722; *Priscilla*, Jan. 24, 1725, d. Jan.

WESTON. 335

7, 1756; *Elnathan*, Sep. 29, 1727 (5); *Nathaniel*, Apr. 30, 1730.

4. ELIPHAS, (s. of —,) Dux.; m. Priscilla Peterson, who d. Sep. 22, 1778, æt. 64; he d. Mar. 18, 1762, æt. 52; had *Daniel*, a. 1739, wrecked on Dux. beach, Nov. 17, 1766; *Eliphas*, a. 1740; *Israel*, a. 1742; *Arunah*, a. 1745; *Joshua*, a. 1748; "Mar. 18, 1762, Eliphas Weston, in his 53d year, and his son Joshua about 14 years old were drowned out of a float in Dux. Bay." Chh. Rec.; *Simeon*, a. 1752; *Ezra* (6).

5. ELNATHAN, (s. of 3,) Dux.; m. Jemima, who d. July 6, 1812, æt. 87; he d. Dec. 29, 1777; had *Nathaniel*, Dec. 27, 1760, a Nathaniel d. in the army, Oct. 19, 1777; *Priscilla*, Jan. 7, 1764; *Samuel*, a. 1753 (7); *Abigail*, a. 1757.

6. EZRA, (s. of 4,) Dux.; m. Silvia Church, Apr. 20, 1767, she d. May 31, 1768, æt. 20; m. 2d, Salumith Wadsworth, Oct. 25, 1770; m. 3d, Mrs. Priscilla Virgin, da. of Richard Cooper of Plymouth, July 4, 1817; had *Silvia Church*, May 13, 1768, m. Capt. Sylvanus Sampson, and d. 1836; *Ezra*, Nov. 30, 1771 (8).

7. SAMUEL, (s. of 5,) Dux.; m. Abigail Bisbee, Mar. 24, 1778; had *Alethea*, May 20, 1778, d. June 16, 1779; *Nathaniel*, Sep. 2, 1779; *Inice*, Dec. 1, 1780, d. May 30, 1781; *Sally*, Mar. 19, 1782; *Susanna*, Feb. 27, 1784.

8. EZRA, (s. of 6,) Dux.; m. Jerusha Bradford, who d. Oct. 11, 1833; he d. Aug. 15, 1842; had *Ezra*, 1796, d. 1805; *Maria*, 1794, d. 1804; *Hon. Gershom Bradford*, Aug. 27, 1799, m. Judith Sprague, who d. Nov. 25, 1845, m. 2d, Deborah B., da. of Edmund Brownell of Little Compton, R. I., Feb. 23, 1848, and had Capt. Gershom B., m. Mary Moore, Maria and Jerusha who d. young, Allyn, Nov. 3, 1825, an attorney of Worcester, Geo. Canning, Mar. 28, 1828, William B., June 20, 1830, Edgar, Aug. 31, 1832, Jerusha, Dec. 19, 1834, Alfred, Jan. 11, 1837, Maria, June 3, 1839, Alden B., Nov., 1844; *Jerusha B.*, 1802, d. 1804; *Alden Bradford*, 1805, a merchant of Boston; *Ezra*, 1809, merchant.

9. THOMAS, (s. of —,) Dux.; b. 1717; m. Mary, who d. May 1, 1765, æt. 41; m. 2d, Martha Chandler, Jan. 15, 1767; he d. May 16, 1766; had *Mary*, 1754, d. Sep. 26, 1776, æt. 22; *Thomas*, July 25, 1760 (10); *June*; *Mercy*; *Peleg*; *Edmund*; *Rebecca*, June 16, 1774, m. Bradford Sampson.

10. THOMAS, (s. of 9,) Dux.; m. Abigail, who was b. Apr. 16, 1765; she d. Aug. 1, 1842; he d. July 29, 1842; had *Thomas*, 1786; *Dura*, 1788; *Stephen*, 1790, d. 1791, *Stephen*, 1792; *Melzar*, 1797; *Galen*, 1797; *Eden*, 1799; *Almira*, 1802; *Seth*, 1804; *George*, 1806.

11. ABNER, (s. of —,) Dux.; m. Sarah Standish, Mar. 2,

1730, she d. Feb. 25, 1779, æt. 74; had *Hannah*, a. 1739, and *Deborah*, a. 1742.

12. MICAH, (s. of —,) Dux.; m. Beriah Oldham, Dec. 3, 1761; he d. Aug. 4, 1816; had *James*, Sep. 24, 1762 (13); *Seth*, Sep. 27, 1764; *Sarah*, Dec. 2, 1766; *John*, Aug. 21, 1769; *Benjamin*, Oct. 27, 1771; *Bethia*, Nov. 2, 1773; *Desire*, Mar. 15, 1777.

13. JAMES, (s. of 12,) Dux.; m. Sarah Sampson, 1785, she d. Dec. 31, 1834, æt. 77$\frac{2}{3}$; had *James*, who m. Abigail, who d. Aug. 8, 1729, æt. 33, m. 2d, Deborah, and had James, 1793, Abigail, 1796, Mary, Sarah, and others.

14. WARREN, (s. of —,) Dux.; m. Mary Bosworth, 1767; she d. Aug. 14, 1778, m. 2d, Martha Weston, 1780; had *Daniel*, Apr. 5, 1772; *Warren; Lydia*, Sep. 17, 1778.

15. JOSEPH, (s. of —,) b. 1692; Dux.; d. Sep. 11, 1778, æt. 86$\frac{1}{2}$; a Joseph m. Mercy Peterson, May 18, 1721; a Mary, wife of Joseph, d. Dec. 27, 1768, æt. 69.

16. JOSEPH, (b. 1753, perh. s. of 15,) Dux.; m. Rebecca; he d. Nov. 21, 1813, æt. 60; had *Thomas*, 1777, d. 1778, *Thomas* 1778, *Polly* 1781, *Joseph* 1783, *Joshua* 1785, d. 1789, *Peleg* 1787, *Mercy* 1789, *Lewis* 1791, *Rebecca* 1793, *Rufus* and *Judith* 1796, and *Joshua* 1798.

17. ASA, (s. of —,) Dux.; m. Jane Brewster, Nov. 20, 1777; Fanny, wife of Asa, d. 1789; Asa b. June 14, 1786, m. Eunice, who was born June 18, 1789, had Bradford, Joshua, George and Simeon.

18. LEVI, (s. of —,) Dux.; m. Patty; had Charlotte 1785, Betsy 1787, d. 1810; Sally 1790, Levi 1793, Ziba H. 1796, Lucy 1798.

19. NATHANIEL C., (s. of —,) Dux.; had *Nathaniel* 1793, m. Abigail Frazar; *Judith* 1796; *Capt. Church* 1799; *Ruby; Lucy; and Sarah*.

20. WILLIAM, (s. of —,) Dux.; m. Ruby Chandler, Oct. 21, 1760; had Ichabod, Lucy and Ruby.

NOTE. *Sarah* m. John Chandler, 1708; *Mary* m. Joseph Simmons, 1709; *Abigail*, 1704, d. Sep. 7, 1766, æt. 62$\frac{1}{2}$; *John* m. Rebecca Peterson, Oct. 1, 1717; *Rebecca* m. Samuel Spooner of Dartmouth, Apr. 10, 1717; *Deborah* m. Benj. Prior, 1723; *Jonathan* m. Mercy Richard, May 8, 1728; *Seth* 1733, kld. by lightning at sea, May 22, 1764, æt. 31; *Sarah* m. John Chandler, 1743; *Geen* m. Tho. Hunt, 1748; *Abigail* m. Enoch Freeman, 1764; *Zadock* m. Mary Peterson, Oct. 8, 1767; *Ichabod* m. widow Mehetabel Soule, Dec. 7, 1769; *Zebdiel* m. Hannah Curtis, Feb. 22, 1769; *Jacob* m. Deborah Simmons, Dec. 25, 1755; *William* m. Elizabeth Sampson, 1781; *Elkanah*, b. Feb. 14, 1781, m. Mary, who was b. Dec. 11, 1781; *Sarah* m. Abel Chandler, 1783; *Jacob* m. Alice Southworth, 1784.

WEYBORNE.

THOMAS, Dux., 1640, land northwest of North hill; same year, had land at Namasakeeset, fifty acres.

WHITE.

Anne, da. of Richard and Katuen of Plymouth, m. Samuel Drew, 1736; *Carpus*, Dux., had Tabitha, b. 1764, d. 1771; *Mehetabel*, m. Samuel Soule, 1756; *Joseph*, m. Rebecca, 1794, and had Joseph, Otis, Briggs, and others.

WILLIAMSON.

1. GEORGE, Dux., lived at Tarkiln pond in Dux.; m. probably a da. of Mr. Crisp; had *Thankful*, May 18, 1702; *Hepzibah*, Apr. 29, 1705; *Beulah*, Nov. 29, 1706; *Mary*, Sep. 10, 1708; *George*, Oct. 1, 1710, probably the one kld. by a highwayman; *Deborah*, Apr., 1713; *Caleb*, July, 1715 (2).

2. CALEB, (s. of 1). This is probably the one who m. Sarah Ransom, and settled in Middleboro', and had 6 sons and 3 das., and only two, George and Caleb, left issue. George, (the 5th son,) b. 1754, a soldier of the Revolutionary war, and Capt. of artillery, removed to Canterbury, Ct., then to Amherst, Mass., and d. at Bangor, Me., 1822, æt. 68, having had by his wife Mary Foster, 4 sons and 4 das., and of these William D. grad. at Brown University, 1804, Judge of Probate, Me., author of a history of Maine, and d. May 27, 1846. New Eng. Hist. & Geneal. Reg. 1. p. 90.

NOTE. *George* (No. 1,) was perhaps a descendant of Mr. George, of whom we only know that he accompanied Capt. Standish on his first interview with Massasoit, Mar. 22, 1621. A Caleb, commanded a company under Col. Church, perhaps the one of Barnstable, who m. Mary Cobb, 3 May, 1687, and had Mary, Sarah, Martha, Timothy, and Ebenezer. (N. E. H. & G. Reg. ii, 198.) George (No. 1) may have been at some time resident in Harwich. Abigail of M., m. Wm. Tolman of Scituate, June 23, 1740; Timothy m. Sarah Peterson, Dec. 3, 1767. Alexander and Timothy *Williams*, were in M., 1643; Timothy *Williamson* kept an ordinary there in 1673, and a Mary Williamson one in 1678.

WILLIS.

1. JOHN, Dux., 1640, had land N. W. of North hill, and 50 acres at Namasakeeset; sold his estate to Wm. Pabodie, 1657;

WINSLOW.

sold land to R. Barker, 1665; removed to Bridgew.; a deacon there; m. Elizabeth [Hodgkins], widow of Wm. Palmer, Jr.; had *John, Nathaniel, Jonathan, Comfort, Benjamin, Hannah* m. Nathl. Hayward; *Elizabeth* m. a Harvey; *Sarah* m. John Ames.

2. NATHANIEL, LAWRENCE, JONATHAN, and FRANCIS were brothers of No. 1. Of Jonathan, we find in the Col. Rec. "Jonathan Willis, who is at Duxbury for cure, shall not be maintained by Duxbury, but by Sandwich, whence he came."

3. RICHARD, servt. of John Barnes, next of Thomas Prence, 1634, then lived in Dux., 1638, m. Amy Glass, Oct. 11, 1639, Plymouth, 1640, and Richard (prob. son) m. Patience Bonum of Plymouth, 1670.

4. JEREMIAH, a youth at Dux. in 1638, brought before the Court for being disorderly, and the same ordered to procure himself a master. Vide Mitchell's Bridgewater.

NOTE. *Eliakim* of Dartmouth, m. Lydia Fish of Dux., July 20, 1738.

WILSON.

RICHARD, Duxbury, able to bear arms, 1643.

WING.

GIDEON, Dux., m. Abigail Ripley, Feb. 25, 1767, had *William*, July 11, 1768; *Allen*, Aug. 27, 1770.

NOTE. *Stephen* was in Sandwich, and had Mercy, 1650; *John*, Yarmouth, had a son, "drowned in the snow," 1648. Col. Rec.

WINSLOW.

1. JOSHUA, Dux., m. Hannah Delano, Dec. 3, 1772, she d. Sep. 16, 1778, æt. 29, m. 2d, Mrs. Salome Delano, 1780, who d. Sep. 23, 1781, æt. 35.

2. EDWARD, (s. of —,) Dux., m. Phebe, and he d. May 29, 1803, and had *Edward*, Nov. 8, 1769, who m. Rebecca, who was b. Dec. 10, 1770, and she d. Sep. 11, 1835, æt. 64, and had George, 1796, d. 1798, Betsy, 1798, d. Sep. 5, 1817, George, Nov. 29, 1800, Polly, Aug. 12, 1802, d. Jan. 30, 1831, Seth, 1805, d. Mar. 7, 1828, Samuel, Sep. 26, 1808, Rebecca E., 1811, d. Dec. 9, 1826.

NOTE. *George* m. Sarah G. Thomas 1781; *Mehetabel* d. March 5, 1791, æt. 66.

WINSOR.

1. JOSEPH, (his name sometimes spelt Windsor) Lynn,* removed to Sandwich 1637, and in 1638 he was presented to the Court "for keeping house alone disorderly, after half a yeares warneing or thereabouts," but was released June 4, 1639; he bought land there of Thomas Chillingworth, and in 1639 was ordered to give it up to public use, the town allowing a fair compensation; he is mentioned in 1641, and in 1643 is able to bear arms in Sandwich, and took the oath of fidelity 1657. —Col. Rec.

2. WALTER. We find this in the Col. Rec. under 1671:— " Walter Winser for selling liquor to the Indians fined five pounds, but on consideration of some particulars about it, it was abated to thirty shillings."—Rec. Vol. IIII.

3. ROBERT, Boston, lived on Ann street, next to John Bateman. In the Suffolk Deeds, II. 343, is his acknowledgment of debt (£64) to Capt. Scottow, and an assignment of his house and land, dated Jan. 24, 1656, and cancelled 1693-4. And on p. 333 is a deed from Capt. S. to R. Winsor, of the estate, having the Conduit street on east and west sides, and towards the flats on the east. This last is dated Jan. 2, 1656. He was a blockmaker and turner. His will is dated April 24, 1679, and gives his property to his wife Rebecca, and was proved on the 15th of the May following, so that he d. in April or May 1679. His estate amounted to £207, including house and land £150. His chd. were *Thomas*, Sept. 30, 1652, d. July 8, 1654; *Rebecca*, Dec. 10, 1654; *Constance*, May 7, 1657; *Thomas*, Oct. 1, 1659 (4); *Sarah*, May 7, 1662; *Samuel*, Sept. 18, 1664; *Lydia*, Aug. 1, 1666, and *John*, April 22, 1669.

4. THOMAS, (s. of 3,) Boston, among the taxable inhabitants of Boston 1695; m. Rachel, and had chd. *Joshua* and *Caleb* (gemini) Dec. 29, 1692; *Rebecca*, March 19, 1697; *Robert*, April 16, 1699; *Mary*,† March 24, 1700.

A Thomas Windsor, Boston, m. Hannah Johnson 12 May,

* Lewis (Hist. Lynn) gives a *John* Winsor, who removed from Lynn to Sandwich 1637.

† Probably the one who m. Solomon Jones of Hull, Nov. 17, 1720. Their chd.— were Rachel July 1, 1723; Sarah Oct. 22, 1724; Elizabeth June 15, 1726; Rebecca Jan. 3, 1727-8; Leah Feb. 12, 1729; Hannah, Dec. 10, 1731; Mercy April 6, 1734; Thomas Jan. 10, 1735-6; Solomon March 17, 1737, d. Dec. 25, 1738.

A widow Mary Jones (prob. of Solomon) m. John Hayden, resident of Long Island (prob. the one in Boston harbor), July 19, 1761, by Rev. Samuel Veazie.—*Information of C. J. F. Binney, Esq.*

1725, had Thomas May 26, 1726, and Hannah July 18, 1729.
—A Thomas Windsor of Boston, m. Elizabeth Moor 24 Sept. 1747. She d. the next year, and he received letters granting administration on her estate Sept. 6, 1748. By the inventory of her estate it appears they owned a house and land at the North-end together, valued at £500. He was a shipwright.

Rachel Winsor (perhaps a da. of 4, or possibly his widow,) m. George Lewis at Boston July 31, 1717.

5. JOHN, Boston; he d. about 1666, and an inventory of his estate (£20) was taken Feb. 15, 1666–7; his wife Mary survived. They had *Martha*, Aug. 22, 1667.

Mary (possibly his widow, or perhaps a da.) m. Benjamin Tour 29 Aug. 1691.

6. JOSHUA, was b. 1648, possibly a son of Robert, No. 3; admitted a freeman May 8, 1678; a member of the 2d church in Boston; constable of Boston 1686; one of the taxable inhabitants 1695; he d. Nov. 1717; his will is dated Nov. 19, 1717, and the inventory taken Dec. 6—the amount was £214. His wife Sarah survived. He had *William* Nov. 26, 1672, d. young; *Sarah*, Nov. 3, 1673, m. Mr. Alexander Sherard,* and d. before her father, leaving a family; *William* Sept. 3, 1679; *Joshua* Nov. 7, 1679, d. young; *Joshua* March 16, 1684; *Elizabeth* Dec. 23, 1689. The father's will names a daughter, *Rebecca* Wilkinson, who was then living in his house. She m. 1st Thomas Leverett, a barber, who d. June 1706, and she m. 2d Edward Wilkinson Dec. 4, 1712. Her first husband is called in the settlement of the estate (£198) Mr. Thomas Hudson Leverett.

7. ROBERT, (s. of —,) according to Hutchinson, he and his wife died in 1717, both aged over 70, and were buried in one grave.

8. PETER Winsor, (s. of -,) Boston, m. 1st, Elizabeth Smith 31 Nov. 1721; m. 2d, Martha Tucker 1 Oct. 1733; m. 3d, Sarah Nottage June 1, 1738.

Sarah Winsor, widow (probably of Peter), died in Boston 1770, and widow Mary Brintnal was chosen to administer on her estate (£52) March 23, 1770.

NOTE. In the Boston Town Records, under date of 1708, *Mr. Winsor's warehouse* is mentioned, as being near the dock, at the end of Fishmarket

---

* He m. a second wife, Bethia, to whom he gave in his will £100 and his negro girl Esther Ned. This instrument was dated June 5, 1721. He mentions his das. Sarah Vering and Hannah, and his sons Windsor, b. 1700, Thomas b. 1703, and Joshua b. 1706. Mr. Sherrar, as the name was sometimes spelt, lived on Cornhill, and also owned a warehouse and land at the Dock, and also land in Windham, Ct. His executors were Jonathan Williams, Nicholas Battolph and Joseph Thorne.

street. The house of Capt. *Winsor* is also mentioned in Ann street, near Mrs. Pemberton's.

9. WILLIAM. I have been able to learn nothing concerning the father of the first of the name in Duxbury, except from vague tradition, which says he bore this name—William, and that he came to Boston from Devonshire, Eng., and soon after m. a second wife, Betsy Smith, and that his chd. were *Samuel* (10), who went to Duxbury, and who was by his first wife, and *William*, who was a jeweller, and remained in Boston, where he d. without children; and *Peter*, who was never married, but went to the West Indies, where he died.

Possibly the tradition may have reference to Peter (8), whose first wife was Elizabeth, *alias* Betsy Smith.

10. SAMUEL, (s. of 9,) was the first of the name in Duxbury, and was born May 14, 1725, settled on Clark's Island in Dux. bay. The site of his house was a few rods northwest of the present building. Here he built several small vessels, and here several of his children were born. He next removed and built a house on the southern slope of Captain's hill. He m. Feb. 18, 1746, Rhoda Delano; she died June 1, 1799; and he died May 22, 1770, æt. 45 years; they had chd. — *Nathaniel*, Jan. 15, 1747 (11); *Joshua*, May 1, 1749 (12); *Samuel*, Aug. 31, 1751 (13); *William*, Jan. 27, 1753 (14); *John*, Aug. 31, 1756 (15); *James*, July 19, 1759, d. Feb. 21, 1767; *Peter*, Aug. 21, 1761 (16); *Rhoda*, June 5, 1764, m. Amos Brown, Jan. 1, 1784; *Betsy*, Feb. 3, 1768, m. Job Sampson; *James*, Mar. 17, 1770 (17).

11. NATHANIEL, (s. of 10,) Dux.; m. Jan. 19, 1768, Olive Soule; she d. Oct. 28, 1833, æt. 85, and he d. Oct. 17, 1839, æt. 93, and was buried in one grave with his wife; had chd. — *Wealthea*, Oct. 17, 1769, m. Isaac Little of Pembroke, and had Wealthea m. Hon. Seth Sprague, Jr. of Dux., Olive m. Rev. Hiram Weston, Sally m. Isaac Barker, Isaac, Lydia, Ann m. Geo. Frazar of Dux., Betsy m. Benj. Standish, Otis m. Betsy Hoskins, and Samuel m. Elizabeth Simmons; *Silvina*, June 19, 1771, m. Capt. Eliphalet Waterman; *Mahala* m. Zenith Wadsworth; *Olive* and *Nathaniel* (18) (gemini), Sep. 8, 1775, Olive d. July 31, 1776; *Sally*, d. Oct. 7, 1778; *Samuel* (19); *Sally* m. 1st, Capt. Thomas Herrick,[*] Sep., 1805, m. 2d, Rev. Thomas Asbury, now living in Columbus, Ohio; *Martin* (20); *Betsy* m. David Turner; *Nancy*, Dec. 27, 1788, m. Capt. John Howland.

[*] He came from Gloucester, was a shipmaster, and d. at Richmond, Va., in 1814, æt. 40. He was the son of Wm. Haskell Herrick, who d. 1806, and who was the son of Thomas (d. 1784), the son of Thomas, Esq. (d. at Gloucester, 1787, æt. 73). His descent can be traced to Robert *Eyrick*, living in England, 1450. — *Herrick Genealogies*, by Gen. Jedediah Herrick, Bangor, 1846.

12. JOSHUA, (s. of 10,) Dux.; m. Olive Thomas, who was b. Dec. 28, 1752, m. 2d, Ruth Thomas, who was b. June 14, 1755, m. 3d, Deborah Fish, who was b. Dec. 11, 1756, and d. May 6, 1843; he d. in 1827, and had chd. — *Lucy*, May 17, 1775, m. Saml. Delano; *Judith*, Sep. 11, 1778, m. Dr. Rufus Hathaway; *Thomas*, July 22, 1780 (21); *Seth*, Apr. 5, 1782, m. Betsy Hunt, Sep. 30, 1802; *Joseph*, May 6, 1788 (22); *George*, Mar. 14, 1790 (23); *Hannah*, May 20, 1785, m. Solomon Washburn; *Ellis*, May 29, 1797. There were two who d. young, *Charles*, Dec. 9, 1776, and *Olive*, June 18, 1786.

13. SAMUEL, (s. of 10,) Dux.; m. Acenith Hunt, Nov. 3, 1774, who d. Sep. 26, 1835; he d. Aug. 26, 1835. He had *John*, Aug. 5, 1775 (24); *Spencer*, May 10, 1779 (25); *Charles*, Sep. 17, 1781 (26); *Abigail*, Oct. 2, 1784, m. Josiah Morton; *Otis*, July 12, 1787 (27); *Lewis*, July 24, 1790 (28); *Alden*, Feb. 2, 1793 (29); *Sarah Barker*, Jan. 13, 1799, m. Henry Louden of Pembroke; and one other *Charles*, b. Oct. 12, 1778, d. young.

14. WILLIAM, (s. of 10,) Dux.; m. Anne Hunt, July 23, 1775; m. 2d, Priscilla Delano, Mar., 1795; had *Melzar; Sally* m. Bartlett Holmes; *Waity* m. Bradford Freeman, Apr., 1802; *Clark*, May 3, 1783 (30); *William*, Sep. 18, 1785 (31); *Nancy* m. Saml. Chandler; *Mary* m. John Alden; *Rhoda* m. Chas. Sampson, m. 2d, Mr. Gerrish.

15. JOHN, (s. of 10,) Dux.; m. Nancy Thomas, Nov. 6, 1778; had *Charlotte, Fanny, Lucy, Susan*, and *William Thomas*, all unm.; *Capt. Isaac* (32); *Nancy* m. Mr. Beals of Abington; *Capt. Benjamin* (33).

16. PETER, (s. of 10,) Dux., removed to K.; m. Deborah Delano, Oct. 27, 1783, who d. Jan. 11, 1785, æt. 21; m. Charlotte Delano; he d. Apr. 19, 1845, æt. 83; had *Zenas* (34); *Charlotte* m. Mr. Coney of N. Carolina, and settled in Medford; and *William*.

17. JAMES, (s. of 10,) Dux.; m. Sarah Gray of Scituate; had *Samuel Gray*, Oct. 30, 1780 (35); *Capt. George*, Nov. 20, 1792 (36); *Capt. Hosea*, Aug. 29, 1794, m. Lucia Prior, and had Charles L., July 4, 1824, d. Sep. 25, 1825, and Sarah J., Dec. 30, 1835; *Sophia*, Dec. 20, 1796; *Sarah*, Feb. 21, 1799, m. Joseph Prior; *James*, Apr. 24, 1801, d. Mar. 4, 1818; *Abigail*, Dec. 23, 1803, m. Josiah Morton; *Eleanor*, Apr. 23, 1804, m. Capt. Church Weston; and *Mary Saunders*, June 17, 1809, m. Mr. Cushing of Scituate.

18. NATHANIEL, (s. of 11,) Dux.; m. Hannah Loring, Dec 9, 1800; and had chd. — *Capt. Gershom*, Nov. 23, 1801, m Jane Winsor, Oct. 14, 1827, and he d. at sea, off Cape Hatteras, Feb. 12, 1841, and had Horace Edwin, May 18, 1829,

Florence Gregory, Aug. 15, 1832, Ada Jane, Aug. 17, 1834, Pauline, Mar. 12, 1836, and Gershom Crayton, Feb. 19, 1840; *Capt. Daniel Loring*, July 7, 1804, m. Sally Bartlett Sampson, and had Georgianna Lloyd, Feb. 24, 1830, d. Aug. 20, 1841, and George Lloyd, Aug. 14, 1843; *Nathaniel*, June 30, 1806, a merchant of Boston, m. Ann Thomas Howland, Apr. 5, 1829, and has had Justin, Jan. 5, d. Jan. 8, 1830, Justin, Jan. 2, 1831, Arthur Herbert, Mar. 2, 1835, d. Dec. 8, 1837, Cordelia Herbert, Mar. 11, 1839, d. Apr. 15, 1842, Cordelia Arthur, May 22, 1842; *Elizabeth*, July 25, 1808, m. Capt. Erastus Sampson; *Mary*, Aug. 18, 1810, m. Lloyd Granville Sampson, who d. July 6, 1838; *Edward*, Apr. 28, 1813, Boston, m. Harriet B. Sprague, Sep. 7, 1835, and has had Parker, Aug. 16, 1836, Gustavus Adolphus, Jan. 15, 1838, Georgiana Lloyd, May 14, 1842, and Edward Sprague, June 22, 1846; *Gustavus*, Dec. 5, 1814, d. Jan. 31, 1836; *Samuel Loring*, Dec. 19, 1816, of Boston; *Capt. Charles Frederick*, May 7, 1819, m. Mary Ann Weston; and *Henry*, Apr. 22, 1826.

19. CAPT. SAMUEL, (s. of 11,) Dux.; m. Olive Chandler, Oct. 22, 1801, and he d. at Jamaica (Kingston), Mar. 24, 1805, æt. 26 years; had *Maria*, Nov. 9, 1800, m. Saml. Frazar; *Eliza*, Oct. 21, 1802, m. John Holmes; *Samuel*, Aug. 1, 1804.

20. CAPT. MARTIN, (s. of 11,) Dux.; m. Hannah Rogers; and has had *Capt. Albert Martin*, Oct. 13, 1807, m. Augusta Merry, and has had Olive Soule, and Lysander, who d. young, and Olive Soule, now living; *Susan*, July 10, 1809, m. Capt. Thomas Winsor; *Caroline*, Aug. 28, 1811, m. Capt. George Prior; *Augusta*, Dec. 2, 1815, m. Elijah Baker; and *Olive Soule*, Nov. 17, 1824, and d. June 14, 1835.

21. THOMAS, (s. of 12,) went to Boston, m. Wealthea Sprague, and had *Henry*, Dec. 31, 1803, merchant of Boston, m. Mary Ann Davis, May 29, 1832; *Jane*, July 31, 1805, m. Capt. Gershom Winsor; *Seth*, Sep. 31, 1807; *Capt. Thomas*, Aug. 22, 1809, m. Susan Winsor, and has Thomas Irving, Sep. 11, 1841, Arthur Austin, Sidney Edgar; *Alfred*, Apr. 9, 1811, merchant of Boston, m. Ann Maria Bird, Apr. 11, 1833, now resides in Brookline, and has Helen, Mary Percival, Alfred, Frank, Rufus; *Edwin*, Nov. 5, 1812, d. Sep. 9, 1813; *Harriet*, May 25, 1816, m. Richard Soule, Jr.; *Elizabeth Hale*, Apr. 14, 1818, m. John Bird; *Judith*, Aug. 1, 1820; *Rufus*, d. Sep. 27, 1842; and *Frederic*.

22. JOSEPH, (s. of 12,) Dux., removed to Boston; m. 1st, Lydia Sampson, m. 2d, Betsy Sprague, m. 3d, —— ——; and has had *Capt. Allen* Sept. 13, 1811; *Ruth Thomas* March 15, 1813, m. Mr. Bird; *Lucia* June 4, 1815; *Maria* Sept. 19, 1817, d. Oct. 3, 1817; *Joseph* May 6, 1819; *Sarah Ann* Sept. 13,

1821; *Frederic Upham* Aug. 6, 1823, d. Nov. 11, 1824; *Sophia*; *Hannah*.

23. CAPT. GEORGE, (s. of 12,) Dux., m. Alice Turner, and has had *George* Aug. 12, 1812, m. Mary Thomas, who d. Jan. 25, 1836, m. 2d, Deborah Thomas, who d. July 23, 1839, m. 3d, Abigail, and has had George A. 30 May, 1834, Henry F. Jan. 1, 1836, Deborah July 23, 1839, d. July 24, 1839, Deborah Dec. 24, 1842; *James* April 14, 1817, m. a Cushing; *Joshua* Sept. 21, 1819, has had Corinda April 13, 1841, and Joshua F. April 21, 1842; *Lorenzo Dow* Jan. 4, 1822; *Lucy Alice* Nov. 11, 1824; *William W.* Aug. 28, 1829.

24. JOHN, (s. of 13,) Dux., m. Martha Howitt of N. Carolina, and had *Sylvanus H.* April 24, 1800, d. Aug. 19, 1836; *Margaret* April 7, 1806; *William W.* Nov. 29, 1811, m. Elizabeth Simmons; *Martha* April 26, 1814, d. Jan. 18, 1834; *Harriet Hall* Sept. 17, 1817, m. Thomas Verge; *Bailey D.* Aug. 24. 1820; *John M.* Aug. 28, 1824.

25. SPENCER, (s. of 13,) Dux., m. Charlotte Howitt of N. Carolina; he d. Oct. 30, 1835; had *Lydia* Jan. 12, 1801, d. Jan. 19, 1836; *Charles* June 18, 1804, d. Oct. 19, 1835; *Alden* Dec. 21, 1806; *Richard* July 4, 1808, m. Deborah Weston, and has had Arabella, March 19, 1843; *Elizabeth Noyes* Dec. 18, 1811, d. Dec. 12, 1815; *Charlotte* May 10, 1815; *Elizabeth Noyes* March 25, 1818, d. Oct. 31, 1835; *Mary Ann* Sep. 4, 1820; *Lucy Ladonia* and *Maria Louisa* (gemini) Feb. 17, 1823, Lucy L. d. Sept. 24, 1835; *Spencer T.* Sept. 14, 1826; *Calvin Gardner* Sept. 17, 1829; and *Harriet*, who d. Sept. 19, 1836.

26. CHARLES, (s. of 13,) Dux., m. Beulah Wadsworth; had *Eden* Aug. 4, 1806, m. Lucy Weston; *Emily* July 15, 1808, m. Thos. Waterman Herrick; *Nancy* July 2, 1810; *Acenith* Aug. 14, 1813, d. Sept. 5, 1835; *Hiram* Nov. 10, 1814, m. Sally Baker, m. 2d Lydia Delano; *Whitman* July 31, 1818; *Ruby Soule* Feb. 17, 1821, d. Mar. 13, 1837; *Abby Otis* April 11, 1823, m. Henry Wadsworth; *Laura Ann* Oct. 28, 1825; *Helen Mar* Oct. 10, 1827, m. Mr. Burbeck; *Clara* Aug. 31, 1829, m. Rufus Holmes.

27. CAPT. OTIS, (s. of 13,) Dux., m. Kesia Sampson; had *Catharine W.* Oct. 4, 1811, d. May 26, 1821; *Ezra Morton* April 2, 1813, d. at sea; *Otis* Oct. 19, 1815, m. Julia Hunt; *Samuel* Oct. 21, 1817, d. at sea; and *Kesia* Jan. 15, 1820, m. Francis Cooper.

28. LEWIS, (s. of 13,) Dux., m. Lydia Howitt; had chd. *Adriana* Oct. 23, 1818, m. Mr. Hutchins; *Lewis* April 31, 1821; *Mahala Allen* Nov. 1823, m. Edwin Peterson; *Henry Otis* Dec. 15, 1825; *Augustus* March 2, 1829; *Lydia* Nov. 23, 1830.

29. ALDEN, (s. of 13,) Dux., m. Eliza Perkins; had *Catharine* Aug. 21, 1821; *Maria* Oct. 31, 1822; *Harvey* July 3, 1824; *Eliza Ann* March 15, 1828; *Susan B.* Feb. 26, 1831; *Samuel Alden* March 22, 1836; *James E.* Sept. 23, 1840.

30. CLARK, (s. of 14,) Dux., m. Mary Chandler, who was b. Sept. 6, 1785; had *Mary Ann* Sept. 2, 1806; *Elbridge* Aug. 20, 1808; *Hiram* July 30, 1810, d. March 19, 1812; *Lydia* Feb. 10, 1813, d. Dec. 17, 1814; *William C.* Nov. 2, 1815; *Elizabeth H.* July 16, 1820; *Samuel T.* June 16, 1826.

31. WILLIAM, (s. of 14,) Dux., m. Sophia Chandler, who was b. Mar. 30, 1789; had *Erastus* July 9, 1809; *Seth* Aug. 6, 1813; *William* Oct. 3, 1806.

32. CAPT. ISAAC, (s. of 15,) Dux., m. Betsy Howitt, and he d. Nov. 28, 1848, and had *Frances* Dec. 28, 1815, m. Rev. (now Elder) William Harlow; *Betsy Sanderson* June 21, 1819; *Lucian* May 15, 1825.

33. CAPT. BENJAMIN, (s. of 15,) Dux., d. June 10, 1842; m. Hannah Freeman, and had *Claudius* Sept. 30, 1828; *Eudora* June 19, 1832; *Edward*, and *Benjamin*.

34. CAPT. ZENAS, (s. of 16,) Dux., m. Lucinda Wadsworth 1806, and has had *Alexander* Aug. 11, 1811; *Zenas* Oct. 8, 1816; *Deborah* Jan. 26, 1808, m. Henry Brooks; *Lucinda* Nov. 7, 1813; *Jerusha R.* Dec. 21, 1819; *Lamelia* June 7, 1825; *Helen C.* Feb. 6, 1823, d. Oct. 8, 1842.

35. SAMUEL GRAY, (s. of 17,) Dux., m. Lydia Delano, and had *Elizabeth* Dec. 10, 1812; *Daniel H.* Oct. 14, 1814; *Maria* June 13, 1817; *Samuel* Jan. 28, 1822; *Elbridge* Feb. 18, 1824; *Harrison Gray* Dec. 28, 1825, d. Dec. 25, 1826.

36. CAPT. GEORGE, (s. of 17,) Dux., m. Hannah Delano; had *Frances James* July 22, 1820, m. John Drew 1848; *George H.* April 8, 1823, d. July 22, 1824; *George H.* July 23, 1826; *Walter* June 11, 1829; *Eugene Adolphus* July 17, 1831; *Julius Augustus* Jan. 17, 1834.

NOTE. The name and family of Windsor, in England, are very ancient. The name of the town (whence comes the family name) is said to have been derived from the winding shore of the river at that place; and we find it early written Windleshore, then Windshore, Windsore, Windsor. In William the Conqueror's time, the town and castle came into the royal possession, and in his reign, we find WALTER FITZ-OTHER, castellan or governor of Windsor castle, and from thence, we are informed, he assumed the name of WALTER DE WINDSOR, and he is the ancestor of the family of Windsor. He is said to have been the son of Sir Other, the son of Othoere, who some say derived his descent from ancestors in the kingdom of Norway, and was living, a powerful prince in K. Alfred's reign. Walter, above, bore arms, as some say, "Gules a saltire argent," or as others affirm, "Argent a saltire gules;" and the different arms of the family down to the present time are but modifications of the same. His sons were William DeWindsor, Robert DeWindsor and Gerald Fitz-Walter. *Gerald's* descendant have not the name of Windsor, but he is ancestor of the family of Fitzgeralds, and the houses of Leicester and Kildare. *Robert* is progenitor of the Windsors, Lords of Estaines. *William DeWindsor* succeeded his father as castellan of Windsor Castle and Berkshire Forest. The family seat was Stanwell, county of Middlesex, until they removed (temp. Henry VIII,) to Bordsley Abbey. He is ancestor of a numerous family, including the Lords of the Barony of Windsor. From this son, it is presumed, (though as yet I have not fixed with certainty their position) are descended the Windsors (Winsors) of Boston and Duxbury. A remarkable similarity of Christian names, between the first American generations, and the cotemporary English families gave rise to the conjecture. The names of Peter, Robert, William and Thomas, appear in both branches.

We learn by a proclamation of King James in 1590, that he returned from Denmark, "honorably accompanied with divers persons of honour," and among this retinue, as one of the "gentlemen of Denmark" stands the name of *Owb Winsour*. — Rymer's Foedera.

In the London directories the names, both of Windsor, and Winsor occur. I think there have been Windsors in Maryland.

JOSHUA WINSOR was the ancestor of the family of Rhode Island, concerning which there appeared in 1847, a pamphlet of twelve pages, entitled "A Genealogical Account of the ancient Winsor family in the United States; collected principally from records in the several branches thereof, introduced by an account of their progenitors in the male line, for several generations previous to the emigration to America. By the late Olney Winsor." By this it appears Joshua arrived at Providence, 1638, and was son of *Samuel,* son of *John*, son of *Samuel*, son of *Robert*, a Roman Catholic knight (temp. Henry VIII). Here again we notice the same names common to the Boston and Duxbury branches. Joshua's children were Samuel, Sarah, Susanna and Mary. This Mary m. Jonathan Cary, son of James Cary, who d. at Charlestown, in 1681. Jonathan was a deacon of the Charlestown church, and d. 1737, æt. 92 years. His children were Jonathan, Samuel, James, Freelove and Abigail. *Vide Alden Epitaphs, ii.*

WITHERELL.

1. WILLIAM, b. 1600, arrived 1634, removed to Dux. 1638; purchased a house and land of Edward Hall, between Rev. R. Partridge's farm and Nicholas Robinson's; had a grant, 1640, northwest of North hill; also had land at North river, and at Namasakeeset; ad. 1658; removed to Scituate, settled there as pastor of the second church, and d. Apr. 9, 1684. Chd.; Samuel, John; Theophilus, Daniel, Mary, Elizabeth, Sarah and Hannah. — See Deane's Scituate.

2. CHARLES, Dux., of late years; m. Anne, and had Ann, Acenith, Sally, Judith, Charles and Reuben.

WORMALL.

1. JAMES, Scituate, 1638; removed to Duxbury; had *Josiah*, Dux., 1670; *John* m. Mary Barrows, Jan. 9, 1698, d. at Bridgewater, 1711.
2. JOSEPH (s. of —,) Scituate, m. Mirriam; d. a. 1661, and had *Josiah; Sarah; Hester.*
A Joseph was a carpenter of Boston, 1650. William of Boston, m. Sarah, and had Mary, May 1, 1704. Sarah m. Wm. Cullove, 14 July, 1715. — Boston Records.
3. JOSIAH, (s. of 1 or 2,) Dux.; m. Patience Sherman, Jan. 15, 1695; had *Josiah*, who d. without issue; *Mehetabel* m. Christopher Wadsworth, 1713; *Mercy* m. Wm. Merry, Oct. 28, 1720; *Samuel* (5); *Ichabod* (6).
4. EBENEZER, (s. of ?) Dux.; m. Elizabeth Briggs, Apr. 22, 1717; had *Kesia*, Feb. 21, 1718, m. Isaac Tinckham, July 26, 1739; *Betty*, Mar. 1, 1720; *Abiah*, May 4, 1725.
5. SAMUEL, (s. of 3,) Dux.; m. Mary Forrest, Jan. 27, 1737, she survived him; had *Azubah*, m. Thomas Delano, Dec. 23, 1762; *Patience* m. John Soule, Jan. 11, 1759.
6. ICHABOD, (s. of 3,) Dux.; m. Lydia Delano, Dec. 13, 1736; had *Ichabod; Desire.*

NOTE. Hannah, 1674, d. July 7, 1758, æt. 84; Grace, 1679, d. Nov. 25, 1757, æt. 78; Lydia m. Ebenezer Delano, May 16, 1745. There was a *John* in Bridgew.; m. Mary Bryant, 1729, and had Joseph, Benjamin, and John; *Sarah* (Bridgew.,) m. Nehemiah Allen, 1707. Hist. Bridgew.

NOTE. The abbreviation *æt.* has in the foregoing pages been used for *aged*, the meaning of the full form *ætatis* being now so generally lost sight of in the abbreviation, that the author has found that the usages of his authorities have so conflicted in regard to it, that discrimination of the true meaning of the authority was in some cases almost impossible. When it has been satisfactorily ascertained that there had been a proper use of the abbreviation, the full form, "in the — year of his age" has generally been given.

APPENDIX.

I.

The Grant of Bridgewater to the Inhabitants of Duxbury, was made to the following persons, at that time (1645) of course residing in Duxbury, and they form the original proprietors of Bridgewater. Many of them removed thither, while others conveyed their grants to their sons, who settled there, and others sold, or otherwise disposed of them.

William Bradford,
William Merrick,
John Bradford,
Abraham Pierce,
John Rogers,
George Partridge,
John Starr,
Mr. William Collier,
Christopher Wadsworth,
Edward Hall,
Nicholas Robbins,
Thomas Hayward,
Nathaniel Willis,
John Willis,
Thomas Boney,
Mr. Miles Standish,
Love Brewster,
Mr. Ralph Partridge,

John Paybody,
William Paybody,
Francis Sprague,
William Basset,
John Washburn,
John Washburn, Jr.,
John Ames,
Thomas Gannet,
William Brett,
Edmund Hunt,
William Clark,
William Ford,
Mr. Const. Southworth,
John Cary,
Edmund Weston,
Samuel Tompkins,
Edmund Chandler,
Moses Simmons,

John Irish,
Philip Delano,
Arthur Harris,
Mr. John Alden,
John Fobes,
Samuel Nash,
Abraham Sampson,
George Soule,
Experience Mitchell,
Henry Howland,
Henry Sampson,
John Brown,
John Haward,
Francis West,
William Tubbs,
James Lindall,
Samuel Eaton,
Solomon Leonard.

NOTE. Those in italics afterwards removed to Bridgewater.

II.

The following list of vessels, which have been wrecked on Duxbury beach, is given, without any pretensions to completeness, and are only such as have been remembered by persons now living.

Nov. 25, 1792, the ship *Rodney*, of London, of between four and five hundred tons, Capt. Whytock, was cast ashore on the Branches ledge in a northeast storm, on her passage from Boston for Martinique, and loaded with lumber and brick, No lives were lost. Capt. Samuel Delano, Jr.,

APPENDIX. 349

of Duxbury, while endeavoring to render her assistance, scarcely escaped drowning, and for his heroic conduct was rewarded by the Humane Society with a gold medal. Her passengers were rescued by a sloop, and among their number were several females, the Captain's family.—*See Delano's Voyages.*

In March, 1792, the ship *Columbia*, of three hundred tons, of Portland, Capt. Isaac Chauncy, was stranded on the beach at the High Pines, and fourteen men lost, and two, the second mate and a boy, were saved.

In April, 1801, a sloop was wrecked, and three men drowned and two saved.

A few years after, a *Swedish* brig was driven upon the beach in a storm, and all the crew saved. By the aid of a force from Duxbury, she was soon got off; but shortly after was again driven on by another gale, when she was again floated and carried into Duxbury for repairs. Her crew remained in Duxbury all winter; and one of their holidays, which they celebrated during their stay, attracted considerable attention, and afforded some delight to the towns-people. This brig was bound for Boston, from the Mediterranean.

A year or two after this, the brig *Pomona* was wrecked on Branches Island, at the north end of the beach.

A *Portland* schooner, loaded with molasses, from the West Indies.

And, a few years ago, a lumber schooner, from the Eastward, when two boys were lost.

III.

SHIP-BUILDING, COMMERCE, FISHERY, ETC.

Mr. Thomas Prince, it is related, established the *first yard*, for building vessels, in the town. This was on the western shore of the Nook, directly opposite to Mr. William Soule's, and here was built the first vessel that was ever raised in the town, now about one hundred and thirty years since. It was a sloop, and constructed mostly of wild cherry, which was considerably used at that time, and found to be very durable. Alexander Weston, the grandfather of the first Ezra Weston, served an apprenticeship with him.

The second was Mr. Israel Sylvester's, where lately was Mr. Frazar's.

The third was conducted by Mr. Benjamin Freeman at Harden Hill.

The fourth was Mr. Perez Drew's.

The fifth was established by Messrs. Samuel Winsor and Samuel Drew, on the Nook shore, to the westward of Captain's Hill, where Mr. Winsor resided, in the house since known as the "Ned Southworth" house. In this yard the first large vessels were built. Mr. Winsor previously resided at Clark's Island, and here on the southern end built several vessels.

The sixth was Mr. Isaac Drew's, who built at the Nook, and carried on the business for upwards of fifty years.

During the last half century or more, the following are those who have been most extensively engaged in this business:—Captains Sylvanus and Joseph Drew, on the north side of Bluefish river; on the south side, Mr. Levi Sampson at the bridge; and adjoining, on the east, Mr. Ezra Weston; and, still further to the east, Capt. Samuel Delano. At the Mill-pond, Mr. Samuel A. Frazar on the north side, and Dea. George Loring on the south. Isaac Drew, James Southworth, and Joseph Wadsworth at the Nook. Benjamin Prior, Ezra Weston and Samuel Hall, near Harden Hill bay. Joshua Cushing and Seth Sprague on the easterly shore; and John Oldham at Duck Hill.

This business has of late years much decreased, owing to want of timber near at hand, and the trouble and expense of procuring the materials from the eastward. At the present time, scarcely more than two or three vessels are built here per annum, and these often of the smaller class. Until of late, vessels of the largest class have been built in Duxbury, and for superiority of model and excellence of workmanship have been justly praised.

Most, if not nearly all of the inhabitants of the town, for the last half century, have been connected directly or indirectly, or at least dependent in some degree on the sea for support. Many of the inhabitants have been large ship-owners, and extensively engaged in the various branches of commerce. The late Mr. Ezra Weston was distinguished as a successful merchant, and enjoyed the reputation of being the largest ship-owner in the country. Others might be named, who have held high rank as merchants, and been of considerable note in the mercantile community.

A very large portion of the inhabitants have been engaged in the merchant service, and a considerable number have been Atlantic ship-masters. Fifteen or twenty years since, there were living in Duxbury forty-three ship-masters; and within the recollection of a person then living, eleven had died.

Although so large a number of vessels have belonged in past times to Duxbury, yet few other than the fishing vessels have ever frequented its harbor, as the port of the metropolis offers far superior advantages.

The *Fishing business* has now engaged the attention of the inhabitants for nearly a century and a half, though of late years the aggregate of tonnage engaged has been considerably less than was employed about ten or fifteen years since.

Among the first who embarked in this enterprise, was Mr. Joshua Delano. Messrs. Joshua and Josiah Soule were also largely engaged in it, and their vessels were constantly employed in the proper season at Cape Sable. Three or four was then the usual number of vessels on the fishing-grounds, and this gradually continued to increase, receiving, however, some detriment during the Revolution, until about the years 1785 or 1786, when there were sent and belonging to Duxbury, sixty-four Bank fishermen, having an average of seventy tons, and an aggregate of about forty-five hundred. At this period Messrs. Nathaniel and Joshua Winsor were probably the most extensively engaged in the business, and for several years continued to be of the most enterprising of the inhabitants.

Schooners, sloops and perhaps larger vessels were engaged in the *whale fishery* from Duxbury as early as the beginning of the last century, and for some years quite a number of the inhabitants were thus employed. Their resort was at first along the shore and between the capes; but by the close of the first quarter of the century they had extended their grounds, and now the coast of Newfoundland became to be generally frequented, and even as late as 1760, or perhaps later, vessels were employed in the Saint Lawrence gulf.

On a blank leaf in the account book of Mr. Joshua Soule of Duxbury, I find the following memorandum. — " Whale vieg begun. elisha cob sayled from hear March ye 4, from Plymouth ye 7, 1729."

It is now about sixty or seventy years since the *first wharf* was built in Duxbury. This was constructed by Mr. Nathaniel Winsor, and was some years after enlarged, though it has since gone to decay. About two years after a second one adjoining was built by Mr. Joshua Winsor, which is now standing. This afterward passed into the hands of Messrs. Levi Sampson, George Loring and Samuel A. Frazar, who sold it to George and Amherst

APPENDIX. 351

A. Frazar, and is now owned by Messrs. Sampson & Knowles. It has been once rebuilt. A few years after Mr. Ezra Weston's at Powder point was built. Ten or more years afterward followed Capt. Samuel Winsor's on the easterly shore, and next Capt. Sylvanus Sampson's at Harden Hill bay. The two next were Capt. John Winsor's at Bluefish, and Samuel Walker's at the Nook, both of which are now decayed. Messrs. Reuben and Charles Drew's on the river was the next. The next one was built by Zadock Bradford and Freeman Loring, near Harden Hill bay.

Nearly seventy years ago, in 1784, the late Major Judah Alden established himself in Duxbury as a trader, and was the first one who carried on regularly that business. Previous to this some had enjoyed a lucrative business in furnishing to the fishermen their stores, provisions and other necessary articles, though in many instances these were provided by the owners themselves, who usually kept on hand a sufficient stock, to enable them also to meet the wishes of their neighbors occasionally, thereby precluding an earlier existence of a regular trader in the town. Alexander Standish is said to have been a trader in Duxbury even as early as the latter part of the seventeenth century. He is said to have made an addition to the house of his father, Captain Standish, and in this part to have conducted his traffic with the Indians and others. In the remains of that part of the house articles have been found, which would serve to strengthen the tradition.

Joshua Soule was also a trader in Duxbury, as early as 1728. The account book of Mr. Soule, now before me, plainly shows that by far the most profitable sales of this period were those of intoxicating liquors. Charges like the following repeatedly occur. " Apr. 21, 1730. Nathaniel Chandler to 1 q. rum 1s. 6d; at weden 2 g. 14s 4d." — " Dec. 5, 1732. Sam. Fish is dr. ¼ p. rum swetened, 8d; ½ p. spised rum, 8d; next morning ¼ p. more, 7d; and at night ½ p. more, 7d." By the same it appears that from September to January, 1730, he laid in a stock of over 450 gallons of rum, and in May following a barrel for his carpenters, and thirty-three gallons more to sell. Mr. Soule owned two sloops, the Seaflower and the Dolphin, which were employed coasting between Virginia, Maryland, the Carolinas and the North.

Maj. Alden was followed soon after by Capt. Seth Sprague, Capt. Sylvanus Sampson, Mr. Parker from Plympton, Mr. Winslow Hooper in 1811, and since that period there have been Messrs. William Sampson, Samuel A. Frazar, Charles Drew, Jr., N. and J. Ford, Eleazer Harlow and others.

FISHING GROUNDS.

In this place it may not perhaps be amiss to give the *marks* of the various *fishing grounds* without the beach, which are the resort of parties of pleasure and others in the proper season. These lie wholly between Branches' Island on the North, and Manomet point on the South. The marks, whose value must be of short duration, in consequence of the temporary character of many of them, are here inserted, if for no other reason, to preserve a record of the present, which may be of some interest in the future.

Ned's ground is a rocky ledge of some length, North and South, but of little breadth, East and West. The water is about ten fathoms. Bring the orchard of Mr. Waterman Thomas in range of the "topsail tree," so called, a large and tall tree on the highlands beyond, which has the appearance of a topsail schooner; and on the other side bring Indian Hill in Sandwich, just out by Manomet on the South. On the westerly edge of this ground is a single rock, called Howland's ledge, which is situated about a mile and a half from a large flat rock, called the Sunk rock, which bears E. by S. from Rouse's Hummock.

Faunce's ledge extends in length N. and S., and is very narrow. The ground is broken, and the water is about ten fathoms. Bring Indian Hill just over the point of Manomet, and Captain's Hill over the South part of the Plumb hills on the beach.

High Pine ledge is a very narrow strip of ground running N. E. and S. W., and about a quarter of a mile in length. Four or five fathoms is the average depth of water. In some places it is so shoal that the fish can be easily seen. When the tide is very low five rocks are left bare. Bring the summit of Manomet just open by the Gurnet, and Captain's hill over the middle of the High pines.

Thump Caps, of which there are said to be three, lying contiguously with a muddy bottom between, called the Outer, the Middle, and the Inner. Bring the northwesterly point of Manomet in range with Warren's orchard in Plymouth, which can quite readily be distinguished, as it is the only considerable clump of trees lying near the shore; and the trees on Clark's Island fairly open by the Gurnet, or Captain's Hill just over the northern declivity of the Gurnet.

Cole's hole. This ground extends N. and S., with about five fathoms of water. Bring the house on Saquish in range with the house on the Gurnet; and the High pines fairly open by the Gurnet.

Marshall's ledge. This is a very small piece of ground, about a mile S. S. E. of the High pine ledge, and an excellent fishing spot, having about twelve fathoms of water. Bring Warren's cliffs open by the Gurnet; and a little sand hill on the beach (the first one South of the High Pines) in range of Captain's Hill.

---o---

ERRATA.

Page 26, line 25, " Typographical " should be " Topographical."
Page 36, line 1, *dele* s in " meadows."
Page 84, lines 8, 12, and last but one, " Ino." should be " Jona."
Page 93, line 18, ditto.
Pages 112, (line 9th from bottom) and 113, (lines 22 and 39,) " Asherst " should be " Ashurst."
Page 153, line 10th from the bottom, " proceeded " should be " preceded."
Page 279, line 3d from bottom, " Mercy " should be " Nancy."
Page 300, line 17, after Dorcas, insert a comma.
Page 325, line 3, " queme " should be " quem."

Other mistakes have doubtless occurred, and if the true reading is apparent to the reader's eye, it is to be hoped that they will be corrected, and viewed with indulgence.

INDEX.

[Every name, which has occurred in the preceding pages, is embraced in the following Index; though, if the same occur more than once on a page, but one reference is made to that page. In case of intermarriages between two members of DUXBURY families, the names of either have not been indexed, as they both occur under the head of their respective family names; and when the full date is not given in connection with the marriage of the female, it will generally be found with that of the male, when both were members of Duxbury families.—Fam. stands for Family, or Families; and Interm. for Intermarriages.]

A.

Abington, 135, 253, 298, 342.
Adams, 305, 321.
Alarm orders, 93, 94, 101, 162, 164; Alarm list, 124; Alarm boats in 1812, 162, 165; Fine for making false alarm, 90, 94.
Alcock, 184.
ALDEN Family, 213; arms, 213. *Hon. John*, at Dux. 10, 17, 32, 35, 70, 77, 92, 109; of the council of war, 101, 102; his biography, 55; his proceedings with the Quakers, 99, 100; his burial-place, 177. —— *Col. Briggs*, at Dux. 19, 78, 118, 119; during the revolution, 124, 141, 143; his biography, 147.—— *Col. Ichabod*, at Dux. during the revolution, 123, 126; his death and character, 132–4. ——*Maj. Judah*, 21, 78, 123, 130-2, 146, 161, 351; a biog. sketch, 147.—— *John*, 20, 73, 92, 115, 118, 163, 185, 187, 191. —— *Jonathan*, 79, 101, 109, 111, 185. —— *David*, 77, 79, 81, 82. —— *Samuel*, 26, 118, 123, 147, 158, 187, 193, 195, 196, 197, 202.——*Benjamin*, 74, 82, 141, 192. —— *Isaiah*, 20, 146. —— *Bezaleel*, 140, 142.—— *Wrestling*, 140, 142.—— *Joseph*, 92. —— *Amherst*, 123. —— *Abiathar*, 144. —— *Caleb*, 205.
Allen, 207, 238, 243, 275, 287, 295, 306, 321, 347.
Allerton, Isaac, 23, 55, 60, 235.
Allyn, Rev. Dr.; outrages on his house, 88; his family, 207–8; his early life, 207–8; his ordination and ministry, 207; his death and character, 208–9.
AMES, 22, 81, 93, 205, 220, 322, 338.
ANDREWS, 22, 81, 221, 328.
Andros, Sir Edmund, 109–10.
Annable, 224.
Appletree, first in N. Eng. 234.
ARDDATON, 221.
ARNOLD, Fam. 221; interm. 226.——*Bildad*, 121, 124, 135, 137, 140, 141, 142, 148.—— *Edward*, 146, 187.——*Ezra*, 118, 135, 137.——*James*, 73, 198, 202.——*Samuel*, 14, 107. ——*Seth*, 15, 44, 115, 185.
Arminian scheme, 194.
Arms, men of Dux. able to bear, in 1643, 92; ordered to be carried to church on the Sabbath, 94, 104, 112, 137. Town voted to buy some, 141.
ARMSTRONG, 221.
Asbury, 341.
Ash, 144.
Ashdod, 12.
Ashurst, Sir Henry, 112.
Assistants, 58, 59, 77.
Atkins, 249.
Attleborough, 217, 237.
Attorneys of the town, 86.
Atwood, 179, 180, 199.
Auger, 192, 196.
Autographs, of Elder Brewster, 48; of Capt. Standish, 51; of John Alden, 63; of Howland and Eaton, 64; of Comfort Starr, 65; of Wm. Pabodie, 67; of C. Southworth, 68; of Alex. Standish, 69; of Col. Church, 107; of Col. Alden, 116.

B.

Babbage, 256.
Babcock, 317, 328.
Bacon, 101, 116, 202.
Bailey, 246, 277, 279.
BAKER, Fam., 222; interm. 231, 277, 279, 280, 288, 344; name mentioned, 86, 124, 141.
Baldwin, 74.
Balfour, Capt., 127–130.
Bandoleers, 89.
Bangs, 10, 282.
Bannister, 265.
Barbor, 288.
BARKER, Fam., 223; interm. 276, 288, 309, 319. *Robert*, 44, 63, 66, 81, 103–4, 182.—— *Francis*, 16, 78, 79, 81, 111. Name mentioned, 81, 116, 117, 136, 169, 182, 341.
Barnaby, 225.
Barnes, 84, 90, 178, 208, 231, 240, 259, 264, 338.
Barnstable Families, 207, 222, 224, 230, 239, 244, 250, 263, 266, 269, 274, 297, 337.
Barrows, 347.
BARSTOW, 224, 245, 278, 307.
BARTIN, 225.
BARTLETT, Fam., 225; interm. 221, 270, 312, 315. *Ebenezer*, 52, 70, 118.——*Benjamin*, 77, 79, 110, 112. —— *Ichabod*, 185.
Bass, 196, 199, 213.
BASSET, Fam., 226; interm. 256, 279. *William*, 17, 46, 64, 66, 70, 77, 93, 172, 173.
Bateman, 339.
BATES, 227, 298.
Batterby, 216.
Battolph, 340.

Bay of Dux., 26.
Beach, Tho, 27. Vessels wrecked there, 348.
Beacon at Captain's Hill, 136.
Beals, 227, 342.
BEARE, 227.
Beaver trade, 84.
Belknap, 219.
Bell, 263, 299.
Bellows, 322.
Benjamin, 274.
Benson, 131.
Bent, 302.
Bestow, 144.
Biddle, 227, 21, 90, 297.
Billington, 34, 90, 221, 257.
Binney, 279.
Biographical Sketches of the men of the Revolution, 147 to 159.
Bird, 178, 343.
BISBEE, 227, 77, 85, 286, 321.
BISHOP, 81, 228.
Black, 318.
Blackmore, 217, 239, 242, 301, 315.
Blake, 224, 315.
Blanchard, 315.
Blasland, 331.
Blinman, 14.
Blossom, 269.
BLUSH, 228.
Boardman, 90.
Boath, 316.
BONNEY, 228; name mentioned, 22, 86, 93, 183.
Boles, 73.
Bonum, 338.
Booth, 229, 244.
Boston mentioned, 135, 180, 201; families, 210, 214–6, 217–8, 222, 224, 229, 233, 239, 240, 247-8-9, 251, 257-8, 260, 268, 271-2, 274-5, 283-4, 298, 299, 304, 305, 309, 313, 321, 322, 323, 324, 326, 329, 331, 332, 339, 340, 347; intm. 219, 225, 265.
BOSWORTH, 229, 290, 314, 331.
Bounds, 13.
Bounties, 45.
BOURN, Fam., 229; interm. 192, 214, 224, 266.
Bowden, 283.
Bowditch, 278.
BOWERS, 84, 230.
BOWMAN, 230.
BRADFORD, Fam., 230; interm. 208, 222, 233, 242, 250, 276, 313, 315.——*William*, 15, 34, 55, 68, 70, 77, 101, 179, 230-1, 234. —— *Samuel*, 115, 126, 130-2, 185.——*Gamaliel, sen.*, 148, 196, 197, 201.——*Gamaliel, jr.*, 124, 126, 135, 149. *Others*, 123, 125, 131, 144, 149, 162, 165, 207, 351.
Braine, 217.
Braintree families, 191, 241, 245, 250, 278, 305, 307, 321. Interm. 213, 260, 263, 269, 287.
Brance, 105.
Brattles, 224.
BRETT, 85, 93, 234.
BREWSTER, Fam., 234; interm. 220, 222, 280, 311, 313.—— *Elder William*, 48, 55, 70, 93, 171.——*Jonathan*, 10, 17, 64, 70, 83, 84, 93, 173, 235.——

Joshua, 143-4, 146, 165, 168.
——*Love*, 90, 93, 228.——
William, 81, 93, 94, 116, 185, 186, 192. *Others*, 185, 118.
Brewster tree, 234.
Bridges, 18, 19.
Bridgewater, 13, 135, 138, 192, 196, 207; families, 214, 220, 234, 241, 261, 266, 268, 282, 295, 297, 306, 309, 310, 321, 322, 323, 324, 338, 347, 349. Interm. 219, 220, 233, 270.
BRIGGS, 81, 237; interm. 217, 258, 281.
Brigham, 131.
Brightman, 216.
Brintnal, 340.
Bristol, 240, 245, 269, 273, 280.
Brooks, 219, 227, 253, 256, 278, 313, 345.
Brooks, *Herring*, 32; *Pine*, 32; *Pudding*, 44; *Mill*, 16, 32; *Stoney*, 16, 32; *Tussocks*, 16, 32.
BROWN, Fam. 238. Interm. 269, 302, 319. *John*, 44, 77, 92, 94, 100, 104. —— *Peter*, 17, 48, 64. *Others*, 206, 264.
Brown's Island, 26, 136.
Brownell, 246, 335.
BRYANT, Fam., 238. Interm. 242, 290. Name mentioned, 93, 139, 347.
Buck, 241.
Bucket, 310.
Bulkley, 14.
Bullard, 283, 288.
BUMFUS, Fam., 239. Name mentioned, 15, 17, 64, 70, 105, 333.
Bunker Hill battle, 130.
Burbeck, 344.
Burchsted, 216.
Burge, 116-7.
BURGESS, Fam., 239. Interm. 262, 297, 318.
Burial grounds. The first at Harden Hill, 176; one near the Methodist church, 177; the second, 183.
Burlington, 205.
Burman, 34.
BURNE, 116, 240.
Burroughs, 204.
Burrows, 105.
Bursley, 269.
BURTON, 240.
Bute, Lord. His effigy burnt at Captain's Hill, 120.
BUTLER, 240, 316.
Byram, 116, 310.

C.

Caliphar, 275.
Cambridge, 210, 222, 230, 263, 271, 274, 281, 297, 322.
Canada Expedition, 110, 112.
Canonacut, 105.
Capron, 217.
Carpenter, 68, 230, 260.
Carriages, 87.
Curver (town), 269.
CARVER, Fam., 240. Gov. *John*, 55, 63, 240. *Others*, 136, 139.
Cary, 69, 241, 324, 346.
Casement, 250.
Caswell, 288.

Cattle, 70, 171.
Cedar Swamp, 33.
Chaddock, 270.
Chaises, 87.
CHAMBERLAIN, 241.
CHANDLER, Fam. 241; interm. 261, 279. Name mentioned, 70, 72, 77, 84, 90, 93, 94, 116, 118, 123, 137, 140, 141, 144, 146, 166, 185, 187, 192, 195, 351.
CHAPMAN, Fam., 244; interm. 284. Name mentioned, 66, 223.
Charter of 1691, 112–15.
Chauncy, 214, 349.
Cheesbrook, 220.
Cherry Valley, 132.
Chickatabut, 75.
Childs, 294.
Chillingworth, 270, 318, 339.
Chilton, 55.
Chipman, 116-7, 231, 269.

CHURCH OF DUXBURY,—History of, 171; letter to it from the General Court, 108; its action upon it, 109; its formation, 171; the second in Plymouth colony, 171; *Rev. Ralph Partridge*, vide; its petition to the Court, 172; the first meeting-house, 177; the church records, 177, 191; *Rev. John Holmes*, vide; tobacco was not to be smoked near the church, 179; *Rev. Ichabod Wiswall*, vide; the second meeting-house, 183; *Rev. John Robinson*, vide; leave given to build pews, 185; votes regarding children on the Sabbath, 186; parsonage, 182, 187; *Rev. Samuel Veazie*, vide; the Great Revival, 192; vote of the chh. respecting communion, 192; votes concerning itinerants, 195; troubles with Veazie, 192-200; the ecclesiastical council's advice to the church, 198–9; it raises money for the ministry, 201; appoints a fast, 201; vote to build a new house, 201; choose a candidate, 201; *Rev. Chs. Turner*, vide; vote concerning the sacrament, 202; communion, 202; a committee to take care of boys, 202; purchase a silver tankard, 203; to build a new house, 203; admissions to the chh., 203; invitations to settle given, 205; *Rev. Zedekiah Sanger*, vide; psalms ordered to be sung without being read line by line, 206; a new house erected, 206–7; the burying ground, 207; invitations extended, 207; *Rev. Dr. John Allyn*, vide; sacred scriptures ordered to be read every Lord's day, 208; church library commenced, 208; *Rev. Benjamin Kent*, vide; *Rev. Josiah Moore*, the present pastor, 210.

INDEX.   355

CHURCH, Fam., 245. Interm., 311, 335. *Col. Benjamin*, 14, 33, 81, 85, 106-7, 110, 226, 245.——*Richard*, 66, 70, 89, 106.
Churchill, 137, 232, 267, 290, 293, 304, 321.
Churchman, 298.
Clapp, 130-1, 306.
CLARK, Fam., 246. Interm. 256, 265, 275, 284. *Thurston*, 22, 76.——*William*, 22, 81, 93, 94.——*Thomas*, 89. *Others*, 205, 228.
Clough, 90.
Cobb, 131, 251, 292, 322, 337, 350.
Cockennehew, 116-7.
COE, 247.
Coffin, 219.
Coggen, 262.
Cohasset, 131.
Colburn, 288.
COLE, Fam., 247. Interm. 260. Name mentioned, 69, 85, 86, 90, 103, 131.
Coleman, 245, 274.
Cole's hole, 352.
COLLIER, *William*, 45, 46, 66, 70, 84, 90, 101, 173, 177, 247, 248.
Collier, Capt., his letter to Duxbury, 163.
Collins, 271.
Commerce, 27, 349.
Committees of correspondence, 124, 137, 142, 143 ; of inspection, 126, 140, 143 ; of safety, 135, 137, 140, 143, in the war of 1812, 162.
Commons of the town, 35.
Concord, 244.
Coner, 116.
Coney, 342.
Congress, Provincial, 126, 135. of Plymouth county, 126.
Conney, 284.
Cook, 34, 89, 90, 249, 255, 257, 266, 282, 309.
COOPER, 179, 232, 240, 248, 302, 303, 335.
Copeland, 99, 319.
Coquish, 116.
Cornelly, 306.
Cornish, 299.
CORVANNEL, 248.
Cotte, 236.
Cotton, 14, 60, 123, 129-31, 199, 221.
Council of war, 91, 92, 94, 101, 102, 107.
Courts of guard, 102.
Crane, 218.
Creeks. Robinson's, 14 ; Careswell, 14 ; Island, 32 ; Eaglenest, 171.
Cripple rocks, 27.
Crisp, 337.
Crocker, 116, 262, 269.
Crooker, 42, 250, 280.
Crosby, 168.
Crowe, 180.
Crows, 45.
Crowswell, 195.
Cudworth, 94, 100, 103.
CULLIFER, 249.
Cullove, 347.
Currency of the Revolution, 143.
Curtis, 42, 249, 202, 255.

CUSHING, Fam., 249. Interm. 224, 238, 240, 276, 293, 301, 318, 344. Mentioned, 123, 196, 349.
CUSHMAN, 60, 144, 188, 203. Fam. 249. Interm. 220, 224, 231-3, 269-70, 309-11, 320-2, 331.
Cuten, 116.

D.

Dabney, 86, 265.
Dace, 257.
DAMMON, 74, 250.
Daniels, 288.
Dark day, 87.
DARLING, 243, 250.
Dart, 236.
Dartmouth, 208, 252, 254, 258, 261, 268, 281-2, 300-1, 307, 321, 336, 338.
DAVIS, 250, 116-7, 131, 343.
DAVY, 251.
DAWES, 116, 123, 146, 251.
Dayes, 316.
Deane, 298, 332.
Dearborn, 164.
Decrow, 139.
Dedham, 217.
Delano, Fam., 251. Interm. 219, 249, 272, 279, 280, 284, 288. *Philip*, 17, 64-5, 70, 82, 90, 185, 187-8, 198.——*Judah*, 82, 135, 137, 140, 141.——*Samuel*, 54, 144, 165, 349. *Others*, 19, 44, 116, 118, 124, 132, 135, 137, 143, 144, 146, 161, 185, 186.
Deputies, 77.
Derby, 309.
DESPARD, 255, 42.
DEVELL, 255.
Dewesbury, 251.
Dickarson, 267, 269.
Dillingham, 257, 290.
Dimmack, 91.
DINGLEY, Fam., 255. Interm. 232, 259, 273, 279, 321. Name mentioned, 20, 130, 161, 165.
Doan, 267.
Dodson, 179.
Dogged, 34.
Dogget, 267.
Dorchester, 180, 184.
Doten, 222, 246, 252, 290, 307.
Dotey, 283.
Doughty, 202.
Douglas, 116.
Dover, 205.
DREW, Fam., 256. Interm. 302. Name mentioned, 20, 44, 123, 131, 141, 144, 150, 162, 322, 349, 351.
Drewry, 216.
Dunbar, 140.
Dunham, 251.
Dutch, war with the, 94, 103.
Dutton, 316.
DWELLEY, 81, 236. Fam. 257.
Dwellings, 70, 172.
Dwight, 233.

E.

Eagle nest, 32, 52.
Eagle tree pond, 57.
Eames, 105, 318.

Eastham, 167, 247, 260, 293, 298, 309.
EATON, Fam., 257. *Francis*, 64, 70.——*Samuel*, 235, 321.
Edgarton, 271.
Edson, 280.
Edwards, 241.
Eedy, 34, 286.
Eells, 116-7, 196.
Eire, 323.
Eliot, 184, 233.
Ellis, 260, 288, 322.
Ellison, 288.
Embargo act, 160.
England. War with U. S. 161. Her cruisers disguised, 167, 168.
ENSIGN, 22, 257.
Epworth, 166.
Everill, 214.
EVESOR, 244, 258.
Ewell, 90, 290.

F.

Fair at Dux. in 1638, 171.
Fairhaven, 169.
Fallowell, 179.
Falmouth, 269, 275.
False alarm of 1814, 165.
Faunce, 264, 266, 267, 268, 297, 322, 331.
Faunce's ledge, 352.
FERNISIDE, 258, 93, 223.
Ferries, 66 ; at Jones River, 224, 298 ; at New Harbor, 235.
Finney, 231.
Firearms, unnecessary discharge of, fined, 104 ; procured by the town, 126.
Fires, 52, 68, 86, 87.
First settlers, 48 ; possessions of, 54.
FISH, 78, 124, 132, 169, 185, 188, 351. Fam. 258. Inter., 222, 243, 342.
FISHER, 258.
Fishing, carried on in Dux., 350. Number of vessels owned there, 27, 350. Vessels captured by the British, 166.
Fishing ground, marks of the, 351.
Fitch, 219, 231, 238.
Fitchburg, 292.
FOBES, 92, 105, 258, 314, 315, 322.
Folger, 270.
FORD, 92, 138, 351. Fam., 259. Interm. 222, 240, 282, 309, 312, 318, 330.
Forrest, 347.
Forster, 329.
Forts at the Gurnet, 136, 162, 165 ; in 1812, 161-2, 170.
Foster, 125, 196, 225, 231, 253, 284, 287, 326, 337.
Fowle, 270.
Fox, 294.
Foxwell, 247.
Francis, 116, 208.
FRAZAR, Fam. 259. *Samuel A.*, 20, 79, 161, 168, 349, 350.
FREEMAN, 77, 82, 102, 118, 124, 140, 141, 165, 194, 195, 205, 349. Fam., 260. Interm., 231, 280, 293, 313, 319, 320.

INDEX.

Freemen, 84-6.
Freetown, 270.
French, 276.
FROST, 261.
Frothingham, 305.
Fryer, 305.
FULLER, 91, 95, 102-3, 199, 230, Fam., 261. Interm., 257. 271, 277, 278, 290, 301-2, 307.
Fullerton, 260, 311, 315.

G.

Gage, Gen., letter from the justices to, 124; address of Marshfield to, and his reply, 128; address of Dux. and five other towns to, 127.
Gaille, 297.
Gainer, 202.
GANNET, 261, 22, 93, 287.
GARDNER, 261, 146.
Garrison, 105.
Gates, 275, 321.
Gay, 202, 232.
Genealogical Registers, 211; plan and abbreviations of, 211-2.
George, 116.
Gerrish, 342.
Gibson, 309.
Gidney, 215.
Gifford, 303.
Gilbert, 232, 319.
Gilson, 278.
GLASS, 81, 118, 123, 132, 143, 144. Fam. 262.
Gloucester, 289.
Goarton, 89, 90.
GODFREY, 92, 241, 263.
Goff, 299.
Gooding, 165, 238, 252, 319.
Goold, 237.
GOOLE, 263, 93.
Gorham, 103, 112, 263.
Goss, 288.
Gouch, 117.
Grants to Duxbury, 86.
Graunger, 235.
Graves, Admiral. His reply to the Marshfield loyalists, 129.
Gray, 34, 219, 276, 314, 329, 342.
Great Britain, war with, in 1812, 161. Neutrality of Dux. in that war, 162.
Green, 248.
Green's harbor, 13.
Grenville's effigy burned at Captain's Hill, 120.
Grosse, 305.
Gulliver, 249.
Gurnet, 253.
Gurnet, 15, 23, 29. Fort, 136, 162, 165. Lighthouse, 30, 136. Meadows, 30.

H.

HADEN, 263, 93.
Halberds, 94.
HALES, 263.
Halifax, 87, 135, 138, 140, 197, 271, 295, 302, 333.
HALL, Fam., 263. Interm. 277, 311. Name mentioned,

93-4, 126, 134-5-7, 141, 223, 346, 349.
Hallet, 214, 247.
Hammond, 131, 300.
HANBURY, 264.
HANDMER, 264.
HANKS, 264, 123.
Hanmore, 267.
Hanover, 87, 135, 196, 197. Fam. 227, 249, 253. Interm. 279.
Hanson, 13, 127.
HARDING, 264, 93.
HARLOW, Fam., 264. Eleazer, 44, 86, 87, 165, 351. Others, 81, 130, 345.
HARMON, 265.
HARRIS, 265, 93.
Harrison, 265, 299.
Hart, 253.
HARTUB, 265, 93.
Harvey, 103, 304, 338.
HATCH, 265, 15, 259, 275, 315, 317, 321.
HATHAWAY, 266. Dr. Rufus, 21, 147.
Hatherly, 46, 90, 94, 100.
Hatton, 260.
Haughton, 316.
Haven, 74, 207.
Hawes, 22, 81, 266, 298.
Hawke, 217, 237.
Hawthorne, 213.
Hayden, 339. Vide Haden.
Hayford, 116.
Hayman, 246.
HAYWARD, Fam., 266. Inter, 216, 219, 220, 283, 307, 338. Name mentioned, 76, 81, 89, 93, 307.
Health of the town, 87.
Hearker, 90.
Hedge, 102.
Henry, 262.
Henshaw, 205.
Hepburn, 116.
Herrick, 162, 333, 341.
Herring fishery, 45.
Herrington, 317.
Hersey, 231, 280.
HEWITT, 266, 161, 290.
HICKS, 266, 64, 179, 293, 310.
Higgins, 244, 298.
Highways, 17.
High pines, 28.
High pine ledge, 352.
HILL, 267, 90, 116, 199.
Hilliard, 207.
HILLIER, 267, 43, 92.
Hills. Allerton's, 23; Captain's, 23, 93, 120, 131, 136, 162, 321; Duck, 26; North, 23.
Hilton, 320.
Hinckley, 101, 103, 116, 232, 233, 320.
Hingham, 202, 222-4-9, 230, 237, 245, 257, 267, 272, 274, 275, 280, 281-3, 296-7, 299, 307, 309, 318.
Hitchcock, 206, 208.
Hitty Tom, 76.
Hoare, 95.
Hobart, 230, 289.
Hobomok, 32, 50, 53.
Hodges, 146.
Hodgkins, 338.
Holloway, 46, 90, 291.
Holly Swamp, 31.

Holman, 90.
HOLMES, 78, 81, 89, 169, 179, 182, 183. Fam., 267. Inter. 221, 293, 295, 299, 312, 318, 320, 330, 343, 344.
Holmes, Rev. John. His ministry, 178; death, 179, and family, 179.
Hooper, 351.
Hopkin, 89, 90, 282, 296.
Hoskins, 341.
Hounds Ditch, 32.
HOUSE, 268.
HOWARD, 268, 144, 254, 295, 302.
HOWES, 288, 293, 296.
Howitt, 344, 345.
HOWLAND, Fam., 269. Interm. 228, 238, 284, 314. Arthur, 96.——Henry, 70, 85, 92, 98. —— Jabez, 107.—— Joseph, 182.——John, 17, 55, 63-4, 70, 84, 99, 267.—— Samuel, 36.——Zoeth, 99, 178.
Howse, 270.
Hubbard, 288.
Huddlestone, 116.
HUDSON, 271, 22, 297, 327.
Hull, 302.
Hull, 196, 199, 237-8, 241, 276, 280, 294, 314, 339.
Humiliation, day of, 86, 101, 102, 104, 111, 112.
HUNT, 22, 81, 92, 105, 107, 118, 144, 146, 162, 167, 173, 223. Fam., 271. Interm. 231, 279, 304, 313, 331, 344.
Huntington, 232.
HUSSEY, 272, 93, 271.
Hutchins, 344.
Hyland, 202.

I.

Incorporation of the town, 11.
Indians, praying, 24, 75; made slaves, 71, 314; allies of the English, 102, 105, 112; selling powder to them fined, 46; do. liquor, do. 339; damage done them, paid for, 85; account of them, 74-6; their name for Duxbury, 13; for Marshfield, 14; their burying grounds, 177.
Ipswich, 228.
IRISH, 272, 43, 90, 92.
Islands, 32; Brown's, 26; Clark's, 14, 23, 349; Little Wood, 14.
Ivey, 225.

J.

JACKSON, 273, 116-7, 248, 318, 321.
Jacob, 276.
Jacobs, 42, 202, 238.
James, 202, 220, 299.
Jaques, 233.
Jenkins, 90, 269.
Jenny, 10, 89, 321.
Johnson, 241, 293, 339.
JOICE, Fam., 273. Interm. 139, 261, 311.
Jonas, 116-7.
Jones, 116, 201, 286, 326, 339.

INDEX. 357

Josselyn, 42, 125, 278.
Jourdaine, 297.
Joye, 66, 294.
Judd, 287.

K.

Kean, 273.
Keen, 116, 224, 273, 280.
KEIN, 273.
Keith, 322.
KEMP, 273, 85, 178.
Kempton, 10, 262.
Kendar, 228.
Kennebec, 68, 85.
Kenneric, 90.
Kenrick, 10.
Kent, 52, 53, 199, 271, 272, 333.
Kent, Rev. Benj., 210.
KIDBYE, 274.
King, 15, 67, 279, 294, 298.
Kingman, 205.
Kingston, 10, 16, 87, 127, 130-1, 135-6, 140, 145, 152, 158, 184, 202, 206. Fam., 231-3, 236, 281-2, 294, 298. Interm. 226, 241, 253-4, 257, 268, 271, 278, 290, 302, 310, 329, 332, 333, 342.
Kinney, 146.
Kitson, 296.
KNIGHT, 274.
Knowles, 167.

L.

LAMBERT, 274.
LAND, 179, 274.
Landmarks, 23.
Lane, 271, 297.
Langdon, 272, 332.
Langton, 316.
LATHAM, 274, 55, 172, 266.
LATHLEY, 274, 299.
LATHROP, 274, 247.
Lattany, 262.
Laughton, 283.
Laveller, 116.
LAWRENCE, 275, 93, 319.
Laws of the colony, revised, 83, 84; concerning marriage, 53.
LAZELL, 275, 333,
Learned, 148.
Leavitt, 280.
Lebanon, 184, 217, 250, 311, 317.
Le Brock, 230.
Lee, 180, 269.
LEONARD, Fam., 275. Interm. 253. Name mentioned, 92, 103, 179, 199, 223.
LEURICH, 275.
Leverett, 340.
Lewis, 131, 239, 269, 300, 315, 340.
LEVHORNE, 276, 17.
Liberty pole, 138; recantations, 138.
Lincoln, 223, 227, 238, 278, 333.
LINDALL, 276, 92, 173.
Liquors, 85.
Little Compton, 67, 106, 137, 226, 245, 271, 273, 285, 286, 299, 315.
Little, 105, 219, 238, 260, 278, 279, 319, 341.

Lobdell, 321.
Long point, 33.
Longevity, 87.
Longfellow, 159.
LORING, Fam., 276. Interm. 224, 237, 238. *Daniel*, 123, 145, 151.——*Jotham*, 151.——*Samuel*, 32, 78, 123, 124, 150, 161.——*Thomas*, 82, 115, 118, 185, 186. *Others*, 20, 124, 126, 135, 137, 140, 141, 144, 151, 194, 349, 350, 351.
LOUDEN, 280, 87, 272, 342.
Low, 105.
Lowell, 324.
Loyalists of Marshfield, 127-9, 138-9.
Lucas, 24.
Lynn, Fam., 230, 240, 255, 260, 263-4, 273, 339. Interm. 216.

M.

Maccane, 288.
Magoon, 266, 281.
Majors Purchase, 15, 33.
Manly, Capt., 137.
Mannamoiet, 18.
Mansfield, 260.
Mantomock, 117.
McCally, 117.
McFARLAND, 281, 42, 265.
McLAUGHLIN, 281, 118, 166, 295.
Map of the town, 87.
Maritime Annals of the Revolution, 144-5; of the war of 1812, 164-9.
Marcy, 205.
Marry, 343.
Marsh, 288.
Marshall, 178, 207, 329.
Marshall's ledge, 352.
Marshfield, 13-5, 18, 35-8, 86, 89, 99, 104-5, 126-30, 135, 138-9, 197, 206. Fam., 221-2, 224, 226-7, 229, 239-40, 247, 255, 259-60, 263, 266-70, 273-5, 282, 291-2, 295, 297-9, 307, 309, 311, 317-18, 324, 326, 327, 330, 332-4, 337. Interm. 217, 225, 243, 262, 271, 278, 290.
Martha's Vineyard, 178.
Martin, 247.
Massachusetts, 139.
Mason, 288.
Mather, Rev. Increase, 112, 113, 184; Rev. Cotton, 114.
Mattakeesett, 13.
Matthew, 131.
Matthews, 278.
May, 116, 230.
MAYCUMBER, 66, 76, 92, 281.
Mayes, 299.
Mayflower, last surviving passenger of the, 60, 63.
Mayhew, 130.
MAYNARD, 281, 22, 323.
Mayo, 167, 293.
Meacock, 235.
Medfield, 277, 288.
MENDALL, 282, 90.
MENDAME, 282.
MENDLOWE, 282.
Mendon, 304.
MERRICK, 282, 22, 81, 93, 260, 282.

Merritt, 282.
Merry, 305, 347.
Miantinomo, 90.
Middleboro', 107, 135, 146, 214, 225-6, 239, 257, 269, 273, 287, 297, 310, 313-4, 329, 337.
Middlecott, 321.
Military discipline, 91, 109.
—— regulations, 101, 104.
Militia officers, 89, 90, 91, 93, 94, 95, 111, 112, 115, 162, 165.
Miller, 116-7.
Mills, 46, 36; defended in war, 105.
Milom, 305.
Milton, 178, 218, 328, 331, 332.
Minute companies, 123, 158.
Miscellany, 83.
Missaucatucket, 14.
MITCHELL, 70, 85, 282, 302, 315.
Mollineaux, 316.
Moody, 254.
MOORE, 105, 205, 228. Fam., 283. Interm. 272, 335, 340.
Moore, Rev. Josiah, 210.
MOREY, 283, 225.
Morgan, 236.
Morley, 323.
Morse, 205, 269.
Mortality, 86, 87.
Mortemore, 216.
MORTON, 283, 24, 64, 108, 294, 342.
Morton's hole, 10, 33, 183.
Mount Hope, 103.
Mountjoy, 216.
Mousall, 271.
Muggs, 279.
MULLINS, 283, 56, 93.
Murdock, 225, 238.
Musquito hole, 33.
Mynne, 316.
MYNOR, 284.

N.

Namasakeeset, 13, 14.
Name of Duxbury, origin of, 11; spelling of, 12.
Nantucket, 219, 270.
Narragansets, 90, 94, 105.
NASH, Fam., 284. Name mentioned, 70, 90, 91, 93-4, 98, 101, 280.
Nauset, 267.
NEAL, 284.
Ned's, ground, 351.
Needham, 217.
NELSON, 34, 180, 225, 284.
Newburgh, N. Y., 219.
Newbury, 226, 287.
New Castle, 184.
Newcome, 285.
New Gloucester, 242.
New Hampshire, 139.
New London, 235, 236.
Newton, 276.
New York, 139.
Niantick, 95.
Nickerson, 256, 333.
Nichols, 246, 267.
Ninnegrett, 95.
Noaks, 117.
Nook, The, 19; topography of, 52.
NORCUT, 284, 42, 117, 244.
Norris, 117, 280.
North Yarmouth, 293, 315.

46

INDEX.

Norton, 99.
Norwich, Ct., 230, 236, 321, 326.
Nottage, 340.
Nowett, 117.

O.

Oakman, 265.
Oales, 326.
Old French war, 117; men of Dux. who served in, 118.
OLDHAM, 285, 81, 92, 123, 349.
Orchard, 69.
Orchards, 17, 57, 70.
Ordinaries, 46.
OSBORN, 285.
Osgood, 279.
Otis, 197.
Otter rock, 31.
Osyer, 123, 295, 326, 327.
Owen, 250, 301.

P.

PABODIE, Fam., 285. Name mentioned, 67, 77, 85, 92, 106, 234, 266.
Packard, 220, 243, 275, 290.
PADDOCK, 286, 248, 214.
Paddy, 90, 260.
Paine, 217, 272, 298, 321.
Palisadoes, 70, 171.
PALMER, 17, 64, 90, 223, 227, 239, 271, 286, 315, 338. Fam. 286.
Parker, 192, 217, 303, 351.
Parks, 235, 248, 321.
Parret, 332.
PARRIS, 42, 79, 287.
Parsons, 203, 204, 322.
PARTRIDGE, Fam., 287. Calvin, 124, 137, 141, 152.—— George, 34, 44, 67, 81, 93, 201. —— Hon. George, 152, 74, 78, 79, 121, 124-6, 130, 135, 140-1, 160, 186. Others, 118, 135, 136, 165, 185, 201, 219.
Partridge, Rev. Ralph. His ministry, 171; his death, character, elegy, 173; will, 177; family, 178.
Pastures required to be fenced, 171.
Pattengell, 228.
Paupers, 86.
Peace in 1815, 170.
Peagon, 118.
PEAKES, 288, 81.
Pecksuot, 51.
PEIRCE, 288, 22, 85, 93, 103, 105, 173, 288, 312, 319.
Pellsant, 316.
Pemberton, 341.
Pembroke, 13, 16, 44, 87, 127, 135, 191, 202, 206, 208. Fam. 223, 240-1, 247, 253, 269, 273, 281, 285, 287-8, 311, 321, 329, 341-2. Interm. 229, 236, 243, 247, 252-3, 257, 271, 278, 280, 315, 327, 334.
Penn, 257.
Penniman, 264.
Pensioners of the Revolution, 146.
Pequot war, volunteers in, 89.

Perkins, 345.
Perry, 117, 222, 260.
Peter, 117.
PETERSON, 44, 118, 143, 188. Fam. 289. Interm. 233, 242, 268, 295.
Philip, 102; his death, 105.
Philip's war, 103-6; loss of the English in, 105; contribution of Ireland after, 106.
PHILLIPS, 90, 93, 105, 108, 118, 130, 138, 139, 186, 214, 282. Fam. 291.
Physicians, 65.
Picknel, 307.
PIDCOCK, 292, 93.
Pidcoke, 292.
Pier, The, 29.
Pine point, 33.
Pitcher, 117, 186, 331.
Plymouth, 10, 13, 16, 126-7, 130, 135-6, 138, 162-3, 166, 171, 179, 197, 202, 207.— Rock, 55. Fam., 213, 221, 225, 230, 233, 235, 239, 240, 246-50, 256-7, 261, 263-4, 267-9, 274, 282, 288, 293, 297, 309-10, 331, 333, 338. Inter. 224, 226, 236, 238, 257, 265, 289, 305, 318, 397.
Plympton, 288.
Plympton, 126, 130, 135, 136, 192. Fam., 273, 301, 302, 310, 322. Interm. 237, 250, 270, 275, 276.
Plummer, 300.
Ponds, 32. Blackwater, 13; Eagle tree, 57; Jones' river, 15.
PONTUS, 293, 34, 262.
Poole, 94.
Pope, 89, 131, 162.
Population of Dux. 16.
Porter, 280.
Portland, 250.
Pound, 83.
Powder point, 16, 27, 33.
Powder mills, 27.
Power, 304.
Powers, 117.
Pownalboro', Me., 223.
Pratt, 10, 180, 260, 294, 298, 309.
PRENCE, 293, 10, 17, 33, 64, 99, 100, 101.
Presland, 89.
Preston, 236, 321.
Price, 209.
PRINCE, 293, 115, 315, 349.
Pring, 321.
PRIOR, 52, 93, 116-7, 118, 135, 141-3, 167, 173, 178, 183, 349. Fam., 294. Interm. 229, 238, 242, 249, 268, 282, 290.
Privateers. The Ash, 144; David Porter, 169.
Punckatocosett, 106.
Putnam, 210.

Q.

Quack, 117.
Quakers, 98. Attending meetings of, punished, 98, 99; entertaining them punished, 98, 99; banished, 99; their meetings in Dux. 99.

Queen's guards, 126.
Quincy, 272.

R.

Ragget, Capt., 166.
Rainer, 178.
Ralph, 117.
Ramsden, 257.
Rand, 202, 206, 232, 233, 268.
RANDALL, 295, 42, 258, 268.
Rankin, 260.
Ransom, 337.
READ, 295, 93, 262.
Records, of the town, 68, 82; of the church, 177, 191.
Redding, 90, 117.
Reed, 116.
Reeves, 334.
Rehoboth, 238, 268, 272, 306.
Representatives, 77; to the conventions of the Revolution, 141.
Revolutionary votes. To encourage home manufactures, 121; to purchase corn for time of need, 134, 136; to stand by congress, 135; about a new constitution, 136, 141, 142, 160; to make a report of tories, 138; to fulfil the resolves of congress, 140; to raise soldiers, 141, 142, 143; to raise money, 142, 143, 145.
Revolutionary Annals, 118-46.
Reply to the committee of Boston, 121; assistance given to Boston, 135.
Rexham, 13.
Reyner, 316.
Reynolds, 296.
RHENOLDS, 296.
Rhode Island campaign, 137.
Rice, 74, 233.
Richard, 336.
RICHARDS, 296, 231, 292, 321.
RICHARDSON, 296, 189.
Richmond, 246, 276, 280, 297, 320.
Rider, 205, 225, 226, 248, 289, 314.
Ring, 34, 246, 301.
RIPLEY, Fam., 296. Interm., 218, 219, 231, 250, 254, 262, 278. Name mentioned, 118, 123, 144, 184.
Rivers, 30-2. Bluefish, 19; Cut, 14; Gotum, 14; Indian Head, 15; Jones, 10; North, 13, 18; South, 13.
ROBBINS, 297, 93, 239.
Roben, 117.
Roberson, 297, 118.
ROBERTS, 297, 286.
ROBINSON, Fam., 297. Name mentioned, 51, 55, 90, 100, 226, 239, 241, 290.
Robinson, Rev. John. His ministry, 184; his salary, 185, 187; his troubles and dismission, 187; anecdotes of him, 187, 189, 190, 191; his family, 184; his wife's death, 185.
Rochester, 130, 135, 221, 225, 239, 268, 281, 317.
ROGERS, Fam., 297. Interm.

INDEX.   359

223, 232, 245, 259, 271, 279, 299, 319, 326, 343. *John,* 17, 69, 77, 81, 93, 234, 241, 294, 299.——*Joseph,* 81, 93, 101.
Rood, 322.
Rose, 298.
Rothbotham, 246.
Rouse, 299, 28, 99, 323.
Row guard of 1812, 162, 165.
Rowe, 299, 84, 217.
Rowles, 322.
Roxbury, 210, 217.
Ruggles, 131.
Rum, use of, 86, 351.
Bussell, 299, 22, 120, 173, 297.

S.

Sachama, 117.
Saco, 214, 218.
Saconet, 102, 299.
Salem, 162, 215.
Salmon, 270.
Samms, 308.
Sampson, 28, 67, 79, 90, 92, 117, 118, 123-4, 131, 136-8, 140-1, 144, 146, 162, 165, 166, 173, 182, 186, 188, 191, 194, 197, 240, 349-51. Fam., 300. Interm. 218, 220, 233, 254, 260-1, 280, 288, 311-2, 320, 331, 343.
Sandwich, 131, 138. Fam., 230, 238, 239-41, 248, 255, 258, 260, 264, 270, 273, 298, 305, 307, 312, 328, 338, 339.
Sanger, Rev. Zed. His ministry, 205; letter of acceptance, 205; his ancestry and family, 205; his ordination and first sermon, 206; his salary, 207; his dismission, 207; his character, 207; settles at Bridgewater, 207; engages in navigation, 207.
Saquish, 15, 23, 26, 29, 66.
Saunders, 305.
Savage, 214, 331.
Saxton, 272.
Scales, 315.
Scammel, 158.
Scarborough, 218.
Schools, 71-4. High school, 210.
Scituate, 13, 14, 16, 87, 90, 92, 127, 135, 168, 178-9, 192, 196, 202-3, 207-8. Fam., 217, 222, 224, 227, 228-9, 237, 241, 248, 253, 261, 266-8, 274-5, 281, 283-4, 294-5, 297-9, 306-7, 316, 322-4, 326, 333, 337, 346, 347. Interm. 219, 220, 225, 230, 236, 239, 256-8, 312, 342.
Scottow, 339.
Scouts, town ordered to maintain a standing, 105.
Seabury, Fam., 305. *Samuel,* 22, 44, 47, 65, 73, 80, 82, 112, 179, 183, 185, 187, 197, 201, 202, 267.
Sea Fencibles, 162.
Sears, 131.
Seaver, 229, 332.
Seaward, 86.
Selectmen, 79.
Sentries at Captain's Hill, 124.
Settlement of the town, 9.
Shaving mills, 145.

Shaw, 22, 123, 192, 205, 206, 207. Fam., 306. Interm. 238, 283.
Shawson, 307.
Sheep, 24, 135.
Shelly, 264.
Shenard, 340.
Sherburne, 205, 206, 279.
Sherman, 307, 22, 92, 245, 259, 267, 279.
Shertly, 291.
Ship-building, 349.
Ship owners and masters, 350.
Shore, 117.
Shrewsbury, 265, 282.
Sides, 252.
Simmons, Fam., 307. Interm. 244, 284, 310, 341. Name mentioned, 64, 65, 70, 116, 162, 167, 179, 185, 186, 188.
Simon, 117.
Skiffe, 199, 230.
Slaves, 70, 71.
Small pox in Dux., 87.
Smith, 14, 117, 131, 136, 202, 206. Fam. 309. Interm. 220, 229, 256, 270, 279, 288, 320, 340, 341.
Snell, 73, 220, 223, 324.
Snow, 118. Fam., 309. Intermarriages, 222, 223, 247, 256, 259, 293.
Sodom, 12.
Sogkonates, 107.
Soldiers' equipments, 92, 94, 111; pay, 92, 102, 103.
Somerby, 316.
Souhegan, 73.
Soule, Fam., 310. Interm. 218, 334. Family arms, 313-4. *George,* 70, 77, 89, 92.——*John,* 99, 182.——*Joshua,* 187, 188, 194, 195, 350.——*Zachary,* 27, 92. Others, 105, 140, 166, 169, 170, 179, 188, 198, 201, 350.
Souther, 91.
Southworth, Fam., 314. Interm. 273. Pedigree in England, 316. *Constant,* 44, 46, 68, 85, 89, 93-4, 102, 185, 234, 310.——*Edward,* 16, 68, 72, 185, 187.——*James,* 28, 135, 137, 142, 349.——*Thomas,* 68, 101, 188, 310.—— Others, 123, 192.
Sparrow, 103, 131, 260, 293.
Speer, 117.
Spooner, 336.
Sprague, Fam., 317. Interm. 225, 278, 309, 343. *Francis,* 17, 46, 47, 70, 93, 172, 276. ——*John,* 105, 183, 188,—— *Samuel,* 82, 123, 184.——*Seth,* 19, 79, 146, 162, 163, 165, 318, 319, 349, 351. Others, 12, 86, 118, 123, 124, 146.
Spring, 204.
Sprout, 314.
Sprout, 320, 123, 129, 285.
Squamaug, 75.
Stacia, 134.
Stamp act, 118. Resolves of the town upon, 119; its repeal, 119; and the rejoicing thereat, 119-20.
Standish, Fam., 320. Interm. 279, 341. Fam. Arms, 96. *Alexander,* 69, 82, 96, 180, 183, 351.——*Josiah,* 77, 95,

101, 102, 109.——*Cpt. Myles,* 10-2, 15, 17, 23, 33, 48, 55-6, 89, 90, 93-5. His house, 52; spring, 53; swords, 54, 98; coat of mail, 54, 98; property, 55, 69, 70, 96.——*Miles,* 197.
Standlake, 324.
Stanford, 322, 217, 219, 135, 137.
Starr, Fam., 322. *Comfort,* 65, 90, 93.——*John,* 22, 69, 93.
Stearns, 210, 260.
Steel, 231.
Stetson, 323, 42, 223, 238, 243, 266, 271, 278.
Stevens, 291.
Stevenson, 233.
Stockbridge, 323, 79, 138.
Stocks, 83.
Strangers, 87; entertaining them, fined, 87.
Studley, 228, 301, 310.
Sturtevant, 131, 260, 333.
Style of dates, 11.
Sudbury, 205.
Sullivan, 137.
Summers, 300.
Swanzey, 102, 238, 240, 247, 269, 272, 286, 297, 334.
Sweetser, 313.
Switzer, 324, 257.
Sylvester, 324, 73, 112, 118, 218, 349.
Synod of 1647, 176.

T.

Tarkiln, 12.
Tarpits, 235.
Taunton, 138, 205, 228, 232, 263, 264, 266, 273, 275, 281, 292, 326.
Taylor, 258, 209, 331.
Temple, 262.
Tenney, 297.
Terrill, 298.
Thacher, 325, 81, 82, 91, 101, 178, 183, 269, 273, 289.
Thanksgiving, 85.
Thaxter, 245, 254.
Thayer, 74, 278, 304.
Thomas, 69, 73, 89, 91, 118, 123, 126, 130-1, 137-8, 184, 199. Fam., 325. Interm. 217, 225, 254-5, 262, 269, 278-9, 291, 300, 302, 317, 319, 342, 344.
Thompson, 131, 256, 296, 331.
Thorne, 340.
Thorp, 326, 223.
Thrasher, 275.
Thresher, 117.
Thump caps, 352.
Tidge, 178.
Tilden, 139, 226, 229, 278, 285.
Tilson, 247.
Tinckham, 347.
Tinkertown, 12.
Tisdell, 326, 93, 205, 297.
Tiverton, 314, 315, 324.
Tobey, 117, 260, 279, 319.
Tolman, 312, 319, 331, 337.
Tompkins, 326, 92.
Topography of the town, 23-35.
Tories, of Marshfield, 127-9, 138. None in Duxbury, 138. Treatment of them, 139, 140.
Torrey, 292.

360 INDEX.

Tour, 144, 340.
Tower, 326.
Town officers. Surveyors of highways, 21; clerks, 68, 82; representatives, 77; selectmen, 79; constables, 81; treasurers, 82.
Townshend, 131.
Tracy, 326, 13, 17, 77, 79, 111.
Trader, the first in Duxbury, 351.
Training-field, 115.
Tray, 117.
Treasurers, 82.
Tree of knowledge, 12.
Treeble, 327.
Trees, 26.
Trewant, 267.
Troop, 244.
Trouest, 327.
Truant, 327, 22, 92.
Trumbull, 185, 189.
Tubbs, 327, 22, 90, 92.
Tucker, 340.
Tupper, 139, 148.
Turfrey, 214.
Turner, 93, 166, 167, 188, 202. Fam., 327. Interm. 222, 225, 232, 236, 266, 271, 299, 304, 323, 341, 344.
Turner, Rev. Charles. His ministry and salary, 202; his family, 202; his dismission, 203; his character, 203-4; anecdotes of him, 203-4; afterwards a senator, 203-4; an ardent whig, 154; prepares young men for college, 74, 152.
Tyler, 304.

U, V.

United colonies, confederation of, 90.
Ussel, 327.
Vassel, 91.
Vaughan, 269.
Veazie, Rev. Saml. His ministry, 191; his family, 191; his troubles with the society, 192; Whitfield converts him, 192; his labors objectionable, 193; his note to the ecclesiastical council, 195; asks his dismission, 196; his law-suit, 197; another council, 197; his dismission, 198; recommended to the chh. of Hull, 199; further accounts of the troubles, 199, 200; anecdotes of him, 201.
Verdie, 329.
Verge, 344.
Vering, 340.
Vermage, 320.
Verren, 276.
Vessels built, 27, 349. Captured in the Revolution, 144 —in the war of 1812, 166.
Viall, 216.
Vicory, 271.
Vinal, 201, 219.
Vincent, 328.
Village, The, 12.
Virgin, 335.
Virginia, 139.
Vobes, 92, 258.
Vose, 151.

W.

Wade, 117, 131.
Wadsworth, Fam., 328. Interm. 224, 272. Fam. arms, 328. *Christopher*, 17, 44, 69, 70, 77, 79, 81, 83, 90.——*John*, 12, 16, 73, 74, 78, 80, 82, 110, 117, 118, 121, 153, 155, 180, 187, 201.——*Peleg*, 80, 121, 124, 126, 130-1, 135-7, 140, 157, 158, 202, 203.——*Wait*, 80, 118, 121, 123-4, 140.. Others, 80, 116, 118, 123, 126, 132, 144, 145, 159, 166, 169, 349.
Waite, 328.
Wakefield, 218.
Walker, 332, 34, 79, 236, 270, 271, 274, 309, 310, 351.
Walley, 214.
Wallis, 332, 43.
Wampanoags, 105.
Wampatuck, 75.
Wannapooke, 76.
Wanton, 333.
Ward, 158-9.
Wards in the day, 104, 105, 112.
Wareham, 135.
Warner, 131.
Warren, 34, 225, 231, 245, 315.
Washburn, 333, 17, 81, 93, 94, 137, 173, 239, 342.
Washington, Gen., 126, 136.
Waste, 243, 248.
Watches in the night, 104, 105, 112.
Waterman, 333, 165, 167, 217, 218, 221, 226.
Waters, 299.
Watertown, 204-5, 208, 222, 260.
Watson, 334, 24, 129, 275, 306.
Wattles, 250.
Wealth of the town, 70, 86.
Wears, 84.
Webb, 73.
Weechertown, 12.
Weed, 117.
Weeks, 117.
Welch, 220.
Weld, 269.
Wells, 327.
Wensley, 260.
West, 334, 22, 34, 47, 70, 80, 81, 83, 86, 185, 188, 190, 208, 227.
West Indies, expedition against, 116-7.
Weston, Fam. 334. Interm. 219, 303, 310, 321, 322, 341. *Edmund*, 69.——*Ezra*, 19, 27, 134, 141, 161, 162, 349, 350, 351. *Others*, 80, 118, 126, 136, 140, 143-4, 146, 165, 169, 187, 349.
Weyborne, 337.
Weymouth, 178, 231, 238, 259, 272, 284, 285, 292, 296, 298, 305, 306, 318, 324.
Whaleboat Expedition. To Sandwich, 131; to Quincy, 148; in Boston harbor, 150.
Whale fishery, 350.
Whales, 86.
Wharf, the first in Dux., 350.
Whetcome, 262.
Whipping-posts, 83.
White, 33, 90, 105, 117, 125, 138, 139, 146, 192. Fam., 337. Interm. 226, 255, 272, 278, 292, 298.
Whitefield, 192.
Whitman, 74.
Whitmarsh, 302.
Whitney, 220.
Whittemore, 222, 290.
Whytock, 348.
Wilbor, 246, 315.
Wilder, 257.
Wilkinson, 340.
Willet, 94, 238.
Williams, 89, 224, 297, 322, 337, 340.
Williamson, 337, 282, 318.
Williard, 214.
Willis, 337, 90, 93, 184, 223, 228, 258, 262.
Wills, 244, 268.
Wilson, 338, 93, 230.
Windham, Ct., 236, 275.
Wing, 338, 312.
Winslow, Fam., 338. Interm. 222, 229, 238, 310. *Gov. Edward*, 55, 70, 99.——*Gov. Josiah*, 34, 101.——*Dr. Isaac*, 128, 138. *Others*, 20, 69, 116, 117, 125, 129.
Winsor, Fam., 339. Interm. 219, 274. Name, its origin, 345; the English family, 345-6; their armorial bearings, 345-6. The Rhode Island family, 346. *Nathaniel*, 26, 80, 87, 144, 162, 167, 169, 350.——*Joshua*, 19, 20, 162, 166, 168, 350. *Others*, 118, 144, 162, 166, 167, 168, 349, 351.
Winter, 74, 217, 266.
Wiswall, 231.
Wiswall, Rev. Ichabod. His ministry, 180; family, 180; his letter to Hinckley, 180; keeps a school, 72; agent to England, 107-9, 112-15; his death and character, 183-4; an astrologer, 184; his salary, 181, 182; his will and estate, 180.
Witchcraft, 215.
Wittowamalt, 52.
Witherell, 346, 90, 102, 103, 263, 273, 285.
Woburn, 296.
Wolcott, 185.
Women gather the crops during the Revolution, 137.
Wood, 131, 179, 180.
Woodberry, 117.
Woodcock, 253.
Woodman, 246.
Woodward, 166, 220.
Woodworth, 302, 307.
Woolwich, 201, 313.
Wormall, 347, 22, 189.
Wright, 86, 146, 230, 237, 303, 305, 310, 322.
Wyman, 315.

Y, Z.

Yarmouth, 214, 222, 225, 263, 264, 266, 273, 323, 338.
Young, 255.
Youths, required to perform military duty, 105.
Zachary, 117.
Zachary's rocks, 27.

www.ingramcontent.com/pod-product-compliance
Lightning Source LLC
Chambersburg PA
CBHW072133220426
43664CB00013B/2227